JOURNAL FOR THE STUDY OF THE NEW TESTAMENT SUPPLEMENT SERIES
104

Executive Editor
Stanley E. Porter

STUDIES IN SCRIPTURE IN EARLY JUDAISM AND CHRISTIANITY
3

Series Editors
Craig A. Evans
James A. Sanders

Sheffield Academic Press

The Gospels and the Scriptures of Israel

edited by
Craig A. Evans
and
W. Richard Stegner

Journal for the Study of the New Testament
Supplement Series 104

Studies in Scripture in Early Judaism and Christianity 3

Copyright © 1994 Sheffield Academic Press

Published by Sheffield Academic Press Ltd
Mansion House
19 Kingfield Road
Sheffield S11 9AS
England

Typeset by Sheffield Academic Press
and
Printed on acid-free paper in Great Britain
by Bookcraft
Midsomer Norton, Somerset

British Library Cataloguing in Publication Data

A catalogue record for this book is available
from the British Library

ISBN 1-85075-497-7

CONTENTS

Preface   9
Abbreviations   10
List of Contributors   13

JOHN J. O'ROURKE
Possible Uses of the Old Testament in the Gospels:
An Overview   15

Part I
JOHN AND JESUS

JEFFREY A. TRUMBOWER
The Role of Malachi in the Career of John the Baptist   28

JAMES D.G. DUNN
John the Baptist's Use of Scripture   42

A.E. HARVEY
Genesis versus Deuteronomy? Jesus on Marriage and Divorce   55

JAMES B. DEYOUNG
The Function of Malachi 3.1 in Matthew 11.10:
Kingdom Reality as the Hermeneutic of Jesus   66

Part II
THE GOSPEL OF MATTHEW

FREDERICK W. DANKER
Matthew: A Patriot's Gospel   94

JAMES A. SANDERS
Ναζωραῖος in Matthew 2.23 116

RUDOLF PESCH
'He will be Called a Nazorean': Messianic Exegesis
in Matthew 1–2 129

D.A. CARSON
Do the Prophets and the Law Quit Prophesying before John?
A Note on Matthew 11.13 179

Part III
THE GOSPEL OF MARK

JOEL MARCUS
Authority to Forgive Sins upon the Earth: The *Shema*
in the Gospel of Mark 196

WILLIAM RICHARD STEGNER
Jesus' Walking on the Water: Mark 6.45-52 212

DEBORAH KRAUSE
Narrated Prophecy in Mark 11.12-21: The Divine
Authorization of Judgment 235

GEORGE WESLEY BUCHANAN
Withering Fig Trees and Progression in Midrash 249

DALE C. ALLISON, JR
Mark 12.28-31 and the Decalogue 270

Part IV
THE GOSPEL OF LUKE

DARRELL L. BOCK
Proclamation from Prophecy and Pattern: Luke's Use
of the Old Testament for Christology and Mission 280

Contents

WILLIAM S. KURZ, SJ
Intertextual Use of Sirach 48.1-16 in Plotting Luke–Acts 308

ASHER FINKEL
Jesus' Preaching in the Synagogue on the Sabbath
(Luke 4.16-28) 325

CRAIG A. EVANS
The Pharisee and the Publican: Luke 18.9-14 and
Deuteronomy 26 342

Part V
THE GOSPEL OF JOHN

A.T. HANSON
John's Use of Scripture 358

MARTIN HENGEL
The Old Testament in the Fourth Gospel 380

STANLEY E. PORTER
Can Traditional Exegesis Enlighten Literary Analysis
of the Fourth Gospel? An Examination of the Old Testament
Fulfilment Motif and the Passover Theme 396

JOHN PAINTER
The Quotation of Scripture and Unbelief in John 12.36b-43 429

J. RAMSEY MICHAELS
Betrayal and the Betrayer: The Uses of Scripture in
John 13.18-19 459

Index of References 475
Index of Authors 499

PREFACE

The present volume is the third in the series Studies in Scripture in Early Judaism and Christianity, a series that has grown out of the Society of Biblical Literature program unit Scripture in Early Judaism and Christianity, founded and currently chaired by Craig A. Evans and James A. Sanders. The series produces occasional volumes that are published as Supplements to the *Journal for the Study of the Old Testament, Journal for the Study of the New Testament* and *Journal for the Study of the Pseudepigrapha*. The first two volumes appeared in 1993: *Paul and the Scriptures of Israel* (JSNTSup, 83; SSEJC, 1) and *The Pseudepigrapha and Early Biblical Interpretation* (JSPSup, 14; SSEJC, 2). As in the case of the first two volumes, *The Gospels and the Scriptures of Israel* represents a collection of studies concerned with the function of Israel's Scriptures in later sacred writings. These studies explore in what ways the Scriptures inform and 'drive' the respective portraits of John and Jesus as we have them in the four canonical Gospels. Four of the papers that make up the present volume were read at the 1992 SBL meeting in San Francisco, while two other papers are revisions of previous publications. The remaining papers were solicited by the editors and were prepared especially for the present volume.

The editors extend their thanks to Mr Geoffrey Green of T. & T. Clark for permission to reprint a revised version of the essay by the late A.T. Hanson,[1] and to Mrs Hanson who called this essay to our attention. We are also grateful to Mr Spencer Stadler, who is currently engaged in doctoral studies at the University of Munich, for translating the essay by Professor Rudolf Pesch.

Craig A. Evans
W. Richard Stegner
Spring 1994

1.   The essay originally appeared in A.T. Hanson, *The Prophetic Gospel: A Study of John and the Old Testament* (Edinburgh: T. & T. Clark, 1991), pp. 234-53.

ABBREVIATIONS

AB	Anchor Bible
ABD	D.N. Freedman (ed.), *Anchor Bible Dictionary*
AGJU	Arbeiten zur Geschichte des antiken Judentums und des Urchristentums
AnBib	Analecta biblica
ANRW	*Aufstieg und Niedergang der römischen Welt*
ArBib	Aramaic Bible
ASOR	American Schools of Oriental Research
AUSS	*Andrews University Seminary Studies*
BA	*Biblical Archaeologist*
BAGD	W. Bauer, W.F. Arndt, F.W. Gingrich and F.W. Danker, *Greek–English Lexicon of the New Testament*
BBR	*Bulletin for Biblical Research*
BDF	F. Blass, A. Debrunner and R.W. Funk, *A Greek Grammar of the New Testament*
BETL	Bibliotheca ephemeridum theologicarum lovaniensium
BEvT	Beiträge zur evangelischen Theologie
Bib	*Biblica*
BJS	Brown Judaic Studies
BNTC	Black's New Testament Commentaries
BSac	*Bibliotheca Sacra*
BT	*The Bible Translator*
BVC	*Bible et vie chrétienne*
BWANT	Beiträge zur Wissenschaft vom Alten und Neuen Testament
BZ	*Biblische Zeitschrift*
BZAW	Beihefte zur *ZAW*
BZNW	Beihefte zur *ZNW*
CBQ	*Catholic Biblical Quarterly*
CBQMS	*Catholic Biblical Quarterly* Monograph Series
ConBNT	Coniectanea biblica, Old Testament
ConNT	*Coniectanea neotestamentica*
CRINT	Compendia rerum iudaicarum ad Novum Testamentum
DBSup	*Dictionnaire de la Bible, Supplément*
DJD	Discoveries in the Judaean Desert
EBib	Etudes bibliques
EKKNT	Evangelisch-Katholischer Kommentar zum Neuen Testament
ETL	*Ephemerides theologicae lovanienses*
EvQ	*Evangelical Quarterly*
EvT	*Evangelische Theologie*

ExpTim	*Expository Times*
FFNT	Foundations and Facets: New Testament
GCS	Griechische christliche Schriftsteller
GNS	Good News Studies
HBT	*Horizons in Biblical Theology*
HDR	Harvard Dissertations in Religion
HeyJ	*Heythrop Journal*
HNT	Handbuch zum Neuen Testament
HTKNT	Herders theologischer Kommentar zum Neuen Testament
HTR	*Harvard Theological Review*
HUCA	*Hebrew Union College Annual*
IB	*Interpreter's Bible*
ICC	International Critical Commentary
IDB	G.A. Buttrick (ed.), *Interpreter's Dictionary of the Bible*
IDBSup	*IDB*, Supplementary Volume
Int	*Interpretation*
JBL	*Journal of Biblical Literature*
JBT	*Jahrbuch für Biblische Theologie*
JewEnc	*The Jewish Encyclopedia*
JETS	*Journal of the Evangelical Theological Society*
JJS	*Journal of Jewish Studies*
JSJ	*Journal for the Study of Judaism in the Persian, Hellenistic and Roman Period*
JSNT	*Journal for the Study of the New Testament*
JSNTSup	*Journal for the Study of the New Testament* Supplement Series
JSOTSup	*Journal for the Study of the Old Testament* Supplement Series
JTS	*Journal of Theological Studies*
MeyerK	H.A.W. Meyer (ed.), Kritisch-exegetischer Kommentar über das Neue Testament
MHUC	Monographs of the Hebrew Union College
NASB	*New American Standard Bible*
NCB	New Century Bible
Neot	*Neotestamentica*
NIBC	New International Biblical Commentary
NICNT	New International Commentary on the New Testament
NIGTC	The New International Greek Testament Commentary
NIV	*New International Version*
NovT	*Novum Testamentum*
NovTSup	*Novum Testamentum* Supplements
NRSV	New Revised Standard Version
NTAbh	Neutestamentliche Abhandlungen
NTD	Das Neue Testament Deutsch
NTL	New Testament Library
NTS	*New Testament Studies*
NumSup	*Numen: International Review for the History of Religions*, Supplements
OBO	Orbis biblicus et orientalis
OTP	J.H. Charlesworth (ed.), *Old Testament Pseudepigrapha*

PG	J. Migne, *Patrologia graeca*
PL	J. Migne, *Patrologia latina*
PW	Pauly–Wissowa, *Real-Encyclopädie der classischen Altertumswissenschaft*
PWSup	Supplement to PW
RB	*Revue biblique*
RevQ	*Revue de Qumran*
RSR	*Recherches de science religieuse*
SBFLA	*Studii biblici franciscani liber annuus*
SBLDS	SBL Dissertation Series
SBLMS	SBL Monograph Studies
SBLSP	SBL Seminar Papers
SBS	Stuttgarter Bibelstudien
SBT	Studies in Biblical Theology
SIDIC	*Service international de documentation judéo-chrétienne*
SIG	W. Dittenberger (ed.), *Sylloge Inscriptionum Graecarum*
SJLA	Studies in Judaism in Late Antiquity
SJT	*Scottish Journal of Theology*
SNT	Studien zum Neuen Testament
SNTSMS	Society of New Testament Studies Monograph Series
STDJ	Studies on the Texts of the Desert of Judah
SVTP	Studia in Veteris Testamenti pseudepigrapha
SWJT	*Southwestern Journal of Theology*
TDNT	G. Kittel and G. Friedrich (eds.), *Theological Dictionary of the New Testament*
THKNT	Theologischer Handkommentar zum Neuen Testament
TLZ	*Theologischer Literaturzeitung*
TS	*Theological Studies*
TU	Texte und Untersuchungen
TynBul	*Tyndale Bulletin*
TZ	*Theologische Zeitschrift*
UBSGNT	United Bible Societies' *Greek New Testament*
VD	*Verbum domini*
VT	*Vetus Testamentum*
WBC	Word Biblical Commentary
WMANT	Wissenschaftliche Monographien zum Alten und Neuen Testament
WUNT	Wissenschaftliche Untersuchungen zum Neuen Testament
ZAW	*Zeitschrift für die alttestamentliche Wissenschaft*
ZNW	*Zeitschrift für die neutestamentliche Wissenschaft*
ZTK	*Zeitschrift für Theologie und Kirche*

LIST OF CONTRIBUTORS

Dale C. Allison, Jr
Friends University
Wichita, Kansas, USA

Darrell L. Bock
Dallas Theological Seminary
Dallas, Texas, USA

George Wesley Buchanan
Wesley Theological Seminary
Washington, DC, USA

D.A. Carson
Trinity Evangelical Divinity School
Deerfield, Illinois, USA

Frederick W. Danker
Lutheran School of Theology
 at Chicago
Chicago, Illinois, USA

James B. DeYoung
Western Baptist Seminary
Portland, Oregon, USA

James D.G. Dunn
University of Durham
Durham, England

Craig A. Evans
Trinity Western University
Langley, British Columbia, Canada

Asher Finkel
Seton Hall University
South Orange, New Jersey, USA

A.T. Hanson
Late Emeritus Professor of Theology
University of Hull
Hull, England

A.E. Harvey
Westminster Abbey
London, England

Martin Hengel
University of Tübingen
Tübingen, Germany

Deborah Krause
Eden Theological Seminary
St Louis, Missouri, USA

William S. Kurz
Marquette University
Milwaukee, Wisconsin, USA

Joel Marcus
University of Glasgow
Glasgow, Scotland

J. Ramsey Michaels
Southwest Missouri State University
Springfield, Missouri, USA

John J. O'Rourke
Old Saint Mary's
Philadelphia, Pennsylvania, USA

James A. Sanders
School of Theology at Claremont
Claremont, California, USA

John Painter
La Trobe University
Melbourne, Australia

W. Richard Stegner
Garrett Evangelical Theological Seminary
Evanston, Illinois, USA

Rudolf Pesch
University of Freiburg
Freiburg, Germany

Jeffrey A. Trumbower
St Michael's College
Colchester, Vermont, USA

Stanley E. Porter
Roehampton Institute
London, England

POSSIBLE USES OF THE OLD TESTAMENT IN THE GOSPELS

John J. O'Rourke

There is no doubt that for the various New Testament authors the Old Testament contained a group of authoritative writings, and we can take this to apply to the people who produced our present canonical Gospels. There is also no doubt that when an introductory formula is found, such as 'Moses said', 'David says', 'it is written', 'as Isaiah prophesies', 'you read', there is an intended use of the Old Testament. When we find words or expressions which may have their source in the Old Testament the question arises: did the individual Evangelists intend the words or expressions to be taken as specific Old Testament references? At least one modern edition of the Greek New Testament does point out the incidences of possible uses of the Old Testament in the New Testament by printing the words which may have an Old Testament basis in italics. The Nestlé–Aland edition finds twenty-eight in Matthew, twenty-two in Mark, fifteen in Luke and four in John. Also to be considered is one recent edition of the Latin Vulgate with similar indications of Old Testament words.[1]

I will in the first instance compare the source of the words or expressions as determined in the edition to the LXX text, since that is the Old Testament text which is primarily reflected in the New Testament. It will also be necessary to look at the Hebrew text.[2]

---

1. E. Nestlé, *Novum Testamentum Graece* (1979), and *Nova Vulgate* (1979); both texts can be found in K. Aland and B. Aland, *Novum Testamentum, Graece et Latine* (Stuttgart: Deutsche Bibelgellschaft, 26th edn, 1984).

2. For general studies on the use of the Old Testament in the New, see B. Lindars, *New Testament Apologetic: The Doctrinal Significance of the Old Testament Quotations* (London: SCM Press; Philadelphia: Westminster Press, 1961); H.M. Shires, *Finding the Old Testament in the New* (Philadelphia: Westminster Press, 1974); R.N. Longenecker, *Biblical Exegesis in the Apostolic Period* (Grand Rapids: Eerdmans, 1975); A.T. Hanson, *The New Testament Interpretation of*

Matthew[1]

In Mt. 7.23 (ἀποχωρεῖτε ἀπ᾽ ἐμοῦ οἱ ἐργαζόμενοι τὴν ἀνομίαν) is taken as a citation of (LXX) Ps. 6.9. The words are the same, save that the LXX has ἀπόστητε instead of ἀποχωρεῖτε. It could be a citation.

In Mt. 9.13 ἔλεος θέλω καὶ οὐ θυσίαν is taken as a citation. The words are verbatim in Hos. 6.6.

In Mt. 9.36 the words ὡσεὶ πρόβατα μὴ ἔχοντα ποιμένα are considered a citation. In Num. 27.17, 2 Chron. 18.28, and Jdt. 11.19 one finds ὡς πρόβατα οἷς οὐκ ἔστιν ποιμήν. The figure is the same although the words are not exactly the same. While it could be intended as a scriptural reference, it seems more likely to have been a rather commonplace expression.

In Mt. 10.35-36 the words ἄνθρωπον κατὰ τοῦ πατρὸς αὐτοῦ καὶ θυγατέρα κατὰ τῆς μητρὸς αὐτῆς καὶ νύμφην κατὰ τῆς πενθερᾶς αὐτῆς, καὶ ἐχθροὶ τοῦ ἀνθρώπου οἱ οἰκιακοὶ αὐτοῦ are taken as a citation of Mic. 7.6. In the corresponding LXX passage we find υἱὸς ἀτιμάζει πατέρα, θυγάτηρ ἐπαναστήσεται ἐπὶ τὴν μητέρα αὐτῆς, νύμφη ἐπὶ τὴν πενθερὰν αὐτῆς, ἐχθροὶ ἀνδρὸς πάντες οἱ ἄνδρες οἱ ἐν τῷ οἴκῳ αὐτοῦ. The LXX is actually closer to the Hebrew than is the Gospel. Obviously it is not a direct citation; however, because of its length it does seem to be an intended reference.

In Mt. 11.5 τυφλοὶ ἀναβλέπουσιν is taken as a reference to Isa. 29.18; 35.5-6; 42.18. Of these the closest in wording is the last, which reads οἱ τυφλοί, ἀναβλέψατε. The Greek takes κωφοὶ ἀκούουσιν as a citation. The closest Old Testament expression seems to be Isa. 42.18 (οἱ κωφοί, ἀκούσατε). The Greek also takes νεκροὶ ἐγείρονται as a

---

Scripture (London: SPCK, 1980); D.A. Carson and H.G.M. Williamson (eds.), *It is Written: Scripture Citing Scripture: Essays in Honour of Barnabas Lindars* (Cambridge: Cambridge University Press, 1988).

1. For general treatments of the use of the Old Testament in Matthew, see K. Stendahl, *The School of St Matthew and its Use of the Old Testament* (Lund: Gleerup, 1954; Philadelphia: Fortress Press, 2nd edn, 1968); R.O. Coleman, 'Matthew's Use of the Old Testament', *SWJT* 5 (1962), pp. 29-39; J.J. O'Rourke, 'Fulfillment Texts in Matthew', *CBQ* 24 (1962), pp. 394-403; N. Hillyer, 'Matthew's Use of the Old Testament', *EvQ* 36 (1964), pp. 12-26; R.H. Gundry, *The Use of the Old Testament in St Matthew's Gospel* (NovTSup, 18; Leiden: Brill, 1967); R.S. McConnell, *Law and Prophecy in Matthew's Gospel: The Authority and Use of the Old Testament in the Gospel of St Matthew* (Basel: Reinhardt, 1969).

citation. In Isa. 26.19 the LXX has ἀναστήσονται οἱ νεκροί. Possibly here references are intended, but there is no direct citation. The Latin takes *pauperes evangelizantur* as a citation. At best the words are reminiscent of various parts of Isaiah.

In Mt. 11.29 εὑρήσετε ἀνάπαυσιν ταῖς ψυχαῖς ὑμῶν is taken as a citation. In Jer. 6.16 we find εὑρήσετε ἁγιασμὸν ταῖς ψυχαῖς ὑμῶν. Possibly it is a citation.

In Mt. 12.7 the words ἔλεος θέλω καὶ οὐ θυσίαν are considered a citation. The words are verbatim in the LXX of Hos. 6.6. Most likely it is an intended citation (as in Mt. 9.13).

The Greek takes τὰ πετεινὰ τοῦ οὐρανοῦ καὶ κατασκηνοῦν ἐν τοῖς κλάδοις αὐτοῦ in Mt. 13.32 as a citation. In Ps. 103.12 of the LXX we find τὰ πετεινὰ τοῦ οὐρανοῦ κατασκηνώσει. Possibly it is a citation, but it could be a normal way of speaking as well. The Greek also takes the words in Mt. 13.42 βαλοῦσιν αὐτοὺς εἰς τήν κάμινον τοῦ πυρός as a citation. In Dan. 7.6 we find ἐμβαλοῦσιν αὐτὸν εἰς τὴν κάμινον τοῦ πυρός. The only thing in common between the New Testament expression and the LXX here is the notion of casting into fire. It is scarcely a citation. The same is to be said of the words in Mt. 13.30.

The Greek takes ἀποδώσει ἑκάστῳ κατὰ τὴν πρᾶξιν αὐτοῦ in Mt. 16.27 as a citation. In Ps. 61.13 there is ἀποδώσεις ἑκάστῳ κατὰ τὰ ἔργα αὐτοῦ, in Prov. 24.12 ἀποδίδωσιν ἑκάστῳ κατὰ τὰ ἔργα αὐτοῦ, in Sir. 35.22 there is some similarity. It is not a citation.

Mt. 17.10-11 refers to the coming of Elias prior to the coming of the messiah. The words Ἠλίαν δεῖ ἐλθεῖν πρῶτον and Ἠλίας μέν ἔρχεται are not a citation from but a reference to Mal. 3.13-14.

The Greek and the Latin take ἐπὶ στόματος δύο μαρτύρων ἢ τριῶν σταθῇ πᾶν ῥῆμα in Mt. 18.16 as a citation. In Deut. 19.15 we find ἐπὶ στόματος δύο μαρτύρων καὶ ἐπὶ στόματος τριῶν μαρτύρων σταθήσεται πᾶν ῥῆμα. It does not seem to be an intended citation. The legal practice would have been well known.

From the context there is a virtual introductory formula for Mt. 19.18-19. The ordering of the first three commandments is that of Deut. 5.17-20 in the LXX rather than that of Exod. 20.13-15.[1]

The song in Mt. 21.9 is a *mélange* of biblical texts. 'Blessed is he who comes in the name of the Lord' is found in Ps. 117.26a; 'in the highest'

---

1. There were several recensions of the commandments by New Testament times; see A. Jepson, 'Beitrage zur Auslegung und Geschichte des Dekalogs', *ZAW* 79 (1967), pp. 277-304.

is found in Ps. 148.1b; 'hosanna' is found in many places and is an obvious Hebrew word.

The Latin of Mt. 23.18 considers *relinquitur vobis domus vestra deserta* a citation. There is some similarity with Ps. 69.26; however, the reference to persons in the LXX is to the third person and not the second. Mt. 23.29 contains words from Ps. 118.26. This does not prove that a citation was intended.

Mt. 24.29 is really a *mélange* of Old Testament texts. Verse 29a has similarity with Isa. 13.10; v. 29b's καὶ οἱ ἀστέρες πεσοῦνται is similar to καὶ πάντα τὰ ἄστρα of Isa. 34.4 in the LXX. There is some analogy in Joel 2.4 to Matthew's καὶ αἱ δυνάμεις τῶν οὐρανῶν.

The Latin takes *plangent omnes tribus terrae* in Mt. 24.30 as a citation. This may recall some of the words in Zech. 12.10-12 but it is scarcely a citation. Both the Greek and the Latin in the same verse take τὸν υἱὸν τοῦ ἀνθρώπου ἐρχόμενον ἐπὶ τῶν νεφελῶν τοῦ οὐρανοῦ as a citation. In Dan. 7.13 we find ἐπὶ τῶν νεφελῶν τοῦ οὐρανοῦ ὡς υἱὸς ἀνθρώπου ἤρχετο. The expressions are similar but the New Testament does not cite the Old Testament here. The same is to be said of Mt. 26.69. However, the New Testament usage may indicate a type of belief held by many at the time which was ultimately based upon Daniel.

The Greek takes περίλυπός ἐστιν ἡ ψυχή as a citation in Mt. 26.38. In Ps. 42.5 we find τί περίλυπος εἶ, ψυχή. It is scarcely a citation.

In Mt. 27.34 the Latin takes *dederunt*, *bibere* and *felle* as citations. This does not seem justifiable.

In Mt. 27.35 διεμερίσαντο τὰ ἱμάτια αὐτοῦ βάλλοντες κλῆρον is taken as a citation. In LXX Ps. 21.19 we find διεμερίσαντο τὰ ἱμάτιά μου ἑαυτοῖς καὶ ἐπὶ τὸν ἱματισμόν μου ἔβαλον κλῆρον. It is scarcely a citation, although it can be classified as a reminiscence.

In Mt. 27.43 πέποιθεν ἐπὶ τὸν θεόν, ῥυσάσθω νῦν εἰ θέλει αὐτόν is found. In Ps. 21.9 the words are ἤλπισεν ἐπὶ κύριον, ῥυσάσθω αὐτόν· σωσάτω αὐτόν, ὅτι θέλει αὐτόν. At best it is an echo and not a particularly strong one.

In Mt. 27.46 we find Θεέ μου θεέ μου, ἱνατί με ἐγκατέλιπες. This is very close to the Hebrew of Ps. 22.2. By the standards of classical Greek it is better than the LXX's Ὁ θεὸς ὁ θεός μου, πρόσχες μοι· ἵνα τί ἐγκατέλιπές με (= 21.2). It is fairly obvious that a citation is intended.

Mark[1]

Mk 4.12 contains words which are similar to Isa. 6.9-10, but in the Gospel the words are in the third person plural while in the LXX they are in the second person plural in the opening clauses. The Old Testament passage is cited with an introductory formula in Mt. 12.14-15; there is agreement between Matthew and the LXX here save that Matthew has some minor omissions. The words in Mark here should not be considered a citation but an expression with Old Testament overtones, perhaps influenced by early targumic tradition (for example, Mark's καὶ ἀφεθῇ αὐτοῖς = the Isaiah Targum's וישתביק להון).[2]

The Greek but not the Latin takes τὰ πετεινὰ τοῦ οὐρανοῦ κατασκηνοῦν in Mk 4.32 as a citation. In Ps. 103.12 we find τὰ πετεινὰ τοῦ οὐρανοῦ κατασκηνώσει. It does not seem to be a true citation. The figure is too common.

The Greek but not the Latin takes ὡς πρόβατα μὴ ἔχοντα ποιμένα in Mk 6.34 as a citation. However, the reference given is to 'Nu 27,17 etc', which shows that the critics did not really consider it a citation but rather the use of a familiar figure of speech. In the LXX of Num. 27.17 we find ὡσεὶ πρόβατα, οἷς οὐκ ἔστιν ποιμήν.

Mk 8.18 has words similar to Jer. 5.21, but the Gospel has the principal verbs in the second person plural and the LXX has them in the third person plural. Perhaps it is an intended echo, but it is not a citation.

The Greek but not the Latin takes Ἠλίαν δεῖ ἐλθεῖν πρῶτον in Mk 9.11 as a citation. Undoubtedly the source of the thought is Mal. 3.22, but the words are not a citation.

ὁ σκώληξ αὐτῶν οὐ τελευτᾷ καὶ τὸ πῦρ οὐρ σβέννυται is taken

---

1. For general treatments of the use of the Old Testament in Mark, see A. Suhl, *Die Funktion der alttestamentlichen Zitate und Anspielungen im Markusevangelium* (Gütersloh: Gerd Mohn, 1965); H. Anderson, 'The Old Testament in Mark's Gospel', in J. Efird (ed.), *The Use of the Old Testament in the New and Other Essays* (W.F. Stinespring Festschrift; Durham, NC: Duke University Press, 1972), pp. 280-309; H.C. Kee, 'The Function of Scriptural Quotations and Allusions in Mark 11–16', in E.E. Ellis and E. Grässer (eds.), *Jesus und Paulus* (Göttingen: Vandenhoeck & Ruprecht, 1975), pp. 165-88; W.S. Vorster, 'The Function and Use of the Old Testament in Mark', *Neot* 14 (1981), pp. 62-72.

2. See C.A. Evans, *To See and Not Perceive: Isaiah 6.9-10 in Early Jewish and Christian Interpretation* (JSOTSup, 64; Sheffield: JSOT Press, 1989), pp. 69-76, 91-99.

as a citation in Mk 9.48. The words are found in Isa. 66.5, but the verbs in the LXX are in the future tense and both nouns are modified by αὐτῶν. The Gospel text is a possible translation of the Hebrew although I would argue that the LXX corresponds better to the Hebrew.

In Mk 10.4 the Latin but not the Greek takes *libellum repudii scribere et dimittere* as a citation. It is not a citation but a generic reference to the way in which Israelite law was interpreted by many.

Most likely, the citations in Mk 10.6b-8a have an introduction because of the mention of Moses and his teaching in the context. ἄρσεν καὶ θῆλυ ἐποίησεν αὐτούς is found in the LXX of Gen. 1.27 (and also Gen. 5.2). The rest of the words are from Gen. 2.24, with the only difference from the LXX being that αὐτοῦ is found after μητέρα in the LXX.

Mk 10.19 contains an enumeration of commandments. There are two differences between the enumeration here and that found in Mt. 19.18-19. Mark adds a further commandment (Μὴ ἀποστερήσῃς) and adds σου after πατέρα. Lk. 18.20 agrees with Mark here, except that it does not have the additional commandment. What was said above applies here and to the Lukan parallel. While the Greek of Mark considers all this an Old Testament citation the Latin does not consider *ne fraudem feceris* such. In Sir. 4.1 the commandment is found.

Mk 11.9b contains essentially Mt. 21.9, but it is fuller by reason of an addition which the editors of the Greek text do not consider an Old Testament citation, 'blessed be the coming kingdom of our father'. Mark also does not have 'to the son of David' in the first part of the hymn. Lk. 19.38 gives the hymn of welcome somewhat differently.

The citation in Mk 12.29-30 is without doubt an intended citation. The parallels in Mt. 22.37-38 and Lk. 10.27 have introductory formulas. Mark does not totally agree with the LXX in its wording; thus the Gospel has διανοίας instead of the δυνάμεως of Deut. 6.3a, 4-5.

In Mk 13.14 βδέλυγμα is taken as a citation. The words are found in Dan. 7.4. While the expression may have originated in Daniel it is highly likely that it had become commonplace in religious speech.

In Mk 13.24b-25 ὁ ἥλιος σκοτισθήσεται, καὶ ἡ σελήνη οὐ δώσει τὸ φέγγος αὐτῆς is quite similar to σκοτισθήσεται τοῦ ἡλίου ἀνατέλλοντος, καὶ ἡ σελήνη οὐ δώσει τὸ φῶς αὐτῆς of Isa. 13.10, but it is not an exact citation. καὶ οἱ ἀστέρες ἔσονται ἐκ τοῦ οὐρανοῦ πίπτοντες, καὶ αἱ δυνάμεις αἱ ἐν τοῖς οὐρανοῖς is similar to πάντα τὰ ἄστρα πεσεῖται of Isa. 34.4; what follows in

Isaiah (ὡς φύλλα ἐξ ἀμπέλου καὶ ὡς πίπτει φύλλα ἀπὸ συκῆς) corresponds in general tenor with the thought of the Gospel here. (Actually the clause is quite similar to Rev. 6.13 whose words the editor did not think were based on the Old Testament!) However, the addition of σαλευθήσονται in Mark (and in the parallel in Matthew) seems to show that a direct quotation was not intended.

In Mk 13.26 τὸν υἱὸν ἀνθρώπου ἐρχόμενον ἐν νεφέλαις and δόξης are considered a citation. The Latin does not consider *gloria* as scripturally based here. In Dan. 7.13 one finds ὁ υἱὸς ἀνθρώπου ἤρχετο and in Dan. 7.12 πᾶσα δόξα αὐτῷ λατρεύουσα. There are certainly echoes of the Old Testament passages, but it does not seem that one should speak of citations in the strictest sense.

In Mk 14.34 the Greek but not the Latin περίλυπός ἐστιν ἡ ψυχή μου and ψυχή are taken as citations. Corresponding words are found in LXX Ps. 41.6, but really one should hold nothing more than that there are similarities of expression.

In Mk 14.62 τὸν υἱὸν τοῦ ἀνθρώπου is found again. The Latin adds to the quotation *videbetis* and *a dextris sedentem Virtutus*. Then both Greek and Latin take as a citation ἐρχόμενον μετὰ τῶν νεφελῶν τοῦ οὐρανοῦ. The full LXX of Dan. 7.13 is ἐθεώρουν ἐν ὁράματι τῆς νυκτὸς καὶ ἰδοὺ ἐπὶ τῶν νεφελῶν τοῦ οὐρανοῦ ὁ υἱὸς ἀνθρώπου ἤρχετο. It is an echo rather than a quotation and the Latin editor's judgment seems better in expanding the Old Testament basis for the words.

What has been said about Mt. 27.35 applies to Mk 15.34. In Mk 15.34 the Hebrew quotation differs slightly from that of Mt. 27.46. Mark's Greek is closer to that of the LXX than is Matthew's, since it has ὁ θεός instead of Matthew's vocative. Mark also has εἰς τί instead of Matthew's ἵνα τί and has μή follow the verb instead of preceding it as in Matthew. It is an intended citation.

Luke[1]

With respect to Lk. 1.15, the Greek takes καὶ οἶνον καὶ σίκερα οὐ μὴ πίῃ as an Old Testament citation. In Num. 6.3 we find καὶ ὄξος

---

1. For general treatments of the use of the Old Testament in Luke, see T. Holtz, *Untersuchungen über die alttestamentlichen Zitate bei Lukas* (Berlin: Akademie Verlag, 1968); H. Ringgren, 'Luke's Use of the Old Testament', *HTR* 79 (1986), pp. 227-35; D.L. Bock, *Proclamation from Prophecy and Pattern: Lucan Old Testament Christology* (JSNTSup, 12; Sheffield: JSOT Press, 1987).

οἴνου καὶ ὄξος ἐκ σίκερα οὐ πίεται. (The editor of the Greek also gives Lev. 10.9 as a reference; this has nothing to do with the matter.) Obviously the words are not a citation.

The Latin takes *ut convertat corda patrum in filios* of Lk. 1.17 as a citation. The expression is close to Mal. 4.6 (LXX 3.23), *ut convertat cor patrum ad filios*, which is close to the LXX's ὅς ἀποκαταστήσει καρδίαν πατρὸς υἱόν. It is at best an echo.

The Latin also takes *non erit impossibile apud omne verbum* as a citation. There is some affinity in meaning with *numquid Deo quidquam est difficile* of Gen. 18.14, but it is scarcely a citation.

The Latin also takes *anima mea Dominum* in Lk. 1.46 as a citation. Only in the broadest sense can it be said to be a reference to the Old Testament. In the next verse it takes *exultant* and *Deo salvatore meo* (which in earlier editions of the Vulgate was *salutari meo*). In Hab. 3.18 we find *in Domino gaudebo et exultabo in Deo meo*. The words are not a citation.

The Latin takes *respexit humilitatem ancillae suae* as a citation in Lk. 1.48. Somewhat similar words are found in 1 Sam. 1.11, *respiciens* and *ancillae*. It is not a citation.

The Latin takes *benedictus Dominus Deus Israel* in Lk. 1.68 as such. The exact words are found in Ps. 41.14. The Greek sees no intended Old Testament reference here. The Gospel text agrees with that of the LXX save for the addition in the Gospel of τοῦ before Ἰσραήλ. It could be an intended citation.

In Lk. 1.76 the Latin takes *ante faciem Domini parare vias eius* as a scriptural reference. In Mal. 3.1 we find *et praeparabit viam ante faciem meam*. It is not a citation.

The Latin of Lk. 1.79 takes *illuminare his, qui in tenebris et in umbra mortis sedent* as a scriptural citation. In Isa. 9.2 there is *qui ambulat in tenebris videt lucem magnam habitantibus in regione umbrae mortis*. It is not a citation, although there is obvious affinity of thought.

Both Greek and Latin take portions of Lk. 7.22 as scriptural; however, they are not in total agreement. They agree with reference to τυφλοὶ ἀναβλέπουσιν, which has some similarity to Isa. 29.18 (ὀφθαλμοὶ τυφλῶν βλέψονται); a citation as such is scarcely intended. The Greek but not the Latin takes κωφοὶ ἀκούουσιν, νεκροὶ ἐγείρονται as a citation. In Isa. 29.18 there is ἀκούσονται...κωφοὶ. Since the order of the words is reversed in the Gospel and the LXX, a citation as such is not intended. The Greek also takes νεκροὶ ἐγείρονται as a citation. Isa.

26.19 has ἀναστήσονται οἱ νεκροί. The idea is the same but the words are not; hence there is not a citation here. The Latin but not the Greek takes *pauperes evangelizantur* as a citation. A possible reference is Isa. 61.1, but Isaiah has *praedicarem captivis*. It is not a citation.

The Latin but not the Greek takes *videntes non videant et audientes non intelligant* in Lk. 8.10 as a citation. The similarity is with Isa. 6.9. While it is not really a citation it seems strange to me that the Greek did not take it as such since the wording is rather similar. LXX Isa. 6.9 reads Ἀκοῇ ἀκούσετε καὶ οὐ μὴ συνῆτε καὶ βλέποντες βλέψετε καὶ οὐ μὴ ἴδητε, while the Gospel has βλέποντες μὴ βλέπωσιν καὶ ἀκούοντες μὴ συνιῶσιν.[1]

The Greek takes Lk. 9.54 (πῦρ καταβῆναι ἀπὸ τοῦ οὐρανοῦ καὶ ἀναλῶσαι αὐτούς) as a citation. The Latin agrees, save for the final pronoun. There are similar words in 2 Kgs 1.10 and 1.12, both of which have καταβήσεται πῦρ ἐκ τοῦ οὐρανοῦ, but both use καταφάγεταί with σε as the object. One can say that the Old Testament story served as a basis for John's words, but there is no direct citation.

The Latin takes *usque in caelum exaltaberis? Usque in infernum demergeris* in Lk. 10.15 as a citation. The Greek does not agree. In Isa. 14.13-15 we find in *coelum conscendam*. There is some similarity but there is no citation.

The Greek takes ὑμῶν αἱ ὀσφύες περιεζωσμέναι in Lk. 12.35 as taken from the Old Testament. In fact, the same words but in a different order are found in Exod. 12.12 (αἱ ὀσφύες ὑμῶν περιεζωσμέναι). While the expression is surely found in the Old Testament, it is scarcely found only there. It is not a citation.

In Lk. 12.53 the Greek takes υἱός, πατρί, θυγάτηρ ἐπὶ τὴν μητέρα and νύμφη ἐπὶ τὴν πενθεράν from the Old Testament. The Latin agrees but also considers the preposition before *patrem* as part of the citation. In Mic. 7.6 such opposition between family members is mentioned but the actual wording is quite different. Thus the verb in the New Testament is διαμερισθήσονται, while in the Old Testament ἀτιμάζει is used with υἱός and ἐπαναστήσεται used with the other subjects. A citation is not intended.

The Greek considers καὶ τὰ πετεινὰ τοῦ οὐρανοῦ κατεσκήνωσεν ἐν τοῖς κλάδοις αὐτοῦ in Lk. 13.19 as a citation. Ps. 113.12 has τὰ

---

1. For discussion of the Latin, see Evans, *To See and Not Perceive*, pp. 148-53; for discussion of the allusion in Luke, see Evans, *To See and Not Perceive,* pp. 115-27.

πετεινὰ τοῦ οὐρανοῦ κατεσκήνωσει. It could be a citation but the idea was—and is—so common that one can doubt this.

In Lk. 13.27 the Greek but not the Latin takes ἀπόστητε ἀπ᾽ ἐμοῦ, πάντες ἐργάται ἀδικίας as a citation. In Ps. 6.9 we find ἀπόστητε ἀπ᾽ ἐμοῦ, πάντες ἐργαζόμενοι τήν ἀνομίας, while in 1 Macc. 3.6 we find πάντες οἱ ἐργάται τῆς ἀνομίας συνεταράχθησαν. The sentiment must have been so common that one cannot argue for a direct citation.

The words εὐλογημένος ὁ ἐρχόμενος ἐν ὀνόματι κυρίου in Lk. 13.35 are taken as a citation. The words are found in Ps. 118.26. It could have been an intended citation, but the expression is rather commonplace. The same can be said in reference to the words found in Lk. 19.38.

Luke 18.20 gives a list of the commandments in a rather unusual order. In accord with Mark the negative used is μή whereas Matthew used οὐ. What has been said in reference to Mt. 19.18-19 and Mk 10.19 applies here.

The words αἱ δυνάμεις τῶν οὐρανῶν in Lk. 21.26 are taken as a citation. The Hebrew of Isa. 34.4 has a similar expression.

In Lk. 21.27 τὸν υἱὸν τοῦ ἀνθρώπου ἐρχόμενον ἐν νεφέλῃ is taken as a citation. In Dan. 7.13 we find ἐπὶ τῶν νεφελῶν τοῦ οὐρανοῦ ὁ υἱὸς ἀνθρώπου ἤρχετο. The expressions are similar.

The Latin takes *Filius hominis sedens a dextris virtutis Dei* in Lk. 22.69 as coming from the Old Testament. In LXX Ps. 109.1 we find no mention of υἱὸς ἀνθρώπου, but we do find κάθου ἐκ δεξιῶν μου. It is obviously not a citation.

In Lk. 22.30 we find the words λέγειν τοῖς ὄρεσιν, πέσετε ἐφ᾽ ἡμᾶς, καὶ τοῖς βουνοῖς, καλύψατε ἡμᾶς. There are similar words in Hos. 10.8 (ἐροῦσιν τοῖς ὄρεσιν καλύψατε ἡμᾶς, καὶ τοῖς βουνοῖς πέσατε ἐφ᾽ ἡμᾶς). Obviously Luke's words here do not constitute a direct citation.

In Lk. 23.34b there are the words διαμεριζόμενοι δὲ τὰ ἱμάτια αὐτοῦ ἔβαλον κλήρους. While it has grammatical differences with Mt. 27.35, it is not much closer to Ps. 22.19.

In Lk. 23.46 we find εἰς χεῖράς σου παρατίθεμαι τὸ μνεῦμά μου. In Ps. 31.6 the same words are found with the verb in the future. This may be an intended citation.

John[1]

In Jn 1.23 the words φωνὴ βοῶντος ἐν τῇ ἐρήμῳ, εὐθύνατε τήν ὁδὸν κυρίου are found. In Isa. 40.3 there is φωνὴ βοῶντος ἐν τῇ ἐρήμῳ ἑτοιμάσατε τὴν ὁδὸν κυρίου. There is certainly a great resemblance and John here could be a translation of the Hebrew.

In Jn 1.51 τὸν οὐρανὸν and καὶ τοὺς ἀγγέλους τοῦ θεοῦ ἀναβαίνοντας καὶ καταβαίνοντας are found. There is no doubt that these are not direct citations, since the story in Genesis 28 refers to Jacob. However, the words could have been intended as an actualization of aspects of the Old Testament story in the life of Jesus. In Hebrew the verbal actions are all expressed by active participles.

In Jn 12.13 we find what is also contained in Mk 11.9 plus, according to the Greek but not the Latin, βασιλεὺς τοῦ Ἰσραήλ, without τοῦ actually found in the Gospel. The expression 'King of Israel' was common in the Old Testament.

In Jn 12.27 the Greek but not the Latin takes ἡ ψυχή μου τετάρακται and σῶσόν με from the Old Testament. In Ps. 6.4 we find ἡ ψυχή μου ἐταράχθη and in Ps. 6.5 σῶσόν με and σῶσον ἡμᾶς in Isa. 37.20. Both expressions would have been too common to warrant calling them scriptural citations.

What has been shown here is that, save where introductory formulas are used, there are few New Testament passages which can be proven to be intended citations from the Old Testament. There is similarity of language at times and almost certainly occasional intended echoes of Old Testament passages. However, these allusions are often as significant for the meaning of the New Testament as are the formal quotations.

---

1. For general treatments of the use of the Old Testament in John, see C.K. Barrett, 'The Old Testament in the Fourth Gospel', *JTS* 48 (1947), pp. 155-69; R. Morgan, 'Fulfillment in the Fourth Gospel', *Int* 11 (1957), pp. 155-65; E.D. Freed, *Old Testament Quotations in the Gospel of John* (NovTSup, 11; Leiden: Brill, 1965); G. Reim, *Studien zum alttestamentlichen Hintergrund des Johannesevangelium* (SNTSMS, 22; Cambridge: Cambridge University Press, 1974); B.D. Schuchard, *Scripture within Scripture: The Interrelationship of Form and Function in the Explicit Old Testament Citations in the Gospel of John* (SBLDS, 133; Atlanta: Scholars Press, 1992).

Part I

JOHN AND JESUS

THE ROLE OF MALACHI IN THE CAREER OF JOHN THE BAPTIST

Jeffrey A. Trumbower

The question has often been raised of the extent to which John the Baptist and Jesus consciously made use of earlier written traditions.[1] We are not even sure of what language(s) they spoke, much less whether either of them was able to read Hebrew, Aramaic or Greek.[2] Echoes of earlier scriptural traditions abound in the surviving accounts of their careers, but these echoes could be solely the result of literate Christian reflection. The purpose of this paper is to make a case for the probability that specific predictions in the text of Malachi, part of the collection known as the 'minor prophets', had a profound influence on the career of the historical John the Baptist. This is not necessarily to claim that John was literate; it is possible that he heard the text expounded by others.[3] Positing John's familiarity with this text, in written or oral form,

---

1. See, for example, B.D. Chilton, *A Galilean Rabbi and His Bible: Jesus' Use of the Interpreted Scripture of his Time* (GNS, 8; Wilmington, DE: Michael Glazier, 1984); R.T. France, *Jesus and the Old Testament: His Application of Old Testament Passages to Himself and his Mission* (Grand Rapids, MI: Baker, 1982).

2. For a discussion of the linguistic picture in Palestine during the first century, see E. Schürer, *The History of the Jewish People in the Age of Jesus Christ (175 B.C.–A.D. 135)* (ed. G. Vermes, F. Millar and M. Black; Edinburgh: T. & T. Clark, rev. edn, 1979), II, pp. 20-28, 74-80.

3. R.A. Horsley ('"Like One of the Prophets of Old": Two Types of Popular Prophets at the time of Jesus', *CBQ* 47 [1985], p. 454) thinks it unlikely that 'oracular prophets' like John the Baptist and Jesus ben Ananias were a product of literate and scholarly groups; rather they were 'clearly a popular phenomenon'. My analysis suggests that Horsley may underestimate the importance of texts in 'popular' circles. Texts such as Josephus, *Apion* 2.17 §175; Philo, *Somn.* 2.127; Acts 13.15 and 15.21 all attest to the fact that the Torah and other sacred books were read weekly in the pre-70 synagogue. See C. Perot, 'The Reading of the Bible in the Ancient Synagogue', in M.J. Mulder (ed.), *Mikra: Text, Translation, Reading and Interpretation of the Hebrew Bible in Ancient Judaism and Early Christianity* (CRINT, 2.2; Assen: Van Gorcum; Philadelphia: Fortress Press, 1988), pp. 137-59.

may help tie together and explain some of the distinctive features of his activities. Of course, later Christians used Malachi and many other texts to interpret and justify John's role in salvation history, but I will attempt to demonstrate that this hermeneutical process began with the Baptist himself. Before turning to John, I will survey some of the evidence for ways in which scriptural traditions provided rationales for concrete action in Second Temple Judaism, with the goal of providing analogous examples that might lead to a deeper understanding of the Baptist.

1. *Texts Used to Spur Concrete Action in Second Temple Judaism*

A number of traditions from Second Temple Judaism witness the importance of textual interpretation in daily life at a variety of social levels, and not just in the legal sphere. In a number of contexts, both eschatological and non-eschatological, ancient texts that had acquired the status of 'scripture' were used to spur action and point the way for decision making. We must keep in mind that the line between eschatologically-focused and non-eschatologically focused action is a thin one; almost everyone thought his or her own time and situation was the crucial one. This was as true of the Maccabees as of John the Baptist. Both expected the intervention of God into history, albeit in different ways.

According to the Hasmonean propagandists who produced 1 Maccabees, Judah the Maccabee and his brothers 'opened the book of the law to inquire into those matters about which the Gentiles consulted the likenesses of their gods' (1 Macc. 3.48); that is, they used the Torah as a source of oracles immediately before equipping themselves for battle. They took courage in their resolve to fight, as Judah said to his men, 'Do not fear their numbers or be afraid when they charge. Remember how our ancestors were saved at the Red Sea, when Pharaoh with his forces pursued them' (1 Macc. 4.8b-9; cf. 2 Macc. 15.8-9). An expectation that God would act decisively again was certainly in view. A similar use of written traditions is seen in Josephus's account of the Jewish revolt of 66 CE, when he reports that 'what more than all else incited [the Jews] to war was an ambiguous oracle, likewise found in their sacred scriptures, to the effect that one from their country would become ruler of the world' (*War* 6.5.4 §312). Here, a text from the past was seen to have contemporary relevance and helped to spur concrete action.

Josephus also gives reports about a number of figures from the first century who appear to have been influenced by biblical prototypes and prophecies. I say 'appear' because it is always possible that Josephus himself is responsible for the connections to earlier biblical patterns, imposing them upon the figures who are the focus of his reports. I shall examine two of these figures in turn: Theudas and Jesus ben Ananias. According to Josephus's account in *Ant.* 20.5.1 §§97-98, not long after the death of Herod Agrippa I in 44 CE, Theudas persuaded a crowd (Acts 5.36 says 'about four hundred men') to take up all their possessions and follow him out to the Jordan River. He promised that at his command the river would be parted and would provide them with easy passage. Fadus sent a squadron of cavalry which killed many of them and took many prisoners. Theudas himself was beheaded and his head was brought to Jerusalem. There are many ambiguities in Josephus's account: for instance, did Theudas and his group stand on the western shore wishing to go miraculously eastward, or had they already crossed at a ford, thereby standing on the eastern shore wishing to gain miraculous entrance into Palestine? Josephus is also silent about the threat perceived by Fadus. Why was he concerned to send cavalry against this group? Josephus does not say that the people were armed. Also, why did they have all their possessions with them? What were they planning to do?[1]

From this extremely sketchy account we must piece together an imaginative reconstruction of the historical Theudas, taking into account what we know of the time in which he lived. Could he have had in mind biblical precedents? There are two places in the Hebrew Bible where a miraculous crossing of the Jordan River is mentioned: Joshua 3 and 4, and 2 Kgs 2.8, 13-14. In Joshua, the Israelites are poised on the eastern shore and they receive miraculous passage westward into the Promised Land. What follows is the conquest of Palestine from its original inhabitants, complete with miraculous aid from God. The 2 Kings episode involves Elijah and Elisha: Elijah touches the Jordan with his mantle and both are able to cross over to the east dry-shod. After Elijah is taken up

---

1. Scholarly speculation about Theudas may be found in a number of places: see P.W. Barnett, 'The Jewish Sign Prophets—AD 40–70: Their Intentions and Origins', *NTS* 27 (1981), pp. 679-97; E.P. Sanders, *Jesus and Judaism* (Philadelphia: Fortress Press, 1985), p. 138; R.A. Horsley and J.S. Hanson, *Bandits, Prophets, and Messiahs: Popular Movements at the Time of Jesus* (San Francisco: Harper & Row, 1985), pp. 164-67; R. Gray, *Prophetic Figures in Late Second Temple Jewish Palestine: The Evidence from Josephus* (Oxford: Oxford University Press, 1993), pp. 114-16.

to heaven, Elisha crosses back over to the west by employing the same technique.

The Joshua story provides a better precedent for Theudas, since both men had a large crowd of followers hoping to cross the river. If we posit that the Joshua account was consciously in Theudas's mind we may begin to resolve some of the ambiguities noted earlier. We may be able to explain why Theudas's followers had their possessions with them: they wanted to be exactly like Joshua's followers who would have had all their possessions with them after the forty-year sojourn from Egypt. We can better explain Fadus's alarm, seeing that he understood quite well the revolutionary political implications of the activities of Theudas and his crowd. We can perhaps begin to understand the aims of the group: they hoped for a re-conquest of Palestine similar to the one accomplished by Joshua. I think that the connection to the Joshua story best explains the details we find in Josephus's account of Theudas. It is also possible that the Elijah traditions played a role in Theudas's thinking, but nothing in Josephus's scanty information allows us to say anything further.

The problem arises, of course, of whether Josephus himself is responsible for painting Theudas in terms of a new but false Joshua. If this is the case, then we have no access to the thinking and actions of the historical Theudas. Several factors lead me away from this conclusion. Josephus's own account of Joshua's crossing the Jordan is very different both from the biblical account and from his narrative about Theudas. Josh. 3.13 and 16, in the MT, the LXX and *Targum Jonathan*, say clearly that the waters of the Jordan coming down from the north stopped completely to allow Joshua and the Israelites to cross over with dry feet. Josephus plays down the miraculous nature of the crossing when he says that 'God promised to make the stream passable by diminishing its volume (μειώσας αὐτοῦ τὸ πλῆθος)' (*Ant.* 5.1.3 §16). This retelling of the biblical story is similar to what Josephus says of Moses' crossing of the Red Sea: he compares it explicitly with a famous 'naturalistic' miracle that happened to Alexander the Great and his men, helping them to defeat the Persians (*Ant.* 2.16.5 §§347-48). In neither case is Josephus sure whether the occurrence was 'by the will of God or by accident' (εἴτε κατὰ βούλησιν θεοῦ εἴτε κατὰ ταὐτόματον). Thus Josephus is not conforming Theudas to his non-miraculous notion of Joshua; it is more likely that Theudas himself was re-enacting the Joshua story as it is found in the book of Joshua and that this is reflected in

Josephus's account. In addition, it is clear that Josephus has a negative evaluation of Theudas and his crowd: he calls Theudas an 'imposter' (γόης) and the actions of the crowd 'folly' (ἀφροσύνη). It is unlikely that Josephus would wish to draw explicit connections between Theudas and the biblical hero Joshua.

If indeed Theudas consciously based his activities on the re-enactment of a biblical narrative, we can say that Scripture was not just the property of scribes, but could also be used to spur action among the masses. The case of Theudas also shows that scriptural traditions were used to inspire confidence in seemingly hopeless causes; that is, if God acted for his people in the past, surely he will act again in the present. The tragic irony is that the Joshua narrative itself is a highly romanticized theological fiction; the living biblical tradition has often been characterized by nostalgia for a past that never was, giving rise to hope for a future that never seems to come.

Another story from Josephus shows an acquaintance with Scripture at an unexpected level of society: the account of the prophet Jesus ben Ananias (*War* 6.5.3 §§300-309). Josephus says that Jesus was a country peasant (τῶν ἰδιωτῶν ἄγροικος) who appeared at the Temple in the year 62 CE with a message of doom. Probably underlying Josephus's account is Jesus' understanding of himself as a new Jeremiah. Like Jeremiah, he was ridiculed and persecuted for his message of doom against the Temple and the city, and, if Josephus can be trusted, he even made use of a refrain found in the book of Jeremiah: 'a voice against the bridegroom and the bride' (Jer. 7.34; 16.9; 25.10; 33.11).[1] Unlike Theudas, who found inspiration in Israel's supposed past triumphs, Jesus found his inspiration in prophetic denunciation; each man, however, thought that an example from the biblical past was occurring again in his own day. Each man consciously based his actions on a particular understanding of that ancient tradition.

A different use of Scripture is found in some of the sectarian documents from Qumran. Much has been written on scriptural interpretation in these texts;[2] here I wish to stress the point that in the Qumran

1. Josephus expresses great sympathy for Jesus; it is clear that Josephus also saw himself as a new Jeremiah, and this may be seen both in how Josephus characterizes his own life and in how he relates the story of Jeremiah. See D. Daube, 'Typology in Josephus', *JJS* 31 (1980), pp. 18-36, esp. pp. 26-27.

2. A summary article with bibliography is provided by M. Fishbane, 'Use, Authority, and Interpretation of Mikra at Qumran', in Mulder (ed.), *Mikra*, pp. 339-77.

pesharim, older texts are used to explain more recent events. The older texts do not so much spur concrete action, as in the cases of Theudas and Jesus ben Ananias, but rather, after dramatic events have taken place, the prophetic texts are understood to have 'predicted' in a hidden way events which have occurred in the life of the sect. In 1QpHab 7.5, it is stated that 'God has made known' to the Teacher of Righteousness 'all the mysteries of the words of his servants the Prophets'. From this insight into the ancient texts, recent events are explained, and the future action of God is predicted, but specific action in the present is not enjoined.

2. *The Case of John the Baptist*

Examining the scant and problematic information about John the Baptist obtained from Josephus, along with the highly tendentious accounts of his career from Christian sources, we can identify a number of points at which biblical texts are used to understand his role in the history of salvation. Isa. 40.3 and Mal. 3.1 are the two most prominent in the Christian texts. The problem is to determine whether John the Baptist himself had those texts or others in mind, or whether their presence is due exclusively to the Christian portrait of John which has molded and shaped him in accord with biblical models. A classic case is John's mode of dress: did he actually dress like the Elijah of 2 Kgs 1.8 in order consciously to imitate that ancient biblical prophet? Did his dress indicate that he was consciously adopting the hairy prophetic mantle as described in Zech. 13.4? Or is it the case that the description of his clothing in Mk 1.6 and Mt. 3.4 was an attempt by Christians to cast John in the mold of Hebrew prophets generally or Elijah specifically?

A number of features in the accounts of John the Baptist, some well known and some not, lead me to conclude that John himself was influenced by the prophecies of the book of Malachi, analogous in some ways to the examples of Theudas *vis à vis* Joshua and Jesus ben Ananias *vis à vis* Jeremiah. The major difference is in the type of text used: Malachi is an explicitly eschatological writing.[1] Theudas took a story from the past and tried to re-enact it as an eschatological event in the present. Jesus ben Ananias took the paradigm of a prophet and pro-

---

1. According to *b. Meg.* 3a, there was a rabbinic tradition that, more so than other books, Haggai, Zechariah and Malachi contained the secrets of God about the eschatological age.

phecy with a specific context in the past and saw it happening again in his own contemporary situation. If I am right, we can say that John took an explicitly eschatological text and thought that its predictions were coming true for the first and only time in his own day. If John's understanding of Scripture was continued by his disciple Jesus of Nazareth and his followers, it may help us to understand why this mode of exegesis was practiced so widely in early Christianity. I am not trying to claim that John was influenced *only* by Malachi, but the echoes of Malachi's vision of the eschaton ring loudly in the surviving accounts of John's career.

Mal. 3.1-3 and 3.19-24 are key texts. They refer to a messenger who prepares the way before Yahweh, a 'lord' (אדון) who will suddenly come into his temple, a messenger of the covenant, the coming fiery day of Yahweh, and the return of Elijah. Many think that the passage about Elijah is a later addition to the original text of Malachi, but we know that it was already there by John's time because the Elijah appendix is present in 4QXII[a], a Qumran scroll of the minor prophets soon to be published by Russell Fuller and dated by him and by Frank Moore Cross to the early Hasmonean period.[1] Bruce Malchow has summarized various proposals about the original meaning of these verses and appendices;[2] here I wish to outline some possibilities for understanding how the texts might have functioned in the career of John the Baptist.

When we look at the Q sermon attributed to John the Baptist, delivered in Luke to 'crowds' and in Matthew to Pharisees and Sadducees, we notice a number of connections to the language of Malachi. Of course, these connections could be due solely to the author(s) of Q, telling us nothing about the historical Baptist. When seen, however, in light of other evidence for Malachi's influence on John (presented below), it appears likely that echoes of the Baptist's original Malachi-inspired message may be found in the Q sermon.[3] John in Q uses the image of fire and burning, presumably both for judgment and for refining:

1.   R. Fuller, 'The Minor Prophets Manuscripts from Qumran, Cave IV' (PhD dissertation, Harvard University, 1988). I wish to thank Dr Fuller for his permission to study this work before its publication.

2.   B. Malchow, 'The Messenger of the Covenant in Mal 3.1', *JBL* 103 (1984), pp. 252-55.

3.   Space does not allow me to enter here into the complex debate about the alleged stratigraphy of Q; see J.S. Kloppenborg, *The Formation of Q: Trajectories in Ancient Wisdom Collections* (Philadelphia: Fortress Press, 1987), pp. 102-107.

You brood of vipers, who told you to flee from the wrath to come? Bear fruit(s) worthy of repentance...Even now the axe is lying at the root of the trees; every tree therefore that does not bear good fruit is cut down and thrown into the fire...I baptize you with water [Matthew adds: for repentance], but one who is more powerful than I is coming after me, whose sandals I am not worthy to untie [Matthew: carry]; he will baptize you with the Holy Spirit and with fire. His winnowing fork is in his hand, to clear his threshing floor, and to gather the wheat into his granary, but the chaff he will burn with unquenchable fire.

A number of well-known exegetical issues have been raised in connection with this sermon. These include (1) the identity of the 'brood of vipers' (Temple officials perhaps; cf. Mal. 3.3); (2) the identity of the 'Coming One' (cf. Mal. 3.1-2); and (3) the function of the second baptism with the Holy Spirit and fire: judgment or purification?[1] In addition to the notion of a 'Coming One', the language of the Q sermon is reminiscent of Malachi in its image of burning with fire—especially Mal. 3.2b-3 and Mal. 3.19-20a which read respectively:

For he [the Coming One] is like a refiner's fire and like fuller's soap; he will sit as a refiner and purifier of silver and he will purify the descendants of Levi and refine them like gold and silver until they present offerings to Yahweh in righteousness.

See the day is coming, burning like an oven, when all the arrogant and all evildoers will be stubble (קַשׁ); the day that comes shall burn them up, says Yahweh of Hosts, so that it will leave them neither root (שֹׁרֶשׁ) nor branch. But for you who revere my name the sun of righteousness shall arise, with healing in its wings.

Needless to say, there are huge methodological problems to consider when one identifies supposed redactional layers in a reconstructed document and then assigns them to various stages in the development of a hypothetical community.

1. These issues and others are discussed in the standard works on John the Baptist: C.H. Kraeling, *John the Baptist* (New York: Charles Scribner's Sons, 1951); J.A.T. Robinson, 'Elijah, John and Jesus: An Essay in Detection', *NTS* 4 (1958), pp. 263-81; W. Wink, *John the Baptist in the Gospel Tradition* (SNTSMS, 7; Cambridge: Cambridge University Press, 1968); J. Becker, *Johannes der Täufer und Jesus von Nazareth* (Neukirchen–Vluyn: Neukirchener Verlag, 1972). Two recent and thorough surveys of the issues are found in J. Ernst, *Johannes der Taüfer: Interpretation—Geschichte—Wirkungsgeschichte* (BZNW, 53; Berlin and New York: de Gruyter, 1989) and R.L. Webb, *John the Baptizer and Prophet: A Socio-Historical Study* (JSNTSup, 62; Sheffield: JSOT Press, 1991).

Fire in these passages serves two purposes: purification *and* judgment; the same is true of the fire imagery in John's Q sermon. In 3.19 the wicked are equated with trees that will be burnt up; I would reiterate John's statements in Q, 'The axe is laid at the root of the trees, every tree therefore that does not bear good fruit is cut down and thrown into the fire'. Isa. 5.24, 33.10-12 and other passages from the prophetic corpus have a similar image of burning roots and leaving stubble for judgment, but only Malachi combines this imagery with talk of a 'Coming One' and with a reference to Elijah.[1]

The Elijah factor is indeed another connection between Malachi and John. According to Mal. 3.24, Elijah comes before the great and terrible day of Yahweh, a role played by Elijah also in Sir. 48.10. In these texts, Elijah himself is neither the fiery judge nor the refiner,[2] but rather he comes *before* the cataclysmic judgment. Therefore, Mal. 3.24 does not identify the messenger of Mal. 3.1b-3 as Elijah, but rather this appendix adds a new character to the eschatological scenario. It is possible that Elijah is to be identified with the preparatory 'messenger' of Mal. 3.1a, but his role is not the same as the judging, purifying 'messenger' of Mal. 3.1b-3. Several aspects of John's career serve to connect him with the Elijah appendix to the book of Malachi and the traditions in Sirach. First, John is supposed to have dressed like Elijah. Secondly, and more importantly, according to the Gospel of John, John the Baptist began his baptizing career in Perea on the eastern side of the Jordan River (clearly in Jn 10.40[3] and also in 1.28, properly understood[4]). According to 2 Kgs

---

1. For more on 'fire' imagery in the prophets, see Becker, *Johannes der Täufer*, p. 28.

2. Pace Robinson, 'Elijah, John and Jesus', p. 265.

3. 𝔓⁶⁶, 𝔓⁷⁵ and most other MSS read πρῶτον ('at first') in Jn 10.40, implying that John began his baptizing on the eastern side of the Jordan. Some other important manuscripts read πρότερον ('previously'). Even the latter reading could refer to the beginning of John's career, especially since the general vicinity is the same as in 1.28, the first verse in the Fourth Gospel to locate spatially John's baptizing.

4. A possible solution to the vexed question of Jn 1.28 is offered by P. Parker, 'Bethany beyond Jordan', *JBL* 74 (1955), pp. 257-61. He reads the verse as follows: 'These things took place in Bethany, which is across from the point of the Jordan where John had been baptizing.' πέραν in 1.28 with an understood 'to be' can mean 'across from', relieving the exegete of having to find an otherwise unknown Bethany (or Bethabara) on the east side of the river. In 10.40 with a verb of motion and εἰς, πέραν clearly means 'to the other side of'. For ancient and modern speculation about the location of sites associated with John the Baptist, see D. Baldi and

2.8, Elijah was taken up to heaven from precisely this spot.[1] Such a connection between Elijah and John the Baptist could be Christian invention, but one important fact suggests otherwise: the only Gospel in which this information is reported, the Fourth Gospel, wishes to deny explicitly that John was Elijah (Jn 1.21). Thus, it is more likely that we have an earlier tradition, not fully appreciated by the author of the Fourth Gospel, which may give us a clue about John the Baptist's own self-understanding: he was somehow Elijah come back to life, dressing like him and beginning his career where Elijah had been taken up to heaven in a whirlwind.

Another piece of evidence arises when we analyze the fact that John baptized people. This action cannot be connected directly with Elijah traditions (cf. 2 Kgs 5.10) or with the book of Malachi, but there may be an indirect connection. Mal. 3.24 states: 'Lo, I [Yahweh] will send you the prophet Elijah before the great and terrible day of the Lord comes. He will turn the hearts of parents to their children and the hearts of children to their parents, so that I will not come and strike the land with destruction (חרם)'. Sir. 48.10 also saw this role for Elijah: 'At the appointed time, it is written, you [Elijah] are destined to calm the wrath of God before it breaks out in fury, to turn the hearts of parents to their children and to restore the tribes of Jacob'. Elijah is not the 'Coming One' who brings the actual judgment; rather, in these traditions, Elijah is to help prepare the people for the coming of God's wrath. In this way, some at least (and perhaps the nation as a whole) will be able to escape the fiery judgment.

This is also the function of the only known parallel to John's eschatological baptism, *Sib. Or.* 4.165. This Jewish text, dating from just after the destruction of the Temple in 70 CE, states:

> Ah, wretched mortals, change these things, and do not lead the great God
> to all sorts of anger, but abandon daggers and groanings, murders and out-
> rages, and wash your whole bodies in perennial rivers. Stretch out your
> hands to heaven and ask forgiveness for your previous deeds and make

B. Bagatti, *Saint Jean-Baptiste dans les souvenirs de sa Patrie* (Studium Biblicum Franciscanus, Collectio Minor, 27; Jerusalem: Franciscan Printing Press, 1980).

1. For this connection I am indebted to J. Murphy-O'Connor, 'John the Baptist and Jesus: History and Hypotheses', *NTS* 36 (1990), p. 360 n. 7. I disagree, however, when Murphy-O'Connor says that John did not think he was Elijah *redivivus*. In my view, John's choice of location is one of the most important factors arguing *for* such a self-consciousness.

propitiation for bitter impiety with words of praise; God will grant repentance and will not destroy. He will stop his wrath again if you all practice
honorable piety in your hearts. But if you do not obey me, evil minded
ones, but love impiety, and receive all these things with evil ears, there will
be fire throughout the whole world.

The function of the baptism in this text is, along with true repentance, to
prevent God from venting his justifiable wrath. This is the same as the
function of Elijah in Mal. 3.24 and Sir. 48.10. In one source we have
baptism and in two others we have Elijah; in all three cases the point is
to prevent God's destruction and calm God's wrath. In the career of
John the Baptist we have a unique combination of Elijah and baptism
together: Elijah returned baptizes in order to stave off God's wrath, at
least for those who are baptized. This idea can be seen in John's Q
question to the brood of vipers: 'Who warned you to flee from the
wrath to come?' (Mt. 3.7 = Lk. 3.7). Somehow the notion was that true
repentance along with John's baptism meant avoiding the wrath. The
idea of an eschatological baptism may have been invented by John; it is
certainly not found in Malachi. It is even possible that the passage from
the *Sibylline Oracles* was influenced by the notions earlier propounded
by John the Baptist. The echo of Malachi is found in that the aim of the
baptism and the repentance is to prevent God's wrath from breaking
out. This was the eschatological role of Elijah in Mal. 3.24 and Sir.
48.10. We should also note that Josephus's account of John stresses his
teaching that true repentance was a necessary prerequisite for baptism
(*Ant.* 18.5.2 §§116-19); this is similar to the idea found in the *Sybilline
Oracles* and in the Q sermon ('Bear fruit[s] worthy of repentance';
Lk. 3.8 = Mt. 3.8).[1]

Faced with this evidence and the evidence from the Fourth Gospel
about John's initial baptizing in Perea, it seems most likely to me that
John saw himself fulfilling the role of Elijah as prophesied in Mal. 3.24
and as described in Sir. 48.10; some later Christian texts (the Gospels of
Mark and Matthew) affirmed this idea by having Jesus state explicitly
that John the Baptist was Elijah (Mk 9.13; Mt. 11.14; cf. Lk. 1.17, 76).
Another Christian text, the Gospel of John, wished to deny this claim,
perhaps because in pre-Christian Jewish tradition Elijah comes before the

1.   This idea is paralleled in 1QS 3.3-9—a wicked person who does not repent is
denied purification by atonement and is denied cleansing with 'purifying waters'. See
W.H. Brownlee, 'John the Baptist in the New Light of Ancient Scrolls', *Int* 9 (1955),
p. 78.

judgment and the end, certainly not before a dying and rising messiah, and thus to allow that John was Elijah made little or no room for Jesus in the history of salvation.[1] John the Baptist likely envisioned a 'Coming One' along the lines of Mal. 3.1-3, but he probably did not foresee a role for Jesus, except perhaps when told about the success of the latter's movement. John is supposed to have sent an inquiry to Jesus, 'Are you the one who is to come, or shall we wait for another?' (Mt. 11.3 = Lk. 7.20). This Q saying does not presuppose any knowledge on John's part of those later Christian traditions wherein John always acknowledges Jesus' superiority (Mt. 3.14; Jn 1.29-36 and 3.28-36). John's query makes sense if the Q author of this saying or the historical John had in mind a version of the 'Coming One' based on Malachi rather than on the later Christian interpretations.

There are still other areas where the echoes of Malachi may be seen in the surviving accounts of John the Baptist. Malachi as a whole clearly attacks corruption in the Jewish Temple establishment; this text would be useful to anyone later who wished to criticize the Temple authorities in Jerusalem. In separate articles, Paul Hollenbach and Craig Evans have pointed out that the accounts of John and Jesus are filled with examples of implicit and not-so-implicit attacks on the Temple establishment of their day.[2] In this way they were standing in firm biblical tradition as represented by Malachi. John's baptism for repentance usurped the traditional role of the priests in mediating God's forgiveness, and we should perhaps take seriously Matthew's notice that John's Q sermon was preached to Pharisees and Sadducees.

In addition, Mal. 2.13-16 is the only place in the Hebrew Bible where

---

1. Although later rabbinic tradition made Elijah the specific forerunner to the messiah, such a notion is not found in Malachi or Sirach. Mk 9.11 only states that Elijah comes 'first'; first before what is not clarified. An Aramaic fragment from Qumran Cave 4, 4QarP, reads:...לכן אשלח לאליה קדם: 'To you shall I send Elijah befo[re...]'. Unfortunately we cannot know before what. This text is discussed in J. Starcky, 'Les quatre étapes du Messianisme a Qumran', *RB* 70 (1963), p. 498. For a summary of the ongoing debate over the relationship between Elijah and the messiah, see J.A. Fitzmyer, 'More About Elijah Coming First', *JBL* 104 (1985), pp. 292-94.

2. P. Hollenbach, 'Social Aspects of John the Baptiser's Preaching Mission in the Context of Palestinian Judaism', *ANRW* 2.19.1 (1979), pp. 850-75; C.A. Evans, 'Jesus' Action in the Temple: Cleansing or Portent of Destruction?', *CBQ* 51 (1989), pp. 237-70.

divorce is criticized, perhaps even prohibited.[1] The text in various versions and recensions is hopelessly corrupt, but most students of Malachi think that the original text did indicate Yahweh's displeasure at the practice of divorce.[2] It is interesting to note in this regard that John the Baptist criticized the marriage of Herod Antipas to Herodias (Mk 6.17-18). No doubt the main problem was that Herodias had been married to Herod's still living half-brother, thereby violating the commands in Lev. 18.16 and 20.21. We must remember, however, that both Herod and Herodias had had to divorce previous spouses in order to marry each other, one of the practices criticized by Mal. 2.13-16. John's disciple Jesus of Nazareth seems to have gone further and prohibited divorce altogether among his followers.

3. *Conclusions*

I think the evidence indicates an appropriation by John of the text of Malachi, perhaps from his own reading of the text or from his having heard it read and interpreted. He saw himself as Elijah, dressing like him and beginning his career at the place where the old prophet had been taken up to heaven. Baptism (perhaps his own novel idea based on the Jewish tradition of periodic cleansings) was a preparation for the imminent judgment, in the hope that at least those who repented and were baptized could avoid the unquenchable fire of God's wrath, ideas which echo Mal. 3.19 and 24. In line with Mal. 3.1-3, John predicted a 'Coming One', either an agent of Yahweh or Yahweh himself. This 'Coming One' (not identical with Elijah) would suddenly come into the Temple, execute judgment and act as a refining fire. The Christians interpreted the 'Coming One' as Jesus of Nazareth, and this idea may go back to Jesus himself (cf. for example his sudden entrance into the Temple in line with Mal. 3.1 [cf. Zech. 14.21]), but it is most likely that John did not accept that Jesus was the one. All of this lends credence to the notion that both John the Baptist and Jesus expected dramatic events which did not occur, similar to the tragic expectations of Theudas.

1.　Two Qumran texts are also critical of the practice of divorce: CD 4.20-21 and 11QTemple 57.17-19. See J.A. Fitzmyer, 'The Matthean Divorce Texts and Some New Palestinian Evidence', *TS* 37 (1976), pp. 197-226. The meaning of Mal. 2.16 (whether it is to be read as pro-divorce or anti-divorce) is debated in *b. Giṭ.* 90b.

2.　See B. Glazier-MacDonald, *Malachi: The Divine Messenger* (SBLDS, 98; Atlanta: Scholars Press, 1987), pp. 113-20.

We have seen that the Maccabees, Theudas, Jesus ben Ananias, Jewish revolutionaries and the sectarians attested to in some of the Dead Sea Scrolls all used Scripture to understand their own times. Some saw events from the biblical past recurring in their own days. Some saw ancient prophecies coming true in their own times. Some consciously did things to help enact or bring about God's new activity in the present based on scriptural paradigms. It should be no surprise, then, that John the Baptist (and no doubt Jesus of Nazareth) did something similar. If we can identify and understand the scriptural traditions most important to them, we can take a step forward in grasping their own self-under-standings as historical individuals caught up in what they saw to be the grand sweep of God's plan for the salvation of the Jewish nation and the world.

JOHN THE BAPTIST'S USE OF SCRIPTURE

James D.G. Dunn

The question seems rarely to have been asked: how did John the Baptist use the Scriptures, in which, presumably, like all Jewish boys, he had been instructed from his youth?[1] It is fairly obvious why the question has not been asked: the traditions regarding the Baptist are so brief, and even then so diverse, as between Q, Mark and John, not to mention Josephus (*Ant.* 18.5.2 §§116-19),[2] that the difficulty of gaining a firm handle on 'the teaching of the Baptist' itself discourages more detailed inquiry. Nevertheless, the Q material is so coherent in itself, and there are sufficient points common to all the Gospel traditions, that we can be fairly confident that a clear and well-rooted memory of the Baptist has been preserved into the written Synoptic tradition.[3] So even if we reword the question, and ask 'How did the earliest Baptist tradition use the Scriptures?', there is a proper and appropriate question to be asked.

It is also true, as we shall see, that there has been considerable sifting of the motifs and themes within Jewish tradition which may have influenced (the record of) the Baptist's preaching. But such discussion has usually been in service of other questions, such as: what was the original form of

---

1. For example, the subject plays only a very minor role in J. Ernst, *Johannes der Täufer* (BZNW, 53; Berlin: de Gruyter, 1989); P.W. Hollenbach, 'John the Baptist', *ABD*, III, pp. 887-99, hardly touches the issue; A.T. Hanson, *The Living Utterances of God: The New Testament Exegesis of the Old* (London: Darton, Longman & Todd, 1983) makes only passing mention of Isa. 40.3; and in D.A. Carson and H.G.M. Williamson (eds.), *It is Written: Scripture Citing Scripture: Essays in Honour of Barnabas Lindars* (Cambridge: Cambridge University Press, 1988), references to John the Baptist are only incidental.

2. On Josephus here, see now J.P. Meier, 'John the Baptist in Josephus: Philology and Exegesis', *JBL* 111 (1992), pp. 225-37.

3. See for example, I.H. Marshall, *Commentary on Luke* (NIGTC; Exeter: Paternoster Press, 1978), p. 138, and discussion in R.L. Webb, *John the Baptizer and Prophet* (JSNTSup, 62; Sheffield: JSOT Press, 1991), ch. 3 and p. 269 n. 14.

the Baptist tradition?[1] Was John influenced by Qumran? Who did the Baptist expect to come after him? And it has been more of a motif exploration through (Jewish) biblical and postbiblical (intertestamental) literature than a study of the Baptist's use of Scripture as such. The question of influence from specific Scriptures has hardly been put.

All this is somewhat surprising since in fact the Baptist tradition, Q material in particular, breathes an intensely scriptural atmosphere. Consequently the question whether the Baptist was influenced by particular Scriptures and what he did with them provides a potentially valuable test case of how Jewish preachers of the late Second Temple period used Scripture. That is not to say or imply that the Baptist was typical of such Jewish use. It is rather to acknowledge that John the Baptist was part of the rich diversity of late Second Temple Judaism and that his presence within that spectrum also tells us something about the spectrum itself.

In the following discussion I shall limit myself to the probably earliest and potentially most fruitful traditions preserved in Q (Mt. 3.7-12 = Lk. 3.7-9, 15-18) and the shared traditions in the introductory material (particularly Mk 1.3 pars).

I

In the introduction to the Baptist's preaching there are two features which cannot escape notice.

Matthew 3.3 = Luke 3.4 (Mark 1.3; John 1.23)
The first is the only explicit scriptural quotation in the Baptist traditions—from Isa. 40.3:

> φωνὴ βοῶντος ἐν τῇ ἐρήμῳ·
> ἑτοιμάσατε τὴν ὁδὸν κυρίου,
> εὐθείας ποιεῖτε τὰς τρίβους αὐτοῦ

As the Synoptic tradition has come down to us, the most obvious explanation is that Mark is the source of the other two, both omitting the misleading insertion of Exod. 23.20 and Mal. 3.1 in Mk 1.2 (the more clearly Christian evaluation of the Baptist—Mt. 11.10 = Lk. 7.27), and Luke extending the Isaiah quotation through to Isa. 40.5, presum-

---

1. My own earlier, more detailed inquiry into the Baptist tradition had this as its primary object; 'Spirit-and-Fire Baptism', *NovT* 14 (1972), pp. 81-92.

ably because of the reference to 'salvation' in Isa. 40.5.[1] Although the evidence of Q material is strong in the rest of the Baptist tradition there is no real indication of such here, and while the possibility of a Q *Vorlage* cannot be excluded (Mt. 11.10 = Lk. 7.27!),[2] it is difficult to reconstruct what a collection of sayings would have contained at this point and how it would have led into Mt. 3.7-10 = Lk. 3.7-9.[3] At the same time we have the alternative version of Jn 1.23, which in its distinctive briefer form is probably independent of the Synoptics, though providing further attestation of Synoptic-like tradition.[4]

The fact that the Synoptic version also uses the LXX, diverging significantly from the MT in the third line ('make straight in the desert a highway for our God'), has also to be weighed. That of itself does not exclude the possibility that there was an Aramaic form of this material derived from memories of the Baptist or from Baptist circles. When such traditions passed into the hands of those whose principal language was Greek it would be understandable if scriptural references were adapted to the more familiar scriptural text. Given the widespread use of Greek within Palestine at the time[5] and the fact that there were not a few Jews (in Jerusalem at least) whose principal language was Greek (Acts 6.1), it is likely that Greek versions of the Baptist traditions were soon circulating in Greek-speaking circles within Palestine, perhaps already within the period of Jesus' ministry.[6]

1. See for example, I.H. Marshall, *Luke, Historian and Theologian* (Exeter: Paternoster Press, 1970), here p. 140.

2. H. Schürmann, *Lukasevangelium* (HTKNT; Freiburg: Herder, 1969), I, p. 160 n. 98; D.C. Allison and W.D. Davies, *The Gospel according to Saint Matthew* (ICC; Edinburgh: T. & T. Clark, 1988), I, p. 294.

3. More confident (perhaps too confident?) is J. Lambrecht, 'John the Baptist and Jesus in Mark 1.1-15: Markan Redaction of Q?', *NTS* 38 (1992), pp. 357-84.

4. In line with the overall findings of C.H. Dodd, *Historical Tradition in the Fourth Gospel* (Cambridge: Cambridge University Press, 1963).

5. M. Hengel, *The 'Hellenization' of Judaea in the First Century after Christ* (London: SCM Press; Philadelphia: Trinity Press International, 1989), particularly chs. 2–3.

6. On the other variation from the MT the evidence is mixed. The MT and Qumran agree in taking 'in the wilderness' with 'prepare the way . . .'. But the Targum and Old Testament Peshitta agree with the Synoptics and the LXX in taking 'in the wilderness' with 'the voice of one crying' (R.H. Gundry, *The Use of the Old Testament in St Matthew's Gospel* [NovTSup, 18; Leiden: Brill, 1967], pp. 9-10). The second line of Jn 1.23 (εὐθύνατε τὴν ὁδὸν κυρίου) seems to be an abbreviated version of the voice's message, but where the abbreviation stemmed from it is now impossible to say.

The most important correlative evidence here, of course, is the quotation of the same passage in 1QS 8.12-14 (alluded to again in 9.19-20) and 4Q176. From this it is clear that the Isaiah passage was formative of the Qumran group's self-understanding:

> And when these become members of the Community in Israel according to all these rules, they shall separate from the habitation of ungodly men and shall go into the wilderness to prepare the way of Him; as it is written, *Prepare in the wilderness the way of...*, *make straight in the desert a path for our God* (1QS 8.12-14 Vermes).

Given the likely proximity of the Baptist and Qumran, it is difficult to dismiss this common appearance of Isa. 40.3 in the traditions of each as wholly coincidental. We do not need to hypothesize that the Baptist had been a member of the Qumran community, though that is certainly possible. It is enough to argue that both were driven to the desert by a similar eschatological expectation and that both (not surprisingly) found in the opening verses of Isaiah 40 inspiration and authority for what they were doing. The distinctive fact that the Baptist went to the wilderness *to preach* at least suggests that Isaiah's talk of a 'voice crying' was a factor in the Baptist's style of eschatological preparation, and may be sufficient to explain how it was that (in the Baptist tradition at least) 'in the wilderness' was linked more naturally with the 'voice crying'.[1]

In the Synoptics the citation does not appear as the spoken words of the Baptist. This suggests that the citation is the evaluation which others made of the Baptist rather than the Baptist's own self-testimony. On the other hand the citation from Isaiah has not been included in the tribute paid by Jesus to the Baptist as recollected in Matthew 11 = Luke 7. And though the self-reference of 1QS 8.12-14 is clear, 4Q176 shows that the alternative pattern of scriptural anthologies allowed Scriptures to be cited without explicit self-reference as simply indicating the well of Scripture from which they drew their inspiration. More directly to the point, Jn 1.23 does have the Baptist using Isa. 40.3 in self-testimony, and this evidence cannot be lightly dismissed, since it is precisely in its Baptist traditions that the Fourth Gospel seems to have strong historical roots and to have been able to draw on traditions unknown to or unused

---

1. Cf. R. Pesch, *Markusevangelium* (HTKNT; Freiburg: Herder, 2nd edn, 1977), I, pp. 77-78. On the influence of Isa. 40.1-5, see K.R. Snodgrass, 'Streams of Tradition Emerging from Isaiah 40.1-5 and their Adaptation in the New Testament', *JSNT* 8 (1980), pp. 24-45.

by the Synoptists.[1] It is quite likely, then, that the association of Isa. 40.3 with the Baptist came down to the first Christians in different forms and that its use by Mark as Christian evaluation of the Baptist is simply the result of Christian editing of earlier tradition.

It is possible to deduce, therefore, that the Baptist had himself been influenced by Isa. 40.3, whether in a derived way through the Qumran community, or in a degree similar to Qumran.[2] We may further hypothesize that this fact was sufficiently well known in his immediate circle and from them it fed directly into Christian evaluation of the Baptist.

Matthew 3.4 = Mark 1.6

The other striking feature of the material introductory to the Q version of the Baptist's preaching as such is the very strong echo of 2 Kgs 1.8 in Mt. 11.4 = Mk 1.6 (cf. Josephus, *Ant.* 9.2.1 §22).

4 Kgdms 1.8	Mk 1.6
καὶ ζώνην δερματίνην	καὶ ζώνην δερματίνην
περιεζωσμένος	περὶ
τὴν ὀσφὺν αὐτοῦ	τὴν ὀσφὺν αὐτοῦ

It can scarcely be doubted that there is a deliberate allusion here. In this case, however, it is hardly possible to trace the allusion back to the Baptist himself with any confidence. It is certainly probable that the Baptist did dress in rough clothing (ἐνδεδυμένος τρίχας καμήλου), as was (and is) typical of those who live in the desert.[3] And he may well have done so in conscious awareness of the tradition which associated 'a hairy mantle (ἐνδύσονται δέρριν τριχίνην)' with the role and status of a prophet (Zech. 13.4).[4] But the particular association of the Baptist with Elijah implied in the echo of 2 Kgs 1.8 is more likely to be a Christian evaluation of the Baptist (Mk 9.11-13 = Mt. 17.10-13; Mt. 11.13-14).[5] On the other hand, the tradition in Jn 1.21 strengthens the likelihood that the coming of Elijah was part of a common eschatological expectation of the time (Mal. 4.5; Mk 6.15 par.; 8.28 pars.) so that such a question put

---

1. Dodd, *Historical Tradition*, pp. 252-53; R.E. Brown, *John* (AB, 29; Garden City, NY: Doubleday, 1966), I, pp. 50-51.

2. Cf. Ernst, *Johannes*, p. 297, though he makes surprisingly little of the Qumran parallel (p. 280 n. 45).

3. Pesch, *Markusevangelium*, p. 81; Allison and Davies, *Matthew*, p. 295; Ernst, *Johannes*, pp. 285-86.

4. So for example, Ernst, *Johannes*, pp. 299-300.

5. See again Ernst, *Johannes*, pp. 284-85.

to a desert prophet ('Are you Elijah?') is entirely conceivable. It remains unclear, however, whether the Baptist's denial ('I am not') is the Baptist's own refusal of the role or a Christian attempt to diminish the role of the Baptist in relation to the Christ (Jn 1.20-27; 3.27-30).[1]

II

When we turn to the record of the Baptist's preaching as such we can divide the most relevant material into two sections, starting with the Q tradition of Mt. 3.7-10 = Lk. 3.7-9. Here we can see at once the strength of the usual motif exploration of the background to or context of John's preaching within Jewish prophetic and apocalyptic tradition, both biblical and postbiblical. For the tone of the passage is thoroughly prophetic-judgmental, and several of its main features can be paralleled immediately or shown to be of a piece with prominent themes in the eschatological reflections present within Second Temple Judaism.

Nothing much can be gleaned from the initial address, γεννήματα ἐχιδνῶν ('brood of vipers'). ἔχιδνα does not occur in the LXX, but it could serve as a variant of ἀσπίς, as Isa. 59.5 (LXX and Aquila) reminds us, and so conjures up such images as Deut. 32.33 and Ps. 140.3. A warning oracle on 'the beasts of the Negeb' speaks of the sand-viper and venomous flying serpent (Isa. 30.6); and the Asp was used as a figure for Belial (Satan) at Qumran (as in 1QH 3.17 and 5.27). Nor does γεννήματα seem to echo any scriptural passage in particular (cf. however, Isa. 14.29 and 57.4),[2] though we may say that a nest of vipers was a natural image for someone who lived much in the desert regions to use (cf. Isa. 11.8). Here talk of scriptural influence may be hard to justify, but we can certainly speak of the prophet coining a vividly powerful metaphor from his immediate environment.

Much more characteristically Jewish is the talk of 'coming wrath'. Although ὀργὴ θεοῦ is not peculiar to Jewish theology, it is a prominent feature thereof. Moreover, most significantly for us here, it is prominent in Jewish prophecy not just as directed against other nations (see for example Isa. 34.2; Jer. 10.25; 50.13; Zech. 1.15), but also as directed against Israel itself, particularly for its failure to live in accordance with

---

1. See particularly W. Wink, *John the Baptist in the Gospel Tradition* (SNTSMS, 7; Cambridge: Cambridge University Press, 1968), ch. 5.

2. Ernst (*Johannes*, pp. 42-43) thinks there may be a reference to the serpent in Gen. 3.1, 4, 13-15.

its covenant obligations and its lapses into idolatry and immorality (see for example Exod. 32.10-12; Num. 25.1-4; Deut. 29.16-28; 2 Chron. 24.18; Isa. 9.18–10.5; Jer. 7.16-20; 25.6; Ezek. 22; Mic. 5.10-15; *Jub.* 15.34; 36.10; 1QS 2.15; 5.12).[1] So too the thought of judgment as eschatological and final is particularly prominent in Jewish thought, not least as a 'day' of wrath (see for example Isa. 13.6-16; 34.8; Dan. 7.9-11; Joel 2.1-2; Zeph. 1.15, 18; 2.2-3; 3.8; Mal. 4.1; *Jub.* 5.10-16; *1 En.* 90.20-27). For eschatological flight in the face of such fearful prospects we may instance Isa. 13.14, 24.18, 30.16-17, Jer. 48.44, Amos 5.19, 9.1 and Obad. 14. In none of these cases can we speak of an immediate parallel or a direct line of influence. But clearly the person who framed this Q material lived and breathed the language of Scripture.

Much the same is true of the rest of this paragraph. It contains a sequence of Semitisms ('making fruit', 'say in yourselves', 'raise up from someone' meaning cause to be born), and there is possibly a Hebrew or Aramaic wordplay in Mt. 3.9 = Lk. 3.8 (אבנים/בנים or אבניא/בניא).[2] 'Fruit' (Mt. 3.8 = Lk. 3.8) as an image of appropriate conduct is fairly universal,[3] but the idea of 'repentance' as moral conversion is thoroughly Jewish (שוב), a prominent feature not least in the Qumran scrolls ('the converts of Israel': CD 4.2; 6.4-5; 8.16; see also for example 1QS 10.20; 1QH 2.9; 14.24; 4QpPs 37 3.1).[4] Again, the idea that the unfruitful tree should be cut down (Mt. 3.10 = Lk. 3.9) sounds like a proverb expressive of age-old rural wisdom (Mt. 7.19; Lk. 13.6-9). But the elaboration of the proverb (axe laid to roots, burnt with fire) provided a powerful image of (final) judgment anticipated in its different elements by the prophets before John. We may instance particularly the oracles of Isa. 10.15-19, 33-34, as well as Jer. 46.22-23, Ezek. 15.1-8, 31.12 and Mal. 4.1.

Within this paragraph as set against the background of Jewish hope and expectation the most striking and innovative feature is the warning against presumption on the basis of descent from Abraham (Mt. 3.9 = Lk. 3.8). But even here we may speak of firm precedents in the warnings

---

1. See particularly J. Fichtner, 'ὀργή', *TDNT*, V, pp. 395-409.
2. For details see M. Black, *An Aramaic Approach to the Gospels and Acts* (Oxford: Clarendon Press, 3rd edn, 1967), pp. 145, 302; Allison and Davies, *Matthew*, pp. 305-308.
3. See BAGD, 'καρπός', para. 2.
4. For the importance of repentance within Jewish theology, see E.P. Sanders, *Paul and Palestinian Judaism* (London: SCM Press, 1977), index 'repentance'.

against abuse of covenant privilege and failure of covenant responsibility as a feature of Jewish covenant theology from Deuteronomy 27–30 onwards. Amos 9.7 is a particularly forceful warning to similar effect.[1] And the factional denunciations, which characterised the different groups within Judaism at the time of the Baptist,[2] amounted in effect to the charge that other Jews had forfeited their covenant standing and inheritance from Abraham by failure to observe the Torah.

In all this it is not possible to identify particular Scriptures which may have influenced the Baptist's proclamation of imminent judgment. At best we might suppose that behind Mt. 3.9 = Lk. 3.8 lies a symbolic contrast between the thought of Abraham as 'the rock from which you were hewn' (Isa. 51.1) and the multitude of rocks and stones which are such a feature of the desert landscape:[3] in contrast to the confidence expressed in Isa. 51.1-3 the possibilities for God to raise up other children of Abraham are as endless as a wilderness of rock and stone. Or if indeed the expectation of a returning Elijah did play any part in the Baptist's self-understanding and preaching we might guess that Mal. 4.1 in particular lies behind Mt. 3.10 = Lk. 3.9.[4] But a fairer assessment would be to speak of variations on scriptural themes, variations which, we may say, in characteristic prophetic fashion reflect the particular concerns and context of the prophet in question.

The final section, Mt. 3.11-12 = Lk. 3.16-18 (Mk 1.7-8; Jn 1.30-33) is the most interesting, particularly because of its talk of baptism and of 'the one coming after me'. If we confine ourselves to the question of possible influence from Scripture, however, we can quickly pass over some of the otherwise fascinating issues. Thus the limits of our inquiry prevent us saying more of John's baptism than that 'baptize, immerse' as a means of purifying would have been familiar enough (2 Kgs 5.14; Sir. 34.25). The importance of ritual purification in Jewish tradition[5] and the increasing archaeological evidence of ritual baths (*mikwaot*), for example, at nearby Qumran and Herod's palace at Jericho,[6] confirm

1. Cf. J. Becker, *Johannes der Täufer und Jesus von Nazareth* (Neukirchen–Vluyn: Neukirchener Verlag, 1972), p. 33.

2. See for example, my 'Pharisees, Sinners and Jesus', in *Jesus, Paul and the Law* (London: SPCK; Louisville, KY: Westminster Press, 1990), pp. 61-88.

3. J. Jeremias, 'λίθος', *TDNT*, IV, p. 271; Marshall, *Luke*, p. 141.

4. So C. Maurer, 'ῥίζα κτλ', *TDNT*, VI, p. 988.

5. See for example Webb, *John the Baptizer*, chs. 4–5.

6. For details, see E.P. Sanders, *Jewish Law from Jesus to the Mishnah*

that a washing ritual would not require a stimulus or authorization from any particular Scripture. That said, however, we cannot ignore the distinctiveness of John's baptism (as indicated by the fact that he was known as 'the Baptist/Baptizer'); and its potent use as a symbol of both judgment and purification must surely be attributed to the Baptist himself.[1]

Much more tangled is the question of who the Baptist might have envisaged 'the one coming after me' (ὁ δὲ ὀπίσω μου ἐρχόμενος) to be.[2] If the phrase itself denotes a particular figure, and not just John's successor, the most obvious possible scriptural influences are twofold. One is Mal. 3.1, taken as a reference to Elijah: '"Behold he is coming [ἰδοὺ ἔρχεται]", says the Lord of hosts'; the thought of Elijah as (the) one who will 'come' is a significant feature of the Synoptic tradition at this point (Mk 9.11-13 = Mt. 17.10-12; Mt. 11.14). The other is Ps. 118.26 taken as a messianic reference: 'Blessed is he who comes [ὁ ἐρχόμενος] in the name of the Lord' (LXX Ps. 117.25); the significance of this Psalms passage in the Synoptic tradition is even more prominent (Mk 11.9 pars.; Mt. 23.39 = Lk. 13.35). In support of a royal messianic interpretation we might note how the sequence of Mt. 3.10-11 is paralleled by the sequence in Isa. 10.33–11.4 (cf. 6.13). The problem here, however, is the further evidence of Mt. 11.3 = Lk. 7.19, that the Baptist had no clear idea of who 'the one coming' was to be, other than as a figure who exercised eschatological judgment.[3] So a search for particular scriptural precedents at this point may be wrong-headed in assuming that 'the one coming' was more clearly delineated in the Baptist's mind.

This leaves us free to focus on the Baptist's description of the coming one's mission. Here motif exploration particularly has tended to obscure the question of whether particular Scriptures were of influence. In particular, it is all too easy to fragment treatment of the Q prediction, 'He will baptize you in holy spirit and fire' (Mt. 3.11 = Lk. 3.16), into

---

(London: SCM Press; Philadelphia: Trinity Press International, 1990), pp. 214-27.

1.   Cf. Becker, *Johannes*, p. 28; Webb, *John the Baptizer*, ch. 6 (conclusion, p. 216).

2.   See discussion for example in Allison and Davies, *Matthew*, pp. 313-14; Webb, *John the Baptizer*, chs. 7–8.

3.   See also Webb, *John the Baptizer*, p. 219 n. 2. On Mt. 11.2-6 = Lk. 7.18-23, see my *Jesus and the Spirit* (London: SCM Press; Philadelphia: Westminster Press, 1975), pp. 55-60.

an analysis of the separate elements—river, רוח/πνεῦμα and fire as instruments or images of judgment.[1] It is also well recognized that precedents for linking two of the three elements can be identified without difficulty—the רוח/πνεῦμα imaged with water metaphors (Isa. 32.15; 44.3; Ezek. 39.29; Joel 2.28-29; *Jub.* 1.23; 1QS 4.21), Isaiah's talk of 'a רוח/πνεῦμα of burning' (Isa. 4.4; see also 29.6 and 66.15), and the powerful apocalyptic vision of a river of fire (Dan. 7.10; 1QH 3.29-32; *1 En.* 14.19; *Sib. Or.* 2.196-97, 203-205, 252-54; 3.54). It is less appreciated, however, that there was already a powerful prophetic oracle which brought all three images together[2]—Isa. 30.27-28:

> Behold, the name of the Lord comes [ἔρχεται] from far away,
> burning with his anger, and in thick rising smoke,
> and his lips are full of indignation [Greek different],
> and his tongue is like a devouring fire
> [καὶ ἡ ὀργὴ τοῦ θυμοῦ ὡς πῦρ ἔδεται];
> his breath is like an overflowing stream [ורוחו כנחל שׁוטף]
> [τὸ πνεῦμα αὐτοῦ ὡς ὕδωρ ἐν φάραγγι σύρον][3]
> that reaches to the neck;
> to sift the nations with the sieve of destruction,
> and to place on the jaws of the peoples a bridle that leads astray
> [Greek again different].

---

1. See for example my 'The Birth of a Metaphor—Baptized in Spirit', *ExpTim* 89 (1977–78), pp. 134-38, 173-75, here pp. 135-36; Marshall, *Luke*, p. 147; Allison and Davies, *Matthew*, pp. 316-17; Ernst, *Johannes*, pp. 305 n. 125 and 307 n. 133; Webb, *John the Baptizer*, pp. 224-27.

2. Webb surprisingly claims that 'wind imagery is [not] linked with water/ ablution imagery' (*John the Baptizer*, p. 225). In my earlier work in this area I had not appreciated the full significance of the Isaiah oracle (30.27-28) (*Baptism in the Holy Spirit* [London: SCM Press, 1970], pp. 11-13), but pointed it out in 'Birth of a Metaphor', p. 136, a point picked up by Allison and Davies (*Matthew*, pp. 316-17). More obvious had been the close parallel of *4 Ezra* 13.10-11—the 'man' of Dan. 7.13 'sent forth from his mouth as it were a stream of fire, and from his lips a flaming breath, and from his tongue he shot forth a storm of sparks. All these mingled together, the stream of fire and the flaming breath and the great storm, and fell on the onrushing multitude which was prepared to fight, and burned them all up...' (C.H.H. Scobie, *John the Baptist* [London: SCM Press, 1964], pp. 68-69)—but this comes from around the end of the first century CE, though it confirms how amenable Jewish apocalyptic thought was to such imagery.

3. The image is of the flash flood that pours down the dry wadis of the desert, overflowing their banks (Hebrew) and carving out new clefts and ravines (Greek).

Given the appositeness of the imagery to a prophet of the desert, reflected already in part also in Qumran thought, and the number of indications in the rest of this paper that Isaiah was a fruitful seedbed of imagery used in the Baptist tradition, it becomes a very attractive hypothesis that the Isaiah oracles, Isa. 30.27-28 in particular, provided a major stimulus to and source for much of the Baptist's emphases and imagery.

Bound up within this complex imagery is the issue of whether the Baptist looked for one to come who would bestow the רוח/πνεῦμα on others. The imagery itself allows this possibility since רוח/πνεῦμα has a range of meanings which can embrace both 'wind' and 'spirit/Spirit', and since the complete image has a redemptive or purgative as well as judgmental character (the 'you' to be thus baptized includes the repentant).[1] I have discussed elsewhere the question of whether there was a Jewish eschatological expectation of one to come who, himself anointed with the Spirit, would anoint others with the Spirit, and concluded that while it is not found in the Jewish Scriptures as such, the association of ideas certainly lies close to hand. We may note the link between one who is anointed with רוח/πνεῦμα and who enacts judgment by means of רוח/πνεῦμα (Isa. 11.1-4). And the Qumran covenanters seem to have been on the verge of making the link in more salvific terms.[2] The key evidence is the Isaiah scroll found in Cave 1 at Qumran which reads at Isa. 52.14-15, 'As many were astonished at him—so did I anoint his face more than man's, and his form beyond that of the sons of men—so shall he *sprinkle* many nations because of himself'. Linked to the allusion to Ezek. 36.25-27 in 1QS 4.21, with its reference to the Spirit under the imagery of the sprinkled water of purification,[3] it is possible that the Qumran covenanters looked for the coming of one who would thus purify with the eschatological Spirit (cf. also CD 2.12).[4] Whatever the precise facts, it does no injustice to the evidence to suggest that the

---

1. See further my *Baptism*, p. 11; *pace* Webb, *John the Baptizer*, pp. 289-95, who argues for two baptisms, one in spirit and one in fire, thus abandoning the Baptist's powerful image of a river of fiery רוח/πνεῦμα.

2. 'Spirit-and-Fire Baptism', pp. 88-91.

3. To the data on p. 90 of 'Spirit-and-Fire Baptism' add now the usage in 11QT 49.18-20 and 50.14-15.

4. Cf. J.A. Fitzmyer, *The Gospel According to Luke I–IX* (AB, 28; Garden City, NY: Doubleday, 1981), p. 474; J. Nolland, *Luke* (WBC, 35a; Dallas: Word Books, 1989), p. 152.

Baptist shared a similar expectation (quite possibly derived from or reflecting Qumran thought). In this case we may conclude that the expectation of the eschatological Spirit's bestowal under water imagery (outpouring/sprinkling) and perhaps Isa. 52.14-15 were particularly significant factors in the Baptist's conceptualization of the ministry of the one to come after him.

Less controversial is the other element of the Baptist's portrayal of the ministry of the one to come—the imagery of winnowing, gathering in the grain and burning up the chaff (Mt. 3.12 = Lk. 3.17).[1] Here we are back to agricultural practices familiar in the hill country above the Jordan and providing self-evident imagery for final restoration and judgment (cf. Jer. 4.11-12). And here again we can speak of scriptural motifs more readily than of influence from any specific texts. As illustration we may instance Ps. 1.4, Isa. 40.24, 41.15-16, Jer. 15.7 and again Mal. 4.1, and particularly noticeable is the positive use of the imagery (restoration) in Isa. 27.12-13 and 30.23-26. Talk of 'unquenchable fire' may echo Isa. 34.10 and 66.24.[2] All this strengthens the suggestion that Isaiah's oracles were of special significance for the Baptist, but the evidence does not encourage the conclusion that there was a more specific reference, with the possible exception of Isa. 66.24.

III

The results are few but relatively clear and not without interest.

1. Our study confirms what was already sufficiently clear: that the tradition of the Baptist's mission and preaching was through and through scriptural, being influenced in both form and content by prophetic emphases and imagery.

2. When we turn to the question of possible direct influence from specific Scriptures an interesting answer has emerged. For in most cases the most obvious specific influence comes from Isaiah, particularly Isa. 30.27-28, 40.3, but possibly also 4.4, 10.15-19, 10.33–11.4, 34.10, 51.1-

---

1.   R.L. Webb ('The Activity of John the Baptist's Expected Figure at the Threshing Floor [Matthew 3.12 = Luke 3.17]', *JSNT* 43 [1991], pp. 103-11, and *John the Baptizer*, pp. 295-300) argues plausibly that what is in view is the cleaning of the threshing floor *after* the winnowing. However, as the following texts indicate, the removal of chaff by wind or by fire are two sides of the same coin, twin aspects of the same process.

2.   Marshall, *Luke*, p. 148; Fitzmyer, *Luke*, p. 475.

3, 52.14-15 and 66.24, with Isaiah prominent among other more diffuse themes and motifs.

3. Given the importance of Isaiah at Qumran (nineteen copies of Isaiah have been found among the Dead Sea Scrolls) and what would appear to be a high degree of correlation between the Baptist and Qumran in their use of Isaiah, our findings must be regarded as strengthening the likelihood of some influence on the Baptist stemming from or mediated through the Qumran community.

4. This also means that it is not possible to draw a hard and fast line (in terms of influence on the Baptist) between scriptural and post-biblical influence. While it is possible to identify a particular scroll (Isaiah) and specific texts which may have exercised major influence on the Baptist, in most cases we have to speak of motifs which run through Scripture and beyond. That is to say, his retreat to a desert ministry notwithstanding, we cannot speak of the Baptist as calling for a return to the primitive Torah purities of the wilderness period of Israel's history ('back to the Bible!'). Rather we have to locate him within a fairly broad prophetic-apocalyptic trajectory extending beyond the Scriptures, presumably influencing other apocalyptic strands but certainly being influenced by such in at least some measure.

5. Equally evident is the Baptist's own creativity, not just in taking up particular scriptural themes and texts, but in the way he developed them. Particularly striking is the manner in which he drew in vivid images from the harshness of his own desert environment—the nest of vipers, the stones of the desert floor, the flash flood spilling over the banks of the wadi, the fiery breath of the desert heat, and the river as metaphor for both judgment and purification. This was a man for whom the environment was a book which spoke about God as much as did the oracles of the prophets.

GENESIS VERSUS DEUTERONOMY?
JESUS ON MARRIAGE AND DIVORCE

A.E. Harvey

An untutored reader of the discussion between Jesus and the Pharisees on divorce (Mk 10.3-12; Mt. 19.2-9) is likely to imagine that the line of argument is fairly straightforward. Challenged to make his own position clear, Jesus asks to be told the relevant provisions in the Mosaic law. Given the apparent permission to divorce implied by Deuteronomy, he responds with two verses of Genesis which may be taken to imply that divorce is contrary to the will of God as revealed in his creation of men and women who become 'one flesh' in marriage. It follows that remarriage after divorce amounts to 'adultery'. Jesus, that is to say, sets one passage of Torah against another. Genesis contradicts Deuteronomy; and Genesis is to be preferred. The fault of the Pharisees was to hold on to the niceties of subsequent Mosaic legislation in preference to the will of God laid down 'in the beginning'.

This straightforward reading gained some scholarly support at a time when the Pharisees were generally characterized as the misguided victims of legalism and casuistry while Jesus proclaimed the grand principles upon which the law was based. 'The letter killeth'—that was the Pharisaic approach—'but the Spirit giveth life'; and it was Jesus who disclosed the 'spirit' of the law. But with the growth, among Christian scholars, of an increasing sympathy for the Pharisaic position (so far as this can be reconstructed) and an increasing respect for the ideals and principles of early rabbinic Judaism, the structure of Jesus' argument with the Pharisees has had to be radically re-assessed. In particular, it has been asked whether *any* Jewish interpreter of Holy Scripture would have pitted one passage of Torah against another. Rabbinic exegetes were of course only too aware of apparent contradictions between different passages in the Bible. But their techniques of interpretation were designed to *resolve* these contradictions: giving precedence to one passage and regarding another as invalid could form no part of a serious approach to divinely inspired writings which also had the force of law. Jesus certainly shared this respect for Scripture as God's word. Are we really to believe that he would have played one text off against another in such a cavalier fashion? Even when it was thought that Jesus placed himself 'above the law' (a view not widely held today[1]), it was hardly to be conceived that he would have believed that the law was actually *wrong*.

Scholars have sought to escape from this quandary in various ways. It is pointed out, for instance, that 'Moses did not command divorce, he permitted it',[2] and that to prohibit something that is legal is not to cancel existing legislation, but merely to make it irrelevant. Alternatively, it is possible to give preference to the Matthaean version of the discussion: this keeps the argument within the limits of the well-known debate between the 'houses' of Hillel and Shammai regarding the permissible grounds of divorce. On this view, Jesus will simply have used Genesis to support the judgment that adultery is the only permissible ground.[3] Or again (still following Matthew rather than Mark), help can be found in the notion of 'concession'. Samuel 'conceded' the institution of kingship to the Israelites even though this was not God's will for them; similarly Jesus could call the Mosaic provision for divorce a 'concession' to Jewish stubbornness, not intended by God 'in the beginning'.[4] It has even been suggested that Jesus (or, more likely, the Evangelist) was following an existing line of interpretation of the Genesis passages, and that he was throwing his weight alongside an existing legal opinion to the effect that there were *no* legitimate grounds for divorce.[5]

1. For recent discussions of this point, see A.E. Harvey, *Jesus and the Constraints of History* (London: Duckworth; Philadelphia: Westminster Press, 1982), pp. 36-65, and E.P. Sanders, *Jesus and Judaism* (London: SCM Press; Philadelphia: Fortress Press, 1985), pp. 245-69. For a Jewish scholarly view, see G. Vermes, *The Religion of Jesus the Jew* (London: SCM Press, 1993), pp. 11-45.

2. Sanders, *Jesus and Judaism*, p. 256.

3. J.D.M. Derrett, *Law in the New Testament* (London: Darton, Longman & Todd, 1970), pp. 377-81.

4. P. Lapide, *The Sermon on the Mount* (Maryknoll, NY: Orbis Books, 1986), p. 67. Cf. CD 5.2: David was permitted to multiply wives despite Deut. 17.17 because Deuteronomy was 'sealed up' until after his time!

5. K. Berger, *Die Gesetzesauslegung Jesu: Ihr historischer Hintergrund im Judentum und im Alten Testament* (WMANT, 40; Neukirchen–Vluyn: Neukirchener

None of these escape routes has found general assent. It continues to be felt that Jesus (or the Evangelist) has treated the biblical texts in an unusual, perhaps unprecedented, way. 'In…these juxtapositions of precepts from the Torah…we have a unique practice unlike anything found in rabbinic custom'[1] is a typical comment. In one sense this is not surprising. Jesus' conclusion from the texts caused amazement at the time; subsequently, it gave the church a notably rigorous marriage discipline. We should not expect to find a precedent or a parallel for his argument. On the other hand, the fact that he (or the Evangelist) based his reasoning on biblical texts implies, at the very least, that the relevance of these texts would have been grasped by his listeners and his method of arguing from them understood. The danger of claiming that Jesus' procedures were 'unique' is that we ascribe to him a form of argument so strange to his contemporaries that they would have been either unable to understand him or unable to see the force of his teaching. In other words, we need to identify the conventions within which he was working before we can measure the degree of his departure from the norm.

There are at least three modes according to which questions of sexual behaviour might have been addressed by someone in Jesus' situation. These are the legal, the sectarian and the moral (or 'wisdom'). Each of these modes would make use of Scripture; but they would do so in different ways. Let us look at each in turn.

Legal

It has often been remarked (though often forgotten by biblical scholars) that laws are not normally passed to *change* social mores but rather to

Verlag, 1972), p. 544. The mass of evidence he presents turns out on examination to be less than convincing. 'The two', added to the MT of Gen. 2.24 in CD, LXX, Samaritan Pentateuch and elsewhere, in the words of J. Dupont (*Mariage et Divorce dans l'Evangile* [Paris: Desclée de Brouwer, 1959], p. 35 n.1) 'favorise le caractère monogamique du mariage: moins clair qu'elle favorise l'indissolubilité'. The search for rabbinic interpretations of Gen. 2.24 in this sense is bound to be fruitless: the rabbis were not looking for support for opinions they did not hold!

1. K.J. Thomas, 'Torah Citations in the Synoptics', *NTS* 24 (1977), pp. 85-96, quotation from p. 88. Cf. R.H. Gundry, *Mark: A Commentary on his Apology for the Cross* (Grand Rapids: Eerdmans, 1993), p. 534: 'the reversal of Moses' law… astonishing in its radicality'.

give proper legal protection to conduct that society already regards as permissible and to identify and punish conduct that society condemns. This was certainly true of rabbinic theory and practice,[1] with the additional constraint that the law, being believed to be of divine origin, was not capable of change or revision: all theoretical activity was devoted to the *interpretation* of existing statutes and the adaptation of old provisions to new circumstances. With respect to divorce, therefore, we should not expect to find lawyers trying to introduce fundamental change. Divorce was fully accepted as a right (for the husband); it was for lawyers to determine how to regulate this right so as to safeguard the natural rights of the wife.[2] There was of course a moral aspect to this. Those who believed (following Mal. 2.14-16) that divorce should be discouraged as much as possible could increase the disincentives by reducing the legitimate grounds of divorce; a man might still divorce on other grounds, but it would cost him the full *ketubah*. But since all legal attention was concentrated on the permissible grounds of divorce and on its consequences, questions of interpretation centred on the only passage in the Torah where these matters are alluded to: Deut. 24.1-4. Genesis 1 and 2 had no immediate relevance, and excited little comment. Gen. 2.24 ('they shall become one flesh') was cited as implying a prohibition of bestiality;[3] and one rabbi is recorded as being of the opinion that the 'one flesh' of Gen. 2.24 should be read in conjunction with Isa. 58.7, 'do not turn away from your own flesh', and obliged him to give financial help to his wife even after he had divorced her and she had married another man![4]

It is inherently improbable that Jesus was concerned to give rulings on legal questions of this kind; and it is significant that in both Mark and Matthew it is the Pharisees, not Jesus, who cite the passage from Deuteronomy. It is true that there are clear signs in Matthew of an attempt to bring Jesus' response within the scope of a halakhic discussion. The phrasing of the Pharisees' question, 'Is it lawful for a man to divorce his

---

1. For an instructive illustration, see the history of Jewish responses to demands for 'handing over' individuals, as told by D. Daube, *Appeasement or Resistance* (Berkeley: University of California Press, 1987), pp. 78-84.

2. Z.W. Falk, *Introduction to Jewish Law of the Second Commonwealth* (AGJU, 11; Leiden: Brill, 1978), II, p. 307.

3. *B. Sanh.* 58a.

4. *Gen. R.* 17.3 (on Gen. 2.19).

wife *for any cause*', appears to refer directly to the debate which we know to have been taking place at the time in Pharisaic circles on the meaning of 'something offensive in her' (Deut. 24.1): what kind of 'offensive' behaviour on the wife's part justified divorce?[1] And the exceptive clause which (in Matthew) qualifies Jesus' reply—'except in the case of unchastity'—could be taken as a contribution to this debate.[2] Nevertheless, in Matthew as in Mark, the emphasis in Jesus' teaching lies on the citations from Genesis, which, for good reason, played no part in rabbinic discussions. The legitimacy of divorce *as such* was not a matter of halakhic concern, and Jesus' teaching on it cannot be construed as a legal opinion intended to influence the judgments of the courts.

Sectarian

If divorce as such, being a recognized institution in Jewish society, was not a matter of debate to those concerned with the interpretation of laws that were deemed to apply to the whole of that society, it could of course be a matter of importance to the leader of a sect. The Jewish sects known to us from Josephus and Philo in some cases accepted a discipline in family and sexual matters that was considerably more rigorous than that of Jewish society as a whole. The Therapeutae obliged their members to total celibacy.[3] The Essenes and the Dead Sea covenanters, though mainly celibate, appear to have had some houses of married members, but made certain regulations which were more severe than normal: the minimum age for marriage was twenty,[4] as opposed to eighteen in the Mishnah (*m. Ab.* 5.21); and marriage between uncle and niece was forbidden on the ground of a specific interpretation of Lev. 18.13.[5] The sect also made a particular criticism of current sexual mores, and condemned 'taking a second wife'—whether polygamously or after divorce is a matter of debate.[6] This last point is particularly significant

---

1. *M. Git.* 9.10.
2. Cf. D.C. Allison and W.D. Davies, *The Gospel according to St Matthew* (ICC; Edinburgh: T. & T. Clark, 1988), p. 532: 'the "exception clause" betrays a halakhic interpretation'.
3. Philo, *Vit. Cont.* 68.
4. 1QSa 1.10-11.
5. CD 5.8-11.
6. CD 4.20–5.2. Cf. G. Vermes, *Post-Biblical Jewish Studies* (SJLA, 8; Leiden:

for our purposes, since the text appealed to is Gen. 1.27 ('male and female created he them'), introduced by the words 'the principle of the creation'. But for the moment we should note that there can be no suggestion that these sectarian disciplines contravened the law. Once again, one does not break the law by *not* doing everything which the law permits. If a sectarian community decides to live in a certain way, it is free to do so as long as it breaks no generally accepted law; and in support of its chosen discipline it may well appeal to texts of no interest to the lawyers of a wider society which accepts no such restraints.

Sectarian legislation of this kind would have been a possible option for Jesus; and the parallel, just noted, with the condemnation of polygamy or divorce in the Damascus Document gives apparent support to the view that this is what he was doing. If so, the Pharisees' question, 'Is it lawful for a man to divorce his wife?', would mean, 'Is it lawful in the community that you are inviting people to join?'. And Jesus' reply to his disciples' concern about the practicability of such a strict discipline could be taken as a warning that by no means everyone should think of joining his sect, but 'only those for whom God has appointed it...let those accept it who can' (Mt. 19.11-12, the case of eunuchs then being not an item of teaching in itself but an illustration of the severity of the requirements for joining the sect[1]). Certainly this is how Jesus' words have been taken by the church, from St Paul onwards: Jesus was laying down a rule to be followed by all who belong to the community he founded. And if this is the case, then we can draw a further analogy with sectarian teaching. It is not a case of contravening or superseding any provision of the Torah. There is no opposition to 'Moses'. It is simply a matter of adopting a tighter discipline than that which is normally held to be permitted. And appropriate biblical texts may be found to support this decision.

Along these lines it is also possible to make good sense of the particular terminology that is employed in Mark. Jesus' question, 'What did Moses command you?', has only one fully appropriate answer: nothing! There is no law either prohibiting or explicitly providing for divorce. But the law does of course take cognizance of the practice of divorce, and

Brill, 1975), pp. 50-56; Sanders, *Jesus and Judaism*, p. 258.

   1.   Accordingly it has been argued that this pericope derives from such a sect, notably by G. Kretschmar, 'Ein Beitrag zur Frage nach dem Ursprung frühchristlicher Askese', *ZTK* 61 (1964), pp. 27-67.

any clause that regulates this practice implies that it is not in itself illegal. The fact that there existed such a regulatory clause fully entitled the Pharisees to reply that 'Moses permitted it'. How is it that Jesus then refers to Moses' 'commandment' (10.5)? There could never be such a thing as a law *compelling* divorce. But the clause referred to, which implied 'permission' to divorce, did of course have the force of law: it made it illegal for a man to remarry his wife after divorcing her (Deut. 24.4). In this sense it was a 'commandment'; and Jesus comments that it was made necessary[1] by people's disobedient obstinacy ('hardness of heart'), presumably because of abuses which the practice of remarriage brought with it.[2] He then goes on to introduce a stricter discipline on the basis of two texts from Genesis.[3]

From a formal point of view, then, Jesus' response is easily comprehensible as the teaching of a sectarian leader. Just as other sectarian groups insisted on a strict code of relationships between the sexes (or even on total separation between them) without any imputation of disregard for the law, and occasionally supported their practice by appeal to passages of Scripture not normally thought to be relevant to the matter, so Jesus may be laying down a rule for his own followers and finding 'support' for it in two verses of Genesis that were normally cited for quite other purposes. But there are two considerations which make it unlikely that this is a correct interpretation.

1. Jesus' formulation of the rule has an unexpected form: 'Whoever divorces his wife and marries another commits adultery against her'. The casuistic structure—whoever does x shall be y—is appropriate for legislation; innumerable clauses of the law have this form. But the purpose of y is to state the penalty which attaches to x. 'Whoever strikes another man and kills him must be put to death' (Exod. 21.12). Jesus

---

1. πρός is normally taken to mean 'in view of'; cf. BDF §239 (8). Gundry (*Mark*, p. 538) prefers the telic use, 'for the purpose of making them hard-hearted'. But this seems contrived.

2. The ground on which it was forbidden was uncleanness contracted by the first husband. But there was presumably a social reason, such as the abuse of loaning one's wife. Cf. Derrett, *Law in the New Testament*, p. 379 and n. 1.

3. In Matthew the terminology is reversed. The Pharisees say 'Why did Moses *command* us to give a bill of divorce', and Jesus replies, 'Moses *permitted* you'. Here it seems that the emphasis is on the necessity of the *get*: Moses (by implication) made a *get* (כט) essential for divorce, which in turn implies that divorce is permissible. Jesus then comments on this 'permission'.

might well have said, 'whoever divorces his wife...must be excluded from the community', or (perhaps) 'must not marry again'. But 'commits adultery' is not legislative language. It belongs in another style of discourse, as we shall see in a moment.

2. Before concluding that in this case Jesus was laying down a disciplinary rule for his followers we have to ask whether it was any part of his purpose to issue such regulations. In other words, was Jesus a sectarian leader? To this the general scholarly consensus replies with a clear negative.[1] Taken as a whole, the teaching of Jesus has a general application, an openness to differing individual responses, a tendency to challenge and inspire rather than to regulate and control, which make it wholly unsuitable for being taken as the rulebook for a closed community.

It is time to consider a third possibility.

Moral

The subject of divorce itself (as opposed to the social and economic consequences of any particular divorce) was of great interest to moral teachers. Given the relative freedom of the husband to divorce his wife—which was considerably greater than that of the wife to divorce her husband[2]—it was left to moralists to add weight to the widely shared sentiment that life-long marriage is the ideal and divorce should be a matter of last resort. For the most part the arguments used were prudential: a good wife is too valuable an advantage to be thrown away lightly,[3] but she can also become so obnoxious that to hold on to her is like allowing 'a leaky cistern to drip' (Sir. 25.25-26) and it may then be wise to divorce. Sometimes, however, the reasoning goes back to first principles. The natural propensity of hyena to prey on dog, or lion on wild ass, explains that of the rich to exploit the poor (Sir. 13.18-19). Similarly, God's having created just one woman to be with the first man

---

1. This is the conclusion of H. Braun's exhaustive study, *Spätjüdischhäretischer and frühchristlicher Radikalismus* (Tübingen: Mohr [Paul Siebeck], 1969).

2. It is inherently probable that a wife had some opportunity for initiating a divorce, even in Jewish law. Cf. Derrett, *Law in the New Testament*, pp. 381-83, 386-88.

3. Prov. 5.18-19; Sir. 36.24 etc.

is a good reason for regarding monogamy as according to his will;[1] and—most significantly for our purpose—the creation narrative is quoted in Tobit (8.6-7) to support a moral view of marriage according to which the wife is to be 'a partner and support' (βοηθὸν στήριγμα). Concentration on the way things were 'in the beginning' as a source of moral enlightenment is common to many cultures. With its strongly international character, the Hebrew wisdom tradition is no exception.[2]

This provides a ready context for Jesus' teaching on divorce. The greater part of Jesus' teaching may certainly be described as moral, rather than legal or sectarian, and in many cases it adopts the forms, and even occasionally the conclusions, of conventional 'wisdom'. There is precedent for an appeal to Genesis in such teaching: the 'one flesh' passage was already used to commend monogamy and to outlaw bestiality, and the creation narrative was used by Tobit (as in Eph. 5.31) to commend the partnership of marriage. It would have been quite in the tradition for Jesus to strengthen his moral line on divorce by appealing to Genesis. For such a purpose it was not required that there be a clear logical progression from the scriptural text to the moral injunction.[3] The union of two beings in a one-flesh relationship was sufficient to suggest that such a union should not be arbitrarily separated. So: no divorce!

The difficulty, of course, is that this is not how Jesus puts it. Instead, he says: 'whoever divorces his wife and remarries commits adultery against her; so too, if she divorces and remarries, she commits adultery'. This sentence has the casuistic form appropriate to law. Whoever does x must expect the consequence y. A string of comparable legal formulations can be found in Num. 35.16-21. 'If anyone strikes his victim with anything made of iron, and he dies, then he is a murderer; the murderer must be put to death. If anyone...he must be put to death.' Such a form was highly appropriate if Jesus was either promulgating legislation (a new interpretation of or supplement to the Torah) or pronouncing a rule to govern his community. But we have seen reason to doubt that he was doing either of these things; and in any case, if it is to be exactly comparable, his teaching needs to be completed: '...commits adultery against her; and the adulterer must be put to death' (Lev. 20.10).

---

1. An argument developed in Ps.-Clem. 13.15.1 (GCS, XLII, p. 200).

2. Berger, *Die Gesetzesauslegung Jesu*, pp. 531-33, 543-45.

3. Cf. D. Daube, *The New Testament and Rabbinic Judaism* (London: Athlone Press, 1956), p. 77: 'there is no need to be so exact in a matter of *haggadah*'.

In its present form, it lacks a statement of the consequences of the act. These of course are there by implication. If the argument is accepted that this form of conduct amounts to adultery, then any instance of it will incur the death penalty. But to complete Jesus' statement in this way sharpens the question: did Jesus really intend to legislate, either for his nation or for his own community? Are we forced by the *form* of his teaching to draw this conclusion?

It is true that the legal or casuistic form (whoever does x incurs y) is typically at home in law codes and community rules.[1] But there is another use of it, infrequent but well established, which belongs in another sphere altogether, that of moral teaching.[2] Moral instruction, of course, usually takes a quite different form: that of a maxim ('A wise son makes a glad father', Prov. 10.1) or of a command ('Listen to your father who begot you', Prov. 23.22). But occasionally a moralist might sharpen the point of his teaching by adopting a pseudo-legal casuistic form. A famous example is in *m. Ab.* 1.5: 'Whoever talks much with a woman...will inherit Gehenna'. Here the form is impeccably legal: whoever does x will incur penalty y. But the content makes it clear that this is not something that could ever occur in a code of law. No human court could ever convict on such a charge or impose such a penalty. It is the moralist, not the lawyer, who is speaking; he is using the casuistic form simply to give solemnity to his teaching and draw attention in a pointed way to the serious consequences which may follow from apparently trivial acts. An exactly similar form of teaching is ascribed to Jesus in the Sermon on the Mount: 'Whoever is angry with his brother shall be liable to judgment...whoever says, "you fool", shall be liable to fiery Gehenna' (Mt. 5.22). Again, no human court could entertain a charge on the basis of a mere angry word or would be competent to impose an eternal penalty. The voice is that, not of a lawyer or disciplinarian, but of a moral teacher.

It is characteristic of this form of teaching that it makes its point by exaggeration: 'He who sends a message by the hand of a fool cuts off his own feet' (Prov. 26.6). This again is characteristic of Jesus, and is illustrated by the next of the 'antitheses' in the Sermon on the Mount:

1. For example 1QS 6.24-27.

2. I have developed this argument in more detail in *Strenuous Commands: The Ethic of Jesus* (London: SCM Press; Philadelphia: Trinity Press International, 1990), pp. 76-89.

'Anyone who looks on a woman with a lustful eye has already committed adultery with her in his heart' (Mt. 5.28). This has the same casuistic form: it points to the seriousness of what is often thought to be a trivial act by exaggerating the consequences; and in this case it betrays the speaker as a moralist, not a lawyer, by adding the words 'in his heart'.

This is the series to which Matthew has assigned Jesus' saying to the effect that divorce amounts to adultery. Its form in Matthew (with the exceptive clause 'except in the case of unchastity') appears to have been influenced by the Matthean presentation of Jesus' discussion with the Pharisees on the subject as an exercise in halakhic definition: on what grounds is divorce permitted? But the fact that it could be felt to run easily alongside two *moral* teachings in pseudo-legal form suggests that we may do well to take it in the same way as the rest of the series. If moreover we have well-grounded doubts whether Jesus ever intended to give halakhic rulings or lay down a code of discipline, we must surely take seriously the possibility that the saying is a *moral* injunction, cast in pseudo-legal form and expressed with a characteristic touch of exaggeration. As such, it is neither an instance of opposition to the law of Moses (for moral teaching is not expected to be identical with law) nor a basis for the rigorous sectarian discipline which some churches have built upon it.[1]

1. I have followed up this implication in two articles in *Theology* 96 (1993), pp. 364-72, 461-68.

THE FUNCTION OF MALACHI 3.1 IN MATTHEW 11.10:
KINGDOM REALITY AS THE HERMENEUTIC OF JESUS

James B. DeYoung

Introduction

Jesus' use of Mal. 3.1 in Mt. 11.10[1] has significant implications for Christian interpretation of Scripture; it is the use of the Old Testament in the New which is the most crucial determiner for solving what is

1. The critical discussion about Mt. 11.10 and its context shows considerable variation. R. Bultmann (*History of the Synoptic Problem* [trans. J. Marsh; New York: Harper & Row, 1968], p. 126) suggests that Mt. 11.2-6 is an independent tradition and that vv. 5-6 may indeed come from Jesus since they lack a 'Christian ring' and no Jewish origin can be conceived (p. 151). To this, various Q sayings about John are added (vv. 7-11, 16-19), along with Matthew's saying (vv. 12-15), all to regulate the conflicting attitudes toward John in the Christian community (pp. 164-65; so also M. Dibelius, *From Tradition to Gospel* [trans. B.L. Woolf; London: Nicholson & Watson; New York: Charles Scribner's Sons, 1934], p. 244). Bultmann allows that 11.7-11a may be a genuine saying of Jesus, while v. 11b may be a Christian addition found early in Q.

More recent criticism is undecided on the issue. K. Stendahl (*The School of St Matthew* [Uppsala: Almqvist & Wiksell, 1954], p. 50), in reviewing the matter of sources, believes that it is difficult to characterize the formula as either Synoptic, Matthean, Lukan or of Q type. More recently, D.M. Smith ('The Use of the Old Testament in the New', in J. Efird [ed.], *The Use of the Old Testament in the New and Other Essays* [W.F. Stinespring Festschrift; Durham, NC: Duke University Press, 1972], pp. 20-25) weighs the support for Jesus versus the early Christian church as the source and leaves it unresolved. See also B.D. Chilton, *God in Strength: Jesus' Announcement of the Kingdom* (Freistadt: F. Plochl, 1979), pp. 203-30, for a discussion of proposed redaction of Mt. 11.12-13.

The quotation of Mal. 3.1 in 11.10 comes within that passage (vv. 7-11a) which even Bultmann allowed to be a possibly genuine saying of Jesus. The introductory formula is unique. I believe that this feature of dissimilarity and the indecision regarding sources (so Smith above) leaves the option of the words being Jesus' own as more viable than others.

probably the number one problem of hermeneutical studies. That problem is how to bridge the gap from the first century to the present one. This is also closely related to what one scholar has called 'the core of the most fundamental problem of biblical theology': the distinction 'between what a text meant and what a text means',[1] and variously expressed as the distinction between meaning and significance,[2] or between what is descriptive and what is normative, or as the question of whether a text has more than one meaning.

A solution to the hermeneutical problem will enable us to do better biblical and systematic theology. As G.K. Beale has written, this problem has a bearing on theology and theological method, 'since the use of the Old Testament in the New Testament is the key to the theological relation of the testaments'.[3] Hence, hermeneutics, exegesis and theology are all involved. Jesus' citation of Mal. 3.1 in Mt. 11.10, with its unique characteristics of form and content, clearly raises the problem of hermeneutics, although many other instances could also serve to highlight the issue.

The Problem of Jesus' Use of Malachi 3.1 in Matthew 11.10

New Testament Context
Matthew 11 begins with the second of the five instances of the formula

---

1.   G.F. Hasel, 'The Relationship between Biblical Theology and Systematic Theology', *Trinity Journal* NS 5 (1984), p. 117. This emphasizes that 'what is at issue' is precisely how exegetical study is related to doing theology' (D.H. Kelsey, *The Uses of Scripture in Recent Theology* [Philadelphia: Fortress Press, 1975], pp. 202-203 n. 18, cited in Hasel, 'Biblical Theology and Systematic Theology', p. 118). Hasel designates this also as the distinction between the descriptive and the normative and cites criticisms of this distinction (pp. 116-19). See also W. Kaiser, *The Uses of the Old Testament in the New* (Chicago: Moody Press, 1985), pp. 1, 145-47, 207, 211, 217. Cf. B.W. Anderson (ed.), *The Old Testament and Christian Faith: A Theological Discussion* (New York: Harper & Row, 1963), p. 1, who says that on the question of the relation of the Old Testament to the New 'hangs the meaning of the Christian faith'. B. Chilton (*A Galilean Rabbi and his Bible* [GNS, 8; Wilmington, DE: Michael Glazier, 1984], pp. 186-98) points to Jesus' use of the Old Testament as strategic for our hermeneutic.

2.   E.D. Hirsch, *Validity in Interpretation* (New Haven: Yale University Press, 1957), p. 8. See Kaiser, *Uses*, pp. 218-20, for application of the distinction to the use of the Old Testament in the New.

3.   G.K. Beale, 'Did Jesus and His Followers Preach the Right Doctrine from the Wrong Texts?', *Themelios* 14 (April 1989), p. 94.

which concludes each section of the Gospel: 'and it came to pass when Jesus had completed...' (καὶ ἐγένετο ὅτε ἐτέλεσεν ὁ 'Ιησοῦς; cf. 7.28; 13.53; 19.1; 26.1). In chs. 8–10 Jesus is presented as the messiah of Israel by virtue of his miraculous works. Chapters 11–13 are meant to explain the rejection of the messianic kingdom by Israel. In 11.2-19 the question from John the Baptist provides opportunity for Jesus to vindicate John's ministry and show its relationship to the kingdom. In 11.20-24 Jesus pronounces judgment on those cities which had witnessed his miracles yet refused to repent. In 11.25-30 Jesus turns his appeal from the nation to the individual who is invited to come to him and take his yoke.

In the section regarding John the Baptist (11.2-19) Jesus first answers John by pointing to the works which validate him (11.2-6). Then he describes the unique place that John holds among the prophets (11.7-15). Finally Jesus describes the response of that generation to John and Jesus (11.16-19).

Clearly there is emphasis on the kingdom here. John has heard about the works of the messiah[1] and asks if Jesus is 'the coming one'.[2] Jesus in his answer alludes to several Old Testament passages regarding the work of the messiah (Isa. 35.5-6; 42.18; 61.1).

The question from John gives occasion for Jesus to comment on John and his role in the kingdom. The people had gone into the desert to see a prophet. Yet he is much more than a prophet—he is the forerunner of the 'coming one' prophesied in Mal. 3.1 (Mt. 11.10). Jesus' own assessment is that there is none greater than John the Baptist, 'yet he who is least in the kingdom of heaven is greater than he'. This paradox of v. 11 suggests that with the arrival of the kingdom, the least person in the kingdom would experience greater benefits or privileges or power than John.

Jesus' assessment of John's greatness is based upon the advancing of the kingdom[3] (v. 12); the fact that 'all the Prophets and the Law

---

1.   This reading appears best among the possibilities ('Christ'; 'Jesus'; or 'our Lord').

2.   ὁ ἐρχόμενος is a messianic title; cf. Ps. 118.26; Dan. 7.13; Mal. 3.1-2; Mt. 3.11; Mk 11.9; Lk. 13.35, 19.38; Jn 1.15, 27, 6.14; Acts 19.4; Heb. 10.37; Rev. 1.4, 8.

3.   The exact force of βιάζεται and βιασταί is debated. It may be passive ('is stormed' positively by the people or 'advanced forcefully' by John and Jesus); or it may be middle (positively, 'forcefully advances' [NIV], or negatively, 'suffers violence'

prophesied until John' (v. 13), so that John begins the era of fulfillment;[1] and the fact that, if the people are willing to accept it, he is 'the Elijah who was to come' (v. 14). The scope of John's ministry is only limited by their response. The wise person should take care to listen correctly (v. 15).

Old Testament Context

Malachi sets forth God's call to the people of Israel to return to the God who has loved them. The Israelites, especially the priests (1.6–2.9), have profaned the covenant of Levi and lived corruptly (2.10-16). By their actions the people of Israel confessed that Yahweh rewards the evil as good and that the God of justice does not exist (2.17). Mal. 3.1 is an answer to this wrong attitude.

Mal. 3.1–4.6 is the prophetic oracle intended to answer this evil attitude by proclaiming that judgment will come suddenly and swiftly. Yahweh will come, preceded by his messenger (3.1). Yahweh will first purify the Levites (3.2-4) and then others who do wickedly (3.5). He does not change and will keep his covenant with their forebears (3.6). Those who are wicked (3.7-15) will be distinguished from the righteous (3.16-18). The former are under a curse for robbing God; the latter will be spared because they fear and serve him. The day of judgment and reward is coming (4.1-4), preceded by the prophet Elijah (4.5).

Mal. 3.1 demonstrates the use of the Old Testament in the Old Testament. The first words are similar to Exod. 23.20-24, where Yahweh promises to send his angel before Israel to bring them to the place he has prepared. The angel has the name of Yahweh in him and has the authority of Yahweh to bring judgment on the inhabitants of the land. The point of Mal. 3.1 is that now a messenger of judgment will come to Israel before Yahweh comes to set up his kingdom.

The second phrase of Mal. 3.1 reflects another earlier promise, Isa. 40.3: 'A voice is calling, "Clear the way for the LORD in the wilderness; Make smooth in the desert a highway for our God"'. The announcement of this messenger rests upon the prophecy in Isaiah, as the

---

[NRSV, NASB?] by the people). It seems best to take it as middle.

1. This is a point that Matthew reporting Jesus wishes to emphasize—that John is in the era of fulfillment, not in the time of prophecy—so he uses a preposition for 'until' differing from the one that Luke uses. See R.H. Gundry, *Matthew: A Commentary on his Literary and Theological Art* (Grand Rapids: Eerdmans, 1982), p. 210.

expression וּפִנָּה־דַרְךָ, which is borrowed from the passage, clearly shows. The person whose voice Isaiah heard calling to make the way of Yahweh in the desert, that the glory of the Yahweh might be revealed to all flesh, is here described as מַלְאָךְ, whom Yahweh will send before him, that is, before his coming.[1]

In Isaiah the message is one of comfort; the sin of Israel has been paid for, Yahweh is coming, and his glory will be revealed (40.1-5). As Sovereign Yahweh will rule over all nations (vv. 10, 15-24) and tend his flock as a shepherd (v. 11). The emphasis on the kingdom is again clearly seen.

Textual Considerations

The textual variations between the New Testament and the Old Testament via both the Masoretic Text (MT) and the Septuagint (LXX) lay the foundation on which hermeneutical considerations will be made. In summary we can say that the quotation in Mt. 11.10 is closer to the MT of Mal. 3.1 than to the LXX due to the New Testament's use of κατασκεύσει rather than the LXX reading of ἐπιβλέψεται. This represents either an error on the part of the LXX or a different tradition regarding the pointing of פנה, taking it as a *qal* rather than a *piel* as in the MT.[2]

When we compare the LXX and the New Testament, we find three differences: (1) the LXX uses ἐξαποστέλλω while the New Testament has ἀποστέλλω; (2) the LXX lacks the article τήν before ὁδόν, which the New Testament supplies; (3) the LXX has πρὸ προσώπου while the New Testament has ἔμπροσθεν. These changes have little significance.

When we compare the Hebrew MT with the LXX and the New Testament, we find that the remaining differences show that the LXX and MT are in agreement against the New Testament: (1) the phrase πρὸ προσώπου μου is added to the end of the first clause in Matthew; (2) the second clause in Matthew begins with ὅς rather than with καί; (3) Matthew adds the personal pronoun σου after ὁδόν; (4) the final σου in Matthew represents a change from the first person μου in the LXX and MT. Again these changes are without *grammatical* significance. Since Jesus apparently cites the Hebrew rather than the LXX, πρὸ προσώπου

---

1. C.F. Keil, *The Twelve Minor Prophets* (Grand Rapids: Eerdmans, n.d.), II, p. 457.

2. See G.L. Archer and G.C. Chirichigno, *Old Testament Quotations in the New Testament* (Chicago: Moody Press, 1983), pp. 164-65.

σου is the only real grammatical difference between the texts.

However, some of these changes may have significance for hermeneutical or theological reasons. The LXX of Exod. 23.20 (except for its initial καί) is exactly the same as the first clause of Mt. 11.10. This leads R.H. Gundry to conclude that Jesus is citing Exod. 23.20, and using ὅς in place of καί as a literary device to connect the quotes from both Exodus 23 and Mal. 3.1.[1]

This could mean that Jesus may have deliberately pointed to himself as the angel sent before Israel in the desert. Yet the problem of whether Jesus is citing Exodus is, in the end, not necessary to resolve, for it seems that Malachi at least alludes to Exodus; so Jesus alludes to Exodus through Malachi. In a sense this means that the first and second 'messengers' of Mal. 3.1 have much in common.

There is some evidence that the texts of Mal. 3.1 and Exod. 23.20 were brought together in rabbinic exegesis. The homiletic literature on Exod. 23.20 shows that the sermon was given on Mal. 3.1-8, 23-24.[2]

Finally there is hermeneutical and theological significance for the uses (three times) of σου in Mt. 11.10: the first two are added (if the quotation is based on Malachi alone); the last represents a change from μου. Thereby Jesus not only changes the text of Malachi from an address about the messiah into an address to him, but also emphasizes the point. In so doing he identifies the messiah with Yahweh, as Exod. 23.20-23 identifies the 'angel' with Yahweh.

Hermeneutical Considerations

The introductory formula, οὗτός ἐστιν περὶ οὗ γέγραπται, occurs only here and in the parallel, Lk. 7.27 (cf. γέγραπται περί in Mt. 26.24). This stresses the significance that the statement has for Jesus. More particularly it stresses the important place of John in prophecy. He is no ordinary prophet in God's kingdom. Indeed, Jesus claims that if Israel would accept this prophecy about John, the kingdom would apparently come and John would be 'the Elijah who was to come' (Mt. 11.14). So Jesus links John to Elijah; he brings Mal. 3.1 and 4.5 together. He reinforces this after the events which occurred on the Mount of Transfiguration where Moses and Elijah appeared with Jesus as he was

---

1. R.H. Gundry, *The Use of the Old Testament in St Matthew's Gospel* (NovTSup, 18; Leiden: Brill, 1967), pp. 11-12.

2. Stendahl, *School*, p. 50. This fusion of texts may point to an Aramaic version used in the synagogues, according to Stendahl.

transfigured. Jesus tells the three apostles that 'Elijah has already come' (Mt. 17.12). The disciples 'understood that he was talking to them about John the Baptist' (17.13). Yet John clearly did not see himself as Elijah. When directly asked if he was, he said 'No' (Jn 1.21). The Pharisees believed his statement (1.25). Thus the Synoptics and John seem to be in contradiction.

So there are two problems.[1] First, why does Jesus make the changes from the first-person pronoun in Mal. 3.1 to the second person pronoun in Mt. 11.10? Secondly, why does he identify the messenger with John the Baptist? The first question concerns Jesus' identification; the second concerns John's.

Part of the resolution depends on the identification of the persons intended in Mal. 3.1. Are there two persons in addition to Yahweh ('I'): the messenger, and 'the Lord' expanded epexegetically by the *waw* as 'Messenger of the covenant'? Or are there three: the messenger, the Lord and the 'messenger of the covenant'?

It seems that there are just two persons: the 'Lord' and the 'messenger of the covenant' are one and the same person. Clearly the

---

1.   There is a prior question, however, which needs to be addressed, for it affects our understanding of Jesus' hermeneutic. It is whether there is any Jewish basis at all in the first century for the belief that Elijah's coming is connected with the coming of the messiah. Some, including M.M. Faierstein and J.H. Hughes, have denied such a connection so that Jesus would be the originator of such a belief; cf. M.M. Faierstein, 'Why do the Scribes Say that Elijah Must Come First?', *JBL* 100 (1981), p. 86; J.H. Hughes, 'John the Baptist: The Forerunner of God Himself', *NovT* 14 (1972), p. 212; both cited in Kaiser, *Uses*, p. 78 n.2. It is sufficient to note here that such a view overlooks Mal. 3.1; 4.4-5 itself, the repeated New Testament allusions reporting current Jewish expectations, possible reference in a Qumran fragment, eighteen rabbinic texts L. Ginzberg analyzed which suggest such a connection (cf. L. Ginzberg, *An Unknown Jewish Sect* [New York: Jewish Theological Seminary, 1976], p. 212; cited in Kaiser, *Uses*, p. 19 n. 4) and modern Judaism's celebration of a cup and seat reserved for Elijah at every Passover. Kaiser (*Uses*) marshalls these supports. In addition, D.C. Allison ('Elijah Must Come First', *JBL* 103 [1984], pp. 256-58) gives five additional reasons for holding to the traditional view rather than following Faierstein, J.A.T. Robinson, J.A. Fitzmyer and J.L. Martyn. He shows how the Elijah of Mal. 4.5-6 can logically be linked to 3.1 and cautions against arguing from silence.

The Mishnah anticipates a return of Elijah in *m. Šeq.* 2.5; *m. B. Meṣ.* 1.8; 3.4, 5; *m. 'Ed.* 8.7; while in *m. Soṭ.* 9.15 the resurrection of the dead comes through Elijah. In light of this and the above there appears to be strong support for the traditional view that the New Testament represents contemporary Jewish belief and practice rather than creating something new.

'Lord' is divine; he is the one described as 'the Lord you are seeking', which answers to Mal. 2.17: 'Where is the God of justice'? Also he is said to 'come to *his* temple', which must be Yahweh's (Zech. 1.16). The last title, 'Messenger [or Angel] of the covenant', is unique in Scripture but reminiscent of Exod. 3.6, 14.19 and especially 23.20. This angel is Yahweh himself, the preincarnate Christ (cf. Exod. 33.15; Isa. 63.9). The covenant must be the New Covenant (Jer. 31.31-34). Hence, the 'Lord' and 'the Messenger of the covenant' are titles for one, divine person.[1] He is also related to Yahweh.

Possible Solutions to the Problem

Various methods have been practiced in interpreting Jesus' use of Mal. 3.1, 4.5 and the New Testament's use of the Old Testament in general.[2] I will now explore some of these briefly.

The Literal Method

The Old Testament quotations in the New generally have the same normal meanings as they did in their original contexts. They are in line with historical, authorial intent. W. Kaiser's view is an example of what is commonly understood as the literal method, namely that meaning is

---

1. B.V. Malchow ('The Messenger of the Covenant in Mal. 3.1', *JBL* 103 [1984], pp. 252-55) argues that there are four persons. He makes the fourth to be a priestly messenger, one of two messiahs. This is based on an alteration of Zech. 4.11-14; 6.9-14 and on reading Onias II as 'the prince of the covenant' in Dan. 11.22, and called a 'messiah' in Dan. 9.26. Hence, 'messenger of the covenant' is an interpolation made after the writing of Daniel in 165 BCE. Yet such textual additions have no support in the manuscript evidence and seem to rest on higher critical presuppositions.

2. There is little uniformity in nomenclature here. I have taken the first five as more or less universally recognized structural models, and then grouped all the remaining motifs or concepts under 'theological methods', loosely defined to include any concept serving as a theme or method that may lead to such a concept, even though this is not entirely satisfactory. See J. Weir, 'Analogous Fulfillment: The Use of the Old Testament in the New', *Perspectives in Religious Studies* 9 (1982), pp. 67-69; R.N. Longenecker, *Biblical Exegesis in the Apostolic Period* (Grand Rapids: Eerdmans, 1975), pp. 28-50, who posits the literal, *pesher*, midrash and allegorical methods. See also D.L. Baker, *Two Testaments: One Bible* (Downers Grove, IL: Inter-Varsity Press, rev. edn, 1991); Kaiser, *Uses*, pp. 6-9, 212-20; P. Verhoef, 'The Relationships between the Old and the New Testaments', in J.B. Payne (ed.), *New Perspectives on the Old Testament* (Waco, TX: Word Books, 1970), pp. 280-303; J. Wenham, *Christ and the Bible* (Downers Grove, IL: Inter-Varsity Press, 1972).

found only in the author's original intention.[1]

Yet is the literal method able to explain this use of the Old Testament and all the others? This example and others seem to go beyond the grammar, history and context of the original author, so that several writers qualify 'literalness'. They acknowledge this extra as the 'plus' in a biblical hermeneutic.[2] For example, F.F. Bruce argues that 'grammatico-historical exegesis is not sufficient for the interpretation of the biblical documents...Theological exegesis is also necessary, although it cannot override grammatico-historical findings'.[3] He goes on to appeal to the part that the Holy Spirit plays in opening the Scripture for us as the risen Christ did for the Apostles. Bruce also shows that medieval doctrine held to a fourfold sense—the literal, allegorical, moral and anagogical sense—which derived heavenly meanings from earthly facts.[4] B.K. Waltke has also advocated a reconsideration of this fourfold sense. The idea is that we are in the heavenlies now and mystically participating in the future age[5] (Gal. 4.26; Eph. 1.3; 2.6, 19; Heb. 12.22-29).

---

1.   See Kaiser, *Uses*, pp. 63-66. More broadly, W.W. Klein, C.L. Blomberg and R.L. Hubbard, *Introduction to Biblical Interpretation* [Dallas: Word Books, 1993], pp. 97-98) write that the goal of hermeneutics is to enable interpreters to arrive at 'the meaning the biblical writers "meant" to communicate at the time of the communication, at least to the extent that those intentions are recoverable in the texts they produced' (see also pp. 133-38).

2.   C.A. Evans, 'The Function of the Old Testament in the New', in S. McKnight (ed.), *Introducing New Testament Interpretation* [Grand Rapids: Baker, 1989], p. 164) puts this in the category of resignification and believes that it witnesses to an exegetical pluralism in the New Testament. But it seems best to keep meaning distinct from significance.

3.   F.F. Bruce, 'Interpretation', in E.F. Harrison (ed.), *Baker's Dictionary of Theology* (Grand Rapids: Baker, 1960), p. 293.

4.   Bruce, 'Interpretation', p. 293. More recently, Bruce ('Interpretation of the Bible', in W. Elwell [ed.], *Evangelical Dictionary of Theology* [Grand Rapids: Baker, 1984], pp. 565-68) goes further and speaks of an 'increment of meaning' which constitutes the 'plenary sense' or *sensus plenior*. It is that supplied by the 'whole of Christian history'; what the Bible 'has come to mean in the experience of Christian readers, generation by generation, has added something to its meaning for Christian readers today' (p. 567). Bruce seems to be combining *sensus plenior* here with a form of reader-response and other approaches. I believe that my proposed solution fits well with Bruce's views.

5.   In an address at the Northwest Section, Evangelical Theological Society, Multnomah School of the Bible, Portland, OR, April 9, 1983. For similar assertions, see B.K. Waltke, 'An Evangelical Christian View of the Hebrew Scriptures', in

E.E. Ellis argues that Pauline exegesis might be termed 'grammatical-historical plus'.[1] Paul assumes grammar and history; his exegesis of the Old Testament begins where these end. Exegesis provides the possibilities for what a text *says*; the *meaning* of the text arises from an 'added factor'—in the meaning of an event for its later fulfillment. Longenecker writes that biblical exegesis has a revelatory stance which took the authors beyond the literal method.[2] Finally, a reader-response approach to Scripture leads to the creation of meaning beyond the original sense.[3]

Now if the Apostles go beyond the original meaning, who taught them this approach? The answer is Jesus Christ.[4] With regard to Matthew, Gundry traces every one of Matthew's hermeneutical principles to Jesus, including the case of Mal. 3.1 in Mt. 11.5, 10, 28 and 29 where Jesus assumed the role of Yahweh.[5]

Gundry further shows that these principles of Matthew and Jesus are consistent with a proper historical understanding of the Old Testament. They are consistent with the exegesis of the Old Testament in its own right and with the interpretation of the New Testament. Gundry shows that the messianic hope arose in the Old Testament itself, from the protoevangelium (Gen. 3.15) onward, especially during the kingdom of

M. Tannenbaum, M. Wilson and J.A. Rudin (eds.), *Evangelicals and Jews in an Age of Pluralism* (Grand Rapids: Baker, 1984), pp. 105-39.

1. E.E. Ellis, *Paul's Use of the Old Testament* (Edinburgh: Oliver & Boyd, 1957), pp. 147-48.

2. Longenecker, *Exegesis*, pp. 218-20. K.R. Snodgrass ('The Use of the Old Testament in the New', in D.A. Black and D.S. Dockery [eds.], *New Testament Criticism and Interpretation* [Grand Rapids: Zondervan, 1991], p. 414) speaks of the tendency of New Testament writers to use the Old Testament 'in ways different from their original intention'.

3. Klein *et al.*, *Biblical Interpretation*, pp. 138-45.

4. So many attest, including Gundry, *Use of the Old Testament*, p. 213; H.M. Shires, *Finding the Old Testament in the New* (Philadelphia: Westminster Press, 1974), pp. 92-95; C.H. Dodd, *According to the Scriptures* (New York: Charles Scribner's Sons, 1953), pp. 110, 126-27; Beale, 'Jesus and His Followers', p. 90 n. 8; R.T. France, *Jesus and the Old Testament* (Downers Grove, IL: Inter-Varsity Press, 1971), pp. 225-26; Ellis, *Paul's Use*, pp. 112-13; N. Hillyer, 'Matthew's Use of the Old Testament', *EvQ* 36 (1964), p. 24, who also suggests that Matthew's peculiar use of the Old Testament may well come from 'a consecrated spiritual mind with the New Testament gift of prophecy'—from Matthew led by the Holy Spirit (p. 25); and Chilton, *Galilean Rabbi*, pp. 167-74. The biblical support is Jesus' own words in Lk. 24.27-44 and also such passages as 1 Pet. 1.10-12; Rev. 19.10.

5. Gundry, *Use of the Old Testament*, pp. 213-15.

the Old Testament. So, historical questions on the horizontal plane and theological questions on the vertical plane are intertwined. This points to direct revelation and divine intention beyond that of Old Testament authors.[1] The Holy Spirit is at work.

It is in Jesus, then, in his use of the Old Testament (for example Ps. 110), that we discover that 'a messianic interpretation heightens the meaning of any passage of Scripture'.[2] There is considerable consensus that Jesus, by identifying John with Elijah in Matthew 11, goes beyond the original intent of Malachi, beyond a literal hermeneutic, defined as grammatical, historical and contextual.[3]

Pesher

To meet the inadequacies of the literal method, some posit the *pesher* method. K. Stendahl analyzed certain Old Testament passages in Matthew and concluded that Matthew's exegetical method was analogous to the

---

1.   Gundry, *Use of the Old Testament*, pp. 216-18. He cites H.H. Rowley as appealing to the 'activity of the Spirit of God in men' as prophecy arose and 'the activity of God in history and experience' to explain the fulfillment (n. 3).

2.   Gundry, *Use of the Old Testament*, p. 229. In n. 2 he adds that underlying 'Jesus' interpretation is the idea that Scripture may contain a divinely intended significance higher (or deeper) than the human author intended'. Terms in Ps. 110.1, 4 are proof of this.

3.   Yet even a literal hermeneutic discovers that a deeper sense may be inherent in Malachi also. Malachi means 'my messenger' and so there is a play on words implicit to Mal. 3.1. Malachi himself is God's sent messenger. Yet Malachi also says that God will 'send' Elijah, and both sendings are followed by references to the coming of the awesome 'day of the Lord' (3.2; 4.5). Malachi himself may not have expected the historical Elijah to reappear. In this sense, at least, Jesus and Malachi are not far apart. Kaiser argues that an actual Elijah was not in Malachi's mind (Kaiser, *Uses*, pp. 82-84).

So in its most narrow form the literal method limits the meaning or significance of the prophecy of Mal. 3.1 and 4.5 to a single actual Elijah to come in the Day of Yahweh. On the other hand, if a broader literal meaning is followed so that meaning can be expanded to significance then more than a single person may be in view, and even a metaphorical Elijah. Yet this approach cannot account for two comings and two or more people fulfilling this, especially since the characteristics attending the promise in Malachi will not be fulfilled as envisioned until the second coming. In addition a literal hermeneutic fails to give certainty or sufficient guidelines for discovering the deeper significance. Even if the literal method were to work here, it does not work everywhere.

pesher hermeneutic of Qumran.[1] This method contextualizes the Old Testament to contemporary events represented by the 'this is that' fulfillment motif, giving little respect for the original intention of the original utterance. Coupled to an apocalyptic orientation it centers on 'the *raz* (mystery) pesher (interpretation) revelational motif'.[2] While *pesher* is not extensive in Paul's writings,[3] according to Longenecker it is Jesus' most characteristic employment of Scripture.[4] Thus when Jesus said in Mt. 11.10, as he did nowhere else, 'This is the one about whom it is written', he may have employed or at least reflected a *pesher* type of interpretation.

Yet an appeal to *pesher* to explain Jesus' use of Mal. 3.1 fails, for *pesher* is unlike what Jesus does. In contrast to Qumran, there is not an attempt to fit a new historical situation to each phrase of the Old Testament regardless of context, nor are there 'far-fetched allegorical interpretations and ingenious word-play'.[5] Further, *pesher* provides no guidelines for what non-literal interpretations are possible, nor can it be the explanation for Malachi's own non-literal meaning hundreds of years before Qumran.

Midrash

Midrashic interpretation is probably the central concept in rabbinic exegesis. It comes from דרש ('to resort to', 'seek', 'study', 'interpret') and denotes an 'interpretive exposition'.[6] It is an exegesis which goes deeper than the literal sense of Scripture and seeks to 'explicate the hidden meaning contained therein by means of agreed upon hermeneutical rules in order to contemporize the revelation of God for the people of God'.[7] It is characterized by the maxim: 'That has relevance to this'.[8] It is claimed that Paul engages in midrashic exegesis more than in *pesher* or allegorical exegesis[9] and that it occurs in

1. Stendahl, *School*, pp. 183-84.
2. Longenecker, *Exegesis*, p. 41.
3. Ellis, *Paul's Use*, pp. 139-47.
4. Longenecker, *Exegesis*, pp. 70-75.
5. Gundry, *Use of the Old Testament*, p. 213. In n. 7 he appeals to Bruce, *Biblical Exegesis*, pp. 11-13, 68-69, as standing in contrast to Stendahl and seeing a wide gulf between Qumran and the New Testament.
6. Longenecker, *Exegesis*, p. 32.
7. Longenecker, *Exegesis*, p. 37. Cf. Ellis, *Paul's Use*, pp. 139-47.
8. Longenecker, *Exegesis*, p. 37.
9. Longenecker, *Exegesis*, p. 126.

Jesus' interpretation of the Old Testament as well.[1]

However, it is difficult to see by what rabbinic rules we can explain Jesus' use of Mal. 3.1 and 4.5 in Matthew 11. As with *pesher*, midrash fails to give adequate place to the author's intended meaning and lacks sufficient controls or parameters for the new meaning. Practicing midrash is complicated by the fact that the similarity between *pesher* and midrash may be too close to distinguish the terms, as I.H. Marshall argues.[2] It may be that the literal and *pesher*/midrash methods overlap and that our categories should not be forced anachronistically. In addition, while there may be parallels between Qumran and rabbinic methods and the New Testament,[3] both Jesus and Paul warned against contemporary Jewish practices of interpretation. Many of the devices employed, such as decoding hidden meanings, are simply not present in the New Testament.[4] Jesus, the example for Matthew, does not use the Old Testament atomistically. Neither searches the Old Testament 'either haphazardly or systematically for isolated proof texts'.[5] It is doubtful that Jesus violates or contradicts Mal. 3.1, 4.5 or any Old Testament passage when the whole context is considered.

Typology

This method is a genuine approach widely practiced in the New Testament and is a possible explanation for what Jesus does in Matthew 11. In seeking to identify whether this is typology, it seems that two extremes must be avoided. One extreme is to force from the text those types and antitypes that have virtually no substantiation from the literal method. While there are some surprising biblical examples ('the rock is Christ', 1 Cor. 10), this as a general approach goes too far. The other extreme does not go far enough, for it makes a type nothing more than

1.   Longenecker, *Exegesis*, pp. 66-70.

2.   I.H. Marshall, 'An Assessment of Recent Developments', in D.A. Carson and H.G M. Williamson (eds.), *It is Written: Scripture Citing Scripture* (Cambridge: Cambridge University Press, 1988), p. 13.

3.   M. Silva, 'The New Testament Use of the Old Testament', in D.A. Carson and J.D. Woodbridge (eds.), *Scripture and Truth* (Grand Rapids: Zondervan, 1983), p. 161. Chilton (*Galilean Rabbi*) shows that targumic material was also used by Jesus and believes it to be the key to his use of the Old Testament.

4.   Marshall, 'Assessment', p. 14.

5.   Gundry (*Use of the Old Testament*, p. 208) says this of Matthew, and he later identifies Matthew's use as derived from Jesus, including a 'deeper sense' (p. 213).

an example or pattern.[1] This seems to ignore a predictive element, the impact of redemption history, and heightening or climax. It denies that typology is an exegetical method, since it is not consistent with a literal meaning which 'embraces essentially one meaning', found by means of grammatical, historical study. Typology, it is said, embraces significance not intended by the author.[2]

Yet I believe with G. von Rad that typology is not to be divorced from historical exegesis, even though it cannot be fully 'regulated hermeneutically, but takes place in the freedom of the Holy Spirit'.[3] This is the 'plus' factor to a literal meaning.

The criteria necessary for a type seem to be present in our problem text: there are several obvious correspondences in the context; there is the historical event; there is predictiveness,[4] and even divine intent and prefiguration.[5] Heightening[6] occurs in Jesus' saying that there 'has not risen anyone greater than John' and that 'all the Prophets and the Law prophesied until John' (Mt. 11.11, 13). Additional characteristics of typology cited by von Rad[7] are also present. In the case that Jesus is practicing typology here, the 'messenger' and 'Elijah' are types of John the Baptist. Indeed, Malachi himself may be.

Yet Jesus seems to go beyond typology when he asserts that John is Elijah (11.14; 17.12-13) and that he fulfills Mal. 3.1 ('This is the one', 11.10). Future fulfillments are yet to come (Mt. 11.11) and perhaps the actual Elijah before the day of judgment (Mal. 4.5). Here, as elsewhere, uncertainty exists in trying to discover typology. In addition, as W. Pannenberg points out, typology tends to undermine the historical

---

1.   Baker, *Two Testaments*, p. 199. He denies that it is exegesis, prophecy, allegory, symbolism or a method or system.

2.   Baker, *Two Testaments*, p. 190. Cf. France, *Jesus*, pp. 41-42.

3.   G. von Rad, 'Typological Interpretation of the Old Testament', in C. Westermann (trans.) and J.L. Mays (ed.), *Essays on Old Testament Hermeneutics* (Richmond, VA: John Knox, 1963), pp. 36-38.

4.   S.L. Johnson, *The Old Testament in the New* (Grand Rapids: Zondervan, 1980), pp. 55-56.

5.   Kaiser, *Uses*, pp. 106-10.

6.   L. Goppelt, *Typos* (Grand Rapids: Eerdmans, 1982), pp. 18, 200-202.

7.   Von Rad, 'Typological', pp. 38-39.

facts connecting the Testaments by being 'a finally unhistorical, purely structural similarity'.[1]

Allegorical Method

In my opinion, it is doubtful that there is a genuine example of allegory in the New Testament. Instances cited, such as Gal. 4.21-31, Heb. 7.1-10 and 1 Cor. 9.9-10, do not sustain the view that the biblical author is nonhistorical or antihistorical. He is respectful of the historical setting and the intention of the author. As von Rad notes, he is concerned with facts, the historical sense, not spiritual truths rigidly attached to the very letter of the text.[2] The instances claimed represent typology better than allegorization as practiced by Philo and the Alexandrian school of the early Christian church. Jesus' method in Mt. 11.10 is not allegorical in that he does not make the messenger or Elijah into an idea or concept or truth. He finds fulfillment in another person.

Theological Methods

Because purely structural relationships have proved inadequate, various theological ideas or motifs have been posited that may be used to explain Jesus' use of Mal. 3.1 and 4.5 in Mt. 11.10-14.

1. *The Purpose of God*. On this view, the New Testament declares that the plan of God has been brought to fulfillment. History, then, is the working out of the divine purpose. This motif may be represented in prophecy by double or multiple fulfillment or sense.

This view means that several successive persons or events fulfilled Mal. 3.1. It would at least include Malachi himself, John the Baptist and a final figure to appear during the final form of the 'Day of the Lord'. In addition, if double sense is meant, Malachi has both a literal sense (the Elijah of the final form of the 'Day of the Lord') and a deeper, double sense which includes John the Baptist.

This motif is a plausible solution to our problem. However, it lacks specificity. We need to know what this divine purpose is in order to use it to discover the full meaning of our text.

2. *Covenant*. The motif of the covenant acts as an integrating theme of continuity throughout Scripture. It ranges from the agreement made

---

1. W. Pannenberg, 'Redemptive Event and History', in C. Westermann (ed.), *Essays on Old Testament Hermeneutics* (trans. J.L. Mays; Richmond, VA: John Knox, 1963), pp. 327-29.

2. Von Rad, 'Typological', p. 21.

with Adam and Eve to that made with Noah, Israel and David. It includes the actualizing of the New Covenant during the present age.

Covenant is a strong emphasis in the context of Malachi (2.5, 8, 10, 14; 3.1; 4.4). Almost all of the references are to the Mosaic covenant which is operative in Matthew. Nevertheless, covenant does not tell us what meaning or fulfillment Malachi had in mind and why—John, multiple fulfillments, or something else. Covenant also fails to encompass all biblical motifs.

3. *Christology*. The significance of Christology as a link between the Testaments can hardly be overestimated. The living presence of Christ is a determining factor in all New Testament exegesis and the Old Testament is to be interpreted christocentrically. It is one of the four major exegetical presuppositions of the earliest Christian use of the Old Testament.[1] Christology seems to explain why Jesus interprets Mal. 3.1 of himself and John. However, this motif or concept is inadequate by itself.[2] Christ is the crux of something broader and the means of achieving it, something which better answers the question 'why the Christ?' Further, the christological approach has been faulted for spiritualizing or allegorizing the Old Testament and thus demeaning the value of the Hebrew religious experience in its own right (and history along with it).

4. *Heilsgeschichte*. Salvation history, or *Heilsgeschichte*, affirms that the Christ-event fulfilled the revelatory acts of God in history. God is sovereign over history and works his purposes in it to accomplish his goals. This concept brings coherence and consistency to all that takes place. However, it is inadequate to explain detailed fulfillments.[3] I am not sure how salvation history helps us understand why John fulfills Mal. 3.1—whether meaning is single or double, with additional fulfillments. The term 'salvation history' and perhaps even the concept itself do not

---

1. Longenecker, *Exegesis*, pp. 93-95. The other three are corporate solidarity, correspondences in history and eschatological fulfillment. Longenecker terms Christology 'messianic presence'.

2. G.F. Hasel (*New Testament Theology: Basic Issues in the Current Debate* [Grand Rapids: Eerdmans, 1978], pp. 155-64) thinks that christocentricity is the center of the New Testament, but that it should not become the structure upon which to write a New Testament theology (p. 164).

3. See Gundry, *Use of the Old Testament*, pp. 215-16. Hasel (*New Testament Theology*, pp. 111-39, 148-53) shows that salvation history seems to be inadequate. In addition, Chilton (*Galilean Rabbi*, pp. 154-65) argues that it is only an assumption that biblical history amounts to salvation.

arise out of the biblical text.[1] More significantly, as Pannenberg has pointed out, *Heilsgeschichte* depreciates history (*Historie*). This is its error, shared with existential theology in its reduction of history to historicity.[2]

5. *Promise-Fulfillment*. The concept of promise-fulfillment is another way to evaluate the use of the Old Testament in the New Testament.[3] This concept shows the proper preparatory nature of the Old Testament. It is essential to history and our concept of God, as Pannenberg shows.[4] It is implicit as well as explicit in Scripture (see for example Jer. 33.14; Heb. 11).

Thus Mt. 11.10, 14 is the fulfillment of the promise that the messenger Elijah will come in the era of judgment. Or is it? Does Jesus exhaust the promise? There appears to be no way to know beforehand what fulfills the promise. While this motif may be a helpful way of viewing the Testaments in relationship to each other and specific passages which are clearly promise-oriented, it is too narrow and limited and fails as a hermeneutic for the rest of Scripture[5] (especially in a genre such as wisdom literature).

6. *Analogous Fulfillment*. J. Weir believes that analogous fulfillment is the overarching model which includes all the above methods. His model is based on the observation that there is 'both a similarity and a difference between one object, event, or idea and another object, event, or idea'.[6] Weir observes that 'fulfillments are normally analogical and only

---

1. It is possible to distinguish between a valid use of *Heilsgeschichte* and an invalid one. R. Allen has defended the moderate view which was, apparently, the position of the originator of the term, J.C.K. von Hofmann. See R. Allen, 'Is There *Heil* for *Heilsgeschichte*?' (paper presented to the Evangelical Theological Society, Reformed Theological Seminary, Jackson, MI, Dec. 30, 1975). Allen goes on to suggest eight considerations or prerequisites for a careful use of *Heilsgeschichte* (pp. 17-20).

2. Pannenberg, 'Redemptive Event', pp. 314-15.

3. See Baker, *Two Testaments*, pp. 203-33; Hasel, *Old Testament Theology*, pp. 181-83; *New Testament Theology*, pp. 127-32, where he cites Goppelt (*Theology of the New Testament*) as limiting salvation history to promise and fulfillment.

4. Pannenberg, 'Redemptive Event', pp. 316-17.

5. Verhoef ('Relationships', pp. 289-90) believes that the whole of the Testaments is to be covered by each term. Yet he acknowledges that this formula must be supplemented by such concepts as unity of perspective regarding the coming of the kingdom of God and continuity/discontinuity (p. 292).

6. Weir, 'Analogous Fulfillment', p. 72. A.B. Mickelsen, H.W. Wolff, von Rad, D.S. Russell and S. De Vries all hint at analogous fulfillment, according to Weir. He

occasionally literal. Even literal fulfillments are analogous due to differences of space and time'.[1] However, the method fails to explain why the analogue of Elijah and John exists and how we today may discover others to contextualize the message for our era.

7. *Generic Promise*. The model of generic promise, originally generic prediction[2] and recently popularized by Kaiser, claims to uphold the original intentional meaning of the author and the later significance of an utterance, supposedly following Hirsch's distinctions.[3] According to generic promise prophecy has one meaning which is of a generic or corporate nature.[4]

As applied to our problem passage generic promise means that not only John the Baptist 'fulfills' Mal. 3.1 and 4.5 (Lk. 1.17, 76-79), but anyone else before or after until the final 'completer' comes before the Day of Judgment. Malachi had in mind not one specific person but a generic messenger who comes in the spirit and power of Elijah throughout time. Yet the meaning is still one.

However, in the present passage Jesus pointed out John specifically, as though he began the era of fulfillment. The prophet Malachi does not appear to have as his authorial intention a whole string of generic 'fulfillments'. It seems that authorial intent has been redefined by a retrospective look at the phenomena in order to protect a literal hermeneutic and to reject dual authorship (*contra* 1 Pet. 1.10-12). Yet divine intention is emphasized by the human authors of prophecy.[5]

---

finds that the analogous fulfillment model meets the four criteria necessary for the fulfillment of the Old Testament in the New Testament (p. 66). Chilton (*Galilean Rabbi*, pp. 184-88) prefers analogy over typology in his process called 'fulfilled interpretation' (involving analogical, critical meditation and experiential steps).

1. Weir, 'Analogous Fulfillment', p. 75.

2. W.J. Beecher, *The Prophets and the Promise* (repr.; Grand Rapids: Baker, 1963 [1905]).

3. Kaiser, *Uses*, p. 204.

4. Thus Kaiser (*Uses*, p. 230) defines generic prophecy as that which 'envisages an event as occurring in a series of parts, often separated by intervals of times, yet, expressed in such a way that the language of the Old Testament may legitimately apply either to the nearest, remoter or climactic event. Thus, the same word, with the same sense or meaning of the Old Testament authors, may apply at once to the whole complex of events or to any one of its parts in any particular era without destroying what the author had in mind when he first gave that word'.

5. This and other reasons lead P. Payne to assert that it is fallacious to equate meaning with the human author's intention. See P.B. Payne, 'The Fallacy of

8. *Sensus Plenior*. Some, especially Roman Catholic writers, appeal to a hidden meaning called *sensus plenior*. It is that fuller, deeper, spiritual sense which lies below or beyond the literal sense. As applied to Mal. 3.1 and 4.5, it means that the fulfillment of Elijah in John the Baptist is a meaning not consciously intended by the human author (Malachi), but is a meaning intended by God and integral to the text and later discerned by Jesus.

D.J. Moo, citing R.E. Brown's defense of *sensus plenior*, shows that this meaning may at times have been dimly perceived by the human author as shown by the context (it need not be a meaning 'reserved by God to himself'[1]); that there is a relationship between the literal sense and the 'fuller' sense; that it differs from typology since it concerns words rather than events; and that it differs from accommodation (God truly intends this meaning).[2]

While *sensus plenior* is helpful, we need to be more certain as to the parameters of control. Considerable subjectivity in identifying the additional meaning in Malachi remains. It seems difficult to practice today. *Sensus plenior* really does not resolve the difficulty,[3] for it fails to delineate the relationship of the senses and to show how one gets from the literal to the deeper meaning.

9. *Canonical Approach*. In order to meet the concerns of the subjectivity of a *sensus plenior* approach to the use of the Old Testament in the New, some have turned to the ultimate canonical context to find the basis for a 'fuller' sense to Scripture and human intention. Moo favors this approach because (1) the meaning is built on the redemptive-historical framework of the Old Testament in the New Testament; (2) it is represented by the use of the Old Testament in the Old Testament; (3) it imparts a meaning not deliberately concealed from a human author

Equating Meaning with the Human Author's Intention', *JETS* 13 (1970), pp. 243-52.

1.　This is an objection raised by B. Vawter and endorsed by Kaiser, *Uses*, p. 209.

2.　D.J. Moo, 'The Problem of Sensus Plenior', in D.A. Carson and J.D. Woodbridge (eds.), *Hermeneutics, Authority, and Canon* (Grand Rapids: Zondervan, 1986), pp. 201-202. See also Baker, *Two Testaments*, pp. 193-94.

3.　J.J. O'Rourke ('The Fulfillment Texts in Matthew', *CBQ* 24 [1962], pp. 402-403) says that 'we should not call a *sensus plenior* something which we cannot otherwise classify; that would be merely labeling a difficulty, not resolving it'. He believes that Matthew viewed his use of the Old Testament as legitimate and proper, but so varied from 'our point of view that no completely satisfactory classifying of them has yet been produced' (p. 403).

but which unfolds as the canon grows; (4) it is open to verification to some extent.[1] Moo seeks to avoid dual meaning by positing that God did not intend or implant additional meaning necessarily hidden from the human author at the point of inspiration, though he knew in his providence that greater meaning would be unfolded.[2] However, J.I. Packer appears to support dual meaning when he writes that

> though God may have more to say to us from each text than its human writer had in mind, God's meaning is never less than his...God's further meaning, as revealed when the text is exegeted in its canonical context, in relation to all that went before and came after, is simply extension, development, and application of what the writer was consciously expressing.[3]

Hence, our understanding of what Mal. 3.1 and 4.5 means is derived from its use in Matthew 11, 17 and elsewhere. The messenger is John the Baptist and he heralds Jesus as the 'Lord to come to his Temple'.

This approach, while having an advantage over *sensus plenior*, cannot tell us how or why the passages are linked, that is, what principles or conceptual center guided Jesus as he unfolded the meaning of Malachi from within his canon. Consequently we cannot pattern our hermeneutic after his in order to discover anything beyond what he (or his disciples) have explicitly unfolded.

10. *Restrained Reader-Response Interpretation.* A final form of theological exegesis used to justify additional or new meaning never envisioned in the original context is that of reader-response. The most legitimate form of reader-response interpretation appears to be that of Klein *et al.*, who, as others above, cite the precedent of the use of the Old Testament in the New Testament. The new or fresh meaning of Jesus beyond the original, historical intention of Malachi is possible yet the historical meaning of the text remains primary.[4]

This approach avoids the usual subjectivity of reader-response criticism while acknowledging the 'creative enterprise' of understanding a biblical text. However, this approach really fares little better than the two preceeding. There are no objective criteria from within Scripture for determining the particulars in the 'creative enterprise'.

In summary, all the approaches as attempts to explain the relationship

1. Moo, 'Sensus Plenior', pp. 205-206.
2. So Moo defines the canonical approach ('Sensus Plenior', p. 210).
3. J.I. Packer, 'Infallible Scripture and the Role of Hermeneutics', in Carson and Woodbridge (eds.), *Scripture and Truth*, p. 350.
4. Klein *et al.*, *Biblical Interpretation*, pp. 138-45.

of Malachi to Jesus' use, and of the Testaments to each other, fall short in one of two ways. First, the more structural methods, while giving some explanation for Jesus' claim of fulfillment in Mt. 11.10, fail to explain why the structures exist, and to give parameters for interpretation of the meaning in the structures. This leads to the search for a theological center. Secondly, all the theological centers or methods as expounded fail to provide guidance for discovering additional meaning and emphases in Malachi and other genres, and fail to encompass all motifs.

A Proposed Solution to the Problem of Jesus' Use of Malachi 3.1 and 4.5: Actualization of Essential Reality

A Kingdom Center

The explanation for Jesus' use of Mal. 3.1 and 4.5 in Mt. 11.10-14 is tied to a proper biblical center or theme.[1] The ultimate reality, the center of the Old and New Testaments, is the kingdom of God. More specifically, it is God's mission to glorify himself by establishing his kingdom through the redemption of humankind. When sin entered human history, a schism erupted, dividing the kingdom of God from the kingdom of the world. Ever since, God has sought to actualize his kingdom in the world by saving (including justifying and sanctifying) humankind and enlisting us in the cosmic war against Satan and his domain. The kingdom of the eschaton was inaugurated on earth by the first advent of Christ. The ongoing work of the church is to actualize the kingdom by living and proclaiming the gospel of Christ and his kingdom. With the second advent of Christ comes the full realization of the kingdom, when the kingdom of the world and God's kingdom are one and the same.[2] Finally, in the

---

1.   See the extensive discussion of other potential centers in Hasel, *Old Testament Theology*, pp. 139-68, 191-93. He argues that the center must be an 'internal key', from within the Bible itself, 'based on the inner biblical witnesses' (p. 159). I think that my approach meets this criterion.

2.   Space does not permit here a thorough discussion of my proposed solution. For this see J. DeYoung, 'Jesus' Use of the Old Testament: Kingdom Reality as a Hermeneutic' (paper presented to the Evangelical Theological Society, Washington, DC, Nov. 18, 1993). For a fuller discussion of the kingdom as center, and the implications for the creation and redemption of humankind, see S. Hurty, 'The Truth Shall Make You Free: A New Model of Sanctification based on a Synthesis of the Models from the Reformed and the Comtemplative Traditions' (ThM thesis, Western Seminary, 1993), pp. 66ff. Hurty's contribution to the present study has been significant and

new heavens and earth, God rules over a people who are truly one with him: he is their God; they are his people (Jn 17; Rev. 21–22).

I am aware of the objections to a kingdom center. However, the key is in one's definition of kingdom. Kingdom is commonly understood as emphasizing the transcendence of God in his rulership (ideas represented by L. Köhler, H. Seebass, R.W. Klein), lacking the emphasis of immanence found in the concept of covenant (W. Eichrodt) or communion (T.C. Vriezen). This tension has led to a positing of a dual center such as rule of God/communion between God and humanity (G. Fohrer).[1] A biblical understanding of the kingdom of God emphasizes both transcendence and immanence, for God is both and relates to humankind from both. Thus the kingdom theme has the dual motifs of rulership and relationship. This kingdom theme seems to meet the various concerns and criteria for a biblical center.[2]

The Paradigm of Reality

I would like to suggest a paradigm of reality as a plausible resolution of the difficulties uncovered in Jesus' use of Mal. 3.1 and 4.5 and the New Testament's use of the Old Testament in general (and indeed the use of the Old Testament by the Old Testament). It is a paradigm or model involving three elements: existential reality, essential reality and a process of actualization involving the concerns for love and truth.[3]

By existential reality I mean those values or concepts that are limited, temporary or transitory. They are accidental in the philosophical sense. By essential reality I mean those values or concepts that are everlasting or eternal which flow from the very essence of God and his kingdom. God himself is ultimate reality. By a process of actualization I mean that there is an ongoing imperative to actualize essential reality in our

pervasive. She originated the core of the paradigm and suggested many of its theological and biblical applications.

1. Hasel, *Old Testament Theology*, pp. 139-71.

2. For examples, see Hasel, *Old Testament Theology*, pp. 139-71, 205-206; G.R. Osborne, *The Hermeneutical Spiral* (Downers Grove, IL: Inter-Varsity Press, 1991), p. 293.

3. For a fuller description of the elements of the paradigm, see Hurty, 'Truth Shall Make You Free', pp. 72-75. For exegetical demonstrations and further applications of the paradigm of reality, see J. DeYoung with S. Hurty, 'Here But Not Yet: A Paradigm toward Understanding the Role of Women in Ministry' (a paper presented to the Evangelical Theological Society, San Francisco, CA, Nov. 20, 1992).

existential reality.[1] Eternal truths and realities must constantly be brought to bear so as to conform existential reality to essential reality. This concern for truth must be tempered by love.

This paradigm of reality corresponds to the actualization of the kingdom as a center. It is a philosophical or 'systematic theological' restatement of the 'biblical theological' theme of the kingdom and its realization. Essential reality roughly corresponds to God and his kingdom, existential reality to the world and its institutions presently oriented away from God, and the process of actualization to the accomplishment of the kingdom on earth.

The Paradigm of Reality as a Hermeneutic

How does the paradigm of reality explain Jesus' somewhat 'non-literal' use of Mal. 3.1 and 4.5 in Matthew 11? The existential reality (basically equivalent to the historical meaning) is that Malachi prophesies a 'messenger' to come (3.1) called 'Elijah' (4.5) to herald the Lord coming to his temple as the 'messenger of the covenant'. The essential reality of Malachi's words (the deeper meaning) is that this messenger will be one in 'the spirit and power of Elijah' embodied in anyone who heralds the Lord's coming with his kingdom. In light of Old Testament usage before and after Malachi we need not understand this as the actual Elijah (or, at least, not as the actual Elijah only); such a messenger was already widely known to precede God's way and his eternal kingdom

---

1.   With regard to actualization, Baker (*Two Testaments*, pp. 304-306) suggests that this may be the unifying concept to bind von Rad's complex solution (involving typology, promise and fulfillment, tradition history and salvation history) together. Von Rad uses the term in a limited way, chiefly to describe how 'the saving events connected with the festivals were "actualized" in the cultic celebration', and how Deuteronomy is 'a unique actualization of God's will to counter specific dangers' in Israel's later history. He also uses the sense of it when speaking of 'the way in which the Old Testament is absorbed in the New' (*Two Testaments*, pp. 304-306). Von Rad writes: 'The question therefore is whether the reinterpretation of Old Testament traditions in the light of Christ's appearance on earth is not also hermeneutically perfectly permissible...The Apostles clearly take the view that the texts of the Old Testament only attain their fullest actuality in the light of their fulfillment' (G. von Rad, *Old Testament Theology* [2 vols.; London: SCM Press, 1965], II, p. 333, quoted by Baker, *Two Testaments*, pp. 305-306). For Baker, this concept is closely related to the idea of 're-presentation' used by M. Noth, C. Westermann and F.-P. Dreyfus. I seek to take actualization more specifically (relating it to kingdom) and more extensively (a central concept).

(for example the Angel of Yahweh, as discussed above). Hence, it is appropriate that Jesus identify John as such a messenger, especially since the various contexts concern the kingdom and its *actualization* (Isa. 40; Mal. 3–4; Mt. 11.12-14): if the Jews receive John and Jesus, the kingdom is realized. If they reject Jesus, they thereby reject John as the final messenger, as 'Elijah' before the 'great and dreadful day of the LORD'.

This interpretation is also commensurate with Malachi's own play on words regarding his name and with the concept that Jesus, as the Angel of Yahweh (Exod. 23.20-23) before him, fulfills the role of 'messenger' before Yahweh. Again, in line with the actualization of essential reality, Jesus fills the role of, in fact is, Yahweh. Indeed, in general it may be said, in light of this aspect of the paradigm, that Yahweh is Jesus in the Old Testament whenever he appears as the one revealed, as coming, as glorified.[1] Hence, Jesus' change of pronouns, from μου to σου, identifies him with Yahweh, the speaker, no longer the addressee, and is appropriate to the actualizing of reality—that Jesus is essentially deity. Jesus and his ministry comprise the key to interpretation (cf. Rev. 19.10).[2]

In light of the additional passages (Exod. 23; Isa. 40) alluded to in Mal. 3.1, it is clear that there is more than one instance of a deeper sense. One concerns the messenger as the angel, another concerns the messenger as Elijah. The paradigm of reality leads us to understand that the messenger is essentially one who goes before Yahweh, who is sent by him, before the kingdom comes. Cannot Jesus, Elijah, John and others yet future all be equated with this 'messenger'? Even Jesus' contemporaries believed that he might be Elijah (Mt. 16.14). So Jesus is (1) the essential 'messenger', (2) the Lord to come to his temple, and (3) Yahweh himself.

The paradigm of reality may also help to explain Jesus' somewhat enigmatic statement that while there is none greater than John among

---

1. So F. Delitzsch (*Commentary on the Epistle to the Hebrews* [2 vols.; repr.; Edinburgh: T & T. Clark, 1978 (1871)], pp. 71-72) writes on the application to Jesus Christ of Deut. 32.43 in Heb. 1.6. This principle that Jesus is Yahweh revealed 'constitutes the innermost bond between the two Testaments', he says. He includes a reference to Mal. 4.5. P.E. Hughes (*A Commentary on the Epistle to the Hebrews* [Grand Rapids: Eerdmans, 1977], pp. 60-61) concurs. See also Gundry, *Use of the Old Testament*, pp. 209, 224-25.

2. Snodgrass ('Use of the Old Testament', p. 427) holds to a related idea when he states: 'We have not completed the interpretive task until we have determined how a text does or does not correspond with Jesus' ministry or the ministry of the church'.

those who are born to women, 'yet he who is least in the kingdom of heaven is greater than he' (Mt. 11.11). According to the actualization of essential reality, anyone who embraces the kingdom and its eternal principles may exceed John in his ministry and person, first, because he or she will have added truth and experience, and secondly, because in the prophetic tradition he or she proclaims in the Spirit and power the coming of the now present and ever approaching kingdom of God.

Summary and Conclusions

In this study of Jesus' use of Mal. 3.1 and 4.5 in Matthew 11, I have suggested that the traditional way of defining or understanding a biblical hermeneutic is faulty or insufficient. Many scholars believe that grammar, history and context are not enough to explain some of the meanings found by later authors of Scripture in previous writings, and that there is a 'plus' in the literal hermeneutic. A number of methods used to account for this 'plus' have been surveyed, including *pesher*, midrash, typology, allegory and various theological motifs and methods. Some of them are plausible solutions to our problem here. When these various solutions are considered for other commonly recognized problems, they seem inadequate as a hermeneutic for all of Scripture. The more 'structural' methods either do not apply to certain genres or phenomena, discount Old Testament historical experience, or lack guidelines to govern the finding of deeper meanings. Theological motifs or methods posited to fill these needs fail to be all-encompassing, lack sufficient specificity and do not provide necessary parameters for finding meaning.

As an attempt to find a better solution to this problem, I suggest that a certain biblical center, namely the actualization of the kingdom (understood as transcendent and immanent) through the redemption of humankind, and its corresponding paradigm of reality provide a promising hermeneutic to explain the 'plus' which goes beyond a strictly literal hermeneutic. Applying the center and its paradigm to our passage, the existential reality is that Malachi prophesies a 'messenger' to come (3.1) called 'Elijah' (4.5) to herald the Lord coming to his temple as the 'messenger of the covenant'. The essential reality of Malachi's words is that this messenger will be one in 'the spirit and power of Elijah' embodied in anyone who heralds the Lord's coming in and with his kingdom. Jesus is indeed deity, so he 'fulfills' the role of Yahweh, and John 'fulfills' the role of the messenger. Had Israel received Jesus, there would be no need for further 'fulfillments'. As it is, the prophecy has not yet been entirely fulfilled, and we are to look for another messenger, possibly Elijah himself, to come before Jesus Christ in the parousia.

The paradigm of reality is another plausible solution to the particular problem taken up in this paper. Preliminary study indicates that it will prove to be helpful as a hermeneutic for all of Scripture, providing the necessary parameters for exegeting meaning following the hermeneutic of the biblical authors. It then has promise for changing the way we do biblical and systematic theology. This remains to be demonstrated in future studies.[1]

1.   I acknowledge the significant contribution of my graduate fellow in New Testament, S. Hurty, to this study. Ms Hurty is presently engaged in graduate study at the University of Sheffield, England.

Part II

THE GOSPEL OF MATTHEW

MATTHEW: A PATRIOT'S GOSPEL

Frederick W. Danker

My aim in this essay is to take note of a feature in Matthew's Gospel that has been submerged under numerous discussions concerning his alleged anti-Judaism. In brief, I hope to demonstrate that Matthew is a patriot, whose book contains a call to the colors under the leadership of Israel's Great Patriot, Jesus Christ.[1] It is a loyalist's reminder that the moment at hand can be Israel's finest hour. The messiah has arrived, and he will keep his people on course. Yet destiny cannot be won without a battle, and there are forces that threaten to impede Israel's movement to their goal. But God is with them, and his name, as prophets predicted, will yet be glorified by all nations. The result will be that Israel's name is also glorified.

Matthew's message is conveyed through a distinctive blend of diction, selection of narrative, structural technique and sensitivity to publics. He endeavors to say something meaningful to those who have not made a commitment to Jesus Christ as well as to those who claim allegiance to him. The former include, first of all, those Israelites who have displayed hostility to Jesus Christ and his followers, and, secondly, Greco-Romans who require some bridging of cultural differences. The latter include Israelites with traditions deeply rooted in Israel's history, and others who find themselves less bound to such traditions. Throughout, Matthew endeavors to develop a sense of peoplehood in the communities that

---

1. This study is a revision and expansion of my article 'God With Us: Hellenistic Christological Perspectives in Matthew', *Currents in Theology and Mission* 19 (1992), pp. 433-39. There is no consensus concerning the authorship of the 'First Gospel'. In this study the term 'Matthew' is therefore used for convenience. I accept a post-destruction-of-Jerusalem date. Unless otherwise specified, as in references to the NRSV (in which case the MT is used) all Old Testament biblical references are cited according to A. Rahlfs, *Septuaginta* (2 vols.; Stuttgart: Württembergische Bibelanstalt, 1935 and reprints).

find God with them in a unique way in Jesus Christ, the messianic deliverer.

Judean Audition

It is a mistake to begin the interpretation of Matthew with modern definitions of nationality or peoplehood in mind. Erroneous methodology is the necessary product of such an approach. Similarly, the retrojection of the adjective 'Jewish' and cognates into the discussion of Matthew's Gospel can interfere with unprejudiced inquiry. In the early decades of the proclamation of Jesus as messianic deliverer, those who claimed allegiance to him constituted one of numerous sects, all of whom would be termed 'Judeans' because of their connection with the cult associated with Jerusalem.[1]

In view of this identification in terms of adherence to basic Mosaic tenets and cultic regulations, the term 'Judean' is more descriptive and also more helpful in scientific discussion than the derived term 'Jew', which in modern parlance is comparatively nebulous, since it is possible to be identified as a Jew without professing any allegiance to the God of Israel. In this essay I shall therefore use the term 'Judean', and the cognates 'Judaism' and 'Judaistic' are also to be understood in the context of Jerusalem's adherence to Mosaic tradition. Indeed, Jerusalem sets the standard for Mosaic observance.[2] Moreover, because early followers of Jesus Christ would be 'Judeans' in cultic practice, some more strictly than others,[3] it is important not to use the terms 'Christianity' and 'Judaism' as antonyms. As stated above, in the earliest decades after the death and resurrection of Jesus, the followers of Jesus would be a sect within the larger body of practitioners of Judean piety, or Judeanism. Espousing Christian practice and belief was therefore not per se the

---

1. On the 'Judean' cult and its outreach, including Galilee, see E. Schürer, *The History of the Jewish People in the Age of Jesus Christ (175 B.C.–A.D. 135)* (ed. G. Vermes, F. Millar and M. Black; Edinburgh: T. & T. Clark, rev. edn, 1979), II, pp. 7-15; for a brief appraisal of the multi-faceted religious picture see R.P. Carroll, 'Israel, History of', *ABD*, III (1992), p. 569.

2. Mt. 15.1-2 points to a broad range in piety, but also to Jerusalem as the elite cultic center. On Jerusalem's prestige, see Schürer, *History of the Jewish People*, II, pp. 195-96.

3. Mt. 1.19 presents Joseph as an 'upright' person (δίκαιος), that is, one concerned about fidelity to Mosaic prescriptions; see BAGD s.v. 'δίκαιος' and 'δικαιοσύνη'.

opposite of Judeanism.[1] Of course, there would be differences in approach, and these would be the subject of intense debate, some of which is reflected in Matthew's book, especially in ch. 23.

Basic to Matthew's perspective is the question of Israel's identity and the manner in which identity is here achieved and maintained. The genealogy cited in ch. 1 roots Jesus Christ firmly in Israel's history, and with the patriotic christological affirmation that Jesus is a descendant of both David and Abraham. The latter is guaranteed a progeny, if necessary out of stone (3.9). At 2.15, Matthew could not fail to elicit deep patriotic feeling with an allusion to the deliverance from Pharaoh of the exodus, and at the same time Jesus is identified as God's son, a term that Hos. 11.1 applies to Israel. Thus Jesus is inextricably associated with the people of Israel. The fact that he is God's Son reinforces the definition of his name 'Immanuel', as 'God with us', the primary boast of Israel. Israel can be certain of permanent identity under the leadership of Jesus. God will never desert Israel. Later in Matthew's story Jesus will be shown to be identifying with his extended family (12.48-50; 23.8). Patriotic feeling would also be aroused with the reference to Bethlehem, David's town, out of which comes the one who will 'shepherd my people Israel' (2.6). Continuity in Israel's peoplehood is here assured.

Jesus' proclamation on a mountain (chs. 5–7) conveys the hallowed aura of illustrious Moses, and the two feeding narratives (14.15-21; 15.32-38) would remind Judeans of notable experiences of divine assistance after the deliverance of their ancestors from Egypt. There would also be remembrance of Elijah's and Elisha's heroic stands against Ahab's misused power, and the transfiguration scene would present Matthew's publics with both prophetic figures (17.3, 5). Resurrection of the name of Solomon (12.42) was calculated to arouse nostalgia and proud identification with one whose greatness exceeded that of the fabulous king who ruled when Israel was at the apex of its

---

1.   I use the term, 'Judeanism', for the word 'Judaism' is weighted with later historical burden and semantic debate. Even less helpful terminology is the opposition of church and synagogue, for not all early Christians were outside the synagogue. On the difference between Matthew and Luke on the question of an 'inter-Jewish affair', see L.M. Wills, 'The Depiction of the Jews in Acts', *JBL* 110 (1991), p. 645; to Wills's thinking, 'whatever Matthew's problems, that Gospel is not guilty of anti-Semitism or anti-Judaism'. Perhaps my new reading of Matthew can also aid in quashing contemporary anti-Jewish sentiment among Christians who have too long sought biblical support for animosity.

prestige. Of the same order is the mention of David at 21.9 and 22.41-46. The selection of twelve apostles, later coupled with a promise that they would sit on twelve thrones judging the twelve tribes of Israel (19.28), also could not fail to kindle patriotic fervor.

Beyond question, Matthew succeeds in drawing attention to themes that would appeal to Judean pride. But the ultimate stimulation needs to be discussed, namely Israel's position as the recipients of divine bounties that gave them an advantaged position over all the nations.[1] This position involved the responsibility of sharing Yahweh's prestige with outsiders. It is necessary to cite only a few of the testimonies. The book of Jonah attests most clearly to an outreach perspective in Israel. According to Zech. 14.16-19 all survivors of the nations that have attacked Jerusalem will be represented at the annual Festival of Booths. Mic. 4.1-4 envisions all nations coming to Jerusalem to be taught the ways of the Lord.[2] From Matthew's perspective, Israel's destiny is achieved when the nations receive proper instruction. The messiah himself transmits it to his eleven apostles (οἱ ἕνδεκα, 28.16), who, despite the loss of one, represent Israel (19.28). Far from denying the future existence of Israel or its privilege as the chosen people of God, Matthew the patriot states that Jesus Messiah ensures Israel's prestigious uniqueness by ensuring that its job gets done through chosen followers. By implication, improper instruction would interfere with the divine objective, and Israel would be the loser. Jesus, the patriot's patriot, would never let that happen, and at numerous stages in his Gospel Matthew is at pains to show that the messiah was engaged in refutation of those who undermined national destiny by improper teaching.

At this point it is necessary to take issue with points raised by Ulrich Luz concerning Matthew's attitudes towards Israel. In an article in *Currents in Theology and Mission*, Luz reaches the conclusion that Matthew 'condemns Israel ' and that his 'anti-Judaism' is 'not without roots in the proclamation and self-understanding of Jesus'.[3] Luz bases

---

1. For prophetic statements concerning Israel's chosen status, see for example Isa. 42.1; 43.20; 45.4; Ezek. 20.5.

2. Mic. 4.2 reads δείξουσιν: 'they [the members of the 'house of Jacob'] will show us the Lord's way'.

3. U. Luz, 'Matthew's Anti-Judaism: Its Origin and Contemporary Significance', *Currents in Theology and Mission* 19 (1992), pp. 405-15, quotation from p. 415. The author notes that this article is in effect a preview of the third volume, 'not yet written', of his commentary on Matthew (the first two volumes form part of the

much of his argument on Matthew's record of the critique Jesus makes of the Judean leadership. After some references to Jesus' words of judgment, Luz comments: 'Thus, Matthew's theology is thoroughly anti-Jewish. His accusations against the Pharisees and the scribes do not only violate the commandment of love, as he himself has proclaimed it in the Sermon on the Mount, but sometimes even the commandment of truth'.[1] It is impossible in brief compass to deal with all aspects of Luz's article, but since Matthew's record about the leadership dominates Luz's discussion most of my critique will relate to this topic.

If Matthew and to some extent Jesus (granting some editorializing by Matthew) are to be charged with judgmental attitudes, one can legitimately ask whether the same charges might not be laid against some of Israel's prophets and even against Yahweh, in whose name the prophets speak. Luz argues that Mt. 21.43 and 27.25 in effect consign Israel to rejection. Granting for the moment that Luz's exegesis is correct, one may well ask whether there is anything like Mal. 2.1-3 in Matthew's record? And what about Mic. 3.9-12, in which Jerusalem is guaranteed to become a heap of ruins because of its complacent leadership? Anyone even slightly familiar with Old Testament prophetic literature knows that these passages are to be taken only as starters for documenting virulent indictment in the Old Testament. By contrast, that of Jesus (or Matthew?) sounds tame.

In his condemnation of Matthew for linking responsibility for destruction of Jerusalem with the leadership, Luz fails to note that in Israelite thought, the fortunes of the total body are linked with the actions of its leadership. Jeremiah (14.13-16) declares that the people of Jerusalem will become victims of the sword because of lying prophets. In Hosea 4, priest and prophet are called to account, for 'my people are destroyed because of lack of knowledge' (v. 6; NRSV). It is quite probable that a passage such as Jer. 23.1-6 specifically inspired some of Matthew's interest in critique of Israel's spiritual leadership.[2]

Matthew's prophetic criticisms of the leadership and somber evaluation of the consequences for the people as a whole also invite comparison with those of Amos, who blasts especially the behavior of the privileged and consigns the 'kingdom of the sinners' to destruction 'from the face

Hermeneia series: *Matthew* [Minneapolis: Fortress Press, 1993]).

1. Luz, 'Matthew's Anti-Judaism', p. 409.

2. Similarity to phraseology in Jeremiah is exhibited at 2.18 (Jer. 38.15); 13.13 (Jer. 5.21); 21.13 (Jer. 7.11); 23.34 (Jer. 7.25 = 25.4); 27.10 (Jer. 18.2-3; 39.7-9).

of the earth' (9.8a). On the other hand, like Amos, who cancels his own dire prediction with an exceptive clause (9.8b), Matthew has survivors from the catastrophe that would overtake Jerusalem, for the disciples of Jesus carry out Israel's destiny by making disciples in all the nations.

It is also to be noted that Matthew's interpretation of the destruction is quite different from that recorded in Jer. 8.1-2 after a prophecy of Jerusalem's fate (7.33-34). Matthew relates a resurrection of pious people after the crucifixion (Mt. 27.52-53). Luz states that he can see no 'interpretation other than the one given in the second century by a Christian redactor of the Testament of Levi' (4.1), who refers to a 'disobedient people...condemned with punishment'.[1] Unfortunately, Luz fails to observe an important difference between the passages from Jeremiah with their explicit judgmental note and Matthew's interpretation of events. According to Jer. 8.1-2, upon the destruction of Jerusalem the bones of the political and spiritual leadership are to be brought out of their tombs and exposed 'like dung on the surface of the ground' (NRSV). In Matthew's account corpses take on new life and enter the 'holy city', a term which not only suggests Matthew's affection for the city but indicates that the city is now purified, despite the terrible travesty of justice that has been perpetrated in its environs.[2] Patriot that he is, Matthew cannot bear to end his story with devastating words. Jerusalem's leadership must bear the responsibility for the destruction that will most certainly come, for even after the series of portents described in Matthew 27, the chief priests and elders engage in bribery (28.12), an echo of their transaction with Judas (26.14-16).[3]

Even if Luz were correct in suggesting that Matthew's view of the leadership is slanted,[4] the Evangelist's prophetic perspective, given the

1. Luz, 'Matthew's Anti-Judaism', p. 408.

2. There may be a suggestion of intercession in response to the terrible self-guilt pronounced earlier. D.M. Crump, *Jesus the Intercessor* (Tübingen: Mohr [Paul Siebeck], 1992), p. 223, does not make reference to our passage, but in support of his *Targum* thesis about Jesus as 'Pray-er' cites a passage preserved only in *Targum Pseudo-Jonathan* (on Gen. 9.19), in which 'the Lord tells Moses to stop praying so that he might destroy the nation, at which point God unleashes five destroying angels against Israel. But when Moses heard this he continued his prayers and immediately "Abraham, Isaac and Jacob arose from their tomb, and stood in prayer before the Lord"'.

3. For prophetic statements about bribery see for example Isa. 33.15; Amos 5.12. See also the Mosaic legislation, Exod. 23.7-8; Deut. 16.19; 27.25.

4. The words of R.S. Cripps, *A Critical and Exegetical Commentary on the*

understanding that Jesus is indeed Israel's messiah, is precisely the kind of interpretation that one would expect within a Judean community. No prophets who made it into the canon were mainstream,[1] and a similar skepticism about the fairness of their descriptions of life in Israel and the character of its leaders could be registered against them.[2]

Greco-Roman Audition

In the preceding section I have endeavored to show that Matthew's christological convictions combine with his concern for the maintenance of Israel's privilege as the one chosen by God for the glorification of God's name among the nations. Hence there is much in Matthew's Gospel that appeals to publics steeped in Israel's traditions. But if his Gospel is also to speak to communities that are being encouraged to move beyond traditional Judean boundaries, there ought to be some indication of points of contact with other publics. In short, one must answer the question of how publics steeped in Greco-Roman traditions might make sense of Jesus' person and work as presented in Matthew's Gospel.

In what follows I shall endeavor to demonstrate Matthew's ability to blend the theme of outreach to the nations with much of his narrative that at first sight might appear to have an appeal limited to 'Judeans'.[3]

Book of Amos (London: SPCK, 1955), p. 208, are significant: 'The student... hardly needs to be reminded that the words of Amos are the bitter rebukes of a reformer, rather than a carefully balanced description of the condition of the nation as by a modern historian sitting in his study chair'. On the special status of Judah and Israel, as recognized by Amos, see A.E. Steinmann, 'The Order of Amos's Oracles against the Nations: 1.3–2.16', *JBL* 111 (1992), p. 687.

1.   See for example the attacks registered by the 'official' prophets in the Mosaic legislation: Isa. 30.10; Jer. 33.7-9; Ezek. 13; Amos 7.10-17; Mic. 3.5-8.

2.   Cripps (*Amos*, p. 228) comments on Amos 7.10-17: 'The narrative provides an illustration of the attitude too often adopted by the leaders of a close-sealed institutional religion towards those in whose spirit God's free Spirit is working'. To which one might add that it is naive to think that a person like Jesus, who manifested extraordinary creativity in his manner and speech, especially in ways that brought him into conflict with cherished traditions, would not incur hostility from some sectors of entrenched position and power.

3.   Numerous references in this section are derived from BAGD. In the course of my reading of Greco-Roman writers for the revision of the latter I have located many more references. Other sources are also indicated in the notes. The translations are my own.

At almost the very beginning, a strong signal beyond Judean boundaries is sent out with the interpretation of the name Immanuel as 'God with us' (1.23). With whom? Does the Judean God think exclusively or inclusively? Matthew will permit no doubt as he develops the theme of the divine presence, a major thread in the texture of his book. God's presence, he maintains, is realized fundamentally in the person of Jesus, the Christ. And where Jesus Christ is, one can count on continuity with Israel.

Inasmuch as Matthew's gospel is written in Greek, with an outreach to the world envisaged at its conclusion (28.19), it is imperative to look first of all for a Greco-Roman cultural model that might have served as a hermeneutical medium for understanding the significance of Jesus. From every direction come figures recognized for their extraordinary merit. Many of them have moved from human to divine status, or are in the process of doing so. In the course of time, rhetorical conventions for appropriate recognition of distinguished persons were developed. In his *Progymnasmata*, the rhetorician Hermogenes lists nationality, place of birth and ancestry as principal topics for the marshalling of items in praise of a notable person.[1] At the beginning of his life of Plato, Diogenes Laertius traces that philosopher's ancestry through his mother Perictione back to the lawgiver Solon and through the latter to Poseidon, god of earthquakes and water. The ancestry of Plato's father Ariston was said to go back through Codrus, an early king of Athens, and it was claimed that Codrus was also able to trace his family back to Poseidon (*D.L.* 3.1).

Matthew presents the ancestry of Jesus in two phases: first, from Abraham forward to Jesus (1.2-17), and then with the involvement of the Holy Spirit (1.18-24). Beyond question, the genealogy recorded in 1.2-17 derives from a Semitic milieu, but what impact might it have had on publics only slightly familiar with or totally ignorant of Israelite tradition? Roman patriotism glowed in the knowledge that the founding ancestors of the great city on the Tiber could be traced to 753 BCE. It is therefore probable that those in Matthew's publics with even minimal Greco-Roman background would have been impressed by Jesus' human

---

1. *Hermogenes Opera* (ed. H. Rabe; Rhetores Graeci, 6; Leipzig: Teubner, 1913): *Progymnasmata* 37, p. 15: τόποι δέ εἰσιν ἐγκωμιαστικοί ἔθνος οἷον ῞Ελλην, πόλις οἷον ᾿Αθηναῖος, γένος οἷον ᾿Αλκαιωνίδης; see also *Nicolai Progymnasmata* (ed. J. Felten; Rhetores Graeci, 11; Leipzig: Teubner, 1913), p. 50, ll. 15-16: ὅπερ λαμβάνεται ἀπὸ ἔθνους, ἀπὸ πόλεως, ἀπὸ προγόνων.

ancestry, which counted centuries before the decline of the Babylonian empire. And after further exposure to Matthew's narrative, they would have been struck by the fact that this Jesus was far larger than life.

In the great epics of the Mediterranean world—the *Iliad*, the *Odyssey* and the *Aeneid*—mighty warriors vied for immortality in a people's memory and adulation. Achilles says that the Trojans worshipped Hector as a god in his lifetime (*Iliad* 22.393-94). In the course of years, distinguished athletes and philosophers, as well as heads of state, qualified for such recognition. Elite human ancestry was an important ingredient in the adulation that was extended, but one would try to reach for divine connections. Pindar, a Greek poet from Boeotian Thebes, mentions many a notable ancestor in odes that commemorate the feats of champions in Olympic, Isthmian, Pythian and Nemean contention, but his highest praise is reserved for victors who could be linked to a family or site that was associated with the exploits of mythological divinities and deities. Thus through his poetry Pindar helped fix the Greco-Roman mindset for patriotic associations.

Matthew does not for a moment forget the interest of Greco-Roman minds, even while winning the attention of tradition-oriented Judeans. Out of the traditions available to him, Matthew selects stories that would also send out a message to Greco-Romans. Some among them might comment about the Semitic quaintness of the narrative, but with one voice they would exclaim: this is the world we know. Rhetoricians recommended including, where possible, evidence of unusual circumstances of birth. Matthew's second phase in the presentation of Jesus' ancestral connections includes two features that meet the highest expectations: Jesus is of divine origin, and marvelous circumstances attended his birth.

Extraordinary conceptions and pregnancies were no novelty in the Mediterranean world, and remarkable portents that might attend them helped focus attention on the emergence of a superstar. Greco-Roman stories of male deities consorting with women are so common that there is no need of recital.[1] It is true, of course, that Matthew's story of the conception of Jesus differs greatly from such accounts, for no sexual connection is even remotely suggested. But of interest is the fact that the

---

1. F. Jacoby, *Die Fragmente der Griechischen Historiker*. I. *Genealogie und Mythographie* (repr.; Leiden: Brill, 1968 [1923]), fragments 1–63, contains essential information in brief space on a variety of matters relating to genealogies from numerous ancient writers.

mere association of Jesus' birth with divine activity would mark Jesus as an exceptional person. In effect, Matthew elevates the story of Jesus' origin above crass Greco-Roman mythology, but with the same strokes of his pen he opens the way for its understanding in a broad cultural environment.[1]

After enumerating the principal topics to be addressed in praise of a distinguished person, Hermogenes advises that one should recite details surrounding the birth itself, including marvelous circumstances and dreams.[2] To highlight the historical significance of Alexander the Great, Plutarch records that a thunderbolt struck the womb of this illustrious general's mother before the consummation of her marriage to King Philip, who then avoided intimate relations with her, either from fear of magical spells or simply because she was now associated with an

---

1.   Plutarch observes that the idea of a deity consorting sexually with a human is difficult to accept. He then notes an Egyptian view that a woman can be made pregnant by a divine spirit; *Numa* 4, 3-4; see also his *Moralia* 718b. For discussions of the two passages and the topic of pneumatic conception, see E. Norden, *Die Geburt des Kindes: Geschichte einer religiösen Idee* (Leipzig: Teubner, 1924), pp. 76-92, and R. Reitzenstein, *Die hellenistischen Mysterienreligion nach ihren Grundgedanken und Wirkungen* (Leipzig: Teubner, 3rd rev. edn), pp. 245-46. See also H. Leisegang, *Pneuma Hagion: Der Ursprung des Geistbegriffs der synoptischen Evangelien aus der griechischen Mystik* (Leipzig: Hinrichs, 1922), pp. 43ff. Reitzenstein praised Leisegang for calling attention to the importance of a discussion of conception by divine influence in Philo, *Cher.* 12-15. For other accounts of extraordinary conceptions and births, see H. Usener, *Das Weihnachtsfest* (Bonn: Cohen, 1889), pp. 69-76; idem, 'Geburt und Kindheit Christi', *ZNW* 4 (1903), pp. 1-21; and the long list cited by E. Petersen, *Die wunderbare Geburt des Heilandes* (Tübingen: Mohr [Paul Siebeck], 1909), pp. 34-37; of the literature cited by H. Almqvist, *Plutarch und das Neue Testament* (Uppsala: Appelberg, 1945), p. 32, see especially L. Bieler, *ΘΕΙΟΣ ΑΝΗΡ: Das Bild des 'Göttlichen Menschen' in Spätantike und Frühchristentum* (Vienna: Oskar Höfels, 1935), I, pp. 24-28. Bieler's observations about later Christian Hellenized associations with the infancy narratives show how readily Matthew's accounts would find a comfortable home in Greco-Roman minds, without a suggestion of borrowing; see also R.E. Brown, *The Birth of the Messiah* (Garden City, NY: Doubleday, 1977), p. 137, with reference to the implications of Dead Sea Scroll evidence, and his comments on Luke's account of the virginal conception, p. 301, especially n. 15. Trypho chided the Christians for reciting stories similar to those recorded by Greco-Roman writers about their deities and heroes. Justin correctly rejected the criticism as invalid, but on invalid grounds: *Dialogue with Trypho* 67.

2.   Hermogenes, *Progymnasmata* 37, pp. 15-16: ἐρεῖς δέ τινα καὶ ἃ περὶ τὴν γένεσιν συνέπεσεν ἄξια θαύματος, οἷον ἐξ ὀνειράτων...ἤ τινων ποιούτων.

exceptional being (*Alexander* 2.1-6).[1] Matthew accentuates the implications of Jesus' conception by noting Joseph's dream concerning Mary's pregnancy (1.20).

As in the Semitic world, reference to dreams was a common medium in the Greco-Roman environment for emphasizing involvement of the divine in human affairs. In his account of Plato, Diogenes Laertius cites writers who claim that Ariston tried to make love to Perictione, who steadfastly resisted him. During a halt in his amorous attempts, he dreamed that he saw Apollo, whereupon he completely desisted from touching Perictione until her child was born (*D.L.* 3.2). An inscription dealing with the founding of a shrine dedicated to the deity Sarapis records that a devotee named Maiistas receives directions in a dream for its erection, along with assurance that dissidents will receive their just due.[2] Significantly, Matthew refers to dreams only at the beginning of his book and near its end.[3] In Matthew's recital the appearance of the angel (1.20a) serves as a portent which sets the stage for the extraordinary pronouncement in 1.20b. Matthew's publics are to sense the import of God's involvement in the destiny of this extraordinary child.

To an Israelite the name 'Jesus' would serve as a reminder of the great deliverer Joshua, but Greco-Romans would be impressed by the role of Jesus as intermediary between God and humankind. Gentiles understood well the importance of right relations with deities. Their cultic systems and personal rituals were designed to retain divine favor.[4] That Jesus would 'save his people from their sins', whether moral offences or cultic inadvertencies, meant that his God would be readily accessible. Matthew's story is therefore replete with evidence of Jesus' outreach to all in Israel, regardless of status. At the very beginning of his public appearance, Pharisees and Sadducees, under a prophetic barrage from John the Baptist, need only repent, evidently of an overemphasis on

1.   For the effect of a portent on marital relations, see also Plutarch, *Alcibiades* 23: a King Agis remains celibate for ten months after an earthquake so terrified him that he left the arms of his wife and ran out of the bedroom.

2.   *Inscriptiones Graecae* XI. 4, no. 1299. For a translation, see F. Danker, *Epigraphic Study of a Graeco-Roman Semantic Field* (St Louis, MO: Clayton Publishing House, 1982), pp. 186-88.

3.   See 1.20; 2.12, 13, 19, 22; 27.19. Dreams are, of course, featured in Old Testament narratives, but the datum only serves to reinforce the fact that Matthew scores points on Semitic and Greco-Roman fronts. The origin of the material is therefore of no immediate interest in the present study.

4.   See BAGD s.v. 'καθαρός', and esp. the ref. *SIG* 983, 5.

legal technicalities and ritual, and order their lives anew so as to be assured of a real connection with Abraham (3.7-10). Tradespeople find a welcome (4.18-22), as do many in need of healing (4.23-25). Many of the marginalized who were called ἁμαρτωλοί in Israel's cultic system, including especially tax collectors, find space in the mainstream of divine consideration (9.10-13).[1]

As in the Semitic world, Greco-Romans were impressed by prophecies connected with extraordinary events or people of heroic proportions.[2] Some concern the the death of heroes. In the *Iliad* (22.358-60) the dying Hector prophesies to Achilles that he must ponder his destined fate at the hand of Paris and Apollo under the walls of Troy. Diodorus Siculus (19.7-9) records that Chaldean astrologers had warned Alexander that he would die if he entered Babylon and that Antigonus was destined to die in conflict with Seleucus. Other prophecies relate to the glorious future that awaits the great one. For example, it was said that Cicero's mother experienced no birth pangs, and his wet nurse was told by some invisible power that he would become a welcome boon to the Roman people (Plutarch, *Cicero* 1–2). Through his reference to Isa. 7.14 (Mt. 1.23), which also elicits his publics' respect for ancient tradition, Matthew reinforces the affirmation made in 1.21: Jesus will save his people from their sins, and thus he will be God-with-us. As the rest of the book proclaims, this last pronoun refers especially to the followers of Jesus Christ. Through them God's invitation into the divine presence is made abundantly audible.

The suggestion of Jesus' greatness and the aura of divine presence find further enunciation, signalled by 'Behold!' in the recital of Herod's encounter with the magi. The reference to a star is meaningful for more than one reason. In his *Odes* (1, 12, 46–48) the Roman poet Horace appealed to popular thinking by connecting a star with Octavian, who, after Alexander, became the brightest light in the political firmament of the Greco-Roman world. And by associating both the star and the magi with the fortunes of Jesus, Matthew further cultivates in his publics a

1. The term ἁμαρτωλός denotes people who lack finesse in dealing with God. They are not necessarily wicked, but they lack the knowledge and skill that Pharisees and Sadducees possess in matters relating to observance of divine precepts; see BAGD s.v.

2. Diodorus Siculus 17.10 epitomizes the general mood. On the subject of prophecy in the Greco-Roman world, see D.E. Aune, *Prophecy in Early Christianity and the Mediterranean World* (Grand Rapids: Eerdmans, 1983), pp. 23-79.

sense of the transcendent significance of this child born in Bethlehem. According to Cicero, magi predicted that Alexander's birth would spell disaster for Asia.[1] Especially striking is the fact that the magi are guided from Jerusalem to Bethlehem by the star. Servius, an ancient commentator on Vergil's *Aeneid*, similarly reports, on the authority of Terentius Varro, that a star guided Vergil to Laurentum.[2]

Like the sailors in Timoleon's fleet, who rejoiced when a star led them to Italy, the magi were 'overjoyed' when they saw the star halt over the place where the child was.[3] Herod's response to the magi's message is in striking contrast and further suggests the cosmic significance of the newborn king. Herod is at a loss in the face of a portent that appears to threaten his reign. So it was with Alexander, who was troubled over Chaldean predictions of his death.[4]

The fact that Jesus was born at Bethlehem evokes a further citation of ancient prophecies (2.5-6). In connection with this birthplace Matthew faces a liability. Matthew knows the Greco-Roman mindset and is probably well aware that one above the common herd ought to be able to claim a famous city. But there are two sides to the matter. After citing the accepted point of view, that birth in an 'important city' spells true happiness, Plutarch offers his own opinion in his life of Demosthenes: 'Being born in a little-known and quite ordinary place is no obstacle to one who wants to enjoy real blessedness, which for the most part consists of character and disposition' (*Demosthenes* 1–2). The fact that Bethlehem could boast of a prophetic promise scored points, and Matthew turns the fulfillment into a further asset by including a combination of statements in Mic. 5.1-3 and 2 Kgdms 5.2 = 1 Chron. 11.2. The catchword ποιμαίνειν ('to shepherd') introduces David, and the demands of appropriate encomium are met. The time of fulfillment requires that Bethlehem no longer be considered unimportant. Hence the revision, 'in no way the least'.

Many in Matthew's publics would agree that Jesus is indeed the 'king of the Judeans', and after having heard the whole story they would note the remarkable contrast in attitude and circumstance involving the

---

1.   Cicero, *On Divination* 1, 23, 47; see BAGD, s.v. μάγος and Usener, *Weihnachtsfest*, p. 37. Ps.-Callisth. 3.33.26 reports that at the death of Alexander a great star plunged into the sea.

2.   Servius on *Aeneid* 2.801; Usener, *Weihnachtsfest*, p. 77 n. 29.

3.   Diodorus Siculus 16.66.3; BAGD s.v. ἀστήρ.

4.   Diodorus Siculus 17.112.2-4; BAGD s.v. ταράσσω.

affirmation recorded in 2.2 and the one in 27.37. But few could fail to grasp Matthew's main objective, that the aura of transcendence developed in the infancy narrative prepare for the ultimate recognition of Jesus' kingship beyond the borders of Israel (28.18-20). Indeed, the infancy narrative projects Jesus as a royal figure, whose birthday merits extraordinary recognition.[1] Expressions of reverence would be dutifully rendered.[2] 'We have come to do homage' (2.2) therefore signals far more to Matthew's publics than a modern reader brought up in democratic institutions can possibly imagine. A potential head of state surrounded by such adulation has the stature of a god.[3] Herod, of course, mockingly adopts the stance of a client king who ordinarily recognizes, as Tiridates III did later, that all power resides in Rome.[4] On the other hand, Herod ironically confirms that the newborn child is greater than his own Roman master. Caesar Augustus was considered a god, but this child is 'God-with-us'.[5] The subsequent gesture of adoration by the magi (2.11) echoes in the recognition of Jesus by the eleven disciples (28.17). Their gifts are appropriate for observance of the birth of a royal personage.[6]

The two portents that follow, both in the nature of a dream (2.12-13), are in harmony with the picture of Jesus' transcendence thus far sketched. As indicated above, warnings are an integral feature of some recitals about superstars. Alexander, who at first was inclined to heed prophetic warning, made the mistake of heeding his philosophers and entered Babylon.[7] Jesus, on the other hand, eluded Herod, thanks to a portent that Joseph took seriously.

In response to the magi's change in travel plans, Herod orders the slaughter of all boys aged two years and under in the environs of Bethlehem. The record of his action, suggesting the presence of a rival to his throne, is the climactic stroke in the portrait of the newborn child

---

1.   See the literature cited in BAGD s.v. βασιλεύς and παρθένος.

2.   See BAGD, s.v. θεός.

3.   See BAGD, s.v. θεός.

4.   Dio Cassius 62.2.4.

5.   On the adulation accorded Augustus see, for example, the well-known inscription of Priene: *OGI* 458 (this inscription in honor of the emperor is abbreviated 'Dit., Or.' in BAGD, by others '*OGIS*').

6.   See BAGD s.v. λίβανον, σμύρνα and χρύσος.

7.   Diodorus Siculus 17.112.4-5.

as a person with an extraordinary destiny.[1] But the image is blurred. The one who is to spell salvation for 'his people' is the ostensible cause of great lamentation, but the calamity will be outweighed by a remarkable circumstance recorded in 27.52-53. Like the magi, who chose an alternate route after being warned in a dream, Joseph obeys an oracle and takes his family to a place outside the jurisdiction of Archelaus. There will be no further mention of dreams until 27.19.

After the infancy narrative, Matthew moves immediately into the public ministry of Jesus. This stage is also introduced by a recital that includes a prophetic citation (3.3). By attaching the citation to the entry of John the Baptist on the scene, Matthew reinforces the importance of Jesus. John is a superstar, but he is so primarily because of his association with Jesus. Hermogenes advises that an encomium should include unusual details connected with the life of honorands, including their τρόφη or diet (*Progymnasmata* 38, pp. 15-16). Judeans would readily catch the allusion to Elijah's diet at 3.4 (see 4 Kgdms 1.8) and would therefore note John's high status, whereas Greco-Romans who lacked intimate acquaintance with Old Testament traditions would catch the message of the text through the prophetic reference and the dietary details. After some rhetorical fanfare by John (3.11-12) Jesus appears on the scene. Two portents attend his inauguration: Jesus sees God's Spirit descending on him like a pigeon, and a voice from heaven affirms him as God's 'beloved son'. In view of the heavenly voice that attends the appearance of the bird, Greco-Romans would be especially impressed by the physical sign. Diodorus Siculus (17.49.5) records that the cawing of crows directed Alexander's entourage to the temple of Ammon.[2]

In the recital of Jesus' temptation, Matthew impresses his publics with the self-discipline displayed by his hero. Jesus fasts for forty days. Diogenes Laertius (4.11) states that the philosopher Xenocrates, noted for his independent spirit and lofty moral principles, spent an hour each day in silence. So esteemed was he for his integrity that Athens made an exception and permitted him to offer evidence in court without taking

---

1.   Usener, *Weihnachtsfest*, pp. 77-78 n. 30, cites other accounts of murder of infants: Pausanias 8.23.6-7; Plutarch, *Greek Questions* 22 (296d).

2.   On the association of a bird with a deity, see Usener, *Weihnachtsfest*, pp. 56-58. The voice from heaven would be the echo of the physical portent. When Alexander entered the temple of Ammon, the deity's prophet greeted him with the words, 'Welcome, son! And accept this greeting as the deity's own' (Diodorus Siculus 17.50.6).

an oath, and Philip of Macedon said that he was the only one whom he could not bribe. Numerous anecdotes about Greco-Romans of exceptional merit recount their skill in repartee. Diogenes Laertius (4.6-11) offers samples of Xenocrates' ready wit: when Alexander, who was an admirer of the arts and philosophy, sent him a rather large sum of money, he kept 3000 Attic drachmas and returned the balance, with the observation that Alexander had so many more people to take care of than he. In the story of the temptation of Jesus, Greco-Romans would be impressed with the Lord's sharp answers and with the fact that he could not be bought off at any price. Xenocrates, who had been dispatched as an envoy to plead for the release of Athenian prisoners, was invited to a banquet by King Antipater and answered the invitation with these words of Odysseus to Circe, straight out of the Hellenic Bible: 'O Circe, what man could call himself upright and eat and drink before he had set his comrades free and seen them with his own eyes?'[1] In his responses to Diabolos Jesus quotes from the Judean Bible, with emphasis on words from Deuteronomy. Israel's Great Patriot is not for sale.

Words backed by deeds marked a person of very special distinction in the Greco-Roman world. As one might expect, the combination is found as early as Homer. In the *Iliad* (9.443), the knight Phoenix addresses Achilles, who remains outraged because of an insult from Agamemnon and therefore unwilling to engage in battle against the Trojans. Phoenix reminds the great warrior that when the latter was but a youth, he had taught Achilles to be proficient in word and in deed.[2] Thucydides (1.139.4) said of Pericles that he was 'the first man of his time at Athens and the most skilled orator and statesman'.[3] In Matthew 5–7 the authoritative words of Jesus are heard, and these are backed up by a series of marvelous deeds (8.1–9.38). In the light of what has been noted above, one can conclude that Greco-Romans would be impressed by the interpretive reference to Isaiah (53.4). The healing narratives and the account of a young girl's restoration to life would be impressive. This Jesus competes well with Isis and Asclepius.[4] The sprightly repartee

---

1. *D.L.* 4.9 = Homer, *Odyssey* (10.383-85).

2. μύθων τε ῥητῆρ' ἔμεναι πρηκτῆρά τε ἔργων (*Iliad* 9.443).

3. ἀνὴρ κατ' ἐκεῖνον τὸν χρόνον πρῶτος 'Αθηναίων, λέγειν τε καὶ πράσσειν δυνατώτατος. Luke makes the point explicitly in connection with Jesus (Lk. 24.19) and Moses (Acts 7.22).

4. On Isis, see I. Bergman, *Ich Bin Isis: Studien zum memphitischen Hintergrund der griechischen Isisaretalogien* (Uppsala: Almqvist & Wiksell, 1968);

interspersed in and among the marvels that Matthew records would further impress Greco-Romans. A prospective student who lacked a basic liberal arts program wished to attend the lectures of Xenocrates. His answer: 'I don't card raw wool' (*D.L.* 4.10). To the scribe who said, 'Teacher, no matter where you go, I will follow you', Jesus replied, 'Foxes have lairs and birds have nests, but the Son of Humanity has no place to lay his head' (Mt. 8.19-20).

It is tempting to sketch many other literary tactics used by Matthew, but space permits only a brief halt at 17.1-8 and 23.37-39, before moving on to Matthew's final two chapters. Numerous features in the transfiguration account would, of course, appeal to readers familiar with stories about Moses, but a Greco-Roman public would also readily see that Jesus was not to be measured by ordinary standards. From Homer on, gleaming garments were associated with superstars and divine involvement. In the *Iliad*, Athena causes Dimodes to shine with the brightness of the star Sirius, and Achilles she crowns with a golden cloud from which a bright flame emerges.[1]

The transfiguration of Jesus could easily suggest to Greco-Roman publics that Jesus was a divine figure, an inference that would find support in what appear to be cultic interests at 17.4. The Mediterranean world was dotted with shrines dedicated to an extensive variety of heroes and deities.[2] But what are the distinctive credentials of Jesus? It takes the voice from heaven to isolate Jesus from Moses and Elijah. The words 'This is my beloved Son' affirm the prophetic pronouncement in 1.23 and echo the voice from heaven at the baptism (3.17).[3] Jesus is, indeed, God-with-us. Yet we await the message of 28.19 to confirm the fact that Jesus has no interest in a limiting cult center.

It is now necessary to deal again with ch. 23 and make one further assessment of the severe criticism that was leveled against the scribes

---

for some of the important texts, see W. Peek, *Der Isishymnus von Andros und verwandte Texte* (Berlin: Weidmann, 1930). On Asclepius and texts, see *Asclepius: A Collection and Interpretation of the Testimonies* (2 vols.; Baltimore: Johns Hopkins University Press, 1945).

1.   *Iliad* 5.4-6 (Diomedes); 18.205-206 (Achilles).

2.   For data see the *Description of Greece* by Pausanias, the Baedeker of the ancient world.

3.   For the routes along which a Greco-Roman public would appreciate the reference to the descent of the pigeon, see BAGD s.v. περιστερά, and the reference to Usener, *Weihnachtsfest*, pp. 56-59.

and Pharisees. As noted above, Judeans would hear the prophetic accent. Thus had prophets ever spoken about those who interfered with God's plan. But what about Greco-Romans? Would such language not conflict with a patriotic strategy? Far from it. The hotter the invective, the more blatant would appear the lack of patriotism on the part of the accused (as in an oration by Lycurgus against an alleged traitor named Leocrates) and the greater the patriotism of the speaker (as in the oration *On the Crown*, by Demosthenes against Aeschines). By attacking those who jeopardize the people's fortunes, the speaker shows his concern for the nation. The scene in Mt. 23.37-39 follows with rhetorical precision. Here Jesus bares his patriotic heart. In diction flooding with tenderness and profound concern, he sees the terrible fate of Jerusalem looming before him, and there is nothing he can do to stop it.

In Jesus' aching words there would be much for Greco-Romans to ponder, for ability to save a city from disaster guaranteed remembrance as a superstar. In his speech against Leocrates, the orator Lycurgus invites his Athenian audience to remember Codrus, an early king of Athens. After a crop failure in the Peloponnesos, the inhabitants of that part of Hellas resolved to march against Athens and take over its territory. But first they consulted the oracle at Delphi. They were told that Athens could be taken only if they spared the life of Codrus. Informed by a certain Cleomantis, who had overheard the oracular response, the Athenians prepared for battle, and King Codrus proceeded to perform his act of valor. Dressed as a beggar he met two men from the enemy's forces and killed one of them. The other in turn killed Codrus. The Athenians then sent out a herald and revealed everything to the Peloponnesians, who then retreated, knowing that heaven was no longer on their side.[1] In Matthew's view Jesus was the last hope for Jerusalem in its struggle for survival as a city in a world dominated by Rome, and the Evangelist shares the patriotic emotion that finds expression in the twofold 'Jerusalem, Jerusalem'.[2] The perplexity of Matthew's Greco-Roman publics would end when they heard the rest of the story.

Between the recital of the transfiguration and the end of Matthew's book appears an episode that seems to conflict with the meaning of Immanuel. Jesus cries out, 'My God, my God, why did you abandon

---

1. Lycurgus, *Against Leocrates* 86 [158].

2. 'The duplication of a name is forceful', observes Pseudo-Demetrius, *On Style* 267. For references, see BAGD, s.v. Ἰεροσόλυμα.

me?' (27.46). But what are the probabilities respecting Greco-Roman interpretation? Some contemporaries of Matthew, accustomed as they were to stories about arbitrary actions of deities, might well have viewed Jesus as a latter-day Prometheus, who maintains his integrity to the last. But those who recalled earlier portions of the book, with its accounts of sage words and helpful deeds, would know that this second-last cry could not be a declaration of defiant impiety. Being Greco-Romans, they would be stirred by the dream ascribed to Pilate's wife (27.19) and by the two descriptions of portents that surround the recital of Jesus' last moments. These latter marvels could mean that someone or something had elicited the wrath of heaven, or that nature itself was affirming the greatness of the sufferer, or both.

Whatever people steeped in ancient biblical lore might have thought, many in Matthew's publics would give the benefit of the doubt to Jesus. Prior to the death of Jesus, 'darkness covered all the land' (27.45). This is the kind of portent that accompanies the death of a superstar. In a work ascribed to Callisthenes, it is reported that the sun was darkened at the death of Alexander.[1] The rending of the temple curtain would have stirred profound emotions: this is one of history's decisive moments.[2] Mention of an earthquake (27.51) was certain to arouse awe and awareness of divine intervention.[3] Also, in the light of the other portents, the disturbance of graves would not sound a jarring note.[4] Nor could the import of the resurrection of unidentified pious people in connection with the death of this crucified man be missed by anyone who followed Matthew's story from its beginning. Once infants died because of his birth (2.16); now his death spells the opening of graves. Unmistakably, this death is an instrument of salvation.

To impress the saving dimension of the moment of Jesus' death, Matthew modifies the resurrection of the nameless pious with the

---

1.   Pseudo-Callisthenes 3.33.26; see BAGD s.v. σκότος.

2.   See for example Polybius 3.112.8 for the Roman point of view. On the political significance of a portent in a shrine, see Dio Cassius 53.1.3; Plutarch, *Demetrius* 12.3 (894).

3.   See BAGD s.v. σείω Dio Chrysostom 80[30], 11; see also references s.v. κόλασις and σημεῖον, and the numerous references on Mt. 27.51 in J. Wetstein, *Novum Testamentum Graece* (Amsterdam: Dommerian's, 1751–52), I.

4.   See the passages cited in Wetstein, ad loc., for example Tibullus 1.2.45; Ovid, *On Love* 1.8.17-18; Ovid, *Metamorphoses* 6.699: Boreas frightens the spirits of the dead and the entire earth with his shaking: *sollicito manes totumque tremoribus orbem.*

observation that they appeared to many after the resurrection of Jesus. This reference to the resurrection seems to be intrusive and inelegantly premature. On the other hand, by apparently dismissing the resurrection as an appendix to his story Matthew maintains the focus on Jesus as saving victor in his death. At the same time, the restoration to life of a notable person surrounded by many portents in the hour of death would further suggest superstar status. In brief, the portents do not signal divine disfavor but verify that this crucified one is indeed God-with-us. Lucan wrote of those who fought in the battle of Pharsalia: 'How great these men, of whom the world took note: all heaven was attentive to their fate'.[1] The centurion knows how to read the signs. He exclaims: 'Indeed, this was God's son'.[2] Unconverted Gentiles would probably have heard his words in the sense: 'This man was more than one of mortal breed'. A superstar of superstars. But Matthew will not let the matter rest. Jesus is far more than a cult hero. To proclaim that fact is the burden of his final paragraphs.

The earthquake, this time a 'great' one, mentioned at 28.2 advances the theme of Jesus as the central figure on the stage of history. The heavenly messenger's visage and extraordinarily white garments (vv. 2-3) constitute a typical motif expressive of divine intervention and presence.[3] Fear is a common response in such contexts.[4] Such was the case when Iris, the messenger of Zeus (Διὸς ἄγγελος) appeared to Priam, 'whose limbs trembled' (*Iliad* 24.169-70). Since deities and divine heroes frequently revealed themselves in manifestations or epiphanies that spelled salvation for their devotees, as in the case of the Dioscuri during the battle at Lake Regillus, Matthew's Greco-Roman publics would anticipate a fuller recital of what he had briefly alluded to at 27.53, together with an appearance of Jesus. Matthew meets the expectation, but a remarkable feature of his concluding paragraph is the absence of any spectacular aspects of Jesus' person.

Matthew's literary economy contrasts, for example, with the legend

---

1. Lucan, *Civil War* 7.205-206.
2. See BAGD, s.v. υἱός 2b.
3. See above on the transfiguration. The term 'angel of the Lord' would be no problem for Greco-Romans familiar with the 'messenger of Zeus', *Iliad* 24.169 (BAGD lacks the reference, s.v. ἄγγελος).
4. On the effects of divine manifestation, see *Iliad* 20.129-31; 24.170; *Odyssey* 16.172-79; F. Pfister, 'Epiphanie', PWSup, IV (1924), pp. 317-18 (see BAGD s.v. ἐπιφάνεια).

about the Dioscuri, who were said to have been far superior in beauty and stature to any mere mortal.[1] Yet his approach is understandable, for he had used epiphany features in the account of the transfiguration. Here, in ch. 28, Matthew does not permit his publics to forget that the death of Jesus is the high moment of the entire story, a veritable epiphany. The women are seeking the 'crucified one' (28.5). But they are looking in the wrong place. In Galilee they will see him. In Galilee Jesus makes still another epiphany. At the transfiguration the disciples 'put their faces to the ground' (17.6). Here they do what was said of the magi (2.11). The beginning and the end come together. And precisely at this point all in Matthew's publics are called to decision. Especially Greco-Romans must know that there are no categories in their experience adequate to assess the significance of Jesus. This is no mere superstar among other superstars. 'All power in heaven and on earth has been given to me', he proclaims (v. 19). It is the definitive answer to Satan's braggadocio (4.9). He goes on to speak as one who holds title to every person on the face of the earth. Thus only a god can speak. But Jesus is not one among many gods. He is one with the Father and the Holy Spirit. How apposite are his concluding words (28.20). They explain why there is no need of an ascension recital in Matthew's Gospel. He does not depart the earth, as was said of certain Greco-Roman heroes who were given divine recognition. Rather, he gives the answer to the question asked in 24.3: what is the sign of your parousia? It is God-with-us, affirms Matthew, the patriot.

Conclusion

In patriotic pride Matthew has presented an account that he hopes will help his various publics appreciate the superstar of superstars, Jesus Christ. A true son of Israel, Jesus is determined to see Israel carry out its destiny, despite the fall of the city. Through his disciples, all of them Israelites, Jesus will preside over the assignment. An Israel without outreach to the world would be unfaithful to its election. As Israel's messiah, Jesus ensures the fidelity of Israel. Any apparently harsh words against the leadership are in effect patriotic expressions of concern for

---

1. On the importance of epiphanies of deities and heroes in Greco-Roman culture, see Pfister, 'Epiphanie', entire article. On the Dioscuri, the sons of Zeus, see BAGD s.v. Διόσκουροι. On the epiphany of the Dioscuri during the battle of Lake Regillus, see Dionysius of Halicarnassus 6.13; Pfister, 'Epiphanie', p. 320.

Israel's destiny. What Israel's leaders fail to accomplish, his disciples will do. Historic Israel has not lost its right to the Gospel, for the Lord's instruction is to teach 'all the nations.' None is excluded. At one moment in history some in Israel accepted responsibility for the death of Jesus. But Jesus is Immanuel, and he saves his people from their sins. Those who pronounced the dreadful curse upon themselves receive a second opportunity through the ministry of Jesus's followers. Woe, therefore, on those teachers, whether in or out of the communities that are committed to the teachings of Jesus, who teach contrary to the messiah's instruction. Matthew's christological contribution is to present a book that speaks to Judeans and at the same time assists Greco-Romans to use their cultural experience as a steppingstone to appreciate the uniqueness of Jesus Christ, the messiah of Israel, the Great Patriot, who includes them in his people.

Ναζωραῖος IN MATTHEW 2.23*

James A. Sanders

The literature available on the quesion of the use of Ναζωραῖος in Mt. 2.23 is considerable, and one who is not a Matthean specialist probably ought to exercise great care before entering so well-treated a field.[1] I am not a Matthean specialist, but I am willing to run the risk of tackling this problem because it affords the opportunity to explore in what ways First Testament patterns and precedence may have contributed to the Evangelist's narrative. It is a context that I believe holds the key to this issue and it is a dimension of the problem that has not been adequately appreciated.

It was Eduard Schweizer's excellent article in the Joachim Jeremias Festschrift, which deals with this problem directly, that served as the point of departure for the present paper in its original form some thirty years ago.[2] The debate has continued in the recent commentaries by

* This study originally appeared in *JBL* 84 (1965), pp. 169-72. It has been revised for this volume. I wish to thank my colleague, Craig Evans, for his assistance in updating the article.

1. I am aware that my brief study is followed in this book by R. Pesch's substantial essay, '"He will be Called a Nazorean": Messianic Exegesis in Matthew 1–2'; cf. Pesch's shorter German version, '"Er wird Nazoräer heißen": Messianische Exegese in Mt 1–2', in F. Van Segbroeck *et al.* (eds.), *The Four Gospels 1992* (F. Neirynck Festschrift; BETL, 100; 3 vols.; Leuven: Peeters, 1992), II, pp. 1385-1401. Pesch's essay does not address directly the problem considered in the present study.

2. E. Schweizer, '"Er wird Nazoräer heißen" (zu Mc 1,24; Mt 2,23)', in W. Eltester (ed.), *Judentum, Urchristentum, Kirche* (J. Jeremias Festschrift; BZNW, 26; Berlin: Töpelmann, 1960), pp. 90-93. Schweizer's study lists the most important relevant studies prior to 1960. Additional studies are noted in an article concerned with the Matthean prologue by E. Krentz, 'The Extent of Matthew's Prologue', *JBL* 83 (1964), pp. 409-14.

Robert Gundry, Ulrich Luz, and Dale Allison and W.D. Davies.[1] I would like to take this opportunity to return to the question, review the evidence that I presented earlier, and interact with recent studies, some of which support my conclusions while others do not.

I

There can surely be no doubt remaining about the geographic validity of Matthew's reference since the massive statement on the subject by William F. Albright, who, following George Foot Moore,[2] showed clearly that the vulgar Aramaic form (Heb. נוֹצְרִי) Nasraya (cf. Syriac) would have become *N^esoraya →*N^ezoraya → (Christian Palestinian) Nazoraya = Ναζωραῖος.[3] That Ναζωραῖος, as well as Ναζαρηνός,

---

1.   R.H. Gundry, *Matthew—A Commentary on his Literary and Theological Art* (Grand Rapids: Eerdmans, 1982), pp. 39-41; U. Luz, *Matthew 1–7* (Continental Commentary Series; Minneapolis: Fortress Press, 1989), pp. 148-50; D.C. Allison and W.D. Davies, *The Gospel according to Saint Matthew* (ICC; 2 vols.; Edinburgh: T. & T. Clark, 1988–91), I, pp. 274-84. Among the most helpful studies, one should see S. Lyonnet, '"Quoniam Nazaraeus vocabitur" (Mt. 2,23)', *Bib* 25 (1944), pp. 196-206; A. Médebielle, '"Quoniam Nazaraeus vocabitur" (Mt. 2,23)', in A. Metzinger (ed.), *Miscellanea Biblica et Orientalia* (A. Miller Festschrift; Rome: Herder, 1951), pp. 301-26; B. Gärtner, *Die rätselhaften Termini Nazoräer und Iskariot* (Uppsala: Gleerup, 1957), pp. 5-36; E. Zolli, 'Nazarenus vocabitur', *ZNW* 49 (1958), pp. 135-36; J. Rembry, '"Quoniam Nazaraeus vocabitur" (Mt. 2.23)', *SBFLA* 12 (1961–62), pp. 46-65; M. Black, *An Aramaic Approach to the Gospel and Acts* (Oxford: Clarendon Press, 3rd edn, 1967), pp. 197-200; R.H. Gundry, *The Use of the Old Testament in St Matthew's Gospel* (NovTSup, 18; Leiden: Brill, 1967), pp. 97-104; H.H. Schaeder, 'Ναζαρηνός, Ναζωραῖος', *TDNT*, IV, pp. 874-79; E. Zuckschwerdt, 'Ναζωραῖος in Matth. 2,23', *TZ* 31 (1975), pp. 65-77; G.M. Soares Prabhu, *The Formula Quotations in the Infancy Narrative of Matthew* (AnBib, 63; Rome: Biblical Institute Press, 1976), pp. 193-216; W.B. Tatum, 'Matthew 2.23—Wordplay and Misleading Translations', *BT* 27 (1976), pp. 135-38; R.E. Brown, *The Birth of the Messiah* (Garden City, NY: Doubleday, 1977), pp. 207-25; R.T. France, 'The Formula Quotations of Matthew 2 and the Problem of Communication', *NTS* 27 (1981), pp. 233-51; H.P. Rüger, 'ΝΑΖΑΡΕΘ/ΝΑΖΑΡΑ ΝΑΖΑΡΗΝΟΣ/ΝΑΖΩΡΑΙΟΣ', *ZNW* 72 (1981), pp. 257-63; D.B. Taylor, 'Jesus— of Nazareth', *ExpTim* 92 (1981), pp. 336-37; G. Allan, 'He shall be Called—a Nazirite?', *ExpTim* 95 (1983), pp. 81-82.

2.   G.F. Moore, 'Nazarene and Nazareth', in F.J. Foakes-Jackson and K. Lake (eds.), *The Beginnings of Christianity* (5 vols.; repr.; Grand Rapids: Baker, 1979 [1920–33]), I, pp. 426-32.

3.   W.F. Albright, 'The Names "Nazareth" and "Nazorean"', *JBL* 65 (1946),

says and means Nazarene in the sense of 'inhabitant of Nazareth' can no longer be seriously questioned.[1]

Krister Stendahl, also in the Jeremias Festschrift, has clearly shown that Matthew 2 has as its primary interest to establish Nazareth as the home of the infant Jesus, and that the chapter is dominated by geographic considerations. The movement of Matthew 2 is from Bethlehem and the question in ch. 1 of who Jesus was, to Nazareth and the fact that he was Galilean: it is a matter of 'christological geography'.[2] One wonders, however, if for Matthew the name Ναζωραῖος is *'purely* [my emphasis] geographic'.[3]

The student of today reads the First Testament quotations in the Second Testament with new respect and genuine excitement.[4]

pp. 397-401. Cf. also Albright's earlier study in *ZAW* 44 (1926), pp. 229-30.

1.   Gundry, *Use of the Old Testament*, p. 103; Soares Prabhu, *Infancy Narrative*, p. 201; Brown, *Birth*, p. 223; Allison and Davies, *Matthew*, I, p. 281. The New Testament MS tradition is divided between Ναζαρέτ (א B D L 33 700 892 1241 1424), Ναζαρέθ (C K N W Γ 28 565), and Ναζαρά (P⁷⁰ᵛⁱᵈ; cf. Lk. 4.16). In the rabbinic literature Jesus is referred to as יֵשׁוּעַ הַנּוֹצְרִי or simply יֵשׁוּ (cf. *b. Sanh.* 43a, 103a; *b. 'Abod. Zar.* 16b).

2.   K. Stendahl, 'Quis et Unde?', in Eltester (ed.), *Judentum, Urchristentum, Kirche*, pp. 94-105, esp. pp. 97-105.

3.   Stendahl, 'Quis et Unde?', p. 98 n. 17. Stendahl does not deal with the question of the Old Testament reference.

4.   For a sampling of the recent literature, see M. Black, 'The Christological Use of the Old Testament in the New', *NTS* 18 (1971), pp. 1-14; D.M. Smith, 'The Use of the Old Testament in the New', in J. Efird (ed.), *The Use of the Old Testament in the New and Other Essays* (W.F. Stinespring Festschrift; Durham, NC: Duke University, 1972), pp. 3-65; H.M. Shires, *Finding the Old Testament in the New* (Philadelphia: Westminster Press, 1974); R.N. Longenecker, *Biblical Exegesis in the Apostolic Period* (Grand Rapids: Eerdmans, 1975); B. Lindars, 'The Place of the Old Testament in the Formation of New Testament Theology', *NTS* 23 (1976), pp. 59-66; E.E. Ellis, 'How the New Testament Uses the Old', in I.H. Marshall (ed.), *New Testament Interpretation: Essays on Principles and Methods* (Grand Rapids: Eerdmans, 1977), pp. 199-219; M. Wilcox, 'On Investigating the Use of the Old Testament in the New Testament', in E. Best and R.M. Wilson (eds.), *Text and Interpretation* (Cambridge: Cambridge University Press, 1979), pp. 231-43; S.E. Balentine, 'The Interpretation of the Old Testament in the New Testament', *SWJT* 23 (1981), pp. 41-57; D. Moo, *The Old Testament in the Gospel Passion Narratives* (Sheffield: Almond Press, 1983); M. Black, 'The Theological Appropriation of the Old Testament by the New Testament', *SJT* 39 (1986), pp. 1-17; D.A. Carson and H.G.M. Williamson (eds.), *It is Written: Scripture Citing Scripture* (B. Lindars Festschrift; Cambridge: Cambridge University Press, 1988); E.E. Ellis,

Intertextuality is an engrossing subject, the old in the new; and every new MS discovery from early Judaism, in which the First Testament is quoted, treated and reflected in multifarious ways, renews and enhances one's interest in how the Second Testament writers used their canon.[1]

'Biblical Interpretation in the New Testament Church', in M.J. Mulder (ed.), *Mikra: Text, Translation, Reading and Interpretation of the Hebrew Bible in Ancient Judaism and Early Christianity* (CRINT, 2.1; Philadelphia: Fortress Press; Assen: Van Gorcum, 1988), pp. 691-725; C.A. Evans, 'The Function of the Old Testament in the New', in S. McKnight (ed.), *Introducing New Testament Interpretation* (Guides to New Testament Exegesis, 1; Grand Rapids: Baker, 1989), pp. 163-93; *idem*, 'Old Testament in the Gospels', in J.B. Green, S. McKnight and I.H. Marshall (eds.), *Dictionary of Jesus and the Gospels* (Downers Grove, IL: Inter-Varsity Press, 1992), pp. 579-90.

For studies specifically concerned with the function of Scripture in the Gospel of Matthew, see R.O. Coleman, 'Matthew's Use of the Old Testament', *SWJT* 5 (1962), pp. 29-39; J.J. O'Rourke, 'Fulfillment Texts in Matthew', *CBQ* 24 (1962), pp. 394-403; G. Barth, 'Matthew's Understanding of the Law', in G. Bornkamm *et al.*, *Tradition and Interpretation in Matthew* (Philadelphia: Westminster Press, 1963); N. Hillyer, 'Matthew's Use of the Old Testament', *EvQ* 36 (1964), pp. 12-26; Gundry, *Use of the Old Testament*; R. Pesch, 'Der Gottessohn im matthäischen Evangelienprolog (Mt 1–2): Beobachtungen zu den Zitationsformeln der Reflexionzitate', *Bib* 48 (1967), pp. 395-420; K. Stendahl, *The School of St Matthew and its Use of the Old Testament* (Philadelphia: Fortress Press, rev. edn, 1968); R.S. McConnell, *Law and Prophecy in Matthew's Gospel: The Authority and Use of the Old Testament in the Gospel of St Matthew* (Basel: Reinhard, 1969); W. Rothfuchs, *Die Erfüllungszitate des Matthäus-Evangeliums* (BWANT, 88; Stuttgart: Kohlhammer, 1969); L. Hartman, 'Scriptural Exegesis in the Gospel of St Matthew and the Problem of Communication', in M. Didier (ed.), *L'Evangile selon Matthieu, rédaction et théologie* (BETL, 29; Leuven: Peeters, 1972), pp. 131-52; F. Van Segbroeck, 'Les citations d'accomplissement dans l'Evangile selon Matthieu d'après trois ouvrages recents', in Didier (ed.), *L'Evangile selon Matthieu*, pp. 107-30; J.M. van Cangh, 'La Bible de Matthieu: Les citations d'accomplissement', *ETL* 6 (1975), pp. 205-11; G. Stanton, 'Matthew', in Carson and Williamson (eds.), *It is Written*, pp. 205-19; O.L. Cope, *Matthew: A Scribe Trained for the Kingdom of Heaven* (CBQMS, 6; Washington, DC: Catholic Biblical Association, 1976); J.H. Neyrey, 'The Thematic Use of Isa. 42.1-4 in Matthew 12', *Bib* 63 (1982), pp. 457-83.

1.   Not only have the Dead Sea Scrolls impacted upon textual criticism of the Hebrew Bible (cf. S. Talmon, 'Aspects of the Textual Transmission of the Bible in the Light of Qumran Manuscripts', *Textus* 4 [1964], pp. 95-132; J. de Ward, *A Comparative Study of the Old Testament Text in the Dead Sea Scrolls and in the New Testament* [STDJ, 4; Leiden: Brill, 1966]), the discovery of 8HevXIIgr has important implications for the form of the Greek Old Testament as well; cf. E. Tov,

What is meant in Mt. 2.23 by τὸ ῥηθὲν διὰ τῶν προφητῶν ὅτι Ναζωραῖος κληθήσεται? The four formula quotations in Matthew to this point employ the singular διὰ τοῦ προφήτου, with Jeremiah specified in 2.17. Since the reference in 2.23 is in the plural, and since the expression 'He shall be called a Nazarene' simply does not exist anywhere in the prophets, nor anywhere in the First Testament for that matter, numerous suggestions have been advanced, often involving ingenious reasoning.[1] Gundry's point that the plural 'prophets' and the absence of λέγοντος imply 'substance' and not 'exact words' is well taken.[2] Others, including Gundry, have rightly called attention to Matthew's haggadic approach.[3] But to what passage's substance has the Matthean Evangelist alluded?

The most fruitful and most probable suggestions have been those

with R.A. Kraft, *The Greek Minor Prophets Scroll from Nahal Hever (8HevXIIgr)* (DJD, 8; Oxford: Clarendon Press, 1990); J.A. Sanders, 'Stability and Fluidity in Text and Canon', in G.J. Norton and S. Pisano (eds.), *Tradition of the Text* (Schweig: Universitätsverlag, 1991), pp. 203-17; *idem*, 'The Dead Sea Scrolls and Biblical Studies', in M. Fishbane and E. Tov (eds.), *'Sha'arei Talmon': Studies in the Bible, Qumran, and the Ancient Near East* (S. Talmon Festschrift; Winona Lake, IN: Eisenbrauns, 1992), pp. 323-36. Fragments of Targums found at Qumran (4QtgLev; 4QtgJob; 11QtgJob) further document the diversity of forms and languages in which Israel's Scriptures were available in the New Testament period.

Twelve centuries ago some manuscripts from the Dead Sea area came to light. Hearing of this, the Nestorian patriarch Timotheus I wrote to Sergius of Elam, inquiring whether the newly discovered Hebrew manuscripts contained readings that agreed with certain problematic New Testament quotations of the Old Testament. Among those specifically mentioned was Mt. 2.23! Cf. de Ward, *Comparative Study*, p. 84. Note also the odd reading preserved in Shem Tov's Hebrew edition of the Gospel of Matthew: 'He came and dwelt in a city called Nazarith [נאזרית] in order to fulfill what the prophet said: "He shall be called Nazareth [נצורה]"'. For text and translation, see G. Howard, *The Gospel of Matthew according to a Primitive Hebrew Text* (Macon, GA: Mercer University Press; Leuven: Peeters, 1987), pp. 8-9.

1.   Such as references to Jer. 31.6; Isa. 11.1; Gen. 49.26; Lam. 4.7. One of the least persuasive options is Isa. 49.6, which has been proposed by Taylor, 'Jesus—of Nazareth', pp. 336-37.

2.   Gundry, *Matthew—A Commentary*, p. 39. So also Soares Prabhu, *Formula Quotations*, p. 202; and Pesch, '"Er wird Nazoräer heißen"', p. 1393.

3.   Cf. M.M. Bourke, 'The Literary Genus of Matthew 1–2', *CBQ* 22 (1960), pp. 60-75; Pesch, 'Der Gottessohn im matthäischen Evangelienprolog', pp. 395-420; E. Nellessen, *Das Kind und seine Mutter* (SBS, 39; Stuttgart: Katholisches Bibelwerk, 1970), pp. 58-80, 89-91; M. Oberweis, 'Beobachtungen zum AT-Gebrauch in der matthäischen Kindheitsgeschichte', *NTS* 35 (1989), pp. 131-49.

which have seen in the Matthean reference some reflection of the birth of Samson; and certainly one of the most attractive to date of all such suggestions is that of Eduard Schweizer. Seeing both Mt. 2.23 and Mk 1.24 in the light of Judg. 13.7 and 16.17, Schweizer notes that the designation ὁ ἅγιος θεοῦ (of LXX[B]: cf. ναζιραῖος θεοῦ of LXX[A]) is the point being made not only explicitly in Mark but implicitly in Matthew. Schweizer's interest in the First Testament Nazirite, specifically Samson, seems to be limited, however, to the fact that a נזיר (MT) could be understood as a Holy One of God (so LXX[B] and the explicit Markan designation of Christ). Schweizer deems it likely that Jesus was first designated as the Nazirite and Holy One of God, and the Greek translation evoked the relation with Nazareth and the peculiar formulation of the adjective Ναζωραῖος.[1]

II

1. Is it not, however, possible that the Evangelist, in establishing his 'christological geography' (Stendahl), and the spectrum Bethlehem–Nazareth in Matthew 2, purposely wanted to call attention to the only wonder-birth in the First Testament in which there is the open possibility of divine conception? Was not Alfred Loisy at least partially right when, at the beginning of this century, he called Matthew's use of Ναζωραῖος a 'jeu de mots'? Loisy was certainly right in his primary observation that Matthew attributed his citation to the 'prophets' because the book of Judges is anonymous and because it belongs to the Former Prophets. And certainly Loisy was also right in saying that nothing proves that the Evangelist did not base his wordplay on the Greek of the Septuagint, or that he would have been so scrupulous about Hebrew etymology.[2] Archaeological discoveries in Palestine long since Loisy's day have clearly shown that Greek existed as a viable vulgate alongside Hebrew and Aramaic in first-century Palestine.[3]

---

1. Schweizer, '"Er wird Nazroräer heißen"', p. 93.
2. A. Loisy, *Les Evangiles Synoptiques* (2 vols.; Ceffonds: Chez l'auteur, 1907–1908), I, pp. 375-76.
3. Cf. R.H. Gundry, 'The Language Milieu of First-Century Palestine', *JBL* 83 (1964), pp. 404-408, and especially the convenient references to archaeological reports in nn. 9-15 on pp. 405-406. For more recent studies, see J.A. Fitzmyer, 'The Languages of Palestine in the First Century A.D.', *CBQ* 32 (1970), pp. 501-31; repr. in *idem*, *A Wandering Aramean: Collected Aramaic Essays* (Missoula, MT: Scholars

122   *The Gospels and the Scriptures of Israel*

Here is a synopsis of the relevant Old Testament passages:

Judg. 13.5 MT כִּי־נְזִיר אֱלֹהִים יִהְיֶה

Judg. 13.7 MT כִּי־נְזִיר אֱלֹהִים יִהְיֶה

Judg. 16.17 MT כִּי־נְזִיר אֱלֹהִים[1]

Judg. 13.5 LXX^A ὅτι ἡγιασμένον ναζιραῖον ἔσται τῷ θεῷ τὸ παιδάριον ἐκ τῆς γαστρός

Judg. 13.5 LXX^B ὅτι ναζὶρ θεοῦ ἔσται τὸ παιδάριον ἀπὸ τῆς κοιλίας

Judg. 13.7 LXX^A ὅτι ναζιραῖον θεοῦ ἔσται τὸ παιδάριον ἀπὸ τῆς γαστρός

Judg. 13.7 LXX^B ὅτι ἅγιον θεοῦ ἔσται τὸ παιδάριον ἀπὸ γαστρός

Judg. 16.17 LXX^A ὅτι ναζιραῖος θεοῦ ἐγώ εἰμι ἐκ κοιλίας μητρός μου

Judg. 16.17 LXX^B ὅτι ἅγιος θεοῦ ἐγώ εἰμι ἀπὸ κοιλίας μητρός μου

Isa. 4.3 MT קָדוֹשׁ יֵאָמֶר

Isa. 4.3 LXX ἅγιοι κληθήσονται

Isa. 4.3 Targ. קדיש יתאמר

Isa. 11.1 MT וְיָצָא חֹטֶר מִגֵּזַע יִשָׁי וְנֵצֶר מִשָּׁרָשָׁיו יִפְרֶה

Isa. 11.1 LXX καὶ ἐξελεύσεται ῥάβδος ἐκ τῆς ῥίζης Ιεσαι, καὶ ἄνθος ἐκ τῆς ῥίζης ἀναβήσεται

Isa. 11.1 Targ. ויפוק מלכא מבנוהי דישי ומשיחא מבני בנוהי יתרבי

2. Let us consider Judg. 13.5b in LXX^A, which reads in full ὅτι ἡγιασμένον ναζιραῖον ἔσται τῷ θεῷ τὸ παιδάριον ἐκ τῆς γαστρός, καὶ αὐτὸς ἄρξεται σῴζειν τὸν Ἰσραὴλ ἐκ χειρὸς ἀλλοφύλων. Several points suggest that this is the principal text to which the Matthean quotation alludes.

Press, 1979), pp. 29-56; G. Mussies, 'Greek in Palestine and the Diaspora', in S. Safrai and M. Stern (eds.), *The Jewish People in the First Century* (CRINT, 1.2; Philadelphia: Fortress Press; Assen: Van Gorcum, 1976), pp. 1040-64; C. Rabin, 'Hebrew and Aramaic in the First Century', in Safrai and Stern (eds.), *The Jewish People in the First Century*, pp. 1007-39; M.O. Wise, 'Languages of Palestine', in Green, McKnight and Marshall (eds.), *Dictionary of Jesus and the Gospels*, pp. 434-44. Fitzmyer's conclusion represents the scholarly consensus: 'By way of conclusion, I should maintain that the most commonly used language of Palestine in the first century AD was Aramaic, but that many Palestinian Jews, not only those in Hellenistic towns, but farmers and craftsmen of less obviously Hellenized areas used Greek, at least as a second language. The data collected from Greek inscriptions and literary sources indicate that Greek was widely used. In fact, there is indication, despite Josephus' testimony, that some Palestinians spoke only Greek, the Ἑλληνισταί. But pockets of Palestinian Jews also used Hebrew, even though its use was not widespread' ('Languages', p. 46). See also Fitzmyer's popular assessment, 'Did Jesus Speak Greek?', *BARev* 18.5 (1992), pp. 58-63, 76-77.

1. The Targum to Judges renders the Hebrew text literally, with the exception that it says Samson will be a Nazirite of 'the Lord' (in place of 'God').

First, both the Nazirites in the Bible for whom we have names, Samson and Samuel, were conceived in their mothers' wombs by divine intervention. Luke, it is recognized, draws heavily in his infancy narrative on the story of the birth of Samuel and on Davidic literature generally. Consider for example the influence of Davidic tradition in the Lukan infancy account:

Luke		2 Samuel	
1.31	καλέσεις τὸ ὄνομα αὐτοῦ Ἰησοῦν	7.9	ἐποίησά σε ὀνομαστὸν κατὰ τὸ ὄνομα τῶν μεγάλων
1.32	οὗτος ἔσται μέγας		
1.32	δώσει... τὸν θρόνον Δαυίδ	7.13	ἀνορθώσω τὸν θρόνον αὐτοῦ
1.32	υἱὸς ὑψίστου	7.14	αὐτὸς ἔσται μοι εἰς υἱόν
1.32	βασιλεύσει ἐπὶ τὸν οἶκον	7.16	ὁ οἶκος αὐτοῦ, καὶ ἡ βασιλεία αὐτοῦ
1.33	εἰς τοὺς αἰῶνας	7.16	εἰς τὸν αἰῶνα

Cave 4 of Qumran has yielded some important materials that have a bearing on the Lukan allusions to 2 Samuel 7. 4QFlor 1.10-12 quotes portions of 2 Sam. 7.11-14, ending with '"I will be a father to him and he shall be a son to me". This is the "Branch of David" [צמח דויד] who will arise with the seeker of the Law and who will sit on the throne of Zion at the end of days'. This interpretation of 2 Samuel is clearly messianic. The title צמח דויד comes from Jer. 23.5; 33.15; Zech. 3.8; 6.12, all of which are paraphrased messianically in the Targum. The Aramaic fragment 4Q246 provides additional evidence of first-century messianic interpretation of this Scripture. What is remarkable is how at certain points the parallels with the Lukan account of the annunciation become even closer:

Luke		4Q246	
1.32	οὗτος ἔσται μέγας	1.7b	ו]רב להוה על ארעא
1.32	υἱὸς ὑψίστου κληθήσεται	2.1b	ובר עליון יקרונה
1.33	τῆς βασιλείας αὐτοῦ οὐκ ἔσται τέλος	2.5a	מלכותה מלכות עלם
1.35	πνεῦμα ἅγιον ἐπελεύσεται ἐπὶ σέ	1.1a	רוחה [ע]לוהי שרת
1.35	κληθήσεται υἱὸς θεοῦ	2.1a	ברה די אל יתאמר[1]

---

1. Cf. J.A. Fitzmyer, 'The Contribution of Qumran Aramaic to the Study of the New Testament', *NTS* 20 (1974), pp. 382-407, esp. pp. 391-94; repr. in *idem*, *A Wandering Aramean*, pp. 85-113, esp. pp. 92-93.

What all of this suggests is that Luke's interpretation of 2 Samuel 7 is not de novo, but is based at least in part on an exegetical tradition current in the first century. This is not, of course, to say that Luke was familiar with writings from Qumran, or even with their specific interpretations. What the Dead Sea Scrolls show is that in Palestinian circles outside of Christianity 2 Samuel 7 was understood in a messianic sense.[1] This aids our understanding of the background when the Lukan annunciation, with its messianic emphasis, incorporates language from this particular First Testament passage.

Observe also how Samuel tradition is echoed in the Lukan story:[2]

Samuel		*Jesus*	
1 Samuel		Luke	
1.22	presentation of child to the Lord	2.22	presentation of child to the Lord
2.1-10	Hannah sings praises of thanksgiving	2.36-38	Anna praises God and gives thanks
2.20	Eli blesses Samuel's parents	2.34	Simeon blesses Jesus' parents
2.26	Refrain A: καὶ τὸ παιδάριον Σαμουὴλ ἐπορεύετο, καὶ ἦν ἀγαθὸν μετὰ Κυρίου καὶ μετὰ ἀνθρώπον.	2.40	Refrain A´: τὸ δὲ παιδίον ηὔξανεν καὶ ἐκραταιοῦτο πληρούμενον σοφίᾳ, καὶ χάρις θεοῦ ἦν ἐπ' αὐτό.
3.1-18	ministry in the Temple (without parents) and a message to Eli the priest	2.41-51	visit to Temple (without parents) and discussion with religious teachers
3.19	Refrain B: καὶ ἐμεγαλύνθη Σαμουήλ, καὶ ἦν Κύριος μετ' αὐτοῦ, καὶ οὐκ ἔπεσεν ἀπὸ πάντων τῶν λόγων αὐτοῦ ἐπὶ τὴν γῆν.	2.52	Refrain B´: καὶ 'Ιησοῦς προέκοπτεν [ἐν τῇ] σοφίᾳ καὶ ἡλικίᾳ καὶ χάριτι παρὰ θεῷ καὶ ἀνθρώποις.

At many points Luke's structure follows that of 1 Samuel. At important points Luke's language has adopted the language of 1 Samuel. The clearest example is Luke's second refrain (B´), which obviously echoes 1 Samuel's first refrain (A). The opening words of the Magnificat (Lk. 1.46-48, 52: μεγαλύνει ἡ ψυχή μου τὸν κύριον, καὶ ἠγαλλίασεν τὸ πνεῦμά μου ἐπὶ τῷ θεῷ τῷ σωτῆρί μου, ὅτι

1. Curiously enough, 2 Sam. 7 is not understood in a messianic sense in the Targum.

2. The following material is adapted from C.A. Evans, *Luke* (NIBC; Peabody, MA: Hendrickson, 1990), pp. 40-41.

ἐπέβλεψεν ἐπὶ τὴν ταπείνωσιν τῆς δούλης αὐτοῦ...καὶ ὕψωσεν ταπεινούς) echo the opening words of Hannah's song of thanksgiving (1 Sam. 2.1 + 1.11 + 2.7: ἐστερεώθη ἡ καρδία μου ἐν Κυρίῳ... εὐφράνθην ἐν σωτηρίᾳ σου...ἐὰν ἐπιβλέπων ἐπιβλέψῃς ἐπὶ τὴν ταπείνωσιν τῆς δούλης σου...ταπεινοῖ καὶ ἀνυψοῖ). In the Targum, Hannah's song becomes a messianic apocalypse (esp. vv. 7-10).[1] Consider, for example, how the Targum rewrites v. 8 (with alterations italicized):

> He raises up the poor from the dust, from the dunghill he exalts the needy one, *to make them dwell* with *the righteous ones*, the chiefs *of the world; and he bequeathes to them* thrones of glory, *for before the Lord the deeds of the sons of men are revealed. He has established Gehenna below for the wicked ones. And the just ones—those doing his good pleasure, he has established the world for them.*[2]

Hannah's apocalypse concludes with the anticipation of final judgment upon Israel's enemies (v. 10, with alterations italicized):

> The Lord will shatter the enemies *who rise up to do harm to his people. The Lord blasts down* upon them *from* the heavens *with a loud voice. He will exact just revenge from Gog and the army of the violent nations who come with him from* the ends of the earth. And he will give power to his king and will magnify *the kingdom of* his Messiah.[3]

Is it not likely that Matthew, who in ch. 2 has clearly established a Mosaic–exodus cadre for his infancy narrative, would want to draw attention to the other Nazirite, the pre-Davidic, perhaps more Mosaic tradition of a wonder-birth? Has not the Matthean Evangelist, like the Lukan Evangelist, attempted to pattern the miraculous birth of Jesus, by using key words and similar narrative structures, after that of the miraculous birth of one of Israel's earlier saviors?

Secondly, the First Evangelist, who alone quotes Isa. 7.14 to support his version of the Christ's birth, would surely not have overlooked the

---

1.   S.H. Levey, *The Messiah: An Aramaic Interpretation* (MHUC, 2; Cincinnati: Hebrew Union College, 1974), pp. 34-35; D.J. Harrington and A.J. Saldarini, *Targum Jonathan of the Former Prophets* (ArBib, 10; Wilmington, DE: Michael Glazier, 1987), pp. 105-106; D.J. Harrington, 'The Apocalypse of Hannah: Targum Jonathan of 1 Samuel 2:1-10', in D.M. Golomb (ed.), *'Working with no Data': Semitic and Egyptian Studies* (T.O. Lambdin Festschrift; Winona Lake, IN: Eisenbrauns, 1987), pp. 147-52.

2.   Harrington and Saldarini, *Former Prophets*, p. 106.

3.   Harrington and Saldarini, *Former Prophets*, p. 106.

story of Samson's mother visited by the angel in the field; for this story in contrast to all other such wonder-birth stories in the First Testament suggests the possibility of divine conception without the benefit of an earthly father—which is, of course, the point of the Christian birth stories (Mary's virginity alone would be meaningless).

Thirdly, it is in Matthew that we hear of Joseph's understandable doubts about Mary's pregnancy, and it is in Judges 13 that we hear of Manoah's concern. The annunciation in each case involves the husband in a dramatic but not biological role; in each it is clear that the husband has not sired the child, but in each he is concerned over his own uncertainties in the situation. Stendahl's point is a good one: 'In *Mt* Joseph is the main person'.[1] And in Judges 13 Manoah plays the principal role. Stendahl continues: 'In *Lk* Mary is the recipient of revelation and Joseph is described as he who stands by'.[2] And in 1 Samuel 1 Hannah is clearly the recipient of revelation and Elkanah is described as he who stands by.[3]

3. A careful comparison of the Lukan and Matthean birth stories shows, furthermore, that the central point of the annunciation of the angel to Mary in each was the pronouncement of the presence of God. In Lk. 1.28 Gabriel says, 'Hail, O favored one, the Lord is with you'. And in Mt. 1.23 the fine point of the quotation of Isa. 7.14 is the meaning of the name Emmanuel, 'God with us'. In each the overriding issue is theophany-epiphany.

4. Stendahl compares Mt. 1.21 and 2.23 and shows how the first two chapters of Matthew end on a similar note and in a similar form: καὶ ἐκάλεσεν τὸ ὄνομα αὐτοῦ Ἰησοῦν // ὅτι Ναζωραῖος κληθήσεται.[4] But one might also go on to point out the similarity between the next phrase in Mt. 1.21 and the concluding phrase in Judg. 13.5 (LXX^A):

Matthew	LXX
αὐτὸς γὰρ σώσει τὸν λαὸν	καὶ αὐτὸς ἄρξεται σῴζειν
αὐτοῦ ἀπὸ τῶν ἁμαρτιῶν αὐτῶν	Ἰσραηλ ἐκ χειρὸς ἀλλοφύλων

1. Stendahl, 'Quis et Unde?', p. 95.
2. Stendahl, 'Quis et Unde?', p. 95.
3. For subtle distinctions between MT and LXX 1 Sam. 1, see S. Walters, 'Hannah and Anna: The Greek and Hebrew Texts of 1 Samuel 1', *JBL* 107 (1988), pp. 385-412.
4. Stendahl, 'Quis et Unde?', p. 100.

5. Since 'holy' has defined נזיר, as Schweizer has shown, it is quite possible that the language of Isa. 4.3 has also made a contribution. It is singular in the Hebrew and the Aramaic ('he will be called holy'), but plural in Greek ('they will be called holy'). The singularity of the Semitic versions suits the Matthean context, while the Greek verb provides an exact parallel.

6. Finally, is it not a fitting transition from the infancy narrative in Matthew 2 to the baptism narrative in Matthew 3 for the Evangelist, who says of Jesus (3.16) καὶ εἶδεν πνεῦμα θεοῦ...ἐρχόμενον ἐπ' αὐτόν, to echo Samson of whom it is similarly said (Judg. 14.6 LXX^A) καὶ κατηύθυνεν ἐπ' αὐτὸν πνεῦμα κυρίου?

III

Ναζωραῖος in Mt. 2.23 clearly means 'inhabitant of Nazareth', no matter how many different meanings and usages נוצרי and its cognates and derivatives have had in later Christian history.[1] But, by an excellent use of biblical paronomasia, the First Evangelist cryptically permits the word, by an indefinite reference to 'the prophets', to convey a second, equally important meaning. Matthew employs a wordplay on a village name, so effectively used by the prophet Micah (1.10-16) and others, to signal the double truth of Jesus' background: the historic home of his youth and the theological grounding of his mission. Like Samson, Jesus was formed of God by an angel in his mother's womb for the purpose of bringing salvation to his people. It was imperative that Matthew argue the case of Christ in terms of the scriptural authority available and compelling to him, in the law and the prophets.

But what about another wordplay, the traditional one that sees Ναζωραῖος as an allusion to the נצר of Isa. 11.1? Gundry opts for this solution, arguing that an allusion to Samson is unlikely, since 'Jesus was anything but a Nazirite'.[2] This is true; Matthew makes no attempt to portray Jesus the 'glutton and friend of sinners' (Mt. 11.19) as an ascetic Nazirite. But is that the only point that can be made in making an allusion to the Samson story? The idea of being God's 'holy one' from

---

1. Cf. O. Cullmann, 'Nazarene', *IDB*, III, pp. 523-24, with Moore, 'Nazarene and Nazareth', pp. 430-32.

2. Gundry, *Use of the Old Testament*, p. 100; idem, *Matthew—A Commentary*, p. 40: 'other views, such as interpretation in terms of Judg. 13:5, 7; 16:17, are less likely...'. Also favoring this option is Rüger, 'ΝΑΖΑΡΕΘ/ΝΑΖΑΡΑ', pp. 257-63.

birth and becoming Israel's savior on whom the Spirit of the Lord descends, complete with an adjectival form that plays on the name of the village in which Jesus is raised, surely provides sufficient grounds for such an allusion.[1] Against Gundry, Soares Prabhu worries that an allusion that only works in Hebrew is suspect.[2] He opts for Judges as the best solution, but fails to compare the respective Samson–Jesus contexts. I hope that the points made above address this omission. In reply to Soares Prabhu, Gundry points out that Matthew assumes that his readers will understand the Hebrew meaning of Jesus' name (1.21: 'because he will save his people') and that the numerical value of 'David' in Hebrew is 14 (1.17).[3] True enough; but this shows only that awareness of the נצר wordplay is a reasonable possibility. It does not militate against the primacy of the allusions to and parallels with the Greek version of the Samson story. These points have in fact persuaded several scholars in recent years that the most likely option is Judges after all.[4]

I wonder why both options cannot be true; they are not mutually exclusive. Priority must be given to the Judges parallels, because we know that the Matthean congregation read the LXX. The closest Greek parallel is to LXX^A Judg. 13.5b. The contextual parallel is also compelling. But if the wordplay happens also to remind the Hebrew reader of Isaiah 11's נצר (which should not be surprising, given the earlier quotation of Isa. 7.14 in Mt. 1.23), Jesus' messianic and Davidic identity is enhanced— yet not at the expense of his identity as the sanctified Ναζωραῖος who will save Israel. In agreement with Brown, Allison and Davies conclude that the primary allusion is Judges 13 (+ Isa. 4.3), while a secondary allusion to Isa. 11.1 is probable and tertiary allusions to Isa. 42.6 (+ 49.6) and Jer. 31.6-7 are unproven and unpersuasive, respectively.[5]

---

1. For more on this, see Soares Prabhu, *Formula Quotations*, pp. 204-207. The points made by Soares Prabhu effectively answer Gundry's objections.

2. Soares Prabhu, *Formula Quotations*, p. 203. Nevertheless, Luz's objection that such a wordplay is 'inconceivable' for the Evangelist's Greek-speaking readers is overdrawn (*Matthew 1–7*, p. 149).

3. Gundry, *Matthew—A Commentary*, p. 40.

4. Schaeder, 'Ναζαρηνός', p. 878; Zuckschwerdt, 'Ναζωραῖος in Matth. 2,23', pp. 65-77; Brown, *Birth*, pp. 211, 223-25 [Isa. 4.3 + Judg. 16.17]; Allan, 'He shall be Called—a Nazirite?', pp. 81-82; Luz, *Matthew 1–7*, p. 149; Pesch, '"Er wird Nazoräer heißen"', p. 1393.

5. Allison and Davies, *Matthew*, I, p. 280.

Rudolf Pesch

1. *Introduction*

At the close of the second chapter of his Gospel, in his account of the childhood of Jesus, the Evangelist Matthew recounts how Joseph, after the flight from the child-murdering King Herod, had brought the child Jesus and his mother Mary back from the Egyptian exile to the land of Israel. He did not return them to Bethlehem in Judea but to Nazareth in Galilee: 'And he came and resided in a city called Nazareth, so that what is spoken through the prophets would be fulfilled: "HE WILL BE CALLED A NAZOREAN"' (Mt. 2.23).

What Kind of Exegesis is This?
The supposed prophetic text from which the Evangelist quotes is nowhere to be found in the Old Testament. Matthew even refers to the prophets, whose prediction was supposed to have been fulfilled in the story of Jesus. This quotation is therefore problematic, as we also learn from the latest commentators on Matthew: 'This citation is a *crux interpretum*, since it cannot be identified in the Old Testament and since the meaning of *Nazaraios* remains unclear'.[1] 'Of what OT text(s) are we to think?'[2] 'We can now only discover with difficulty the details of the argument containing this "scripture quotation" as is indicated by the host of suggestions for its interpretation.'[3] Does Matthew refer 'only in

1. U. Luz, *Das Evangelium nach Matthäus.* I. *Mt. 1–7* (EKKNT, 1.1; Zurich and Neukirchen–Vluyn: Neukirchener Verlag, 1985), p. 131.
2. D.C. Allison and W.D. Davies, *The Gospel according to Saint Matthew.* I. *Introduction and Commentary on Matthew I–VII* (ICC; Edinburgh: T. & T. Clark, 1988), p. 276.
3. J. Gnilka, *Das Matthäusevangelium.* I. *Kommentar zu Kap. 1,1–13,58* (HTKNT, 1.1; Freiburg: Herder, 1986), p. 55.

general terms to "what is spoken of through the prophets"' because
'an exact text from the Old Testament...cannot be discerned'?[1] Or
does 'the general nature of the statement "through the prophets"...'
reveal 'that Matthew does not know the source of the short sentence,
but that he probably held it to be a true quotation'?[2]

What kind of exegesis is this, which cannot withstand historical-critical
examination at any point? A source for the alleged quotation cannot be
found. If Matthew is taken at face value, the prophecy contained in the
as yet undetected quotation would have had to have been proclaimed by
a number of 'prophets'! The meaning of Ναζωραῖος remains unclear,
even if Matthew does connect the term with Jesus' upbringing in
Nazareth.

What kind of exegesis would portray a contemporary fact (i.e. Jesus'
coming from Nazareth and being called a 'Nazorean') as the fulfillment
of prophetic oracles? Is not the reference to a story which fulfills prophecy discredited if the original prophecy is missing or lost in obscurity?

A survey of the first two chapters of Matthew's Gospel indicates that
in every other case in which one encounters quotations which are to
indicate the fulfillment of prophecy, the use of the Old Testament,
specifically the use of alleged predictions by the prophets, is also in dispute. The alleged 'fulfillment' of the various prophetic words (Isa. 7.14;
Mic. 5.1, 3; Hos. 11.1 and Jer. 31.15) are hardly dealt with more merci-
fully in light of historical-critical research. Let us listen to some of the
voices from the choir of recent critics.

Regarding Isa. 7.14 (in Mt. 1.23): 'The traditional Christian interpretation, which points to the Messiah Jesus, is not tenable as an exegesis of
Isa. 7.14, and at most is worthy to be considered a pneumatic exegesis.
Matthew 1.22-23 confronts the church paradigmatically with the problem of the hermeneutic of the Old Testament.'[3] 'The content of the
prophetic word of Isa. 7.14 is enigmatic. One almost gets the impression
that it was understandable only for Isaiah, king Ahaz and others of their
time.'[4]

Regarding Mic. 5.1, 3 (in Mt. 2.6): 'The wording of the quotation

1.   R. Schnackenburg, *Das Matthäusevangelium 1,1–16,20* (Die Neue Echter
Bibel, 1.1; Würzburg: Echter Verlag, 1985), p. 28.
2.   E. Schweizer, *Das Evangelium nach Matthäus* (NTD, 2; Göttingen:
Vandenhoeck & Ruprecht, 1973), p. 20.
3.   Luz, *Matthäus*, p. 107.
4.   Gnilka, *Matthäusevangelium*, p. 20.

differs from all known textual variants of Mic. 5.1. It is a mixed citation...which could go back to Matthew.'[1] Who would doctor alleged prophetic utterances in this way? What does this statement mean: 'The composition of the reflective quotation was primarily the result of christological deliberation'?[2] Is this speaking of arbitrary exegesis?

Regarding Hos. 11.1 (in Mt. 2.15): 'The total disassociation of the quotation from its context is completely at odds with our own exegetical preferences.'[3] 'Matthew naturally understands his quotation from Hosea as prophetic; he did not share the insight, common since Zwingli...and Calvin...that his interpretation does not correspond to the original meaning.'[4]

Regarding Jer. 31.15 (in Mt. 2.18): 'It seems far-fetched to quote the text as fulfillment of prophecy.'[5] 'According to Jer. 31.15-20, Rachel, Jacob's favorite wife, laments over her sons which have been carried off into exile...In Matthew 2, the optimistic viewpoint is not mentioned; instead everything concentrates upon the disaster.'[6]

We need to ask how Matthew could speak in a responsible manner of fulfillments of prophecies in his account of Jesus, if these prophecies were not extant, if they were not spoken by the prophets, and if they were not even derived from the Jewish exegetical traditional of prophetic texts? Is Matthew not guilty of arbitrary, ideological interpretation of Scripture? Should *we* even allow his exegesis to be given the meritorious adjective 'messianic'?

Intensifying the Question

Before we can attempt to justify the Evangelist and rehabilitate his canonical book, we must first intensify our criticism.

If measured by the standards of the historical-critical method, Matthew not only receives little credit as an exegete but also has to bear our criticism of him as a historian. Not only do his 'prophecies' stand on feet of clay if we are allowed to employ the historical-critical method, but also his 'fulfillment of *events*'. The genealogy of Jesus is incorrect, the story of the virgin birth is a legend—as is the whole narrative of the

---

1. Luz, *Matthäus*, p. 113.
2. Gnilka, *Matthäusevangelium*, p. 39.
3. Gnilka, *Matthäusevangelium*, p. 51.
4. Luz, *Matthäus*, p. 129.
5. Schnackenburg, *Matthäusevangelium*, p. 27.
6. Gnilka, *Matthäusevangelium*, p. 53.

magi, Herod, the flight of Joseph with the child and his mother to Egypt, the killing of the children in and around Bethlehem and the return of Joseph with the child and his mother to Nazareth. How then could the Evangelist speak of the fulfillment of events ('All of these things happened, in order to fulfill') if he did not really want to transmit actual history? Let us again listen to some of the voices from the choir of current critics.

Regarding the genealogy (Mt. 1.1-17): 'Too many things speak against the historicity of the genealogy in order to seriously take it into consideration.'[1] 'The genealogy compiled for Jesus Christ serves...not an historical but a theological purpose; the "arithmetic" is also obscure. If evaluated historically the list is problematic in other ways as well.'[2]

Regarding the announcement of the birth (Mt. 1.18-25): 'In the face of the many parallels, the question of historicity is hopeless.'[3] 'The form and structure of this Christian faith-affirming narrative do not allow us to assume a historical scenario.'[4] 'The question regarding the historicity of the virgin birth must also remain unanswered.'[5]

Regarding the story of the magi (Mt. 2.1-12): 'The second chapter... is wrought with considerable difficulties for a modern audience, used to viewing an account as a historical report.'[6] 'Our story is a legend, told succinctly and soberly, which is not concerned with the laws of historical probability...In short, a historical core can no longer be retrieved.'[7]

Regarding the story of the flight and return (Mt. 2.13-23): 'The story, whose deeper meaning can be found...through the citation dealing with prophetic fulfillment...should not be understood as a biographical account.'[8] The pericope is 'in its essential parts unhistorical...Neither the notorious cruelty of Herod nor the fact that Egypt has been a sanctuary for the persecuted of Israel in the past is very helpful, since every legend or myth is found attached to some historical event.'[9] If the commentaries are correct—if Jesus' life is not due to a virgin birth, if he

1. Luz, *Matthäus*, p. 92.
2. Schnackenburg, *Matthäusevangelium*, p. 17.
3. Luz, *Matthäus*, p. 102.
4. Schnackenburg, *Matthäusevangelium*, p. 19.
5. Gnilka, *Matthäusevangelium*, p. 30.
6. Schnackenburg, *Matthäusevangelium*, p. 21.
7. Luz, *Matthäus*, p. 116-17.
8. Schnackenburg, *Matthäusevangelium*, p. 25.
9. Luz, *Matthäus*, p. 128.

was not born in Bethlehem, if no children were killed on his account, if Joseph did not flee with Jesus and Mary to Egypt and also did not move to Nazareth (and all of this we must reckon to be historically most unlikely if we are to rely upon the most recent commentaries on Matthew)—then just as there had been no prophetic promises, there had been no historical fulfillments!

But what then? How has Matthew interpreted the Scripture?

The Present Situation of the Evangelist and his Congregations

One key to exploring the exegesis in Matthew 1–2 is provided by the text itself; particularly in the prophetic fulfillment passages in which Christology and ecclesiology are inseparably linked. The Matthaean language of 'fulfillment' has eschatological quality, in as far as it is based on the messiah who has already come: its reasoning 'begins with the historical event and understands this event to be the fulfillment of prophecies' and 'originates in the present and reflects on it in light of the Bible'.[1] Matthew could already have discovered from the writer of Chronicles this method of viewing history (cf. 2 Chron. 36.21-22). However, for Matthew an eschatological dimension is added, since the New Testament congregations understand prophetic fulfillment as messianic-eschatological fulfillment.

In a number of key texts, the present situation of the Evangelist, of his congregations, of the *ecclesia*, is addressed directly and in a revealing manner. The Christian community is the messianic people which had been saved through Jesus the messiah, who redeemed from their sins all those who repented and believed (Mt. 1.21). The name 'Jesus' (*Yeshua*, 'Salvation' = Yehoshua, 'Yahweh is salvation') is interpreted in terms of popular etymology; the messiah, the Immanuel, acts in place of God, as the allusion to Ps. 130.8 ('He will redeem Israel from all his sins') demonstrates.

The forgiveness of sins came about through the death of the messiah and continues to be active in the community to whom the power to bind and to loose has been given. The congregation (but only when it is assembled[2]) has become the place where the knowledge of Yahweh, no

---

1. Luz, *Matthäus*, p. 136.
2. Compare with this R. Pesch, '"Wo zwei oder drei versammelt sind auf meinen Namen hin..." (Mt 18.20): Zur Ekklesiologie eines Wortes Jesu', in L. Schenke (ed.), *Studien zum Matthäusevangelium* (W. Pesch Festschrift; SBS; Stuttgart: Katholisches Bibelwerk, 1988), pp. 227-43.

longer obstructed by sin, has become accessible and in that way also the understanding of his plan and his deeds in the past, present and future. The congregation is the place where Jesus of Nazareth is recognized as the 'Immanuel'. Altering Isa. 7.14, the Evangelist no longer has the virgin mother but the members of God's people calling her son Immanuel: 'They will call his name Immanuel' (Mt. 1.23), and this name means 'God is with us', that is, with his people. The congregation is promised God's assistance. It is also in the church's history that the sayings of the prophets, and the promises of God which have been transmitted by them, are fulfilled. This historical event, being a 'fulfillment event', a 'miracle', allows for the 'messianic interpretation of Scripture'.

How the miracle occurred can be discovered in the person of Joseph, the protagonist of the legend told by Matthew: 'He did as the angel of the Lord had commanded him' (Mt. 1.24). With this Old Testament obedience formula[1] the nature of faith is described. For the congregation, the miracle occurs when the disciples of Jesus keep everything that Jesus the messiah had commanded them in his authority as the Immanuel through their actions: 'Teach them to observe all things which I have commanded you. And behold, I am with you [as the Immanuel] all the days to the completion of the age' (Mt. 28.20). To the Evangelist his own time is also the time when 'all the ruling priests and scribes of the people' in Israel are frightened about the birth of their messiah-king. These, along with many who belong to this people, did not come to believe in their messiah. They did not see Jesus as the one of whom Yahweh (along with 2 Sam. 5.2) had said: 'He will shepherd my people Israel' (Mt. 2.4-6).

In light of the miracle of the fulfillment of the promises given to the people, the confessional apologetic of the Evangelist and his congregation is confronted with the puzzle, the mystery, of the blindness of a portion of Israel. Matthew aggravates this mystery: as the life of Jesus corresponds to the plan of God, so also does the eschatological renewal of Israel within the New Testament community through the addition of those Gentiles who allow themselves to be made into disciples. Matthew seeks to demonstrate to both Jewish and Gentile Christians that the messianic prophecies have been fulfilled in the story of Jesus, and that at the present time the *ecclesia* has become the place of fulfillment.

The Evangelist's own time is also the time when Jesus, the man from

---

1.   Compare with this R. Pesch, 'Eine alttestamentliche Ausführungsformel im Matthäusevangelium', *BZ* 10 (1966), pp. 220-45; 11 (1967), pp. 79-95.

Nazareth, is 'called a Nazorean' (Mt. 2.23), in accordance with the prophets' message. It is the time when he is rejected by some as the one originating from an insignificant village from which no good thing is expected to come (cf. Jn 1.46), and welcomed by others as the 'shoot from the stump of Jesse' (Isa. 11.1). As Luz says,

> The 'Nazorean' has as his community 'the Nazarenes', as the Christians were called in the Syrian region where the Matthaean congregations existed. Since the one who hears or reads the Gospel is told that, exactly like his own congregation in Syria, Jesus will be called a 'Nazorean'... he senses thus a part of the movement of Israel's Messiah towards the Christian congregation, in fulfillment of Israel's Scripture[1], in fulfillment of the whole of the prophets' message.

The Key to Understanding the 'Messianic Exegesis' of Matthew

The contemporary situation of the Evangelist and his congregation is reflected explicitly in Matthew 1–2 and is the hermeneutical key to understanding Matthew's method of scriptural interpretation which I have termed 'messianic exegesis'. Matthew perceives the Old Testament on the basis of the experience of his congregation; and this perception is shaped 'messianically'. This now would mean that if 'a text is to be understood as it wants to be understood, i.e. as it understands itself'[2], then more precisely, it must be understood as the messianic community (in which the veil of incomprehension can be taken from everyone's heart) understood it by way of its messianic interpretation of Scripture. The New Testament (messianic) community of Christians (messianists) gradually discovers its and the messiah's 'foundation in the whole of biblical tradition'[3]. How does this become apparent in the exegesis of Matthew?

In Matthew 1–2, the church views its own origin in the light of the 'origin of the Messiah Jesus, the son of David, the son of Abraham' (Mt. 1.1), who at the same time is also 'God's son'. Its descent, its genealogy is found with those who 'have built up the house of Israel', as it says in the story of Ruth with regard to David's genealogy and in reference to the matriarchs Rachel and Leah (Ruth 4.11). The community, because of

---

1. Luz, *Matthäus*, p. 133.
2. H. Gese, 'Hermeneutische Grundsätze der Exegese biblischer Texte', in A.H.J. Gunneweg and H. Schroer (eds.), *Standort und Bedeutung der Hermeneutik in der gegenwärtigen Theologie* (Bonn: Bouvier, 1986), pp. 43-62, esp. p. 43.
3. Gese, 'Hermeneutische Grundsätze der Exegese biblischer Texte', p. 52.

its trust in God's word, views the miracle of its own existence in the light of the wonderful account of the fulfillment of prophetic promises. As with Israel it also has grown from people of various backgrounds: from those who are by nature both related and estranged, from Jews and Gentiles.

The community is also aware of the fear concerning the messiah and his congregation which is found not only in the world generally but also among God's people (that is, the Jews) themselves. The congregation notes names and places which mark the 'red thread' of salvation history and which do not only connect Zerah and Rahab in the genealogy (the former, brother to Perez, stretched forth his hand from Tamar's womb first and a crimson thread was tied to it [Gen. 38.27-30], and the latter, a prostitute of Jericho, let down the spies on a crimson rope from the city wall [Josh. 1.15-18]): by describing a Christian as a 'Nazarene' and 'Galilee' as the 'land of the Gentiles', further descriptions of the contemporary situation of the Matthaean congregation are given. This community probably came about as a result of the flight of the 'Hellenists' (the Greek-speaking Jewish Christians) from Jerusalem to Antioch, and it was strengthened by Peter who had also fled from Jerusalem.

The following will explore how the key, the contemporary situation of the Evangelist and his congregation, can unlock the 'messianic exegesis' in Matthew 1–2. Why was it possible for Matthew to interpret the Scripture in the way he did? Can we agree with him against his critics? By using the genealogy, which introduces the Gospel, as the means of looking back upon the messiah's origin, the Matthaean community can claim the whole history of Israel as its own messianic (pre-)history. Israel's history is seen as the miracle of a history of fulfilled prophecies which, in response to the faith and trust of humanity and despite all human failure, is continually being directed by God—right up to its eschatological fulfillment. In light of the special origin of the messiah from God, an origin which exceeds all former concepts and the whole of former history, the community understands its own origin and being in the birth announcement of the 'Immanuel'. Although its beginning does not, like that of the messiah, need the symbol of the virgin birth, it does require the idea of procreation through God, through the Holy Spirit (cf. Jn 1.13).[1] The questions 'who is the messiah?' and 'from where does he

---

1. Compare with R. Pesch, 'Gegen eine doppelte Wahrheit: Karl Rahner und die Bibelwissenschaft', in K. Lehmann (ed.), *Vor dem Geheimnis Gottes den Menschen*

come?'[1] are also coded questions regarding the community: who is part of it, whence do the believers come? 'Who' is the community itself, whence does it come?

Since the narrative contains the magi, Herod, the flight to Egypt and the return to the land of Israel, the community recognizes in the messiah's history its own history, as well as the history of God's people from its very beginning. This history has been, since Abraham, the history of God's choice and of the free 'yes' of those who are called, each of whom allowed his or her whole being to be led into the exodus; it has been the history which led to the constitution of a new, free, united community, which God wanted to have for his people, who would be a blessing to the whole world. The connection with this narrative, in which the present situation of the 'messianic synagogue' (a valid term for the church) is anchored, opens eyes and increases the ability to perceive the witnesses in the whole history which are preserved in the traditions of Israel, in the Scripture, and in their interpretation.

'Messianic exegesis', therefore, presupposes a 'tradition-historic structure to the biblical text' and includes 'the dimension of a historically unfolding purpose'[2] to Scripture, thereby unlocking its meaning.

Historical-critical exegesis is in danger of narrowing down its interpretation to the so-called original meaning of the text which it is called upon to discover. However, in the process of discovering this original meaning, if possible, historical-critical exegesis can focus our attention on the dynamic of the texts and their meaning within the living tradition history of God's people.

Modern exegesis has attacked the exegesis of Matthew in two ways, claiming that it is arbitrary and that it lacks any basis in historic facts. I am attempting to interpret Matthew from a new viewpoint, based on the key found above.

---

verstehen (K. Rahner Festschrift; Munich and Zurich: Schnell & Steiner, 2nd edn, 1984), pp. 10-36.

1. See K. Stendahl, 'Quis et unde? An Analysis of Mt 1–2', in W. Eltester (ed.), *Judentum, Urchristentum, Kirche* (J. Jeremias Festschrift; BZNW, 26; Berlin: Töpelmann, 1960), pp. 94-105; also see A. Vögtle, 'Die Genealogie Mt 1,2-16 und die matthäische Kindheitsgeschichte', in *idem, Das Evangelium und die Evangelien* (Düsseldorf: Patmos, 1971), pp. 57-102.

2. Gese, 'Hermeneutische Grundsätze der Exegese biblischer Texte', p. 49.

2. *The Genealogy (Matthew 1.1-17)*

The Text

1 The book of the origin of Jesus Christ, son of David, son of Abraham
2 Abraham (1) begat Isaac,
   and Isaac (2) begat Jacob,
   and Jacob (3) begat Judah and his brothers,
3 and Judah (4) begat Perez and Zerah from Tamar,
   and Perez (5) begat Hezron,
   and Hezron (6) begat Aram,
4 and Aram (7) begat Amminadab,
   and Amminadab (8) begat Nahshon,
   and Nahshon (9) begat Salmon,
5 and Salmon (10) begat Boaz from Rahab,
   and Boaz (11) begat Obed from Ruth,
   and Obed (12) begat Jesse,
6 and Jesse (13) begat David (14), the king.
   And David (14) begat Solomon from the one of Uriah,
7 and Solomon (1) begat Rehoboam,
   and Rehoboam (2) begat Abijah,
   and Abijah (3) begat Asa,
8 and Asa (4) begat Jehoshaphat,
   and Jehoshaphat (5) begat Joram,
   and Joram (6) begat Uzziah,
9 and Uzziah (7) begat Jotham,
   and Jotham (8) begat Ahaz,
   and Ahaz (9) begat Hezekiah,
10 and Hezekiah (10) begat Manasseh,
   and Manasseh (11) begat Amos,
   and Amos (12) begat Josiah,
11 and Josiah (13) begat Jechoniah (14)
   and his brothers at the time of the banishment to Babylon.
12 And after the banishment to Babylon:
   Jechoniah (14) begat Shealtiel,
   and Shealtiel (1) begat Zerubbabel,
13 and Zerubbabel (2) begat Abiud,
   and Abiud (3) begat Eliakim,
   and Eliakim (4) begat Azor,
14 and Azor (5) begat Zadok,
   and Zadok (6) begat Achim,
   and Achim (7) begat Eliud,
15 and Eliud (8) begat Eleazar,
   and Eleazar (9) begat Matthan,
   and Matthan (10) begat Jacob,

16 and Jacob (11) begat Joseph (12), the husband of Mary,
   from whom was begotten (13) Jesus (14), who is called the Christ.

17 So all the generations from Abraham to David are fourteen
   generations, and from David to the banishment to Babylon fourteen
   generations, and from the banishment to Babylon to the Christ
   fourteen generations.

The Interpretation

The genealogy, as 'book of the origin of Jesus Christ, son of David, son of Abraham', follows as much as possible the biblical tradition concerning the history of Israel since Abraham. This history can be encoded in condensed form through the succession of generations. The division into three times fourteen generations (Mt. 1.17)—the point being that in each epoch fourteen begetters, that is, fourteen begotten, are named—is oriented on the number of generations between Abraham and David, the decisive epoch which is framed by the messianic prototypes. At the same time, the number fourteen, according to gematria (the system of assigning to each letter a numerical value), represents the sum of the digits in the name of David. The symbolism of the numbers is based on the divine providence in the history of origins.

Matthew read in Mic. 5.1-3 that the messiah, the son of David, has 'his origin in the distant past, in days long gone by'. This is the prophetic word that the assembly of chief priests and scribes, having been gathered by King Herod, used in order to answer the question where the 'king of the Jews' was to be born.

The reason why the Matthaean genealogy begins with Abraham, in contrast to the Lukan genealogy which ends with Adam and God (Lk. 3.38), is that the history of the people of God and his promises commenced with Abraham. Analogously to Luke, Matthew makes clear in his own way that the origin of the messiah is to be found completely with the (believing) person and completely with God.

Son of Abraham—Son of David

'Abraham begat Isaac': already the first birth in the first epoch from Abraham to David reminds us of the miracle of the founding of God's people, which took place through the fulfillment of God's promises because of the believers. Matthew assumes what is verbalized in the letter to the Hebrews: 'By faith even Sarah received the power, despite her age, still to become a mother, because she considered him faithful who had given the promise' (Heb. 11.11). Since in the title at the beginning of the genealogy (Mt. 1.1) Jesus is deliberately called 'son of Abraham', he is not only being introduced as a 'Jew'. In the early Jewish-Christian understanding (as in the understanding of the early Gentile Christians who were educated, prepared and trained in the synagogue), one can assume that an association with an Isaac typology would be made. Paul even uses a dual Isaac typology in Galatians 3–4: the messiah is the 'seed' promised to Abraham (Gal. 3.16 from Gen. 22.17), and the messianic people consist of the 'children of promise like Isaac' (Gal. 4.28) who was born 'by virtue of the promise' (Gal. 4.23), that is, 'by virtue of the Spirit' (Gal. 4.29). As the 'son of Abraham', Messiah Jesus resembles Isaac. Isaac, as the son who was born by virtue of the promise or the Spirit, has become a messianic representative. Early Jewish traditions also demonstrate this: the promise of seed to Abraham and the promise of a son of David were already combined in Jer. 33.21-22. The connecting link was the common terminology of the 'eternal covenant' which Yahweh would make with Abraham and with David's descendants respectively.

This connecting link is used also in the Targum to Ps. 89.4, as can be seen when additions and substitutions to the canonical text are bracketed: 'I have made a covenant [with Abraham], my chosen one, I have sworn to David, my servant: I will establish your house [your seed] for ever, and set up your throne [the throne of your kingdom = 2 Sam. 7.13] from generation to generation'.

In early Jewish tradition, Isaac is one of the few, besides Moses, Solomon and Josiah, as well as the messiah, whose name is preexistent. According to *Jub.* 16.3, the 'angels of the presence' who visited Abraham by the grove of Mamre revealed to Sarah 'the name of her son, just as it was ordained and written in the heavenly tablets: Isaac'. According to *Jub.* 16.16-17, Abraham is promised: 'And from the sons of Isaac will come one holy seed…'

The Isaac typology can also be found in the birth announcement in Mt. 1.18-25 since the miraculous birth of the messiah is prefigured in Isaac's miraculous birth. The end of the genealogy (1.16) already prepares for the birth announcement of the Immanuel which is told as a footnote to the genealogy.

The Genealogy from Abraham to David
The messianic genealogy from Abraham to the second messianic figure, 'David, the king', is marked and arranged by four extra branches or

additions to the genealogical pattern 'A begat B'. The first fourteen generations are comprised of 4 generations from the time of the patriarchs to the formation of the nation of twelve tribes: from Abraham to 'Judah and his brothers'; 6 generations during the time of the Egyptian slavery, the exodus and the conquest of the land: from the twins 'Perez and Zerah', who were born to Judah 'from Tamar', to Salmon who took the prostitute Rahab as his wife; and 4 generations from the time of the judges to the reign of David, beginning with David's great grandfather Boaz who was born 'from Rahab' and who married Ruth, the matriarch of the messianic house, thereby making a Gentile woman the carrier of the promise. The fourteen generations are divided according to the numeric value of the name of *David* (4 + 6 + 4); they cover the decisive period of Israel's history, which can be arranged in many different ways due to its rich nucleus: the period to the exodus contains seven generations, as does the period to David's reign. (Philo of Alexandria also numbered seven generations from Abraham to Moses.)

The first three generations cover the time of the patriarchs, who laid the basis for Israel's history as the history of the people who were chosen and led by the God of the fathers, 'the God of Abraham, the God of Isaac and the God of Jacob' (Exod. 3.6; cf. Mt. 22.32). Isaac was the son of promise, Jacob, the younger of the twins (after Esau), was the son of election. His salvation-historical preference was announced by Yahweh to their mother Rebecca (Gen. 25.23: 'the elder shall serve the younger') and was interpreted by the prophet Malachi as referring to Yahweh's unfounded love: 'Jacob I have loved, but Esau I have hated' (Mal. 1.1-2; cf. Rom. 9.12-13). Judah also was at the head of his brothers, the 'twelve sons' of Jacob (Gen. 25.32), not as the first-born but as the fourth (of the sons of Leah). In the early Jewish *Testament of Judah* Judah says himself: 'As the fourth son I was born to my father' (*T. Jud.* 1.3).

With Judah, however, the royal tribe which would lead to 'David, the king' begins. Another reason why Judah advanced to his prominent position is the replacement of Reuben and Simeon by Ephraim and Manasseh (Gen. 48.5) and the transition of Levi into the priestly tribe. This can be seen in the blessing by Jacob:

> Judah, your brothers praise you; your hand is on the neck of your enemies. Your father's sons bow down before you... The scepter will never depart from Judah, the ruler's staff from his feet, until he comes to whom it belongs, whom the obedience of the nations is due (Gen. 49.8-10).

The 'coming one' was, in a first fulfillment of the prophecy, David. In the last, the surpassing, fulfillment, the 'coming one' is the messiah, who also fits the messianic prophecy regarding his mount: 'He binds his mount to the vine, his donkey to the choice vine' (Gen. 49.11; cf. Mt. 21.2).[1]

In the stricter sense the Davidic genealogy begins with Perez, the son of Judah, as can be seen at the end of the book of Ruth (4.18-22). Here David appears tenth in the genealogy. Perez is emphasized in Mt. 1.3 by the second addition to the genealogical pattern as the brother of Zerah, whom he preceded, and as the son of Tamar, Judah's daughter-in-law.

Tamar, the messianic matriarch, like Mary the mother of Jesus, was suspected of sexual immorality: 'And behold, she is pregnant by harlotry' (Gen. 38.24). The 'house of Perez whom Tamar has born to Judah' (Ruth 4.12) is also remembered in the book of Ruth because of Boaz's, David's grandfather's, Levirate marriage to Ruth. This was denied to Tamar by Judah (at the insistence of his wife) when he would not give her his third son in marriage (Gen. 38.6-14). The Jewish tradition describes Judah as a 'lover' who 'was rewarded': 'for from him sprang Pharez and Hezron, who were to give to us David and the King Messiah who will redeem Israel. See what devious ways God must follow before He can cause the King Messiah to arise from Judah'.[2]

With Perez and Zerah (who later in the Midrash were equated with the spies), Judah moved to Egypt as a part of the emerging nation of the twelve tribes. In the early Jewish book of *Jubilees*, where ancient and patriarchal history is retold, the births of Perez and Zerah are dated as follows: 'And after this the seven years of full harvest which Joseph had promised Pharaoh were completed' (*Jub.* 41.22; cf. Gen. 41.29, 53).

Hezron, Aram, Amminadab and Nahshon were born in Egypt, the place where Yahweh had promised to make Jacob 'into a great nation' (Gen. 46.3). With Amminadab and Nahshon we have already reached the generation of the exodus. In the genealogy of 1 Chron. 2.1-10, which, from Aram to Jesse, agrees almost word for word with Ruth 4.18-22, Nahshon is set apart with an additional clause: 'Amminadab begat Nahshon, the head of the sons of Judah'. Nahshon is an outstanding individual of the exodus generation. According to Exod. 6.23 he is a brother-in-law of Aaron: 'Aaron married Elisheba, daughter of Amminadab and sister of Nahshon'. In the time of the wilderness he is

---

1.   Compare with R. Pesch, *Das Markusevangelium*. II. *Kommentar zu 8,27–16,20* (HTKNT, 2.2; Freiburg: Herder, 4th edn, 1991), p. 179.

2.   From S. Buber, as cited in G. Kittel, 'θαμάρ, κτλ', *TDNT*, III, p. 3.

the 'commander of the people of Judah' (Num. 2.3), an assistant at the census (Num. 1.7), and the tribal leader who offered Judah's donation for the altar dedication (Num. 7.12-18). At the departure from Sinai he commands Judah's army: 'So they set out for the first time, as the LORD had commanded them through Moses. The standard of the camp of Judah set out first, ordered according to companies. Nahshon, the son of Amminadab, commanded the army of Judah' (Num. 10.13-14). Through Nahshon, 'the head of the sons of Judah', Moses can also be seen in the history of Israel as it is remembered by the genealogy. After the forty-year wilderness period, the time of the conquest of the land begins with Nahshon's son Salmon. Especially Rahab, the prostitute from Jericho, mentioned as the mother of Boaz, reminds us of this time. According to Joshua 6, Rahab and her family were spared at Jericho's destruction: 'The harlot Rahab and her father's family and all that belonged to her Joshua let live. So her family lives to this day in the midst of Israel; because Rahab had hidden the messengers whom Joshua had sent out to spy out Jericho' (Josh. 6.25). The letter to the Hebrews also knows that Rahab had settled 'in the midst of Israel': 'By faith Rahab the harlot did not perish together with the disobedient: because she had taken in the spies in peace' (Heb. 11.31). According to rabbinic tradition, Rahab became the matriarch of a large number of priests and prophets.[1] She belongs to the righteous proselytes like Ruth, beside whom she is placed.[2] Rahab is added to the messianic genealogy only in the Matthaean genealogy. Here she is named with Tamar, to whom she corresponds within the structure of the genealogy, in that the construction of the house of Israel is not a matter of morals but of courageous faith (which of course includes works, as Matthew knows—along with the author of the letter of James, who praises Rahab for her works [Jas 2.25]).

The last section of the list of the first fourteen generations deals with the succession from Boaz to David. It focuses attention on the time span beginning with the judges and ending at the height of the kingdom, at the same time reminding us of Bethlehem, the birthplace of the messiah. Boaz lives 'at the time when the judges ruled' (Ruth 1.1); Bethlehem's people and elders voice their wish for him:

1.   See B.J. Bamberger, *Proselytism in the Talmudic Period* (New York: Ktav, 2nd edn, 1968), p. 194.

2.   See J. Zakowitsch, 'Rahab als Mutter des Boas in der Jesusgenealogie', *NovT* 17 (1975), pp. 1-5.

> May the LORD make the woman who is coming into your house like Rachel and Leah, those two who have built the house of Israel. May you come to riches in Ephrathah and to high esteem in Bethlehem! May your house be like the house of Perez whom Tamar bore to Judah, through the offspring which the LORD shall give you by this young women (Ruth 4.11-12).

David's greatgrandmother Ruth, as a daughter of Abraham (being a proselyte as he was), is called to become the matriarch of the messiah. Boaz says to her '…how you have left your father and your mother, your land and your relations and have come to a people that previously was unknown to you. May Yahweh, the God of Israel, to whom you have come in order to seek refuge under his wings, repay your action and richly reward you' (Ruth 2.11-12). She is marked out on account of her trust, her obedience. She answers her mother-in-law: 'All that you say I will do', and the text then says: 'And she went to the threshing floor and did exactly what her mother-in-law had instructed her' (Ruth 3.5-6). Joseph, Mary's husband, would follow her in this kind of obedience (cf. Mt. 1.24)! Jewish tradition represented Ruth as the daughter of a Moabite king.[1] Her son Obed, David's grandfather, had been given to Boaz by God 'from this young woman': 'Yahweh made her conceive, and she bore a son' (Ruth 4.12-13). This process also points ahead to the birth of the messiah.

The name of Jesse establishes a link with the messianic promises regarding the shoot in Isaiah 11. The name of David, the king, establishes a link with the more extensively witnessed expectation regarding the 'son of David', the messiah, who would be God's son. These names come to the fore in the birth announcements.

The Genealogy from David to the Babylonian Exile

The list of the second fourteen generations from Solomon to Jechoniah covers the whole period during which Israel was ruled by kings. The genealogy emphasizes the beginning and the end of the list by means of additions: 'from the one of Uriah'; 'and his brothers at the time of the banishment to Babylon'. It follows in most points the genealogy of the kings of Israel in 1 Chronicles (1 Chron. 3.10-16), except that in Mt. 1.9 the kings Ahaziah, Joash and Amaziah are missing between Joram and Uzziah and at the end it seems that those between Josiah and Jechoniah, Jehoiakim were omitted. But all of this has its place in the salvation-

---

1. Bamberger, *Proselytism*, p. 195.

historical view of messianic exegesis. Bathsheba, the wife of Uriah, supplements the list of the Gentile matriarchs of the messiah: Tamar is Aramean (*Jub.* 4.1), Rahab Canaanean, Ruth a Moabite and Bathsheba presumably, like her husband, a Hittite. God's nation is built up by people from other nations, so unlike the planning of narrow human expectation, but according to God's plan which reveals itself fully only in retrospect. The kings who were omitted, Ahaziah, Joash and Amaziah, did not build Israel up but tempted it to idolatry; they did not support the coming of the messiah. Jehoiakim and Jechoniah were otherwise also occasionally confused with each other, and the curses which were placed on them in Jer. 22.30 and 36.30 did make them extremely alike. At the end of 2 Kings and 2 Chronicles, the exile of both kings to Babylon is recounted (cf. 2 Kgs 24.1-5; 2 Chron. 36.6). Perhaps Matthew also drew his inspiration for his exegesis from 2 Chron. 36.21 where we read: 'So the word was fulfilled, which the LORD had proclaimed through Jeremiah'.

Just as the fulfillment of the prophecy regarding David's kingdom is found at the end of the first list of fourteen, so the fulfillment of the prophecy of disaster concerning the exile is found at the end of the second. According to 2 Chron. 36.22, the end of the exile is to be interpreted also as a fulfillment of God's prophecy through Jeremiah: 'But in the first year of King Cyrus of Persia it was fulfilled what the LORD had spoken through Jeremiah'.

The Genealogy from the End of the Exile to the Messiah

The third list of generations, which leads up to the messiah, does not follow the genealogical table of 1 Chron. 2.19-24 after it names Zerubbabel, the leader of those Jews who returned from the exile (cf. Ezra 2.2; 3.2; 5.2). According to *4 Ezra* 3.1, the composer of the book of Ezra, which describes the beginning of the post-exilic period, was Shealtiel. According to Neh. 12.1 Zerubbabel was a priest, and he was proceeded by Abiud and (later) Eleazar as those carrying priestly names. Should these names characterize the time of the temple community under priestly rule which followed the time of the kings?

At the conclusion of the list Matthew abandons the genealogical pattern of 'A begat B' and names Joseph, 'the husband of Mary'. He then points in veiled terms, through the use of the theological passive, to God, that is to the Holy Spirit, as the 'begetter' of Jesus: 'from whom was begotten Jesus, who is called the Christ' (Mt. 1.16). The reduction of the third list to only thirteen names, despite the Evangelist's insistence that there are fourteen generations, should probably also be understood as a hidden clue pointing to God as the 'father' of the messianic 'son of God'. In this way Matthew makes it very clear at the end of his genealogy that the messiah is not simply the product of Israel's history, but at the same time God's pure gift of grace—of course in fulfillment of prophecies and predictions, as can be recognized now in the time of fulfillment and in the place of fulfillment, in the church.

The break in the genealogical pattern and the veiled description of the fathering of Jesus begs for an explanation. It is found in the story of the miraculous origin of Jesus in Mt. 1.18-25: 'begotten of the Holy Spirit' (Mt. 1.20).[1] This is a footnote to Mt. 1.16 which refers back to the prophecy of Isa. 7.14: 'behold, the virgin shall be with child...' (Mt. 1.23).

Prior to this explanation Matthew first notes explicitly (1.17) that his genealogy contains three times fourteen generations, organized to correspond with the history of Israel: from Abraham to David: the decisive period of promise; from David to the nadir of Israel's exile: the period of the exemplary blunder in the attempt by God's people to form a state; finally the almost meaningless third epoch, which did not produce expectations but which leads to the surprising arrival of the messiah.[2]

This History is Constellated by God

Seen from the present historical-critical exegetical standpoint, a number of questions arise concerning the genealogy, even with regard to the first sentence: 'Abraham begat Isaac'. Was Abraham even Isaac's father, whatever the precise meaning of this statement may be? Was not the nomadic group which honored Abraham as its patriarch younger than the obviously unrelated group which honored Isaac as its patriarch? Was not Isaac the older, Abraham the younger legendary figure? If this should be considered probable according to the historical-critical insight which is possible at present, this would surely indicate to us that we can emphasize and develop in an even greater way the genealogy of the

---

1. Compare also with R. Pesch, 'Der Gottessohn im matthäischen Evangelienprolog (Mt 1–2): Beobachtungen zu den Zitationsformeln der Reflexionszitate', *Bib* 48 (1967), pp. 395-420.

2. Regarding the number 42, compare also O.H. Lehmann, 'Number Symbolism as a Vehicle of Religious Experience in the Gospels, Contemporary Rabbinic Literature and the Dead Sea Scrolls', in F.L. Cross (ed.), *Studia Patristica* (TU, 79; Berlin: Akademie Verlag, 1961), IV, pp. 125-35, esp. p. 127.

messiah and the messianic people as a history of grace (which nature presupposes and brings to completion), a history of faith and, through faith, a history of the fulfillment of prophecies. We can discern more readily that Abraham stands at the beginning of the genealogy as the one who, according to the word of Moses ben Maimonides (*Morek Nebukim* 2.13), 'came to a knowledge of God by virtue of his reason'. He stands as the one who started the history of the religio-critical differentiation between God and the gods, thereby initiating the history of revelation. He was the one who received the promise of the messiah, the 'son of Abraham' (Mt. 1.1), and the promise of the messianic nation and its land (that is, the earth, in the light of the fulfillment!), in order to be a blessing to all the nations.

The Matthaean congregation places itself within a history which began with Abraham and which reached its *telos* with Jesus, the promised 'messianic' son of Abraham. The history, represented in condensed form through the genealogy, is the unusual history of the nation of God. Only a view through the eyes of faith, only a theological interpretation and historiography, can do it justice. Why? Because this history is constellated by God, as is the witness regarding it, being a witness of faith, an 'inspired document', in Israel's tradition.

'Messianic exegesis' has to do justice to the above. It has to correspond with this kind of history, by discovering, illuminating and verbalizing its parallels in the eschatological event of the messiah's arrival and the renewal of his people.

3. *The Immanuel (Matthew 1.18-21)*

The expectation of the reader (or hearer), conditioned as it was by the previous monotony of the genealogical pattern 'A begat B', was not met in Mt. 1.16. It does not say, as would be expected: 'And Joseph begat Jesus'. *Interruption despite continuity, something new as the surpassing fulfillment of the tradition*: this is the personal experience of the community with itself and with its messiah. Contrary to our expectations, but in fulfillment of prophecy, the end of the genealogy states: 'From her [Mary] was begotten Jesus, who is called messiah' (1.16). At the end of the genealogy the Evangelist makes it very clear that the messiah is not simply the product of Israel's history, but is also God's gift of grace, of course in fulfillment of all prophecies.

The Text

18 But the origin of Jesus Christ took place in this way: When his mother
    Mary was engaged to Joseph, before they had come together, she
    found herself to be pregnant from the Holy Spirit.
19 But Joseph, her husband, was righteous and did not want to disgrace
    her; he considered dismissing her secretly.
20 But while he was considering this, behold: An angel of the Lord
    appeared to him in a dream and said: 'Joseph, son of David, do not be
    afraid to take to yourself Mary as your wife! for that which is begotten
    in her is from the Holy Spirit.
21 But she will bear a son, and you will call his name Jesus. For he will
    save his people from their sins.'
22 But all of this took place, so that it might be fulfilled what had been
    spoken by the Lord through the prophets, who said:
23 'BEHOLD, THE VIRGIN WILL BECOME PREGNANT AND
    SHE WILL BEAR A SON, AND THEY WILL CALL HIS NAME:
    IMMANUEL [Isa. 7.14], which translated means: GOD (is) WITH
    US.'
24 But when Joseph had arisen from sleep, he did as the angel of the
    Lord had commanded him: And he took his wife to himself.
25 And he did not know her, until she had given birth to a son, and he
    called his name Jesus.

An Explanation Concerning the Genealogical Table
In Mt. 1.16 Matthew employs the theological passive, which early Judaism
(including Jesus), used to circumlocute the actions of God. In the footnote to the genealogy, introduced by the clarifying annotation, 'But the
origin of Jesus Christ took place in this way' (1.18), the circumlocution
'Jesus was begotten' is decoded: Mary 'found herself to be pregnant [lit.
with child] from the Holy Spirit' (1.18); and: 'that which is begotten in
her is from the Holy Spirit' (1.20).

The theological passive, therefore, announces God in his creative
power, in his Holy Spirit, as the procreator of Jesus. The origin of the
messiah Jesus is his 'genesis' from Mary and from the Holy Spirit.

In his own legendary narration, which I will consider later, Matthew's
exegesis discovers and considers to what extent the completely
unexpected advent of the messiah takes place in fulfillment of the
promises of God. That God acts anew in the present is surprising, even if
his activity can be seen as his faithfulness to his promises. Matthaean
exegesis considers and formulates how God's absolutely free action,
performed through his Spirit, would realize the objective: the fulfillment

of his promises within his people, through the faith and obedience of his righteous ones.

In the legendary text this is indicated thus: the messiah would not have come as 'son of David' to his people had not righteous Joseph, the 'son of David', done everything exactly as the angel of the Lord had commanded him. What is said of Mary in the Lukan introduction (or 'prehistory') is by analogy also true of Joseph in the prologue to the Matthaean Gospel: 'Blessed are you who have believed that there would be a fulfillment of the words which were spoken to you by the Lord' (cf. Lk. 1.45).

The clarifying footnote to the Matthaean genealogical table deals first, of course, with Mary, the mother of the messiah. It was said of her, that Jesus 'was begotten...from her', that she was engaged to Joseph 'her husband' (1.16) and that, prior to her being taken home and prior to the consummation of the marriage through sexual union, she was found to be pregnant, specifically 'from the Holy Spirit'. The theological 'conclusion', which in didactic manner the narrator himself conveys beforehand, he then repeats by placing it, in the form of an explanation, on the lips of the angel of the Lord who appears to Joseph in a dream: 'for that which is begotten in her is from the Holy Spirit'! The angel predicts the birth of a son, and the exegesis of Matthew recognizes in this event, which deals with the origin of the messiah, the fulfillment of the prophecy of Isa. 7.14: 'Behold, the virgin will be with child and she will bear a son'! The legendary, theologically highly subtle and exact scenario recounts how the mother of the messiah conceives and bears her son as a virgin.

Seen as a whole, however, the annotation to the genealogy is a narrative concerning Joseph: how he, in light of the pregnancy of his fiancée, sought to dismiss her secretly; how in a dream he is instructed by the angel of the Lord not to be afraid to take Mary as his wife and, after the birth of the son who was begotten in her by the Holy Spirit, to name him Jesus (according to the right of the father); and how Joseph, in obedience to these instructions and beyond, also fulfilled the prediction of the prophet regarding the virgin birth of the Immanuel.

As we have already discovered, the large degree to which Matthew's exegesis originates in the current experience of the congregation is demonstrated by the changes made to the quotation from Isaiah: while Joseph performs the task of naming the child with the predetermined name of Jesus as it was revealed by the angel, it is no longer the virgin who names her son Immanuel but the nation which has been redeemed from its sins by Jesus. These people have recognized and personally experienced him, the Nazorean, as the Immanuel. This personal experience, that God has taken his eschatological residence in the midst of the assembly of the *ecclesia* through Jesus, has also directed attention to the prophecy concerning the birth of the Immanuel.

However, was the recourse to Isa. 7.14 justified? Was not the Old Testament text violated? Was not a meaning pressed from it which was not its own? Did not modern biblical scholarship proclaim that the Matthaean exegesis of Isa. 7.14 was 'untenable'?

The Prophecy of the Birth of the Messiah

As I have already said, 'messianic exegesis' does not know of coincidence but is instructed to interpret and explain the constellation of history. To this constellation also belongs the history of the biblical texts with regard to tradition and redaction, as well as effect. It is not coincidence that Isa. 7.14 has been transmitted with the characteristic announcement formula, 'behold, she will conceive and bear', in the midst of the birth announcements of other great men of God. This is despite the fact that Immanuel's birth was seen as yet unfulfilled prophecy while the other births were recounted consistently as historical events. It is also not coincidence that the Septuagint renders the *'almah* (young woman) of Isa. 7.14 with *parthenos* (virgin), thereby strengthening the messianic overtones of the old oracle. Assuredly it is not coincidence that in the interpretation of Isa. 7.14 by Mic. 5.1-3 the announced Immanuel was connected, on the one hand, with the promised 'prince of peace' found in Isa. 9.5-6 and, on the other hand, with the messianic 'shoot' of Isaiah 11 to whom the name 'Nazorean' already pointed.

The messianic oracle in Isa. 9.5-6 reads:

> A child will be born to us,
> a son will be given to us.
> The government rests upon his shoulders,
> and he is called:
> 'Wonderful Counselor, Mighty God, Eternal Father and Prince of Peace.'
> His rule is great, and peace has no end.
> He rules on the throne of David over his kingdom;
> he establishes and upholds it with justice and righteousness, now and for
>   all times.

A tradition-historical plain[1] extends from this text, by way of Isa. 7.10-14 (with v. 14!) and Mic. 5.2, to Mic. 5.1. It stretches from the re-establishment of the Davidic kingship, past the physical birth and enthronement of the eschatological Davidide and Son of God, to the question concerning his initial, protological origin, the origin of the messiah in his preexistence. Mic. 5.1-3 (the text is quoted in Mt. 2.6) not only is reminiscent of Isa. 7.14 and Isa. 9.5-6, but also of the messianic son of David prophecy found in 2 Sam. 7.12-16. The latter is a part of the total constellation of messianic texts.

The oracle found in Mic. 5.1-3 (5.2-4 English) reads:

> But you, Bethlehem Ephrathah,
> for the thousands of Judah a small tribe,
> from you will come forth for me the future ruler over Israel.
>   → Isa. 9.5-6
> His origin goes back to ancient times,
> to days long gone by.
> Therefore he (God) will surrender them until the time,
> when she who is in labor has given birth
>   → Isa. 7.14
> and the rest of his brothers return to the sons of Israel.
> And he will appear and shepherd in the strength of Yahweh,
> in the glorious name of his God Yahweh,
> and they will live securely, for now he will be great to the ends of the earth.

The reference to 'ancient times' (*Vorzeit*) is meant to remind us of David but also of the time of creation. The current plight comes to an end with the birth of the messiah. 'Through the re-interpretation of Mic. 5.1-3, the promised Messianic figure appears in the light of the Immanuel-prophecy of Isa. 7.14 and the announcement of Isa. 9.5.'[2]

The Targum, the early Jewish translation and exposition of Mic. 5.1-3, adds to Mic. 5.1 the words: 'from you will come forth for me the Messiah'. Mic. 5.3 is also expanded: 'For now his name will be great'. The Targum presupposes the theologumenon concerning the preexistence of the name of the messiah—as do the narratives in the New Testament

---

1. H. Gese, 'Natus ex Virgine', in H.W. Wolff (ed.), *Probleme biblischer Theologie* (G. von Rad Festschrift; Munich: Chr. Kaiser Verlag, 1971), pp. 73-89; repr. in H. Gese, *Vom Sinai zum Zion: Alttestamentliche Beiträge zur biblischen Theologie* (BEvT, 64; Munich: Chr. Kaiser Verlag, 1974), pp. 130-46.

2. G. Schimanowski, *Weisheit und Messias: Die jüdischen Voraussetzungen der urchristlichen Präexistenzchristologie* (WUNT, 2.17; Tübingen: Mohr [Paul Siebeck], 1985), p. 118.

which have angels proclaiming the name of Jesus.

We can recognize that the Matthaean narrative which deals with the origin, the genesis, the source of the messiah, was inspired by prophetic promises. But how exactly does this take place? To begin with, it is clear that the constellation of Old Testament texts, which were linked by the history of tradition and related to each other by distinct key terms, lay ready like hidden embers, so that the living breath of the Christology which roared through the New Testament congregations would fan it into flame. Should one take a closer look, it is possible to demonstrate that the 'messianic exegesis' of Matthew came to its production of texts as well as to its formation of legends through the illumination of the Old Testament by the coming of the messiah.

Who gives the Son?

The passive construction in Isa. 9.5, 'will be born, will be given', raises the question regarding those individuals who are actually acting: who is bearing the child to us? Who is giving the son to us?

The first question is answered by the cluster of messianic texts in the book of Isaiah (chs. 7, 9 and 11), especially by Isa. 7.14: the virgin, who is to become pregnant, will bear to us the child, the son, whose throne-names will include also the name 'Immanuel'.

The second question is answered in the manner in which the text of Isa. 9.5 itself is formulated. Here, 'will be given' can and should be read as a theological passive. God, whose 'zeal' (Isa. 9.6) for Israel brings about his promises, gives to us the son. In the Old Testament tradition, God's 'giving' the son who is to be born is a stereotypical image, especially in the narratives dealing with the miraculous births of great men of God:

> Gen. 17.16: God is speaking to Abraham concerning Sarah who would give birth to Isaac: 'I will bless her and also *give you a son* by her'.

> Gen. 30.6: Rachel says after the birth of Dan: 'God has vindicated for me; and has also listened to my voice and *given me a son*'.

> Ruth 4.12: The people and the elders have this wish for Boaz, David's ancestor: 'May your house be like the house of Perez, whom Tamar has borne to Judah, through the offspring which *the Lord will give to you* from this young woman'. (The phrase 'from this young woman' also points ahead to the phrase 'from Mary'.)

> Ruth 4.13: '*The LORD gave* her conception'.

1 Sam. 1.6: Hannah's 'rival provoked and humiliated her severely, because *the LORD had given* her no children'.

1 Sam. 1.11: Hannah prays (concerning Samuel): *'LORD* of hosts, if you ... would *give me a son'.*

Narratives in Genesis also use the formula 'God gives seed', which can refer either to many or to one offspring (cf. Gen. 15.3; 38.9). The passive construction in Isa. 9.5, 'a son will be given us', is therefore to be correctly translated: 'God gives us a son'. In the context of the messianic texts of Isaiah 7, 9 and 11 it is clear: as the promised messiah, this announced son is the 'Son of God'.

The Matthaean exegesis takes seriously the constellation of the history of tradition and effect of the Old Testament texts (and the Old Testament as the context for interpretation). Therefore we can see that an awareness of the textual constellation of Isa. 7.14 and Isa. 9.5-6 leads the Matthaean exegesis to the recognition of the theological origin, the genesis, of the messiah from the virgin who bears him, and from God, that is, his Holy Spirit, who gives or 'begets' him.

The Constellation of the Prophetic Texts of the Old Testament

A textual analysis, not only of Matthew but also of the Gospel of Luke, demonstrates that those narrating the birth announcement of Jesus in the New Testament were indeed aware of the constellation of the messianic prophetic texts, probably already in the tradition prior to the actual writing of the Gospels. These texts included Isaiah 7 and 9 (also Isa. 11), as well as Mic. 5.1-3 and 2 Sam. 7.12-16. The discovery of such clusters of Old Testament texts was also cultivated in the liturgy of the synagogue, in whose tradition the first Christian congregations arose. In the Gospel of Matthew, the following sequence of Old Testament texts is in view:

Mt. 1.1 (Son of David):	2 Sam. 7.12-16
	Ps. 2.6-7
	Ps. 89.27-30
	Ps. 110.1-3
Mt. 1.21 (announcement formula):	Gen. 17.19
Mt. 1.23 (quotation):	Isa. 7.14
(phrase 'with us'):	Isa. 8.8, 10
Mt. 2.6 (quotation):	Mic. 5.1-3
	2 Sam. 5.2; 7.8
	1 Chron. 11.2
Mt. 3.17:	Ps. 2.7
Mt. 4.15-16:	Isa. 9.1-2

In the Lukan birth announcement the constellation of texts is available in an even more closely confined space:

Lk. 1.27:	Isa. 7.14
Lk. 1.32:	Isa. 9.6
	Ps. 89.27-28
	2 Sam. 7.12-16
Lk. 1.33:	Mic. 4.7; 5.1-3
Lk. 1.37:	Gen. 18.14
Lk. 1.38:	Gen. 21.1

In the Matthaean and the Lukan childhood stories, the messianic clusters of texts, which are foundational to both compositions, seem to be the same despite the many differences in the details of the legendary stories. This indicates decisively that the choice of messianic texts was definitive in the formation of the Christologumena in the Gospel narratives.

From the synagogal liturgy, the composition of the following related texts can be compared:[1]

> Gen. 21 with 1 Sam. 2–3; Ps. 110; Hab. 3.17-18; Ps. 123.9; Isa. 66.9.
> Or: Gen. 16 with Isa. 54.1-10.
> Or: Gen. 18 with Jer. 33:7-8.
> Or: Gen. 25.19 with Isa. 65.23–66.8.[2]

The question whether or not Isa. 9.5 influenced Matthew 1–2 in its careful differentiation between παιδίον (child; cf. Isa. 9.5a: 'A *child* will be born to us'), used each time in connection with the mother Mary who had borne the child (cf. Mt. 2.8, 9, 11, 13, 14, 20, 21), and υἱός (son; cf. Isa. 9.5b: 'A *son* will be given us'), which is used each time in the sayings of God (Mt. 1.23 = Isa. 7.14; Mt. 2.15 = Hos. 11.1)[3], cannot be answered with any certainty.

God 'Gives'—God 'Begets'—God 'Creates'

The New Testament speaks in legendary-haggadic narratives of Jesus' sonship to God, his procreation by the Holy Spirit and his birth by the virgin. An analysis of the Old Testament sources which are used in these New Testament texts guides our attention more directly to the messiani-

---

1. C. Perrot, 'Les récits d'enfance dans la Haggada', *RSR* 55 (1967), pp. 481-518.

2. See also J. Mann, *The Bible as Read and Preached in the Old Synagogue* (repr.; New York: Ktav, 1971 [1940]).

3. See Pesch, 'Der Gottessohn in matthäischen Evangelienprolog'.

cally interpreted prophecies concerning the son of David and the Son of God, and to his relationship to Yahweh as father. These sources make clear that the divine 'giving' of the son could be interpreted as 'begetting', that is, 'creating' (or even 'forming', *plasmare*), just as, inversely, the 'begetting' could be seen as creative 'giving'. Therefore, we can understand that the procreation by the Holy Spirit (God gives the son) was linked to the birth by the virgin (Mary bears the child) if we are aware that the textual clustering of Isa. 7.14 and Isa. 9.5-6 has been combined with the promises concerning the Son of David/Son of God.

In Ps. 2.6-7 a 'model' is given which exemplifies how the nature of the messiah could be determined by his origin with God:

> But I was *created* (in a miraculous manner)
> as his king on Zion, his holy mountain.
> The decree of the LORD I will proclaim:
> You are my son. Today I have *begotten* you!

It is not coincidence that the messianic exegesis of Matthew, guided by its Old Testament sources, reserves the declaration of Jesus as Son of God for the proclamation of the heavenly voice at Jesus' baptism (where of course Isa. 42.1 is emphasized since Matthew exchanges the Markan predicate formula 'you are' with the identification formula 'this one is'). God identifies this Jesus from Nazareth as his beloved son: 'And behold, a voice spoke from the heavens: "This one is my beloved Son whom I have chosen"' (Mt. 3.17). The messiah is the Son who has been miraculously created, begotten, by Yahweh, by the Lord. Next to Ps. 2.7, Ps. 110.1 plays an outstanding role within early Christology (as it already had in early Jewish messianology). In Ps. 110.1 the messiah, as God's representative, is appointed to his right hand. In Ps. 110.3, as in Ps. 2.7, the messiah's divine nature is determined by his origin. Here Yahweh speaks to the messiah-king: 'I have *begotten* you even prior to the morning star, just like the dew in the morning'.

According to the declaration of Ps. 110.4, which makes reference to Melchizedek who was regarded as a type of messiah in early Judaism, the messiah, the Son of God, is a priest-king. This point of view was also taken up by the Matthean genealogy, which connected the names of kings with the names of priests. This implies that the messiah-priest-king is the founder of the messianic nation which is made up entirely of priests and kings.

The messianic prophecies found in 2 Sam. 7.14 and Ps. 89.27 strengthen the idea of a special, exclusive, relationship that God has with his son. This is the God who, according to Isa. 9.5, gives the messiah to us as his son and whom he, according to Ps. 2.7 and 110.3, has begotten, that is, created by his Holy Spirit. Ps. 89.27 (89.26-27 English) reads:

> He will declare to me: 'You are my father, my God, the rock of my
>   salvation.'
> I will make him the firstborn son, the highest among the rulers of the earth.

And in 2 Sam. 7.14 God prophesies: 'I will be a father to him, and he will be a son to me'.

Within early Jewish literature, probably in an interpretation of Ps. 2.7, a text from the pious ones of Qumran mentions 'that God *begets* the Messiah' (1QSa 2.11). In light of these texts, Jesus' use of the Abba-address, whose originality no one doubts, appears indeed to be an expression of his messianic self-awareness as the son of God.

The Son—Son of David and Son of Abraham

Isa. 9.5 raised the question: 'Who is giving the son?' We have discovered how this question can be answered with the messianic traditions about the son of David. However, the traditions about Abraham also provide us with the same answer: God gives the son! Indeed, the genre of the birth announcements used in Mt. 1.18-25 leads us back to Abraham, Sarah and Isaac. In Genesis 17, 18 and 21 statements are collected which describe the miracle of the gift of a promised son, a miracle impossible for human beings, possible only for Yahweh. Paul will proclaim that this son was conceived by a barren woman according to promise and Spirit (Gal. 4.23, 29).

In Gen. 17.14-15, 19, 21 we read:

> Then God said to Abraham:
> 'Your wife Sarai you shall no longer call Sarai but Sarah (mistress) she
>   shall be called.
> I will bless her *and also give you a son by her.*
> I am blessing her, so that nations shall come forth from her...
> *Your wife Sarah shall bear you a son* and you shall call him Isaac.
> I will establish a covenant with him as an eternal covenant for his
>   descendants...
> But my covenant I will establish with Isaac, *whom Sarah shall bear to you*
>   at this time next year.'

The parallels to the prophetic texts regarding the messianic son of David are apparent: God gives the son, the previously barren woman (Sarah) gives birth to him. In Gen. 18.10, 14 Yahweh says:

'Next year I will come to you again, your wife Sarah will then have a
son...
Is anything impossible with the LORD?'

In Luke, the angel Gabriel takes up this question again in the scene
dealing with his announcement to Mary.

Finally, in Gen 21.1-3 we are told:

The LORD took heed of Sarah, as he had said, and he *did, as he had
promised.*
Sarah became pregnant and *bore a son to Abraham* even in his old age, at
the time which had been appointed by God.
Abraham named *the son, whom Sarah bore to him,* Isaac.

The texts from the three chapters of Genesis identify the connection (a
connection which comes to light on the basis of the questions raised by
Isa. 9.5) as a hypothesis which could be taken up in the Matthaean
exegesis:

God gives the son,
the woman bears him,
the father gives him the name.
The birth is a miracle!

Early Jewish Witnesses to the Tradition
The surviving sources of those early Jewish writings which repeat the
Old Testament narratives indicate that this connection is present in early
Judaism and therefore at the time of the New Testament.

For instance, *Jub.* 16.12-13 repeats Gen. 21.1 as follows:

In the middle of the sixth month the Lord visited Sarah and did for her as
he had said. [According to *Jub.* 15.16 the Lord had said: 'I will bless her,
and *give to you a son from her'*.] She became pregnant and gave birth to a
son in the third month, to be exact, in the middle of the month...

The time indicators date Isaac's birth as having taken place at the time
of the Passover feast. This birth was thanks to the miraculous action of
God, whose 'activity' is emphasized greatly in the retelling.

According to Pseudo-Philo's *Liber Antiquitatum Biblicarum,* God
promises Abraham that he will give him offspring from the barren
woman, from her 'closed womb'; Sarah belonged to those women
'whose womb I will open, and they will give birth' (*LAB* 23.5, 7).

In *LAB* 23.8, God reports about his deeds on behalf of Abraham:
'And *I gave him Isaac* and *formed him* in the womb of the one who

gave birth to him, and I commanded it, that it would produce him quicker and give him back to me in the seventh month'. See also *LAB* 32.1 where we are reminded concerning Yahweh's action on behalf of Abraham: 'And *he gave him a son* in his highest old age and brought him forth from a barren womb'. The fact that God gives sons is also pointed out with regard to Rebecca's children in *LAB* 23.8: '*And I gave to Isaac Jacob and Esau*'. The early Jewish writing *Cave of Treasures* recounts in 29.1-2:

> Abraham was ninety-nine years old;
> then God went into his house and *gave Sarah a son.*
> Abraham was one hundred years old when Isaac was born to him.

Philo of Alexandria, who utilized such texts allegorically, notes explicitly that God had taken the place of the patriarchs, the fathers, in the Old Testament accounts: opening the womb should be a matter for the husband. The *Liber Antiquitatum Biblicarum* of Pseudo-Philo has demonstrated that early Judaism could understand God's 'begetting' as his creative 'forming' (*plasmare*).

A clearly noticeable tradition-historical trail leads from the miraculous conception of Sarah right to the virginal conception of Mary. 'The theme of the miraculous conception of Sarah gives rise to delicate questions, given its implications with the theme—connected, but distinct—of the virgin birth.'[1] Like Pseudo-Philo, Philo himself witnesses to a corresponding tradition: God himself has formed Isaac, 'the Lord has begotten Isaac' (Philo, *Leg. All.* 3.219).

Finally, Paul also knows of this tradition. To him, Isaac is the one begotten by the Spirit.

In early Jewish literature we can also find evidence, even if sparse, for the idea of miraculous procreation in the traditions concerning Cain, Lamech, Noah and Melchizedek[2]. 'The anti-Christian Jewish polemic certainly tried to eliminate them.'[3]

The traditions could easily be placed next to each other: God as the one who forms, and the human father as the procreator. This was an early expression of the 'totus-totus' model needed to define the 'together' and 'within one another' of divine and human action.

LAB 8.4 combines the statements:

1. Perrot, 'Les récits d'enfance dans la Haggada', p. 489.
2. Perrot, 'Les récits d'enfance dans la Haggada', pp. 490-91.
3. Perrot, 'Les récits d'enfance dans la Haggada', p. 492.

And Abraham knew Sarah his wife, and she conceived and gave birth to
    Isaac.
God opened the womb of Sarah and gave Abraham a son from Sarah.

Philo of Alexandria as a Witness to Early Jewish Traditions

Early Jewish exegesis recognized and contemplated the relationship and
the meaning of such texts, their formulation and their genre-bound
patterns. This fact is especially indicated by Philo in his work *De
Cherubim* (*Cher.* 42-52), where he presents an allegorical interpretation
of Old Testament texts with a view to the divine procreation of the
virtues by the unspotted virgin soul. Philo bases such allegories on the
literal meaning of the following texts:

> But Abraham and Sarah were old people, advanced in days,
> It no longer happened to Sarah after the manner of women (Gen. 18.11).

> And the LORD visited Sarah, as he had said, and the Lord did for her as he
> had spoken, and she conceived and gave birth to a son to Abraham in her
> old age, at the time when the Lord had told her. And Abraham called the
> name of the son who was born to him, whom Sarah had borne to him:
> Isaac (Gen. 21.1-3; Paul picked up the expression 'having become' with
> reference to the son [in Rom. 1.3-4]).

Philo develops the (new) virginity of Sarah from the fact that 'it no
longer happened to Sarah after the manner of women'. He then interprets God's 'visiting' and 'doing for her' as his 'giving' or 'begetting'
the son, that is, the virtue, from the unspotted virgin soul for which
Sarah allegorically stands:

> *Therefore God gives the seed*, but the strange fruit which he brings forth
> with the seed *is a gift*; For God *begets* nothing for himself since he is
> completely without needs, but everything for the one who needs to receive.
> Concerning that which is said, I can list as a fully adequate witness Moses
> the very holiest. For he shows us Sarah becoming pregnant when God
> looks upon her in her solitude [Gen 21.1], but he does not allow her to
> give birth for the one who looked upon her, but for the one who strives to
> reach for wisdom, whose name is Abraham (*Cher.* 44-45).

It is clear that Philo's allegory presupposes a literal reading of the Old
Testament text, according to which God 'begets' the son of promise.
This is just as clear in Philo's commentary to the following text:

> But Isaac pleaded to the LORD on account of Rebecca his wife, because
> she was barren. And God heard his prayer, and his wife Rebecca became
> pregnant (Gen. 25.21).

Philo comments: 'After the all-wise Isaac had pleaded with God, *Rebecca,* persistent virtue, *became pregnant from the one being pleaded to* [i.e. God] (*Cher.* 47)'. Philo again reads the Old Testament text literally, so that he can interpret it allegorically as pointing to the procreation of the virtues in the virgin soul through God.

A further example is the exegesis of Gen. 29.31-32:

> But the LORD saw that Leah was despised; he opened her womb...
> And Leah conceived and bore a son to Jacob.
> And she called his name Reuben; she said:
> 'The LORD has looked upon my humiliation'.

Philo comments:

> Even more clearly he [Moses] taught us with Leah, by saying, that God opened her womb—opening the womb is surely a matter for the husband—but she conceived and gave birth, not for God—since this one is complete by himself and totally sufficient—but for Jacob who took upon himself the troublesome concern for good. Therefore, while virtue receives the divine seed from the Creator, she gives birth to it for one of her lovers (*Cher.* 46).

This much is clear: the prerequisite for the allegory of Philo of Alexandria is a literal reading of his reference texts from the stories regarding the fathers. As with the early Jewish haggadah, the book of *Jubilees,* and the *Liber Antiquitatum Biblicarum* of Pseudo-Philo, the narratives dealing with the birth of the men of God were understood to be miracles performed by God.

Taken literally, the texts indeed appear to put God in the place of the patriarchs, to whom he 'gives a son', a son to whom the wives give birth for the patriarchs. 'Philo derived the virginity of the patriarchal wives from the conviction that God would only associate with the virgin soul. Looked at differently this would mean that the one whom God seeks must be at his complete disposal.'[1]

Of course the virgin birth of the messiah Jesus is not to be explained with reference to Philo. Instead, Mary's virginity suggested itself to the messianic exegesis of Matthew or his communities during the study of the tradition-historical constellation of messianic texts, among them especially Isa. 7.14 and 9.5-6. This took place independently, in a new way—and indeed not until after the arrival of the messiah as Jesus of Nazareth.

---

1.   Gnilka, *Das Matthäusevangelium,* p. 26.

That the New Testament communities and churches were stimulated and enabled to such a reading of the Old Testament texts was probably also connected with the fact that, in their experience, it required a miracle for the believing community to receive brothers and sisters, sons and daughters, who form the 'body of Christ', which is the eschatological miracle.

The Genre of 'Birth Announcements'

Both the birth announcement formula in Isa. 7.14 and the 'God gives a son' formula in Isa. 9.5 point ultimately to the Old Testament and the early Jewish genre of 'birth announcements'. This is widely witnessed to outside of the Abraham–Isaac tradition, and is used in the formation of the narrative concerning Jesus' birth announcement in Mt. 1.18-25 (as it is with regard to John the Baptist and Jesus in Lk. 1). The following narratives can be compared:

Gen. 16 (Ishmael)	=	*Jub.* 14
Gen. 17 (Isaac)	=	*Jub.* 15
Gen. 18 (Isaac)	=	*Jub.* 16
Gen. 21 (birth of Isaac)	=	*Jub.* 16
Judg. 13 (Samson)	=	*LAB* 42-43
1 Sam. 1 (Samuel)	=	*LAB* 50-51
Isa. 7.10-15 (Immanuel)		
(cf. Isa. 9.5-6 as a proclamation of birth)		
Josephus, *Ant.* 2.9.2-4 §§205-23 (Moses) =		*LAB* 9

Genres are characterized by 'formulas', by set literal expressions. In Mt. 1.18-25 we meet a number of formulas typical of the genre of 'birth announcements': the statement concerning the 'angel of the Lord': Gen. 16.7-8, 11; Judg. 13.3; the indicative formula 'Behold': Gen. 16.11; Judg. 13.3, 5; Isa. 7.14; the announcement 'to be pregnant': Gen. 16.11; Judg. 13.5; Isa. 7.14; the instruction 'to call his name': Gen. 16.11; 17.19; Isa. 7.14; cf. Judg. 16.13; the statement 'to bear a son': Gen. 16.11; 17.19; Judg. 13.5; Isa. 7.14. All contacts of the reflexive citation of Isa 7.14 in Mt. 1.23 with the remaining verses in Mt. 1.18-25 are at the same time contacts with the formula language of the 'birth announcement' genre. This genre has moved beyond the original intention of recounting a miraculous birth, through the early Jewish interpretation of the Old Testament narratives which placed the emphasis on the actions of God.

The Moses Typology

A particular surprise of the messianic exegesis in the footnote to the genealogy is its reference back to Moses typology when it is dealing with the narrative of the origin of the son of Abraham and son of David, the messianic Son of God. This we can understand, not only because Jesus is measured against Moses, but also if we recognize to what degree the congregations saw their own fortune reflected in the fortune of the messiah-child.

The haggadah concerning Moses offers the material for the narration regarding the eschatological prophet and the second savior and liberator, who repeats and renews the fate of the first savior in a structurally congruent yet surpassing way, thereby opening up a new history for the people of God.

In the footnote to the genealogy of Jesus, the genre of 'birth announcement' is transformed into a fable, a narrative thread, of which almost all important features have been characterized previously in the Moses tradition. All motives in the birth announcement of Jesus can be compared to motives in the narrative of Moses' birth announcement:

Mt. 1.18b Mary is pregnant	*Josephus, Ant. 2.9.3 §§210-16* Amram, the father of Moses, is worried (in view of Pharaoh's order to kill all new-born males) because *his wife is pregnant*.
Mt. 1.19a Joseph is righteous	*Num. R. 13.2 (on Num. 7.12); Exod. R. 1.13 (on Exod. 1.15)* Amram is *a righteous one*. Miriam, Moses' sister, says to Amram: 'You however are *a righteous one*'.
Mt. 1.19b Joseph wants to dismiss Mary	*Exod. R. 1.13 (on Exod. 1.15)* 'Immediately he *dismissed Jochebed* [his wife] from the house and denied himself use of the marriage bed. He *turned out his wife* when she was pregnant in the third month.'
Mt. 1.20a Appearance of angel in a dream	*Sefer-ha-Zikkronot; Josephus, Ant. 2.9.3 §§210-16* An *angel* appears (the angel of the birth announcement is Gabriel) or God speaks *in a dream* to Amram.

Mt. 1.20b-21	*Chronicle of Moses; Mek. Exod. 15.17-21*
	(Shir. §10); Sefer-ha-Zikkronot; Josephus,
	Ant. 2.9.3 §§210-16
Speech of the angel, birth	The prophetess Miriam says: 'Behold, this
announcement, explanation of the	time *a son will be born to my father and*
son's meaning	*mother who will save the children of Israel*
	out of the hand of Egypt'.

Mt. 1.24-25	*Chronicle of Moses; Sefer-ha-Zikkronot;*
	Exod. R. 1.19 (on Exod. 2.1); Josephus,
	Ant. 2.9.4 §217
Joseph follows the instructions	'When Amram heard the words of the girl
of the angel	[Miriam], *he took his wife to himself.'*
	'So Amram left the house of Levi and *took*
	Jochebed, the daughter of Levi, *to*
	himself.' Amram said: 'I will therefore
	go to my wife'.
	'And Amram of the tribe of Levi went *to*
	take his wife Jochebed to himself.'
	'Because this had been revealed to him
	by the face, Amram *awoke from sleep* and
	made it known to Jochebed.'

When focusing upon the second chapter of the infancy narrative it becomes obvious that Mt. 1.18-25 is intended to bring the Moses tradition to mind. The fate of the messiah-child, who is persecuted by King Herod, is paralleled to the persecution of Moses by Pharaoh, as is the fate of God's people, Israel and the church, saved each in its turn by the first and the second redeemer.

Isaiah 7.14 and the Miracle of the Birth of the Messiah

Considering the cloud of Old Testament and early Jewish witnesses, it is no longer possible to say that Matthew, and the early church tradition which predates him, has interpreted Isa. 7.14 in contradiction to the meaning it has received through the constellation of the tradition. It cannot be said that the Christian exegesis of Isa. 7.14 is 'untenable'. To the contrary. The absolute miracle of the birth of the messiah and Son of God is interpreted by means of this excellent prophetic promise-text, whose prophecy can thus be proclaimed to have been fulfilled.

Already since Isaac's miraculous birth, the messianic 'son', who was expected to come from Abraham and from his and David's descendants, has been hoped for as a *gift of God*! Isa. 7.14 has shown itself to be the outstanding text among the birth announcements and *the* messianic prophetic text, beginning with the cluster of messianic texts in chs. 7–11 of the book of Isaiah, but especially in the combination of these texts with Micah 5 and the messianically-interpreted Psalms (primary among them Pss. 2 and 110). The concept of faith in the early church could not transcend this verse; it had to take it up and in fact did so in the haggadic narrative of the birth of Messiah Jesus.

Isa. 7.14 was moreover the only text in the Old Testament dealing with a birth announcement whose fulfillment had not already been reported within the Old Testament itself; in Isa. 9.5-6, and likewise Mic. 5.1-3, the fulfillment was only announced. The first New Testament congregations could proclaim the fulfillment, because they had recognized Jesus as the messiah. Their messianic exegesis is interpretation based upon the fulfillment of the prophecies.

4. 'And You Bethlehem...' (Matthew 2.6)

The narrator, or Evangelist, confirms that 'Jesus was born in Bethlehem' (Mt. 2.1). Historical-critical exegesis has established that, in all likelihood, Jesus was not born in Bethlehem. But what does it mean when criticism declares Bethlehem as the 'theological birthplace', as the birthplace of the messiah which in Judaism had already been discovered from the Scriptures?

The Text

1 But when Jesus was born in Bethlehem in Judea in the days of king Herod, behold: magi from the east appeared in Jerusalem and said:

2 'Where is the new-born king of the Jews? For we have seen his star in the east and have come to pay him homage.'

3 But when King Herod heard this,
   he was frightened and all Jerusalem with him.

4 And he gathered all the ruling priests and scribes of the people and wanted to know from them where Messiah was to be born.

5 But they said to him:
   'In Bethlehem in Judea!
   For so it is written by the prophets:

6 *and you, Bethlehem, land of Judah,*
   by no means are you the least among the ruling clans of Judah:
   because from you shall come forth a ruler; who will shepherd my
   people Israel' [Mic. 5.1, 3; 2 Sam. 5.2].

7 Then Herod secretly called the magi to himself
   and learned from them the exact time of the appearing star.

8   And he sent them to Bethlehem and said:
    'Go and ascertain exactly where the child is!
    But when you have found it report it to me,
    so that I also can come and pay him homage.'
9   After the audience with the king they set out.
    And behold, the star, which they had seen in the east
    went before them until it came and stood above the place where the
    child was.
10 When they saw the star they rejoiced much with great joy.
11 And when they came in the house, they saw the child with Mary his
    mother.
    And they fell down and paid him homage.
    And they opened their treasure chests and brought him gifts:
    Gold and frankincense and myrrh.
12 And since they received instruction in a dream not to return to Herod,
    they set out on another way to their land.

Concerning the Interpretation

The newer commentaries have directed attention to questions which
cannot be suppressed in light of the text. As Luz puts it,

> Once again the interpreter is confronted with the problem of how he
> should deal with a story whose historicity seems improbable. Since one of
> its most fundamental concerns is the proclamation of God's providential
> leading, the problem is intensified: A leading which is only proclaimed is
> close to being an illusion. Where does this leave God's work, which is
> what the story wants to relate?[1]

Quite correctly, Luz has referred to the experiences of the first congregations as a historical prerequisite for the legendary narrative and has
demanded that 'The preacher who uses it is questioned about his own
experiences which correspond to this witness'.[2]

The legendary staging in Mt. 2.1-12 seems to be based upon the
following logic: if Jesus is the messiah, the 'king of the Jews'—as the
statement of his crime above his cross proclaimed!—then he had to be
born in Bethlehem. In Jn 7.41-42 this is used as a passage from
Scripture to oppose Jesus of Nazareth: 'Again others said: "Is Messiah
to come out of Galilee? Does not the Scripture say: 'The Messiah comes
from the seed of David and from the village of Bethlehem where David
lived?"' ' Similar is the objection to Jesus found in Jn 6.42: 'And they

1.   Luz, *Matthäus*, p. 116.
2.   Luz, *Matthäus*, p. 116.

said: "Is this not Jesus the son of Joseph, whose father and mother we know? How can he say now: 'I have come down from heaven'?"

According to the theology of the Gospel of John, Jesus can say this, because God's actions cannot be placed on the same level with human cooperation. The contradictions—from heaven or the son of Joseph; from Bethlehem or from Nazareth—draw attention to the fact that the messianic quality of Jesus can only be apprehended by faith. The contradiction regarding the locale also serves as a hint regarding the paradox of faith.

In Jn 7.27 objections are once again raised against Jesus: 'Concerning this one here we know whence he is; however when the Messiah comes, no one knows whence he is!' This objection is both valid and invalid. That Jesus came from Nazareth is possible to know and verify. That Jesus 'came from God'—and in its place 'from Bethlehem' hints of fulfillment—is not possible to know and verify, although by faith it is possible to experience and to tell others through one's witness. Further, the credibility of the community guarantees it!

The Gospel of John therefore helps us in our understanding of Matthew's messianic exegesis: Jesus, though born in Nazareth, comes as the messiah from Bethlehem. Jesus is Joseph's son, yet as messiah he is God's Son. Joseph's son, Jesus of Nazareth, is known according to his place of birth (*Herkunft*), and yet, as messiah, he is unknown regarding his place of origin (*Ursprung*). The messianic exegesis presupposes the paradox of the unexpected and completely unanticipated arrival of the messiah and the paradox of the renewal of his people into the *ecclesia*.

The legend found in Mt. 2.1-12 makes it clear that only the one who, like the magi, sets out to worship the king of the Jews, who can be found with his mother, has personally discovered that Jesus is born 'in Bethlehem', that is, that he is the messiah who has been foretold by the prophets.

King Herod, who 'was frightened and all Jerusalem with him' (instead of breaking forth in jubilation), wants to kill the messiah-child. He does not find the child in Bethlehem because God delivered him from his grasp by taking him to Egypt. For the unbeliever there is no 'Bethlehem', only an 'Egypt'.

The assembly of all the ruling priests and scribes of the people, while able to answer the hypothetical question of where the messiah is to be born, is not interested in the real question of the magi: 'where is the new-born king of the Jews?' Unbelief does not expect either his birth or the renewal of God's people in the church.

Such were the experiences of the Matthaean community, which condensed them into the so-called legend of the three kings. Only Bethlehem, the 'theological place of birth', allowed for the narrative to be composed in its present form, since with Bethlehem the congregation claimed the Davidic-messianic tradition of Israel for itself, for its messiah, for the Nazorean Jesus.

Mic. 5.1, the prophetic text quoted by the scribes, has also been interpreted in early Judaism as indicating that the messiah should come from Bethlehem. The Targum to Mic. 5.1b reads: 'From you will come forth the Messiah in order to rule over Israel, whose name is named since the beginning, from eternal times'. The legendary storytelling of the New Testament communities could appropriate this tradition for its narrative Christology, even if the storytellers also knew that Jesus came from Nazareth.

5. *'Out of Egypt I Called my Son'* (Matthew 2.15)

The initial problem is found here anew: in all likelihood, Jesus was never in Egypt, neither as a child, nor as a young man, nor as a grown adult. Joseph never did flee to Egypt with the 'child and his mother' (an expression used four times in Mt. 2.13-23). Then why does the legend speak of this?

The Text

13 But when they had departed,
     behold, an angel of the Lord appeared to Joseph in a dream and said:
     'Get up, take the child and his mother, and flee to Egypt!
     And remain there until I tell you!
     For Herod will search for the child in order to destroy it.'
14 And he got up, took the child and his mother by night
     and departed for Egypt.
15 And he was there until the death of Herod.
     So that what was spoken by the Lord through the prophet would be
     fulfilled, who says:
     'From Egypt I called my Son' (Hos. 11.1).

Concerning the Interpretation

Why does this Matthaean text say that Joseph had fled to Egypt with Jesus and his mother? The genre of the 'narrative of the persecuted and rescued child-king'[1] does not demand this geographic specificity. Also, the parallels from the Moses-haggadah, where Moses flees Egypt, rather point in the opposite direction. However, Egypt is mentioned specifically four times in Mt. 2.13-23, while the 'land of Israel', with which it is contrasted, is mentioned only twice. In the original text of Hos. 11.1, 'the son' who had been called 'by the Lord' out of Egypt was Israel, God's people, which Yahweh, in Exod. 4.22, had called his 'first-born son'.

It is important to Matthew that God himself identifies Jesus as the Son of God. However, has not his exegesis now indeed become 'wild exegesis'? Also noteworthy is that while both Isa. 7.14 and Mic. 5.1, 3 were spoken in the future tense, as prophecies should be, the prophet Hosea, who is not named, instead recorded a word from Yahweh, which speaks of his call at the time of Israel's youth: 'When Israel was young, he became dear to me, out of Egypt I called my son' (Hos. 11.1).

Probably long before the Gospel of Matthew was penned, the legend recounted the flight to Egypt of the 'newborn king of the Jews', of the 'savior' of God's people. Matthew interprets this narrated event as a fulfillment of Old Testament prophecy: even the persecution identifies the messiah as God's Son, in the same way that persecution acts as a qualifying sign of the messianic community (cf. Mt. 5.12-13).

Matthew implies at the same time that the exodus from Egypt is repeated and completed in Jesus and in the community which is gathered around him: 'The redemptive event is happening again. The reader acquainted with the Bible senses that God's action through his son has elementary character, tying into Israel's foundational experience yet realizing it anew'.[2]

The quotation of Hos. 11.1 is used in a context where the reigning King Herod persecutes the boy-messiah, where the assembly of all high priests and scribes remains at a distance while all Jerusalem is gripped with messianic fear. It is therefore valid to ask if Matthew's account was meant to reflect the context of Hosea 11 as well. Has not Israel failed as the son?

> But he must return to Egypt (Hos. 11.5; cf. 8.13; 9.3).
> The more I called them, the more they ran away from me (Hos. 11.2).
> But they did not realize that I wanted to heal them (Hos. 11.3).
> My people persist in unfaithfulness (Hos. 11.7).

---

1.   See the table in Luz, *Matthäus*, p. 84.
2.   Luz, *Matthäus*, p. 129.

The next quotation in Matthew (2.18) which is understood as the fulfillment of Old Testament prophecy is taken from Jeremiah 31. This proximity of the two prophetic texts, Hosea 11 and Jeremiah 31, helps to demonstrate the correctness of the assumption that Matthew wanted to have the original context of the quotation taken into consideration. Even more importantly, however, the whole context of the Gospel of Matthew supports this interpretation. What is said with regard to the hostility of Herod toward the child-messiah is later repeated with regard to the hostility of the Pharisees, ruling priests and elders toward Jesus:

Mt. 2.13:	Herod will look for the child to destroy it.
Mt. 12.14:	The Pharisees conspired against him to destroy him.
Mt. 27.20:	The ruling priests and the elders persuaded the crowds that they... should destroy Jesus.

And the same fate awaits the disciples, the congregation (cf. Mt. 10.16-25; 24.9-14).

Rev. 11.8 says of Israel or Jerusalem, which persecutes and kills its prophets, that the city would 'spiritually' be called 'Sodom and Egypt'. Whether Matthew was aware of the depth of such a spiritual dimension to the text must remain open. He does imply in Mt. 2.20, with the use of the plural, that he did see beyond the persecutor Herod, who indeed resided in Jerusalem, to all those persecuting the cause of God. As in Exod. 4.19, the Evangelist speaks of the death of those 'who were seeking the child's life' (thereby alluding to the prototypical fate of Moses). It is paradoxical that now, at the messiah's coming, the persecutors are to be found 'in the land of Israel' (Mt. 2.20-21) while the Gentile country has become the place of refuge for the messianic child.

Matthew's community, at home in Syria, probably in Antioch, would have understood the structural congruence between their own personal experience and the experience which had been fabricated within the legend. The founders of the Antiochian community consisted of Hellenists who had been banished from Jerusalem, and Peter. Peter's rescue from the hands of the other Herod, Agrippa I, his liberation from the dungeon in Jerusalem (cf. Acts 12), was recounted with obvious allusions to Israel's rescue from Egypt.[1]

It is possible to recognize that Matthew, through his 'messianic exegesis', has read the prophetic books in their entirety as prophecies,

---

1. See R. Pesch, *Die Apostelgeschichte*. I. *Apg 1–12* (EKKNT, 5.1; Zurich and Neukirchen–Vluyn: Neukirchener Verlag, 1986), pp. 359-70.

not only those passages which are formally identified as such. In doing so he agrees with the common view of the earliest church, as it was expressly stated for example by Paul: 'And everything which was written beforehand, was written for our instruction, that we may have hope through patience and through the comfort of the Scripture' (Rom. 15.4).

6. 'A Voice was Heard in Ramah' (Matthew 2.18)

The first narrators who told the story of the killing of the children at Bethlehem through Herod, and of Jesus' return from Egypt when Joseph's fear of Herod's son, Archelaus, prompted the move to Galilee, were presumably Palestinian Jewish Christians who were still familiar with contemporary history. Herod was indeed a brutal murderer, at least of his own children. And his son Archelaus, who would follow him as regent of Judea, Idumea and Samaria (4 BCE to 6 CE), was exiled in Gaul by Caesar Augustus due to the combined complaint of Jews and Samarians in Rome:

> When Archelaus had taken possession of the ethnarchy, in remembrance of past quarrels, he treated not only the Jews but the Samaritans as well with such brutality, that both parties sent deputations against him to Caesar. Thereupon, in the ninth year of his reign, he was banished to Vienna, a city in Gaul, and his property was confiscated in favor of the imperial treasury (Josephus, *War* 2.7.3 §111).

Despite the references to the contemporary situation, the Matthaean text constitutes a legend in which the narrators could make free with the actions and adventures of their characters. They were only bound by the objective of their narrative and by the experiences which helped to determined it. Historical-critical exegesis, through its critical analysis of the transmission, comes to the conclusion that in all probability the killing of the children at Bethlehem never took place. And again the question is raised regarding the relationship between prophetic promise and end-time fulfillment.

The Text

16 Then, when Herod saw that he had been tricked by the Magi,
he became very angry.
And he had all boys in Bethlehem and in all of its districts,
from two years and under killed, according to the time,
which he had inquired exactly from the Magi.

17 Then was fulfilled what was spoken by Jeremiah the prophet, who
     said:
18 a voice was heard in Ramah
     much wailing and lamenting.
     Rachel is weeping for her children,
     and she would not be comforted,
     because they are no more (Jer. 31.15).

Concerning the Interpretation

To what should we refer this quotation which was meant to point to
fulfillment of prophecy, if the killing of the children at Bethlehem never
took place? Conspicuous in Mt. 2.17 is the change from 'so that' to
'then' in the formula of the citation. The fulfillment-event, while no
longer depicted as having been intended by God, remains as a prophecy
by Jeremiah, making him appear as a prophet of doom.

Oddly enough Jer. 31.15 (LXX 38.15) has been transmitted as direct
speech from Yahweh: 'Thus says the Lord', although Yahweh's answer
to Rachel's complaint has not been transmitted until Jer. 31.16. Exegetes
therefore think that 'the announcement formula should stand properly in
v.16'.[1] But should not Yahweh indeed be seen as the one hearing
Rachel's complaint?[2]

Mt. 2.18 deviates from the Hebrew and Greek texts of Jeremiah when
it speaks of 'much wailing and lamentation' and of Rachel's 'children'
instead of her 'sons'. According to Jer. 31.15, Jacob's favorite wife, the
matriarch of Israel, laments over those sons who were carried off to
Babylon and who are passing by her grave at Ramah to the north of
Jerusalem.

Already the Old Testament tradition had relocated Ramah to the
vicinity of Bethlehem (cf. the gloss in Gen. 35.19; 48.7: 'on the way to
Ephrath [or: Ephrata], that is, Bethlehem'), where Rachel's grave is
exhibited and venerated to this day. This tradition is also found in *Jub.*
32.34: 'And Rachel died there. And she was buried in the land of
Ephrath [or: Ephrata], that is Bethlehem. And Jacob built a pillar upon
the grave of Rachel, on the road above her grave'. Rachel's lament, as
transmitted by Jeremiah, is applied by Matthew to all the boys in
Bethlehem and the surrounding area, whom Herod ordered killed.

---

1.   J. Schreiner, *Jeremia II* (Die neue Echter-Bibel; Würzburg: Echter Verlag,
1984), p. 183.
2.   See LXX[A], where 'in the heights' instead of 'in Ramah' is translated.

However, he also makes the lament clear, or audible, to the children of Rachel who are dead among the people of God:

> Child/children is already in the 'Logienquelle' a designation for the 'children' of the people of God (Mt 3.9; 11.19; 23.37) as it is in Mk. 7.27 = Mt. 15.26. Mt. 27.25 ('His blood be upon us and our children') uses the term with a meaning related to that of Mt. 2.18. At risk is the loss of the status of childhood, which here is equaled with membership in God's people.[1]

Matthew prophetically interprets 'Israel's "No" to Jesus as being inconsistent with that which makes it into Israel'.[2] The 'wailing' (together with the 'gnashing of teeth') characterizes the expulsion from God's kingdom (Mt. 8.11-12; 13.42, 50; 22.13; 24.51; 25.30).

In the messianic exegesis of Matthew the result is a multiple typology: (1) like the first redeemer Moses, the second redeemer, the messiah Jesus, is already persecuted as a child and saved through God's providence; and (2) just as Rachel's children were destroyed instead of the messiah, so many children of the people of God would come to ruin because of him.

The Scripture, the word of the prophet Jeremiah, interprets the messianic story of Jesus since within it is mirrored the history of the messianic people. This is true where the story of Jesus has been been molded by the faith-experience of the community. As the fate of the messiah is already prefigured in the Old Testament since the prophecy concerning him has already been given, so the history of his community is already sketched in the story of the messiah.

When the community follows in the steps of righteous Joseph by obeying the instructions of the angel of the Lord, it allows for the fulfillment of all still outstanding prophecies. When the arrival of the messiah and the existence of the messianic community produces 'fear' and 'rage', or leaves those who have been informed indifferent, then former children of Rachel 'are no more'.

Matthew could not have failed to notice the affinity between the words of God in Jer. 31.15-22 and Hos. 11.1-11. Yahweh has freed his children from Egypt and from Babylon, or from the exile:

> Is Ephraim such a dear son to me or my favorite child?
> For as often as I reprove him I still must always remember him.
> Therefore my heart beats for him, I must have mercy on him (Jer. 31.20).

---

1. Gnilka, *Das Matthäusevangelium*, p. 53.
2. Luz, *Matthäus*, p. 130.

How can I abandon you Ephraim, how can I surrender you Israel?
(Hos. 11.8).

According to Mt. 1.21, the persecuted child-messiah is appointed to
save his people from their sins. The adult Jesus gave his life for the
establishment of the new covenant through the forgiveness of sins (cf.
Mt. 26.28 with Jer. 31.31-34). Through him, Israel's history has been
taken up in the church. Through him, the interpretation of Israel's
Scripture in its eschatological-universal depth has also been developed
within the church.

7. *'He will be Called a Nazorean'* (Matthew 2.23)

I have already discussed the difficulties with the 'Nazorean quote' in the
introduction. A text which corresponds to the one quoted by Paul
cannot be traced to the Old Testament.

The Text

19 But after the end of Herod,
    behold: An angel of the Lord appears in a dream to Joseph in Egypt
    and says:
20 'Arise, take the child and his mother and go into the land of Israel!
    For those who seek the child's life have died.'
21 But he got up, took the child and his mother
    and came into the land of Israel.
22 But since he heard that Archelaus is king of Judah in place of his
    father Herod, he was afraid to go there.
    But he received instruction in a dream and departed for the region of
    Galilee.
23 And he came and settled in a city which is called Nazareth.
    So that it might be fulfilled what was spoken through the prophets:
    'He will be called a Nazorean.'

Concerning the Interpretation

The first (or last?) reason why Jesus is called a 'Nazorean' is that he
grew up in Nazareth and that he was distinguished from others who
carried his common name with this hometown designation: Jesus of
Nazareth. The Christians in Syria were considered to be 'Nazarenes'.
They were a part of the sect which had been founded by this Nazarene

and which also had been joined by Gentiles who had led them beyond their Jewish beginnings.[1]

Nonetheless, the first (or last?) reason why Jesus is called a 'Nazorean' is that 'the prophets' had predicted him, that he came in fulfillment of prophetic predictions as the messiah and as none other than the man from Nazareth. After all, the reason why Jesus is spoken of as a 'Nazorean' does not have to do so much with the fact that he is a Nazaretene [*Nazaretaner* rather than the usual *Nazoräer*] but rather with the fact that *this* Nazaretene is the messiah who was predicted by the prophets, in contrast to the many other people from this town who were not 'called Nazoreans'. Jesus' being called a 'Nazorean' is not coincidence to the believers of the community of the 'Nazarene', it is providence, divine providence if seen within the history of revelation, the history of God's people.

According to Amos 3.7, Yahweh's providences as a whole are foretold by his prophets, and these prophecies are illuminated by their fulfillments. The community of the Nazareans came upon Scriptures which, to them, announced the Nazorean, because of the living process of their reflection, which is a part of their Scripture-related theology.

That the *neser*, the messianic shoot announced in Isaiah 11, came from Nazareth was not something which was expected! It can only be recognized as part of a meaningful constellation if there is a historical concrete fulfillment of the prophets' probing attempts at prediction.

Although only Isa. 11.1 speaks of the *neser*, its equivalent expression *semah* can be found in the proclamations of other prophets as well:

Isa. 11.1:	A shoot will come forth from the trunk of Jesse and a scion (*neser*) will bear fruit from his roots.
Jer. 23.5:	Behold, days are coming, says the LORD, when I will awaken for David a righteous shoot (*semah*).
Jer. 33.15:	In those days and at that time I will cause a righteous shoot (*semah*) to arise for David.
Zech. 3.8:	For I am going to have my servant, the shoot (*semah*), brought in.
Zech. 6.12:	There is a man, his name is shoot (*semah*).

Early Jewish tradition also is aware of this prophecy, as is seen for example in *T. Jud.* 24.5-6: 'Then the sceptre of my kingdom will light up, and from your root *a shoot* will arise. And through him a sceptre of

---

1. See Luz, *Matthäus*, pp. 131-33 (as well as the literature on pp. 124-25).

righteousness will rise for the nations, to judge and to save all who call upon the Lord'.

The exegesis of Matthew presumes that the equivalent expression *neṣer* also carries the messianic meaning of the 'title' *shoot* (*ṣemaḥ*). Because of this the Evangelist can speak of 'the prophets' (in the plural). The use of the expression 'shoot' takes for granted that the family is envisioned like a tree, whose power lies within its roots.

In Isa. 60.21 the messianic nation is understood to be the shoot growing from that which had been planted by Yahweh. Matthew may also have kept in mind that Jesus, the 'Nazarene', was understood to be the 'Holy One of God' (Mk 1.24). Such an association could have been drawn from Judg. 13.7 and 16.17 where the LXX had changed *Nazaraios* to the 'holy one of God'.[1]

In any case, Matthew 1–2 remembers Jesus as the 'shoot' when he is named for the third time (Jesus, Immanuel, Nazorean). This ties together the textual unit, beginning with the genealogy, in such a way that the questions 'who?' and 'from where?' truly seem fitting. As I have already noted, the community of the Nazarenes understands its own origin as an end-time planting by God.

What has been discovered in Mt. 2.23, at the very end of Matthew 1–2, is valid also with regard to the whole of the textual complex: the question regarding the origin of the messiah and his community is answered consistantly with material handed down concerning the history of God's people and with the verbal material used in these traditions. The truly 'new' material, which could not be derived from the earlier history of Israel, is from what has become the prehistory of the church. All of it is articulated by a new constellation of the traditional motifs and pictures, of old genres and their narrative structures, and of their connection to the present end-times. These include the arrival of the messiah, the salvation of God's people from their sins through his death, and the addition of the Gentiles to the eschatologically constituted Israel, the church. It was necessary to use the verbal material of Israel's tradition for the articulation of these events since Jesus was the messiah of

---

1. Compare with this R. Pesch, *Das Markusevangelium. I. Kommentar zu 1,1–8,26* (HTKNT, 2.1; Freiburg: Herder, 5th edn, 1989), pp. 122-23. See also the studies by E. Schweizer, '"Er wird Nazoräer heißen" (zu Mc 1,24; Mt 2,23)', in Eltester (ed.), *Judentum, Urchristentum, Kirche*, pp. 90-93; J.A. Sanders, 'ΝΑΖΩΡΑΙΟΣ in Matt 2:23', *JBL* 84 (1965), pp. 169-72; rev. and repr. in this volume.

Israel, the 'king of the Jews', and because the church was the renewed Israel.

It is not only the quotations dealing with the fulfillment of prophecy, but also the genealogy and the narrative cycle which follow it, which draw their life from the tradition of the people of God, from its historical enrichment and messianic culmination. Therefore, it has now become clear that the eschatological situation of the community and its personal experience allow the Matthaean exegete to recognize prophecy on the basis of its fulfillment. The prophets have announced that Jesus of Nazareth, the messiah, the messianic shoot, will be called a Nazorean.

8. *Messianic Exegesis*

Part of the essence of the literary category of 'legend' is the construction of a 'narrated world', built upon facts found in the historical world, and the introduction of 'stories' within this narrated world, whose truth is fed by the personal experience of the narrator or the community within which he or she is active. While a 'legend' reshapes history, a legend based on faith will reshape revelatory history. 'All biblical texts are witnesses of faith and proclaim a personal experience of God within history, life and thought as event and instruction, judgement and salvation.'[1]

Only our own superficial one-dimensional understanding of reality causes us difficulties. It only seems to recognize shallow truth, hardly deeper truth, and cannot grasp the content of truth particular to texts of a legendary or mythical kind. However, precisely because of the deeper dimension of its truth, the biblical tradition appropriates such extraordinary genres. The experience of the people of God in the past, the present and the future can best be portrayed in a legendary narrative, in which, to the one who experiences, the structural congruity of his or her experience becomes apparent.

The difficulties that exist for our understanding of reality because it has not been opened and widened by the personal experience of the one universal history of God's people are encountered by us only at those places where this experience re-emerges in the text. 'Biblical realism is not oriented on an objective, detached factuality but on the farther and deeper reaching reality of one's own experiences. A basic hermeneutical

---

1. Gese, 'Hermeneutische Grundsätze', pp. 44-45.

principle must be to direct oneself towards the truth taken up by a text and not towards the truth we are accustomed to seeing',[1] unless we are moved by the same truth which is found in the text, and are thereby empowered to a structurally congruent interpretation.

Like other canonical documents dealing with revelatory history or the history of revelatory faith, the whole of the Gospel of Matthew, not just Matthew 1–2, demonstrates that the Evangelist (as the speaker for the common experience of his communities) is neither guided by nor especially interested in an objective factuality which can be evaluated, validated and measured in a detached way.

A comparison between the Gospel of Matthew and its *Vorlagen*, especially the Gospel of Mark (but also Q), demonstrates that the Matthaean interpretation of the tradition does not allow itself to be enslaved by the transmitted facts. Instead it is free to reinterpret the tradition and with it the whole of history—the beginning, the present and the future—according to the present eschatological experience of the community.

At the end of Jesus' parable discourse, in Mt. 13.51-52, Matthew himself has pointed out the qualifications for scribes in the New Testament community consisting of Jesus' disciples. The disciples, clearly distinguished from the crowds and from those outside of the community who hear but do not understand (cf. Mt. 13.10-17), can answer Jesus' question, if they have understood everything, with 'Yes'. Jesus then says to them: 'For that reason every scribe who has become a disciple for the kingdom of heaven is like the head of the household who brings forth out of his treasure things new and old'.

One is made a disciple for the kingdom of heaven by being called into the church, into that which succeeded the disciples' community of learning. In the history of the church, things old and new have eschatological explosiveness, and the scribe tells of its history in 'parables', just as Jesus was said to have done. As the prototype of the community he fulfilled even in this point the prophecies:

> All of this Jesus spoke in parables to the multitudes, and he said nothing to them without parables, so that it might be fulfilled what was spoken through the prophet, who says:
> 'I will open my mouth in parables,
> I will utter things hidden since the foundation of the world!' (Mt. 13.34-35 and Ps. 78.2)

---

1.   Gese, 'Hermeneutische Grundsätze', p. 46.

Matthew is a scribe, an exegete, who has become a 'disciple for the kindom of heaven', or, as the text can also be translated, 'has been made knowledgeable and experienced through the *Basileia*'; through its arrival, through the community of living and learning which is consti-tuted by it. The community of the disciples as the place where the Torah—the community rule of God's people—is brought to fulfillment by Jesus, is the place of learning, the place of experiencing, which makes it possible that the interpretation of history by means of experienced history is congenial, that is, structurally congruent; it corresponds to reality and personally experienced truth. The *regula proxima* of biblical hermeneutics is the present faith-experience of the people of God, the personal faith-experience of the church, which formed and continues to form the portrayal of history.

The 'community theology' in Matthew's Gospel, composed into legends in Matthew 1–2, has to be understood at that place where today's 'community theology' corresponds to it—within the historical connection of the eschatologically renewed, universal people of God.

In conclusion, we may ask: what, then, is 'messianic exegesis'? A succinct answer, based upon the preceding exposition, may be: an inter-pretation of Scripture which recognizes and formulates the full meaning (*sensus plenior*) of the Scripture (and the tradition) on the basis of the miracle of the eschatological fulfillment of all messianic prophecies in the history of the messiah and his messianic community. In short: messianic exegesis is exegesis in the fullness of time and at the place of the messianic miracle![1]

1.   I wish to join the editors of this volume in expressing my thanks to Mr Spencer Stadler for translating this paper.

DO THE PROPHETS AND THE LAW QUIT PROPHESYING
BEFORE JOHN? A NOTE ON MATTHEW 11.13

D.A. Carson

> It would seem that, if 11.12 includes John the Baptist in the time of the
> kingdom... then 11.13 places him outside the time of the law and the
> prophets; for 11.13 supplies the explanation (γάρ) for v. 12, and, if the
> latter statement includes John in the new time, then evidently the latter must
> exclude him from the old time. ἕως will then be inclusive in v. 12 but
> exclusive in v. 13.

So write Davies and Allison,[1] and their opinion is shared by many. To
the question posed by the title of this essay, they are then bound to reply
in the affirmative. Yet in the next paragraph, they strongly insist that
neither Jesus nor Matthew could rightly be called antinomian, and prefer
to speak of the kingdom displacing the Mosaic law from central stage.
They conclude: 'What that means for the Mosaic Torah is an open
question not answered by Mt 11.12-13 par.'.[2]

The questions relating to the interpretation of Mt. 11.13 are especially
complex because each decision generates a new permutation of
possibilities. None of the interrelated exegetical and historical judgments
can be tackled in isolation; each has an effect on all the others. In what
follows, I propose to lay out rather briefly a series of exegetical judgments that shed some light on this saying (and its parallel in Lk. 16.16).
Although each point could be discussed at much greater length, there
may be some advantage in stating them briefly and tying them together
in this way so as to explore whether or not this interpretation can
command broader assent.

---

1.   D.C. Allison and W.D. Davies, *A Critical and Exegetical Commentary on the
Gospel according to Saint Matthew* (ICC; Edinburgh: T. & T. Clark, 1988–), II,
p. 257. They here cite R.H. Gundry, *Matthew: A Commentary on his Literary and
Theological Art* (Grand Rapids: Eerdmans, 1982), p. 210.
2.   Allison and Davies, *Matthew*, II, p. 258.

I shall begin with Matthew's portrait, and then progressively introduce considerations from Luke and Q.

I

Matthew insists that there is something about Jesus' ministry that John the Baptist does not understand, and is ill prepared to accept (Mt. 11.2-6). To the question 'Are you ὁ ἐρχόμενος?' Jesus responds by describing his ministry in terms that allude to several passages in Isaiah, notably 35.5-6 and 61.1, but probably also 26.19; 29.18-19; 42.7, 18. Certainly Isaiah 61 was regularly interpreted in an eschatological framework;[1] it is widely recognized that the influence of the Isaiah texts on Mt. 11.5 extends beyond mere vocabulary to the very structure of the sentence. Almost as widely recognized is the fact that Jesus' use of the Isaiah texts, according to Matthew, omits any mention of judgment: 'the day of vengeance of our God' (Isa. 61.2); 'he will come with vengeance, with divine retribution he will come to save you' (Isa. 35.4).[2] What this suggests is that the Baptist had questions about Jesus' identity because he could see in him no powerful work of judgment. Whether or not Matthew understands the baptism 'with Holy Spirit and with fire' (3.11) to be one baptism (the fire exercising a purifying role) or two (the fire indicating judgment), the images of the winnowing fork, the gathering of the wheat into the barn and the burning of the chaff (Mt. 11.12) leave no room for doubting that in Matthew's view John the Baptist preached, *inter alia*, impending judgment.[3] Jesus' reply, then, studiously avoiding mention of judgment even when citing texts that intermingle blessing and judgment, suggests that the judgment is delayed, even while the promised blessings are being fulfilled in his ministry. In its context, the macarism

1. Cf. J.A. Sanders, 'From Isaiah 61 to Luke 4', in J. Neusner (ed.), *Christianity, Judaism and Other Greco-Roman Cults* (SJLA, 12; Leiden: Brill, 1975), pp. 75-106; M.P. Miller, 'The Function of Isa 61:1-2 in 11QMelchizedek', *JBL* 88 (1969), pp. 467-69.

2. See J. Jeremias, *Jesus' Promise to the Nations* (London: SCM Press, 1958), p. 46; J.D.G. Dunn, *Jesus and the Spirit: A Study of the Religious and Charismatic Experience of Jesus and the First Christians as Reflected in the New Testament* (London: SCM Press, 1975), p. 60; Davies and Allison, *Matthew*, II, p. 245.

3. Whether or not this judgment took on apocalyptic overtones (denied by J. Ernst, *Johannes der Täufer: Interpretation—Geschichte—Wirkungsgeschichte* [BZNW, 53; Berlin and New York: de Gruyter, 1989]), or was simply directed against the ungodly, is irrelevant to my case.

of 11.6 confirms this point: John the Baptist has begun well, and must not fall away at this juncture. If he can see the messianic blessings fulfilling Scripture, he must be content to wait for the judgments still to come.

The point to bear in mind, then, when we try to decide whether or not Matthew places John the Baptist in the kingdom, is that he has already made clear how little the Baptist understood. Matthew and his readers know that Jesus is going to the cross, that the eschaton is delayed, that judgment is not on the immediate agenda—but John the Baptist does not.

II

In the next verses, John is presented as a prophet, but also as more than a prophet. The distinction is important, and turns on two elements. First, the term 'prophet' is notoriously slippery in the first century. Until a decade or two ago, it was a truism in much New Testament scholarship that Palestinian Jews in the first century believed that the age of prophecy had passed, and if God wished to speak he did so indirectly via the בת־קול. In 1982, Aune protested that the use of 'prophet' in Josephus demonstrates that when prophecy is studied 'historically' instead of 'theologically' one must conclude that the phenomenon continues right through the disputed period.[1] But Aune himself is forced to draw attention to important distinctions between canonical prophecy and prophecy of a later period.[2] Some of the distinctions have been nicely teased out by Horsley, who shows that in the first century the word 'prophet' could refer to a diviner, that is, someone who predicts the future (cf. *Ant.* 13.11.2 §311; 15.10.5 §§373-78; *War* 2.8.12 §159), to an 'oracular prophet' who, like many of the biblical prophets, preached a message of judgment and repentance against the social and religious sins of their age (cf. *War* 6.5.3 §§300-309), or to certain eschatological figures such as Elijah (cf. Mal. 3; Sir. 48.10) or Moses (cf. Deut. 18.15-18; 1QS 9.11; 4Q175; Jn 1.45). In the New Testament a minor pagan poet can be labelled a 'prophet' (Tit. 1.12), presumably because he is inspired by the Muse. Clearly John was considered by many to be an eschatological prophet.[3] That made him 'greater' than popular diviners;

---

1. D.E. Aune, 'The Use of προφήτης in Josephus', *JBL* 101 (1982), pp. 419-21.

2. D.E. Aune, *Prophecy in Early Christianity and the Ancient Mediterranean World* (Grand Rapids: Eerdmans, 1983), pp. 106-21, 139, 153, 195.

3. Aune, *Prophecy*, pp. 129-32.

it even made him 'greater' than oracular prophets.

Secondly, the quotation of Mal. 3.1 in Mt. 11.10 is clearly meant to explain the assertion that John the Baptist is a prophet who is more than a prophet. Like Mal. 4.5-6, Matthew interprets Mal. 3.1 as a prophecy about Elijah. But the effect is to make John the Baptist (i.e. Elijah) the messenger who is preparing the way for Jesus. Matthew is saying, then, that John's greatness is tied not only to his role as an eschatological prophet, but to his role as an eschatological prophet who prepares the way for another, that is, Jesus.

If this delineation of the flow of Matthew's argument is sound, then before we conclude that John the Baptist joins Jesus in the kingdom, and the ἕως in 11.13 is exclusive, we must factor into our assessment Matthew's insistence, in this pericope, on the preparatory nature of John the Baptist's role.

III

Rightly understood, v. 11 heightens the distinction between John and Jesus. We may usefully observe four things.

First, although it is common to treat v. 11a in isolation, it is almost impossible to think of v. 11b circulating on its own. The two halves of the verse are cast in antithetic parallelism; it is simplest to assume that they always belonged together.

Secondly, as to its authenticity, it is difficult to imagine any context in which Christians would have articulated a gentle 'put-down' of the Baptist by beginning with such effusive praise as that which is recorded in v. 11a.[1]

Thirdly, although it does not follow that the present setting of v. 11 is authentic, and most modern scholars deny it, that does not relieve us of the obligation to determine what Matthew meant by the saying in this context. In the light of the flow of the argument from v. 2 to v. 10, the first part of v. 11 must not be pressed to mean that John the Baptist is greater than everyone without exception, *including Jesus*. John the Baptist's superiority over other prophets (of whatever kind) rests on the fact that, as an eschatological prophet, he prepares the way for Jesus. The inevitable assumption is that Jesus is greater than he. Verse 11a must therefore mean that John the Baptist is the greatest born of

---

1.   On the unity and authenticity of v. 11, cf. J. Schlosser, *Le règne de Dieu dans les dits de Jésus* (2 vols.; EBib; Paris: Gabalda, 1983), I, pp. 159-61.

woman, that is, the greatest person ever, *up to that time*. That makes him greater than Moses, greater than David, greater than Solomon, greater than Isaiah, and so forth. But if v. 11a is read with the preceding verses, he is less than Jesus, for he prepares the way for him.

This reading is entirely in line with Matthean theology—indeed, with the theology of all four canonical Evangelists. They read the Scriptures as pointing to Jesus, as preparing the way for him, but there is no doubt in their mind as to his relative status as compared with any of the antecedent witnesses. Thus in the next chapter we are assured that Jesus is greater than the temple (12.6), greater than Solomon (12.42). Son of David Jesus may be, but, on the appropriate exegesis of Ps. 110, he is also David's Lord (Mt. 22.41-46). Matthew is steeped with fulfillment passages that assure us that the focus of antecedent revelation was to point the way to Jesus. John the Baptist is now declared to be part of that train.[1] But because he is the last part, the eschatological prophet who immediately prepares the way of the Lord, he is declared to be greater than any other person.

Thus the first part of v. 11, while declaring that John the Baptist is the greatest person who has ever lived (implicitly: *up to that point*), is, in the context of this chapter, astonishingly christocentric. The 'greatest' John the Baptist may be, but he derives such greatness from his unique eschatological role in preparing the way for Jesus.

Fourthly, if this is a correct delineation of the flow of Matthew's argument, we are in a better position to understand the second half of v. 11. There is little merit in the suggestion that the meaning of v. 11b turns on a distinction between the kingdom now and the kingdom in its consummated form, as if the passage were saying that the least in the kingdom *then* will be greater than John is *now*.[2] Quite apart from the fact that this interpretation seems unbearably trite,[3] it is irrelevant to the context. In a pair of comparisons between 'A' and 'B' and between 'B' and 'C' such that 'B' is declared to be greater than 'A' and 'C' to be

---

1. Similarly in the Fourth Gospel: John's entire significance is tied to his truthful witness to Jesus (Jn 10.40-42).

2. So, *inter alios*, W.C. Allen, *A Critical and Exegetical Commentary on the Gospel according to St Matthew* (ICC; Edinburgh: T. & T. Clark, 1912), pp. 115-16; A.H. McNeile, *The Gospel according to St Matthew* (London: Macmillan, 1915), p. 154; J.C. O'Neill, *Messiah: Six Lectures on the Ministry of Jesus* (London: Cochrane, 1980), pp. 10-11.

3. So, rightly, Gundry, *Matthew*, p. 208.

greater than 'B', the basis on which the comparison is made must be preserved from one pair to the next, or all coherence is lost.

The same weakness forces us to dismiss another interpretation of v. 11b that has drawn significant support. On this reading ὁ μικρότερος refers to Jesus: he is not 'the least' but 'the younger', that is, 'the lesser' in a purely temporal sense.[1] This view assumes that John the Baptist, like Jesus, is in the kingdom, and therefore nudges the interpreter to a similar reading of v. 13. Very frequently this view draws strength from a comparison of the respective ministries of John and Jesus, in particular from a comparison of Mt. 3.2 and 4.17: both John and Jesus preach, 'Repent, for the kingdom of heaven is near'. Should one not on this ground conclude that both the Baptist and Jesus are in the kingdom?[2]

It must be admitted, however, that the primary reason why ὁ μικρότερος is read this way is because the passage as a whole is difficult; the expression itself does not cry out to be taken this way. Moreover, the appeal to Mt. 3.2 and 4.17 to establish the proposition that both John the Baptist and Jesus were in the kingdom is misguided. It fails to recognize their respective redactional settings. John the Baptist preaches the nearness of the kingdom in the context of being identified as the one who prepares the way for the Lord (3.3), and who announces the imminent arrival of one whose sandals he is not fit to carry (3.11). It is this later figure who will baptize in the Holy Spirit and fire (3.12). By contrast, Jesus preaches repentance and announces the nearness of the kingdom (4.17) in the context of being identified as the one who fulfills Isaiah 9 by the onset of his ministry in Galilee: 'the people living in darkness have seen a great light; on those living in the land of the shadow of death a light has dawned' (4.16). Thus despite the formal similarity of the one-line summaries of the respective ministries of John and Jesus, Matthew has taken pains to distinguish those ministries. Perhaps more importantly, it is surely incongruous to think of Jesus as

---

1. This view goes back to the church fathers: cf. Chrysostom, *Hom. on Matt.* 37.3; Tertullian, *Adv. Marc.* 4.18. In more recent times it has been adopted, with varying degrees of certainty, by O. Cullmann ("Ὁ ὀπίσω μου ἐχόμενος', *ConNT* 11 [1947], p. 30), M. Brunec ('De Legationi Ioannis Baptistae [Mt 11.2-24]', *VD* 35 [1957], pp. 262-70), BDF §61(2), and M. Zerwick (*Biblical Greek* [Rome: Pontifical Biblical Institute, 1963], §149). We need not linger over interpretive curiosities, for example that ὁ μικρότερος refers to angels (Ambrose).

2. See, for instance, W. Wink, *John the Baptist in the Gospel Tradition* (SNTSMS, 7; Cambridge: Cambridge University Press, 1968), pp. 33-35.

merely '*in* the kingdom' (ὁ μικρότερος ἐν τῇ βασιλείᾳ). Finally, there is no commonality between the comparison in v. 11b and the comparison in v. 11a. On this reading it becomes necessary to read v. 11b as a declarative pronouncement of Jesus' superiority over John, while the evocative comparison of v. 11a is left dangling.

But if 'the least in the kingdom' refers to the least of Jesus' followers, the least Christian (from Matthew's perspective), without any reflection on whether the kingdom is present or future,[1] the basis of the comparison between John the Baptist and all who were before him returns in the comparison between the least in the kingdom and John the Baptist. He bore witness to Christ most immediately, as the eschatological prophet, so he supersedes Abraham or David or Ezekiel. But the least in the kingdom bears witness to Jesus, more clearly, immediately and knowledgeably than could John the Baptist; so in this regard the least in the kingdom is greater than John.

Apart from the fact that this seems the most natural way to take the Greek, this interpretation has several advantages. 1. It continues the defense of John begun at 11.2. The Baptist's query, sent by emissaries (11.2-3), does not spring from fickleness or weakness (11.7-8), nor does it cause him to forfeit his primacy among all those who preceded Jesus and pointed to him. It springs, rather, from his place and role in redemptive history. 2. This interpretation also continues the important theme of witness among the followers of Jesus (10.32-33). The least in the kingdom points to Jesus more clearly than all Jesus' predecessors, not excluding John, for either they live through the tumultuous events of Jesus' ministry, passion and resurrection (from which John was excluded), or they enter the kingdom after them (like many of Matthew's readers), and with the same understanding as that enjoyed by those who passed through them. Thus the ground is laid for the 'great commission' (28.18-20): clear witness to Christ before men and women is not only a requirement of the kingdom (10.32-33) and a command of the resurrected Lord (28.18-20) but the true greatness of the disciple (11.11). 3. This interpretation is also in line with Matthew's subtly expressed interests in explaining 'how we moved from there to here', that is, in closing the gap between what was understood 'back then' in Jesus'

---

1. So, rightly if cautiously, U. Luz, *Das Evangelium nach Matthäus* (EKKNT, 1.2; Zürich: Benzinger Verlag; Neukirchen–Vluyn: Neukirchener Verlag, 1985–), II, pp. 175-76.

ministry and what was understood only later.[1] Neither Matthew nor the modern interpreter can long think about such matters without pondering the redemptive-historical developments. 4. Above all, this interpretation is in line with the paramount concern of all four canonical Evangelists, that is, to articulate the supremacy of Jesus Christ in various ways. All the other cast members bear witness to him: John the Baptist and all those who, like him, came before Jesus, and all others who come after, including the very least in the kingdom.

The result of this exegesis, however, is that John the Baptist was not in the kingdom. That is in line with my first two points, and clearly has a bearing on how we interpret v. 13.

IV

We must venture a few observations on v. 12. If we dismiss the idiosyncratic interpretations of this extraordinarily difficult verse,[2] the remaining options turn primarily on two exegetical decisions. 1. Is the verb βιάζεται a deponent middle (the kingdom 'forcefully advances' or the like), or passive—and in this case is it being attacked (in a negative sense), or forcefully advanced (by God[3])? 2. Should βιασταὶ ἁρπάζουσιν be taken negatively, of those who are trying to pillage the kingdom (whether people or demons), or positively, of those who are (rightly) entering it by storm?

The studies of Moore[4] and others[5] have convinced many that the verb must be taken as a passive, *in malem partem*, in line with the distinctly

1. Cf. D.A. Carson, 'Christological Ambiguities in the Gospel of Matthew', in H.H. Rowdon (ed.), *Christ the Lord: Studies in Christology* (D. Guthrie Festschrift; Leicester: Inter-Varsity Press, 1982), pp. 97-114.

2. For example, J. Swetnam, Review of *Notes de lexicographie néotestamentaire*, by C. Spicq, *Bib* 61 (1980), pp. 440-42, argues that the kingdom of heaven has been suffering the violence of (faulty) interpretation; F.W. Danker ('Luke 16:16—An Opposition Logion', *JBL* 77 [1958], pp. 231-43) thinks that 'the violent ones' was a term that was first applied to Jesus and his disciples by the Pharisaic opposition (which could in theory allow for Jesus' ironic use of the expression, though Danker does not seem to explore the possibility).

3. Cf. G. Schrenk, 'βιάζομαι', *TDNT*, I, pp. 610-11.

4. E. Moore, 'Βιάζω, ἁρπάζω and Cognates in Josephus', *NTS* 21 (1975), pp. 519-43.

5. For example, C. Spicq, *Notes de lexicographie néotestamentaire* (2 vols.; Göttingen: Vandenhoeck & Ruprecht, 1978), s.v.

evil overtones of βιασταὶ ἁρπάζουσιν: 'the kingdom of heaven is suffering violence and violent men are seizing it', or the like. Nevertheless some scholars argue that βιάζεται is most naturally taken as a middle, probably in a good sense, and conclude that the second line therefore must also be read in a good sense: 'the kingdom of heaven is forcefully advancing and forceful men lay hold of it'.[1] Part of the debate has turned on the common assumption that both lines must be taken in a good sense or in a bad sense—an assumption which turns on the intrinsic parallelism and on the obviously cognate relationship of βιάζεται and βιασταί. The assumption comes under strain when we discover that, if controlled word studies mean anything, ἁρπάζουσιν almost has to be taken in a bad sense, while a strong case can be mounted for taking βιάζεται as a deponent middle in a good sense. Although not usually mentioned as an option, taking both parts in their most obvious ways results in *antithetic* parallelism; the verse also then boasts a form of antanclasis (a figure of speech in which the same word is repeated in a different or even contradictory sense), based in this instance not on exactly the same word but on a cognate.

But whether the kingdom is forcefully advancing (which seems to be the case, judging by the miracle stories of chs. 8–9) while evil men are attacking it (note the warnings of ch. 10), or is univocally presented as being under attack, for our purposes the critical phrase in this verse is the first: ἀπὸ δὲ τῶν ἡμερῶν Ἰωάννου τοῦ βαπτιστοῦ ἕως ἄρτι. Because the ἕως in the next verse (v. 13) is so often taken in an exclusive sense, making John belong to the period of the kingdom and not to the period of the law and the prophets,[2] the crucial phrase in v. 12 is commonly understood to mean that John himself inaugurates the days of which Jesus speaks. But nothing we have discovered in the flow of the passage supports that conclusion; everything we have looked at so far militates against it. The expression 'from the days of John the Baptist' simply means 'from the time of the activity of John the Baptist'; the *terminus a quo* is thereby established. It was during that time that

---

1. The most recent support for this minority view is from G. Häfner, 'Gewalt gegen die Basileia? Zum Problem der Auslegung des "Stürmerspruches" Mt 11,12', *ZNW* 83 (1992), pp. 21-51.

2. Indeed, J.P. Meier ('John the Baptist in Matthew's Gospel', *JBL* 99 [1980], pp. 383-405) makes this the crux of Matthew's presentation of the Baptist, over against Lk. 16.16, which, in common with most interpreters, he understands in an inclusive way.

Jesus was baptized and began his public ministry; the text says nothing about the Baptist's participation in it, still less of his inauguration of it. The expression does not even assume John's death; it merely insists that it was during the period of John's ministry that the kingdom pressed forward (or was attacked). Comparison of the contexts of 3.2 and 4.17 puts Jesus' ministry, and Jesus' ministry alone, in a 'fulfillment' category. Perhaps that is one of the reasons why 4.17 is presaged by a short pericope that mentions that John has been put in prison. He does not belong to the period of Jesus' messianic, kingdom-revealing ministry. The words ἕως ἄρτι, whether they refer, as cast on Jesus' lips, to this point in his ministry, or, as many contemporary scholars think, to Matthew's period in the church,[1] do not constitute a *terminus ad quem* at which the forceful advance of the kingdom (or the passive suffering of the kingdom) comes to an abrupt halt, but simply signals the continuous advance of (or attack upon) the kingdom until the *now* in view.

Thus far in the chapter, then, there is still no reason whatsoever for thinking that the prophets and the law should not prophesy 'until John' (v. 13) in an *inclusive* sense.

V

Before turning to Mt. 11.13, perhaps I should draw attention to what is obvious to any reader of a Gospel synopsis, that although the closest parallel to Mt. 11.12-13 is Lk. 16.16 (where the two verses from Matthew appear in reverse order, and in slightly different form), the closest parallel to Mt. 11.2-19 as a whole is Lk. 7.18-35. These passages end in an aphorism that is different in the two accounts: Mt. 11.19b: καὶ ἐδικαιώθη ἡ σοφία ἀπὸ τῶν ἔργων αὐτῆς. Lk. 7.35: καὶ ἐδικαιώθη ἡ σοφία ἀπὸ πάντων τέκνων αὐτῆς. The most common explanation of the redactional differences is that Matthew has transformed the Q saying to support his Wisdom-Christology. If that interpretation is right, then in Matthew's form of the aphorism ἡ σοφία refers to Jesus as incarnate Wisdom, and Wisdom's 'works' are Jesus' works (an exegesis that is often tied to the mention of 'works' in 11.2). By contrast, in Luke's form of the saying John the Baptist and Jesus are clearly tied

---

1.   See for example O.L. Cope, *Matthew: A Scribe Trained for the Kingdom of Heaven* (CBQMS, 5; Washington, DC: Catholic Biblical Association, 1976), pp. 75-76; W.F. Albright and C.S. Mann, *Matthew* (AB, 26; Garden City, NY: Doubleday, 1971) *in loc.*

together. If this more-or-less standard exegesis of Q7.35 is correct, then in Matthew's account there is additional reason for thinking John the Baptist must not be lumped together with Jesus—and once again this may have some bearing on how we interpret Mt. 11.13.

I have argued at some length elsewhere, however, that this interpretation of Mt. 11.19b // Lk. 7.35 is probably wrong.[1] For reasons that cannot be rehearsed here, I think that 'wisdom' in Mt. 11.19b is used much as in the canonical Wisdom literature, and has nothing directly to do with Christology. *Both* John the Baptist *and* Jesus are justifed by their works—or, put more poetically, Wisdom is always justified by what she does. In the life of the Baptist, this issued in asceticism; in the life of the Christ, this issued in conviviality (11.16-19a). Both were justified; that is, wisdom was justified in both cases, even if 'this generation' does not appreciate either of them.

Although at first glance this may sound as if I am arguing against myself because John and Jesus are being bracketed together, in reality such a reading of 11.19b does not at all jeopardize the line of thought I am developing toward an exegesis of 11.13. Although John the Baptist and Jesus are linked together as both contributing to the justification of wisdom, they do so in very different ways. That is the point of the 'parable' in 11.16-19a, capped by the aphorism of 11.19b. All this is very much in line with the flow of the argument in 11.2-19: John the Baptist is praised and exonerated, but his significance is located in his witness to and preparation for Jesus Messiah. That is exactly the tone of 11.16-19.

Thus, whether the 'standard' exegesis of 11.19b is adopted, or the exegesis that I have supported, in both cases there are strong reasons for thinking that Matthew is interested in maintaining some strong *distinctions* between the Baptist and Jesus. In the second case, although their works are linked together in the justification of wisdom, the two men are so strongly distinguished in their respective roles in redemptive history that there is very little warrant left for thinking that Matthew presents John the Baptist as in the kingdom.

---

1.   D.A. Carson, 'Matthew 11:19b / Luke 7:35: A Test Case for the Bearing of Q Christology on the Synoptic Problem', in J.B. Green and M.M.B. Turner (eds.), *Jesus of Nazareth: Lord and Christ* (I.H. Marshall Festschrift; Grand Rapids: Eerdmans, 1994), pp. 128-46.

VI

We come to the critical verse, Mt. 11.13. It may help to set it out with its parallel in Lk. 16.16:

> Mt. 11.13: πάντες γὰρ οἱ προφῆται καὶ ὁ νόμος ἕως Ἰωάννου
> ἐπροφήτευσαν
> Lk. 16.16: ὁ νόμος καὶ οἱ προφῆται μέχρι Ἰωάννου

In Matthew, the Sinaitic Syriac and one manuscript from the Bohairic version omit ὁ νόμος. This almost certainly springs from (1) the oddity of the order 'the prophets and the law'—as far as I know, the only text in the ancient world with this order, while 'the law and the prophets' is commonplace; and (2) the apparent incongruity of supposing that the law prophesies. In Luke, ἕως replaces μέχρι in several codices and in the Byzantine tradition; the verb ἐπροφήτευσαν is appended to the verse by D and Θ and a few minor witnesses. Both variants doubtless stem from assimilation to Matthew.

If we assume that Q stands behind both texts—a probable but by no means certain inference—then it is unmistakeable that all four of Matthew's distinctive readings lean in the same direction: (1) the order 'the prophets and the law' tends to emphasize the prophetic function of Scripture; similarly (2) the modifier πάντες and (3) the verb ἐπροφήτευσαν; (4) the γάρ ensures that this logion be read either as the explanation or as the summary of vv. 11-12, and thus a further articulation of the relationship between John the Baptist and Jesus.[1]

All sides recognize that ἕως can function either inclusively or exclusively; the context must decide. If one were to read this verse only in the light of 11.9-10a, one might well be warranted in thinking that, since both John and Jesus are the objects of prophecy (John in 11.9-10a, and Jesus throughout this Gospel), 'all the prophets and the law' exercise their prophetic function up to but not including the period of the Baptist, at which point those to whom they point—John and Jesus—put in their appearance. In other words, ἕως (11.13) is taken in an exclusive sense. But we have seen that element after element in the context argues against this interpretation. Moreover, whatever the function of γάρ, it certainly does not skip over intervening verses and tie v. 13 to vv. 9-

---

1. In other words, γάρ smoothes out the transitions once there is a new order in the clauses: cf. E. Klostermann, *Das Matthäusevangelium* (HNT, 4; Tübingen: Mohr [Paul Siebeck], 2nd edn, 1927), p. 98.

10a. If John the Baptist is not only a prophet but a person about whom prophetic words have been spoken, it is important to note what those prophetic words are: that is, v. 10b is not less important than v. 10a. John the Baptist still remains a prophet, but more than a prophet: he is the one who immediately prepares the way before Jesus. In that he points to Jesus, he is at one with 'all the prophets and the law'; his unique greatness consists in the clarity and immediacy of his ministry vis-à-vis Jesus the messiah, not in terms of his performing something radically different. It is worth noting that Matthew does not include the words ἀπὸ τότε ἡ βασιλεία τοῦ θεοῦ εὐαγγελίζεται (Lk. 16.16). Had he done so, it would have been slightly harder to deny that Matthew was thinking of Mt. 3.2, despite the peculiar redactional distinctions between 3.2 and 4.17, already noted. Matthew's silence in this regard removes even the possibility of misconstruing the ministry of the Baptist.

The logical links that connect vv. 10, 11, 12 and 13 seem fairly clear. And if this line of interpretation is right, then ἕως is inclusive: all the prophets and the law prophesy up to and including (the time of) John the Baptist. What all of them, including John, are prophesying, is the coming of Jesus and the dawning of the kingdom.

VII

All of this is surely in line with Matthean theology. Jesus has not come to abolish the law and the prophets, but nor has he come to maintain them or to intensify them: he has come to 'fulfill' them, and πληρόω in Matthew (16 occurrences) always has a prophetic or predictive meaning. Nor is it a question of the prophets prophesying and the law legislating: both the law and the prophets 'prophesy'.[1] Thus obeying Moses' commands becomes a testimony to who Jesus is (8.1-4); exercising faith in Jesus associates the believer, whether Jew or not, with the patriarchs in the long-awaited kingdom (8.5-13); Jesus' healings fulfill Isa. 53.4 (Mt. 8.14-17). Unlike John's disciples, who fast, Jesus' disciples enjoy the presence of the bridegroom (9.14-15)—yet another piece of evidence that Matthew does not regard John as already in the kingdom.

---

1. I here follow the essential point of R. Banks (*Jesus and the Law in the Synoptic Tradition* [SNTSMS, 28; Cambridge: Cambridge University Press, 1975], *in loc.*), even though I cannot adopt his exegesis of 5.17-20 in every particular.

Much more evidence could be adduced, but the basic line is surely well established: Matthew views the coming of Jesus and the dawning of the kingdom as that to which the law and the prophets point. Whatever function 'law' has in its nature as *lex*, its primary function, in Matthew's emphasis, is prophetic and predictive. True, judging by his actual exegesis of scriptural passages, Matthew frequently makes this predictive function of Scripture depend on complex typologies rather than on simple verbal predictions. But that, of course, is part of what enables the early Christians to insist that the Jewish Scriptures are so christocentric. Whatever this means or does not mean for the continued observance of 'law' as *lex* is not Matthew's chief interest, especially not in Matthew 11—though admittedly he does drop some interesting hints elsewhere.

The chief point to observe, then, is that one of Matthew's central themes is the way in which antecedent revelation points to Jesus and the kingdom he announces and inaugurates. He does not allot the same honor to the Baptist, however careful he is to say positive things about him. In short, my exegesis of Mt. 11.13 is entirely in line with some of the main thrusts of Matthean theology.

VIII

It would take us too far afield to subject Lk. 16.16-17 to detailed study, but three things may usefully be said.

1. The presence of the clause ἀπὸ τότε ἡ βασιλεία τοῦ θεοῦ εὐαγγελίζεται helps to clarify the relationship between the time of 'the law and the prophets' and the 'now'. There is no verb ἐπροφήτευσαν (in the best witnesses) to help to establish the relationship (as in the Matthean parallel), but the ἀπὸ τότε clause signals a major redemptive-historical transition at the time of John. Until his time, the law and the prophets (were proclaimed?); from his time on, the kingdom of God is preached. Partly because there is no Lukan parallel to Mt. 3.2, fewer scholars have been tempted to place John on the kingdom side of the transition.[1]

2. The connection between v. 16 and v. 17 is far from transparent. Scholars debate whether the two verses were connected in a pre-Lukan

---

1.   See esp. J.A. Fitzmyer, *The Gospel according to Luke* (AB, 28, 28a; Garden City, NY: Doubleday, 1981–85), II, pp. 1115-16.

source (Q?),[1] and whether or not v. 16 is dominical.[2] There is at present another debate over Q's view of the law.[3] From our perspective the most intriguing element in the text is the tension between an apparent relegation of 'the law and the prophets' to the past (v. 16) and the massive support for the law in the next verse (v. 17)—a tension that cries out for an explanation.

3. If we try to resolve the tension within the framework of Lukan theology as a whole (however difficult the setting of this passage is in ch. 16), we immediately stumble across familiar themes. It is Luke's Gospel, after all, which says of the resurrected Jesus: 'And beginning with Moses and all the Prophets, he explained to them what was said in all the Scriptures concerning himself' (Lk. 24.27). 'He said to them,

---

1. Thus H. Schürmann (*Traditionsgeschichtliche Untersuchungen zu den synoptischen Evangelien* [Düsseldorf: Patmos, 1968], pp. 126-36) judges that 16.14-18 constituted a unity in Q; P. Hoffmann (*Studien zur Theologie der Logienquelle* [NTAbh NS, 8; Münster: Aschendorff, 2nd edn, 1972], pp. 53-56) denies it.

2. Many deny it: for example S. Schulz, *Q: Die Spruchquelle der Evangelisten* (Zürich: Theologischer Verlag, 1972), p. 263; G. Braumann, 'Dem Himmelreich wird Gewalt angetan', *ZNW* 52 (1961), pp. 104-109. E. Bammel ('Is Luke 16,16-18 of Baptist's Provenience?', *HTR* 51 [1958], pp. 101-106) answers in the affirmative to the question he raises; as we have seen, F.W. Danker thinks that the saying originates in the opposition charge. But many insist that both the 'enigmatic nature of the saying' and its 'positive estimate of the Baptist' argue for an origin in the ministry of Jesus: so I.H. Marshall, *The Gospel of Luke: A Commentary on the Greek Text* (Exeter: Paternoster Press; Grand Rapids: Eerdmans, 1979), p. 627; similarly W.G. Kümmel, *Promise and Fulfilment* (SBT, 23; London: SCM Press, 1957), pp. 121-24; E. Percy, *Die Botschaft Jesu: Eine traditionskritische und exegetische Untersuchung* (Lund: Gleerup, 1953), p. 199; N. Perrin, *Rediscovering the Teaching of Jesus* (London: SCM Press, 1967), pp. 74-77.

3. The most commonly accepted view is that of Schulz (*Q: Die Spruchquelle*), who holds that Q represents the theology of a Torah-observing Jewish Christianity, intensified under the impact of charismatic experience. By contrast, H. Merklein (*Die Gottesherrschaft als Handlungsprinzip* [Würzburg: Echter Verlag, 1981]) insists that the ethics of Q do not at all derive from Torah. Texts apparently contradicting his view (including Lk. 16.17) are judged to be late interpolations. More recently D. Kosch (*Die eschatologische Tora des Menschensohnes: Untersuchungen zur Rezeption der Stellung Jesu zur Tora in Q* [Göttingen: Vandenhoeck & Ruprecht, 1989]) takes a mediating line: in Q Jesus does not derive his ethics from Torah, but sees no opposition between his teaching and that of Torah. Lk. 11.41 and 11.42d are judged interpolations (even if fairly early ones). Cf. the first major rejoinder: G. Dautzenberg, 'Tora des Menschensohnes? Kritische Überlegungen zu Daniel Kosch', *BZ* 36 (1992), pp. 93-103.

"This is what I told you while I was still with you: Everything must be fulfilled that is written about me in the Law of Moses, the Prophets and the Psalms"' (24.44). Whatever we think of the details of Conzelmann's thesis, it is Jesus who is rightly characterized by the label *Die Mitte der Zeit*;[1] John the Baptist belongs to the first period, the period of the law and the prophets, however transitional a character he is.

All of this suggests that Mt. 11.13 is not as far removed from Luke (or, for that matter, from Q and even from Jesus) as is often supposed. Matthew does not lump the Baptist together with Jesus in the kingdom. He assigns him the highest honor among those who pointed the way to Jesus. The prophets and the law do not quit their prophetic function with the arrival of the Baptist; rather, he caps them, for it is during his watch, during the course of his witness and preparatory ministry, that the kingdom of heaven begins its forceful advance or comes under attack. Whatever continuing validity the prophets and the law still enjoy now that the one to whom they have pointed has arrived and inaugurated the kingdom is not spelled out; what Matthew insists is that such validity and continuity as persist do so in reference to that which they anticipated. In such glories John the Baptist never participated; the least in the kingdom does.

---

1.   H. Conzelmann, *Die Mitte der Zeit* (Tübingen: Mohr [Paul Siebeck], 5th edn, 1964).

Part III

THE GOSPEL OF MARK

AUTHORITY TO FORGIVE SINS UPON THE EARTH: THE *SHEMA* IN THE GOSPEL OF MARK

Joel Marcus

The Shema *in Mark*

There are three passages in the Gospel of Mark that conjoin the adjective εἷς, 'one', with the noun θεός, 'God': 2.7, 10.18 and 12.29 (cf. 12.32). The last of these passages, 12.29, is a clear citation of the *Shema*, the famous passage in Deut. 6.4 which today forms 'the very center of the synagogue liturgy',[1] and which probably already had a pivotal place in the worship of the Second Temple.[2] In this passage Israel is called to 'listen' (Hebrew שְׁמַע) to a message of vital importance: κύριος ὁ θεὸς ἡμῶν εἷς ἐστιν, 'The Lord our God is one'. Jesus goes on to quote the second verse of the *Shema*, the command to love the Lord with all one's heart (Deut. 6.5), as well as the Levitical exhortation to love one's neighbor as oneself (Lev. 19.18). This study, however, will concentrate on the *Shema*'s affirmation of God's oneness, which seems to be crucial for Mark, since in v. 32 he has the sympathetic scribe second it and drive home the point with an allusion to Deut. 4.35: 'That's a good reply, Teacher; you have truthfully said that God is one, and there is no other but he'.[3]

---

1. A.F. Segal, *Two Powers in Heaven: Early Rabbinic Reports about Christianity and Gnosticism* (SJLA, 25; Leiden: Brill, 1977), p. 139.

2. On the antiquity of recital of the *Shema* see S.C. Reif, *Judaism and Hebrew Prayer: New Perspectives on Jewish Liturgical History* (Cambridge: Cambridge University Press, 1993), pp. 83-84, who cites its presence on *mezuzoth* and *tefillin* found at Qumran and in the Nash papyrus, as well as its linkage with the blessing mentioned below.

3. In their redaction of Mk 12.28-34, both Matthew and Luke, perhaps in reliance on another source, omit the reference to Deut. 6.4 as well as the scribe's seconding of it, though they retain the reference to Deut. 6.5. For them, apparently, the emphasis on the oneness of God is not as important as it is for Mark. They also

The Markan context for the reference to the *Shema* is consistent with two of the passage's associations in first-century Judaism. First, the discussion takes place in the Temple (cf. Mk 11.27; 12.35), and as I have just noted recitation of the *Shema* was a central part of the Temple worship. Secondly, Jesus ends the discussion with a reference to the royal power of God (βασιλεία τοῦ θεοῦ, Mk 12.34), and the following pericope, with its portrayal of a figure exalted to co-regency with God, continues this theme (12.35-37).[1] This linkage of the *Shema* with the βασιλεία reflects first-century Judaism; in the synagogue liturgy, for example, recitation of the *Shema* is followed by the words, 'Blessed be the name of his glorious kingdom for ever and ever', and S.C. Reif argues plausibly that this linkage goes back to the Temple liturgy.[2] Not only is the *Shema* cited in Mk 12.29, then, but it is cited in a doubly appropriate context.

Although the *Shema* is not explicitly cited in the other two Markan passages, it is probably implicit.[3] Both stress God's uniqueness by means of the identical clause εἰ μὴ εἷς ὁ θεός:

> 2.17 τίς δύναται ἀφιέναι ἁμαρτίας εἰ μὴ εἷς ὁ θεός;
>   Who is able to forgive sins except one, namely God?

> 10.18 οὐδεὶς ἀγαθὸς εἰ μὴ εἷς ὁ θεός.
>   No one is good except one, namely God.

In neither case is the word εἷς really necessary for the sense; in 2.7 the scribes could just as easily, and less awkwardly, have asked, 'Who is able to forgive sins except God?', and in 10.18 Jesus could have declared,

---

leave off Jesus' commendation of the scribe in 12.34, with its reference to the kingdom of God; this omission is of a piece with the others, since the *Shema* is linked with the theme of God's kingdom in Jewish liturgy (see below).

1. See J. Marcus, *The Way of the Lord: Christological Exegesis of the Old Testament in the Gospel of Mark* (Louisville, KY: Westminster Press/John Knox, 1992), pp. 134-36.

2. Reif (*Judaism*, p. 83) points out that this blessing is a Temple response in origin, citing *m. Yom.* 4.1-2 and *b. Ta'an.* 16b. On the linkage between the *Shema* and the βασιλεία, see R. Kimelman, 'The *Shema'* and its Blessings: The Realization of God's Kingship', in L. Levine (ed.), *The Synagogue in Late Antiquity* (Philadelphia: ASOR, 1987), pp. 73-86.

3. See R. Pesch, *Das Markusevangelium* (2 vols.; HTKNT, 2; Freiburg: Herder, 1976), I, p. 159; II, pp. 138-39; J. Gnilka, *Das Evangelium nach Markus* (2 vols.; EKKNT, 2; Zürich: Benzinger Verlag; Neukirchen–Vluyn: Neukirchener Verlag, 1978), I, p. 100.

'No one is good except God'. If an adjective were felt to be necessary to underline God's unique goodness and power to forgive sins, the natural candidate would be μόνος ('alone'), as in Lk. 5.21, rather than εἷς. Why then does Mark have εἷς in these two places? The most logical response would seem to run: because it is the key-word of the *Shema*. The hypothesis that the usage of εἷς in Mk 2.17 and 10.18 brings the *Shema* into view is further strengthened by the similar language of 1 Cor. 8.4 (οὐδεὶς θεὸς εἰ μὴ εἷς, 'there is no God but one'), which also seems in context to be a *Shema*-reference (cf. 8.6).[1] Indeed, the *Shema*-associations of εἷς appear to be so important for the Markan narrative that the word is thrown in a few extra times for good measure in 10.17-22 and 12.28-34.[2]

Why is oneness, and more particularly the oneness of God, such an important theme in Mark? And while we are posing exegetical questions, a few related ones may be added:

1. In what way does Jesus' response to the scribes in 2.9-11 meet their objection that he is arrogating to himself a prerogative of God?

2. Does the Markan Jesus' assertion in 10.18 that 'no one is good except one, namely God' mean that the term 'good' is *not* an appropriate one for Jesus?

3. Most fundamentally, how does the emphasis in 12.28-34 on the unity of God—upon which both Jesus and his scribal interlocutor agree—square with the portrait in the very next passage (12.35-37) of a figure enthroned at God's right hand?[3]

The *Sitz im Leben* for Mark's emphasis on the unity of God, I would suggest, is revealed in the first passage, where it is Jesus' opponents, the scribes, who introduce the topic of the *Shema* into the narrative. Hearing Jesus declare the sins of the paralytic forgiven, they become bewildered,

---

1. On the allusion to the *Shema* in 1 Cor. 8.6, see below.

2. Each passage contains three usages of the word. Mk 10.17-22 begins with εἷς ('one man') running up to Jesus and kneeling before him, continues with Jesus' retort that no one is good except εἷς ('one'), and reaches its climax with Jesus' pronouncement that the man lacks ἕν ('one thing'). Mk 12.28-34 not only contains two applications of εἷς to God, but also begins with the introduction of Jesus' interlocutor as εἷς τῶν γραμματέων ('one of the scribes').

3. I raised this question in *Way*, pp. 145-46. The present study further develops and branches out from the answers I sketched there.

then indignant: 'Why does this man speak thus? He is blaspheming! Who can forgive sins except one, that is, God?' If, as many scholars think, the whole discussion of forgiveness of sins in 2.5b-10 is a secondary intrusion into the miracle story, one that reflects not the ministry of the historical Jesus but the concerns of the early church,[1] then the scribes' *Shema*-based objection may very well mirror acrimonious first-century debates in which Jewish religious authorities accused Christians of blasphemy because of their claims about Jesus, which in these authorities' eyes threatened the unity of God.[2]

Such debates are reflected elsewhere in the New Testament in Johannine passages in which Jesus is accused of blasphemy and threatened with stoning for making himself equal to God (5.18; 10.33; cf. 19.7). In response, John implies in a number of passages that Jesus' exalted status does not infringe God's unity, utilizing a novel interpretation of God's oneness to do so.[3] Paul, too, alludes to the *Shema*, and gives it some novel twists, in at least three passages (Rom. 3.30; 1 Cor. 8.6; Gal. 3.20);[4] it is possible that in so doing he, too, is responding to

---

1. See for example Gnilka, *Evangelium*, I, p. 96. Omission of 2.5b-10 results in a classic miracle story and eliminates the awkwardness of 2.10, including the repetition of λέγει τῷ παραλυτικῷ from 2.5. The scribes, moreover, suddenly pop into view in 2.6, whereas no indication of their presence has been given previously, and this presence creates some tension with 2.12, in which all—including the scribes?—are amazed and say that they have never seen anything comparable to the miracle Jesus has performed. The question the scribes raise, moreover, can be plausibly related to early Christian convictions about human access to forgiveness through Jesus (cf. for example 1 Cor. 15.3; Rom. 3.25; Mt. 26.28). For all these reasons 2.5b-10 is probably secondary. Is it a Markan or a pre-Markan insertion? Gnilka thinks the latter, but the use of Mark's typical method of intercalation (cf. M.D. Hooker, *The Gospel According to St Mark* [BNTC; London: A. & C. Black, 1991], p. 84), as well as the stylistic similarity of 2.10 to 7.5, in which Mark takes up his narrative thread again after the awkward insertion of 7.3-4, inclines me toward seeing 2.5b-10 as Markan.

2. These debates may very well have been triggered by the awareness of non-Christian Jews that Christians baptized and pronounced forgiveness in the name of Jesus, sang hymns to him and even prayed to him. See L.W. Hurtado, *One God, One Lord: Early Christian Devotion and Ancient Jewish Monotheism* (London: SCM Press; Philadelphia: Fortress Press, 1988), pp. 99-114.

3. See C.K. Barrett, 'The Old Testament in the Fourth Gospel', *JTS* 48 (1947), pp. 161-62; W.A. Meeks, 'Equal to God', in R.T. Fortna and B.R. Gaventa (eds.), *The Conversation Continues: Studies in Paul and John* (J.L. Martyn Festschrift; Nashville: Abingdon Press, 1990), pp. 309-21.

4. On 1 Cor. 8.6 as a reference to the *Shema* see J.D.G. Dunn, *Christology in*

Jewish objections to Christianity based on the *Shema*. It is certain, at any rate, that the *Shema* continued to be a flashpoint for Jewish–Christian debate into the second century and beyond, for in rabbinic traditions Jewish Christians are routinely charged with believing in 'two powers in heaven' (i.e. God and Christ) and thus compromising the unity of God.[1]

Does Mark give us hints as to how he would answer such charges? I believe that he does. First, it is clear that he would deny them! In his mind the Christian conviction about Jesus' quasi-divine status[2] in no way compromises the unity of God. This is clear from the juxtaposition already mentioned between 12.28-34, in which the unity of God is affirmed by means of the *Shema*, and 12.35-37, in which Ps. 110.1 is cited. The latter verse pictures a figure, 'my Lord', who is told by *the* Lord, that is God, to sit at his right hand until God subdues his enemies. Jesus' exegesis of this verse makes it clear that for him the object of this heavenly enthronement is the messiah. For Mark, however, Jesus is the messiah, and so he is speaking about himself when he exegetes Psalm 110. It is evident, then, that Mark experiences no embarrassment in portraying Jesus both as one who claims a quasi-divine status for himself, as in Ps. 110.1, and as a faithful upholder of the unity of God, as in Deut. 6.4.[3]

But this reference to the juxtaposition of two different scriptural passages merely begs the question: *how* does Mark reconcile the different conceptions that these Old Testament passages embody? It is not enough to say that he believes both in the *Shema* and in Psalm 110; it is

---

the Making: A New Testament Inquiry into the Origins of the Doctrine of the Incarnation (London: SCM Press, 1980), p. 180, who notes that here Paul 'splits' the *Shema* between God the Father and Christ the Lord. On Rom. 3.30 see *idem*, *Romans 1–8* (WBC, 38A; Dallas: Word Books, 1988), p. 189, and on Gal. 3.20, see R.N. Longenecker, *Galatians* (WBC, 41; Dallas: Word Books, 1990), p. 142. See also the allusions to the *Shema* in the textually suspect Rom. 16.27 and the deutero-Pauline Eph. 4.6;1 Tim. 1.17; 2.5; 6.15-16, as well as in Jas 2.19 and Jude 25 (see Dunn, *Parting*, p. 316 n. 22).

   1.   See Segal, *Two Powers*, *passim*.

   2.   On Mark's ascription to Jesus of a status close to that of God in Mk 12.35-37 and 14.62, see J. Marcus, 'Mark 14.61: "Are You the Messiah-Son-of-God?"', *NovT* 31 (1989), pp. 125-41.

   3.   As Hurtado (*One God*, p. 2) shows, this is a general pattern in early Christianity; Christians 'apparently felt thoroughly justified in giving Jesus reverence in terms of divinity and at the same time thought of themselves as worshipping *one* God'.

necessary to elucidate the thought processes that enable him to throw together these seemingly contradictory passages with such apparent unconcern.

A starting point in answering this question is the recognition that even Ps. 110.1, which speaks of a figure exalted to God's right hand, implies the subordination of that figure to God. He is called 'my Lord', not *the* Lord, a term that is reserved here, and in Mark's Gospel in general, for God himself.[1] Moreover, it is not by his own active power that the exalted figure's enemies are subdued, but by the power of God, who says to him: 'Sit at my right hand until *I* put your enemies under your feet'. As the Midrash on the Psalms comments on this verse: 'The Holy One, blessed be he, declared, "He will sit, and I will make war"'.

In consonance with this psalmic picture, the Markan Jesus is not one who acts by his own power, but by the power of God; he proclaims, not his own royal power, but the royal power of God (1.15). Several Markan passages, accordingly, imply his subordination to God (10.40; 13.32; 14.36; 15.34). The other side of this modesty, however, is equally important: when Jesus acts, it is not a mere human being acting, but the sovereign God (5.19-20), for Jesus is the one who comes 'in the name of the Lord' (11.9).

Authority on Earth

So far we have been concentrating on the juxtaposition in 12.28-37 between a scriptural assertion of God's oneness and a scriptural portrayal of a figure enthroned alongside God. The same sort of juxtaposition is implicit in the first *Shema* passage in the Gospel, 2.1-12. Here, however, the scriptural background that speaks of the exalted figure is not Psalm 110 but Daniel 7—a passage which may indeed be based on Psalm 110.[2]

Daniel 7 comes into view in Mk 2.1-12 through Jesus' reference to

---

1. Mk 11.3 is not an exception, since for the characters in the story κύριος probably means simply the master of the colt, although Mark is probably punning on the use of κύριος for God and Jesus in early Christianity; see Marcus, *Way*, pp. 37-40.

2. See D.M. Hay, *Glory at the Right Hand: Psalm 110 in Early Christianity* (SBLMS, 18; Nashville: Abingdon Press, 1973), p. 26. Hay points out that Ps. 110 and Dan. 7 are the only Old Testament passages that speak of a figure enthroned beside God.

himself in 2.10 as 'the Son of Man', the first such self-reference in Mark. Although the whole question of the meaning of the Son of Man title in Mark is a complex one, it is hard to deny that at least part of its background lies in Daniel's description of 'one like a son of man' who is presented to the Ancient of Days and given power, dominion and authority by him (Dan. 7.13-14). This passage is cited in the Son of Man sayings in 13.26 and 14.62 and already alluded to in the Son of Man saying in 8.38. That it is also alluded to in our passage is made more certain by the reference in 2.10 to the Son of Man's authority (ἐξουσία), since Dan. 7.14 LXX lists ἐξουσία as one of the things given by the Ancient of Days to the 'one like a son of man'.[1]

In order to understand Mark's way of reconciling the unity of God with the exalted role of Jesus, it is important to keep in mind the overall context of Daniel 7. The chapter first describes Daniel's vision of four evil earthly kingdoms, symbolized by four beasts that arise from the sea and succeed each other. The fourth beast, as we read later in the chapter, symbolizes a kingdom that will 'devour the whole earth, and trample it down, and break it to pieces' (7.23 RSV). Daniel next sees a vision of the heavenly throne-room that counterbalances the vision of the four beasts ravaging the earth. Here 'thrones were placed, and one that was ancient of days took his seat' (7.9 RSV). The plural 'thrones' here may be significant, as some later rabbinic commentaries suggest,[2] for immediately a human-like figure, 'the one like a son of man', is presented before the Ancient of Days, who gives him 'dominion and glory and royal power, that all people, nations, and languages should serve him'.[3] The implication would seem to be that, as in Psalm 110, this

---

1.   Cf. Pesch, *Markusevangelium*, I, p. 169; W.D. Davies and D.C. Allison, *A Critical and Exegetical Commentary on the Gospel according to Saint Matthew*. II. *Commentary on Matthew VIII–XVIII* (Edinburgh: T. & T. Clark, 1991), p. 93.

2.   See for example *b. Sanh.* 38b, on which see Marcus, 'Messiah-Son-of-God', pp. 140-41.

3.   On the identity of this figure in Daniel, see the discussion and bibliography in J.J. Collins, *The Apocalyptic Imagination: An Introduction to the Jewish Matrix of Christianity* (New York: Crossroad, 1989), pp. 80-85. The main alternatives are to see it as a corporate symbol for Israel, as Yahweh's chief angel or as the messiah. Collins himself argues for the angelic interpretation, more specifically identifying the angel as Michael, 'the great prince who has charge of your people' (Dan. 12.1; cf. 10.13, 21). It does not seem to me that the corporate interpretation necessarily excludes either of the other two possibilities; the 'one like a son of man' could be both a symbol for Israel and a reference to the angel who fights for it or to the king who will lead it to victory.

human-like figure is enthroned at God's side (hence, perhaps, the plural 'thrones') and thus shares in his royal authority.[1]

Two points about this picture are important for our consideration of Mk 2.1-12. First, the royal authority of the 'one like a son of man' is a *derived* one; he has it not by virtue of his own power but by royal grant from the true, heavenly king, the 'one that was ancient of days'. That Mark is aware of the subordinationism implicit in Daniel 7 and applies it to Jesus' relation to God is clear from 8.38, where we hear of the Son of Man 'com[ing] in the glory of *his Father*'. Here Mark draws directly on the language of Dan. 7.13-14 ('one like a son of man...came to the Ancient of Days...and to him was given...glory'), and his phrasing implies that the returning Son of Man will come bearing not his own glory but that of God.

The second reason for the importance of Daniel 7 as background to Mark 2 is that, despite the picture of enthronement beside God in heaven, the authority of the 'one like a son of man' is exercised not in heaven but *on earth*. Stretching a point, one might even speak of a division of labor in Daniel 7 between the Ancient of Days and the 'one like a son of man'; the Ancient of Days rules in heaven, where millions of angels serve him (7.10), while the human-like figure rules on the earth as his plenipotentiary. The earthly sphere of action of the Son of Man figure is revealed in three ways. First, this figure, by his human-likeness, is the counterpoise to the four beasts, and the latter are described as wreaking havoc *on the earth* (Dan. 7.23). It is logical to assume, then, that his everlasting dominion and royal power (7.14), like their temporary dominion, will be exercised on the earth. Secondly, the royal prerogatives given to him in 7.14 include the obedience of 'all peoples, nations, and languages', clearly implying an earthly sphere of action. Thirdly, these royal prerogatives (dominion, royal power, the obedience of all peoples) are almost identical with those given in 7.27 to 'the

---

1. J.J. Collins ('The Son of Man in First-Century Judaism', *NTS* 38 [1992], pp. 457-58) sees the enthroned position of the Son of Man in *1 En.* 62.5 and 69.29 as a natural inference from the plural 'thrones' in Dan. 7.9. This implication, however, could be deemed blasphemous if the 'one like a son of man' was interpreted as a human being; see for example *b. Sanh.* 38b (discussed in Marcus, 'Messiah-Son-of-God'), where R. Jose accuses R. Akiba of profaning the divine presence for applying Dan. 7.9 to the messiah (i.e. Bar Kochba?).

people of the saints of the Most High',[1] and the authority of the saints is obviously exercised on earth, since they become masters of 'the greatness of the kingdoms *under the whole heaven*'.[2]

When we return to Mk 2.1-12 with this Danielic background in mind, the phrase 'upon the earth' in 2.10, and the description of the crowd's reaction to the cure in 2.12, gain new significance. The Son of Man has the authority to forgive sins *on earth*, acting as the earthly plenipotentiary of the one who forgives them *in heaven* (cf. Mt. 18.18).[3] When he acts on earth in this way, he does not claim to be doing so by his own power but by the power of God; any charge that Christians worship two gods, therefore, is misguided.[4] Similarly, the miraculous power displayed in the paralytic's cure is not Jesus' own possession but the gift of the One God who is now acting on earth through him. It is fitting, therefore, and very possibly a reflection of the derived nature of the authority of the 'one

1. This parallelism is the main support of the corporate interpretation of the figure in Dan. 7.13-14; see above.

2. Cf. Hurtado (*One God*, p. 56) on Enoch as the Son of Man in *1 En.* 71: he is 'a chief agent whose primary work and authority appear to be exercised *upon the earth*, although he is described in heavenly scenes' (emphasis added). The Son of Man in *1 Enoch* is based on the human-like figure in Dan. 7; see Collins, 'Son of Man', pp. 452-53.

3. Cf. A.M. Ambrozic, 'New Teaching with Power (Mk 1:27)', in J. Plevnik (ed.), *Word and Spirit; Essays in Honor of David Michael Stanley, S.J. on his 60th Birthday* (Willowdale, Ont.: Regis College, 1975), p. 123. But this concept of the Son of Man exercising on earth the authority of the heavenly God is somewhat in tension with Mk 12.36//Ps. 110.1, where 'my lord' (which for Mark means Jesus) is enthroned in heaven at God's right hand, and 'the Lord' (= God) subdues this enthroned figure's enemies, who are presumably on earth. This tension is reduced, though not eliminated, by the realization that since the resurrection, Jesus can be present both in heaven (12.36) and on earth (2.10). This is in line with Dan. 7, where the human-like figure is both enthroned beside God in heaven and the representative for his authority on earth. For Mark, moreover, the salient point of 'until I put your enemies under your feet' in Ps. 110.1 is not that Jesus remains in heaven while God conquers his enemies on earth but that Jesus subdues his enemies through God's power rather than his own; see above.

4. In Mk 2.6 the scribes ask, 'Who can forgive sins except one, namely God?' This is vaguely reminiscent of the name of the archangel Michael, which means 'Who is like God?', and which is probably a double entendre implying both the incomparableness of God and Michael's approach to divine status. Since both ideas are consonant with Mark's Christology, and since some scholars identify Michael with the Son of Man figure in Dan. 7 (see above), it is just possible that Mark has Michael at the back of his mind as he formulates 2.7.

like a son of man' in Daniel 7, that the onlookers in Mark should glorify God when they witness the stunning miracle that *Jesus* has performed (2.12).[1]

Authority to Forgive Sins

But the 'one like a son of man' in Daniel 7 is not explicitly said to receive the authority to forgive sins. Does that mean that this aspect of Mk 2.10 lacks Danielic background?

Not necessarily. The statement about the Son of Man forgiving sins may reflect midrashic activity by which other Danielic texts have been linked with Daniel 7. In Dan. 9.9, for example, we read, 'To the Lord our God belong mercy and forgiveness'. This is just one of a number of Old Testament texts that ascribe forgiveness to God (see for example Exod. 34.6-7; Isa. 43.25; 44.22) and thus provide the scriptural basis for the scribes' objection, 'Who can forgive sins except one, namely God?'[2] For our purposes the passage from Daniel 9 is a particularly interesting expression of this theme, because it appears only a couple of chapters after the 'Son of Man' vision and is part of a well-known passage in which Daniel prays for the forgiveness of his people's weighty sins. Since the 'one like a son of man' in Daniel 7 is given the authority of the Ancient of Days, it is not hard to imagine that a reader of Daniel would have assumed that this included the authority to forgive sins.

Or the midrashic process may have been somewhat more complicated. There exists evidence that various figures from Daniel 7 and 10 were linked by later exegetes with the angel in whom God's name dwells from Exod. 23.20-22. The discussion in *b. Sanh.* 38b, for example, links Dan. 7.9 with Exod. 23.21. In *Apocalypse of Abraham* 10, moreover, the angel Iaoel, apparently the angel of Exodus 23, is sent to Abraham 'in the likeness of a man', and he 'comes' to him. Both the verb 'comes'

---

1. The Matthean parallel ends with the amazed crowd glorifying God, 'who had given such authority to human beings' (Mt. 9.8). The added phrase is probably an allusion to Dan. 7.27, where royal power, dominion and so on are given to 'the people of the saints of the Most High'—a grant parallel to that bestowed on the 'one like a son of man' in 7.14 (see above). Matthew, then, seems to be cognizant of the Danielic background of Mk 2.1-12 and the parallel between Dan. 7.14 and 7.27.

2. The latter three texts are mentioned by V. Taylor in his treatment of Mk 2.7 (*The Gospel according to St Mark* [Grand Rapids: Baker, 2nd edn, 1981 (1966)], p. 196). Dan. 9.9 is mentioned by Allison and Davies in their treatment of the Matthean parallel (*Matthew*, II, p. 91).

and the phrase 'the likeness of a man' are reminiscent of the 'one like a son of man', who 'comes' to the Ancient of Days in Daniel 7. Also, in *Apoc. Abr.* 11.1-4 Iaoel is described in ways that echo the description of the Ancient of Days in Dan. 7.9 ('the hair of his head [was] like snow') as well as the description of the mighty angel in Dan. 10.5-6.[1]

This linkage of the figures in Daniel 7 with the angel in Exodus 23 is significant because that angel, in turn, is associated with forgiveness of sins in the Old Testament original:

> Behold, I send an angel before you, to guard you on the way and to bring you to the place which I have prepared. You shall give heed to him and hearken to his voice, you shall not rebel against him, *for he will not pardon your transgression*; for my name is in him. But if you hearken attentively to his voice and do all that I say, then I will be an enemy to your enemies and an adversary to your adversaries (Exod. 23.20-22 RSV altered).

Although phrased negatively ('he will *not* pardon your transgressions'), this passage at least links the angel in whom Yahweh's name dwells with the theme of forgiveness. The dwelling of God's name in the angel, moreover, gave rise to speculation in later Judaism that he—in many ways like the Son of Man figure in Daniel 7—was a semi-divine being who represented the authority of God in the earthly sphere. *Apocalypse of Abraham* 10–11 is a relatively early example of this development;[2] *Exodus Rabbah* contains some later examples of it. One tradition recorded in the latter, for example, notes the alternation of personal pronouns in Exod. 23.22 and draws a logical conclusion from it:

> 'But if you hearken attentively to his voice and do all that I [God] say.' It is not written here, 'that *he* says,' but 'that *I* say'—if you accept [a word] from him, you are accepting it from me (*Exod. R.* 32.4 [on Exod. 23.22]; my trans.).

---

1.   See Hurtado, *One God*, p. 80. It should come as no surprise that Iaoel combines elements of both the Ancient of Days and the 'one like a son of man', since a similar amalgamation occurs in Rev. 1.13-14. Hooker (*Mark*, p. 216) sees a parallel process in Mk 9.3, where Jesus is pictured in a glorified state in garments of shining white, and thus is reminiscent of the Ancient of Days in Dan. 7.9, a few verses after his prophecy that the Son of Man will come 'in the glory of his father' (Mk 8.38).

2.   As Hurtado notes (*One God*, p. 87), Iaoel's name is a contraction of the names Yahweh and El, both names for God in the Old Testament, and this detail 'clearly sets the angel apart as given special, likely surpassing, authority in the administration of God's rule'. *Apocalypse of Abraham* probably dates from the end of the first or beginning of the second century; see Segal, *Two Powers*, p. 196; R. Rubinkiewicz in *OTP*, I, p. 683.

For this interpretation, the alternation of 'his voice' with 'I say' indicates that the angel speaks with divine authority.

For some exegetes, moreover, the divine authority of the angel of Exodus 23 apparently included the authority to forgive sins. This would be a logical inference, since the Exodus passage warns that the angel will not pardon the transgression of those who disobey him; it would make sense, then, to assume that if they *do* obey him, he *will* pardon them. Although several rabbis warn against this conclusion because in their eyes it amounts to a divinization of the angel, this polemic is itself evidence that the conclusion was being drawn by others.[1] This is particularly clear from *Exod. R.* 32.4 [on Exod. 23.22]:

> Another interpretation: 'You shall not rebel against him (אל תמר בו).' You shall not exchange me [God] for him (אל תמירוני), and you shall not substitute him for me. For perhaps you will say: 'Since he is our prince, we will worship him, and he will pardon our transgressions.' No!—on the contrary, 'He will *not* pardon your transgression.' He is *not* like me, for of me it is written: 'Forgiving iniquity and passing over transgression' (Mic. 7.18). But *he* shall not pardon your transgression (my trans.).

The emphases here are mine, but they reflect the polemical tone of the passage, which is strenuously concerned to deny to the angel the God-like role of forgiving sins. It is a reasonable inference that this strenuous denial is a response to scriptural interpreters who were claiming the opposite, namely that the angel described in Exodus 23 was like God, could pardon transgression, and even should be worshipped. As A. Segal argues, these exegetes were probably Christians who identified the angel in Exodus 23 with Jesus and used the passage as a scriptural support for the high status they ascribed to him—including the authority to forgive sins.

This argument, to be sure, proves neither that the Son of Man was amalgamated with the angel of Exodus 23 in Mark's time nor that the prerogative to forgive sins was ascribed to this amalgamated figure. All it shows for certain is that some later traditions fused the 'Son of Man' figure from Daniel 7 with the angel indwelt by God's name from Exodus 23, and that certain other traditions gave the latter figure the divine prerogative of forgiving sins. It does, however, provide a plausible exegetical process by which Mark or his precursors *might* have arrived

---

1. See Segal, *Two Powers*, pp. 68-70, who refers to *b. Sanh.* 38b. Similar arguments appear in *Tanḥuma, Mišpaṭim* §18 and *Exod. R.* 32.4 (on Exod. 23.21).

at a justification for the statement in Mk 2.10 that the Son of Man has
authority to forgive sins on earth,[1] and in its favor is Mark's awareness
of Exod. 23.20-21 (see Mk 1.2)[2] and his view of Jesus as 'the one who
comes in the name of the Lord' (see Mk 11.9).[3]

One way or another, then, Mk 2.10 employs the theme of the
authority of the Son of Man, which is drawn from Daniel 7. Yet it
should not be overlooked that Mark's use of Daniel 7 here contains an
element of paradox. The 'one like a son of man' in Daniel 7 is strongly
associated with the theme of judgment that pervades the chapter (Dan.
7.10, 22, 26), and the *Similitudes of Enoch*, drawing on this Danielic
background, presents the Son of Man himself as a judge (*1 En.* 45.3, for
example). For Mark, on the other hand, Jesus' authority as Son of Man
is expressed not by judging but by forgiving sins on the earth. No
matter that, as we have seen, this authority could be exegetically derived
by combining Daniel 7 with other scriptural passages; the paradoxical—
perhaps even polemical[4]—element remains.[5]

The One Good One and the One God

In 2.1-12 as well as 12.28-37, then, Mark is engaged in a creative
struggle to reconcile exegetically the *Shema*'s affirmation of God's unity

1.   In his treatment of rabbinic polemic against a 'high' interpretation of Exod.
23.20-22, Segal (*Two Powers*, p. 70) mentions Mk 2.7, though he is rightly cautious
about reading a third-century debate back into a first-century text.

2.   Mark is aware of Exod. 23.20, since he cites its beginning in 1.2, although
there the angel/messenger is interpreted as John the Baptist rather than Jesus.

3.   This is a citation of Ps. 118.26, but in the original 'in the name of the Lord'
modifies 'blessed', and the sentence is merely a ritual blessing extended to all
pilgrims approaching the Temple. Mark, however, interprets the psalm citation as a
messianic acclamation; for him 'in the name of the Lord' modifies 'he who comes'.
This christological reinterpretation may be partly due to the influence of Exod. 23.21.

4.   It is possible that here as elsewhere Mark is polemicizing against Jewish
apocalypticists in his *Sitz im Leben* in the Jewish War who eagerly embrace the
judgmental aspect of the Danielic Son of Man figure and understand it to be directed
against the Roman 'beast'; see Marcus, *Way*, pp. 167-69.

5.   Later in the Gospel, Mark will use Dan. 7 in a similarly paradoxical manner.
Hooker (*Mark*, p. 250) points out that the οὐκ...ἀλλά ('not...but') structure
clearly presents 10.45 as a paradox, and this paradox is plausibly rooted in Dan. 7.14
(cf. 7.27), where the Son of Man is served by others. Jesus, on the other hand, says in
10.45 that the Son of Man came not to be served but to serve, and to give his life as a
ranson for many.

with scriptural passages that speak of exalted figures with great, even God-like authority. Something similar probably explains the problem posed by the third *Shema*-reference, Mk 10.18.

The problem is this: what, in Mark's mind, is the meaning of Jesus' retort to the rich man, 'Why do you call me good? No one is good except one, that is God'?[1] At first glance the implication would seem to be that Jesus thinks that the adjective 'good' is as inappropriate for him as it is for other human beings, and this indeed may have been what the reply meant in the mouth of the historical Jesus. But it is difficult to see how it could bear this meaning for Mark. The passage as a whole, on the contrary, seems to be deliberately shaped to emphasize Jesus' benevolence, a quality often associated with goodness; in 10.21 Jesus looks at the man, loves him and graciously shows him the way to enter into the kingdom of God. Elsewhere in the Gospel, too, Jesus' 'goodness' is assumed, for example in 3.4, where he asks his opponents whether it is permitted on the Sabbath 'to do good or to do evil (ἀγαθὸν ποιῆσαι ἢ κακοποιῆσαι)'. This question suggests that Jesus' subsequent act of healing is an example of doing good and thus, one would suppose, an indication of his goodness. And if, as seems incontrovertible, Mark believes that the demon in 1.24 is correct in acclaiming Jesus as 'the holy one of God', it is difficult to see how Mark could think that Jesus *was* holy but was *not* good.

The alternative is to see Jesus' question in 10.18 not as rhetorical but as a real question: '*What is your basis* for calling me good, seeing that no one is good except God?' The Markan Jesus, in other words, is challenging the man to attain a christological insight, the realization that Jesus is good because God is good,[2] and that Jesus as the Son of God,

---

1. As E. Lohmeyer points out (*Das Evangelium des Markus* [MeyerK; Göttingen: Vandenhoeck & Ruprecht, 1957 (1936)], p. 209), it is an Old Testament commonplace that God is good (see for example Ps. 118.1; 1 Chron. 16.34; 2 Chron. 5.13), but it is not a common conclusion that only God is good; see however Philo, *Mut. Nom.* 7 and *Somn.* 1.149 (cited by Pesch, *Markusevangelium*, II, p. 139). The latter is a particularly interesting passage for comparison with Mk 10.18, because it seems to be an allusion to the *Shema*, and it contains both the idea that God is the One who is good and the implication that a human being can incorporate his goodness. This is very close to the interpretation of Mk 10.18 proposed in what follows.

2. As Hooker notes (*Mark*, p. 241), this interpretation was popular among the church fathers; cf. Gnilka, *Evangelium*, II, p. 89 n. 33, who cites Theophylact (*PG* 123.600), Bede (*PL* 92.231), and Calvin's comment on the passage in his *Gospel Harmony*.

the earthly representative of the heavenly king, and the one indwelt by God's name, participates in the goodness of God's reign and manifests it eschatologically upon the earth.[1] His goodness does not impugn the radicalized form of the *Shema* that attributes goodness only to God, because his goodness *is* God's goodness.

Because of the Markan Jesus' role of establishing God's goodness on earth, moreover, it might even be said that he becomes the ultimate instrument for the realization of the divine unity. For according to a suggestive Old Testament passage, God's oneness is not just a matter of present reality but also a matter of future hope, a hope related to the restoration of his goodness, his gracious royal rule, in the world he has created: 'And the Lord will become king over all the earth; on that day the Lord will be one and his name one' (Zech. 14.9). For this passage the Lord cannot truly be 'one' while a pocket of resistance to his salvific will remains;[2] his oneness will only be fully restored when he becomes all in all, on earth as in heaven, through the re-establishment of his kingship in the world he created (cf. 1 Cor. 15.28). And for Mark, Jesus' life, death and resurrection, which extend the royal rule of God from heaven to earth, are the means for the restitution of this oneness.

For Mark, then, the *Shema* and God's royal power are inseparably linked, and it is therefore no surprise that Jesus' last words in Mk 12.28-34 concern the βασιλεία: 'You are not far from the royal power of God'. This linkage between the *Shema* and God's royal power, we have seen, has background in the Judaism of the first century, as the blessing after the *Shema* reveals. This blessing and the theme of God's sovereignty, moreover, are linked with the *Shema* in a later rabbinic tradition that sheds an interesting light on the Markan editorial comment that concludes 12.28-34:

> This is the voice that silences both celestial and terrestrial beings...When Israel say, 'Hear O Israel,' the angels are silent and then drop their wings. And what do they proclaim? 'Blessed be the name of his glorious kingdom for ever and ever' (*Gen. R.* 65.21 [on Gen. 27.22]).[3]

---

1.   The eschatological manifestation of God's goodness upon the earth restores the original goodness of creation, which is emphasized throughout Gen. 1 and especially in the 'it was very good' of 1.31.

2.   Cf. J.C. Beker, *Paul the Apostle: The Triumph of God in Life and Thought* (Philadelphia: Fortress Press, 1980), p. 194.

3.   Translation slightly altered from H. Freedman, *The Midrash Rabbah* (5 vols.; London, Jerusalem and New York: Soncino, 1977), I, pp. 597-98.

Here the *Shema*'s call to listen has an immediate result: heavenly and earthly beings fall silent as the sovereign power of the One God manifests itself. Mark may be making a similar linkage when he has Jesus silence his opponents through a reference to the *Shema*, to the royal power of God and to the love of neighbor that manifests that power on earth and thus actualizes Deut. 6.4. He may believe that, when Jesus spoke the awesome and power-laden words that begin 'Hear, O Israel', the consummation of God's unity in the arrival of the βασιλεία was prefigured, the rebellious cosmos fell silent before its conqueror, and thereafter 'nobody dared to ask him anything anymore' (Mk 12.34). In that moment Israel did indeed listen, and thus anticipated—if only, in some cases, unwittingly, or even unwillingly—the future day when the Lord would become king over all the earth and his name would be truly one.

JESUS' WALKING ON THE WATER: MARK 6.45-52

William Richard Stegner

Anyone who has worked with the narrative of Jesus' walking on the water finds tremendous diversity among interpreters. The following sampling illustrates that diversity as well as the speculative nature of the scholarly attempts to analyze the story.

According to Rudolf Bultmann the narrative is a nature miracle in form, and the 'original motif' is 'the walking on the water'. The 'storm motif has been added to it...as a secondary feature'.[1] The presence of two motifs is probably due to a 'mixture of sources' in the story.

Perhaps the most influential line of interpretation has been that of Dibelius and Lohmeyer. Martin Dibelius classifies the narrative as a 'tale' and stresses its epiphanic character. In an epiphany 'the divine power of the divine wonder-worker becomes manifest'.[2] Thus, walking on the water reveals the God-like nature of Jesus.[3] Ernst Lohmeyer also held Jesus' walking on the sea to be an epiphany. However, in addition to the epiphany motif, the narrative stresses the stilling of the storm. Both motifs are present because Mark combined two originally independent stories in his account. Lohmeyer argues for two originally independent pieces on the basis of conflicting geographical notes both within the narrative and in its immediate context.[4]

---

1. R. Bultmann, *History of the Synoptic Tradition* (trans. J. Marsh; New York: Harper & Row, 1963), p. 216. See also pp. 215 and 230.

2. M. Dibelius, *From Tradition to Gospel* (trans. B. Woolf; New York: Charles Scribner's Sons, 1971), p. 94. See also p. 95.

3. Among more recent authors John Heil also strongly supports the classification of the pericope as an epiphany: Jesus' walking on the water recalls God's mastery of the sea both in creation and in the exodus (*Jesus Walking on the Sea* [AnBib, 87; Rome: Biblical Institute Press, 1981]).

4. E. Lohmeyer, *Das Evangelium des Markus übersetzt und erklärt* (MeyerK, 1.2; Göttingen: Vandenhoeck & Ruprecht, 1957), pp. 131-32.

Writing in conscious opposition to such a two-source theory, Thierry Snoy asks how one separates the epiphany from the stilling of the storm. Where is the seam in the narrative? Apart from Markan redactional activity at the beginning and the end, the story is a unity.[1]

Some British scholars have tended to emphasize the historicity of the narrative while, at the same time, rejecting its miraculous character. Vincent Taylor is a good example. He does not attempt to classify the form of the story, but cites its 'homiletical and doctrinal interests'. He suggests that originally Jesus was 'wading through the surf near the hidden shore...'[2]

Writing from a Jewish perspective, Pinchas Lapide points to similarities with the story of Jonah. However, in the pre-Markan tradition Jesus does not walk upon the water: rather, he is seeking refuge from political persecution. Lapide stresses Jesus' connections with the Zealots. Bethsaida, which was outside Herod Antipas's jurisdiction, was a haven for Jesus and his disciples. Whatever the narrative meant in Jewish Christianity, Mark and the Gentile church changed it significantly.[3]

Diverse views concerning this narrative do not end with questions of form and meaning: they extend to the story in its pre-Markan phase. Did the narratives of the feeding of the five thousand and the walking on the water circulate in the pre-Markan tradition in the present order? While a majority of scholars would answer affirmatively, a minority feel that Mark is responsible for the present order.[4]

Further, which Old Testament passages may have influenced the wording of this brief narrative? Surely, the narrative does not allude to all the passages cited by various authors! Closely related to the issue of relevant Old Testament passages is the diversity of translations offered for key terms in the pericope. For example, is the Greek word

---

1. T. Snoy, 'La rédaction marcienne de la marche sur les eaux', *ETL* 44 (1968), pp. 205-41. See esp. pp. 224-25.

2. V. Taylor, *The Gospel according to Mark* (London: Macmillan, 1955), p. 327. So also J.D.M. Derrett, 'Why and How Jesus Walked on the Sea', *NovT* 23 (1981), pp. 330-48.

3. P. Lapide, *Er wandelte nicht auf dem Meer* (Gütersloh: Gerd Mohn, 1984), pp. 16-50. See also *idem*, 'A Jewish Exegesis of the Walking on the Water', *Concilium* 138 (1980), pp. 35-40.

4. Snoy, 'Rédaction marcienne', p. 232. See also P.J. Achtemeier, 'The Origin and Function of the Pre-Marcan Miracle Catenae', *JBL* 91 (1972), p. 200. Achtemeier cites evidence indicating that the sea miracle was thought to precede the feeding miracle in some circles.

παρέρχομαι in Mk 6.48 better translated 'pass by' or 'save'?[1]

Why is there such diversity of results in dealing with the critical issues of this narrative? One reason is the failure of the early form critics to classify its form adequately. Since these critics were working with a limited number of forms, they tended to force forms onto narratives which eluded their categories. Also, early exegetes were not looking for Old Testament allusions and words cited from Old Testament stories, and were unaware of the *Sitz im Leben* of certain Gospel narratives within Jewish Christianity and, consequently, contemporary Judaism. Given such handicaps, early exegetes practiced more eisegesis than exegesis. Clearly, the diversity of results and the speculative nature of the scholarly attempts to understand the narrative argue for a new approach to the analysis of this story.

Since my approach presupposes the widespread scholarly agreement on two critical issues, those issues must be discussed. Today, nearly everyone agrees that Mark incorporated a pre-Markan account into his Gospel. Secondly, nearly everyone agrees that the conclusion in v. 52 was written by Mark and that some or all of the introduction in v. 45 is the result of Markan redaction.[2] The consensus of modern scholarship on these two points is sound and I presuppose it in my analysis of the narrative.

Let us look further at the issue of Markan redaction in these verses. Verse 52 shows the familiar Markan theme of the disciples' misunderstanding; further, it binds this narrative to the preceding story. Some argue that the confusing geographical notes in v. 45 must be due to Mark's ignorance of Palestinian geography. On the other hand, Snoy and others who believe that 6.45-52 originally circulated by itself, or preceded 6.35-44, do not regard the geographical notes as redactional.[3]

My approach also presupposes what seems to be known about the pre-Markan history of this narrative. Albert-Marie Denis finds that the

---

1. H. Fleddermann, '"And He Wanted to Pass by Them" (Mark 6:48c)', *CBQ* 45 (1983), p. 392. Fleddermann offers the following free translation: 'And he wanted to save them'.

2. W. Kelber, *The Kingdom in Mark* (Philadelphia: Fortress Press, 1974), p. 57 n. 43. According to Kelber, the last seven words in 6.51 are probably Markan also. In v. 45 the words are Markan except for 'he made' and 'Bethsaida'. See Kelber, *Kingdom in Mark*, pp. 57-58.

3. Snoy, 'Rédaction marcienne', pp. 222-24.

pre-Markan version was already written in Greek.[1] In his discussion of
the pre-Markan miracle catenae Paul Achtemeier finds a 'pattern for the
catenae in Jewish traditions', but not 'in the Hellenistic milieu'.[2] In
particular, he traces the sea miracles and the feeding miracles to the
Moses tradition. The Old Testament also gives precedent for the
wondrous intervening acts.

Further, Bertil Gärtner traces the walking on the water and the
feeding of the five thousand to a Christian Passover haggadah in which
Christ was pictured as the fulfillment of the 'types' or foreshadowings
seen in the manna and the deliverance at the sea.[3] While Gärtner and
Achtemeier differ about the function that the narratives played in the
pre-Markan tradition, they are not far apart concerning their *Sitz im
Leben*. Certainly Gärtner, and possibly Achtemeier (although he is not
asking the question concerning Jewish Christianity), would trace the
narrative to the activity of Jewish Christians. In my proposal I shall build
on the insight that Mark was working with a pre-Markan Greek account
first formulated by Jewish Christians.

My Proposal and a Methodology

I can now present my proposal and a methodology for interpreting the
narrative of the walking on the water. The form critics were not able to
classify the form of this narrative because none of the conventional
forms employed by them 'fit' Mk 6.45-52. This narrative is modeled on
the story of the deliverance of Israel at the sea found in Exodus 14. It is
'modeled' in the sense that key words, phrases, emotions and structural
parallels from the Old Testament story are reused and reenacted in the
narrative of the New Testament. One narrative is told with the other 'in
mind' so that the audience who heard the story about Jesus would recall
the familiar story from the Septuagint.

However, the story of Israel's deliverance at the sea, as recorded in
Exodus 14, was not static, but continued to grow and change with the

---

1. A.-M. Denis, 'La marche de Jésus, sur les eaux: Contribution à l'histoire de
la péricope dans la tradition évangélique', in I. de la Potterie (ed.), *De Jésus aux
Evangiles* (Gembloux: Duculot, 1967), p. 247. So also H. Kee, *Community of the
New Age* (Philadelphia: Westminster Press, 1977), p. 33.

2. Achtemeier, 'Origin', pp. 200-202.

3. B. Gärtner, *John 6 and the Jewish Passover* (ConNT, 17; Lund: Gleerup,
1959), pp. 30 and 37.

addition of new exegetical traditions. One such tradition was the visible presence of God in the event. Consequently, the thrust of the Markan narrative is complex. On the one hand, it tells of Jesus' mastering the sea by walking on it and rescuing his followers. On the other, it is 'modeled' on the central event in the life of the Jewish people, *as that event was understood in the first century*. Theologically, then, this narrative depicts Jesus in a manner similar to Yahweh in mastering the sea and rescuing his people from it. Jewish Christians would believe that the power of God, which had once delivered their ancestors, was now working through Jesus to deliver them.

Fortunately, the description of the narrative implies a methodology for interpreting it. The narrative is composed of three and probably four elements. First, there are the words, phrases and structural parallels that this narrative shares with Exodus 14. Secondly, the narrative was shaped by first-century exegetical traditions that interpreted Exodus 14. We often forget that in the first century the Old Testament was already an interpreted book: Jewish Christians did not read their Bible with modern critical eyes. Thirdly, someone had to formulate, shape and write the narrative that Mark used. I will discuss this further under the role of Jewish Christians.

A fourth element is the possible historical event, the point of departure for the story. As Albert-Marie Denis observed, this is difficult to determine.[1] While many would look upon this narrative as a purely literary creation, I do not want to prejudge that question by the terminology I use. Therefore, I prefer to use the awkward term 'formulate' in speaking of the work of the Jewish Christian formulators of the story. Nevertheless, this paper does not seek to answer the historical question.

One other observation needs to be made. The above methodology was first advanced by Birger Gerhardsson in his analysis of the temptation narrative in Matthew and Luke.[2] In the following discussion I have used his three categories, but prefer to use my own terminology, such as 'Jewish tradition' and exegetical traditions.

Let us now turn to our first category: phrases, words and structural

---

1. Denis, 'Le marche de Jésus', p. 247.

2. B. Gerhardsson, *The Testing of God's Son: An Analysis of an Early Christian Midrash* (Lund: Gleerup, 1966), p. 12. Also see W.R. Stegner, *Narrative Theology in Early Jewish Christianity* (Louisville, KY: Westminster Press/John Knox, 1989), where I have applied Gerhardsson's methodology to the narratives of the baptism, the temptation, the feeding of the five thousand and the transfiguration.

parallels from the Greek Bible. (Of course, this category can also be seen as an element of form in that words quoted from Exodus 14 constitute a considerable part of the vocabulary of the narrative.)

Phrases, Words and Structural Parallels from the Greek Bible

A prominent literary characteristic of Exodus 14 is the repetition of key words and phrases in the narrative. This literary characteristic offers a natural place to begin our analysis: key words and phrases from one narrative would be recalled if another narrative were being modeled upon it.

Let us begin by focusing on the formula-like expression found in God's command to Moses to 'stretch out your hand over the sea' (ἔκτεινον τὴν χεῖρά σου ἐπὶ τὴν θάλασσαν) in Exod. 14.16. This expression is repeated in vv. 21, 26 and 27. It contains the prepositional phrase 'over the sea' (ἐπὶ τὴν θάλασσαν: ἐπί with the accusative). This same prepositional phrase is found twice in Mk 6.48 and 49 with reference to Jesus' walking 'on the sea'. Of course, the case is changed to genitive with ἐπί because of the different usage.[1]

Another prepositional phrase is repeated three times in Exodus 14. In 14.16 the Lord commands Israel to enter '*into* midst of the sea' (εἰς μέσον τῆς θαλάσσης) in order to escape the Egyptians. In this prepositional phrase εἰς (into) with the accusative is used. In 14.22 Israel actually enters the sea and in 14.23 the Egyptians enter after them.[2] Then in 14.29 the phrase '*in* midst of the sea', the preposition ἐν with the dative being the only variant, describes the deliverance of Israel: 'But the people of Israel walked on dry ground through the sea [in midst of the sea], the waters being a wall to them on their right hand and on their left'. Significantly, the same phrase and case is found in Mk 6.47: 'the boat was out on the sea [in midst of the sea]'. Thus, the same phrase is used to describe the disciples in the boat before the sea rescue, and it echoes a repeated phrase from Exodus 14.

The approximately fifteen usages of the word 'sea' (θάλασσα) indicate its importance in Exodus 14.[3] We should not be surprised that it

---

1. The phrase follows the participle 'walking' in Job 9.8b (καὶ περιπατῶν ὡς ἐδάφους ἐπὶ θαλάσσης) but lacks the article.

2. In 14.27 the phrase 'midst of the sea' (μέσον τῆς θαλάσσης) without the preposition is used.

3. In vv. 1, 2, 9, 16 (2×), 21 (3×), 22, 23, 26, 27, 28, 29, 30.

is repeated three times within our narrative. Indeed, Mark's usage of the term 'sea' throughout his Gospel is unusual, since the more common designation for this body of water is the term 'lake' (λίμνη). In her study of the name 'Sea of Galilee' in Mark, Elizabeth Malbon makes the following observation:

> At this point it is clear that the Marcan application of the term *thalassa* rather than *limne* to the Lake of Galilee serves well its narrative and theological purposes. Though *limne* is more geographically precise, the more ambiguous *thalassa* is rich in connotations from the Hebrew scriptures. Mark presupposes the connotation of the sea as chaos, threat, danger, in opposition to the land as order, promise, security.[1]

Another frequently repeated term in Exodus 14 is the verb 'to see' in its various tenses and persons. Thus, in Exod. 14.13 Moses tells the people, 'Fear not...and *see* the salvation of the Lord' (θαρασεῖτε... καὶ ὁρᾶτε τὴν σωτηρίαν τὴν παρὰ τοῦ θεοῦ). Then in 14.30 and 31 the verb is repeated: 'and Israel *saw* (εἶδεν) the Egyptians...and Israel *saw* (εἶδεν) the great work which the Lord did...' (these three references are not at all exhaustive[2]). Is it then surprising that in Mk 6.49 and 50 the same tense and the same root as are found in the Septuagint of 14.30 and 31 are used twice to say the disciples *saw* Jesus walking on the water? Of course, Greek, like English, can use several different words for 'see'. For example, St John uses a different word for 'see' in 6.19 in his account of Jesus' walking on the water.

The verb 'tell' is repeated four times in the Greek translation of Exodus 14. In Exod. 14.1 (and 2) the Lord *tells* Moses what he should in turn *tell* the people of Israel. Then in 14.12 the people remind Moses what they *told* him in Egypt. Again in 14.15 the Lord commands Moses to *tell* the people to enter the sea. In two of these four occurrences the present tense of the verb 'to say' is coupled with the verb 'to tell'. A literal translation of 14.1 would read: 'And the Lord *told* Moses *saying*...' (ἐλάλησεν κύριος πρὸς Μωυσῆν λέγων). In 14.12, where the people speak, the same aorist tense for 'tell' is followed by the present tense for 'say' (ὃ ἐλαλήσαμεν πρὸς σὲ ἐν Αἰγύπτῳ λέγοντες). That same coupling of the present tense of the verb 'to say' with the aorist tense of the verb 'to tell' is found in Mk 6.50!

---

1. E. Malbon, 'The Jesus of Mark and the Sea of Galilee', *JBL* 103 (1984), p. 376. See also p. 364 for a further discussion on λίμνη.

2. Note one occurence in 14.10, three in 14.13, βλέπω with preposition in 14.10 and 24.

In Mk 6.50 after Jesus 'told' them and 'says' to them, we read the words: 'it is I; have no fear' (ἐγώ εἰμι. μὴ φοβεῖσθε). Of course, these words are also found in Exodus 14. In Exod. 14.10 the Israelites 'fear' the Egyptians who encamp behind them. Then in 14.31 the people 'fear' the Lord. Jesus tells his disciples not to fear, using the same word found twice in Exodus 14. This particular word for 'fear' did not have to be used, as the parallel expression 'were terrified' (6.51a) indicates. Thus the same emotion is indicated in both scenes: in Exodus the people 'fear' the Egyptians and God and in Mark the disciples 'fear' the sight of Jesus' walking on the water. However, this is not all. The two Greek words translated 'it is I' also occur twice in Exodus. In Exod. 14.4 and 14.18 the same sentence is repeated: in that sentence God identifies himself as the Lord: 'and *all* the Egyptians shall know that *I am* the Lord' (καὶ γνώσονται πάντες οἱ Αἰγύπτοι ὅτι ἐγώ εἰμι κύριος).

In order to make the point clearer let us summarize what we have found concerning the wording of Mk 6.50: 'for they all *saw* him, and were terrified. But immediately he *spoke to* them and *said*, "Take heart, *it is I*; *have* no *fear*"'. We have learned that the Greek words for 'saw', 'he spoke (told)', 'said', 'it is I' and 'fear' have all been used twice or more in the Exodus story. Further, we have learned from the last paragraph that the word 'all' is repeated in Exodus 14 (actually, it is used eleven times[1]). Even more striking is the coupling of the word 'all' with the formula 'I am the Lord' (or 'it is I' in Mark). While we have not yet turned our attention to the words used only once in Exodus 14, we can say that the term 'take heart' (θαρσεῖτε) is found in Exod. 14.13 in the same person, number and tense as occurs in Mk 6.50. In Exodus, Moses tells the people to 'take heart' and *see* the salvation from God. What is the result? Every major word in Mk 6.50, including 'were terrified', is also found in Exodus 14. The Greek word translated 'were terrified' is found in the aorist passive voice in Mark. In Exod. 14.24 it occurs in the aorist active voice: the root ταράσσω is the same, but the preposition σύν has been added to the root. It should be translated as 'throw into confusion'; 'and [the Lord] threw into confusion the camp of the Egyptians...'.[2] The only words in the Greek not found in Exodus 14 are 'for', 'immediately' and 'not'. If those who wrote the pre-Markan narrative had not been modeling their narrative on Exodus 14, what are the mathematical probabilities for such an occurrence as we have found?

---

1. In vv. 4 (2×), 6, 7 (2×), 9, 17 (2×), 18, 23, 28.
2. *BAGD*, p. 805.

Only four other words need be mentioned before citing the words that occur only once in the Exodus account. The word 'night' (νύξ) is emphasized by being repeated three times (twice in v. 20 and once in v. 21). Then the Markan account uses 'night' in connection with 'the fourth watch' (περὶ τετάρτην φυλακὴν τῆς νυκτός) in 6.48. The word 'heart' is also repeated four times.[1] God hardens the 'heart' of the Egyptians and of Pharaoh. Surprisingly enough, the word 'heart' is used in v. 52 which is usually ascribed to Mark. The word 'land' is found twice in Exod. 14.3, 11 and once in Mk 6.47. Finally, the words translated 'against' (ἐναντίος) in Mk 6.48, 'for the wind was against them', is found twice in an idiomatic expression in Exod. 14.2 and 9, 'in front of Baalzephon'.

Perhaps of equal significance in establishing a relationship between the two passages are the words that occur only once in Exodus 14. I have already mentioned 'take heart' and 'were terrified'. Also, the word 'wind' occurs only once. Indeed, the Exodus account emphasizes the 'strong east wind' by which the Lord parted the sea. Perhaps for this reason the Markan account mentions the wind twice in 6.48 and 51. Also, the word 'watch' occurs once in both accounts. Exod. 14.24 mentions the 'morning watch' while Mark speaks of the equivalent 'fourth watch of the night' in 6.48.

The Greek of Mk 6.47 shows an artistically satisfying juxtaposition by contrasting the location of the boat 'in midst of the sea' and the location of Jesus 'alone on the land'. The next verse mentions that Jesus 'saw that they were distressed in rowing'. This juxtaposition has a parallel in Exodus 14. Here, Israel is in the midst of the sea with the Egyptians in hot pursuit. From the land God sees the Egyptians in pursuit: 'the Lord in the pillar of fire and of cloud looked down upon the host of the Egyptians, and discomfited the host of the Egyptians...' (14.24).

We may summarize the above by saying that the Markan account of the walking on the sea shares a significant number of words with Exodus 14. By my count 32 words in Mark's account are also found in Exodus 14. Thus of the 139 Greek words in Mk 6.45-52, as many as 32 may be quoted from Exodus 14.

However, the picture changes dramatically if we focus our attention upon the pre-Markan narrative. In the paragraph immediately below I have reproduced the Greek text of Mk 6.45-52. In doing so I have

---

1.   In 14.4, 5, 8, 17.

followed Kelber's summary of recent redaction criticism on this narrative by separating vv. 45 and 52 and the last seven words in 6.51 from the rest of the narrative. I have also highlighted the words common to Mark and Exodus 14.

45 καὶ εὐθὺς ἠνάγκασεν τοὺς μαθητὰς αὐτοῦ ἐμβῆναι εἰς τὸ πλοῖον καὶ προάγειν εἰς τὸ πέραν πρὸς Βηθσαϊδάν, ἕως αὐτὸς ἀπολύει τὸν ὄχλον.
46 καὶ ἀποταξάμενος αὐτοῖς ἀπῆλθεν εἰς τὸ ὄρος προσεύξασθαι.
47 καὶ ὀψίας γενομένης ἦν τὸ πλοῖον **ἐν μέσῳ τῆς θαλάσσης**, καὶ αὐτὸς μόνος ἐπὶ **τῆς γῆς**. 48 καὶ **ἰδὼν** αὐτοὺς βασανιζομένους ἐν τῷ ἐλαύνειν, ἦν γὰρ ὁ **ἄνεμος ἐναντίος** αὐτοῖς, περὶ τετάρτην **φυλακὴν τῆς νυκτὸς** ἔρχεται πρὸς αὐτοὺς περιπατῶν **ἐπὶ τῆς θαλάσσης**· καὶ ἤθελεν παρελθεῖν αὐτούς. 49 οἱ δὲ **ἰδόντες** αὐτὸν **ἐπὶ τῆς θαλάσσης** περιπατοῦντα ἔδοξαν ὅτι φάντασμά ἐστιν, καὶ ἀνέκραξαν: 50 **πάντες** γὰρ αὐτὸν **εἶδον καὶ ἐταράχθησαν**. ὁ δὲ εὐθὺς **ἐλάλησεν** μετ' αὐτῶν, καὶ **λέγει** αὐτοῖς, **θαρσεῖτε, ἐγώ εἰμι** μὴ **φοβεῖσθε**. 51(a) καὶ ἀνέβη πρὸς αὐτοὺς εἰς τὸ πλοῖον, καὶ ἐκόπασεν ὁ **ἄνεμος**.
51(b) καὶ λίαν [ἐκ περισσοῦ] ἐν ἑαυτοῖς ἐξίσταντο, 52 οὐ γὰρ συνῆκαν ἐπὶ τοῖς ἄρτοις, ἀλλ' ἦν αὐτῶν ἡ **καρδία** πεπωρωμένη.

Now the picture is quite different. If the 41 words ascribed to Markan redactional activity in vv. 45, 51b and 52 are subtracted from the 139 total, 98 Greek words are left. Of these 98, 30 are also found in Exodus 14.[1] The pre-Markan narrative, then, echoes recurring phrases from Exodus 14, repeats key words from Exodus 14, and shares a few less than one third of its 98 words with Exodus 14! Could this be coincidence? If one story is not quoting another, this heavy concentration of words is difficult to explain.

Yet this is not all. There is evidence that the pre-Markan account is citing another Old Testament passage from the Septuagint. A number of scholars attribute the key term 'walking' to Job 9.8b.[2] While 'walking' is not found in Exodus 14, the same participial form of the same Greek

---

1. How does one count the eight uses of the pronoun 'them' and three of the pronoun 'he' in various cases since both also occur in Exod. 14? When does one count the article and words like καὶ and δέ? I have counted the article only when it appears in the Septuagint with the same noun. The same is true of the καὶ appearing before 'were terrified' in v. 50. I did not count 'them' or 'he', although 'them' is sometimes used for the people of Israel in Exod. 14.

2. See Heil, *Jesus Walking*, pp. 38ff. for an exhaustive discussion. Also Fleddermann, 'Pass By Them', p. 393 n 21.

word as in Mk 6.48 is found in Job 9.8b. Although other Old Testament passages speak of God's dominance over the sea, they do not use the word 'walking'. Further, the context furnishes a reason why Jewish Christians might choose Job 9.8b rather than another passage. In Job 9.8b 'walking' is associated with the recurring phrase ἐπὶ τὴν θάλασσαν that we found in Exodus 14. Only in Job the article (as I noted) is lacking and the case is genitive because God is walking 'on sea as if on ground'. Rabbis would recognize this connection at once as a *gezera shava*, an 'analogy of expressions…based on identical or similar words occurring in two different passages of Scripture'.[1] According to exegetical practice, if one of the passages in which the word is found is obscure, its meaning can be learned from the other passage. Thus, the passage from Job would simply *supplement* the description of God's activity in the deliverance at the sea according to Exodus 14.

The Septuagint of Job may also account for the difficult term 'pass by' in Mk 6.48, since this verb is found in the immediate context of Job 9.8b. In Job 9.11 the RSV reads: 'Lo, he passes by me, and I see him not; he moves on, but I do not perceive him' (ἐὰν ὑπερβῇ με, οὐ μὴ ἴδω. καὶ ἐὰν **παρέλθῃ** με, οὐδ᾽ ὡς ἔγνων). However, this attribution is controversial.

If the formulators of the pre-Markan account associated the passage from Job 9.8b with the Exodus narrative by *gezera shava*, the number of words in common with the Septuagint accounts for exactly one third of the total words used to tell the story.

In addition to common words, phrases and emotions (fear), there are also structural parallels between the pre-Markan account and Exodus.[2] In the preceding discussion I have used the term 'juxtaposition' to describe one such structural parallel. Just as God in Exod. 14.24 'looked down' from 'the pillar of fire and of cloud' and saw the distress of the people of Israel, so Jesus from the mountain or hill 'saw' the distress of the disciples.

A second and more significant structural parallel is the rescue at sea. Just as God rescued the people of Israel from the threatening Egyptians, so Jesus rescues the disciples from the tormenting and harassing wind

---

1.   M. Mielziner, *Introduction to the Talmud* (New York: Bloch, 1968), p. 143.

2.   For a discussion of structural parallels in ancient and biblical narratives see H. Hommel, 'Per aspera ad astra', *Würzburger Jahrbücher für die Altertumswissenschaft* 4 (1949–50), pp. 157-65. Also see C. Westermann, 'Sinn und Grenze religionsgeschichtlicher Parallelen', *TLZ* 90 (1965), cols. 489-96.

(Mk 6.47). Both rescues occur 'in midst of the sea'. Also, both rescues occur at the same time: in the watch preceding the dawn.

A third structural parallel is the life-threatening nature of their respective situations. While no one questions the danger of the people of Israel from Pharaoh, a significant number of New Testament scholars doubt that the disciples were experiencing real danger. Unfortunately most biblical scholars have never sailed a boat or witnessed the effect of wind on the Sea of Galilee. Even today with sophisticated modern sailing equipment it is difficult to enter a harbor or make headway against contrary winds. How much more difficult would have been the plight of first-century sailors in rowing against contrary winds. How severe were the winds and consequent waves? Mark seems to tell us by tying this story to Mk 4.35-41 by the use of four identical words in both narratives: 'and the wind ceased' (Mk 6.51 and 4.39). No one doubts the life-threatening nature of the wind and waves in the story of the stilling of the storm. A *gezera shava* consisting of the four common words ties the two narratives together.

A fourth structural parallel involves the visible presence of God in the Exodus narrative. As the people of Israel saw God in the deliverance at sea, so the disciples saw Jesus walking on the sea. This fourth structural element will be discussed in the following section. Of course, these structural parallels further strengthen the argument that the pre-Markan account was modeled on Exodus 14.

While the usage of common words and structural parallels may seem far-fetched to the modern mind, the Jewish Christians seemed to be following midrashic technique in employing precisely such methods. A good example of this technique is found in a later rabbinic text which makes this kind of comparison between Abraham's gracious actions toward the three angels in Genesis 18 and God's gracious actions toward Israel in the wilderness:

> Thus what Abraham did for God, God did for the children of Israel in the desert. Abraham brought water, and so God gave water to the people to drink through the rock in the desert. Abraham served bread, and the people received manna, bread from heaven. Abraham escorted 'the three men' down toward Sodom, and so God went with the people in the pillars of fire and cloud.[1]

In this careful interplay of words and scenes the actions of God are modeled on the actions of Abraham. So also the Jewish Christians told

---

1. Gärtner, 'John 6', p. 16. For the rabbinic texts see Gärtner's note 1.

of Jesus' mastering the sea by using key words and phrases, emotions and structural parallels from Exodus 14. In listening to the story about Jesus the audience would recall the familiar story of the deliverance at the Reed Sea.

However, while Exodus 14 furnished words and phrases, emotions and structural parallels for the New Testament narrative, its influence went beyond that. The next section will deal with other dimensions of the influence of this passage as well as that of other passages which tell of Israel's deliverance at the sea.

I have said (above) that the story of Israel's deliverance at the sea was not static, but grew and changed with the addition of new exegetical traditions. One such tradition was the visible presence of God in the event. Let us turn now to the Jewish traditions behind the narrative.

The Jewish Tradition

The Exodus story is essentially a theophany in that the presence of God is asserted. For example, in Exod. 14.24 we read: 'the Lord in the pillar of fire and of cloud looked down upon the host of the Egyptians and discomfited the host'. While God is not visible, the effects of his presence, such as the strong east wind and the destruction of Egypt's army, are visible. How do we get from a theophany to a visible presence?

It seems that we need to look here at Deut. 4.34, and that what began with this passage became an exegetical tradition associated with other passages about the deliverance at the sea. Let us begin with the translation of Deut. 4.34 into the Septuagint and the Targums. The RSV translates the Masoretic Text of Deut. 4.34 as follows: 'Or has any god ever attempted to go and take a nation for himself from the midst of another nation, by trials, by signs, by wonders, and by war, by a mighty hand and an outstretched arm, and by great terrors?' However, instead of 'by great terrors' the Septuagint and the Targums read 'by great visions' (ἐν ὁράμασιν μεγάλοις).[1]

The wording of Jer. 32.21 is quite similar to that of Deut. 4.34 and should be considered along with that passage, for the same phenomenon

---

1.   Arndt and Gingrich, *Greek–English Lexicon*, pp. 580-81. The word is used 'of supernatural visions'. The same translation is found in the Targums. For example, M. McNamara and M. Maher also translate the Aramaic with 'with great visions'. See A. Díez Macho, *Neophyti 1*. V. *Deuteronomy* (Madrid and Barcelona: Consejo Superior de Investigaciones Cientificas, 1978), p. 460.

occurs. The RSV translates Jer. 32.21 as follows: 'Thou didst bring thy people Israel out of the land of Egypt with signs and wonders, with a strong hand and outstretched arm, and with great terror'. Instead of 'with great terror' the Septuagint reads 'with great visions' and the Targum 'with a great vision'. Was the Hebrew translated by the Septuagint and the Targums different from the present Masoretic reading?

The use of Deut. 4.34 in the Passover haggadah sheds further light upon the problem. A midrash gives a running commentary on Deut. 26.5-19 to explain the significance of the festival. Louis Finkelstein translated the midrash on the phrase 'with great terror' (Deut. 26.8) as follows:

> This refers to the visible manifestation of the Divine Presence, as it is said, 'Or hath God essayed to go forth to take Him a nation from the midst of another nation, by trials, signs, and by wonders and by war, and by a mighty hand, and by an outstretched arm, and by great terrors' (Deut. 4.34).

In the above comment on the phrase 'with great terror' Deut. 4.34 is cited to support 'the visible manifestation of the Divine Presence'. The midrash 'works' because 'vision' (מראה) and 'terror' (מורא) are very similar to each other in spelling.

Then Finkelstein goes on to say that the appearance of God in visible form was one of the two theological emphases in the haggadah:

> The assertion that God appeared in visible form at the Exodus is a second theological statement of great importance. Like the question of the angels, so the question of the possibility of the appearance of the Deity in visible form was long disputed during the Second Commonwealth.[1]

Finkelstein argues that the original reading of the above passages was 'vision' and not 'terror' on the basis of translations in the Septuagint, the Targums and other versions. He also suggests that, since the tradition of a visible presence was a subject of dispute between the Pharisees and the Sadducees, the rabbinic successors of the Pharisees suppressed the reading 'visions' in the Scripture.

He dates the suppression of the older reading before 100 CE on the basis of Aquila's new Greek translation of the Bible. Aquila, who translated around 100 CE, departs from the Septuagint and renders the

---

1. L. Finkelstein, 'The Oldest Midrash: Pre-Rabbinic Ideals and Teachings in the Passover Haggadah', *HTR* 31 (1938), p. 309. The translation of the midrash is found on p. 297.

phrase as the present Masoretic Text does. Thus 'the controversy regarding God's appearance in visible form is a most ancient one'.[1]

Accordingly, Finkelstein dates the midrash, embedded in the haggadah, far earlier than the suppression of the older reading. However, in a subsequent article S. Stein criticizes Finkelstein's dating and, on the basis of symposia literature from the Greco-Roman world, claims that 'no fixed Seder liturgy was in existence before the second third of the second century CE'.[2]

While Stein confines himself to dating the liturgy, he does not attempt to refute Finkelstein's reasoning. Therefore, the argument that minor changes in the spelling of 'vision' in order to change it to 'terror' were made around 100 CE appears to stand. Also, the exegetical tradition found in the midrash of the haggadah can probably be dated to the first century CE.

I want now to present two later examples of the exegetical tradition that God visibly appeared in the deliverance at the sea. Note how closely the second example approximates the New Testament story.

In commenting on the passage 'this is my God, and I will praise him' (Exod. 15.2c) the *Mekilta deRabbi Ishmael* reads:

> R. Eliezer says: Whence can you say that a maidservant saw at the sea what Isaiah and Ezekiel and all the prophets never saw?...To give a parable for this, to what is this like? To the following: A king of flesh and blood enters a province surrounded by a circle of guards; his heroes stand to the right of him and to the left of him; his soldiers are before him and behind him. And all the people ask, saying: 'Which one is the king?' Because he is of flesh and blood like those who surround him. But, when the Holy One, blessed be He, revealed Himself at the sea, no one had to ask: 'Which one is the king?' But as soon as they saw Him they recognized Him, and they all opened their mouths and said: 'This is my God and I will glorify Him'.[3]

In commenting on Ps. 77.19 the late *Pirke deRabbi Eliezer* reads:

> Rabbi Eliezer said: On the day when He said, 'Let the waters be gathered together' (Gen. 1.9), on that very day were the waters congealed, and... (the people) could see one another, and they saw (ראו) the Holy One,

---

1. Finkelstein, 'Oldest Midrash', p. 311.
2. S. Stein, 'The Influence of Symposia Literature on the Literary Form of the Pesach Haggadah', *JJS* 8 (1957), p. 15.
3. J.Z. Lauterbach, *Mekilta deRabbi Ishmael* (Philadelphia: Jewish Publication Society, 1933), II, pp. 24-25.

blessed be He, walking before them (מהלך לפניהם), but the heels of His feet they did not see, as it is said, 'Thy way was through the sea, thy path through the great waters; yet thy footprints were unseen' (Ps. 77.19).[1]

How much of the above could the early Jewish Christians have known in modeling the pre-Markan account on Exodus 14? If they read Greek, they would know the reading 'with great visions'. If they spoke Aramaic, they might have known the reading 'with great visions' from some early form of the Targums, although such suppositions are precarious. If Finkelstein is correct in stating that a tradition of the visible presence was a subject of dispute between the Pharisees and the Sadducees, they probably knew an early version of the above exegetical tradition. If Gärtner is correct in locating the *Sitz im Leben* of the pre-Markan account in a Christian Passover celebration, they probably knew both the reading 'with great visions' and the exegetical tradition based upon it.

What is the significance of Jewish Christians' knowing about the visible presence of God in the deliverance at the sea? This tradition makes the parallel between the Old Testament narrative and the pre-Markan account even more complete than the interplay of words and structural parallels described in the previous section. As the Israelites saw their God in the midst of the deliverance at the sea, so the disciples saw Jesus in delivering them from the windswept sea.

In Jewish tradition the sea is also understood in ways quite alien to the modern mindset. In referring to the sea, the tradition could view creation and redemption together. Perhaps Isa. 51.9-10 is the classic example: 'Was it not thou that didst cut Rahab in pieces, that didst pierce the dragon? Was it not thou that didst dry up the sea, the waters of the great deep; that didst make the depth of the sea a way for the redeemed to pass over?' Here the creation myth and the exodus are mentioned together. Similarly, the pre-Markan account juxtaposes words from Exodus 14 with Job 9.8b, 'a hymnic description of God's power as creator'.[2]

This juxtaposition tells us how the sea was viewed and understood. Rahab and Leviathan are the sea monsters God slew in creation. In creation God brought order out of chaos. Hence the sea 'represents the

---

1. G. Friedlander, *Pirqe deRabbi Eliezer* (New York: Benjamin Blom, 1971), p. 330. Also see Heil, *Jesus Walking*, p. 51.

2. Heil, *Jesus Walking*, p. 38. So also the comment on Ps. 77.19 in *Pirke deRabbi Eliezer*.

powers of chaos'.[1] Creation, then, is linked with redemption. Again, God mastered the chaotic sea so that his people could escape.

What, then, is the narrative saying when Jesus masters the sea by walking on it and frees his followers from their distress in rowing against it? Here Jesus masters 'the powers of chaos' represented by the windswept sea. Indeed, the use of the verb κοπάζειν in both Markan sea narratives (4.39 and 6.51) also points to the chaos motif. In the Septuagint of Gen. 8.1 this verb describes the subsiding of the flood waters.

In the next section we will see that Jewish Christians saw two additional motifs in the sea-rescue. First, however, we must define with some precision the Jewish Christians to whom we are referring.

The Work of Jewish Christians

To which level of the tradition are we referring? We are concerned with the pre-Markan Greek version of the narrative. If Mark was written in 68 CE or 70 CE we are referring to the Jewish Christians who formulated the account sometime before that date.

Can we know anything further about the situation of these Jewish Christians? With the help of the insights of cultural anthropology, Jerome Neyrey has sketched the *Sitz im Leben* of a comparable group of Jewish Christians behind the Gospel of John. Of course, he is speaking of the Johannine Christians who produced the Signs Gospel. While no one knows the relationship between the pre-Markan account and the pre-Johannine account of the same story in the Signs Gospel, we are concerned with Jewish Christians (whether two groups or the same group) at approximately the same time and perhaps in the same geographical area. Neyrey's comments shed light on the situation of these Jewish Christians. He describes their missionary activity as 'preaching about Jesus, arguments on his behalf from the Scriptures, and the proclamation of his signs'.[2] They retain their memberships in the Synagogue and look upon themselves as faithful Jews. Still, they are different from other Jews in that they see Jesus as the new focus of God's activity and find in Jesus the fulfillment of their Scriptures.

---

1. P.J. Achtemeier, 'Person and Deed: Jesus and the Storm-Tossed Sea', *Int* 16 (1962), p. 174.

2. J. Neyrey, *An Ideology of Revolt* (Phildadelphia: Fortress Press, 1988), p. 122. I am following Neyrey's description on pp. 122-25.

Neyrey's sketch of the Johannine community behind the Signs Gospel supplies a context for a Jewish Christian Passover in that those Jewish Christians remained within the Synagogue and considered themselves to be Jews. Of course, Neyrey's sketch then strengthens Gärtner's suggestion that the *Sitz im Leben* of the pre-Markan narrative was a Christian Passover celebration. What further evidence is there for such a *Sitz im Leben*? First, there is the centrality of the story of the exodus from Egypt in the celebration of Passover. Certainly, a key part of that story is the deliverance through the sea. Secondly, Finkelstein shows that the tradition of the visible presence was known in the first century and earlier. In such a setting, modeling a story about Jesus upon a contemporary understanding of Exodus 14 would be quite natural. On the other hand Achtemeier posits a variant (that is, from the Gospel accounts) Eucharistic celebration as the *Sitz im Leben* of the miracle catenae. This variant celebration may have focused on the miraculous feedings rather than the Passover as the constituting event. In any case, the variant celebration pictured Jesus as the epiphany of a divine man. In addition to the highly speculative nature of the proposal, its primary weakness lies in reading a divine man Christology into the narrative. At the end of this section I shall show that a 'divine man' interpretation of the narrative presents more exegetical problems for the interpreter than it solves. Finally, the whole thrust of our research—modeling one narrative upon another, the meaning of the sea, the apocalyptic background (see below)—points away from any 'divine man' hypothesis!

Further, the Jewish Christian context, as sketched above, enables us to make additional observations about the pre-Markan account. Jewish Christianity apparently linked the chaos motif with the demonic and the powers of darkness. In the Revelation to John, Satan is pictured as a dragon (recall Isa. 51.9) who collaborates with the beast from the sea (Rev. 13.1-10). Recent scholarship has linked the dragon (Satan) with three Old Testament figures: Leviathan, Rahab and another dragon, the enemy of Yahweh mentioned in Isa. 27.1. Thus, the dragon of Revelation is 'the embodiment of chaos'.[1] Characteristically, the dragon fights against the woman with a flood of water (Rev. 12.15). After the dragon is defeated, John pictures a new creation in which 'the sea was no more' (Rev. 21.1). The new creation is safe from the demonic and the chaotic power of the sea.

---

1. J.M. Ford, *Revelation* (AB, 38; Garden City, NY: Doubleday, 1975), p. 199.

In the stilling of the storm (Mk 4.35-41)[1] the connection between the sea and the demonic is quite explicit. In rebuking the sea, Jesus employs a technical term for exorcism.[2] 'In short, Jesus is combating and defeating the demonic powers when he stills the storm just as he does when he exorcises a demon.'[3]

In view of the connections between the two Markan sea stories, such as four identical Greek words in sequence (καὶ ἐκόπασεν ὁ ἄνεμος) in 6.51 and 4.39, the linkage between the demonic and the sea also may be assumed. Nevertheless, no term for exorcism is found.

The narrative of Jesus' mastering the sea (Mk 6.45-52) probably also reflects the apocalyptic mindset of Jewish Christianity.[4] We have seen how this narrative quotes many words from and draws parallels with Israel's deliverance at the sea in Exodus 14. This theological method of drawing parallels (typology) is thoroughly apocalyptic because it presupposes a doctrine of two ages. This present evil age is being superseded by the age of deliverance. Thus, Jesus' temporary mastering of the chaotic, demonic sea both refers back to the first deliverance from Egypt and anticipates the coming great deliverance when the sea will be no more. Like Jesus' whole ministry, mastering the sea is a proleptic realization of the full coming of the kingdom of God.

Finally, in reconstructing the work of early Jewish Christians we face the most difficult issue of all: what were Jewish Christians teaching about Jesus through this narrative? Did they intend this narrative to be an epiphany in which 'the divine power of the divine wonder-worker becomes manifest'?[5] Did they see this as a nature miracle which proved Jesus to be some kind of 'divine man'? I think not.

If the research of Neyrey and others[6] is correct, such a conclusion would be strangely at odds with the context in which it was formulated. Rather, I have argued that this narrative belongs to the world of Jewish

1. Lohmeyer, *Evangelium des Markus*, p. 89. Lohmeyer long ago recognized the Semitic nature of the idiom and parallelism of the narrative.

2. H.C. Kee, 'The Terminology of Mark's Exorcism Stories', *NTS* 14 (1967–68), pp. 232-46.

3. Achtemeier, 'Person and Deed', p. 176. See also T. Suriano, '"Who then is This?"... Jesus Masters the Sea', *The Bible Today* 79 (1975), pp. 449-456. See esp. pp. 450-51.

4. Stegner, *Narrative Theology*, esp. pp. 107-12, for the apocalyptic orientation of early Jewish Christianity.

5. Dibelius, *From Tradition to Gospel*, p. 94.

6. Stegner, *Narrative Theology*, pp. 107-12.

apocalyptic with its exorcisms and wonders. There, exorcisms and wonders do not prove the divinity of the wonder-worker so much as they reveal the power of God working through him. Similarly, in Judaism the rain-making capabilities of Honi, the Circle-Drawer, did not point to his divinity so much as his being a channel for God's actions.

In his exhaustive study of this narrative, John Heil says the following about the phrase ἐγώ εἰμι in Mk 6.50:

> But Jesus is not revealing himself to be God, nor attributing to himself the divine name. Rather, as Yahweh's agent of revelation Jesus reveals Yahweh's will to save his people here and now in the concrete situation of saving his disciples from distress in crossing the sea. The ἐγώ εἰμι, then, signifies the self-identification of Jesus as the revealer of Yahweh.[1]

What further indications confirm Heil's analysis of the Christology of the narrative? The words for 'ghost' (Mk 6.48) and 'pass by' (Mk 6.48) point to a similar conclusion and away from any 'divine man' concept.

The word 'ghost' (φάντασμα) does not seem to support a 'divine man' interpretation for this narrative. In the Septuagint of Job 20.8 the word is translated as 'vision' in the phrase 'a vision of the night'. Although this word is found only in Mk 6.49 and its parallel in Mt. 14.26, Bultmann and Lührmann define it as 'ghost'.[2] The context confirms that translation. Jesus seeks to alleviate the fears of the disciples by identifying himself: 'it is not an unreal φάντασμα whom they see walking on the sea, but Jesus himself'.[3] Let us paraphrase: 'Don't be afraid. I am not a ghost, but Jesus whom you know'. Then, Jesus climbs into the boat! Strange words and stranger activity for a 'divine being'. Further, if walking on water defines a 'divine man', then Peter also belongs to that category (see Mt. 14.29).

Similarly, the term 'pass by' (παρελθεῖν) seems to have lost its epiphanic quality in recent research. Note the context in Mk 6.48. The disciples are distressed in rowing. Jesus comes to them 'walking on the sea'. Then, we read that enigmatic sentence: 'He meant to pass by them'. Why? Lohmeyer turned to the Septuagint and found that the verb 'pass by' designated the action of God in the theophanies to Moses and Elijah recorded in Exod. 33.18-23; 34.5-9 and 1 Kgs 9.9-18. However, H. Fleddermann found that the Septuagint usage was more complex

---

1. Heil, *Jesus Walking*, p. 59.
2. R. Bultmann and D. Lührmann, 'φαντάζω, φάντασμα', *TDNT*, IX, p. 6.
3. Heil, *Jesus Walking*, p. 59.

than Lohmeyer had suspected. 'Pass by' can also mean 'to rescue from disaster' and 'to save'.[1] Fleddermann considers that the latter usage in Amos 7.8 and 8.2 (an infinitive with an object) is much closer to Mk 6.48 than is that of the theophanic passages. Accordingly, Fleddermann translates the sense of the sentence: 'And he wanted to save them' (as already noted).

Pinchas Lapide also challenges the epiphanic interpretation of the word 'pass by' with the following question: 'How can the words "he meant to pass them by" (6.48) be reconciled with his obvious intention to bring them help in their distress?'[2]

Finally, Lapide challenges the 'divine man' theory of interpretation with another question: 'Does not the assertion that Jesus withdraws, as on so many other occasions, in order to "pray" (6.46), conflict with the view, common in later interpretations of the walking on the water, that the incident is to be regarded as a theophany?'[3] If a redaction critic asserts that the withdrawal to pray is a Markan redactional touch (as it probably is), then are we to assume that Mark misunderstood the major thrust of the story he redacted and incorporated into his Gospel? Rather, I would argue that the Jewish Christians did not formulate the story to be an epiphany and Mark did not understand it as such.

From the above we can conclude that interpreting Mk 6.45-52 as an epiphany which reveals Jesus as a 'divine man' raises more questions than it answers. These questions arise because the Jewish Christian formulators did not intent the narrative to be so understood.

Further, if my interpretation of the work of Jewish Christians is correct, significant exegetical problems are resolved. For example, consider the issue of the unity of the narrative. On the one hand, Bultmann projected an 'original motif' and a 'storm motif' that was later added to it, and Lohmeyer projected two independent stories that were combined. On the other hand, the narrative is a unity if Jewish Christians were modeling a story about Jesus on Exodus 14 as that passage was understood in the first century. Exodus 14 emphasizes 'a strong east wind all night' (14.21) and Jewish tradition added a visible presence of God in the event. Also, a number of interpreters have wondered whether there was a real storm. Since the same Greek words for 'and the wind ceased' (with the same word order and tense) in 6.51 are found in the other sea

1.   Fleddermann, 'Pass By Them', p. 391.
2.   Lapide, 'A Jewish Exegesis', p. 35.
3.   Lapide, 'A Jewish Exegesis', p. 35.

rescue narrative in Mk 4.39, we may be sure that there was. Accordingly, Jesus wanted to save or rescue the disciples, not to pass by them. He did save them because as soon as he climbed into the boat 'the wind ceased' (6.51).

Other points of interpretation are also solved. The location of the boat 'in midst of the sea' (6.47) need no longer trouble exegetes since it is quoted from Exodus 14. The disciples are terrified because they think that Jesus is a ghost. Why does Jesus wait until the fourth watch to save them? Again, Exodus 14 supplies the answer. If the form of the story is correctly ascertained, one exegetical problem after another finds its solution.

The Theological Significance of the Story

We are now ready to articulate the theology that the story seeks to convey. Since early Jewish Christians conveyed their theology in narrative form it has been necessary to work through the constituent elements of the story. What then is the narrative saying?

As I have said above, the thrust of the story is complex. On the surface the narrative tells that Jesus walked on the sea to rescue his disciples from the storm that was tormenting them. However, the story about Jesus has been modeled upon Exodus 14 as that passage was understood in the first century. Since key words and phrases from Exodus 14 are quoted the audience would recall the familiar Passover story. Thus, the central thrust of the New Testament narrative is complex and shimmering. In addition to telling about Jesus, it recalls the central event in the life of the Jewish people. Theologically, the main thrust of the story lies in the association of Jesus with the central event of Israel's past. Since the narrative depicts Jesus in a manner similar to Yahweh in mastering the sea by walking on it and by rescuing his people from it, Jewish Christians were saying that the power of God, which had once delivered their ancestors, was now working through Jesus to deliver them. This was a Jewish Christian 'updating' of Passover.

Further, we should note that the Jewish Christians' theology was based on the drawing of parallels (that is, typology) between Jesus and the deliverance at the sea. As Gärtner has noted: 'The salvation of the people out of Egypt is the pattern for the coming salvation'.[1] Jesus then

---

1. Gärtner, 'John 6', pp. 17-18.

reenacts the deliverance at the sea. As Paul writes in 1 Cor. 10.11: 'Now these things...were written down for our instruction, upon whom the end of the ages has come'. Indeed, typology points to the apocalyptic mindset of the people behind the story.

Finally, the rescue of the disciples from the windswept sea indicates more than modern eyes see. In this narrative the defeat of the chaotic and demonic forces associated with the sea is a partial realization of the full salvation that will be finally achieved when the sea is no more.

NARRATED PROPHECY IN MARK 11.12-21:
THE DIVINE AUTHORIZATION OF JUDGMENT

Deborah Krause

Introduction

Recently a variety of biblical critics have called for an expanded examination of the early Christian use of the Jewish Scriptures. In considering the origins of christological confessions, Donald Juel has argued that Scripture was the literature *through* which early Christians understood their faith, not merely what they used to argue on its behalf.[1] In advocating the literary aspects of the Gospels, Frank Kermode has claimed that the Old Testament allowed for 'the creation of fictive history or historicized fiction by the development of ancient narrative germs'.[2] Such suggestions posit that Scripture may have served a generative as well as an apologetic role in the formation of the New Testament literature. Furthermore, such suggestions provide a call to reexamine Scriptural allusions and quotations in the New Testament for their potential function in the formation and organization of New Testament texts as well as their christological significance.

Against this backdrop I seek to examine the presence and function of an Old Testament oracle (Hos. 9.10-17) in Mk 11.12-21. I contend that Mark employs the oracle in order to give form to the narrative of the cursing of the fig tree and the clearing of the temple.[3] I name the

---

1. D. Juel, *Messianic Exegesis: Christological Interpretation of the Old Testament in Early Christianity* (Philadelphia: Fortress Press, 1988), p. 1.

2. F. Kermode, 'New Ways with Bible Stories', in *Poetry, History and Narrative* (Cambridge, MA: Basil Blackwell, 1990), p. 49.

3. The precise nature of the event in the temple as either a reformative cleansing or a prophetic act foreshadowing its doom has long been argued (cf. C.A. Evans, 'Jesus' Action in the Temple: Cleansing or Portent of Destruction?', *CBQ* 51 [1989], pp. 237-70). I use the term 'temple clearing' as it seems to adhere closely to the sense of the verb ἐκβάλλειν, which describes Jesus' actions in Mk 11.15.

appropriation of this oracle 'narrated prophecy'.[1]

The phrase 'narrated prophecy' represents a use of the Old Testament in the New Testament that is distinct from the more commonly discussed hermeneutics of 'prophecy-fulfillment'.[2] The distinction lies in the use of the Old Testament as a poetic means toward characterization and description rather than the use of the Old Testament to underscore a single point: namely, the fulfillment of God's preordained plan in Jesus.

In narrated prophecy an Old Testament oracle is expanded and transformed into the actions and speech of the Gospel story. In this, narrated prophecy does more than prove the fulfillment of an oracle. First, it draws on the tradition of Israel's Scripture to characterize and give form to the narrative. Secondly, it places the narrated oracle in relationship with other Old Testament appropriations in the larger narrative. Hence, the larger narrative works to comment not only on the fulfillment of the received tradition, but to impel the reader to see the Old Testament prophecies in new relationship with one another. The placement of traditions in the narrative functions as an implicit commentary on the characters and situations in the Gospel story.

In this reading I seek to demonstrate how Mk 11.12-21 instances the narration of Hos. 9.10-17. Moreover, I seek to show how a reading of 11.12-21 in light of the oracle addresses some of the traditional problems of form- and redaction-critical interpretations of the unit. First, I will trace the dominant interpretation of the unit as the intercalation of two Jesus traditions and outline a few of its prominent problems. Secondly, employing the methodological categories of Michael Fishbane, I will

---

1.   C.A. Evans has used the phrase 'prophetic narrative' to characterize Acts 2 in light of the Old Testament ('The Prophetic Setting of the Pentecost Sermon', *ZNW* 74 [1983], pp. 148-50). My observations of narrated prophecy in Mk 11 share points of contact with Evans's reading. Like Evans, I understand the Old Testament text (Hos. 9.10-17) to share not only words and themes with the New Testament narrative, but also occasion. Like Evans, I understand that the Old Testament appropriations in Mark have a certain sense of enacting the predicted events of the prophets of old. However, I understand the phrase 'narrated prophecy' to catch the fact that Mk 11.12-21 is infused with prophetic imagery and form, but also the dynamic that in Mark the Hosean oracle has been rendered from one genre (oracle) into another (narrative).

2.   The interpretive tradition of 'prophecy-fulfillment' has been traced in this century to C.H. Dodd's *According to the Scriptures* (London: Nisbet, 1952), and R. Harris's two-volume work *Testimonies* (Cambridge: Cambridge University Press, 1916, 1920).

propose a method for reading Mark in light of the Old Testament and establish the narration of the Hosean oracle. Thirdly, I will suggest how this new reading of Mk 11.12-21 in light of the oracle offers a fresh review and perhaps some resolution of the unit's traditional interpretive problems.

Mark 11.12-21 as a Sandwich: The Form- and Redaction-Critical Examination of the Unit

In 1928 Ernst von Dobschütz described the composition of Mk 11.12-21 as the intercalation of one tradition with another.[1] Since that time the fig tree–temple–fig tree construction has been held to be the premier example of Markan intercalation, or 'sandwiching technique'.[2] The sandwich metaphor describes the insertion of one tradition (in this case, the temple story) in another tradition (in this case, the fig tree cursing, and the report of its withering).[3] The observation of the 'sandwich' construction of Mk 11.12-21 has encouraged the separate examination of the traditions of Jesus' cursing of the fig tree and the clearing of the temple by both form and redaction critics. Some of the interpretive problems that have plagued these examinations are as follows:

1. What is the significance of Jesus' seemingly cruel curse on an inculpable fig tree?[4] Or, why does Mark add the troubling γὰρ

---

1. E. von Dobschütz, 'Zur Erzählerkunst des Markus', *ZNW* 27 (1928), pp. 193-98.

2. W. Telford, *The Barren Temple and the Withered Tree: A Redaction Critical Analysis of the Cursing of the Fig Tree Pericope in Mark's Gospel and its Relation to the Cleansing of the Temple Tradition* (JSNTSup, 1; Sheffield: JSOT Press, 1980), pp. 15-25; J.A. Edwards, 'Markan Sandwiches: The Significance of Interpolations in Markan Narratives', *NovT* 31 (1989), p. 196; and T. Shepherd, 'The Definition and Function of Markan Intercalation as Illustrated in a Narrative Analysis of Six Passages' (PhD dissertation, Andrews University, 1991), p. 209.

3. My contention in the observation of the fig tree and temple stories is not that Mark does not use intercalation or sandwiching as a technique, but rather that in Mk 11.12-21 the traditional formal influence derives from the Old Testament oracle, not merely the manipulation of separate Jesus traditions.

4. The curse of the out-of-season tree has engaged historical speculation by both rationalist and skeptical critics. For example, J.N. Birdsall ('The Withering of the Fig Tree', *ExpTim* 73 [1961–62], p. 191) argues that the disciples misunderstood Jesus' motivation as hunger, and his words to the tree as a curse. Bertrand Russell, on the other hand, in his 1927 essay 'Why I am not a Christian', in R.E. Egner and

clause 'for it was not the season for figs?'[1]

2. What is the relationship between the fig tree units and the temple unit? What is the relationship between the temple actions and the temple teachings?[2]
3. What is the larger relationship between Mk 11.12-21 and the teaching regarding prayer in 11.22-25?[3]

Overall, the examination of Mk 11.12-21 along the lines of the 'sandwich paradigm' has inhibited the interpretation of the formative presence of Scripture in the unit. Although many have noticed the numerous allusions and the quotes of the prophets in Mk 11.12-21 (for example, Hos. 9.10, 16; Mic. 7.1; Jer. 8.13; Isa. 56.7; Jer. 7.11), none have considered how the presence of Scripture might influence the form of the unit, and thereby inform its content.[4]

L.E. Denonn (eds.), *The Basic Writings of Bertrand Russell* (New York: Simon & Schuster, 1961), p. 595, argues that the story of Jesus and the fig tree (along with the Gerasene demoniac) demonstrates Jesus' lack of virtue and wisdom, and thereby makes a dubious reason for following him.

1. For example, L.A. Loise, 'The Cursing of the Fig Tree: Tradition Criticism of Mark 11:12-14, 20-25', *Studia Biblica et Theologica* 7.2 (1977), p. 11; W.J. Cotter, 'For it was not the Season for Figs', *CBQ* 48 (1986), p. 66; R.A. Culpepper, 'Mark 11:15-19', *Int* 34 (1980), p. 179.

2. R. Bultmann is representative of the form-critical position on these problems which he addresses by noting seams and citing editorial activity (*The History of the Synoptic Tradition* [trans. J. Marsh; Oxford: Basil Blackwell, 1963], pp. 36, 218).

3. The relationship of the temple action and teaching to the teaching on prayer is a problem for both Telford (*The Barren Temple*, p. 239) and S.E. Dowd, *Prayer, Power and the Problem of Suffering: Mark 11.22-25 in the context of Markan Theology* (Atlanta: Scholars Press, 1988), pp. 37-55.

4. For example, Telford, *The Barren Temple*, pp. 128-75; H.C. Kee, 'The Function of Scriptural Quotations and Allusions in Mark 11–16', in E.E. Ellis and E. Grässer (eds.), *Jesus und Paulus* (W.G. Kümmel Festschrift; Göttingen: Vandenhoeck & Ruprecht, 1975), pp. 165-88; C. Myers, *Binding the Strong Man: A Political Reading of Mark's Story of Jesus* (Maryknoll, NY: Orbis Books, 1988), pp. 297-306. In particular, Telford and Myers both note that the parallels between Hos. 9.10-17 and Mk 11.12-21 are striking. Myers even refers to Mark's use of Hos. 9.10-17 as 'midrashic'. Yet both maintain the 'sandwich' construction of the unit and ultimately argue for the presence of two separate Jesus traditions. In this they note the Hosean oracle as 'background' material, but miss the significance of the formal similarities between the texts.

Mark 11.12-21 and Hosea 9.10-17: The Narration of Prophecy, or Michael Fishbane's Mantalogical Midrash

As the sandwich metaphor implies, Mk 11.12-21 is composed in such a way that Jesus' actions of casting out and teaching in the Jerusalem temple in 11.15-17 are framed by his cursing of the fig tree in 11.13-14, and a report of the withered fig tree in 11.20-21. Hos. 9.10-17 contains a similar structure in which the prophet's report of YHWH's speech (1) compares seeing Israel to seeing the first fruit on the fig tree in 9.10, (2) threatens to cast Israel out of the Lord's house in 9.15, and (3) claims that Ephraim is withered to its root, and will never bear fruit again in 9.16. When they are compared side by side, the content and structures of the texts correlate roughly as follows:

Hos. 9.10-17	*Mk 11.12-21*
Fig tree	Fig tree
Cast out of the house	Cast out of the temple
Withered root (fig tree)	Withered root of the fig tree

In light of the observation of the structural similarity between Hos. 9.10-17 and Mk 11.12-21, I challenge the 'sandwich' model for the construction of Mk 11.12-21. In response, I propose the presence of exegetical activity in the unit similar to the mantalogical exegesis observed by Michael Fishbane in the Hebrew Bible.[1] Fishbane understands that

---

1. In *Biblical Interpretation in Ancient Israel* (Oxford: Clarendon Press, 1985). The appropriation of Fishbane's methods and criteria into the examination of relationships between Old Testament oracles and Mk 11 requires a caveat. Fishbane himself might well reject the entire project. He argues that the Gospel and Pauline writings use the Hebrew Bible in a decidedly 'unbiblical' way in that 'the dominant thrust of the documents... is that they have fulfilled or superseded the ancient traditum' (*Biblical Interpretation*, p. 10). Fishbane's distinction between the exegetical activity of the Testaments is important from a confessional as well as a historical standpoint. However, methodologically, two points may offer an apology for using his categories within the study of the New Testament. First, Fishbane himself has provided a compelling analysis of Paul's exegesis of Ezek. 43.3 and Num. 12.8 in 1 Cor. 13.8 ('Through the Looking Glass: Reflections on Ezek. 43.3, Num. 12.8 and 1 Cor 13:8', *HUCA* 10 [1986], pp. 63-75). Secondly, in the particular area of mantalogical exegesis, Fishbane presumes the predisposition of later literature to 'fulfill' or resolve the unresolved oracles of earlier literature (*Biblical Interpretation*, p. 465). With regard to mantalogical exegesis, therefore, he establishes a point of similarity if not a point of contact between exegesis of Scripture within both of the Testaments.

Israel's Scripture reflects an exegetical tradition in which older authoritative literature (*traditum*) is appropriated and reworked (*traditio*) in order
to address crises and new situations in which the authoritative tradition
no longer bears the weight of Israel's experience.[1] Mantalogical exegesis
in particular is the appropriation and reworking of oracular literature in
order to present the voice of the deity or prophet speaking anew to a
new situation.[2]

The argued appropriation of Hos. 9.10-17 by Mark is not an explicit
one. It is not introduced or concluded by a formula. Nor is it a direct
quotation. Rather the unit contains an implicit narration of the events
proclaimed in the divine oracles of Hos. 9.10, 15 and 16. Fishbane's
method for establishing exegesis between texts when there are no
objective criteria entails the demonstration of lexical and thematic links,
as well as a rethematization or reorganization of the earlier text.[3] Using
Fishbane's criteria, the method for establishing the presence of Hos.
9.10-17 in Mk 11.12-21 now requires an examination of the form and
content of Hos. 9.10-17, and a demonstration of the lexical and thematic
links between the units. The LXX text of Hos. 9.10-17 will be used to
compare Hosea and Mk 11.12-21, since an examination of Mark's use
of the Old Testament demonstrates that Mark follows a text closely akin
to or identical with LXX text traditions.[4] Overall the comparison will
demonstrate how the divine oracle is reorganized into the speech and
actions of the Gospel narrative.

---

1. *Biblical Interpretation*, p. 15.
2. In terms of Mark's mantalogical midrash on Hos. 9.10-17, it is important to
note that Hos. 9 is an oracle, and Mk 11.12-21 is a Gospel narrative. In Mark the
oracle is transformed into a different genre (prophecy-narrative). Fishbane (*Biblical
Interpretation*, p. 465) claims that mantalogical exegesis which transforms oracles
into non-oracles is 'radical'; however, he offers no specific examples. C. Newsom
('Merkabah Exegesis in the Qumran Sabbath Shirot', *JJS* 38 [1987], pp. 11-37)
demonstrates the appropriation of the Merkabah oracle of Ezek. 1 into the Sabbath
Shirot (the Angel Liturgy) of Qumran, employing Fishbane's categories of analysis.
In this, she provides an early Jewish example of the appropriation of an authoritative
oracle into a non-oracular genre (a liturgical text). Perhaps Fishbane's understanding
of the 'radical' nature of such appropriations may be seen in Newsom's example in
that not only is the Ezekiel oracle transformed into a new historical setting, it is
ascribed a new function.
3. *Biblical Interpretation*, p. 285.
4. Kee, 'Scriptural Quotations', p. 174.

The Form and Content of Hosea 9.10-17

The form of Hos. 9.10-17 is highly problematic in that it contains no introductory formulas. Most commentators maintain that the unit is an audition account similar to those found in Isa. 6.5, and Amos 7.2-3, 5-6.[1] The precise nature of this text as an audition account has been questioned.[2] However, it does present alternating divine speech and prophetic interjection: divine speech in 9.10-13, 15-16; prophetic interjection in 9.14, and perhaps in 9.17. For this investigation it is essential to note that the proposed verses appropriated by Mark are all from the divine speech units (9.10, 15, 16). Hence, Jesus' actions both in cursing the tree and clearing the temple are narrated from divine oracles.

Not only is the form of Hos. 9.10-17 problematic, its content is allusive as well. The references in the unit are highly metaphorical and difficult to clarify (for example the image of Ephraim as a flighty bird, and the references to children as prey). For this reason, it is difficult to discern the exact nature of YHWH's complaint against Israel in the unit. There are, however, two concrete historical references in the text which point toward the judgment of Israel's cultic malpractice. The citation of Baal Peor in 9.10 alludes to Numbers 25 which describes Israel's first apostasy in the Canaanite fertility cult. In 9.15 the reference to Gilgal alludes to Joshua 3–4, in which Gilgal is clearly an important amphictyonic cult center. Hos. 9.15 may also allude to 1 Samuel 11–15. Here Saul is rejected as king at Gilgal, because he used the booty of the Amalekites (against YHWH's will) as sacrifice to YHWH.[3]

In Hos. 9.10-17 the divine and prophetic response to Israel's cultic malpractice is one of unmitigated judgment. The entire account of historical remembrance, cultic malpractice and judgment is framed by

1. For example, H.W. Wolff, *Hosea* (trans. G. Stansell; Hermeneia; Philadelphia: Fortress Press, 1974), p. 162; J.L. Mays, *Hosea* (Philadelphia: Westminster Press, 1969), p. 134; and W. Rudolph, *Hosea* (Gutersloh: Gerd Mohn, 1966), p. 183.

2. Cf. M. Buss, *The Prophetic Word of Hosea* (BZAW, 111; Berlin: Töpelmann, 1969), p. 69; and D. Krause, 'A Blessing Cursed: The Prophet's Prayer for Barren Womb and Dry Breasts in Hosea 9', in D. Nolan Fewell (ed.), *Reading between Texts: Intertextuality and the Hebrew Bible* (Louisville, KY: Westminster Press/John Knox, 1992), p. 193.

3. G. von Rad claims that the 'apparent split between religion and politics in Hosea is a modern distinction' ('Hosea', in *The Message of the Prophets* [trans. D.M.G Stalker; London: SCM Press, 1967], p. 114). This is especially clear in 1 Sam. 15, as the political overtones are clearly mixed with the impropriety of Saul's sacrifice (1 Sam. 15.21).

the metaphor of the fruit on the fig tree (9.10), and the withered root of Ephraim that will bear no fruit (9.16). Overall the fig tree metaphor functions both to recall the rich relationship between YHWH and Israel and to comment upon the barrenness which has resulted from Israel's transgression of that relationship.

The Lexical and Thematic Links between Mark 11.12-21 and Hosea 9.10-17

There are three general points of lexical contact between Mk 11.12-21 and Hos. 9.10–17: (1) the fig tree's being seen and cursed, (2) the casting out of the house, and (3) the report of the withered root of the fig tree. The first observation of lexical connection between the two texts may be seen in Mk 11.13 and Hos. 9.10. Between these verses there are similar verbs of finding and seeing, and connections between the noun for 'figs' or 'fig tree'. In Mk 11.13 Jesus sees (ἰδών) the fig tree (συκῆν), and Jesus finds (εὗρεν) nothing on it. In Hos. 9.10 YHWH remembers finding (εὗρον) Israel like desert grapes, YHWH remembers seeing (εἶδον) their ancestors like the yield of the fig tree (σκοπὸν ἐν συκῇ). In Hosea YHWH is the agent of finding and seeing. In Mark Jesus is the agent.

In Jesus' cursing of the fig tree another lexical link may be seen between Hos. 9.10-17 and Mk 11.12-21. In the narrative of Mk 11.14 Jesus actively curses the tree: 'No one will ever eat fruit from you again'. In the Hosean oracle YHWH reports in Hos. 9.16b that 'Ephraim will not bear fruit'. In each case the line acts as a curse. The Markan appropriation merely acts in the narrative to make the causal connection between the curse and its consequence (the withered root) clearer. Hence, the oracular material of Hos. 9.10-17 is reorganized to fit the new genre of narrative.

A potential thematic connection of the time for figs may also be seen between Hos. 9.10 and Mk 11.13. In Hos. 9.10 a relationship between the fig tree and its season is mentioned in the phrase 'the fig tree...in its pre-season/first season (πρόιμον)'. In Mk 11.13d the lack of figs is explained by the tree's being out of season in the enigmatic γάρ clause: 'for it was not the season/time (καιρός) for figs'. In each case the fig tree is described in relation to its season. In Hosea the fig tree is exceptional on account of its season. In Mark, an exception is made for the fig tree on account of its season. Again, there is a reorganization of the concept of surprising season; however, the idea of the season is maintained between the Hosean oracle and the Gospel narrative.

The second group of lexical and thematic connections between Hos. 9.10-17 and Mk 11.12-21 consists in the connection between YHWH's threat to drive Israel/Ephraim out of YHWH's house (ἐκ τοῦ οἴκου μου ἐκβαλῶ αὐτούς), and Jesus' action of casting out those who sell and buy in the temple (ἤρξατο ἐκβάλλειν). It is true that the reference to 'house' in Hos. 9.15 cannot be equated with the Jerusalem temple. However, interpretations of Hos. 9.15 in the targumic and midrashic literature apply the reference of 'my house' to the sanctuary in Jerusalem.[1] Hence, Mark's association of οἴκου μου in Hos. 9.15 with the Jerusalem temple is not without contemporary analogues.

The lexical connection between Hos. 9.15 and Mk 11.15 is expanded further in Mark's presentation of Jesus' teaching in the temple. Here, Jesus is portrayed as citing two prophecies regarding the temple: Isa. 56.7 ('My father's house shall be a house of prayer for all the nations'), and Jer. 7.11 ('but you have made it a den of robbers'). In light of Hos. 9.15, it is striking that each of the three texts in their larger context share the lemma οἴκου μου. As such, a case may be made that Jesus' teachings in Mk 11.17 are keyed with the Hos. 9.15 oracle around the issue of the house of the Lord. In this, the underlying structure of Hos. 9.15 serves as a bridge for the introduction of the two citations from Isa. 56.7 and Jer 7.11. The overarching midrash concerns the issue of the Lord's house.

The third point of contact between Hos. 9.10-17 and Mk 11.12-21 comes in the report of the withered root. In the Hosean oracle (Hos. 9.16a) YHWH reports: 'Ephraim is sick, its roots (τὰς ῥίζας) are withered (ἐξηράνθη)'. The condition of the withered roots is then associated with the tree's ultimate effect: it will never bear fruit again. In Mk 11.20 the narrative reports the seeing of the tree: 'And they saw the fig tree withered to its root (ἐξηραμμένην ἐκ ῥιζῶν)'. Peter is then reported as having remembered the earlier event and he remarks: 'Look, Rabbi, the fig tree which you cursed has withered (ἐξήρανται)'. In the oracle and the narrative lexical links are evident in the root and its withered condition. Thematic links are evident in the association of the

---

1.   In the Targum the seemingly generic 'house' of Hos. 9.15 is rendered 'Sanctuary'; cf. K.J. Cathcart and R.P. Gordon, *The Targum of the Minor Prophets* (ArBib, 14; Wilmington, DE: Michael Glazier, 1986). In *Lamentations Rabbah*, Proem 4 Hos. 9.15 is employed in a study of the fall of the temple to demonstrate how the Lord drives out those who are unfaithful from the Lord's presence.

withered root and the description of its ultimate effect, rendered in the narrative as a curse.

The Questions of Form and Redaction Criticism in Light of Narrated Prophecy in Mark 11.12-21

As promised earlier, I now move to suggest how a reading of Mk 11.12-21 in light of Hos. 9.10-17 might serve to clarify some of the traditional problems in the interpretation of the unit.

1. Why does Jesus curse an inculpable tree? Or, why does Mark add: 'for it was not the time for figs'? In Mark's story, Jesus is portrayed as physically carrying out the judgment of divine metaphorical speech. Therefore, his actions have a literary, and not a historical, rational basis. For those with ears to hear the Old Testament allusions at work in Mk 11.12-21, Jesus' actions seem less humanly irrational than divinely judgmental. Mark's exegesis places Jesus' actions in continuity with the judgment of YHWH, and the temple cult and its leaders in continuity with apostasizing eighth-century Israel.

Although it is only a thematic connection, the reference to 'early season' or 'pre-season' in the LXX version of Hos. 9.10 might have something to do with Mark's maintenance of the awkward phrase.[1] H.W. Bartsch and E. Schweizer (among others) have argued that Mark's use of καιρός in 11.13 is an eschatological reference.[2] In this understanding, the tree is cursed because it should always bear fruit in the new age. Perhaps this element is present. But if Mark is maintaining a reference to Hos. 9.10 with the phrase, the tree is cursed, not because it is not a 'new age' tree, but rather because it is unlike the surprising tree which YHWH found long ago in the wilderness.

2. What is the relationship between the fig units and the temple unit, and is there any relationship between the temple actions (Mk 11.15-16) and the temple teaching (Mk 11.17)? When Mk 11.12-21 is read in

---

1.   The connection between Hos. 9.10 and Mk 11.13d has been made before by B. Bauer, *Kritik der Evangelischen Geschichte der Synoptiker* (Hildesheim and New York: Georg Olms, 1974 [1842]), III, p. 111.

2.   H.W. Bartsch, 'Die Verfluchung des Feigenbaums', *ZNW* 53 (1962), p. 257; E. Schweizer, *The Good News according to Mark* (trans. D.H. Madvig; Atlanta: John Knox Press, 1970), pp. 232-33. Specifically, Bartsch includes 11.13d in his original apocalyptic sayings, which he understands to have been reframed in terms of Markan eschatology.

relationship with Hos. 9.10-17 the fig tree narratives are of a piece with the temple narrative. Just as in Hosea's prophecy, the references to the fig tree serve to bind the judgment of cultic malpractice with the metaphor of Israel's abundance and blessing. Thereby they help paint a stark contrast between YHWH's care and YHWH's judgment.

Bultmann insists on seeing a seam between Mk 11.16 and 11.17.[1] However, Mark's midrash on 'my house' demonstrates that although there is a shift from judgment to instruction in the verses, there is not necessarily evidence of editorial activity. Instead, the shared lemma of οἴκου μου demonstrates a fundamental connection between the act of judgment and the teaching. The entire complex of tradition serves to reflect on the house of the Lord: both what it is and what it is intended to be.

3. What is the larger relationship between Mk 11.12-21 and the teaching on prayer in Mk 11.22-25? Holding fast to the 'sandwich' construction, Telford maintains that vv. 24-25 are secondary additions.[2] Dowd uses the sandwich construction as well, but challenges that the reference to 'house of prayer' in 11.17 is picked up in 11.24 in Jesus' teaching on prayer.[3] A reading of Mk 11.12-21 outside of the sandwich construction and in light of Hos. 9.10-17 underlines the fact that the house of the Lord has been extended beyond the confines of the Jerusalem temple. The introductory 'house' from Hos. 9.15 provides a bridge whereby Mark can move from the complete condemnation of the temple cult, to the extension of hope for a house of prayer for all the nations through Isa. 56.7.

Conclusion

The narrated prophecy of Hos. 9.10-17 in Mk 11.12-21 functions on several levels. First, the appropriation of the divine speech units of the Hosean oracle and their reorganization into the narrative connects the judgment of Israel's malpractice in the ancient tradition with the situation in Jerusalem during Mark's time. In this sense, the narrated prophecy may work to address the crisis in the temple around 70 CE by historicizing the curse of the oracle. Here, Fishbane's understanding of how authoritative tradition is appropriated and reworked in times of

---

1. *History of the Synoptic Tradition*, pp. 36, 218.
2. *The Barren Temple*, p. 239.
3. *Prayer, Power and the Problem of Suffering*, pp. 37ff.

social, religious and political crisis is particularly pertinent. The precise relationship between Mark's community and the Jerusalem temple cannot be known. However, Mark's appropriation of an ancient tradition regarding the judgment of cultic malpractice and his narration of this tradition in Jesus' actions may be seen as connecting the crisis in the temple with the tradition of YHWH's judgment of the cult.

Secondly, Mark's portrayal of Jesus' enactment of the divine speech units aligns Jesus' authority in the judgment with that of YHWH. In this light, the portrayal of the chief priests, scribes' and elders' question in Mk 11.28 ('By what authority do you do these things? Or who gave you the authority to do them?') functions as a self-indictment. Anyone with ears to hear or eyes to see the scriptural tradition in Jesus' actions knows precisely within whose authority he acts.

Finally, the narrated oracle functions as a bridge for the presentation of the direct quotes from Isa. 56.7 and Jer. 7.11 through the shared lemma οἴκου μου. In this, the oracle serves to connect the judgment against the temple cult with the vision of the temple as a house of prayer for all the nations. To this end, Hos. 9.10-17 connects the actions in the temple with the teaching on prayer in Mk 11.22-25. This combination of Old Testament tradition through the Hosean oracle finally serves a function beyond curse and judgment. It is an implicit commentary which extends hope. The temple is portrayed as withered and dry in Jesus' enactment of the oracle; however, the power of prayer is extended in its stead through the midrash on the Lord's house.

APPENDIX

Hosea 9.10-17[1]

10   Like grapes in the wilderness, *I found Israel.*
      Like the first fruit on the fig tree,
      in its first season, I saw your ancestors.
      But they came to Baal Peor,
      and consecrated themselves to a thing of shame,
      and became detestable like the thing they loved.

11   Ephraim's glory shall fly away like a bird—
      no birth, no pregnancy, no conception!

12   Even if they bring up children,
      I will bereave them until no one is left.
      Woe to them indeed when I depart from them!

13   Once I saw Ephraim as a young
      palm planted in a lovely meadow,
      but now Ephraim must lead his children for slaughter.

14   Give them, O Lord—what will you give?
      give them a miscarrying womb and dry breasts.

15   Every evil of theirs began at Gilgal;
      there I came to hate them.
      Because of the wickedness of their deeds
      I will drive them out of my house.
      I will love them no more;
      all their officials are rebels.

16   *Ephraim is stricken,*
      their root is dried up,
      they shall not bear fruit.
      Even though they give birth,
      I will kill the cherished offspring of their womb.

17   Because they have not listened to him,
      my God will reject them;
      they shall become wanderers among the nations.

---

1.   Translation from the NRSV.

Mark 11.12-21[1]

12 On the following day, when they came from Bethany, he was hungry. 13 Seeing in the distance a fig tree in leaf, he went to see whether perhaps he would find anything on it. When he came to it he found nothing but leaves, for it was not the season for figs. 14 He said to it, 'May no one ever eat fruit from you again'. And his disciples heard it.

15 Then they came to Jerusalem. And he entered the temple and began to drive out those who were selling and those who were buying in the temple, and he overturned the tables of the money changers and the seats of those who sold doves; 16 and he would not allow anyone to carry anything through the temple. 17 He was teaching and saying, 'is it not written, My house shall be a house of prayer for all the nations? But you have made it a den of robbers.' 18 And when the chief priests and the scribes heard it, they kept looking for a way to kill him, because the whole crowd was spellbound by his teaching. 19 And when evening came Jesus and his disciples went out of the city.

20 In the morning as they passed by, they saw the fig tree withered away to its roots. 21 Then Peter remembered and said to him, 'Rabbi, look! The fig tree that you cursed has withered.'

1.   Translation from the NRSV.

WITHERING FIG TREES AND PROGRESSION IN MIDRASH

George Wesley Buchanan

Christians have traditionally claimed that the promises that were made in the Hebrew Scripture had been fulfilled in the New Testament. Indeed, much of the New Testament was written in midrashic form, based on the belief that the Hebrew Scripture was the word of God that contained numerous promises that either had been fulfilled or would be fulfilled in the days of the authors. This belief was not a new design of early Christians. It was a belief at least as old as Isaiah of Jerusalem in the eighth century BC. Many parts of the Hebrew Scripture were composed as commentaries on earlier texts, and by New Testament times there were long series of literary compositions that were interrelated. It is important to discover where each midrash fits into the series in order to interpret that text accurately. This essay is designed to show how the identification of midrashic background contributes to the understanding of one New Testament passage. It will help explain why Jesus was so badly disappointed that he cursed a fig tree for not bearing ripe fruit out of season. Preparation for that analysis involves a rapid survey of the historical exegesis of the text on which Jesus depended, showing the way that earlier authors used scriptural texts that had been composed still earlier. At first Jeremiah 17 will be compared to Psalm 1, showing that Ezekiel based his prophecy on Psalm 1 and Jeremiah 17. Summarily, passages from Joel and Zechariah will be shown as prophecies based on Ezekiel 47, but the main emphasis will be given to the New Testament illustration of the expectation that Ezekiel's prophecy would soon be fulfilled in the Kidron Valley, east of the temple area, and that the Mount of Olives would be split in two, just as Zechariah prophesied. In the text that follows the words or their synonyms that exist in both texts are italicized.

Jeremiah's Use of Psalm 1

Text

Jeremiah 17

7 *Blessed* (ברך) *is the man* (גבר) *who* trusts in Yahowah, and Yahowah has been his trust.

Psalm 1

1 *Blessed* (אשרי) *is the man* (האיש) *who* trusts in Yahowah, who does not walk in the council of the wicked; in the way of the sinners he does not stand, and in the meeting of the scornful does not sit, 2 but his desire is with the Torah of Yahowah; with the Torah he meditates day and night.

8 *He will be like a tree planted by water; by* a stream (יובל) it sends out its roots. It is not afraid when heat comes. *Its leaves* will be green. *In* the year of drought it will not worry, and will not cease producing *fruit.*

3 *He will be like a tree planted by* streams of *water* that produces its fruit *in* its season, and *its leaves* do not wither (יובל). All that he does will succeed.

Commentary

Although most scholars[1] have presumed that the Psalmist used Jeremiah, it is not certain from these brief passages alone whether the Psalm is the text used by Jeremiah or whether it was Jeremiah that was the source for the Psalm.[2] Many words are identical, but others are synonyms. For

1.   M. Dahood (*Psalms I* [AB, 16; Garden City, NY: Doubleday, 1965], p. 2) argues that the correct translation Ps. 1.1 is 'How blest is the man who has not entered the council of the wicked/Nor in the assembly of sinners stood'. He rendered דרך 'assembly' rather than 'way' on the basis of Ugaritic.

2.   Dahood (*Psalms I*, p. 4), W.R. Taylor ('The Book of Psalms', *IB*, IV, p. 18) and N.M. Sarna (*The Psalms* [New York: Schocken Books, 1969], p. 851) followed C.A. Briggs (*A Critical and Exegetical Commentary on the Book of Psalms* [ICC; Edinburgh: T. & T. Clark, 1914], I, p. 6) in thinking that the author of this Psalm was adapting material taken from Jer. 17, neither noticing the midrashic characteristics of Jeremiah's narrative. On the basis of his conviction that the Psalmist used Jer. 17, Sarna classified Ps. 1 among the post-exilic Psalms. A.F. Kirkpatrick (*The Book of Psalms* [3 vols.; Cambridge: Cambridge University Press, 1917], I, pp. 3-4) did not even notice a relationship between the two passages. J. Bright (*Jeremiah* [AB, 21; Garden City, NY: Doubleday, 1965], p. 119) did not try to discern which text was the source of the other. He noted that Jer. 17 contained 'a bit of poetry (vss. 5-8) contrasting the righteous and the wicked, very similar in thought to Ps I'. He thought it was impossible to date any of the parts used in Jer. 17, and he believed that there were several small fragments involved. This suggests the midrashic character of that chapter. J.P. Hyatt ('The Book of Jeremiah', *IB*, V, p. 951) followed H. Gunkel (*Die*

example, Jeremiah has different Hebrew words for 'blessed' and 'man' than the Psalm has. The same root is employed by Jeremiah to mean 'stream' and by the Psalm to mean 'wither'. The high percentage of identical words and synonyms shows that one is dependent upon the other without determining which way the dependency lies. Further insight, however, appears in the following verses which continue the passages from Jeremiah quoted above:

Text

Jeremiah 17	Psalm 1.3
9 The heart is more deceptive than anything; it is dangerously corrupt. Who can understand it? 10 I, Yahowah, search the heart and test the emotions, giving to each according to his way, according to the *fruit* of his work. 11 [Like] a partridge [that] broods on its eggs but hatches none of them; [so is one] who makes wealth unjustly. When he has finished half of his days it will abandon him, and, at the end, he will be a fool [a *withered* one, נבל]. 12 A glorious throne, exalted from the beginning, the place of our sanctuary, 13 the hope of Israel, Yahowah. All who forsake you will be put to shame. Those in the land who turn away from me will be recorded, because they have forsaken the source of living *water*, Yahowah. 14 Heal me, Yahowah, and I will be healed. Save me, and I will be saved, for you are my praise.	that produces *fruit* in its season its leaves do not *wither* (יובל) like a tree planted by streams of *water*

Commentary

These last verses from Jeremiah[1] show that Jeremiah quoted and commented on Psalm 1 rather than vice versa. He not only quoted from the Psalm initially, but he also picked up the words 'fruit', 'wither' and 'water' from Ps. 1.3 and commented on them further. His was a narra-

---

Psalmen [Göttingen: Vandenhoeck & Ruprecht, 1926], p. 3) in concluding that 'the poem here [in Jer. 17] is more original and more spiritual than Ps 1'. He did not say why he thought that.

  1.   The translation of v. 11 follows the argument given by J.F.A. Sawyer, 'A Note on the Brooding Partridge in Jeremiah xvii 11', *VT* 28 (1978), pp. 324-29.

tive midrash. This is a normal way for rhetoricians, preachers or rabbis to exegete a text. Jeremiah paraphrased the Psalm, using synonyms for 'blessed' and 'man'. He also paraphrased Ps. 1.3. The Psalmist had said the man would be like a tree that 'produces its fruit in its season'. Jeremiah said it would not cease bearing fruit, by which he meant the same thing. It would not dry out from hot summers; it would survive and produce, year after year. The fact that Jeremiah used the expression לא ימיש, 'will not cease', justified Ezekiel in spelling out further the significance of this wonderful performance. Reasoning like a lawyer studying a contract, he argued that if it did not cease it would bear fruit all the year around, twelve months of the year. This was his claim in his midrash on Jeremiah.

Ezekiel's Midrash

Text

Ezekiel 47

1 He returned me to the door of the temple. Now look! *Water* was flowing out from under the temple toward the eastern threshold of the temple, because the face of the temple was east. The *water* went down under the south side of the threshold, south of the altar. 2 He brought me out by *way* of the north gate, and he brought me around by *way* of the north gate, and he brought

me around by the outside *way* to the outer gate in the *way* that faces east. Now look! Water was running from under the south threshold.

3 The man went eastward with a line in his hand, and he measured a thousand cubits. Then he brought me across through *the water* ankle-deep. 4 Then he measured a thousands cubits, and he brought me across through the water. It was knee-deep. He measured a thousand cubits, and he brought me through [the water]. It was hip-deep. 5 Then he measured a thousand, [and it was] a river which I was not able to cross, because the water had risen. The water [in

Psalm 1 and Jeremiah 17

He will be like a tree planted by *water* (Jer. 17.8)
He will be like a tree planted by streams of *water* (Ps. 1.3)

In the *way* of sinners he does not stand (Ps. 1.1)

I, Yahowah, search the heart, testing the emotions, giving to each one according to his *way*, according to the *fruit* of his works (Jer. 17.10)

which] they could swim, a stream that could not be crossed.

6 He said to me, 'Do you see, son of man?' Then he led me and brought me back to the bank of the river. 7 When he brought me back, Look! On the bank of the river were very large trees on both sides.

8 He said to me, 'This water goes out to the eastern region and goes down along *the Arabah* (בערבה) and goes seaward, to the sea. *The water* which goes out *is healed*.

He is like a shrub in *the Arabah* (בערבה) (Jer. 17.6).
Heal me, Yahowah, and I will be *healed* (Jer. 17.14).

9 Every living soul which squirms will be wherever the river goes, [and] it will live, and there will be very many fish because this water will come there, and it will heal [them]. There will be life wherever the river goes. 10 It will happen that fishermen will stand alongside it from Ain Geddi to Ain Egliam. They will be spreading nets for very many kinds of fish, like fish of the Great Sea. 11 Its swamps and marshes [the water] will not heal. They will be left for salt. 12 Alongside the river will grow up along its banks on both sides every *tree* for food. Its *leaf will not wither*, and *its fruit* will not fail. It will produce (יבכר) every month, because its *water* from the temple goes out, and there will be *fruit* for food and *leaves* for *healing*.

He will be like a *tree* planted by *water* (Jer. 17.8; Ps. 1.1). that produces *its fruit* in its season, and *its leaf will not wither* (Ps. 1.3).

In the year of drought, it will not worry, and will not cease producing (מעשות ימיש) *fruit* (Jer. 17.9).

Commentary

Psalm 1 is a wisdom Psalm. It narrates in parallel, however, the opposite effects of opposite character. The good man will receive blessings and the evil man will be cursed. Jeremiah was concerned for the future of Judah. He feared that the people were so wicked that the Lord would remove their heritage and make them slaves in a foreign land (Jer. 17.1-4). Paraphrasing Psalm 1 he justified his prophecy on this text. He even introduced his message with: 'Thus said Yahowah' (Jer. 17.4),[1] meaning

1. For a justification for this pronunciation of the Tetragrammaton, see G.W. Buchanan, 'Some Unfinished Business with the Dead Sea Scrolls', in F. Garcia

that his message was from the Lord. He knew that, because he had taken it from Scripture.[1] Just as the Psalmist said, those who trusted in human flesh would perish, and those who trusted in the Lord would be blessed (Jer. 17.5-7). Jeremiah called special attention to the curses that were promised for the wicked.

Ezekiel had a different purpose in mind for his message. His message was not just one of basic wisdom. Nor was it a prophecy of doom. He had a vision of the new, restored promised land, especially the area around the temple. Whereas Jeremiah compared the wicked man to a shrub in the Arabah, Ezekiel visualized the Arabah not as a dried-up wilderness but as a prosperous land watered by a river that streamed from the temple. It was not the curses from Psalm 1 in which Ezekiel was interested; it was the blessings. The restored land would be blessed by water just as the Psalmist said a tree would be blessed with an abundance of water. He was already thinking of the new blessed land before he began to think of Psalm 1 and Jeremiah 17.[2] Therefore he did not analyze the text objectively, but took only those words and promises that supported his convictions. He took words like 'tree', 'water', 'fruit' and 'Arabah' to describe the blessings associated with Psalm 1 and Jeremiah 17.[3]

Martínez and E. Puech (eds.), *Mémorial Jean Carmignac* (*RevQ*, 49–52; Paris: Gabalda, 1988), pp. 411-20.

1. For a demonstration of the way Jeremiah quoted earlier Scripture, using such documentary phrases as 'thus said Yahowah' or 'said Yahowah', see G.W. Buchanan, 'The Function of Agency and the Formation of Canon', *Explorations* 8 (1990), pp. 63-79.

2. S. Niditch ('Ezekiel 40-48 in a Visionary Context', *CBQ* 48 [1986], pp. 208-24) followed J.D. Levenson (*Theology of the Program of Restoration of Ezekiel 40–48* [Missoula, MT: Scholars Press, 1976] in relating Ezek. 47 to Gen. 2. Neither scholar, however, noted the midrashic connection between Ezekiel and either Jeremiah or Ps. 1. Several scholars think Ezek. 40–48 is a separate unit, distinct from the rest of the book, and not all of them consider Ezekiel to have been its author. M. Greenberg ('The Design and Themes of Ezekiel's Program of Restoration', *Int* 38 [1984], pp. 181-208), however, is one of those who think that Ezekiel wrote the entire prophecy, even though it was composed at different times. He even thinks that chs. 40–48 consist of several individual units, all of which were written by Ezekiel. For this essay, it does not matter whether Ezekiel wrote Ezek. 47 or not. The phenomenon that is important is that it was developed midrashically, using Ps. 1 and Jer. 17 as sources. By the New Testament times Ezek. 47 was accepted as the word of Ezekiel and the word of God, and Matthew reported that Jesus considered it valid prophecy.

3. H.G. May ('The Book of Ezekiel', *IB*, VI, pp. 325-28) did not notice any

Ezekiel planned his essay on the basis of both Psalm 1 and Jeremiah 17. Some words occurred in both Jeremiah and in Psalm 1. Others were unique to one or the other. Ezekiel began his midrash commenting on the words 'water' and 'way', both of which occurred in both of his sources. Continuing to emphasize the word 'water', Ezekiel next used the word 'heal', which appeared only in Jeremiah's text. Ezekiel's third step was to comment on 'tree', 'wither', 'fruit' and 'leaf'. 'Fruit', 'tree' and 'leaf' come from both Jeremiah and the Psalm, but the term 'wither' occurs only in Psalm 1. 'Healing' comes only from Jeremiah. Ezekiel could not have prepared this entire midrash as he did if he had not had both Scripture passages at his disposal. Without Jeremiah he would not have had a basis for his message on healing. Transformation of salt water to fresh water does not automatically call for the word 'healing'. Jeremiah told of this tree that survived the drought, but he did not call its survival 'not withering', as the Psalmist did. Jeremiah's interpretation of Psalm 1 was important to Ezekiel. The Psalmist said that this well-irrigated tree would produce fruit 'in its season'. This means that it would produce every year. It would not dry up and die for lack of moisture. Jeremiah paraphrased that sentence to say that it would 'not cease bearing fruit'. By that he meant it would keep on bearing even in dry years. The legalist Ezekiel, however, took that to mean that the tree would have green leaves and fruit all the year around. If it never ceased, and its leaf would always be green, as Jeremiah said, then there must be fruit and leaves every month of the year.

For Jeremiah, all of this description was given to characterize the man who trusted in Yahowah. The same was true of his source, Psalm 1. Ezekiel, however, took these texts as bases for his prophecy on the way life would be in the restoration of the kingdom of Israel. At that time the water would follow the river beds from the temple to the Dead Sea and would perform miracles all along the way. The water in the Dead Sea would become fresh, all except a few small ponds which would produce the necessary salt for the nation. The stream from the Kidron Valley to the Dead Sea would have trees on its banks that would be nourished like the tree about which the Psalmist and Jeremiah spoke. It was Jeremiah's slight change in words that permitted Ezekiel to visualize the trees that would grow in the new Judah.[1] Ezekiel thought Jeremiah was right

relationship between Ezek. 47 and either Ps. 1 or Jer. 17.

1.   K.P. Darr ('The Wall around Paradise: Ezekelian Ideas about the Future', *VT* 37 [1987], pp. 271-79) correctly observed that Ezekiel's vision was not universal. The

when he said that the leaf would be green, and the trees would continue to produce. Ezekiel's interpretation of Jeremiah provided the basis for Jesus to look for signs of the new age in the Kidron Valley just before Passover. If this was the beginning of a new age the trees should be green and there should be an abundance of fruit at any time of the year.

Ezekiel's Commentators

The identification of the productive stream, flowing from the temple area, seems to have been widely accepted on the basis of Ezekiel's authority. For example, Joel anticipated a great battle in the Kidron Valley where the Lord would lead the Jews in their battle against all of the Gentile nations which would be gathered there to destroy Jerusalem. At that time the Lord would annihilate the wicked Gentile soldiers, including the destruction of the Edomites and the Egyptians (Joel 4.19-20). The Jews would regain possession of the promised land and the new age would begin. The sign of its beginning would be the productiveness of the land which would flow with milk and wine. Stream beds would be filled with water, and, following Ezekiel, there would be a fountain of water that would flow from the temple area and fill up the river of Shittim into which the Kidron stream would flow (Joel 4.18). That was evidently the river of which Ezekiel spoke that would run southeast into the Dead Sea.

Following Ezekiel, Zechariah also looked forward to the time when the water would flow from the temple. Half of this water would run eastward, as Ezekiel promised, but the other half would run toward the Mediterranean Sea. This stream would not dry up in the summer as many streams did. It would flow all the year around (Zech. 14.8). Zechariah did not say that there would be fruit trees all the year around producing fruit, as Ezekiel had, but on the basis of the ever-present water and the Psalmist's observation about the way trees grew by streams of water, that would be the natural sequel. These aspirations were based on earlier Scripture upon which Ezekiel, Joel and Zechariah depended. It was not a reality in their own day. In the age during which all of these prophets lived, the stream in the Kidron Valley did not flow all the year around, and trees in Jerusalem did not produce fruit every month of the year, but since there were promises in the Hebrew Scripture that could be understood that way, these prophets prepared

blessings were to be fulfilled within the boundaries of the promised land for Jews alone.

their prophecies on the assumption that the Scripture would all be fulfilled in the age to come, that is, in the days of the messiah. Their eschatology was based on the written word of God.

The Expectations of Jesus

Introduction

No one has ever explained the narrative about the fig tree incident in a way that is pleasing to Christians. According to the Gospel report, Jesus seems to have behaved as if the tree were personally responsible for its condition. This seemingly impulsive behavior on Jesus' part seems less than mature, and the idea that it could happen seems ridiculous. The text is as follows:

> Early the [next] morning after he had gone into the city, he was hungry, and he saw a fig tree along the way; he came to it; he found nothing on it but leaves; and he said to it, 'No longer will any fruit come from you in the age [to come].' Then the fig tree suddenly withered. When the disciples saw [it] they were surprised and said, 'How [could] the fig tree be withered suddenly?' Jesus answered and said to them, 'I tell you under oath,[1] if you have faith and do not doubt, you will not only do that [which happened] to the fig tree, but even to this mountain you will say, 'Be taken up and thrown into the sea,' and it will be done, and everything which you ask in prayer, believing, you will receive' (Mt. 21.18-22; doubled in 17.20).

Scholarly Reactions

Comparatively few scholars have written extensively about Jesus' reaction to the fig tree, and those who have written about it at all have reacted in different ways. Some have bypassed the historical problem to offer ethical or theological explanations; others have tried to defend the narrative's reliability; still others have frankly said that they are puzzled by the report. Many[2] followed Victor of Antioch in saying that this was

---

1. The word 'amen' is a court term, used when taking an oath (see Num. 5.1-22; b. Šeb. 29b).

2. R.H. Gundry (*Matthew: A Commentary on his Literary and Theological Art* [Grand Rapids: Eerdmans, 1982], p. 416), W.L. Lane (*The Gospel according to Mark* [Grand Rapids: Eerdmans, 1974], p. 400), L. Sabourin (*The Gospel according to St Matthew* [Bandra, Bombay: St Paul's Press, 1982], p. 765), J.P. Meier (*Matthew* [Wilmington, DE: Michael Glazier, 1980], p. 237), A.W. Argyle (*The Gospel according to Matthew* [Cambridge: Cambridge University Press, 1963], p. 159), and T.H. Robinson (*The Gospel of Matthew* [London: Hodder & Stoughton, 1928], pp. 173-74) followed the same course. For a thorough study of secondary sources

an acted parable which Jesus used to set forth the judgment that was about to be inflicted in Jerusalem. Taylor[1] thought that a parable had been transformed into a legend and attached to a withered fig tree on the way to Jerusalem. Others[2] said that it was not figs Jesus was looking for but 'fruits of righteousness in the holy city'. Bartsch[3] thought that this was a symbolic miracle intended to instruct the nearness of the passion and resurrection. Schweizer also thought that it was symbolic.[4] McLaughlin[5] suggested that Jesus was angry because the tree had been deceptive: 'So the fig tree was not punished for not having fruit primarily but for falsely professing to have it.' Mounce thought that the words of Jesus were more of a prediction than a curse: 'History has demonstrated repeatedly that dead formalism leads to institutional decay'.[6] Meyer suggested that when Jesus saw the tree had leaves he naturally expected to find fruit, and when there was none he was disappointed.[7] Hyvernat and Slater[8] both said that there were figs that

see W.R. Telford, *The Barren Temple and the Withered Tree* (JSNTSup, 1; Sheffield: JSOT Press, 1980), pp. 1-18.

1.   V. Taylor, *The Gospel according to Mark* (London: Macmillan, 1955), pp. 458-59.

2.   D.J. Harrington, *The Gospel according to Matthew* (Collegeville, MN: Liturgical Press, 1983), p. 84; F.W. Beare, *The Gospel according to Matthew* (San Francisco: Harper & Row, 1981), p. 419; H.N. Ridderbos, *Matthew* (trans. R. Togtman; Grand Rapids: Zondervan, 1987), p. 390; R.V.G. Tasker, *The Gospel according to Matthew* (Grand Rapids: Eerdmans, 1976), p. 201.

3.   H.W. Bartsch, 'Die "Verfluchung" des Feigenbaums', *ZNW* 53 (1962), pp. 256-60. Bartsch's major point was his attempt to prove that Bultmann was wrong in considering the Matthaean version of this pericope to be original and the Markan unit secondary. He correctly noted that the Markan version was much like a *chreia*, but he failed to observe that Matthew's was nearer to that form, lacking the interpretive comment 'For it was not the season for figs'.

4.   E. Schweizer, *The Good News according to Mark* (Atlanta: John Knox, 1970), pp. 230-35.

5.   G.A. McLaughlin, *Commentary on the Gospel according to Saint Matthew* (Chicago: Christian Witness, 1909), p. 293.

6.   R.H. Mounce, *Matthew* (San Francisco: Harper & Row, 1976), p. 203.

7.   H.A.W. Meyer, *Critical and Exegetical Hand-Book to the Gospel of Matthew* (repr.; Winona Lake: Alpha, 1970 [1883]), p. 366. Meyer listed other scholars who followed Chrysostom in holding that Jesus was not fooled by the tree, but only acted as he did to provide the occasion for a miracle.

8.   W.F. Slater, *St Matthew* (Edinburgh: T.C. and E.C. Jack, n.d.), pp. 263-64; H. Hyvernat, 'Fig and Fig-Tree', *JewEnc*, V, p. 382.

remained on the tree after the leaves had fallen. Tasker pleaded that *'Some* fruit usually appeared on the fig trees *before* the leaves',[1] but gave no evidence for his belief. The best basis for this argument would have been Pliny the Elder, who said that the fig tree was peculiar in that it produced fruit before leaves (*Hist. Nat.* 16.40), but he did not claim that the fruit at Passover time would be ripe enough to eat.

New Testament scholars sometimes overlook Jewish customs, expectations and literature of New Testament times. For example, it is unlikely that figs of the previous season would have continued to hang on the tree after the new leaves had appeared, especially in a country where gleaners were allowed to pick the fruit left after the tree had been shaken once. Furthermore, Rabbi Shimon ben Gamaliel said that normally 50 days elapsed between the time when fig leaves appeared and the time when there was green fruit. Other rabbis said that there were either 40 or 50 days between the time of the first appearance of leaves and the trees' blooming; it took another 40 or 50 days for the green fruit to appear and still another 40 or 50 days until there was ripe fruit—a total of about 120–150 days from the first appearance of leaves until there would be ripe fruit (*y. Šeb.* 35d). Even if the rabbis were not exactly accurate in the number of days they prescribed, there certainly was a period of time between the appearance of leaves and the harvesting of figs. Since Jesus was a native Palestinian it is reasonable to assume that he knew that normally there should be several weeks between the first leaves and the first ripe fruit. Therefore Jesus should not have been deceived by the leaves into thinking there was fruit on the tree, ready to eat. Some figs ripened in June, but the largest harvest of figs came in August.[2]

Johnson was correct in saying that 'The story has raised many questions in the minds of the readers'. He asked: 'Was it like Jesus to curse the fig tree, particularly if, as Mk 11.13 says, "it was not the season for figs"?'[3] Patte agreed that it was not, but neither Patte[4] nor Johnson had

1. Tasker, *Matthew*, p. 201.

2. Hyvernat, 'Fig and Fig-Tree', p. 382.

3. S.E. Johnson, *The Gospel according to St Matthew* (New York: Abingdon Press, 1951), p. 506.

4. D. Patte, *The Gospel according to Matthew* (Philadelphia: Fortress Press, 1987), p. 292. Patte later strained to relate this story to the tenants (Mt. 21.34-35) since the latter did not pay rent when it was due. He said, 'The servants are sent while it is not quite "the time for fruit"' (p. 299). M.-J. LaGrange (*Evangile selon Saint Matthieu* [Paris: Gabalda, 1948], pp. 404-405) also had more questions than answers.

a satisfying answer to the problem. Cotter said that 'The tree was in harmony with nature! So then, Jesus' curse appears to be judged by [Mark] v. 13d as quite unjustified, and frankly strange'.[1] Albright and Mann said that it was impossible to know 'What historical background lies behind the narrative of these verses',[2] and Beare argued that the event could not have really happened.[3] Meyer, already in 1883, was amazed at the ways in which this narrative had been distorted by scholars.[4] Most scholars have assumed that Jesus was looking for figs, because he was hungry. That seems like a trifling reason for the anger that was expressed. Nevertheless, this is where the problem is left unless some new insight is found to make sense of this event. There seem to be more questions than answers. Why would any later writers, such as Matthew, Mark or their sources, falsely attribute such action to Jesus? If they recorded a historical event, why did Jesus do it?[5]

Both Hiers and Derrett noted the miraculous fruitfulness expected in the messianic age.[6] These views will be considered in detail after the literary questions are taken into account.

Literary Questions

Bartsch was correct in observing that the Markan version is very much like a *chreia*.[7] The Matthaean version appears to be a responsive *chreia* that has been expanded, and the Markan version expanded still more. A responsive *chreia* is a literary form distinguished in the following ways:

1. W.J. Cotter, '"For it was not the Season for Figs"', *CBQ* 48 (1986), p. 62.
2. W.F. Albright and C.S. Mann, *Matthew* (AB, 26; Garden City, NY: Doubleday, 1971), p. 260.
3. Beare, *Matthew*, p. 84; W. Grundmann (*Das Evangelium nach Matthaus* [THKNT, 1; Berlin: Evangelische Verlagsanstalt, 1968], pp. 450-52) thought it was a pious legend.
4. Meyer, *Hand-Book*, p. 143.
5. Cotter ('Season', pp. 62-66) wrestled with this question vigorously. She finally concluded that the Markan addition was a backward explanation, telling why Jesus might have been looking for figs rather than why he did not find any. This, however, does not explain why he became angry enough to curse the tree.
6. R.H. Hiers, 'Not the Season for Figs', *JBL* 87 (1968), pp. 394-400; C.S. Mann (*Mark* [AB, 27; Garden City, NY: Doubleday, 1986], pp. 439-41) denied all of the other explanations that had been given earlier and followed J.D.M. Derrett ('Fig Trees in the New Testament', *HeyJ* 14 [1973], pp. 253-55) in holding that in the new age there would be natural wonders not known in this age.
7. Bartsch, 'Verfluchung', pp. 256-60.

(1) a speaker or actor is identified, (2) the situation that prompted the speaker to speak or the actor to act is given, (3) a summary of the speaker's saying or the actor's action is given, and (4) the entire unit is very brief.[1] The Matthaean *chreia* is as follows:

1. The context shows that the speaker was Jesus.
2. The situation that prompted him to speak was as follows: 'Early the [next] morning after he had gone into the city, he was hungry, and he saw a fig tree along the way; he came to it; he found nothing on it but leaves'; and he said to it,
3. "No longer will any fruit come from you in the age [to come]"'—that was the summary quotation.
4. The entire unit is brief.

Mark made the addition 'For it was not the season for figs',[2] and Matthew and Mark (11.20) both reported that the tree withered,[3] but these statements are not a part of the *chreia*. When the *chreia* is compared with 28 other *chreias* it seems coherent with other teachings of Jesus.[4] It belongs to a Palestinian setting around Passover time. There is nothing in the *chreia* to suggest a later date or a different location. There is an extensive collection of evidence showing the reliability of *chreias* in reporting fairly events related to great teachers or leaders, so we cannot rule out the possibility that Jesus himself actually cursed the fig tree. No matter how the literary form came into existence, however, there is the problem of making sense of the report. How can be event be explained? The answer to this question becomes clear when the series of midrashic texts to which this New Testament passage is related are identified.

The Mood of the Times

Jesus and his disciples, like other Jews before, during and after New Testament times, seemed to be confident that they were living in the last days of the old Roman age. People thought Jesus was the one who would redeem Israel (Lk. 24.21). Jesus reportedly said there were some of his hearers who would not die before the kingdom came (Mt. 24.24;

---

1. For a list of these literary forms in the Gospels, their definitions and their critical analyses see G.W. Buchanan, *Jesus: The King and his Kingdom* (Macon: Mercer University Press, 1984), pp. 45-74, 127-28, 165, 221, 238-39.
2. V. Taylor (*Mark*, p. 460) thought this was a Markan addition.
3. Hiers ('Figs', p. 394) and others think Mk 11.21 is a legendary addition.
4. Buchanan, *Jesus*, pp. 45-74, 127-28, 165, 221, 238-39.

Mk 13.28-30). He also assured his disciples that within their own life-
times they would sit on twelve thrones governing the twelve tribes of
Israel (Mt. 19.28).

Jews reached these conclusion on several bases. First, they thought
that history would be repeated. What had happened after the exile in
Egypt, the exile in Babylon and the exile under the Syrian Greeks would
happen again after the exile under the Romans. They studied carefully
the events that were supposed to take place at the very end of the old
age before the kingdom came. They thought they were close to the very
time when the ages would change. At any moment their whole situation
would be different. The first would become last and the last first (Mt.
19.30).[1] The cycle was predestined to turn over into an antitype of the
age of Solomon, Nehemiah and the Hasmoneans, so Jews were looking
everywhere for signs of the end of the age.[2] There probably had never
been a time in previous history when Jewish eschatological excitement
was as high as during the fifty-year period before the fall of Jerusalem in
AD 70.

The second ground is really an extension of the first: a new redemption
would be like the redemption from the Greeks reported by Daniel. If
Jews could only identify parts of the current history with parts of the last
three-and-a-half-year period of Daniel's calendrical account (the
'tribulation' or the 'birth pangs of the messiah'), they could tell where
they were then in the cycle and when the three and a half years would
be over.

The third point is that Jews believed that all prophecy was prophesied
only for the days of the messiah (*b. Ber.* 34b), and that these were the
days of the messiah. This is probably what was meant by the statement
'All the prophets and the law prophesied until John' (Mt. 11.13). That

---

1.   Hiers ('Figs', pp. 398-99) gave still more reasons for thinking that Jesus was
expecting the ages to change: his entrance on a donkey in fulfillment of Zech. 9.9, his
healing of Bartimaeus openly (Mk 10.46-52) and disciples asking for seats in the
kingdom (Mk 10.35-40).

2.   On the cycles of time and eschatological expectations see Buchanan, *Jesus*,
pp. 253-83; on sabbatical eschatology see G.W. Buchanan, *The Consequences of the
Covenant* (Leiden: Brill, 1970), pp. 9-18. The term 'sabbatical eschatology' has been
recognized, accepted and used by such other scholars as A.Y. Collins, 'Numerical
Symbolism in Jewish and Early Christian Apocalyptic Literature', *ANRW* II.25.1,
pp. 1228-32, S. Bacchiocchi, 'Sabbatical Topologies of Messianic Redemption', *JSJ*
17 (1986), pp. 153-76, and R.M. Johnston, 'The Eschatological Sabbath in John's
Apocalypse: A Reconsideration', *AUSS* 25 (1987), pp. 39-50.

was when the messianic age began, so Jews had only to read all of the prophecies related to the changing of the ages and look for signs related to these events to learn how close they were to the crucial change. Matthew interpreted many events in the life of Jesus as current fulfillments of Hebrew Scripture. Luke thought Jesus was the one through whom Isaiah 61 was fulfilled (Lk. 4.21).[1]

These methods of calculating the time of the end of Jewish exile were applied many times throughout Jewish history, from the Jubilee following the North Israelite captivity (Isa. 27) until the present day.[2] There are many indications that these were also applied at the time of Jesus.

Unfulfilled Promises
Fresh Figs at Passover. As reported, both the fig tree incident and the promise to be able to move mountains took place in the Kidron Valley, as Jesus and the apostles were returning to the temple area from their overnight lodging in Bethany. This was a crucial time, just before Passover, and a critical place, between the Mount of Olives and the temple area at Jerusalem. While they were all seated near the Kidron Valley on the Mount of Olives, disciples asked Jesus when all of these expected things would take place: what would be the signs that could prompt Jesus to declare his position openly? When could they shout these secrets from the rooftops? When would the end of the Roman age take place, followed by the succeeding messianic age (Mt. 24.3)?

Jesus may have been looking for such signs as these himself. Those Jews who calculated the end of the Roman era studied, primarily, those Hebrew Scriptures that dealt with promises related to the end of the 'captivity'. These were Jeremiah, Ezekiel, Second Isaiah, Zechariah and Daniel. Since all prophecy was prophesied only for the days of the messiah, and these were the days of the messiah, Jesus and his disciples had only to read all of the prophecies related to the changing of the ages and look for current signs related to these events to learn how close they

---

1. Although they did not use the same terms, Jeremiah also interpreted Ps. 1 in a way that applied to his own time. Ezekiel also interpreted Ps. 1 and Jer. 17 in a way that was applicable to his own day. The author of the Habbakuk Commentary applied the text of Habakkuk to his own day. New Testament Jews and Christians were not unique in their use of Scripture.

2. See further G.W. Buchanan, *Revelation and Redemption* (Macon: Mercer University Press, 1978), *passim.*

were to the crucial change. Two of the great prophets of change were Ezekiel and Zechariah. Ezekiel prophesied that in the new age the Kidron Valley, between the Mount of Olives and the temple area, would carry a stream of water of life from the temple that would run all the way down through the Wadi Qumran to the Dead Sea,[1] near Ain Eglaim, now called Ain Feshka (Ezek. 47.1-12). When this stream is followed topographically it runs through Wadi Qumran past the monastery near the sea (Ezek. 47.10). On both sides of this stream there would be trees bearing all kinds of fruit, every month of the year, so there would be no time which was 'not the season for figs', as Mark had said (Mk 11.13) was the case when Jesus approached the fig tree. Citizens of Palestine would never be without fruit for food (Ezek. 47.1-12).

That which Jews of New Testament times expected to take place at the introduction of the new age was not the normal but the miraculous. They did not expect things to be as they had been customarily in the old age under Roman control. One of the first miracles of the new age would be fresh fruit all the year round in the Kidron Valley. Jesus evidently expected to see some of the signs of change at that particular feast. One certain sign available for testing the calendar was the condition of the fruit trees near the Kidron stream. If they produced fruit out of season, the new age had already begun. When Jesus found no fruit he was understandably disappointed, so he cursed the fig tree.[2] Since it had not produced fruit of the new age at that time when Jesus wanted the new age to begin, Jesus asked that it not be one of the trees blessed with the ability to bear fruit out of normal season 'in the age [to come]' (εἰς τὸν αἰῶνα; Mt. 21.19). That was the curse. According to the *chreia*, Jesus did not ask that the tree dry up. That was a later addition, employed by a later scribe who misunderstood the curse and misinter-

---

1.   On this see W.R. Farmer, 'The Geography of Ezekiel's River of Life', *BA* 19 (1956), pp. 17-22.

2.   Hiers ('Figs', pp. 396-97) listed Ezek. 47 as only one of many indications of the fruitfulness expected of the new age. Irenaeus (*Adv. Haer.* 5.33.3) said that Papias remembered that Jesus taught that in the days to come the vine would produce ten billion, billionfold. Rabban Gamaliel said that trees were destined to yield fruit every day (*b. Ket.* 111b; *b. Šab.* 30b). These were all part of the atmosphere, but Ezek. 47 was the direct prophecy to which Jesus seems to have responded. These later reports were probably based on Ezek. 47.

preted it to prove that Jesus' curses were effective.[1] The curse was suitable in a scriptural context, such as that of Psalm 1, which describes rewards and punishments in terms of blessings and curses. That which was not a blessing was a curse. The blessing would have been the provision of ripe fruit at Passover time, the announcement of the new age; the curse would have been the withering of the fig tree. The blessedness that Jesus had anticipated was not based on Psalm 1, but on Ezekiel's interpretation of Jeremiah's interpretation of Psalm 1. This was a midrash upon a midrash, but like Ezekiel, Jesus seems to have recognized both the midrashim and their earlier texts.

Not only the Gospel writers but the New Testament seer and later rabbis expected Ezekiel's promise to be fulfilled in the new age. The seer thought that in the new age the river would flow at Jerusalem where the Garden of Eden would be restored, and there would be fruit trees on its banks (Rev. 22.1-12). When this happened the land would be restored and salvation would take place.[2] This was also part of the Scripture expected to be fulfilled at the national redemption according to the 'Book of Zerubbabel'.[3] A narrative attributed to Rabbi Akiba said: 'There is no city except Jerusalem, because it is said, The city which I have chosen (1 Kgs 11.13). From this [passage] you learn that the holy One blessed be He will not raise the dead [anywhere] except in the land of Israel'.[4] This belief has been so pervasively held that the Mount of Olives today has become a Jewish cemetery. Jewish corpses from all over the world have been buried there, because Orthodox Jews believe that the resurrection will take place only here, when the Mount of Olives splits in two as Zechariah promised, and the corpses are raised alive. Eschatological expectations were closely tied to Jerusalem and to the time of feasts.

1. Hiers ('Figs', pp. 397-98) correctly related the expression εἰς τὸν αἰῶνα to refer to the age to come, the age when the messiah would rule, but he interpreted the passage to say that the tree would not bear fruit *until* the age to come, just a few months later. That would not have been any curse at all. All other trees would bear fruit at the same time. Jesus said that in the age to come, when other trees would be bearing fruit all the year around, this tree would not bear at all.

2. Buchanan, *Revelation*, p. 58.

3. Buchanan, *Revelation*, p. 380.

4. From 'The Midrash Alpha Beta according to Rabbi Akiba', in A. Jellinek (ed.), *Beth ha-Midrash: Sammlung kleiner Midraschim* (4 parts; Leipzig: Teubner, 1853–57), III, p. 31; Derrett ('Fig Trees', pp. 255-56) correctly related the moving of mountains to the Mount of Olives, but he did not develop the point in detail.

Miracles and Mountains

Another miracle expected at the change of the ages was promised by Zechariah. Zechariah had promised that on Judgment Day the Lord would stand on the Mount of Olives, and the mountain would split in two, part of it moving in one direction and part in the other (Zech. 14.4). Like other faithful Jews, Jesus probably expected this to happen, because this is what was said in the Lord's word. If the disciples had faith they could hasten the judgment when the mountain would move. 'Then the Lord would come, and all of the holy ones [would come] with him' (Zech. 14.5). According to Matthew Jesus, as the Son of Man, expected to come into his glory bringing all of his angels with him (Mt. 25.31); and if he asked his Father, God would send him more than twelve legions of angels (Mt. 26.53). This shows Jesus' familiarity with the relevant passage in Zechariah, according to Matthew.

While Jesus and his disciples were in the Kidron Valley, Jesus told the disciples that if they had faith they could command 'this mountain' to move, and it would. 'This mountain' was obviously the Mount of Olives, the place where Jesus had spent the night (Mt. 21.17), the mountain adjacent to the Kidron Valley where Jesus tested the fruit tree, and the very mountain where the disciples asked Jesus about signs of the end of the age (Mt. 24.3). The Judgment Day was to take place just at the end of the Gentile age and the beginning of the Jewish age to come. The Judgment Day was on New Year's Day, and according to the old Pentacontad Calendar, New Year's Day was the first Sunday after Passover.[1] The time when Matthew reported Jesus and his disciples to have discussed these things would have been very close to the time when the judgment should have taken place, the mountain should have moved and the trees should have born fruit out of season. The site was also very close to the place where all these things should have taken place when the ages changed.

Postponed Optimism

When signs like these did not occur, Jesus became convinced that this was not the feast at which the kingdom of Heaven would be restored.[2]

---

1.   H. Lewy and J. Lewy, 'The Origin of the Week and the Oldest West Asiatic Calendar', *HUCA* 17 (1942–43), pp. 1-152a; J. Morgenstern, 'The Calendar of the Book of Jubilees', *VT* 5 (1955), pp. 34-76.

2.   Hiers ('Figs', pp. 397-98) took the saying that Jesus would not drink of the fruit of the vine again until he drank it anew in the kingdom of God to be parallel to

This was a disappointment to the apostles, who apparently expected Jesus to initiate some action to take possession of the kingdom at that particular feast. It was only after they were sure that he would not lead some rebellion against the Romans that Judas betrayed him, and Peter denied him, but Jesus refused to act without God's approval, and the sign he hoped for was not given.

If the fig tree really had produced fresh ripe fruit at Passover time when Jesus looked for it, if the mountain had moved to announce the Judgment Day and if the holy ones had come down from heaven to support Jesus' movement (Zech. 14.5; Mt. 25.31; 26.53), Jesus probably would have acted as the apostles anticipated, but that was not the case. Since no sign had been given at this feast, Jesus promised that it would happen before *next* Passover.

Perhaps the sign would come before the New Year's Day that was observed by popular Judaism in the autumn, and the Day of Atonement, as it had for Judas the Maccabee, many years earlier. In any case, there was not much time left in this Roman age, in Jesus' judgment, but there was still some. His new revision of timetables suggested that the age to come would begin before the next Passover, which he and his apostles would celebrate in the new kingdom of his Father (Mt. 26.28-29).

Conclusions

The author of Matthew seemed not to think that there was anything abnormal about Jesus expecting fresh fruit at Passover time in the Kidron Valley. Like other religious Jews, he was familiar with Jewish expectations and Jewish understandings of biblical texts. The author of Mark was probably the first to express surprise. At Passover, of course, there would be no ripe figs on the fig tree, because it was not the season for figs (Mk 11.13)! Scholars ever since have had difficulty with this passage because they did not know know how important Hebrew Scripture was to Jews and early Christians in their attempt to understand what God had in mind for them in the future.

It is clear that Matthew thought that there was nothing abnormal about Jesus' action. This means that Matthew or one of his sources might have composed this pericope and attributed it to Jesus. Another

the curse of the fig tree. They seem related, but one is a curse against the fig tree, and the other is a promise that the kingdom would come before the next Passover. There is a difference between a curse and a promise or a vow.

possibility, however, is that Jesus might actually have cursed the fig tree and told the disciples that if they had faith they could make the Mount of Olives move. Although there is no proof that this is a historical report there are some arguments in its favor.

The fact that the report is contained in a *chreia*, and the further fact that the message of the expansion is different from the meaning of the *chreia* itself, shows that the interpretations were later additions by someone other than the author of the *chreia*. This is the typical way in which midrash is formed, and it is the normal use made by commentators and editors of *chreias* as texts. This alone speaks for the validity of the *chreia* report. Another consideration is the content: why would any Christian in the later church compose this *chreia* after the fall of Jerusalem in AD 70, falsely showing that Jesus became angry and took out his hostility by afflicting violence on a fig tree? The fact that some members of the church did not like the implication of this character portrayal is shown by the addition whereby later editors 'corrected' the content of the curse and the emphasis of the pericope. The scribe who made this interpretive addition did not want people to think that Jesus was a false messiah who had been mistaken in his expectations, so he added a sentence to show that Jesus' curse was effective. The tree withered and died.

The unknown scribe who made this addition did not do it frivolously. Ezekiel, following Jeremiah 17 and Psalm 1, said that the tree would produce fruit all the year around, and that its leaf would not *wither*. That would happen because it was planted by this mighty river of water flowing out from the temple. When Jesus cursed the tree he asked that it *not* produce fruit in the age to come, as Ezekiel had prophesied. Since it did not produce fruit in its time (Ps. 1.3)—namely, every month, as Ezekiel promised—then it would suffer the alternative consequence: it would perish (Ps. 1.6). The scribe assumed that this curse would have been effective. Therefore, not only would the tree not produce fruit, but its leaves would wither (Ps. 1.3; Ezek. 47.12), and the tree itself would wither up and die, so he presumed that it must have done just that.

This study has added five new considerations to the information necessary for interpreting Mt. 21.18-22. First, it has shown the importance of earlier texts that had been accepted as the word of God to the composers of later literature. For example, it has demonstrated the way in which Jeremiah used Psalm 1 and the way in which Ezekiel used both Psalm 1 and Jeremiah, and the study has shown further how Jews of New Testament times held the same traditional view of Hebrew Scripture that earlier prophets and Psalmists did. There is a continuity of exegesis at least from the sixth century BC to the first century AD. This is basic to the understanding of Mt. 21.18-22. Secondly, this research has recognized the limitations in the Matthaean text of the literary unit, the *chreia*. Thirdly, it has called attention to three neglected articles and further developed and sharpened the theses suggested by Hiers, Farmer and Derrett. It has noted in greater detail than any of these, however, the relationship of the Hebrew Scripture and the geography of the area to the Jewish expectations of Jesus' time and to Jesus' expectations as reported in the Gospels. Fourthly, it has shown how the expectations of the Gospels reflect cyclical time and sabbatical eschatology. Finally, it has explained Jesus' anger and the associated curse. The fact that the tree did not have ripe figs was a serious matter which justified Jesus' anger and disappointment. The curse came in the context that was opposite to the blessing given in Psalm 1. Like Ezekiel, Jesus evidently knew not only his immediate text, but the texts upon which that was based. Jesus' disappointment was not just because of his own momentary hunger. The absence of ripe fruit meant that Ezekiel's prophecy had not been fulfilled at the time and in the way he had expected. He and his disciples had miscalculated. This meant that the new age had not yet begun. This was not the end of the birth pangs of the messiah. The kingdom of heaven would not come at this feast. Jews would still remain in their foreign 'captivity' at least a short time longer. When Jesus realized that he did not have scriptural support for any action he had planned, he refused to act. Instead he passively accepted crucifixion at the hands of the Romans, fulfilling the prophecy of Isaiah 53, since the prophecy of Ezekiel 47 was evidently not going to be fulfilled at that time.

MARK 12.28-31 AND THE DECALOGUE

Dale C. Allison, Jr

In Mk 12.28 a certain scribe asks Jesus this question: 'Which commandment is the first of all?' Jesus responds with these famous words: 'The first is, "Hear, O Israel: The Lord our God, the Lord is one; and you shall love the Lord your God with all your heart, and with all your soul, and with all your mind, and with all your strength"'. Jesus then adds: 'The second [commandment] is this: "You shall love your neighbour as yourself". There is no other commandment greater than these'.

Despite recurrent attempts to find something unique in Mk 12.28-31 par., it is widely acknowledged that Jesus' double commandment to love cannot be reckoned unprecedented.[1] This is because there are a number of near parallels, among which the following are most frequently cited:

> *T. Iss.* 5.2: ἀγαπήσατε τὸν κύριον καὶ τὸν πλησίον.
>
> *T. Iss.* 7.6: τὸν κύριον ἠγάπησα καὶ ἄνθρωπον ἐξ ὅλης καρδίας.
>
> *T. Dan* 5.3: ἀγαπήσατε τὸν κύριον ἐν πάσῃ τῇ ζωῇ ὑμῶν καὶ ἀλλήλους ἐν ἀληθίνῃ καρδίᾳ.
>
> Aristeas, *Ep.* 229: 'Piety is the first degree of beauty; its power is love.'
>
> Philo, *Virt.* 51: 'humanity' (φιλανθρωπία) and 'piety' (εὐσέβια) are twin virtues.
>
> Philo, *Virt.* 95: 'piety' and 'humanity' are the queens of the virtues.
>
> Philo, *Spec. Leg.* 2.63: 'among the vast number of particular truths and principles there [in the Torah] studied, there stood out... high above the others two heads: one of duty to God as shown by piety and holiness, one of duty to men as shown by humanity and justice.'
>
> Philo, *Abr.* 208: 'Holiness to God and justice to men.'[2]

---

1. The fact seems already implicit in both Mark and Luke. In the former the scribe approvingly quotes Jesus' answer back to him (Mk 12.32-33). And in Lk. 10.27 the commandment to love God and one's neighbour is spoken not by Jesus but by a lawyer.

2. More distant parallels include *T. Naph.* 8.9-10; *T. Benj.* 3.3; *Jub.* 7.20; 20.2;

C. Burchard has urged that these texts—all of them, in his judgment, of non-Palestinian origin—indicate that the words attributed to Jesus in Mk 12.28-31 were not spoken by him; rather, they were produced by Hellenistic Jewish Christianity.[1] Whether in this he persuades is not an issue I shall here pursue. My aim instead is to direct attention to some parallels which, to my knowledge, have not been discussed in the secondary literature—parallels which are in important respects closer to Mk 12.38-41 than any of those just cited and which suggest a line of interpretation not adopted in modern commentaries on Mark.

In his volume on the decalogue Philo more than once gave it as his judgement that the ten commandments summarize the rest of the Torah's legislation.[2] For example, in *Dec.* 19-20 the ten words are characterized as 'heads summarizing the particular laws'.[3] The same thought appears again in ch. 154, where we read that 'the ten covenants are summaries of the laws which are recorded in the sacred books and run through the whole of the legislation'.[4] In other words, the decalogue outlines the laws of Moses and contains them *in nuce*. This idea, which reappears in *Spec. Leg.* 1.1, comes as no surprise; for already the Pentateuch itself arguably presents the decalogue, which is not law in the strict sense,[5] as the *foundation* of Israelite legislation, as a sort of heading for its corpus of ordinances.[6] We should note that the ten commandments

36.7-8; Josephus, *War* 2.8.7 §139; 7.8.1 §260. Are the unspecified 'two commandments' of *T. Naph.* 8.9 love of God and love of one's neighbour?

1. C. Burchard, 'Das doppelte Liebesgebot in der frühen christlichen Überlieferung', in E. Lohse *et al.* (eds.), *Der Ruf Jesu und die Antwort der Gemeinde* (Göttingen: Vandenhoeck & Ruprecht, 1970), pp. 39-62.

2. Cf. *Targ. Ps.-J.* Exod. 24.12 ('I [God] will give to you [Moses] the tablets of stone upon which are hinted the rest of the law and the six hundred and thirteen commandments') and *Cant. R.* 1.2 §2 (the 613 commandments are implied by the decalogue).

3. νόμων τῶν ἐν μέρει κεφάλαια.

4. οἱ δέκα λόγοι κεφάλαια νόμων εἰσὶ τῶν ἐν εἴδει παρ'ὅλην τὴν νομοθεσίαν ἐν ταῖς βίβλοις ἀναγραφέντων.

5. That is, not 'case law'. The decalogue is 'categorical law', if by that is meant an expression of broad principles.

6. So P.D. Miller, 'The Place of the Decalogue in the Old Testament and its Law', *Int* 43 (1989), pp. 229-43. Only the ten commandments are delivered directly to the people by God's own voice.

of Exodus 20 are placed before all the other Pentateuchal imperatives delivered through Moses.[1]

If Philo believed that the decalogue is a précis of the entire Mosaic legislation, he also believed that the decalogue itself can be summarized, that the ten words can in fact be reduced to two. As have so many since, our philosophical exegete divided the ten commandments into 'two sets of five, which he [God] engraved on two tables' (*Dec*. 50; cf. 106). The first set of five contains the 'monarchical principle', the ban on graven images, the interdiction against taking the Lord's name in vain, the injunction to keep the Sabbath and the command to honour one's father and mother. The second set consists of the prohibitions of adultery, murder, theft, false witness and covetousness or lust (51). Philo's division is more than formal, that is, more than just an assignment of each group of five to a separate stone table: the partitioning is also thematic. The first (πρωτεῖα) set of injunctions, which is 'superior' (ἀμείνων, 51) and 'most sacred' (ἱερώτατα, 106), 'is more concerned with the divine' (121) whereas the 'second' (δευτέρα) set has to do with 'the duties of man to man' (106). This dividing of the decalogue into duties to God and to humanity reminds one of Mk 12.38-31 as well as of the parallel passages cited earlier.[2]

But there is more. For *Dec*. 108-10 reveals how the duties to God and humanity are to be summarily characterized—and here we read of love. Those who observe the first five words are 'lovers of God' (φιλοθέοι). Those who observe the second five words are 'lovers of men' (φιλανθρώποι). This interpretation, which is offered as though well-known and obvious, makes plain that the summary of the Torah, the decalogue, may itself be summarized by two demands, the demand to love God and the demand to love one's neighbour. The parallel to Mk 12.38-41 is all the closer in that, in Philo, the set of commandments concerning love of God is the 'first set' and the set concerning love of humanity the 'second set', while Mark's Gospel designates Deut. 6.4 ('and you shall love the Lord your God') as the 'first' commandment and Lev. 19.18 ('you shall love your neighbour as yourself') as the 'second' commandment.

---

1.   On the centrality of the decalogue for Deuteronomy, see E. Nielsen, *The Ten Commandments in New Perspective* (SBT NS, 7; London: SCM Press, 1968), pp. 44-51.

2.   Recall also the rabbinic distinctions between commandments concerning persons and God and commandments concerning persons and persons.

It is plain that the double commandment of Mk 12.38-41 has a very close parallel in Philo's commentary on the decalogue, *Dec.* 106-10. But it may well be that the parallelism stretches even further than I have indicated. Philo understood the first half of the decalogue to demand love of God, the second half to enjoin love of one's neighbour. I should like to suggest that Mark's first-century Christian readers would in all likelihood have construed Jesus' commandments to love God and one's neighbour as Philo surely would have, namely, as together constituting a synopsis of the decalogue. In other words, the quotations of Deut. 5.6 and Lev. 19.18 were intended to be brief résumés of the two tables given to Moses. What, beyond Philo, is the evidence for this?

1. The ten commandments, which throughout Jewish and Christian history have been regarded as the quintessence of proper religious and moral behaviour, have conventionally been divided into two parts. To begin with, the Old Testament itself informs us that Moses carried the ten words down from the mountain on two tablets of stone (Deut. 32.15; 34.1; cf. *LAB* 12.10); and Josephus, like Philo, believed that there were five commandments on each (*Ant.* 3.5.8 §101)—a belief we may assume to have been as popular in antiquity as in our own day.[1] The Pentateuch does not, to be sure, indicate that each tablet had, as it were, its own theme; but this idea has been a commonplace. Very much like Philo, Gerhard von Rad urged that the decalogue falls into two sections, the first having to do with 'man's duties to God', the second with 'man's duties towards man'.[2] The same notion appears in Justin, *Dial.* 44,[3] and Irenaeus, *Adv. Haer.* 4.16.3.[4] From a later time reference may be made to Aquinas, *De decem parae.* 4.11, and Calvin, *Inst.* 2.8.52-53. I spare the reader additional documentation, which would be superfluous. The point is simply that it is altogether natural to think of the ten commandments as composed of two groups of imperatives, one having to do primarily

---

1. Augustine, however, and after him much of Roman Catholic tradition, assigned the first three to the first table, the final seven to the second; see Nielsen, *Ten Commandments*, pp. 33-34.

2. G. von Rad, *Old Testament Theology* (New York: Harper & Row, 1962), I, p. 191.

3. 'A certain commandment [that is, the decalogue] is for service of God and neighbour.'

4. 'The righteous fathers had the meaning of the decalogue written in their hearts and souls, that is, they loved the God who made them, and did no injury to their neighbour.'

with God, the other primarily with human relationships. And Philo's testimony shows us that the generalization reaches back at least to first-century Judaism.[1]

2. Paul, in Rom. 13.9, wrote: 'The commandments, "You shall not commit adultery, You shall not kill, You shall not steal, You shall not covet", and any other commandment, are summed up in this sentence, "You shall love your neighbour as yourself"'. Here, to quote Charles Cranfield, 'the particular commandments of the "second table" of the Decalogue are all summed up in the commandment to love one's neighbour as oneself (Lev. 19.18)'.[2] This is exactly what I suggest is implicit in Mk 12.31. The point gains force because (1) Rom. 13.9 probably depends upon the tradition passed on in Mk 12.28-31[3] and (2) Paul was far from being the only early Christian to associate Lev. 19.18 with the final four or five commandments. Mt. 19.18-19 cites the same commandments as does Paul, adds the imperative to love father and mother, and then cites Lev. 19.18 as the general rule that contains the preceding particulars. Similarly, Jas 2.8-13 (here I think dependent upon the Jesus tradition[4]) refers to Lev. 19.18 as 'the royal law' and then cites the prohibitions of adultery and murder as instances of that law.[5] And then there is the *Didache*. It opens by citing Deut. 5.6 (love God) and Lev. 19.18 (love one's neighbour) and then instances, in illustration of the latter, commandments from the second half of the decalogue.[6] The same exegetical tradition, that is, the use of Lev. 19.18 to characterize the final four or five commandments, appears also in Aristides, *Ep.* 15.3-5; Tertullian, *Adv. Jud.* 4; Gregory of Nyssa, *Vit. Mos.* 2.48; and

---

1. It is pertinent that early Christian paraenesis sometimes made use of only the final four or five commandments, thus probably implying awareness of a distinction between the two parts of the decalogue; see for example Mt. 19.19 par.; Eph. 6.1-3; Pliny, *Ep.* 10.96.

2. C.E.B. Cranfield, *A Critical and Exegetical Commentary on the Epistle to the Romans* (Edinburgh: T. & T. Clark, 1979), II, p. 677.

3. Cf. J.D.G. Dunn, *Romans 9–16* (WBC, 38b; Dallas: Word Books, 1988), p. 779.

4. P.H. Davids, 'James and Jesus', in D. Wenham (ed.), *The Jesus Tradition Outside the Gospels* (Gospel Perspectives, 5; Sheffield: JSOT Press, 1984), pp. 72-73.

5. L.T. Johnson, 'The Use of Leviticus 19 in the Letter of James', *JBL* 101 (1982), p. 48.

6. I presume that *Did.* 1.3-6 is an interpolation and that the connexion between Lev. 19.18 and the decalogue was even closer in an earlier form of the document.

Benedict, *Regula* 4.2-7, to name four later sources. Obviously the commandment to love one's neighbour, quoted in Mk 12.41, was widely regarded among early Christians as a summary of the second half of the decalogue.[1]

3. Unlike Mt. 22.37 and Lk. 10.27, Mk 12.39 introduces the double commandment to love with these words from Deut. 6.5: 'Hear, O Israel: The Lord our God, the Lord is one'. This reminds us that the commandment to love God is from the *Shema*, a liturgical text for ancient as for modern Jews. Indeed, the sources tells us that the *Shema*, consisting of Deut. 6.4-9 + 11.13-21 + Num. 15.37-41, was recited every day at sunrise and sunset,[2] which is interesting for our purposes because of the solid evidence that the *Shema* was, in some circles, firmly linked with the decalogue.

As preface it should be observed that already in the Tanakh the *Shema* follows closely Deuteronomy's version of the ten words (in ch. 5), and, further, that commentators often take the great imperative in the *Shema* (Deut. 6.4-5) to be a positive restatement of the decalogue's first commandment.[3] That in any case a close connexion between the decalogue and the *Shema* was perceived around the turn of the era is evidenced by the Nash papyrus (first or second century BCE, from Egypt, in Hebrew). This combines, on a single sheet (perhaps used for lectionary purposes), the decalogue and the *Shema*.[4]

No less importantly, the rabbinic sources inform us, and in this particular there is no reason to disbelieve them, that in the Second Temple period recitation of the *Shema* followed recitation of the decalogue.[5] Thus the liturgical creed of Jews in the New Testament

1. It was probably common in Judaism to associate Lev. 19 with the decalogue; see for example Ps.-Phoc. 3–21, along with the commentary of P. van der Horst, *The Sayings of Pseudo-Phocylides* (SVTP, 4; Leiden: Brill, 1978).

2. Aristeas, *Ep.* 106; Philo, *Spec. Leg.* 4.141; Josephus, *Ant.* 4.8.13 §212; *b. Ber.* 47b.

3. Observe that the theme of loving God unites the *Shema* with the second commandment (Exod. 20.6 = Deut. 5.10: 'showing steadfast love to thousands of those who love me and keep my commandments').

4. W.F. Albright, 'A Biblical Fragment from the Maccabean Age: The Nash Papyrus', *JBL* 56 (1937), pp. 145-76.

5. See for example *m. Tam.* 5.1; *b. Ber.* 12a. Cf. the prohibition of reciting the decalogue with the *Shema* in *Sifre Deut.* §34 (on Deut. 6.5-6). The traditional association of the *Shema* and decalogue is also reflected in Christian literature; see for example Methodius of Olympus, *Symp.* 8.13.

period summarized the faith by quoting the ten commandments and the *Shema*. This is closely analogous to what I postulate for Mk 12.38-41: 'Hear, O Israel' and so on prefaces a summary of the decalogue. In other words, the profession in Mark is a restatement of the common Jewish profession, Jesus' creed the Jewish creed.

4. The 1928 *Book of Common Prayer* contains, in its Catechism, the following question and answer sequence:

> *Question*: You said that your Sponsors did promise for you, that you should keep God's Commandments. Tell me how many there are?
> *Answer*: Ten.
> *Question*: Which are they?
> *Answer*: The same which God spake in the twentieth Chapter of Exodus, saying, I am the LORD thy God, who brought thee out of the land of Egypt, out of the house of bondage.

There follows a recitation of the ten commandments, after which is this exchange:

> *Question*: What dost thou chiefly learn by these Commandments?
> *Answer*: I learn two things; my duty towards God, and my duty towards Neighbour.
> *Question*: What is thy duty to God?
> *Answer*: My duty towards God is To believe in him, to fear him, and to love him with all my heart, with all my mind, with all my soul, and with all my strength [cf. Deut. 6.5]...
> *Question*: What is thy duty to thy Neighbour?
> *Answer*: My duty towards my Neighbour is To love him as myself [cf. Lev. 19.18]...

The *Book of Common Prayer* clearly sets forth what I believe to be implicit in Mark, namely, a division of the ten commandments into two parts, the first part summarized by Deut. 6.5, the second by Lev. 19.18. That is to say, the *Book of Common Prayer* interprets the decalogue in terms of the double commandment to love.

This interpretation is by no means confined to the 1928 *Book of Common Prayer*. On the contrary, the mutual explication of the double commandment to love and the decalogue is a commonplace of Christian literature throughout the centuries. It can be found, for instance, in the systematic theologies of Thomas Watson (1692) and John Gill (1769–70),[1] in the works of Matthew Henry (1662–1714) and Jonathan

---

1. T. Watson, *A Body of Divinity*, question 42; J. Gill, *A Body of Divinity* 4.6.

Edwards (1703–58),[1] in the Heidelberg Catechism (1562) and the Westminster Confession (1646–47),[2] and, still earlier, in the writings of John Calvin (1509–64) and Thomas Aquinas (1225–74).[3] That we have here to do with a very old tradition is established by its appearance in the *Apostolic Constitutions*, a fourth-century compilation of earlier sources. In 2.5.36 of this old collection of ecclesiastical law, the faithful are enjoined to keep the ten commandments. An incomplete list of them, mixed with other exhortations, follows. The catalogue is prefaced by 'Love the one and only God with all your strength', words from Deut. 6.5. Moreover, the commandment to love one's neighbour (Lev. 19.18) is inserted immediately after 'Honour your father and mother'. Here, then, the tradition later taken up by the *Book of Common Prayer* is already in place.

Attention should perhaps also be directed to Benedict's *Regula* (c. 540). This, in enumerating the so-called 'instruments' of good works, cites, first, the commandment to love God, secondly, the commandment to love one's neighbour, and thirdly, the second half of the decalogue (*Reg.* 4.1-7).

An even earlier witness to the tradition under review is almost certainly to be found at the end of the second century, in Irenaeus, *Adv. Haer.* 4.16.3. Here we read that 'the meaning of the decalogue' was 'written in the hearts and souls' of the patriarchs, which means that 'they loved the God who made them and did no injury to their neighbour'. For Irenaeus, as for Philo, the substance of the decalogue could be reduced to two items, duty to (that is, love of) God and duty to one's neighbour. Moreover, 'to love the God that made them' is a variant of Deut. 6.5 known also from the *Didache* (1.2; cf. Justin, *1 Apol.* 16.6), and 'do no injury to their neighbour' is a free rendering of Lev. 19.18, influenced by a negative form of the so-called 'golden rule'.[4] It is difficult

---

1. M. Henry, *Exposition of the Old and New Testaments ad* Mt. 22.34-40; J. Edwards, *Charity and its Fruits* 1.2.2.

2. Westminster Confession §21; Heidelberg Catechism 3.14-16 (questions 93-112).

3. Thomas Aquinas, *De decem parae.* 4 and 11 (the first three commandments concern love of God, the last seven love of one's neighbour); Calvin, *Inst.* 2.8.11.

4. Cf. Irenaeus, *Epideixis* 87: 'the love of neighbour adds no evil to a neighbour'. Both the positive and negative forms of the golden rule were regarded as synonymous with Lev. 19.18 in ancient Christianity as well as ancient Judaism; see *Did.* 1.2; Ps.-Clem. *Hom.* 12.32; Cyprian, *De dom. orat.* 28; *Targ. Onq.* Lev. 19.18. Note that the Evangelist Matthew could identify both the golden rule and Lev. 19.18

to avoid concluding that Irenaeus understood the double commandment to love in the same way as does the *Book of Common Prayer*.

The one place I have not found the combination of Deut. 5.6 and Lev. 19.18 construed as a summary of the decalogue is in twentieth-century critical commentaries on the canonical Gospels. Or so at least my memory tells me; and a recent examination of twelve major commentaries on Mark—those of H.B. Swete (1913), B. Harvie Branscomb (1937), Ernst Lohmeyer (1937), Vincent Taylor (1952), C.E.B. Cranfield (1959), Sherman E. Johnson (1960), D.E. Nineham (1963), Eduard Schweizer (1970), William L. Lane (1974), Hugh Anderson (1976), Rudolf Pesch (1977) and Joachim Gnilka (1979)—confirms my recall.[1]

The same negative yield has come from my review, also admittedly less than exhaustive, of recent commentaries on Mt. 22.34-40 and Lk. 10.25-28. The fact is cause for some puzzlement. How could such a plausible and richly attested interpretation go unnoticed? Whatever the explanation for the omission, it does seem that we have here proof of the ever-present need for what the Germans call *Wirkungsgeschichte*. We are wont to imagine that correct or credible exegetical insights will be preserved in the commentaries. But with regard to Mk 12.38-41 and its parallels, we have seemingly forgotten what many before us, with good reason, took for granted: that the double commandment to love is a summarizing exposition of the decalogue.

as the sum of the law and the prophets; see Mt. 7.12 and 22.39.

1.   Swete, however, was aware that Lev. 19.18 is 'a recapitulation of the second half of the Decalogue'; see his *The Gospel according to Mark* (London: Macmillan, 1913), p. 285. Cf. G. Salmon, *The Human Element in the Gospels* (London: John Murray, 1908), pp. 411, 455 (Jesus taught that Lev. 19.18 is 'the compendium of the whole second table of the Law').

Part IV
THE GOSPEL OF LUKE

PROCLAMATION FROM PROPHECY AND PATTERN: LUKE'S USE OF THE OLD TESTAMENT FOR CHRISTOLOGY AND MISSION

Darrell L. Bock

Introduction

The Lukan use of the Old Testament in the New concentrates on two themes: Christology and mission.[1] Most studies of the Lukan use of the Old Testament focus on hermeneutics, text, or the issue of sources for the material.[2] One significant essay by Charles Talbert has dealt with the basic issue of 'proof from prophecy' as the underlying theme of Luke–Acts.[3] Talbert's goal is to clarify how the theme was used.

---

1. 'Old Testament' is a term of convenience for the Law, Prophets and Writings, texts which were read with respect and reflection in first-century Judaism. To use the term says nothing about the extent of the canon in the first century. I must thank the Luke–Acts study group at SBL (1991) and the Seminar on Biblical Studies for the Southwest region, which met in 1993 at Brite Divinity School, Texas Christian University, Fort Worth, Texas, for their interaction with earlier drafts of this essay.

2. For example, T. Holtz (*Untersuchungen über die alttestamentliche Zitate bei Lukas* [Texte und Untersuchungen zur Geschichte der altchristlichen Literatur, 104; Berlin: Akademie Verlag, 1968]) concentrates on the Old Testament text Luke used. M. Rese (*Alttestamentliche Motive in der Christologie des Lukas* [SNT, 1; Gütersloh: Gerd Mohn/Gütersloher Verlagshaus, 1969]) concentrates on hermeneutics and on the issue of the sources in the Jesus tradition behind Luke's use. He challenges the prophecy-fulfillment approach to Luke–Acts and emphasizes the 'hermeneutical' (explanatory) function of Scripture. In my judgment, Rese is right in what he affirms, but wrong in what he denies. C.K. Barrett's article takes sources for the Jesus tradition in Luke, while he takes a more thematic approach in Acts. In addition, in the Gospels he compares how the citations are used in Luke versus the parallels, while in Acts most comments are limited to introductory formulae and the naming of the passage cited; C.K. Barrett, 'Luke–Acts', in D.A. Carson and H.G.M. Williamson (eds.), *It is Written: Scripture Citing Scripture: Essays in Honor of Barnabas Lindars* (Cambridge: Cambridge University Press, 1988), pp. 231-44.

3. C. Talbert, 'Promise and Fulfillment in Lucan Theology', in *idem* (ed.), *Luke–Acts: New Perspectives from the Society of Biblical Literature Seminar* (New York:

Talbert makes three basic points. First, he argues that the theme of 'proof from prophecy' is not as dominant as some have suggested, a point, Talbert argues, that Rese's work *Alttestamentliche Motive in der Christologie des Lukas* demonstrates. Secondly, he argues that the goal of all the texts is not simply continuity with holy history, since certain texts do not emphasize continuity, but other aspects of mission (Acts 18.9-10, 12-17; 27.23-25; 20.23; 21.11; 11.27-30; 12.25). Thirdly, Talbert deals with ancient readers' expectations upon encountering such a theme. He argues that the prophetic motif has three elements: (1) divine necessity controls the course of history: (2) history's course fulfills oracles, both written and oral, whether through understanding or through misunderstanding; and (3) the motif has many functions. Such prophecy legitimates a person's religious status, legitimates other things that the prophet of the oracle said, points to continuity, and shows, in its Jewish form, the providence of God in human affairs, since God rewards virtue and punishes vice. Talbert's conclusion is that this use of prophecy and fulfillment fits the ancient Mediterranean milieu and that there is 'no justification for the claim that the prophecy-fulfillment motif in Luke–Acts functions to assist Gentile followers of Paul in their struggle with Jews'.[1] In fact, he doubts that promise-fulfillment is the major Lukan theme under which all other themes can be subsumed.

Now one of the problems with Talbert's critique at this point is that he appeals to texts that do not use Old Testament promise, but divine promise through fresh revelation. This mixing of categories can confuse the discussion, if one is trying to see how Luke uses Old Testament promise. In short, Talbert's essay, by broadening the discussion on promise, helps to show the variety of ways in which Luke appeals to that theme, both in old promises and new, but his study risks obscuring how the ancient texts are used by Luke.

In this essay I seek to challenge an aspect of Talbert's thesis and to rehabilitate the theme of promise and fulfillment, at least as it relates to Luke's use of the Old Testament. I am here building on my earlier work

Crossroad, 1984), pp. 91-103. This essay examines the basic theme of proof from prophecy and then presents three areas to help place this theme in its proper perspective. The burden here is to show that proof from prophecy is not as dominant as some suggest, since it can be shown that many texts lack this emphasis. In making this point, Talbert follows some of the points raised initially by Rese.

1.   Talbert, 'Promise and Fulfillment in Lucan Theology', p. 101.

and seeking to bring the discussion up to date.[1] In addition, this essay will add a brief discussion of the theme of mission as a way of showing that Talbert's approach to the issue, though providing a major qualification, ultimately fails to deal with the vast amount of material on continuity and mission as related to Christology.

In looking at this topic I shall spend very little time on hermeneutics, since this was a major theme of my earlier work. Nonetheless, one introductory point about hermeneutics from that study needs to be made here. When one speaks of the theme of Old Testament promise in Luke–Acts, one is speaking of the appeal to both prophecy and pattern. But the appeal to pattern is still to be seen as prophetic, because the God behind the history is unchanging. What God did in one era to move covenant promise along, he can and will do in those times when he again becomes actively involved in directing and completing his program. This is a major theological supposition of Luke's use of the Old Testament, which allows him to appeal to such a variety of texts. It is the axiomatic background for his declaration that certain things 'must' take place. Thus while many texts Luke uses are not exclusively prophetic, they are 'typological-prophetic' in that the pattern of God's activity is reactivated in ways that mirror and enhance his acts of old. Such mirroring allows the events to be seen as part of God's plan and shows that he is active in the events, which recall the great days of old and which show God designing the movement of history along parallel lines. In the repetition is the presence of design and thus of prophecy. Such mirroring and what it represents about God's presence gives comfort (Lk. 1.4).

I shall also depart from the normal procedure for examining this material by proceeding in literary order, rather than by sources. This enables us to hear Luke speak as he tells the story in his own way. I will examine Christology first and then mission, since this is the way in which Luke himself proceeds. I will concentrate on the use of citations in Luke–Acts, noting that a full study of this area would also include allusions. But citations, being explicit, are more obvious and less debatable than allusions, so this is a good place to begin a consideration of what Luke does with the Old Testament. I shall begin with a brief discussion of my method.

---

1.   D.L. Bock, *Proclamation from Prophecy and Pattern: Lucan Old Testament Christology* (JSNTSup, 12; Sheffield: JSOT Press, 1987).

Method

Before beginning the survey of Luke's usage, a note about method is appropriate. The basis of this overview in my previous work was a historical-literary survey of the Lukan citations. By 'historical' I mean that both the Old Testament text and the New Testament text were evaluated in terms of their historical message before I analyzed how the later writer used the earlier text. The merit of such study is that one can investigate the history of the tradition and interpretation of a passage that may well inform how the text is being used and what assumptions existed about its meaning when the later author used the earlier text. This approach proved helpful in the Lukan debate because many texts were shown to be eschatological in the first century when Luke used them. One did not need to note a prophetic fulfillment because the text was understood within Judaism as having at least an aspect of prophetic significance. The key to such study is to be sure that the parallels noted from Judaism represent evidence that was available in Luke's time.

Since that study, a new approach has emerged, the formal literary study of the reuse of texts, or intertextuality.[1] Some have argued that this is a better approach than the historical-literary approach.[2] I would

1. For an intriguing study of this question in Jewish midrash and a good introduction to the literary discussion, see D. Boyarin, *Intertextuality and the Reading of Midrash* (Bloomington, IN: Indiana University Press, 1990).

2. See R.L. Brawley, 'Canon and Community: Intertextuality, Canon, Interpretation, Christology, Theology, and Persuasive Rhetoric in Luke 4.1-13', in E. Lovering (ed.), *Society of Biblical Literature Seminar Papers 1992* (Atlanta: Scholars Press, 1992), pp. 419-34, esp. 420-22. He argues that the historical-literary method, what he called the 'conventional method', separates texts too much, failing to recognize that when a text is reused, it impacts on the understanding of texts at both points. But this critique, though generally correct, ignores the conclusion made in my *Proclamation from Prophecy and Pattern*, p. 273: 'We have shown in several texts that the relationship between text and event is two way'. It is 'two-way' in that a later event can fill out the meaning of a text, making an implied sense more explicit. The reading of such texts is a decidedly two-way process. The choice to use an earlier text is a way of making it speak anew, of declaring its ongoing value, because the text is seen not as deficient but as informative about the event described. What was said in a more descriptive way in this earlier method, intertextuality explains more forcefully and with a focused eye on how such reuse works. But to be complete, intertextuality should continue to glance at the historical interpretive tradition behind an Old Testament text.

acknowledge the immense value of this new wave of study, but would argue that it is a complementary method. What this approach recognizes is that a text has a life (or a voice) beyond its original author. When it is reused, new meaning results simply because of the application of the text into a new context. This extends the message of the original text. An author sets the parameters for helping the reader appreciate the nature and force of his or her use of the Scripture, but he or she also assumes the cultural expectations of his or her audience. This means that both literary features and an awareness of historical context, where it is possible to determine, can inform usage and meaning. In terms of method I refuse to allow the dictatorship of any one approach to our study of the text. Turning to Luke, then, why and in what ways does he use the Old Testament?

The Basic Christological Category: Messiah-Servant-Prophet

The Lukan infancy material mostly contains allusions to the Old Testament and works with ideas, rather than with explicit citations. Nevertheless the unit is important as the overture to Luke–Acts. These chapters paint an initial portrait of Jesus using ideas which come from texts with eschatological and dynastic images. John the Baptist is described as the eschatological prophet who prepares the way for God (Lk. 1.14-17). The appeal to Malachi's image immediately brings to the surface expectations of God's great act of salvation. John the Baptist becomes the frame for the portrait of Jesus and serves as the bridge figure into the new era.

The first key allusion to Jesus comes in the birth announcement. Here regal images dominate. Here is the 'Son of the Most High' and the one who will be called 'great' (Lk. 1.32). The Lord God will give to him the throne of David, and Jesus 'will rule over the house of Jacob forever' (Lk. 1.32-33). Of his kingdom there will be no end. In Luke 1, John the Baptist is the prophet and Jesus is the king. Here also is an example of the escalation of Old Testament imagery. David was promised an ever-lasting dynastic line. Jesus is an everlasting king.

Unlike Matthew, Luke makes little of the connection to Isa. 7.14. The language of the birth announcement simply parallels other such announcements (Gen. 16.11 LXX), but with one exception. John the Baptist is born from a previously barren couple, as many great Old Testament saints were; but Jesus is born of a virgin. There is parallelism and escalation with the Old Testament acts of old. Patterns of God's activity are renewed and there are also new developments.

The title 'Son', which is introduced in Luke 1, is a key one for Luke. It will reappear in Lk. 3.22 at the baptism, be a key title in Lk. 4.41, and also make an appearance in Lk. 9.35. It has Old Testament background from Psalm 2, as the baptismal scene makes clear. It is wrong to call it an exclusively messianic title. Rather it is dynastic. However, Luke's use will make clear the fact that it is a messianic title for him. The clearest evidence of this emphasis is in Lk. 4.41. Here there is a uniquely Lukan remark, which clarifies the way that Luke sees the title. It comes after a sequence of texts in which the emphasis has been on Jesus, the Son (Lk. 3.22; 4.3, 9). The demons confess that Jesus is the 'Son of God'. Luke goes on to explain that this was because they knew him to be 'the Christ'. The title 'Son' appears in one other encounter with the forces of evil in Lk. 8.29. Thus sonship pictures rule, but the rule is escalated. Not only does Jesus sit over Jacob, he has power over the demonic. Pattern and escalation mark Luke's use of the Old Testament. Here is a new era figure, who surpasses those of the old age. Jesus' sonship is Old Testament hope and more.

The rest of the infancy imagery tied to Jesus is similar in thrust. In the hymns of Luke 1, eschatological hope is placed side by side with dynastic hope. Mary's hymn in Lk. 1.46-55 is a personal psalm of praise, which starts out largely personal in focus. As the hymn develops, Mary represents a type of person for whom God is concerned. The hymn concentrates on the patterns of God's activity for the poor and hungry against the powerful. The hymn raises covenant promise as the key to these actions and as such raises notes of eschatological hope, since God is said to remember his mercy to Abraham and his posterity. In contrast, Zechariah's hymn is less personal and more national in thrust (Lk. 1.67-79). Here the imagery is very explicit. The God of Israel has visited his people (1.68). God has 'raised up a horn of salvation for us in the house of David' (1.69). In fact, this was promised in the prophets of old (1.70). Here regal claims are placed beside divine design and prophetic promise. The initial notes about Jesus in Luke are played with the choruses of pattern, escalation, divine design and prophetic hope. The refrain is one of continuity and advance. In fact, Lk. 1.72-73 continues the emphasis on continuity by speaking of mercy promised, remembering the covenant, and of an oath sworn to Abraham. On the other hand, the remarks are very nationalistic. The goal for this regal ruler is to free God's people from their enemies and those who hate them (1.71).

The reference to the house of David in Lk. 1.69 is another specific use of an Old Testament idea. The idea of 'raising up' someone onto the scene of history describes how God is active behind the events (Deut. 18.15, 18; Judg. 3.9, 15; 1 Sam. 3.35; 2 Sam. 23.1). God brings the key figures of covenant history onto the scene. The allusion to the house of David recalls dynastic imagery from the 'Davidic covenant' of 2 Sam. 7.13-14. The description of the 'horn' of salvation describes a powerful figure who can fight off foes and bring victory (Deut. 33.17; 2 Sam. 22.3; Ps. 75.5, 6, 11; 148.14). The association of the horn with the dynastic house is also common (1 Sam. 2.10; Ps. 132.17; Ezek. 29.21). The Lukan focus on the Davidic connection will continue when Bethlehem is called the city of David (Lk. 2.4, 11). The fundamental christological category Luke draws from the Old Testament is that of ruler. The escalation of the imagery shows that Jesus is a unique ruler. Thus the term 'messiah' is appropriate.

If there were any doubt about the foundational role of the messianic function, one need only look at the set of titles used in Lk. 2.11. This passage speaks of a 'Savior born in the city of David, Christ the Lord'. The Davidic connection is made explicitly in the unusual allusion to Bethlehem as David's city.[1] The image of savior was described in the hymn of Zechariah, as Jesus was proclaimed to be the delivering Davidic horn. The image of the Christ recalls the sonship of Jesus noted in Lk. 1.31-35, as well as his rule. The only title unprepared for through Old Testament infancy allusion is 'Lord'. But this is precisely because this is the title Luke will come to define as he tells the story of Jesus. Lk. 2.11 is a major 'choral-like' refrain in the infancy section, which summarizes who Jesus is and which prepares for the account of Jesus' life which follows.

The eschatological imagery continues in the brief remarks of Simeon. Again the emphasis is on the 'messianic' character of the child (Lk. 2.26). In fact, the child represents the presence of God's salvation (Lk. 2.30) with a universal role. Jesus is light. Lk. 1.78-79 introduced this image

---

1. Normally 'the city of David' would be Jerusalem. 2 Sam. 5.7, 9; 16.10 are but a few examples of this use. The use is even more exceptional if one considers the LXX. Nowhere in the LXX is Bethlehem called the 'city of David', though 1 Kgdms 20.6 and 16.18 are close. Note especially the omissions of 1 Sam. 17.12 and 58 LXX. Mic. 5.1-2 may be behind the allusion, but it is hard to be sure.

with the Old Testament picture of the 'rising star', a passage in which a wordplay between the morning light and the 'branch' is possible in Semitic ('branch': Jer. 23.5; 33.15; Zech. 3.8; 6.12; Isa. 11.1-10; 'light': Num. 24.17; Mal. 3.20 MT).[1] In Luke 1 the image of light dominates. So also in Luke 2. Simeon speaks of Jesus' universal mission as revelation to Gentiles and glory for Israel.

In this image of revelation and glory, the appeal to imagery from Isaiah begins (Isa. 60.1-3). Here the use associates Jesus with the eschatological hope of deliverance which Isaiah's texts describe. This association also represents a mixture of prophetic and deliverance images. Isaiah 60 is not technically speaking a Servant Song, but in thrust it is like the salvation theme tied to the songs. More importantly, Isaiah 60 is part of a larger complex of texts from Isaiah, which appear in the synagogue speech of Lk. 4.17-19 (Isa. 61.1). Luke simply introduces this theme in Luke 2.

But not everything about this 'servant-like' figure is positive. There is pain coming as well. Simeon's note to Mary in Lk. 2.34-35, using images like those in Isa. 8.14-15 and 28.13-16, shows that Jesus will create a division among people and bring pain to Mary. Simeon's portrait of Jesus' authority presents the child in servant-like terms in Lk. 2.29-31. Simeon represents the Lukan emphasis on the authority and role of this servant-like figure, rather than concentrating on Jesus as the sufferer as much of the New Testament servant tradition does. For Luke, Jesus is a victorious servant, but that victory comes through pain and suffering. So here are the first ominous notes that the eschaton does not come easily and that the messiah is not embraced universally with open arms. On the other hand, the note of hope continues in a second prophet, Anna, who sees in Jesus someone who is related to the hope of the 'redemption of Jerusalem'. Here the Old Testament portrait of Jesus in the infancy material ends.

The infancy narrative's fundamental christological category from the Old Testament is that of a regal deliverer, the messiah. In Jesus the hope of covenant, as expressed in various covenants, is realized. Both Abrahamic promise and Davidic hope receive attention. The Old Testament brings a note of continuity and design. Promise and pattern are wed together as one in Jesus. But there is also escalation. The new era is greater than the old. There are hints of other basic categories, such

1. This image became decidedly messianic in many strands of Judaism: CD 7.18-19; 1QM 11.6; 4QTest 12; 4QFlor 1.11; *T. Levi* 4.4; 18.3.

as servant and prophet, but these have a minor role. There is one title, 'Lord', which is simply introduced without explanation. Luke will develop this title later, so he says next to nothing about it now.

When one comes to the body of Luke's Gospel, the categories of messiah, servant and prophet dominate the Old Testament discussion until the events of Jesus' ministry approach their turning point during Jesus' last week in Jerusalem.

As with the infancy material, John the Baptist is the frame of the Old Testament portrait, as Lk. 3.4-6 appeals to Isa. 40.3-5. This eschatological passage raises the theme of the approach of God's salvation in the activity of the forerunner. God's great deliverance, which was promised in this prologue to the salvation section of Isaiah 40–66, always raised great hope within Judaism that God would one day bring to pass all that he promised.[1] To such hope Luke now appeals. Again the note is one of design and continuity. Luke makes clear that all flesh will see this salvation, to underline the fact that Jesus appears before all nations of human beings. Only Luke notes these points. Christology and mission appear side by side.

The next text, Lk. 3.22, is the complex set of allusions associated with the voice from heaven at Jesus' baptism. Many issues are bound up in how one sees the Old Testament used here.[2] However, it seems most likely that the reference to 'Son' is an allusion to the regal title of sonship in Ps. 2.7, while the allusion to 'in whom I am well pleased' is an allusion to the portrait of the Servant of Isa. 42.1.[3] Here regal, national and covenant images are all combined. Israel was called the 'servant' in Lk. 1.54, an allusion which shows the sensitivity and diversity of Luke's usage of the servant image. The 'beloved one' is one on whom God's special favor rests. Jesus is like the nation, a special object of God's love. He also is the promised Son, who begins his mission shortly. It is the

---

1. For the history of interpretation for this text in Judaism, see K.R. Snodgrass, 'Streams of Tradition Emerging from Isaiah 40.1-5 and their Adaptation in the New Testament', *JSNT* 8 (1980), pp. 24-45.

2. For details and a defence of the position taken here, see Bock, *Proclamation from Prophecy and Pattern*, pp. 99-105.

3. In fact, it may be that a third allusion is encased in this remark. Isa. 41.8 places the ideas of the servant, love and God's appointment side by side in describing the nation's special relationship to God. Parallels would again be the point of contact here. For this connection is the fact that the parallel announcement to the baptismal voice at the transfiguration in Lk. 9.35 uniquely speaks of Jesus as the chosen.

messiah-servant who is baptized by John.

A text that I ignored in my previous study was the temptation narrative. However, it does make significant points and should be included in such any overview. Robert Brawley has studied this passage in terms of intertextuality and has emphasized the ways in which Luke portrays Jesus and recalls the story of Israel in the process.[1] Such identification with the history of the nation extends the story of God's acts to save people. It retells the story of the origin of the people of God and introduces a new phase in that history by retelling the story and recalling the founding days. It shows the use of Scripture for a theocentric reason, rather than for a merely christological one.

But another theme is here as well. The juxtaposition of Lk. 4.1-13 after the genealogy which ends with Jesus, the Son of Adam, Son of God (Lk. 3.38) makes another key point. The theme of the temptations is the issue of vice-regency and who Jesus will serve. Will he, as Son of God, serve God through miraculous self-provision? No, he will live by the Word. Will he be Satan's vice-regent and worship him? No, he will worship and serve God alone. Will he test God's faithfulness and force God to act miraculously on his behalf as Satan suggests Psalm 91 teaches? No, he will not test, and thereby doubt, the will and goodness of God. All these texts from Deuteronomy in the context of this struggle indicate that Jesus is not only representative of Israel but a worthy, faithful vice-regent of all humanity. This will be reinforced after the temptations when Jesus is called the 'Holy One of God' (Lk. 3.34) and the Christ, the Son of God, in Lk. 4.41 (a text unique to Luke).

Another text which involves a complex use of the Old Testament is Lk. 4.16-30. Here we may need to distinguish between how the pericope functions in isolation and how it functions in Luke. The text clearly raises prophetic categories. This is suggested not only by the use of Isa. 61.1, but also by the appeal to the patterns of the past in Elijah and Elisha. Jesus announces the fulfillment of a task that the anointed prophet performed in days of old. There is pattern and continuity. But there is also escalation. Within Luke's Isaiah 61 citation is an allusion to Isa. 58.6, a text which pointed to the failure of the nation to bring justice. In contrast Jesus does bring justice. In fact, Jesus not only proclaims salvation, he brings it.

In Luke's view what is fulfilled here is not just a prophetic task, but

---

1. Brawley, 'Canon and Community', pp. 419-34. This is a fine example of an intertextual study of the use of the Old Testament by a New Testament author.

also a regal, messianic one. The 'anointing' to which Lk. 4.18 alludes must, in the narrative development of Luke, refer to the anointing of Jesus by God with the Spirit at his baptism (Lk. 3.22). At the baptism, the emphasis was on a messianic-servant role, a special covenant relationship to God. Now in Luke 4 it may appear that the allusion itself, considered as an independent pericope in the isolation of the synagogue scene, is only to a prophetic function. If the original remark was only a prophetic point, it must be to a unique eschatological prophetic role, given the eschatological imagery present. But when the remark is placed alongside Jesus' baptism, Luke's emphasis is clearly greater.

In fact, the literary evidence for a messianic focus is even stronger, when one notes that the genealogy of Luke ends with Jesus as 'Son of God' and that the debate of the temptations, the previous event, is about Jesus as 'Son'. Luke 4 keeps the focus on the fundamental regal category of the messiah, while bringing in additional imagery, which associates Jesus' work with the office of prophet and eschatological prophet. Jesus is many things in one package.

Lk. 7.22, 27 represent a return to the emphasis on the presence of the eschaton, but again the messianic function of Jesus is not absent. The remarks in Luke 7 come in response to a question about whether Jesus is 'the one who comes'. This alludes back to the remarks of John the Baptist in Lk. 3.15-17, where the Baptist speaks of 'one who comes' who brings the Spirit, a new covenant allusion. In comparison to this coming figure John, as God's appointed messenger, is not worthy to do the slave's work of tying a master's sandal. The reader of Luke's Gospel is well aware of whom John is asking about in Luke 7 when the Baptist raises the question about the 'one who comes'.

Jesus does not answer the question directly; rather, he describes what he is doing in Old Testament terms. Lk. 7.22 appeals to numerous texts which describe events of the period of salvation, events which Jesus performs (Isa. 35.5-7; 29.18-19; 61.1). Jesus' answer is that his ministry speaks for itself. If one knows the Old Testament, one knows what time he brings, and thus who he is. Lk. 7.27 appeals directly to Mal. 3.1 to describe John's role. In this pericope, John is viewed from the perspective of the old era, as Lk. 7.28 makes clear. He is the greatest man born of woman, but he is less than anyone who is in the kingdom. The presupposition behind the remark is that the kingdom comes with Jesus and belongs to those who associate with him. Again there is the working out of promise, but there also is the escalation which comes with the presence of a new era. The Old Testament is the ground for describing how Jesus functions and is the launching point for describing the surpassing greatness of the new era. The Old Testament texts, though eschatological in origin, when combined with the remark about John the Baptist have a christological point. Jesus is the one who comes. Jesus brings the kingdom. So, Jesus must be the king. The fundamental messianic category is still present, though only implied, even in these fundamentally eschatological remarks.

Lk. 9.35 represents essentially a repetition of Lk. 3.22, but with three important differences. First is the narrative context of the remark. The voice from heaven represents an essential endorsement of Peter's confession of Jesus as the Christ in Lk. 9.20, a confession which itself contrasts with the popular view that Jesus is merely a prophet (Lk. 7.16; 9.7-8, 18-19). Secondly, within the declaration is a change from the earlier endorsement at the baptism. Jesus is now the 'chosen' one. Design is stressed here, and the baptismal phrase 'the one in whom I am pleased' is explained by the change. Thirdly, there is an additional reference within the heavenly remarks. The disciples are to 'listen to him'. This is an allusion to Deuteronomy 18 with its promise of a prophet like Moses. Here again the two eras are connected and yet are contrasted. The disciples have much to learn. The new era, though promised, is not entirely like the old. A new revelator is necessary to make the difference clear. The categories of messiah and prophet combine here, but this is not just any prophet. The inadequacy of the popular view of Jesus makes it clear that Jesus' prophetic function is unique. The prophet in view here is the messenger of eschaton, not like the Baptist, who merely announced its approach. The prophet like Moses announces the foundations of the new era and functions much like a ruler of the new people, as Moses did for the nation. Acts 3.14-26 will elaborate on this imagery.

Lk. 13.35 is part of a larger complex of texts in which Jesus speaks as a prophet and is presented as a regal figure. Jesus' lament over Jerusalem speaks of God's constant desire to gather the nation under his cape, like a bird protecting her young. This first-person language represents Jesus revealing the desire of God to protect the nation. The first-person remarks are reminiscent of prophetic declarations, where the prophet brings God's message directly.[1] Then follows a declaration of a

---

1. On the image of God as a bird see Deut. 32.11; Ruth 2.11; Isa. 31.5; Ps. 17.8; 36.8 (v. 7 Eng.); 57.2 (v. 1 Eng.); 61.5 (v. 4 Eng.); 91.4; 2 Bar. 41.3-4; *4 Ezra* 1.30. On God speaking in the first person through the prophet see Amos 8.11-14;

covenant judgment on the nation like the judgment of exile. Israel's house is desolate. This language recalls Jer. 12.7 and 22.5.[1] Here is judgment for a nation which has failed to act properly (Jer. 22.5-6). In Luke 13, the failure is to respond to the 'one who comes in the name of the Lord' (Ps. 117.26 LXX [118.26 Eng.]). Jesus says that their house is desolate until they recognize this one. Now it is not entirely clear in the Luke 13 context what office the 'one who comes' possesses. In the Lukan literary flow, however, it is clear that the reference recalls the description of John the Baptist in Lk. 3.15-17 and the Baptist's question of Lk. 7.20, and it also anticipates the reuse of the Psalm in Lk. 19.38. The phrase in Luke has clear regal, messianic overtones. In fact, in the Old Testament the Psalm itself looked to the priests' welcome of an entourage of pilgrims into the worship at the temple. This entourage was led in all likelihood by the king. So the passage from the Psalm simply represents an acknowledgment that the people coming to God's house are acceptable to him. Jesus says that until the nation recognizes the same truth about him and accepts him as 'sent by God' for their deliverance and protection, no protection exists for the nation. Again, the image is regal and messianic, though it is not as explicit as the next use of the Old Testament. Psalm 118, though a text which has some regal implications, is largely a descriptive text in its usage here. It is clearly not as prophetic a usage as is the next use of Psalm 118.

In Lk. 19.35-38, Jesus enters Jerusalem. He rides a donkey, an act which recalls Zech. 9.9, though Luke's appeal to this text is less explicit than Matthew's in that Luke does not note the text directly. Luke's allusion is grounded in the combination ἐπιβιβάζω ('to set') and πῶλον ('on a donkey') in Lk. 9.35. In fact, only Luke uses a direct reference to the colt at this point in his story, thus strengthening the allusion. This is regal imagery, since the Zechariah text pictures a delivering king. In Lk. 19.38 comes the reuse of Psalm 117 LXX. Here, however, there is one important addition, which serves as an explanation. Now the declaration is 'Blessed is "the King" who comes in the name of the Lord'. The regal emphasis is direct and explicit. This text is not the fulfillment of Lk. 13.35, as some have claimed. It is the disciples who make this declaration in Luke, not the people as a whole. In fact, the challenge of the Pharisees in the next pericope shows that a national acceptance is not

9.7-15; Mic. 5.10-15; 7.15. Often these texts are introduced with the statement that 'the Lord declares' what is said, but the introduction is not always present.

1.   The imagery also appears in Ps. 69.26; Ezek. 8.6; 11.23.

the point. Jesus is again a regal figure sent by God. The praise is for miracles, which Jesus performed (v. 37), the last of which in Luke was the healing of the blind beggar, who cried out to Jesus as the 'Son of David' (Lk. 18.38, 40).

One other use of Psalm 118 remains in Luke's Gospel. It comes at the end of the parable of the wicked tenants in Lk. 20.17. Here the historical indictment is set forth against the nation. Just as the nation had rejected many messengers before, so now it rejects 'the only son'. Again continuity is present, the theme of the constant rejection of God's messengers picking up the Deuteronomistic note of the nation's unfaithfulness, which is so much a part of the Old Testament historical books.[1] There is continuity with the events of old. But the use of the Psalm has an irony to it. The rejected king of the Psalm was a figure rejected by the nations which surrounded Israel. In Jesus' time, the enemy comes from within. Nonetheless, the principle of the Psalm remains. Though the chosen king is rejected by people, he is exalted by God. This is the pattern of God's activity. The reference to the 'only son', who is heir, is a regal image, since the vineyard itself pictures the blessing associated with the promise of the kingdom. In fact, the image of the stone which crushes points to the regal authority which this 'son' possesses to issue judgment. Its imagery represents a conceptual fusion of Isa. 8.14 and Dan. 2.34, 44 LXX. The parable itself is a warning about such a judgment. It is a regal Jesus who enters Jerusalem and teaches there. The point about his authority is one which Luke will develop in the transition from Luke to Acts.

The fundamental category of Lukan Old Testament Christology is a regal one. Sometimes it is suggested that Luke's Christology is rather patchwork in character, but this is not the case with his presentation through the Old Testament.[2] Luke has kept the fundamental portrait of

---

1. Though Luke does not directly cite the historical books from Joshua to Chronicles, he is aware of their presentation of divine history, as the allusions to 1 Samuel in Acts 13 show. For what portions of the Old Testament Luke uses and in what forms, see J. Fitzmyer, 'The Use of the Old Testament in Luke–Acts', in E. Lovering (ed.), *Society of Biblical Literature Seminar Papers 1992* (Atlanta: Scholars Press, 1992), pp. 524-38. He also notes most interestingly that Luke's introductory formulae are closer to the eschatological Qumran material and unlike the Mishnah.

2. C.F. Evans (*Saint Luke* [TPI New Testament Commentaries; Philadelphia: Trinity Press International, 1990], p. 65) calls Luke's Christology the 'most variegated in the NT' and argues that no title is dominant.

Jesus as the regal, Davidic hope in the forefront of almost every text. Other functions also are tied to him. The image of the servant and of the prophet also appear in places, but the messiah dominates. No wonder that, when Luke summarizes his presentation in Lk. 24.26, 43-47, he speaks of what the Old Testament predicts of 'the Christ'. What Jesus does is portrayed in a variety of texts from the Old Testament. There is continuity in what God promised, much of what the nation hoped for, and what Jesus does. If there is patchwork in Luke's portrait, it comes from the wide variety of texts he draws on as he presents the account of Jesus. Eschatological texts, dynastic texts, praise passages and prophetic declaration are all used to show how Jesus brings the time of salvation and performs the acts of deliverance. Important to this discussion are texts which Luke alone presents or which he presents in fresh ways. These include Lk. 4.16-18, 9.35, 13.35 and 19.38. These texts in one way or another strengthen the regal portrait of Jesus. They continue the refrain found in the unique overture of Luke 1–2. Yet as Jesus enters Jerusalem, the portrait will change. Luke's picture of Jesus expands in the midst of the drama which sends Jesus to his death. As events pull Jesus down to his death, Luke raises him higher. This is not just any death, as events after the death make clear.

One other point needs mention. In citing these texts Luke does not generally use the 'this was done so it might be fulfilled' introductory formula, nor does he use 'thus it stands written' to point to these texts. He simply lays the text out by the event, much as a title is placed under a great painting. He lets the event speak for itself and declare its fulfillment. Even in Luke 4, where such a point is made, it comes from within the event. Divine design as reflected from the Old Testament is seen *in* the events themselves. This heightens the prophetic emphasis, since it is not the narrator but the narrative itself which points to fulfillment.

The Climactic, Comprehensive Christological Category: Lord

The movement from Luke to Acts is especially important. Old Testament texts cluster in these chapters. They begin the movement to what are for Luke definitive descriptions of Jesus. Naturally there is interplay between Jesus' death and his exaltation. For Luke, the emphasis is always on what these events show Jesus to be, rather than on what his death accomplished.

Lk. 20.41-44 introduces the use of Psalm 110. This text is part of a triad of references to the Psalm in Luke–Acts, which are at the heart of Luke's christological development. Lk. 22.69 and Acts 2.30-36 are the other uses. In Luke 20, Jesus concludes a series of controversy accounts with a messianological question of his own, a question which is not answered here, but which is answered later. The dilemma is this. Why should the great king David call his promised messiah 'Lord', if the definitive title for the messiah is 'Son of David'? The question is a riddle of sorts. It is not an attempt to say that the title 'Son of David' is wrong, but to say that this is a less than comprehensive description of this figure. In fact, the question as Jesus raises it is simply a messianological inquiry. Jesus makes no attempt here to identify himself with this figure, though the reader is aware of the implication, given the Lukan description to this point. Luke is simply noting that Psalm 110 raises an interesting note about the respect David had for this promised one. Other imagery from Psalm 110 is totally ignored here. The right hand image, which will be so important later, is not noted. Only the introduction of the title 'Lord' is the point. This title was introduced in Lk. 2.11. It has also appeared occasionally in the narrative as a title of address for Jesus, usually as a common title of respect. More important are narrative uses of the title 'Lord', which are unique to the Synoptics. These Lukan descriptions of Jesus appear as Luke narrates certain events (7.13; 10.1, 39, 41; 11.39; 12.42a; 13.15; 17.5-6; 18.6; 19.8). Luke is saying that the key title for the messiah is 'Lord', though he has yet to fill in its content.

Luke 21.27 is an important text, because it contributes to the image of authority which Jesus bears. Here is the only Lukan use of the title 'Son of Man', which ties the title to its use in a specific Old Testament text. The text is Dan. 7.13. The image of the Son of Man on the cloud depicts the authority of this appointed figure as he returns to judge humanity. The cloud image is important. In the Old Testament, only God rides the clouds (Exod. 34.5; 14.20; Num. 10.34; Isa. 19.1; Ps. 104.3). The image is of a figure of suprahuman majesty and state. Here Jesus bears the presence and authority of the heavens. The nature of the messiah is clarified in this association with the Son of Man. In fact, the title will be reused in the key text of Lk. 22.69 to describe authority. The picture of 'the Lord' is being filled out.

But before the return comes death. A brief remark in Lk. 22.37 is the only use of Isaiah 53 in the Gospel. Here a simple point of divine design is made. Jesus will be reckoned among the transgressors. He will die as a criminal. It must be so. The picture of Jesus as the innocent martyr appears here, and it will dominate the Lukan portrait of Jesus' death on the cross.

Lk. 22.69 is a crucial text. Here Jesus is on trial and yet he issues a warning about who the real judge is. When asked if he is the Christ, Jesus responds by speaking about the 'Son of Man'. Jesus says that 'From now on' his accusers will see 'the Son of Man seated at the right hand of the power of God'. It is hard to overestimate the importance of this text for Luke. It is the remark which condemns Jesus. It also encapsulates the issue of his identity. Jesus claims to be able to go directly into God's presence, to sit at his side, and thus to exercise God's power. Jesus is telling his accusers that God accepts him and that from now on he will be the one who represents God and shares his presence. The reply combines the Son of Man title and its emphasis on authority with an allusion to Psalm 110.

The figure of the 'right hand' is a figure for rule (Exod. 11.15; 12.29— of Pharoah; 1 Kgs 1.17; 3.6; 8.25; 1 Chron. 17.16). The figure of the hand is also used of God's power (Josh. 4.24; 1 Chron. 12.23 LXX; Wis. 7.25; 2 Macc. 3.24, 38; 9.8; 1QM 1.11, 14; 4.4, 12; 6.2, 6; 10.5). The idea of going into God's presence and sitting at his side was offensive to Jews. An incident recorded in the Talmud (*b. Sanh.* 38b) shows a second-century dispute between Rabbi Akiba and others, where Akiba is rebuked for suggesting that the great king David could have such a session with God. Akiba is warned not to profane the Shekinah. The warning makes it clear that he risks being guilty of blasphemy.[1] Jesus' claim is one of sharing authority with God, being his confidant and mediator. Here is the essence of Jesus' Lordship for Luke, as Acts 2 will make even clearer. For Luke, Jesus' role is described in the Old Testament. It is often asked why Luke uses no texts when he speaks of the Old Testament fulfillment in Lk. 24.26-27, 43-47. The answer is simple. The texts are presented throughout his two volumes as Luke builds his portrait of Jesus from 'the earth up'. Luke has used the Old Testament to present the promise of Jesus. The promise is laid next to events, so the reader can see that what happened was also described in the Old Testament. Luke begins with categories to which his readers can relate: categories such as messiah, prophet, servant. Then he expands the

---

1. D.R. Catchpole, 'You have Heard his Blasphemy', *TynBul* 16 (1965), pp. 10-18; F. Neugebauer, 'Die Davidssohnfrage (Mark XII.35-37 Parr.) und der Menschensohn', *NTS* 21 (1974–75), p. 107 n. 1.

limits of what those categories mean as he presents Jesus as Lord, the one who bears authority as the Son of Man. The answer to another christological dilemma may be found in Luke's approach. The reason the title 'Son of Man' disappears and is not used by the church is that it comes to be regarded as equivalent to the title 'Lord'.

For completeness, we must touch on the allusions to various Psalms in Luke 23. As Jesus dies various images are used to show him as the innocent, faithful, righteous one who dies unjustly at the hands of those who ignore God's ways. Most of these allusions come from lament psalms (Ps. 22.8-9 in Lk. 23.35; Ps. 22.19 in Lk. 23.34; Ps. 69.22 in Lk. 23.36; and Ps. 31.5 in Lk. 23.46). His death was unjust, but it fitted the pattern of rejection which the righteous face.

The Lukan Psalm 110 triad is completed in Acts 2.14-40. Here eschatological texts like Joel 2 are placed alongside texts of hope like Psalm 16 and dynastic texts like Psalm 110 to explain the death and resurrection of Jesus. The argument of the speech is complex and a detailed treatment here is beyond the scope of a synthesis.[1] The essential linkage is this. God promised the coming of the Spirit and now in the 'last days' this has come (Joel 2). God promised David that his seed would sit on his throne and not be left to decay in Sheol (Pss. 16.8-10 and 132.11). The resurrection fulfills the promise of an immediate, bodily resurrection. The resurrection means that Jesus is exalted to God's right hand and distributes the Spirit which God promised would come. The one promised to David has come. The presence of the Spirit is evidence of Jesus' position of authority at the right hand of God. Psalm 110 describes this 'co-regency' rule of Jesus. In fact, Joel calls upon people to call upon the Lord. Psalm 110 makes it clear that Jesus is both Lord and messiah. One who is baptized now is baptized in the name of Jesus. In short, to call upon the Lord is to call upon Jesus, who distributes the blessing of the Spirit. This is the essential argument of Acts 2, which as the inaugural post-resurrection speech has a central importance in Luke–Acts. It argues that God is at work through Jesus. Christology serves to explain the divine plan and activity. God pours out the Spirit, raises Jesus from the dead and shows Jesus to be Lord and Christ by doing so.

The key to the speech is that it presents the imagery of fulfillment for both Davidic and new covenant promise. The linkage occurs through Joel 2, the allusion to Psalm 132 and the use of Psalm 110. The key is

---

1. The details can be found in Bock, *Proclamation from Prophecy and Pattern*, pp. 156-87.

not just that Jesus is messiah, but that he is Lord (note that 'Lord' is in the emphatic position in Acts 2.36). Religious rites are performed, not in the name of Yahweh, but the name of Jesus. In Acts 2 all the limits on Christology are broken as Jesus' function is totally equated with that of God. Jesus has become the authoritative mediator of divine blessing. Jesus is 'Lord', and for Luke this is the central christological truth and function. Again Luke says that to understand Jesus we must look to the Old Testament and its promise. What Jesus does is described there. He parallels the functions of the time of salvation and represents the hoped-for figure of salvation. He breaks the limits of earth and performs his tasks from heaven, from the right hand of God. Jesus' death was not a roadblock to hope, but it was the door through which exaltation and hope could be realized. The death was not the end of the road; it was the road to heaven. With the completion of this Psalm 110 triad, Luke's christological portrait has reached its height. Subsequent references only fill out the basic picture.

Acts 3 is a defense from the Torah of Jesus as the eschatological prophet like Moses. He brings covenant blessing or cursing, depending on the response. The comparison to Moses is not lacking in regal overtones, since Jesus is a revelator and an authoritative leader around whom a new community is present. Acts 4.11 has two uses of the Psalms. Psalm 118 returns in the image of the rejected stone who is exalted and bears authority, while the prayer of the community in Acts 4.25-26 appeals to Psalm 2 to show how everyone has opposed God's messiah. An allusion to Psalm 110's exaltation and to Deuteronomy 21 with its curse for one who hangs on a tree appears in Acts 5.31. Acts 8 discusses whether Isa. 53.7-8 describes the prophet or another. Philip presents Jesus from this text.

The next key text comes in Acts 10, because it is a clue as to how Lordship relates to mission. Here Peter speaks to a Gentile audience. There are no Old Testament citations, only allusions, as is the case with the other speech to pure Gentiles in Acts 17.[1] But the theme is clear. Jesus is 'Lord of all' (Acts 10.36). This remark, though syntactically parenthetical, introduces the theme of the speech. Everything Peter describes in the following verses describes Jesus' Lordship authority. He has authority over demons (v. 38). He is judge of the living and the dead (v. 42). The theme of prophetic hope is appealed to as the speech closes.

---

1.   The allusions here are to Isa. 61.1 in Acts 10.38 and to Deut. 21.22-23 in Acts 10.39. Both of these texts have already been developed in Luke.

To him all the prophets bear witness that everyone who believes in him receives forgiveness of sins through his name (v. 43). Salvific authority resides in Jesus. In short, Jesus is Lord of all, so the gospel can go to all. 'Everyone who believes' can receive forgiveness. Here Christology and mission merge. Luke is making a transition. The Old Testament describes who Jesus is; now it will help to explain how mission will proceed.

One other purely christological speech exists in Acts. It comes in Acts 13. Here Paul presents Jesus as the promised Davidic messiah. Luke returns to his basic category. But Luke can also portray Jesus' authority in the speech. The Son (Ps. 2.7) has been given the 'holy things of David' (Isa. 55.3 LXX) and has been raised as promised (Ps. 16). The Pauline refrain for response is little different from Peter's announcement except for one Jewish touch: forgiveness of sins comes through this man and liberation from that which the law could not do is available for the one who believes. The text closes with a warning not to reject the message (Hab. 1.5 LXX).

This is the last explicitly christological Old Testament text in Luke–Acts. Three quarters through the two volumes, these citations stop, never to be resumed. The christological portrait is complete. What the Old Testament described (and therefore promised) has taken place. Jesus is the messiah, the servant, the prophet, and the prophet like Moses. But beyond all of this he is the Son of Man, which means that he is Lord. There is continuity between Jesus' life and Old Testament hope. What was promised has come. This is the point of Luke's use of the Old Testament. It is proclamation, not proof. The proclamation comes as events speaks for themselves, when placed beside Old Testament texts. The proclamation comes through prophecy and pattern.[1] God is at work in Jesus. For Luke, looking at the Old Testament and looking at the events will show that it is so.

Christology serves to reveal the divine plan. Luke's use of the Old Testament is not a repudiation of its message about Israel's hope, but is

---

1. This is where I would alter slightly the emphasis made famous by Paul Schubert. Luke's use of the Old Testament for Christology is not proof from prophecy. It is not mere apologetic. It is setting forth Jesus in proclamation. The use of the Old Testament is not dominated by texts which are merely read as prophetic. Rather a variety of texts are appealed to and the appeal comes both through prophecy and through the reappearance of patterns of God's activity. In short, Luke's use of the Old Testament for Christology should be described as 'proclamation from prophecy and pattern'.

a challenge and appeal to hear it anew in the light of recent events. God speaks through those events tied to Jesus and through the reading of Scripture which explains them. He appropriates Israel's history and shows how that nation can obtain greatness for itself and for all humanity through Jesus. The entire argument assumes an audience well versed in the Scripture. The dispute Luke writes about seems to involve both the Jew and the Greek. They are the implied readers of Luke's appeal.

But why does Christology stop? How is the Old Testament used from here on in Acts? It is to this final question that we now turn, since almost all of the explicit Old Testament citations in Acts from this point on treat either Gentile mission or Jewish rejection.[1] Is there a relationship between Christology and mission, which helps not only to explain this shift of focus, but Luke's task as well?

Gentile Mission and Israelite Rejection

As attention is turned to a new set of themes, it would be well to review their narrative development to this point in Acts 13. Luke treats the concept of Gentile inclusion in a variety of texts, some of which have already been noted. Lk. 2.32 begins to raise this note with its use of imagery from Isaiah, showing that Jesus the messiah will be light for revelation to the Gentiles. The use of Isaiah for missionary hope is significant to Luke, as will become clear. Isaiah 40 is the base for the remark that all flesh will see the salvation of God (Lk. 3.6). In Lk. 7.9 it is the faith of a foreigner, a centurion, which is cited as exemplary by Jesus. Lk. 13.29 and 14.23 contain allusions to Gentile inclusion in the midst of parables. In Luke 13 people will come from north, south, east and west to be in the kingdom, while those who expected to be included are excluded. In Luke 14 a double set of invitations is issued so that the banquet table will be full. The second invitation goes outside the city. Luke alone has this double invitation for this parable. An allusion to Gentile inclusion is likely here.[2] Lk. 20.16 also includes a parabolic reference, when Jesus notes that the vineyard, which now is in the hands of wicked tenants, will go to others after they slay the only son. In Acts, the mission to the Samaritans (Acts 8) and to Cornelius (Acts 10) open

---

1.   The only exception is found in Acts 23.5, where Paul notes that he should show respect for the high priest (Exod. 22.7).

2.   T.W. Manson, *The Sayings of Jesus* [London: SCM Press, 1949], p. 130) even suggests an allusion to the message of Isa. 49.6 here, but this is less than clear.

up this expectation into reality. The first missionary journey, which is where the Acts 13 speech comes, is Luke's initial description of an active mission into such regions.

The theme of Israelite rejection also comes into play in the Gospel. In fact, one could argue that one of the major burdens of the unique Jerusalem journey section, especially Luke 9–13, is to show that the way of official Judaism is not the way to God. These chapters are built on a series of contrasts between how Jesus approaches God and how the leadership does. Implied in all of this is that this leadership fails to provide guidance in how to find God.

But more explicit texts also underscore this point. A hint of trouble comes in the infancy narrative when Mary is told that Jesus' ministry will bring her pain, an allusion to the division Jesus will bring. The first clear warning comes from John the Baptist, when he warns his audience not to rely on their Abrahamic roots (Lk. 3.7-9). Lk. 4.25-27 warns of the nation experiencing another period like that of Elijah and Elisha, when Gentiles were blessed and the nation starved. A stinging rebuke comes in Lk. 11.37-52, where Pharisees and lawyers are criticized for their hypocrisy. Rather than having the key to heaven these leaders function like open graves for the people. These remarks are hardly an endorsement of Israel's security. Another recognition that Jesus brings division comes in the pericope about divided families in Lk. 12.49-53.

In Luke 13 the warnings become explicit. Lk. 13.6-9 contains a parable in which the uprooting of the fruitless fig tree is graciously postponed. The passage stresses that the nation's time to respond is short. Lk. 13.34-35 has the first prophetic declaration that Israel's house is desolate. The nation is guilty of covenant unfaithfulness and is headed for judgment. Lk. 19.41-44 is even more specific, as the fall of Jerusalem is described in detail. Covenant unfaithfulness has led to judgment which parallels the old siege of the capital by the Babylonians. Again, parallelism with the days of old becomes the basis for how God will act in the present (Ps. 137.9; Nah. 3.10; Jer. 6.6-21; 8.13-22; Isa. 3.26; 29.1-4; Ezek. 4.1-2). Lk. 20.16 was mentioned above. The nation is losing the vineyard. Finally, on the way to the cross, Jesus tells the 'women of Jerusalem' not to weep for him (Lk. 23.28-31). He then cites Hos. 10.8. The image is of approaching judgment, which is so great that the people will cry for relief.

The theme of potential rejection appears in Acts in the form of warnings in the speeches. Acts 2.40 and 3.23 warn the people of impending judgment. Acts 2, with its use of Joel, invokes imagery of cosmic signs to suggest the approach of the Day of the Lord, while Acts 3 uses Lev. 23.39 to warn of the dire consequences of covenant unfaithfulness. So both the concept of mission and of Israelite rejection form sub-themes in Luke–Acts up to Luke 13.

The last half of Acts deals with the fate of Paul in mission. But there are very few missionary speeches of Paul in these chapters. Most of his speeches are speeches of defense. Acts 13 represents the only detailed speech made to a Jewish audience by Paul. After presenting Jesus as the promised Davidic hope, this speech closes with a warning to his audience. It is first of four remaining Old Testament texts which treat either the consequences of rejection or mission.

The citation is from Hab. 1.5 LXX. The LXX version is an expanded citation of the MT, which develops the Old Testament context. The references to scoffers and to 'perishing' (so RSV) are not in the MT, but the tone of rebuke and warning is the same in both versions. The remarks in the Old Testament constitute a divine rebuke to Habakkuk for questioning God's justice in the exercise of exilic judgment. Paul again creates a parallel. He appeals to a pattern. Do not scoff, and risk perishing, as those of Habakkuk's generation did. God is at work, and do not deny that he is present. The parallel is particularly appropriate, since Habakkuk's charge was that God was absent and unconcerned. The prophet claimed that God was not involved in the events of Israel. The Jewish charge in Paul's time was similar. God was not present in the activities surrounding Jesus. Paul warns his audience not to make the mistake of those who experienced exile. Paul says, in effect, 'Do not be among those who do not believe'. There is a pattern to God's actions, and unbelief in God's new acts will meet with God's rejection. The divine reply in Habakkuk has conceptual parallels in Isa. 28.21-22 and 29.14. The warning is similar to Peter's warning using Lev. 23.29 in Acts 3.23. Of course, God's acts, which are to be believed, are those tied to the coming of Jesus, which Paul has outlined in Acts 13.16-39.

The 'necessity' of Paul's mission is developed even later in the chapter. Two Sabbaths later, Paul is challenged by the Jews and so he declares the necessity of going to the nation first and then to the Gentiles. The basis of his view of mission is the command of the Lord cited in Acts 13.47. Here Paul cites Isa. 49.6. Paul and Barnabas are 'light for the Gentiles', that they might 'bring salvation to the uttermost parts of the earth'. The interesting thing about the citation is that it is an application of Isaianic servant imagery not to Jesus but to his followers. Also interesting is the introductory formula. Here Paul speaks of the Lord giving this command. This appears to be an allusion back to the Lord's report to Ananias about Paul's mission to the Gentiles in Acts 9.15. Acts 22.15 also suggests as much, as does especially Acts 26.17-18. Acts 26 even uses the image of light to make the point. Thus the commission is both a command from God (as seen in the Old Testament allusion) and from the Lord Jesus, who is the source of the commission. The mission is directed from heaven and is subject to the commission of the Lord Jesus. Here Christology and mission come together as they did in Peter's speech in Acts 10. Yet the link of continuity to the Old Testament is also still present. Paul takes up the task of the Servant. His task is like the messenger of old. There is design, direction and pattern in Paul's activity. There is unity between what God spoke in days of old and what the Lord Jesus commands his disciples now. What Jesus was (Lk. 2.32), his disciples now become.

The next citation comes in Acts 15.16-17. This is the citation of Amos 9.11 LXX. It is clear that Christology and mission come together here. The rebuilt Davidic house is the ground upon which the rest of humanity may seek God. Gentiles who are called by God's name may come. Acts 15.11 describes the offer of salvation as coming through the grace of the Lord Jesus in Peter's remarks, to which James adds assent with his citation of Amos. James regards this text as fulfilled in the current activity of the church. His introductory formula is also important, since he says 'the words of the prophets agree' with Peter's remarks and the testimony of Paul and Barnabas. The plural suggests that James is citing but one text of several he might note. He is also portrayed as citing a particularly Hellenistic version of the passage, possibly to show goodwill, as well as to make use of a particularly explicit text, where Christology and mission are put together. The rebuilding of the house of David recalls remarks in Acts 2.28-36 and Lk. 1.32-33. So yet again Christology is the ground for mission and the use of the Old Testament links the two together.

The final passage is Acts 28.26-27. In between Paul has made one key summary description of his mission in Acts 20.21. In Acts 20 Paul says to the Ephesian elders that his call was to testify to 'both Jews and Greeks of repentance to God and faith in our Lord Jesus Christ'. Acts 20.24 says that he received this ministry from the Lord Jesus. Paul preaches the kingdom (v. 25). This commitment brings him to Rome, after a long and dangerous journey.[1] As many have noted, Paul's journey to Rome is like Jesus' to Jerusalem. But there is one difference. Jesus goes to Jerusalem to die. Paul goes to Rome to preach.

Here Paul again shares with the Jews and again defines his mission in terms of Isaiah, when he meets with rejection. Paul places the remarks of Isaiah in their historical frame when he says that the 'Holy Spirit was right to say to your fathers' what was spoken through the prophets. Then Paul cites Isa. 6.9-10. Here is the pattern appearing one last time. Paul knows what happened long ago and what is happening now. What happens to the church today happened to God's great messengers of old. There is continuity and design in God's plan. The passage itself is part of Isaiah's commission and warned the ancient prophet that the people would not hear his message. Paul is saying that a similar thing happens when he preaches the gospel. So Paul says that the message goes to Gentiles. They, he says, will listen. The passage, and indeed the book, concludes with Paul preaching the kingdom of God and the Lord Jesus Christ openly. Mission and Christology close the book. Appropriately enough, the two key titles for Jesus appear at the end. Christ, the foundational title, and Lord, the climactic title, summarize well who Jesus is as he brings in the kingdom (Acts 28.31).

Summary

It is my contention that promise as expressed in pattern and prophecy explains how the Old Testament is used in Luke–Acts. Pattern points to design and allows Luke to make associations between what happened to the messengers of old and what happened to Jesus and the church. Behind the promise and the pattern is the God who is the same, yesterday, today and forever. The Old Testament is designed to show continuity and the presence of fulfillment. Luke's use of the Old Testament seeks ultimately to explain God's plan. Such use has a theo-centric goal. The new community is involved in events that are divinely directed and inspired, and the venerated historical record of God's

---

1.   A major function of the sea journey in Acts 27 is, in my judgment, to show that Rome belongs to the 'uttermost parts of the earth'. The journey also shows divine protection. Although Rome was the center of activity in the ancient world, as E.E. Ellis has shown ('"The End of the Earth" [Acts 1.8]', *BBR* 1 [1991], pp. 123-32), in the narrative world of Luke–Acts it is on the fringe, since the center of the world for the Luke–Acts narrative is Jerusalem.

people shows that this is so. In addition, the two major themes of Old Testament fulfillment are Christology and mission. Old Testament Christology is presented from 'the earth up' as the portrait moves from Jesus as messiah to Lord. Other portraits also have a significant role. Jesus is like the Servant, like the prophet and like the prophet like Moses.[1] In his Lordship, Jesus bears the authority of the Son of Man. A variety of texts are appealed to and brought together to paint this portrait. Dynastic, eschatological and prophetic descriptions unite in Jesus.

However, Christology is not unrelated to mission. Jesus is Lord of all, so the message can go to all (Acts 10.36-43). Mission has two expected elements: Gentile inclusion and Israelite hardening and rejection. This too parallels the days of old and was anticipated in God's previous activity and promise. In the realities of the nation's exile and the past treatment of the prophets lies the prediction of how the nation responds to God's messengers. In the hope of salvation as described by the ministry of Isaiah and the picture of the servant comes not only the reality of Israelite hardening, but also of Gentile inclusion. Davidic salvation was to encompass the world. The rule of the returning Davidide would know no national boundary. In the rebuilding of the dynastic line, the kingdom would extend to the uttermost parts of the earth.

Here is Luke's use of the Old Testament for Christology and mission. It is a theodicy and more. It is a declaration and proclamation of hope and comfort to those who will hear. I disagree with those who would challenge either the presence of promise or the importance the Old Testament plays as the supposition for mission in Luke–Acts. But can one fix a setting for this emphasis?

The conclusion one draws from this vast array of textual data is that Luke was presenting and defending salvation in Jesus, particularly as it is extended to the Gentiles. This is not to be seen as a defense of Pauline mission per se, but of what his mission represents, the activity of God on behalf of all humanity. Luke is saying that the way to God is not found

---

1. Another significant christological theme is Jesus as a suffering figure, but this motif emerges more from allusions than citations. See D. Moessner, ' "The Christ Must Suffer": Rethinking the Theology of the Cross in Luke–Acts', in D.J. Lull (ed.), *Society of Biblical Literature Seminar Papers 1990* (Atlanta: Scholars Press, 1990), pp. 165-95. Also to be considered with regard to Luke's use of Old Testament allusion and story is D. Moessner, *Lord of the Banquet* (Philadelphia: Fortress Press, 1988), which highlights the use of the 'prophet like Moses' motif and the appeal to the patterns of the Deuteronomistic History in Lk. 9–19.

in Israel, but in the church which offers the gospel to all. In fact, Israel is heading for (or has already experienced) judgment for its lack of piety and rejection of Jesus.[1] This Israelite concern is a major burden of Luke 9–19, along with detailing how the new community should live in relation to human beings. The attention paid to Paul in Acts only makes sense in the light of a concern to justify Gentile mission. The same can be said for the role Peter has in taking the gospel to Cornelius. I see Theophilus as a Gentile who either is considering, or more likely has responded to, the Christian faith. In all likelihood, Theophilus had been a proselyte of Judaism or a 'God fearer', who had turned to Christ. The depth of the use of Scripture and the assumption that a reader of Luke would appreciate it suggests contact with Judaism. But he now, and many others like him, need reassurance that he belongs in this move-ment. Simply put, his question might be: 'What is a Gentile doing in what was essentially a Jewish movement, especially when Jews around the world are reacting negatively to it?'; 'Is God really in this work?'; 'Do I really need to be prepared to suffer for this belief?'

On the other hand, Luke is also dealing with charges that raise doubts, such as: 'God is judging those in this new community for making salva-tion too broad. The evidence of persecution is evidence of God's rejection.' Luke's reply is that God's activity and the testimony of the Old Testament show that Gentiles were always to be included. Christology teaches it as well. In fact, persecution is not a sign of judgment. It reflects the repetition of the patterns of old. The church is like the prophets of old, being rejected by the people to whom they were sent (Lk. 6.23, 26). But persecution is also, paradoxically, the means by which the message is spread to the ends of the earth. As for the claims of the nation, they can be challenged, for the nation stands in judgment. This newly emerging community did not seek to be separate

---

1.   Whether one reads the text or the parenthesis depends on how one dates Luke–Acts. Those who are convinced that Lk. 19.41-44 evidences knowledge of the fall of Jerusalem in AD 70 will see Luke's explanation as applying to a nation which has already fallen. Although this is possible, I am not sure that so much can be made to rest on these descriptions, which repeat themes form the Old Testament for covenant unfaithfulness. The concern to justify salvation to the Gentiles, explain the response of disciples in the church, exhort the disciples to faithfulness and present Gentile inclusion and recent events as God's doing would seem to presuppose an earlier time-frame in the sixties, but the case for the use of the Old Testament does not hinge on the dating of the book. The themes remain regardless of when the two volumes were written.

from the nation; it was forced out of the synagogue and temple. The new community of God was forged out of the fires of a large national rejection of Jesus. Its presence and the pressure it is under do not suggest divine rejection. This recent history fits a pattern of activity that reaches back into the days of old. The church goes to Gentiles, because the promise of the Scriptures said it should and because God and Jesus directed that it be so. In short, Jesus is Lord of all, so the gospel can go to all. It is God who has done all of this, just as Scripture shows. It is a theodicy about the relationship of Israel to this new community that we today know as the church. The way to God comes though the Lord Jesus. Luke proclaims this truth by laying events next to Old Testament texts and letting the reader see that it is so. It is proclamation from prophecy and pattern.

INTERTEXTUAL USE OF SIRACH 48.1-16 IN PLOTTING LUKE–ACTS

William S. Kurz, SJ

Introduction

Suggestions about Lukan resonances with the Elijah and Elisha stories are commonplace, but the possible special influence on Luke–Acts of the Elijah–Elisha segment in Sirach 48 has not been emphasized.[1] In this essay I will propose and argue the thesis that the basic plotline of Luke–Acts was influenced by the plot structure of Sir. 48.1-16. This passage underscores a pattern of God's λαός refusing to repent despite the powerful ministries of both Elijah and his successor Elisha, and therefore being plundered and scattered from their land. Luke–Acts exhibits intertextual use of this pattern in plotting the account of the wonder-working prophet Jesus and his wonder-working successors, the apostles in Acts.

The argument for this thesis is built not only on standard approaches to allusions and influences from the Jewish Scriptures on New Testament passages, but also on literary insights both into intertextuality and into how disparate episodes are plotted into a continuous narrative. Arguing this thesis promises further insight into how the Lukan author organized the materials that went into his Gospel and Acts, which comprise one quarter of the New Testament, and deeper understanding of how the Old Testament is used in the writing of New Testament narratives, and the relevance of this comprehension for source criticism, historical questions, questions about the nature and genre of Gospels and Acts, canonical approaches and the like.

It is important to situate this approach among contemporary studies of functions of the Old Testament in the Gospels and other New Testament narratives. This intertextual approach allows more explicitly for multiple influences on a New Testament narrative plot (in this case Luke–Acts),

---

1. For an overview and critique of theories about the influence of the Elijah-Elisha cycle on Luke–Acts, see C.A. Evans, 'Luke's Use of the Elijah/Elisha Narratives and the Ethic of Election', *JBL* 106 (1987), pp. 75-83.

with less insistence on conscious Lukan imitation of only this particular Old Testament text (Sir. 48.1-16).[1] This literary approach to inter-textuality, however, differs from that of deconstruction, where inter-textuality is a springboard for associative speculations about semiotic or cultural matters in general,[2] or a way to dissociate concepts from their references so as to rewrite history according to contemporary ideologies and agendas.

My intertextual approach studies the ways in which ancient written texts like Luke–Acts utilize within their cultural matrices the conven-tions, vocabulary, concepts, even plots and other narrative elements of classics (especially the Greek Old Testament and some other Hellenistic classics) to narrate the new account at hand, the story of Jesus and the rise of the church.[3] On this general foundation, I argue the plausibility of the thesis that the plot-structure of the Elijah–Elisha segment of Sirach 48 functioned as the model for a similar plot-structure in the two-volume narrative of Luke–Acts.

This approach presupposes some methodological cautions. To argue

---

1. This continues the direction taken by Evans, 'Elijah/Elisha Narratives': after recalling earlier debates between those arguing Deuteronomistic or Kings influence on Luke–Acts, he notes that extensive Lukan use of one Old Testament text increases the possibility that he similarly used other portions of the Old Testament (p. 77).

2. Hans-Peter Mai warns us about possible confusion from conflicting defini-tions of inter-textuality in use today: 'A poststructural approach uses the concept as a springboard for associative speculations about semiotic and cultural matters in general. On the other hand, traditional literary studies have seized upon the term to integrate their investigative interests in structures and interrelations of literary texts under a comprehensive, and fashionable sounding, catch-all term. These divergent interpreta-tive interests cannot be reconciled theoretically' (H.-P. Mai, 'Bypassing Intertexuality: Hermeneutics, Textual Practice, Hypertext', in H.F. Plett (ed.), *Intertextuality* [Research in Text Theory/Untersuchungen zur Texttheorie, 15; Berlin and New York: de Gruyter, 1991], pp. 30-59; Summary, p. 51). My use of intertextuality is that of traditional literary studies, not a poststructural deconstruction. It is based on observa-tions of how written texts, especially in the ancient world, work within a cultural matrix of classics, in this case especially the Jewish Scriptures.

3. Compare J. Culler, *The Pursuit of Signs: Semiotics, Literature, Deconstruction* (Ithaca, NY: Cornell University Press, 1981), p. 103. Culler remarks about the double focus of intertextuality: first as calling 'our attention to the importance of prior texts', because 'a work has the meaning it does only because certain things have previously been written'. But intertextuality also 'becomes less a name for a work's relation to particular prior texts than a designation of its participation in the discursive space of a culture' (in Luke's case that dominated by the LXX).

that the basic outline of the overall plot is based on the peculiar plot thrust of Sir. 48.1-16 is not to deny the influence of other Old Testament occurrences of the Elijah–Elisha cycle on the plotting of Luke–Acts. It is to argue that along with the Elijah–Elisha accounts in Kings and their echoes in Malachi, Sirach 48 has certain characteristic emphases that correspond to emphases found especially in Lukan *Sondergut* or distinctively Lukan redaction of source material. Although some clear allusions are needed to point to the Sirach perspective in distinction from other versions, the data for establishing the credibility of this hypothesis are generally not found in verbatim quotations or echoes of Sirach 48 in Luke–Acts. What we know of the Greco-Roman rhetorical and educational practice of *imitation* of earlier sources indicates, rather, a concern to apply traditional material creatively to new situations and themes. One aspect of this in historiography is the expectation that new authors will rewrite their sources in their own style.[1] Influence from Sirach 48 is rather in patterns in the *plotting* of Luke–Acts, which is undoubtedly less easy to substantiate than verbatim quotations.

It is clear that in its short summary narrative of Elijah and Elisha, which is based on the longer accounts in Kings, Sir. 48.1-16 has imposed on several distinct episodes a plot structure of double rejection by God's λαός: the people reject first the prophet Elijah and then his successor Elisha, which leads to their removal from their land. If one can demonstrate similar Lukan use of Old Testament plot patterns for the short narratives commonly agreed to be his own creations, such as the reviews of Israel's history in speeches in Acts, this will add plausibility to the hypothesis that the Lukan author was aware of such a pattern in Sir. 48.1-16 and used that pattern for his overall plot ordering of source materials into his two-volume narrative of Luke and Acts.

Literary-Critical Intertextuality, Allusion and Writing with Scripture

Before we turn to the specific arguments and evidence for positing Sir. 48.1-16 as plot outline for Luke–Acts, some new applications of secular

---

1.   Cf. T.L. Brodie, 'Greco-Roman Imitation of Texts as a Partial Guide to Luke's Use of Sources', in C.H. Talbert (ed.), *Luke–Acts: New Perspectives from the Society of Biblical Literature Seminar* (New York: Crossroad, 1984), pp. 17-46. See his extensive discussion and references, esp. T.M. Greene, *The Light in Troy: Imitation and Discovery in Renaissance Poetry* (New Haven: Yale University Press, 1982), ch. 4, 'Themes of Ancient Theory', pp. 54-80, and the notes on pp. 305-308.

literary criticism and other distinctions from previous classical treatments of this problem may help provide a broader context than those supposed by earlier arguments.

Principles of intertextual writing, patterning later biblical accounts after earlier ones and rewriting earlier narratives in subsequent versions for later situations all imply complexity in the way allusions, typologies and patterns from earlier texts are used in later narratives. Looking for a one-to-one correspondence, especially a verbal one, between a New Testament text and a single Old Testament text often seems overly narrow a search.

Robert Brawley remarks 'how scriptural precursors and their successors resonate against each other to form allusive meanings that elude literal explanations'.[1] He reminds us of this in his criticism of Thomas Brodie:

> In a series of articles Thomas Brodie has argued that the Elijah–Elisha narratives provide literary source material for the composition of portions of Luke–Acts. But the evidence he marshals is meager and untested by authenticating criteria. Further, theories of composition from literary sources are far different from noting allusions.[2]

Daniel Boyarin also refers to the ways in which later writings use earlier scriptural words, expressions and patterns in new contexts (in midrashic fashion) to express new concerns: 'If I wish to pray, argue with God, interpret, or read, all I have is God's words with which to do so.

---

1. R.L. Brawley, 'Canon and Community: Intertextuality, Canon, Interpretation, Christology, Theology, and Persuasive Rhetoric in Luke 4.1-13', in E.H. Lovering (ed.), *Society of Biblical Literature Seminar Papers 1992* (SBLSP, 31; Atlanta: Scholars Press, 1992), pp. 419-34, here p. 419.

2. Brawley, 'Canon and Community', p. 424 n. 27. Brawley adds that overt biblical citation requires 'a common understanding of canon with the authorial audience', whereas 'covert allusions constrain the reader to recognize the intertext, and the reader presumes a community of interpretation with shared values and conventions' (p. 433). Therefore one can postulate that the Lukan community had the LXX in its cultural repertoire, so that it could recognize allusions to the LXX (p. 434). 'Scripture constitutes a conspicuous part of the knowledge Luke–Acts presumes of its readers' (p. 420). Brawley (p. 421 n. 11) also cites O. Steck ('Theological Streams of Tradition', in D. Knight [ed.], *Tradition and Theology in the Old Testament* [Philadelphia: Fortress Press, 1977], pp. 183-214) as understanding uses by later Hebrew biblical books of earlier texts 'as adaptations of streams of tradition to concrete events in order to interpret new historical experiences'.

Midrashic reading is discovery of meaning through the interanimation of recontexted verses'.[1]

Another methodological nuance to be mentioned is the notion of 'writing with Scripture' as elucidated by Jacob Neusner and William Scott Green. As Neusner puts it:

> When Judaic and Christian authorships proposed to compose their statements, they of course appealed to scripture. But it was an appeal to serve a purpose defined not by scripture but by the faith—the Judaic or Christian system—under construction and subject to articulation. Scripture formed a dictionary, providing a vast range of permissible usages of intelligible words. Scripture did not dictate the sentences that would be composed through the words of that (limited) dictionary...It [the Church] spoke through those [Old Testament] writings. It appealed to their facts...Its life and faith were nourished by those writings. But the Church came first, then the scriptures, and, ultimately, the Bible, Old and New Testaments forming one complete and wholly harmonious, seamless statement and document. And so it was with the Judaism of the dual Torah, in its framework and within its inner logic and discipline.[2]

My claim—that the Lukan author made his overall plotline resonate with that contained in Sir. 48.1-16—functions in this context of the LXX as a prominent component of the Lukan cultural repertoire and in the context of 'writing with Scripture' which is common to both rabbinical and Christian first- and second-century authors. The pattern of God's people rejecting both prophet and successor and hence being evicted from their land becomes part of the Lukan 'vocabulary' with which he makes his own statement about Jewish reaction to Jesus and his apostolic successors.[3]

---

1. D. Boyarin, 'Old Wine in New Bottles: Intertextuality and Midrash', *Poetics Today* 8.3-4 (1987), pp. 539-56, here p. 546. Cf. D. Boyarin, *Intertextuality and the Reading of Midrash* (Indiana Studies in Biblical Literature; Bloomington and Indianapolis: Indiana University Press, 1990).

2. J. Neusner, 'Judaic and Christian Uses of Scripture: "As it is Said" or "The Old Testament in the New"', in *idem* with W.S. Green, *Writing with Scripture: The Authority and Uses of the Hebrew Bible in the Torah of Formative Judaism* (Minneapolis: Fortress Press, 1989), pp. 1-6, here p. 3.

3. W.S. Green sees the application of the term 'intertextuality' as more appropriate to later Old Testament and intertestamental and New Testament texts than to rabbinic use of the Jewish Scriptures: 'Indeed, in obvious contrast to the "inner biblical exegesis" described by Fishbane, in which later expansions and modifications are intricately embedded in earlier texts, and contrary to early Christian materials such as Luke's infancy narrative or the Book of Revelation, which subtly appropriate

To articulate the process of allusion to Sirach 48 I am suggesting for Luke–Acts, I find especially helpful an article 'On Alluding' by Carmela Perri. She characterizes allusion *semantically* as a species of the genus reference, and *pragmatically* as a speech act used to do things with words.[1]

Her semantic approach defines 'allusion' as 'the marker in the alluding text, the sign...that points to a referent by echoing it in some way. Allusion markers are possible to recognize and echoes are sufficiently overt to be understood' (p. 290). Allusion markers not only denote unique source texts but 'they also tacitly specify the property(ies) belonging to the source text's connotation relevant to the allusion's meaning' (p. 291). Referents in allusion must be recognized and their relevant connotations applied, but this is only the primary level in alluding. 'Its great power of signification resides in the additional inter- and intra-textual patterns of associated attributes it can evoke once the primary sense is comprehended' (p. 293). Unlike the specific ways of referring in allegory, allusion is more recondite, assuming a knowledgeable reading public not only to recognize the referent of the allusion marker, but to know the source text's intension enough to grasp and complete the allusion's unstated significance (p. 299).

In her pragmatic approach to allusion, Perri's following illocutionary observations seem particularly helpful for our topic. The alluding author and audience share a cultural tradition. The allusion marker has its own meaning in the world of the alluding text, but echoes a source text. This echo can be recognized as such, and is intended to identify the source text for the audience, who can know what the source text is. Merely identifying the source text is insufficient to make sense out of the marker. This insufficiency, combined with the part of the source text echoed and the context of the alluding text, suggest the properties from the source text needed to complete the sense of the allusion marker in its own context. Further reflection on the source text can provide further properties for the alluding text (p. 300). Perri summarizes the perlocutionary aspects of allusion thus: 'Recognizing, remembering, realizing, connecting: these are the effects of a successfully performed allusion for its audience' (p. 301).

---

various Old Testament images, the rabbi's use of scripture is explicitly referential' ('Writing with Scripture', in Neusner with Green, *Writing with Scripture*, pp. 7-23, here p. 17).

    1.   C. Perri, 'On Alluding', *Poetics* 7 (1978), pp. 289-307.

Perri's approach to allusion sheds particular light on Sir. 48.15 and Lk. 21.23-24. Sir. 48.15 enunciates the following principle of interpreting the historical phenonemon of exile as punishment for the people's rejection of both the prophet and his successor: 'For all this the people did not repent, and they did not forsake their sins, till they were carried away captive from their land and were scattered over all the earth...' (RSV). Lk. 21.23b-24 refers to the suffering of God's people thus: 'For great distress shall be upon the earth and wrath upon this people; they will fall by the edge of the sword, and be led captive among all the nations...' (RSV). The echo in Luke 21 is not verbatim, but the pattern of God's people refusing to repent (implied by the reference to wrath in Lk. 21.23 as well as by the clear rejection of Jesus and of the apostles in the plots of Luke and Acts respectively) and being consequently scattered from their land is recognizable, and points beyond this primary link to the context of double rejection in Sir. 48.1-16. It is this fuller context which completes the fullness of the allusion and deepens the intertextual resonance behind the basic plot of Luke–Acts.

Old Testament Plotlines in Speeches of Acts

It will not be too difficult to point out similarities between the summary plotline in Sir. 48.1-16 and the overall plotting of Luke–Acts (as the chart below does). However, more confirmation is needed to argue that Sirach 48 influenced the Lukan plot. For supporting evidence, one can first show from the prologue prima facie indications that the Lukan author did indeed order separate episodes within an overall plot structure, and the likelihood that this plotline would be grounded in his Bible. Secondly, indirect confirmation about Lukan awareness of Old Testament plotlines in general can make more plausible the influence of the particular plot in Sir. 48.1-16 on Luke–Acts. Finally, evidence of actual Lukan plotting of historical surveys according to Old Testament plot patterns can add further probability for this particular influence.

The Lukan prologue (Lk. 1.1-4) indeed provides prima facie evidence for self-conscious Lukan ordering of often unrelated smaller episodes into a persuasive narrative plot. The prologue compares this narrative to previous attempts to form many episodes into a continuous account. It remarks that 'many have undertaken to compile a narrative of the things which have been accomplished among us...' (Lk. 1.1 RSV). 'It seemed good to me also...to write an orderly account for you...that you may know the truth concerning the things of which you have been informed' (1.3-4 RSV). The notion of ordering episodes is especially implied in the words 'compile a narrative' (ἀνατάξασθαι διήγησιν), and 'to write an orderly account for you' (ἀκριβῶς καθεξῆς σοι γράψαι). To compile or order a narrative (ἀνατάξασθαι διήγησιν) requires placing episodes in order, as does writing in order (καθεξῆς... γράψαι).[1]

The desire for certainty or assurance (ἀσφάλειαν) in the clause ἵνα ἐπιγνῷς περὶ ὧν κατηχήθης λόγων τὴν ἀσφάλειαν (Lk. 1.4) seems to have been addressed especially by writing the narrative against the background of God's Old Testament plans, saving actions and future promises. Showing the congruence of what actually took place 'among us' with the way God worked in the Old Testament lends assurance that those events 'among us' were accomplished or fulfilled (πεπληροφορημένων) according to God's plan.[2] The attempt to show this would prompt the use especially of Old Testament plotlines in ordering the Lukan episodes, as well as the more direct and standard proofs from prophecy.

Therefore it is reasonable to anticipate that some of this Lukan plotting of episodes would be modelled upon Old Testament plotlines. In fact, the influence of Old Testament plots can be demonstrated in speeches in Acts, which are commonly held to bear the heavy redactional imprint of, if not complete composition by, the Lukan author. Those speeches provide summary plots of parts of Israel's history, especially in Acts 3, 7 and 13. If the Lukan author used summaries of Old Testament histories to structure his historical overviews in Acts speeches, this adds to the plausibility of his using similar Old Testament summary plotlines to structure the overall plot of Luke–Acts.

Thus, the correspondence between the peculiar plot of the Elijah–

---

1. Cf. ch. 4, 'The Prologue to Luke's Gospel: Narrative Questions', in my monograph *Reading Luke–Acts: Dynamics of Biblical Narrative* (Louisville, KY: Westminster Press/John Knox, 1993), pp. 39-44, and the bibliography in the notes, pp. 193-95.

2. Cf. F. Bovon, *Das Evangelium nach Lukas*. I. *Lk 1,1-9,50* (EKKNT, 3.1; Zürich: Benzinger Verlag; Neukirchen–Vluyn: Neukirchener Verlag, 1989), pp. 29-43, esp. p. 35; J.A. Fitzmyer, *The Gospel according to Luke (I–IX): Introduction, translation, and notes* (AB, 28; Garden City, NY: Doubleday, 1981), pp. 287-302, esp. pp. 289-90, 292-93, 300-301; R.C. Tannehill, *The Narrative Unity of Luke–Acts: A Literary Interpretation*. I. *Luke* (FFNT; Minneapolis: Fortress Press, 1990), p. 12.

Elisha segment of salvation history in Sir. 48.1-16 and the overall plot of double rejection by God's people of the messiah and his successors, with their resulting punishment in the Gospel and Acts, may plausibly be attributed to more than coincidence. In the light of his comparable use of other short plotlines from Israel's history in some speeches in Acts, especially in chs. 3, 7 and 13, it is likely that the Lukan author could also be using just such a short plotline as that in Sir. 48.1-16 (which has such striking correspondences to the overall plot of his two-volume work) as an organizing pattern for Luke–Acts.

Acts 7 provides particularly impressive evidence of Lukan use of typological patterns from his Greek Bible to organize historical surveys into plotlines that recall those LXX patterns. The Stephen speech contains a widely recognized Moses–Jesus typology in its short plotline of the story of Moses, along with explicit reference to heeding the prophet like Moses on pain of being cut off from the λαός (Deut. 18.15; Acts 3.22-23; 7.37).[1] The Moses–Jesus typology in the Acts 7 speech parallels the Elijah–Elisha typology from Sirach 48, in that both involve a double rejection of the prophet like Moses (in Kings first Elijah then Elisha, in Luke–Acts the earthly and risen Jesus). A key pattern of similarity between Moses in Acts 7 and Jesus in Luke–Acts is their *double rejection* by the λαός.[2]

This is prepared for in Luke's plotting by reference in Acts 1.1 to the Third Gospel as describing what Jesus *began* (ἤρξατο) to do and teach, with the implication that the risen Jesus (through his successors, the apostles) *continued* his work in Acts.[3] In terms of plotting and ordering of episodic source materials, there is a close relationship between

---

1. See esp. L.T. Johnson, *The Literary Function of Possessions in Luke–Acts* (SBLDS, 39; Missoula, MT: Scholars Press, 1977), pp. 70-76. Cf. E. Richard, *Acts 6.1–8.4: The Author's Method of Composition* (SBLDS, 41; Missoula, MT: Scholars Press, 1978).

2. Johnson, *Literary Function of Possessions*, esp. pp. 71-75.

3. With G. Schneider, *Die Apostelgeschichte. I. Kommentar zu Kap. 1,1-8,40* (ed. A. Wikenhauser, A. Vögtle and R. Schnackenburg; HTKNT, 5.1; Freiburg: Herder, 1980), pp. 191-92; F.F. Bruce, *The Acts of the Apostles: The Greek Text with Introduction and Commentary* (Grand Rapids: Eerdmans, 3rd edn, 1990), p. 98; and R.C. Tannehill, *The Narrative Unity of Luke–Acts: A Literary Interpretation. II. The Acts of the Apostles* (FFNT; Minneapolis: Fortress Press, 1990), p. 23; against F.J. Foakes Jackson and K. Lake (eds.), *The Beginnings of Christianity, Part I: The Acts of the Apostles. IV. English Translation and Commentary* (ed. K. Lake and H.J. Cadbury; Grand Rapids: Baker, 1979 [1932]), p. 3.

showing the double rejection of Jesus (first in his earthly ministry in the Gospel, and secondly as risen and acting through his apostles in Acts), and showing an Elijah–Elisha pattern of rejection first of the Moses-like prophet Jesus and then of his successors, the wonder-working prophetic apostles.

A partial confirmation of the plausibility of the influence of the Elijah–Elisha plotline from Sirach 48 on the plotting of Luke–Acts is the fact that the treatment of Moses in Sir. 45.1-5, another part of the 'Praise of the Ancestors' in Sirach 44–50, also finds allusive echoes in the Lukan narratives.[1] In addition, Brawley mentions Luke's intertextual treatment of the Abraham covenant, in which we can find further evidence of allusive links between Sirach's 'Praise of the Ancestors' and Luke–Acts, this time vis-à-vis Abraham.[2] Not only does Luke–Acts use short summary Old Testament plotlines similar to that for Elijah and Elisha in Sir. 48.1-16, but we have seen Lukan resonances also with the Moses and Abraham sections of the 'Praise of the Ancestors' in Sirach 44–50.

1.   Among these Moses echoes in Luke–Acts from Sir. 45.1-5, note the similarities between Sir. 45.1 and Acts 13.23 and Lk. 2: καὶ ἐξήγαγεν ἐξ αὐτοῦ ἄνδρα ἐλέους εὑρίσκοντα χάριν ἐν ὀφθαλμοῖς πάσης σαρκὸς ἠγαπημένον ὑπὸ θεοῦ καὶ ἀνθρώπων Μωυσῆν...; Sir. 45.5 and the Lukan baptism, transfiguration and emphasis on the cloud: ἠκούτισεν αὐτὸν τῆς φωνῆς αὐτοῦ καὶ εἰσήγαγεν αὐτὸν εἰς τὸν γνόφον καὶ ἔδωκεν αὐτῷ κατὰ πρόσωπον ἐντολάς, νόμον ζωῆς καὶ ἐπιστήμης, διδάξαι τὸν Ιακωβ διαθήκην...; Sir. 45.4 and the Lukan emphasis on Jesus as chosen (ἐκλεκτός) messiah in his mocking in Lk. 23.35: ἐξελέξατο αὐτὸν ἐκ πάσης σαρκός.

2.   Intertextual allusion to the Abraham covenant is seen in the expanded promise to inherit the earth (γῆ [eretz]), which in Gen. 12.1-3 is indeterminate and associated with universal blessing (only later in Gen. 17.8 limited to Canaan). In tradition the promise was seen unfulfilled in Canaan and projected into the whole earth in the future, as in Sir. 44.19-21; Jub. 17.3; 19.21; 22.14; 32.18; Rom. 4.13; Mek. on Exod. 14.31 (Bešallah §7). Cf. Philo, Vit. Mos. 1.155; Heb. 2.5. See Brawley, 'Canon and Community', p. 427 and n. 35. Note also the following similarities between Sir. 44.19-21 and Luke–Acts, especially Lk. 1–2 and the speeches in Acts: Sir. 44.19, Αβρααμ μέγας πατὴρ πλήθους ἐθνῶν...; Sir. 44.20, ὃς συνετήρησεν νόμον ὑψίστου καὶ ἐγένετο ἐν διαθήκῃ μετ' αὐτοῦ· ἐν σαρκὶ αὐτοῦ ἔστησεν διαθήκην καὶ ἐν πειρασμῷ εὑρέθη πιστός; Sir. 44.21, διὰ τοῦτο ἐν ὅρκῳ ἔστησεν αὐτῷ...καὶ ὡς ἄστρα ἀνυψῶσαι τὸ σπέρμα αὐτοῦ καὶ κατακληρονομῆσαι αὐτοὺς ἀπὸ θαλάσσης ἕως θαλάσσης...

Resonances between the Content of Sirach 48.1-16
and the Plot of Luke–Acts

Positing the modeling of the Lukan plot on Sir. 48.1-16 helps to explain several peculiarities of Luke's plot, either when it is compared to Matthean and Markan use of similar source material, or in the Lukan *Sondergut*, both of which have been widely discussed in redactional studies (see the chart below).

1. In my opinion, the most unambiguous allusion by the Lukan plotline to Sirach 48 comes in the rejection by the λαός of both Jesus in Luke and his apostolic prophetic successors in Acts, and the people's consequent exile predicted in Luke 21. Sir. 48.15 concludes Sirach's account of the people's reaction to Elijah and Elisha with this rationale for their consequent punishment: ἐν πᾶσιν τούτοις οὐ μετενόησεν ὁ λαὸς καὶ οὐκ ἀπέστησαν ἀπὸ τῶν ἁμαρτιῶν αὐτῶν, ἕως ἐπρονομεύθησαν ἀπὸ γῆς αὐτῶν καὶ διεσκορπίσθησαν ἐν πάσῃ τῇ γῇ. As noted above, the wording of this principle is not identical to that in the prediction of Jerusalem's fall and the people's scattering in Lk. 21.23-24, but the images and patterns are comparable. The biblical pattern in Sirach 48 is given a new expression in the Lukan rewriting. The plotline of Sirach 48 not only receives a new application in Luke–Acts, but it in turn gives intertextual richness and meaning to Luke–Acts.

2. The ascension and Pentecost in Acts 1–2 allude to the prophetic succession motif which is also found in Sirach 48, but not verbatim. Sir. 48.8 says of Elijah vis-à-vis Elisha: ὁ χρίων...προφήτας διαδόχους μετ᾽ αὐτόν. Sir. 48.11 calls blessed those who see Elijah (μακάριοι οἱ ἰδόντες σε), and Sir. 48.12 refers to Elisha's receiving Elijah's spirit: Ηλιας ὃς ἐν λαίλαπι ἐκεπάσθη, καὶ Ελισαιε ἐνεπλήσθη πνεύματος αὐτοῦ. Sir. 48.9 refers to Elijah's exaltation with the same verb that Luke uses for Jesus' ascension, ὁ ἀναλημφθεὶς ἐν λαίλαπι πυρός (cf. v. 11, Ἰησοῦς ὁ ἀναλημφθείς).

Acts 1.9-11 emphasizes that the disciples were watching and witnessed Jesus being taken up and removed by the cloud from their sight, and that he would return the same way he left (that is, on a cloud; Lk. 21.27). With intertextual resonance to both the Kings account and the Sirach summary, just as Elisha saw Elijah taken up and thus received his spirit, so the disciples saw Jesus taken up and therefore (at Pentecost in Acts 2) received his spirit. Further, the first statement that Sir. 48.12

makes about Elisha after his reception of Elijah's spirit is that Elisha was not intimidated or overcome by any ruler: οὐκ ἐσαλεύθη ὑπὸ ἄρχοντος, καὶ οὐ κατεδυνάστευσεν αὐτὸν οὐδείς. Acts has a similar motif about neither the apostles nor Paul fearing any ruler despite a series of trials and imprisonments. Acts ends on the triumphal note of Paul preaching (despite house arrest) in Rome μετὰ πάσης παρρησίας ἀκωλύτως.

3. The generally mixed Jewish reactions to Jesus and Paul in Luke–Acts also have a close correspondance to Sirach 48. Sometimes, as in the three turnings from Jews to Gentiles after mixed or negative reactions in Acts 13.45-46, 18.16 and 28.24-28, the pattern seems awkward enough to appear like rather artificial Lukan redaction.[1] That otherwise awkward plot pattern may well be influenced by Sir. 48.16, which appears in a similar context of judgment on the λαός because of their mixed reaction to Elijah and his successor Elisha: τινὲς μὲν αὐτῶν ἐποίησαν τὸ ἀρεστόν, τινὲς δὲ ἐπλήθυναν ἁμαρτίας.

4. Some particular incidents may also suggest the influence of the Elijah–Elisha cycle as interpreted in Sirach 48. The Samaria episode in Lk. 9.51-56 recalls Elijah's calling down fire on the first two of three groups of soldiers sent to bring him to the king, recapitulated (inaccurately) in Sir. 48.3b: κατήγαγεν οὕτως τρὶς πῦρ. James and John ask Jesus, κύριε, θέλεις εἴπωμεν πῦρ καταβῆναι ἀπὸ τοῦ οὐρανοῦ καὶ ἀναλῶσαι αὐτούς; Unlike Elijah, Jesus emphatically disavows this approach.

5. The Nain raising echoes a phrase from the LXX account of Elijah raising a widow's son, καὶ ἔδωκεν αὐτὸν τῇ μητρὶ αὐτοῦ (Lk. 7.15; 1 Kgs 17.23). But its emphasis on the people responding to the raising by praising God, ὅτι προφήτης μέγας ἠγέρθη ἐν ἡμῖν, correlates to Sir. 48.1 and 5, καὶ ἀνέστη Ηλιας προφήτης, and ὁ ἐγείρας νεκρὸν ἐκ θανάτου.

6. Thematic motifs from the Canticles of Zechariah and Mary also allude to Sirach 48, especially Lk. 1.52, καθεῖλεν δυνάστας ἀπὸ θρόνων, to Sir. 48.6, ὁ καταγαγὼν βασιλεῖς εἰς ἀπώλειαν. The Lukan difference in wording would correspond to the Greco-Roman principle of imitation by paraphrasing one's source in one's own style.

---

1.   Cf. R.C. Tannehill, 'Rejection by Jews and Turning to Gentiles: The Pattern of Paul's Mission in Acts', in J.B. Tyson (ed.), *Luke–Acts and the Jewish People: Eight Critical Perspectives* (Minneapolis: Augsburg, 1988), pp. 96-101; Tannehill, *Narrative Unity*, II, pp. 172-75.

Lk. 1.17, that the Baptist will go before the Lord in the spirit and power of Elijah ἐπιστρέψαι καρδίας πατέρων ἐπὶ τέκνα, alludes more closely to the wording of Sir. 48.10, ἐπιστρέψαι καρδίαν πατρὸς πρὸς υἱόν, than to Mal. 3.23, ἀποκαταστήσει καρδίαν πατρὸς πρὸς υἱόν.

7. The Elijah–Elisha cycle in Sirach 48 also helps to explain the dropping in Luke of the Markan/Matthean reference to the Baptist as Elijah returned (Mk 9.14-29 = Mt. 17.14-21). Though Lk. 1.17 had predicted that the Baptist would turn the hearts of fathers to their children in the spirit and power of Elijah, this is not the same as *identifying* the Baptist with Elijah returned. An actual identification of the Baptist as Elijah would obscure the major Lukan theme of an Elijah–Elisha type of succession between Jesus and the apostles.

Sirach 48.1-16 as Plot Outline for Luke–Acts

Within a perspective of narrative plotting, therefore, Sir. 48.1-16 can be read to function as a plot outline for Luke–Acts.[1] In Sir. 48.1-16, the wonder-working prophet Elijah was followed by his disciple Elisha who worked similar miracles. Likewise, in Luke and Acts, Jesus the wonder-working prophet like Moses was followed by his wonder-working disciples in Acts.

Sir. 48.15-16 summarizes the reaction of the people to Elijah and Elisha (and thus the plotline of Sir. 48.1-16) thus: 'For all this the people did not repent and they did not forsake their sins, till they were carried away captive from their land and were scattered all over the earth... Some of them did what was pleasing to God, but others multiplied sins' (RSV). This same plotline undergirds Luke and its sequel Acts. In the Gospel, despite the wonders of Jesus, the prophet like Moses, the Jewish people did not repent but rejected Jesus, who (because of this repudiation) foretold the destruction of their city and their captivity among all the nations (Lk. 21.20-24).[2] A similar mixed reception of

---

1. W.S. Kurz, 'Narrative Models for Imitation in Luke–Acts', in D.L. Balch, W.A. Meeks and E. Ferguson (eds.), *Greeks, Romans, and Christians* (A.J. Malherbe Festschrift; Minneapolis: Fortress Press, 1990), pp. 171-89, here p. 184.

2. Cf. W.S. Kurz, 'Acts 3:19-26 as a Test of the Role of Eschatology in Lukan Christology', in P.J. Achtemeier (ed.), *Society of Biblical Literature Seminar Papers 1977* (SBLSP, 11; Missoula, MT: Scholars Press, 1977), pp. 309-23, here pp. 314-16.

believing and unbelieving runs throughout Acts, but ultimately spells rejection by the λαός of the disciples and Paul, culminating in the Acts ending (28.24-28): καὶ οἱ μέν ἐπείθοντο τοῖς λεγομένοις, οἱ δὲ ἠπίστουν... Paul responds by quoting the condemnation by Isa. 6.9-10 of the people's hardheartedness, declaring that henceforth the message would be preached to the Gentiles.[1]

Thus a pattern in Sir. 48.1-16 becomes a typology for a similar plot pattern in Luke–Acts.

Conclusion

This evidence suggests that the plot of Luke–Acts was modeled after Sir. 48.1-16, with its pattern of the λαός refusing to repent despite the powerful ministries of both Elijah and his successor Elisha, and therefore being plundered and scattered from their land. The plot of Luke and Acts manifests intertextual use of this pattern found in Sirach 48. The Gospel and its sequel use the same pattern of God's people failing to repent despite the powerful ministries of Jesus and his apostolic successors for plotting the account of the wonder-working prophet Jesus and his wonder-working successors, the apostles in Acts.

This plotline provides a principle of putting 'order' into the many episodes in the Gospel and Acts (Lk. 1.3). Based as it is in Luke's Greek Bible, it makes sense of the otherwise almost incomprehensible rejection by God's λαός of their messiah Jesus, by grounding it intertextually in previous accounts of the double rejection of Moses, and of the rejection of the first prophet like Moses, Elijah, and then his successor Elisha. As the λαός had rejected Moses twice, as well as rejecting Elijah, his successor Elisha, and 'all the other prophets' (Lk. 11.47-51, 13.33-35; Acts 7.51-52; cf. Lk. 16.29-31), so they have now rejected Jesus (the prophet like Moses) both before and after his resurrection (Acts 3.22-23; 7.37), and his successors the apostles and Paul in Acts. Because of this double rejection, the prophecies of Jesus and earlier prophets about the destruction of Jerusalem and scattering of the λαός among the Gentiles have taken place by the time of writing Luke and Acts.

By grounding in a biblical plotline (evidenced in Sir. 48) the rejection

---

1. This corresponds to a retributive logic common in Old Testament and Hellenistic Jewish writings, as noted by G.W. Trompf, *The Idea of Historical Recurrence in Western Thought: From Antiquity to the Reformation* (Berkeley: University of California Press, 1979), pp. 156-70; regarding Luke–Acts, pp. 170-74.

by God's people of their messiah Jesus and of the prophetic witnesses to
his resurrection, the Lukan author has not only put order into disparate
episodes, but has also provided his narratee Theophilus with ἀσφάλειαν
about the otherwise seemingly far-fetched accounts and claims about
Jesus he had heard (Lk. 1.1-4). The rejection of Jesus and of his disciples
by the λαός does not undermine his claim to be messiah and savior of
the λαός. The λαός had similarly rejected Moses as their savior both
before and after his vindication by God (Acts 7.23-29, 35, 38-41), as
well as both Elijah and his successor Elisha. Intertextuality provided
meaning to an otherwise inexplicable fate of Jesus. It articulated that fate
in a biblical plotline that demonstrates that his rejection by the people
was part of God's plan and already foreshadowed in the fates of Moses,
Elijah and Elisha.

Chart
Sirach 48 and Luke–Acts

Sirach 48

48.3: κατήγαγεν οὕτως τρὶς πῦρ

48.4: ὡς ἐδοξάσθης, Ηλια, ἐν θαυμασίοις σου·

48.5: ὁ ἐγείρας νεκρὸν ἐκ θανάτου

48.6: ὁ καταγαγὼν βασιλεῖς εἰς ἀπώλειαν

48.7: ἀκούων ἐν Σινα ἐλεγμὸν καὶ ἐν Χωρηβ κρίματα ἐκδικήσεως·

48.8: ὁ χρίων βασιλεῖς εἰς ἀνταπόδομα καὶ προφήτας διαδόχους μετ' αὐτόν·

48.9: ὁ ἀναλήμφθεὶς ἐν λαίλαπι πυρός

48.10: ὁ καταγραφεὶς ἐν ἐλεγμοῖς εἰς καιρούς... ἐπιστρέψαι καρδίαν πατρὸς πρὸς υἱὸν καὶ καταστῆσαι φυλὰς Ιακωβ

Luke–Acts

Lk. 9.54 (Samaria): κύριε, θέλεις εἴπωμεν πῦρ καταβῆναι ἀπὸ τοῦ οὐρανοῦ καὶ ἀναλῶσαι αὐτούς;

Acts 3.13? (ὁ θεός... ἐδόξασεν τὸν παῖδα αὐτοῦ Ἰησοῦν)

Lk. 7.14-15 (Nain): ἐγέρθητι. καὶ ἀνεκάθισεν ὁ νεκρός...

Lk. 1.52 (Magnificat): καθεῖλεν δυνάστας ἀπὸ θρόνων

Lk. 9.28, 30-31 (Moses– Transfiguration): ἀνέβη εἰς τὸ ὄρος προσεύξασθαι... συνελάλουν αὐτῷ... Μωϋσης καὶ Ἡλίας... ἔλεγον τὴν ἔξοδον αὐτοῦ...

Acts 1–2: λήμψεσθε δύναμιν ἐπελθόντος τοῦ ἁγίου πνεύματος ἐφ' ὑμᾶς (1.8); καὶ προφητεύσουσιν... (2.17-18) + Lk. 22.29-30: κἀγὼ διατίθεναι ὑμῖν... βασιλείαν... καὶ καθήσεσθε ἐπὶ θρόνων τὰς δώδεκα φυλὰς κρίνοντες

Acts 1.9-11: νεφέλη ὑπέλαβεν αὐτόν... Ἰησοῦς ὁ ἀναλημφθείς...

Acts 3.20-23 (?)

Lk. 1.17: ἐν πνεύματι... Ἡλίου, ἐπιστρέψαι καρδίας πατέρων ἐπὶ τέκνα... ἑτοιμάσαι κυρίῳ λαὸν κατεσκευασμένον.

48.11: μακάριοι οἱ ἰδόντες σε καὶ οἱ
ἐν ἀγαπήσει κεκοιμημένοι· καὶ γὰρ
ἡμεῖς ζωῇ ζησόμεθα.

48.12: Ηλιας ὅς ἐν λαίλαπι
ἐσκεπάσθη, καὶ Ελισαιε ἐνεπλήσθη
πνεύματος αὐτοῦ·

...οὐκ ἐσαλεύθη ὑπὸ ἄρχοντος,
καὶ οὐ κατεδυνάστευσεν αὐτὸν
οὐδείς.

48.15: ἐν πᾶσιν τούτοις οὐ
μετενόησεν ὁ λαὸς καὶ οὐκ
ἀπέστησαν ἀπὸ τῶν ἁμαρτιῶν
αὐτῶν, ἕως ἐπρονομεύθησαν ἀπὸ
γῆς αὐτῶν καὶ διεσκορπίσθησαν ἐν
πάσῃ τῇ γῇ.

48.16: καὶ κατελείφθη ὁ λαὸς
ὀλιγοστός, καὶ ἄρχων ἐν τῷ οἴκῳ
Δαυιδ· τινὲς μὲν αὐτῶν ἐποίησαν τὸ
ἀρεστόν, τινὲς δὲ ἐπλήθυναν
ἁμαρτίας.

Acts 1.9-11 (?): βλεπόντων αὐτῶν
ἐπήρθη, καὶ νεφέλη ὑπέλαβεν αὐτὸν
ἀπὸ τῶν ὀφθαλμῶν αὐτῶν. Lk. 10.23,
25, 27-28 (?): μακάριοι οἱ ὀφθαλμοὶ
οἱ βλέποντες ἃ βλέπετε...
᾽Αγαπήσεις κύριον τὸν θεόν
σου...καὶ τὸν πλησίον σου...
τοῦτο ποίει καὶ ζήσῃ.
Acts 1–2: νεφέλη ὑπέλαβεν αὐτὸν
ἀπὸ τῶν ὀφθαλμῶν αὐτῶν (1.9);
λήμψεσθε δύναμιν ἐπελθόντος τοῦ
ἁγίου πνεύματος ἐφ᾽ ὑμᾶς (1.8);
ἐπλήσθησαν πάντες πνεύματος
ἁγίου (2.4).
Acts (Peter and John, Stephen, Paul vs.
various authorities):...μετὰ πάσης
παρρησίας ἀκωλύτως (28.31).
Acts 3.23: ἔσται δὲ πᾶσα ψυχὴ ἥτις
ἐὰν μὴ ἀκούσῃ τοῦ προφήτου
ἐκείνου ἐξολεθρευθήσεται ἐκ τοῦ
λαοῦ. Lk. 21.20-24: ὅταν δὲ ἴδητε
κυκλουμένην ὑπὸ στρατοπέδων
᾽Ιερουσαλήμ, τότε γνῶτε ὅτι ἤγγικεν
ἡ ἐρήμωσις αὐτῆς...ὅτι ἡμέραι
ἐκδικήσεως αὗταί εἰσιν...ἔσται
γὰρ ἀνάγκη μεγάλη ἐπὶ τῆς γῆς
καὶ ὀργὴ τῷ λαῷ τούτῳ, καὶ...
αἰχμαλωτισθήσονται εἰς τὰ ἔθνη
πάντα.

Acts 3.23: ἔσται δὲ πᾶσα ψυχὴ ἥτις
ἐὰν μὴ ἀκούσῃ τοῦ προφήτου
ἐκείνου ἐξολεθρευθήσεται ἐκ τοῦ
λαοῦ. Paul turns to Gentiles: Acts
13.45-46; 18.6; 28.24-28; 28.24: οἱ μὲν
ἐπείθοντο τοῖς λεγομένοις, οἱ δὲ
ἠπίστουν·

JESUS' PREACHING IN THE SYNAGOGUE
ON THE SABBATH (LUKE 4.16-28)

Asher Finkel

Synagogue and Scripture Reading on the Sabbath

The oldest witness to synagogue worship, with its focus on the liturgy of the Word, that is, prayer and scriptural reading, occurs in Nehemiah 8. This biblical account from the Second Temple period describes a public gathering for worship on the holy day of the New Year. Strikingly, the assembly (*qahal*) gathers in the city square of Jerusalem and not in the Temple area. It participates in a Torah reading, for which purpose a wooden pulpit was especially erected (v. 8). The people did not gather at a sacrificial service conducted by priests at the altar, as is usually depicted in similar biblical accounts, for the scribal work of Nehemiah wishes to describe a parallel development in the religious life of the Judean community of the Second Temple time. He is presenting the synagogal model of worship that in all probability emerged during the exilic period.[1] συναγωγή in Greek renders the Aramaic *kenista* for *qahal* and *keneset* becomes the mishnaic equivalent in the postbiblical development of the Hebrew language. It denotes a formal assembly gathered for worship or convened to deliberate on critical issues.[2] Such

---

1.   See W. Schrage, 'συναγωγή', *TDNT*, VII, pp. 798-852; E. Schürer, *The History of the Jewish People in the Age of Jesus Christ* (rev. and ed. G. Vermes, F. Millar and M. Black; 3 vols.; Edinburgh: T. & T. Clark, 1973–87), II, pp. 423-63; J. Gutmann (ed.), *The Synagogue: Studies in Origins, Archaeology and Architecture* (New York: Ktav, 1975); F. Huttenmeister and G. Reeg, *Die antiken Synagogen in Israel* (2 vols.; Wiesbaden: Reichert, 1977); E.M. Meyers, 'Synagogues of Galilee', *Archaeology* 35.3 (1985), pp. 51-58; L.L. Grabbe, 'Synagogues in Pre-70 Palestine', *JTS* 39 (1988), pp 401-10; R. Hachlili, 'Synagogue', *ABD*, VI, pp. 251-63.

2.   *keneset hagedolah* refers to a deliberating body of the Persian and early Greek periods (cf. *m. Ab.* 1.1). See L. Finkelstein, *The Pharisees and the Men of the Great Synagogue* (Hebr.; New York: Rabbinic Bet haMidrash of America, 1950).

religious gatherings originally met in the town square or in the market place. Eventually, they gathered in a house (*bet hakeneset*) specifically built for collective worship. Unquestionably, such buildings existed in addition to the Jerusalem Temple throughout the world of Jewry, as the archaeological and literary evidence clearly establishes, at least for the first century.[1]

Lk. 4.16 relates that Jesus 'went to the synagogue as his custom was on the Sabbath day'. In the first century this practice was already seen as an old established custom, which the rabbinic traditions attributed to the oral legislation of Moses' and Ezra's special enactments.[2] Similarly, Luke transmits in the name of James, the head of the Jerusalem church (Acts 15.21), that 'Moses had from early generations in every town those who preach his [book]; for it is read every Sabbath in the Synagogue'. Nehemiah of the Persian period portrays a Torah reading followed by a prophetic lection (the Haftarah, the concluding reading). Apparently, two forms of lectionary evolved in the synagogue of the Hasmonean period that paralleled the liturgical side of the Temple service.

One lectionary form developed out of the practice of completing the reading of the Pentateuch on successive Sabbaths. The cycle of readings conformed to the Sabbatical calendar of the agrarian society. At the end of the septennial cycle, the Deuteronomic text was read by the head of the state to a large gathering of pilgrims in the Temple area during the Tabernacle festival.[3] In this manner the synagogue readings culminated in a Temple pilgrimage service (Deut. 31.10-13, *Haqhel*). Similarly, the Temple daily service was presided over by a representative group of the Israelite community. Such a group (called *Ma'amad*) gathered in different towns on the weekdays to read selections from the story of creation. This early practice was a parallel development of Torah reading in con-

---

kenista renders the Hebrew *qahal* in *Targ. Ps.* 107.32; 109.6.

1. See H. Shanks, *Judaism in Stone* (New York: Harper, 1979); L.I. Levine (ed.), *Ancient Synagogues Revealed* (Jerusalem: Israel Exploration Society, 1981); G. Foerster, 'The Ancient Synagogues of the Galilee', in L.I. Levine (ed.), *The Galilee in Late Antiquity* (New York and Jerusalem: Jewish Theological Seminary of America, 1992), pp. 289-319; L.I. Levine, 'The Sages and the Synagogue in Late Antiquity: The Evidence of the Galilee', in Levine (ed.), *The Galilee in Late Antiquity*, pp. 201-22.

2. Cf. *m. Meg.* 4.6; *b. B. Qam.* 82a. Compare *Mek. Ishmael* and *Mek. SbY.* to Exod. 15.22.

3. Cf. *m. Soṭ.* 7.8, in view of Deut. 31.10-13. See A. Finkel, *The Pharisees and the Teacher of Nazareth* (AGJU, 4; Leiden: Brill, 1974), pp. 143-49.

nection with the Temple. It was not the prototype of synagogal service but rather a corresponding development effected by the established Torah-reading practice outside the Temple.[1]

The other lectionary form existed as an early practice to relate the ritualistic aspect of the annual festivals to selected readings drawn from the Pentateuchal text. They detail the laws of the particular holiday with its sacrificial service or they present a narrative on the religio-historical significance of the sacred time.[2] Such a development is already indicated by the account of Nehemiah and indeed serves as the exegetical background to the cycle of festivals appearing in the Gospel of John.[3]

The septennial cycle of scriptural readings on the Sabbaths was determined by two triads of the tithe years culminating in a Sabbatical year. Thus, the Torah readings for successive Sabbaths were greater in number than those of the post-destruction Palestinian triennial cycle.[4]

---

1. The *Ma'amad* model of worship described in *m. Ta'an.* 4.2-3 is not the historical background to synagogue service as claimed by J. Heinemann, *Prayer in the Talmudic Period* (Hebr.; Jerusalem: Magnes, 1966), but a parallel development effected by the synagogue reading service. Similarly, Heinemann's claim that the lectionary was not determined by a fixed cycle ('The Triennial Lectionary Cycle', *JJS* 19 [1968], pp. 41-48) is based on the erroneous observation of the *Piyyutim*'s material on the Sabbath portions, which refer to the sessional petition for rain or dew. These Palestinian texts included their mention throughout the year as part of the daily second praise formulation of God's powers.

2. Cf. *m. Meg.* 4.5, 6; *b. Meg.* 31a, 32b.

3. See A. Guilding, *The Fourth Gospel and Jewish Worship* (Oxford: Oxford University Press, 1960). Similar work has been done with respect to the Gospel of Matthew; cf. M.D. Goulder, *Midrash and Lection in Matthew* (London: SPCK, 1974); *idem, The Evangelists' Calendar: A Lectionary Explanation of the Development of Scripture* (London: SPCK, 1978). Goulder thinks that Matthew's five major discourses correspond to major Jewish feasts and holidays: (1) the Sermon on the Mount (chs. 5–7)—Pentecost; (2) the Sending of the Twelve (ch. 10)—Rosh Hashanah and Yom Kippur; (3) the Parables of the Kingdom (ch. 13)—Sukkah; (4) Rules for Church Order (ch. 18)—Hanukkah; and (5) the Eschatological Discourse (chs. 24–25)—Pesahim. Guilding and Goulder have been criticized, however, for overinterpreting the evidence; cf. L. Morris, 'The Gospels and the Jewish Lectionaries', in R.T. France and D. Wenham (eds.), *Studies of History and Tradition in the Four Gospels* (Gospel Perspectives, 1; Sheffield: JSOT Press, 1980), pp. 129-56; C. Perrot, *La lecture de la Bible dans la synagogue* (Hildesheim: Gerstenberg, 1973), p. 287. The evidence of *b. Meg.* 31b, possibly reflecting second-century tradition, suggests that there was no uniform Jewish lectionary prior to that time.

4. See C. Perrot, 'The Reading of the Bible in the Ancient Synagogue', in

The early division of Pentateuchal pericopes was the work of scribes, who apparently transmitted the biblical texts for lectionary usage. From the days of Ezra, the Torah was carefully transcribed for the sake of study and reading, thus leading to the development of rabbinic Massorah.[1] The Synagogue gave rise to an authoritatively transmitted text and eventually produced an official translation. It also provided the natural setting for preaching. The pedagogical and paranaetic sides of Torah reading necessitated a public address on the biblical selection in order to move the congregation to a deeper commitment to God's words.

During the Hasmonean time, a further extension of the synagogal reading emerged in the form of Haftarah, the concluding selection from the Prophets. It came to establish the canonicity and unity of Torah and Prophets, the two parts of the Hebrew Bible, for the worshipping community. The prophetic selection, most probably, was determined by a correlative principle, similar words or themes.[2] The authoritative word and the theological link between the two bodies of Scriptures were made public through reading followed by preaching. The Mosaic law proclaimed God's teaching, revealed in the past, that comes to guide the present community in thought and practice. Hearing the Torah selection read in the synagogue represents the communal acceptance of the Sinaitic covenant. The prophetic words were read in acknowledgment of the supremacy of the Mosaic law. This extended to the community a comforting hope in the future that holds the divine promise of final judgment and reward.

The scribes appended a canonical statement (Mal. 3.22-24) to the closing verse of the Prophets. Malachi ends with the characteristic prophetic signature, 'thus saith the Lord of Hosts'. To this is added an exhortation to 'remember the law of my servant Moses'. Remembrance denotes not only obedience to the covenant in a general sense but also a

---

M.J. Mulder (ed.), *Mikra: Text, Translation, Reading and Interpretation of the Hebrew Bible in Ancient Judaism and Early Christianity* (CRINT, 2.1; Assen: Van Gorcum; Philadelphia: Fortress Press, 1988), pp. 137-59.

1.   See M.J. Mulder, 'The Transmission of the Biblical Text', in *idem* (ed.), *Mikra*, pp. 87-136.

2.   See J. Mann, *The Bible as Read and Preached in the Old Synagogue* (2 vols.; Cincinnati: Hebrew Union College, 1940–66 [vol. 2 with I. Sonne]). Refer also to J.J. Petuchowski (ed.), *Contributions to the Scientific Study of Jewish Liturgy* (New York: Ktav, 1970), Part 2.

liturgical commemorative reading in particular.[1] The law of Moses is to enter the mind and heart of the community through a proper hearing. The time for reception of Torah appropriately coincided with the Sabbaths and festivals; times set apart for public religious assembly (*miqra qodesh*). These sacred times provided the pedagogical opportunity that Neh. 8.8 so eloquently describes. 'They read from the book, from the Law of God, with translation giving the sense so that the people understood the reading.' The rabbis (*b. Meg.* 3a) see in this description the seminal development of scribal rules for transmitting the written text with its authoritative Targum.

Malachi's canonical ending concludes with reference to the coming of Elijah that will usher in the final awesome Day of the Lord. This statement maintains that prophecy has ended but will be restored through a future advent of Elijah.[2] It expresses a hope in a future return of the people as prelude to universal peace. This formulates an eschatological teaching that can be embraced by the present biblically oriented community. Thus, the canonical ending of Malachi presents a coalescence of the eschatological hope with the covenantal obedience in the present hearing of Scriptures. The emergence of a worshipping community in the Second Temple period is related directly to the introduction of canonical Scriptures for reading and instruction.[3]

The gathering of the worshipping community on the New Year, as described in Nehemiah 8, has resulted in enthusiastic celebration of the festival of Tabernacles, in accordance with the reading and the explanatory instruction. This custom prevailed in the Jewish community to introduce the people to a proper understanding of the laws and meaning of the holidays through special reading and instructive preaching. The community of Ezra and Nehemiah enjoyed a deepened awareness of providential care and God's presence in the celebration of Tabernacles.[4]

---

1. *Zakhor* indicates the liturgical practice of commemorative recitation; cf. *Sifra Lev.* §260 (on 26.3); *b. Pes.* 106a; Maimonides, *Yad, Hilkhoth Sabbath* 29.1.

2. See L. Frizzell, 'Elijah the Peacemaker: Jewish and Early Christian Interpretations of Malachi 3.23-24', *SIDIC* 17.2 (1984), pp. 19-25.

3. See J.A. Sanders, *Canon and Community* (Philadelphia: Fortress Press, 1984).

4. This theme is offered in Lev. 23.43 as a reason for the celebration of Sukkoth, which the rabbis explain in light of the providential manifestation of divine clouds (cf. Exod. 14.20-21). See *Sifra* and *Mekilta* on the above texts (*Sifra Lev.* §239 [on 23.43]; *Mek.* on Exod. 14.16-21 [Bešallaḥ §5]).

Thus, this sacred period resulted in a climactic event of communal acceptance of the Torah covenant (Nehemiah 10). The heads of this theocratic state, representing the three classes of Jewry (Kohen, Levi and Israel), affix their signatures to a covenant document (*ketav'amanah*). This decisive religious act for the Second Temple period suggests that the very experience of Torah reading was rooted in a liturgical re-enactment of the Sinaitic covenantal event. Coming together on the Sabbaths and the festivals offered the spiritual opportunity for the biblically oriented community to engage seriously in a covenantal reception of God's words. These days designated sacred time of affective remembrance and closeness to God's presence in history, for they were specially set apart as days of rest. The community abstained from all secular work and instead was involved in spiritual activities of collective prayer, scriptural readings and familial table fellowship.[1]

The Liturgical Experience of Scriptural Readings

Torah reading provided a dramatic religious setting of a liturgical re-enactment of the Sinaitic covenantal event. Through a meticulous reading of God's words and a reverential hearing by the congregants, the very sense of God's presence is deepened. The community expresses its response in the act of doxological prayer. Nehemiah (8.6) describes the blessing of God's name and the collective response of 'Amen', accompanied by reverential prostration. The words of the Sinaitic covenant, namely the Torah of God, enjoy an effective reception by the community in compliance with the Deuteronomic exhortation: 'Take heed lest you forget the things which your eyes have seen...and make them known to your descendants how on that day you stood before the Lord your God at Horeb [i.e. Sinai]' (Deut. 4.9-10). Furthermore, the Covenant is made 'not with our fathers but with us who are all of us here alive today' (Deut. 5.3). The purpose of such a sacred gathering is to instill in the congregants a reverential experiencing of standing in God's presence and hearing his words, as well as the pedagogical willingness to transmit this to their children (Deut. 9.10).

The Sabbath morning, therefore, offered the community a spiritual opportunity to hear God's words in awe within a liturgical setting. From early days, the rabbis have formulated specific benedictions in connection

---

1.   See A.J. Heschel, *The Sabbath* (New York: Meridian, 1952).

with the public reading of Scriptures.[1] They reflect the theological meaning of this very act. It opens with a doxological invocation, 'Let us bless the Lord who is blessed'. The community responds, 'Blessed be the Lord, who is blessed for ever and ever'. This doxological antiphony can only be said in a sacred gathering,[2] and Torah reading requires at least ten male adults in attendance (the basic quorum of the synagogue). Moreover, at least seven members representing the three classes of Jewry are to be called up on the Sabbath to read from the Scriptures. This act of 'going up' (*aliyah*) to the *bema* remains even today an honorific act of religious participation of a male adult in the worshipping community, the historical background to *Bar Mitswah* celebration on the Sabbath.

Nehemiah's model of worship points to reverential determinants during a Torah reading event. The scroll is lifted in the view of the congregation while they are standing in awe. Ezra the scribe offers a doxological invocation and the people respond with 'Amen', while raising their hands as a sign of acceptance and commitment.[3] Then the congregants bow and fall on the ground in a reverential posture. Lifting the scroll (*Hagbahah*) is a cultic act that points to the holy presence of God. The scroll itself, therefore, becomes a sacred object to be revered. Accordingly, the rabbis declare that biblical writings contaminate the hands upon contact, a concrete sign of their canonical worth.[4] The contemporary Sephardic custom of lifting the Torah in its case before the scroll is read appears to evolve from this ancient practice. *hagbahah* was viewed by the rabbis as a high point during the Torah reading event.[5]

Special benedictions were recited before and after the readings. They reflect a particular consciousness of God as the giver of the Torah (the benedictory signature). The opening benediction speaks of the covenant made with Israel 'who is chosen from all the people'. At Mount Sinai the same relationship is expressed in a reciprocal formulation of the covenant. Israel is 'God's own treasure among all people' and it accepts its role as 'a kingdom of priests and a holy nation' (Exod. 19.5, 6). This

---

1.   They are recorded in the Geonic work of *Soperim* (ed. M. Higger), ch. 13. Refer to its early development in view of *Sifre Deut.* §306 (on 32.3).

2.   Cf. *b. Ber.* 21b.

3.   The tradition carried over into some early Christian communities; cf. 1 Tim 2.8.

4.   Cf. *m. Yad.* 4.6 (a Pharisaic decision).

5.   Cf. *b. Meg.* 32a; compare *Sop.* 14.14.

very condition for Israel's becoming a theocratic nation serves as the guiding principle of Pharisaic teachings.[1] The benediction following the reading speaks of the very nature of Torah as God's words. They are 'true, planting in our midst everlasting life'. This is a formal recognition by the congregants that accepting the covenant is a free human act in choosing life. 'Behold, I place before you today life and good, death and evil…choose life', through 'loving God, hearing his voice and cleaving to him' (Deut. 30.15, 19, 20). Through proper hearing of the Pentateuchal text, the community acknowledges in the 'Amen' response to the blessings the fact that God's voice will be obeyed and his presence embraced. This appears to be the liturgical intention for a Torah reading as a reverential experience in accepting God's law.

The rabbis eventually introduced another set of benedictions to accompany the Haftarah, the additional reading at the end of the Torah reading. It proclaimed the theological unity of Torah and Prophets. God 'has chosen the Torah and his servant Moses', as he also has 'chosen his people Israel and the true and righteous prophets'. Thus, all words heard in the reading are equally true, including the prophetic promises that will be historically fulfilled. This theme is elaborated in the concluding benediction, a prayer that was originally meant to be recited responsively while standing: 'You are faithful and your words are faithful, for not one of your words spoken in the past shall remain unfulfilled'. The following relates effectively what the prophetic promise holds for the present covenantal community. On the Sabbath morning the faith of the worshipping community was expressed eschatologically in its acceptance of scriptural fulfillment. The Haftarah came to shape their sense of historical movement towards final redemption. In light of this, the rabbinic liturgists later appended their eschatological vision for Israel in petitionary form after the Haftarah's concluding benediction. First, it appeals to God's mercy on Zion 'who is so painfully grieved for her exiled inhabitants' and is in need 'for a speedy redemption in our own days'. It then calls for the coming of Elijah and the establishment of the Davidic kingdom. 'For no "stranger" shall sit upon his throne nor let "others" any longer inherit his glory. For you did swear unto him by

---

1. See Finkel, *Pharisees*, p. 42, and J. Neusner, *From Politics to Piety* (Englewood Cliffs, NJ: Prentice Hall, 1973). The latter examination fails to see the distinctive nature of the Pharisaic teachings that relate to the entire nation. They seek to emulate the priestly community and they aspire to the establishment of a holy nation (Pharisee means 'holy' in Aramaic).

your holy name that his "light" shall not be quenched forever.'

The prophetic promises of the past determine the eschatological expectation for Israel. The first theme explores the present condition of Jewish exile with its dispersed people. The Prophets promise the ingathering of Israel in its homeland Zion.[1] The second theme points to the new redemptive time in the future to be ushered in by prophetic restoration through Elijah *redivivus* and the establishment of the Davidic rule under the messiah.[2] It is the promise that was made to David as formulated in Ps. 132.11: 'God promises to David in truth...that also his descendants will sit upon his throne...in Zion, which God chose as his abode'. Thus, the rabbinic references for the Haftarah prayer to 'stranger' or 'others' suggest particular false types, who claimed kingship and messiahship in Israel.[3] The 'stranger' may point even to Herod of the end of the first century BCE or Bar Kokhba in the beginning of the second century CE. 'Others' connote *minim*, heretical followers of a Gnostic redeemer. Thus, in the post-destruction time, the rabbinic liturgists have formulated an eschatological vision in their interpretive view of scriptural fulfillment. Furthermore, they came to reject other claims to messiahship or heretical views of eschatology.

It appears then that the liturgical reading of Torah and Haftarah on the Sabbath provided the religious forum for public response to teaching authority and eschatological claims. The biblically oriented community, whose covenantal consciousness was deepened by an eschatological orientation, was open to effective preaching. Similar liturgical determinants affected the Sabbath reading in the days of Jesus, even though the prayer formulations and the lectionary system were not fixed yet by the rabbinic authority. Preaching following the Haftarah offered the opportunity to move the worshipping community dramatically to obedient acceptance of God's demands and to an acknowledged commitment

---

1. Cf. Isa. 56.8; Jer. 23.3; Mic. 2.12. The former formulates the tenth petition of the Jewish daily prayer that begins with this eschatological expectation. The hope of the ingathering of the Jewish exiles is a prominent feature in the Targums, esp. that to Isaiah; cf. B.D. Chilton, *The Glory of Israel: The Theology and Provenience of the Isaiah Targum* (JSOTSup, 23; Sheffield: JSOT Press, 1983), pp. 28-33.

2. The appearance of the Davidic messiah who will restore Israel is another prominent theme in the Targums. With respect to the Isaiah Targum, see Chilton, *The Glory of Israel*, pp. 86-96. For a survey of most of the messianic passages in the Targums, see S.H. Levey, *The Messiah: An Aramaic Interpretation: Messianic Exegesis of the Targum* (MHUC, 2; Cincinnati: Hebrew Union College, 1974).

3. See J. Herz (ed.), *Daily Prayer Book* (New York: Bloch, 1957), p. 497.

to an eschatological realization. This is the phenomenological background to Jesus' preaching or fulfillment of scriptures on the Sabbath in the synagogue of Nazareth.

Luke's Account of Jesus' Preaching Fulfillment in the Synagogue

Only Luke offers the liturgical setting of reading and preaching in the synagogue for the initial proclamation of the kingdom of God by Jesus on the Sabbath.[1] The other Synoptic Gospels (Mt. 4.7 and Mk 1.15) simply relate succinctly the message of Jesus without any particular setting for its delivery. Keeping in mind that this was the historical way in which Jesus first disclosed his redemptive presence in a biblically oriented and eschatologically directed community, Matthew and Mark refer generally to Jesus teaching in the synagogues (Mt. 4.23, 25; Mk 1.39). It seems, however, that Luke intended also to present a *vorgeschichtlich* (historical prefiguration) account for the later development of missionary preaching that he is describing in the second part of his work, the Acts of the Apostles. Peter preaches on the Festival

---

1.   There is an extensive body of scholarship concerned with Luke's version of Jesus' Nazareth sermon. I can only offer a selected sample of the literature: A. Finkel, 'Jesus' Sermon at Nazareth (Luk. 4,16-30)', in O. Betz *et al.* (eds.), *Abraham unser Vater: Juden und Christen im Gespräch über die Bible* (O. Michel Festschrift; Leiden: Brill, 1963), pp. 106-15; H. Anderson, 'Broadening Horizons: The Rejection of Nazareth Pericope of Lk 4,16-20 in Light of Recent Critical Trends', *Int* 18 (1964), pp. 259-75; A. George, 'La prédication inaugurale de Jésus dans la synagogue de Nazareth: Luc 4, 16-30', *BVC* 59 (1964), pp. 17-29; H. Schürmann, 'Zur Traditionsgeschichte der Nazareth-Perikope Lk 4, 16-30', in A. Descamps and A. de Halleux (eds.), *Mélanges bibliques en honnage au R.P. Béda Rigaux* (Gembloux: Duculot, 1970), pp. 187-205; D. Hill, 'The Rejection of Jesus at Nazareth (Luke iv 16-30)', *NovT* 13 (1971), pp. 161-80; W. Eltester, 'Israel im lukanischen Werk und die Nazarethperikope', in *idem* (ed.), *Jesus in Nazareth* (BZNW, 40; Berlin: de Gruyter, 1972), pp. 76-147; R.C. Tannehill, 'The Mission of Jesus according to Luke iv 16-30', in Eltester (ed.), *Jesus in Nazareth*, pp. 51-75; B. Reicke, 'Jesus in Nazareth—Lk 4.14-30', in H. Balz and S. Schulz (eds.), *Das Wort und die Wörter* (G. Friedrich Festschrift; Stuttgart: Kohlhammer, 1973), pp. 47-55; J.A. Sanders, 'From Isaiah 61 to Luke 4', in J. Neusner (ed.), *Christianity, Judaism and Other Greco-Roman Cults, Part One: New Testament* (M. Smith Festschrift; SJLA, 12; Leiden: Brill, 1975), pp. 75-106; B.D. Chilton, 'Announcement in *Nazara*: An Analysis of Luke 4:16-21', in R.T. France and D. Wenham (eds.), *Studies of History and Tradition in the Four Gospels* (Gospel Perspectives, 2; Sheffield: JSOT Press, 1981), pp. 147-72.

Haftarah (Joel 3.1-5) for the Pentecostal gathering of pilgrims in the Temple area,[1] at the time for synagogal reading (Acts 2.14-37; note the third hour in the morning). Paul preaches at Antioch of Pisidia on the Sabbath, following the reading of Torah and Haftarah (Acts 13.14-41), for the apostles pursued the way of Jesus in proclaiming their message of good news, especially in their appeal to synagogal Jews on the Sabbaths or Festivals.

The dual composition of Luke offers parallel accounts of preaching in the synagogue within the historical frame of the time of Jesus and the time of his apostles, for the Jewish world with its Sabbath reading in the synagogue provided the natural affective setting for the initial proclamation of scriptural fulfillment in their days. The eschatological meaning of Jesus' coming can only be disclosed in the biblically oriented community, and the similar liturgical setting of reading and preaching was presented by the early church in connection with the eucharistic service revealing his presence, for Luke wishes to transmit the early experiential setting that actually moves the worshipping community to relate the person of Jesus to scriptural fulfillment. In his historiographical manner, Luke relates eschatological fulfillment to both Scriptures of the past and actual events of the present.

The appearance of John ushers in a new redemptive era with the coming of Jesus. Most significantly, Luke offers a detailed synchronized date for the preaching activity of John the Baptist, who ushers in the messianic ministry of Jesus (3.1-3), for that year, the fifteenth of Tiberius's reign (27–28 CE) was a Sabbatical year, a year of national redemption. The actual dating of the 'year of release' (*Semitah*) in the Jewish calendar is linked in Luke with a scriptural fulfillment of Isa. 40.3-5. This text is cited in full only here in the Gospel (3.4-6).[2] John the Baptist is the promised 'voice' that prepares the way for the manifestation of 'God's salvation'. Luke changes the Hebrew text to read this paronomastic phrase *yesu'at Elohim*, signifying Jesus,[3] for in the

---

1.   The Prophetic lection correlates to Exod. 19. On the structure and homiletic forms of the ancient synagogue, see Finkel, *Pharisees*, pp. 143-72, and 'Jesus' Sermon at Nazareth', pp. 106-15.

2.   See K.R. Snodgrass, 'Streams of Tradition Emerging from Isaiah 40.1-5 and their Adaptation in the New Testament', *JSNT* 8 (1980), pp. 24-45.

3.   This is probably an instance of *pesher*, which Jesus and his disciples evidently employed. Consult W.H. Brownlee, 'Biblical Interpretation among the Sectaries of the Dead Sea Scrolls', *BA* 14 (1951), pp. 54-76; F.F. Bruce, *Biblical Exegesis in the*

appearance of John a new era has dawned; the promise of Elijah's coming has been realized. 'He will go before him in the spirit and power of Elijah "and he will preach" to turn the hearts of the fathers to the children' (Lk. 1.17, as fulfillment of Mal. 3.23-24). The new era will be the promised 'great awesome year of the Lord', which is proclaimed in Jesus' inaugural preaching at Nazareth as the 'acceptable year of the Lord'.

The historical linkage of John and Jesus is presented as the eschatological fulfillment in Luke. Moreover, the heavenly voice in the hearing of John-Eliah recalls the coming of the Servant of God, 'with whom God is well pleased', as promised in Isa. 42.1. The verse continues to explain his very nature, for 'I have placed my spirit upon him'. Luke, however, relates the actual 'descent of the Holy Spirit upon him in bodily form as a dove' (3.22). Thus, the sign of *Jonah* (in 11.29 without 'the prophet') implies the initial testimony by the 'dove' (in Hebrew *yonah*), as well as the scriptural example of Jonah the prophet in Luke. This is characteristic of Lukan duality in presenting both the symbolic and typological aspects of *Yonah*, for Lukan redaction stresses the significance of the Holy Spirit in the Acts of the Apostles. He therefore depicts its actual manifestation in Jesus at the beginning of his ministry. His Gospel refers to 'Jesus full of the Holy Spirit returned from the Jordan' (4.1) and 'Jesus returned in the power of the Spirit into Galilee' (4.14). The inaugural preaching at Nazareth offers the occasion on which Jesus proclaimed that 'the Spirit of the Lord is upon me' (4.18) and, therefore, that the promise of 'scripture has been fulfilled in your hearing today' (4.21). Moreover, Jesus appeals also to the eschatological restoration of prophecy as a historical fulfillment in his proverbial comment 'no prophet is acceptable in his own country',[1] for the synagogal setting in Luke relates both to Jesus' authority in teaching the Torah and his eschatological fulfillment in pointing to the Haftarah. Jesus reads from

---

Qumran Texts (Grand Rapids: Eerdmans, 1959); O. Betz, *Offenbarung und Schriftforschung in der Qumransekte* (WUNT, 6; Tübingen: Mohr [Paul Siebeck], 1960); K. Stendahl, *The School of St Matthew and its Use of the Old Testament* (Philadelphia: Fortress Press, 2nd edn, 1968); R.N. Longenecker, *Biblical Exegesis in the Apostolic Period* (Grand Rapids: Eerdmans, 1975); G.J. Brooke, *Exegesis at Qumran* (JSOTSup, 29; Sheffield: JSOT Press, 1985); M. Fishbane, 'Use, Authority and Interpretation of Mikra at Qumran', in Mulder (ed.), *Mikra*, pp. 339-77.

1. Compare Mt. 13.57 and Mk 6.4 with Jn 4.44 and *Gos. Thom.* §31.

the scroll of Isa. 61.1-2 with an interpolated comment, which reflects the very teaching of Jesus.

Jesus proclaims 'the acceptable year of the Lord' with the preceding explanation, 'to set at liberty those who are oppressed'. This interpolated comment assumes practical meaning in the Jewish community of Nazareth. It announced a Sabbatical time[1] with its Pentateuchal demands to convert the feudal society to a community sharing with the poor. The 'acceptable year of the Lord' comes 'to proclaim liberty throughout the land to all its inhabitants', as Lev. 25.10 prescribes. During the Sabbatical period people are released from their subjugation to land ownership (Lev. 25) and from bodily and monetary enslavement to other human beings (Deut. 15). In this manner, the entire community enters a new experience in living under providential care and with a deep sense of altruistic concern. 'The land shall not be sold in perpetuity, for the land is mine' (Lev. 25.23). 'The silver is mine and the gold is mine, says the Lord of Hosts' (Hag. 2.8). 'Have we not all one Father? Has not one God created us?' (Mal. 2.10). A closeness to God's presence in awe and love can be experienced by people who have released themselves from an egoistic attachment to land properties and from oppressive control of others through slavery and debt. Such a community is open to an invitation to God's reign, and Jesus' initial proclamation that the 'time is fulfilled and the kingdom of God is at hand' is directed toward a Sabbatical life in the community of the poor.

The Sabbatical demands assumed redemptive meaning on socioeconomic, national and cosmic levels. Messianic stirrings were associated with the Sabbatical year. The zealotic movement, which led to the war against Rome, began on a Sabbatical year, when Quirinius imposed a census on the Jewish people (6 CE). It proclaimed God's rule in rejection of imperial Rome's authority. The Temple itself was destroyed on a post-Sabbatical year,[2] which prompted Jewish circles to raise the question of divine retribution. Luke is clearly aware of these messianic

---

1. See J.H. Yoder, *The Politics of Jesus* (Grand Rapids: Eerdmans, 1972); R.B. Sloan, Jr, *The Favorable Year of the Lord: A Study of Jubilary Theology in the Gospel of Luke* (Austin, TX: Schola Press, 1977); S.H. Ringe, *Liberation and the Biblical Jubilee* (Philadelphia: Fortress Press, 1985).

2. See B.Z. Wacholder, 'The Calendar of Sabbatical Cycles during the Second Temple and Early Rabbinic Period', *HUCA* 44 (1973), pp. 153-96; *idem*, 'Sabbatical Chronomessianism and the Timing of Messianic Movements', *HUCA* 46 (1975), pp. 201-18; *idem*, 'Sabbatical', *IDBSup*, pp. 762-63.

movements in Judaism (Acts 5.36-37: Judah the Galilean during the census) and especially the catastrophic event of the fall of Jerusalem (Lk. 21.20). Luke's *heilsgeschichtlich* (salvific history) work offers the Christian response to Sabbatical time.

According to Luke, the early church emerged as the realization of the kingdom that was announced by Jesus. The beginning of Acts (1.3, 6-8) clearly indicates that the Jewish hope in the coming of the kingdom is not to be realized through the establishment of the Davidic monarchy and the restoration of the Temple in Jerusalem. These expectations were uppermost in the mind of the synagogue Jews as reflected in their prayer.[1] The Christian response was directed towards a universal redemption through the gradual emergence of apostolic communities in different lands, beginning with 'Jerusalem, all Judea and Samaria and even to the remotest part of the earth' (Acts 1.8). This development is depicted in the Acts of the Apostles. A new socio-religious reality in redemptive time is coming into being as the translation of God's kingdom into a Sabbatical context for the world. Accordingly, Luke[2] presents teachings of Jesus on the kingdom with reference to selling properties, sharing with the poor, renewal and release of both men and women from *mammon* and abhorrence of arrogance. All these points converge on a Sabbatical reality for the Lukan community that promotes the interpersonal acts of love and maintains diligent participation in the transpersonal act of prayer (Lk. 11.37; 18.1-14).

Jesus' Inaugural Proclamation on the Sabbath

The Sabbath day of rest provided Jesus with an interpretive link with the Sabbatical year of release. In Jesus' teachings particular to Luke (13.10-17; 14.1-6), rest on the Sabbath is conditioned by the release from Satanic bondage or from a pit. The dramatic events of healing during his ministry come to demonstrate the messianic reality of his initial proclamation, 'to release the captives'. This is seen in the reply to John the Baptist (7.22) that Jesus' activities openly fulfill the scriptural program of his synagogue reading on the Sabbath. In this manner, Jesus proclaimed his Sabbatical intention at the outset of his ministry with a manifest program of healing and redemptive acts by God's anointed. He effectively

---

1. Compare the eschatological petitions of the daily prayer with the themes in the Pharisaic *Pss. Sol.* 11, 17, 18 and the Hasmonean prayer in 2 Macc. 2.27-29.

2. See Lk. 12.33; 13.6; 14.5, 13; 16.13, 15; 18.22.

linked his ministry of release with the Sabbatical demands directed to those invited into the kingdom.

Jesus announces also that he is 'anointed to preach the good news to the poor (*'ebyon*)'. The concern for 'the poor' is indeed the explicit concern of the Deuteronomic legislation for the Sabbatical community:

> Take heed lest there be an evil thought in your heart, and you say, 'The seventh year, the year of release is near', and your eye be hostile to your poor (*'ebyon*) brother... you shall give to him freely, and your heart shall not be grudging when you give to him; because for this the Lord your God will bless you... For the poor (*'ebyon*) will never cease to exist in your country (Deut. 15.9-11).

The Sabbatical demand comes to evoke a genuine response in the altruistic pursuance of charity and interpersonal acts of love. The realization of the love commandment[1] is effectively translated in the Sabbatical acts to 'open your hand widely to your brother, to the needy and to the poor (*'ebyon*) in your country' (Deut. 15.12).

According to Luke (6.20), Jesus too offered the Beatitude of entry into the kingdom to the poor (*ptochos* = *'ebyon*). He coupled them with those who are hungry and weep now. These groups are also referred to in the Isaiah lection (61.2-3). The Sabbatical year became a year of divine blessing: 'I will command my blessing upon you in the sixth year, so that it will bring forth fruit (on the seventh year) for three years' (Lev. 25.21). The blessing of plenty parallels the multiplication of manna for the Sabbath (Exod. 16.22). Thus, the redemptive time is dramatically blessed by Jesus' multiplication of one loaf for a thousand in Lk. 9.13-17. This sole pericope on multiplication in Luke suggests a *Vorgeschichte* to the apostolic time. Seven deacons are appointed for the distribution of food in the community (Acts 6.3) and there are five loaves and two fish. In a brilliant redactional arrangement of his dual composition, Luke eliminates the other pericope on feeding the four thousand (cf. Mt. 15.32-39 = Mk 8.1-10), for the community of the five thousand is clearly identified in Acts 4.4. Thus, the twelve baskets represent the twelve apostles, who were originally responsible for food distribution.

At Jesus' inaugural address of 'gracious words' in the synagogue, the Nazareth community is said to have questioned Jesus' role: 'Is not this

---

1. 'Open your hand' is the Torah formulation for the act of charity, which comes to express altruistic love. The commandment to love the neighbor guides the Sabbatical society and becomes appropriately the principal teaching of Jesus.

Joseph's son?' (Lk. 4.22). In contrast to Mark's reference to 'son of Mary', the rejection is based on the Lukan special tradition that Joseph left for Bethlehem to be enrolled (2.1-5). Joseph is compelled to leave for his Davidic ancestral town to be assessed for property tax by the Romans. Joseph was the landowner, as the apocryphal sources corroborate.[1] Thus, the Galilean community of Nazareth, with whom Jesus and his family live, questioned Jesus' intent in his inaugural proclamation. His Sabbatical demand was faced with a challenge to his own family in the release of their land. Jesus replies, 'Doubtless you will quote to me the proverb, "physician, heal thyself"'. (A similar challenge regarding properties faces Jesus later in Galilee, according to Luke only [12.13-21.] Jesus refuses to act as a judge and arbiter in a property dispute due to inheritance. He admonishes them, 'Take heed and beware of all covetousness, for a man's life does not consist in the abundance of his possessions'.) This Lukan special tradition indirectly provides the historical circumstance that resulted in a rift between Jesus and his own country people. Thus, Luke concludes his remark on the proverbial physician with reference to Jesus' work in Capernaum where his teaching authority was challenged. For the people only seek a demonstration by Jesus of his prophetic healing; since Jesus' preaching presented originally both the Pentateuchal demand of Sabbatical life and the prophetic fulfillment of Jesus' redemptive nature.

Luke, therefore, places the logion 'a prophet is not acceptable in his own country' at the beginning of Jesus' preaching in Nazareth. In conrast to Mt. 13.54-58 and Mk 6.1-6, Luke presents it at the outset of Jesus' ministry, for this oblique identity of Jesus' person is viewed christologically[2] in Acts 3.23 and 7.37. Jesus is the 'prophet like Moses', whose coming is an epiphanic event like the revelation at Mount Sinai (Deut. 18.16). The eschatological Moses does not supply a sign but his ministry of the word becomes his testimony (contrast 11.2). In the Lukan style of duality, Jesus supplies two examples of the prophet who came in the past, Elijah and Elisha. Initially, they too were not acknowledged by Israel.

The widow of Zarephath declares: 'Now I know that you are a man of God and the word of the Lord in your mouth is true' (1 Kgs 17.24).

---

1.   Cf. *Prot. Jas* 9.2; 13.1; 16.1. Joseph of Bethlehem is a carpenter or builder, who may have been connected with the Temple renovation under Herod.

2.   See O. Cullmann, *The Christology of the New Testament* (Philadelphia: Westminster Press, 1963), pp. 13-50.

Similarly, all who were present at the resurrection of the widow's son in Nain declare: 'a great prophet has arisen among us' (Lk. 7.16).[1] Naaman the Syrian centurion was healed so that he 'will acknowledge that there is a prophet in Israel' (2 Kgs 5.8). Similarly, the Roman centurion's slave is to be healed at the request of the Jewish elder (Lk. 7.4-5). All these parallels are to be found in Luke only. Jesus' reply can only suggest *vorgeschichtlich* guidelines for apostolic mission, to be directed towards the poor and the oppressed (such as the widows of Zarephath and Nain) as well as towards the ruling class (such as the Syrian or Roman centurion). These apostolic efforts are depicted in Acts with a mission directed both to Israel and to other people. The apostles proclaim Jesus' redemptive presence and the Sabbatical invitation to the kingdom. The initial act of preaching in the synagogue of Nazareth, with its dual aspects of the coming of Jesus and the demands of the kingdom, has been pursued fully by his followers after his death.

The Lukan religio-experiential setting is first to be located in the event of the synagogal reading and preaching. It provides the religious dynamics for the proper understanding of Jesus' person and his teaching. Thus, the eschatologically oriented church has translated this understanding for its own, according to the Lukan presentation of the apostolic life in Acts. The worshipping Christian community has entered the sacred time of the kingdom through a Sabbatical realization of its socioeconomic existence.

1. The parallel is even closer when the targumic reading of 1 Kgs 17 is taken into account: 'You are the prophet of the Lord'.

THE PHARISEE AND THE PUBLICAN:
LUKE 18.9-14 AND DEUTERONOMY 26

Craig A. Evans

According to the Deuteronomy hypothesis propounded by C.F. Evans in 1955, Luke's Central Section (Lk. 9.51–18.14) was arranged to match the order and contents of Deuteronomy 1–26.[1] Though largely neglected by Lukan scholars, this intriguing hypothesis has of late received some favorable attention.[2] According to this scheme the parable of the Pharisee and the publican[3] (Lk. 18.9-14), the last pericope of the Central

---

1. C.F. Evans, 'The Central Section of St Luke's Gospel', in D.E. Nineham (ed.), *Studies in the Gospels* (R.H. Lightfoot Festschrift; Oxford: Basil Blackwell, 1955), pp. 37-53.

2. J.D.M. Derrett, *The Law in the New Testament* (London: Darton, Longman & Todd, 1970), pp. 100, 126-55; J. Bligh, *Christian Deuteronomy (Luke 9–18)* (Langley: St Paul, 1970); J.A. Sanders, 'The Ethic of Election in Luke's Great Banquet Parable', in J.L. Crenshaw and J.T. Willis (eds.), *Essays in Old Testament Ethics* (J.P. Hyatt Festschrift; New York: Ktav, 1974), pp. 247-71; rev. and repr. in C.A. Evans and J.A. Sanders, *Luke and Scripture: Essays on the Function of Sacred Tradition in Luke–Acts* (Minneapolis: Fortress Press, 1993), pp. 106-20; J. Drury, *Tradition and Design in Luke's Gospel: A Study in Early Christian Historiography* (London: Darton, Longman & Todd, 1976), pp. 138-64; M.D. Goulder, *The Evangelists' Calendar: A Lectionary Explanation of the Development of Scripture* (London: SPCK, 1978), pp. 95-101; C.A. Evans, 'Luke's Use of the Elijah/Elisha Narratives and the Ethic of Election', *JBL* 106 (1987), pp. 75-83; rev. and repr. in Evans and Sanders, *Luke and Scripture*, pp. 70-83; R.W. Wall, '"The Finger of God": Deuteronomy 9.10 and Luke 11.20', *NTS* 33 (1987), pp. 144-50; *idem*, 'Martha and Mary (Luke 10.38-42) in the Context of a Christian Deuteronomy', *JSNT* 35 (1989), pp. 19-35; C.A. Evans, 'Luke 16:1-18 and the Deuteronomy Hypothesis', in Evans and Sanders, *Luke and Scripture*, pp. 121-39.

3. As is frequently noted by contemporary commentators, 'publican' and 'tax collector' are not good translations for τελώνης. See J.R. Donahue, 'Tax Collectors and Sinners: An Attempt at Identification', *CBQ* 33 (1971), pp. 39-61; F. Herrenbrück, 'Wer waren die "Zöllner"?', *ZNW* 72 (1981), pp. 178-94. The τελῶναι of the

Section, was situated by the Lukan Evangelist to fall opposite Deuteronomy 26, the passage prescribing the 'Confession' that is to be made when one presents first fruits to the Temple.[1]

To facilitate discussion it will be helpful to provide the parallels that Evans proposed (with a few larger groupings subdivided and other minor adjustments enclosed in square brackets):

Deuteronomy	Subject	Luke
1.19-25	sending of emissaries	10.1-3, 17-20
2.1–3.3	inhospitable kings and cities	10.4-16
[3.3-7, 23-27	conquest of evil	10.17-20]
4.5-8, 32-40	the source of wisdom	10.21-24
5.1–6.24	the Great Commandment	10.25-28
7.1-16	attitude toward foreigners	10.29-37
8.1-3	God's Word as food	10.38-42
8.4-20	God provides for the needs of people	11.1-13
9.1–10.11	God's enemies dispossessed	11.14-26
10.12-15; 11.26-28	blessings for the obedient	11.27-28
10.16–11.7	stubbornness and signs	11.29-36
12.1-16	clean and unclean	11.37–12.12
12.17-32	warning against selfishness/idolatry	12.13-34
13.1-5	time tests the faithful	12.35-48
13.6-11	faithfulness divides families	12.49-53
13.12-18	danger of judgment	12.54–13.5
[14.28	fruit every third year	13.6-9]
15.1-18	release from debt and slavery	13.10-21
[15.19-23	eating in God's presence	13.22-30]
16.1–17.7	feasts in Jerusalem	13.[31]22-35
17.8–18.22	justice and the law	14.1-14
20.1-9	excuses for exemption from holy war	14.15-24
20.10-20	terms of peace/counting cost	14.25-35
21.15–22.4	families and restoration of lost	15.1-32
23.15–24.4	slaves, usury, divorce	16.1-18
24.6–25.3	laws against oppressing the poor	16.19–18.8
26.1-19	tithes and obedience	18.9-14

Gospels should probably be understood as toll collectors, and I shall refer to them as such in this essay.

1. Evans, 'Central Section', p. 50. The Confession is sometimes called the Avowal or the Declaration. Words used include קרא, which literally means reading or reciting (cf. קורין in *m. Bikk.* 1.1), and ידי (= Hebr. ידה), which in the *ithpaʿal* means to confess (cf. מתודין in *m. Maʿas. Š.* 5.10). For early rabbinic discussions of the ritual of the Confession commanded in Deuteronomy 26, see *m. Maʿas. Š.* 5.10-15 and *m. Bikk.* 1.1–3.12.

The purpose of this present brief study is not to mount a defense of the Deuteronomy hypothesis itself (that has been attempted in a preliminary fashion and will receive a fuller treatment sometime in the future[1]), but to probe the relationship between the parable of the Pharisee and the toll collector and the Confession prescribed in Deuteronomy 26.

This parable, one of several found only in Luke, describes two men who went to the Temple to pray. The parable reads as follows (my translation):

> 9 But he also spoke this parable to those who despised others and had confidence in themselves that they were righteous. 10 'Two men went up into the Temple to pray, one a Pharisee and the other a toll collector. 11 The Pharisee stood by himself and prayed these things: "God, I thank you that I am not like the rest of men—robbers, unjust persons, adulterers, or even as this toll collector. 12 I fast twice a week. I tithe all that I earn." 13 But the toll collector stood at a distance and was unwilling to lift his eyes to heaven, but beat his breast, saying, "God, be merciful to me a sinner!" 14 I say to you, this one went down to his home justified, rather than the other; because every one who exalts himself will be humbled, and the one who humbles himself will be exalted.'

The proposed parallel passage from LXX Deuteronomy (26.1-19) reads as follows (my translation):

> 1 And it will be when you should enter the land, which the Lord your God gives to you to inherit, that you should inherit it and should dwell upon it, 2 that you should take of the first of the fruits of your land which the Lord your God gives to you, and you should put (them) into a basket and go to the place which the Lord your God shall choose to have his name called upon. 3 And you shall come to a priest who shall be in those days, and you will say to him: 'I testify this day to the Lord my God, that I have

---

1.   Evans, 'Luke 16:1-18 and the Deuteronomy Hypothesis', pp. 121-39. In this study I propose criteria for assessing the presence and meaning of Deuteronomistic traditions in the Lukan Central Section. A future study is being planned that will treat every pericope in detail. The weightiest criticism brought against the Deuteronomy hypothesis is that offered by C.L. Blomberg, 'Midrash, Chiasmus, and the Outline of Luke's Central Section', in R.T. France and D. Wenham (eds.), *Studies in Midrash and Historiography* (Gospel Perspectives, 3; Sheffield: JSOT Press, 1983), pp. 217-59, esp. pp. 228-33. Blomberg's criticisms have persuaded J. Nolland, *Luke* (WBC, 35a, 35b, 35c; 3 vols.; Dallas: Word Books, 1989–93), II, p. 529. His criticisms are especially on target with reference to some who have exploited the Deuteronomy hypothesis in support of the questionable theory that much of the material in the Central Section represents freely created midrash. In the aforementioned study I attempt to answer Blomberg's criticisms.

entered the land which the Lord swore to our fathers to give to us.' 4 And the priest shall take the basket out of your hands and shall place it before the altar of the Lord your God. 5 And answering he will say before the Lord your God, 'My father abandoned Syria and went down into Egypt, and sojourned there with a small number, and became there a mighty nation and a great multitude. 6 And the Egyptians treated us badly and humbled us, and placed on us hard tasks. 7 And we cried for help to our Lord God, and the Lord heard our voice and saw our humiliation, our labor, and our affliction. 8 And the Lord brought us out of Egypt with his great strength, with his mighty hand and his exalted arm, and with great visions, signs, and wonders. 9 And he brought us into this place, and gave us this land, a land flowing with milk and honey. 10 And now, behold, I have brought the first of the fruits of the land, which you, O Lord, have given to me, a land flowing with milk and honey.' And you shall leave it before the Lord your God, and you shall worship before the Lord your God. 11 And you shall rejoice in all the good things which the Lord your God has given to you, you and your house, and the Levite and the stranger who is with you.

12 But when you should have completed tithing all the tithe of your fruits in the third year, you shall give the second tenth to the Levite, the proselyte, the orphan, and the widow; and they shall eat (it) in your cities and be merry. 13 And you shall say before the Lord your God, 'I have collected the holy things out of my house, and I have given them to the Levite, the proselyte, the orphan, and the widow, according to all the commandments which you commanded me. I did not transgress your commandment, nor did I forget it. 14 In my distress I did not eat of them; I have not gathered from them for uncleanness; nor have I given of them to the dead. 15 Look down from your holy house, from heaven, and bless your people Israel, and the land which you have given to them, as you swore to our fathers, to give to us a land flowing with milk and honey.'

16 On this day the Lord your God commanded you to do all just ordinances and judgments; and you shall observe and do them from your whole heart, and from your whole soul. 17 This day you have chosen God to be your God, and to walk in all his ways, and to observe the just ordinances and the judgments, and to obey his voice. 18 And the Lord has chosen you this day that you should become to him a peculiar people, as he said, to observe his commandments; 19 and that you should be above all nations, as he has made you renowned, a boast, and glorious, that you should be a people holy to the Lord your God, just as he spoke.

We shall consider several aspects of the relationship between this parable and its Lukan and Deuteronomistic contexts. First, we shall consider the verbal parallels. Do the proposed parallel pasages have in common significant vocabulary? Is there verbal (or dictional) coherence?

Secondly, we must look for thematic coherence, if any.[1] That is, do the proposed parallel passages speak to common themes or issues? Thirdly, we must examine evidence of exegetical coherence. That is, do ancient interpretive traditions of Deuteronomy 26 heighten the parallels between this Old Testament passage and the Lukan parable? Finally, we must ask about the parable's meaning in the context of Luke's Central section. In what sense, if any, does this parable bring the Central Section to a fitting conclusion? Does its interpretation against the background of Deuteronomy 26 and its interpretive traditions clarify its function as the concluding pericope of the Central Section?

Verbal Coherence

There are a few significant verbal parallels that should be noted. First, the Pharisee of Luke's parable 'tithes all (ἀποδεκατῶ πάντα)' that he earns (Lk. 18.12). This is what the Israelites are commanded in Deut. 26.12: 'to tithe all the tithe (ἀποδεκατῶσαι πᾶν τὸ ἐπιδέκατον)'. The verb ἀποδεκατοῦν is quite rare in both Testaments, occurring but twice in Deuteronomy (cf. Deut. 14.22; 26.12; only four other places in the LXX) and three times in the Gospels (cf. Mt. 23.23 = Lk. 11.42; 18.12). The rareness of this word lends additional support to the Deuteronomy hypothesis and its proposal that Lk. 18.9-14 has been deliberately placed in a sequence so as to be viewed against Deuteronomy 26.

A second significant verbal parallel is found in the complementary pair of words ταπεινοῦν/ὑψοῦν and their cognates. The Israelites are reminded that the 'Egyptians humbled (ἐταπείνωσαν)' them (Deut. 26.6). But when God saw Israel's 'humiliation (ταπείνωσιν)', he 'brought [Israel] out of Egypt with his mighty hand and his exalted (ὑψηλῷ) arm' (Deut. 26.7-8). Through God's intervention, Israel's humiliation is transformed into exaltation. This humiliation–exaltation language may have been the reason why the Lukan Evangelist appended the

---

1.   B.D. Chilton (*A Galilean Rabbi and His Bible: Jesus' Use of the Interpreted Scripture of his Time* [GNS, 8; Wilmington, DE: Michael Glazier, 1984], also published as *A Galilean Rabbi and His Bible: Jesus' Own Interpretation of Isaiah* [London: SPCK, 1984]) has developed the criteria of 'dictional coherence' and 'thematic coherence'. My first two criteria parallel these.

saying in 18.14b to the parable: πᾶς ὁ ὑψῶν ἑαυτὸν ταπεινωθήσεται, ὁ δὲ ταπεινῶν ἑαυτὸν ὑψωθήσεται.[1]

Finally, two weaker verbal parallels are worth considering. The first is seen in the cognates δικαίωμα and δικαιοῦν. The former occurs in Deut. 26.16, 17: 'the Lord your God commanded you to do all the just ordinances (δικαιώματα) and judgments'. In Luke's parable the Pharisee exemplifies those who regard themselves as 'just (δίκαιοι)' (Lk. 18.9); but it is the toll collector, we are told, who left the Temple 'justified (δεδικαιωμένος)' (Lk. 18.14). The second parallel involves 'heaven'. The righteous Israelites are to pray that God will look down 'from heaven (ἐκ τοῦ οὐρανοῦ)' and bless their people and the land (Deut. 26.15). But in the Lukan parable, the toll collector, because of his sense of sinfulness, is unwilling to lift his eyes 'to heaven (εἰς τὸν οὐρανόν)' (Lk. 18.13).

The verbal coherence grows even stronger when we consider Josephus's version of Deuteronomy 26:

> And when any man, after having done all this and having offered tithes of all, along with those for the Levites and for the banquets, is about to depart to his own home, let him stand (στάς) opposite the sacred precincts and render thanks to God (εὐχαριστησάτω μὲν τῷ θεῷ)... let him ask God ever to be favorable and merciful to himself (ἵλεων αὐτῷ) (*Ant.* 4.8.22 §§242-43).

According to the Lukan parable, the Pharisee, who 'stood (σταθείς) by himself', has done the first part: 'God, I thank you (ὁ θεός, εὐχαριστῶ σοι)' (Lk. 18.11), while the toll collector, who 'stood (ἐστώς) at a distance', does the second: 'God, be merciful to me (ἱλάσθητί μοι) the sinner!' (Lk. 18.13).[2] Josephus has employed three words (εὐχαριστοῦν, ἱστάναι, ἵλεως) in his paraphrase of the passage that occur in the Lukan parable (but do not occur in Deut. 26). This fact should not, of course, be taken as evidence of literary dependence, but it

---

1. This saying is found in other contexts (Mt. 23.12; Lk. 14.11) and may have been placed here by the Lukan Evangelist; cf. J.A. Fitzmyer, *The Gospel according to Luke* (AB, 28, 28a; 2 vols.; Garden City, NY: Doubleday, 1981–85), II, p. 1044, who thinks that the saying comes from Q and was introduced into the Evangelist's 'L' material. Originally, of course, the saying had nothing to do with Deut. 26.7-8; it reflects LXX Ezek. 21.31.

2. ἵλεως and ἱλάσκομαι are cognate; cf. F. Büchsel, 'ἵλεως κτλ', *TDNT*, III, pp. 300, 314.

does draw Deuteronomy 26 and the Lukan parable into closer verbal alignment.

Thematic Coherence

Of more significance than dictional coherence is thematic coherence. If the Deuteronomy hypothesis is valid, then we should expect the parallel passages to clarify one another. Does Deuteronomy 26 shed light on the parable? It appears that it does.

Deuteronomy 26 constitutes the command to all Israelites to present a tithe of their first fruits and a tithe of third-year produce. Along with the presentation of these tithes, the Torah-observant Israelites are to confess their allegiance to the Sinai Covenant. They are to acknowledge their descent from Jacob, God's subsequent dramatic and powerful rescue of Israel from Egyptian bondage, and the gift of the promised land. After presenting the tithe, the Israelites are to aver that they have performed all the tithing commandments, neglecting none.

Both the Pharisee and the toll collector have gone to the Temple, 'the place' to which Israelites are commanded to go (Deut. 26.2) and worship (26.10). The Pharisee in the Lukan parable appears to be acting out the liturgy prescribed by Deuteronomy 26.[1] As a man who has been faithful to the Sinai Covenant, he is 'not like the rest of men' who have broken the laws of the covenant. And for this, he thanks God. He is not a sinner; he is a Torah-observant Jew who fasts twice a week[2] and tithes all that he earns. He appears to exemplify the description offered by Josephus: 'the Pharisees, an order of Jews held to be more pious than others (εὐσεβέστερον εἶναι τῶν ἄλλων)' (War 1.5.2 §110).

The Pharisee's prayer, moreover, parallels other prayers preserved in later rabbinic sources:

> I thank you, O Lord, my God, that you have assigned my portion with those who sit in the house of learning, and not with those who sit at street corners; for I am early to work on the words of the Torah, and they are early to work on things of no importance. I weary myself, and they weary

---

1. One of the very few commentators to observe this is J. Lightfoot, *Horae Hebraicae et Talmudicae* (4 vols.; 1658–78; ET Oxford: Oxford University Press, 1859), III, p. 185.

2. According to *b. Ta'an.* 12a, the two days may have been Monday and Thursday. According to *Did.* 8.1, these are the days on which 'hypocrites' fast. The author of this work enjoins his readers to fast on Wednesdays and Fridays instead.

themselves; I weary myself and profit from it, while they weary themselves to no profit. I run and they run. I run towards the life of the Age to Come, and they run towards the pit of destruction (*b. Ber.* 28b; cf. *y. Ber.* 4.2).[1]

In contrast to the Pharisee, the toll collector cannot recite the Confession. He has not obeyed the commandments of the covenant. He cannot boast of having tithed his earnings. Echoing the language of Psalm 51, he confesses, instead, that he is a 'sinner'.[2] All that he can do is beg for God's mercy.

The actions of the characters in the parable make good sense against the background of Deuteronomy 26. What appears at first blush to be shameless boasting on the part of the Pharisee is in reality his obedience to Torah. He acknowledges his election, which is the result of the covenant, and he avers that he has paid his tithes. Because of his disobedience, the toll collector cannot make the Confession. The irony in the Lukan parable is that it is not the Pharisee who leaves the Temple justified, but the toll collector. How this idea functions in Luke's Central Section will be further considered below.

Exegetical Coherence

Several significant features of the parable are found to cohere with ancient interpretive traditions concerned with Deuteronomy 26. Such coherence adds important support to the Deuteronomy hypothesis.

First of all, the parable's depiction of the Pharisee and toll collector going up to the Temple to pray coheres with interpretations of various particulars that relate to Deuteronomy 26. The 'place' (Deut. 26.2, 9) is understood to refer to the Temple of Jerusalem (*Sifre Deut.* §298 [on 26.2]; §301 [on 26.9]; *m. Ma'as. Š.* 1.5; 5.12; *m. Bikk.* 2.2), which

---

1. The passage is cited by J. Jeremias, *The Parables of Jesus* (New York: Charles Scribner's Sons, rev. edn, 1963), p. 142. Fitzmyer (*Luke*, II, p. 1187) rightly criticizes Jeremias for claiming that the prayer 'has come down to us from the first century'. Nevertheless, the affinities with the Pharisee's prayer in the parable suggest that prayers like the one preserved in the fifth-century Babylonian Talmud must have existed in some form in the first century. For a concise discussion of the problems and possibilities of utilizing rabbinic and targumic sources for New Testament interpretation, see G. Vermes, *Jesus and the World of Judaism* (London: SCM Press; Philadelphia: Fortress Press, 1983), pp. 74-88; *idem, The Religion of Jesus the Jew* (London: SCM Press; Minneapolis: Fortress Press, 1993), pp. 6-9.

2. 'Have mercy on me, O God, according to your great mercy... wash me thoroughly from my iniquity, and cleanse me from my sin' (LXX Ps. 50.1-2).

agrees with the setting of the parable (Lk. 18.10). According to the parable, the Pharisee and the toll collector went up to the Temple to 'pray' (Lk. 18.10, 11: προσεύχεσθαι). But in the Greek and Hebrew versions of Deuteronomy 26, the Torah-observant Israelite is to 'worship' (Deut. 26.10: προσκυνεῖν/ שׁחה). Neither version says anything about prayer. But prayer is introduced into the text by the Pentateuch Targums, through their expansion of the Exodus recital: 'But the Egyptians dealt harshly with us, and imposed hard labor on us. So we prayed before the Lord God of our fathers, and the Lord accepted our prayer' (Deut. 26.6-7 in *Onq.*, *Ps.-J.*, and *Neof.*: pa'el of צלי).[1] The opening line of the parable, 'two men went up to the Temple to pray' (Lk. 18.10), which occurs elsewhere in Luke–Acts (cf. Acts 3.1), echoes rabbinic diction: 'Rabbi Ishmael ben Rabbi Yose went up to pray (לצלאה) in Jerusalem' (*Gen. R.* 81.3 [on 35.4]).[2]

Secondly, there are important points of exegetical coherence that clarify certain aspects of the Lukan parable. Commenting on the phrase 'of the ground' (Deut. 26.2), a Tannaitic tradition maintains that 'tenants, lessees, holders of confiscated land, and robbers (גזלן)' are excluded from the law of first fruits and the Confession (*Sifre Deut.* §297 [on Deut. 26.1-2]). The same interpretation is found in *Mek.* on Exod. 23.19 (*Kaspa* §5): 'This is to exclude tenants on shares, tenants on fixed rents, the holder of confiscated fields, and the robber (גזלן)'.[3] This interpretation coheres with the Pharisee's statement, thanking God that he was not a 'robber (ἅρπαξ)' (Lk. 18.11).[4] If he were, he would be ineligible to make the Confession. But it is different in the case of the toll collector. In the rabbinic literature, tax collectors and toll collectors are frequently associated with thieves and robbers (cf. *m. Toh.* 7.6; *m. B. Qam.* 10.1-2; *m. Ned.* 3.4; *Der. Er. Rab.* 2.11). Certain things are susceptible to uncleanness if touched by tax collectors and robbers

---

1. See B. Grossfeld, *The Targum Onqeolos to Deuteronomy* (ArBib, 9; Wilmington, DE: Michael Glazier, 1988), p. 75.

2. See also *Targ. Joel* 1.14: 'enter the sanctuary of the Lord your God and pray before the Lord'. The phrase may very well represent Lukan redaction (Lk. 2.4-5; 9.28; Acts 10.9), as Fitzmyer (*Luke*, II, p. 1186) suggests, but it is a phrase very much at home in Jewish piety.

3. According to *Sifre Deut.* §301 (on Deut. 26.5-11), various other persons are excluded from the Confession, but not from the tithe of first fruits (cf. *m. Bikk.* 1.5). The principal issue here is ownership of the land.

4. In the LXX, ἅρπαξ occurs but once (Gen. 49.27), but the cognates ἁρπαγή and ἅρπαγμα occur several times, almost always translating גזל and its cognates.

(*t. Ṭoh.* 8.5-6). Rabbi Simeon ben Yohai (c. 150 CE) is remembered to have declared that there is no family in which there is a tax collector 'unless they are all robbers (ליסטים)'[1] (*b. Šebu.* 39a). The 'robbers' (אנסין) to which reference is made in *m. Sanh.* 3.3 are probably tax (or toll) collectors. The significance of this is that no 'robber' (גזלן) is permitted to present first fruits and make the Confession (*m. Bikk.* 1.2).[2] Consistent with this teaching, the toll collector in the Lukan parable does not claim to have tithed, nor does he make the Confession.

The outcome of the parable is surprising, as is often the case with the parables of Jesus. It is the toll collector, not the Pharisee, who departs from the Temple 'justified' (Lk. 18.14a). What makes this conclusion especially surprising is the commonly held belief that 'for tax collectors and toll collectors, making repentance is difficult' (*t. B. Meṣ.* 8.26). This negative view of revenue farmers contributes significantly to the effectiveness of the parable. Contrary to conventional wisdom, the toll collector's prayer is more pious than that of the Pharisee.

Even the parable's secondary conclusion, 'Everyone who exalts himself will be humbled' (Lk. 18.14b), appears to parallel interpretation of Deuteronomy 26. According to rabbinic law, the Confession of Deut. 26.5-10 is to be discussed during the celebration of Passover: 'He begins with the disgrace [גנות] and ends with the glory [שבח]; and he expounds from "A wandering Aramean was my father…" until he finishes the whole section' (*m. Pes.* 10.4). The father is to tell his family of Israel's disgrace and eventual glory. The 'disgrace' refers to Israel's humiliation (cf. LXX Deut. 26.6-7), while the 'glory' refers to Israel's mighty deliverance through God's exalted arm (LXX Deut. 26.8). It is interesting that this aspect of the Confession is underscored. It is an aspect that coheres with the saying appended to the parable, namely, that the one who is humbled will be exalted.

Luke 18.9-14 in Context

Does the parable of the Pharisee and toll collector find a meaningful place with the context of the Central Section? Is it intended, in fact, to

---

1.   ליסטים is a Greek loanword (cf. λῃστής).

2.   The assumption that tax collectors and toll collectors were thieves and robbers may explain why Zacchaeus, a chief toll collector, repaid fourfold anyone overcharged (Lk. 19.8). Fourfold restitution was required of thieves (cf. Exod. 21.37 [22.1 Eng.]: 'four sheep for a [stolen] sheep').

be the conclusion of the Central Section? I believe that both of these questions can be answered in the affirmative.

James Sanders has tentatively concluded that every pericope in Luke's Central Section in one way or another touches the theme of election: what one must do or be to enter or remain within the company of the elect.[1] Not all of the pericopes that make up the Central Section contribute to this theme in an obvious way, but many do. One thinks of the good Samaritan, Martha and Mary, the great banquet, the prodigal son, the rich man and Lazarus, and the ten lepers. All of these passages, most of them parables found only in Luke, advance and clarify in significant ways Luke's theology of election; and all of them cast significant light on the proposed parallels with Deuteronomy, and have light cast upon them by these parallels. It will be helpful to review these examples, in order to appreciate better how the parable of the Pharisee and the publican contributes to the context of the Central Section.

According to the Deuteronomy hypothesis, the parable of the good Samaritan (10.30-37) has been arranged to lie opposite Deuteronomy 7. In this chapter Israelites are commanded not to make covenants with or show any mercy upon the foreigners whom they are to drive from the promised land (Deut. 7.2). If they show them mercy and allow them to remain, the Israelites might become ensnared in foreign religion (Deut. 7.4, 16) and fail to honor the covenant (Deut. 7.11). The issue that occasioned the parable of the good Samaritan had to do with what was 'written in the Law' (Lk. 10.26). In response to Jesus' question, the lawyer recites the 'Great Commandment' (Lk. 10.27), the first part taken from Deut. 6.5, the second from Lev. 19.18. The parable is given in order to clarify what is meant by 'neighbor'. As the lawyer himself confessed, the man who fulfilled the commandment was the Samaritan, the man who 'showed mercy on him' who fell among the robbers (Lk. 10.36-37). In dramatic contrast to the command to 'show no mercy' on foreigners, the Samaritan, a foreigner, shows mercy and so fulfills the commandment and, by implication, has fulfilled the covenant, as summarized by Deut. 6.5. He has done the right thing, and so 'will live' (Lk. 10.28).

According to the Deuteronomy hypothesis, the Martha and Mary pericope (Lk. 10.38-42) lies opposite Deuteronomy 8, especially vv. 1-3. Martha busies herself with serving; Mary sits at the Lord's feet to hear

---

1.   Sanders, 'Election in Luke's Great Banquet Parable', p. 255 (p. 110 in rev. edn).

his word. The Evangelist has illustrated what it means not to 'live by bread alone, but...by everything that proceeds out of the Mouth of the Lord'. Martha illustrates the first part, Mary the second.[1]

The parable of the great banquet (Lk. 14.15-24) provides a dramatic challenge to popular assumptions regarding election. The very people thought blessed by God make excuses, which appear to lie opposite the excuses for not participating in holy war (Deut. 20.5-7), and so fail to attend the banquet. Instead, the very people thought cursed by God and disqualified for religious service, including holy war as Qumran understood it (cf. Lev. 21.17-23; 1QM 7.4-6; 1QSa 2.5-22), attend the banquet.[2]

The parable of the prodigal son (Lk. 15.11-32) underscores the possibility of restoration and the proper response to it. According to the Deuteronomy hypothesis, the legislation concerning primogeniture (Deut. 21.15-17) and the rebellious son (Deut. 21.18-21) parallels this parable.[3] Although the law allows for the stoning of a disobedient son, who is a 'glutton and a drunkard', the father of the parable is willing to forgive the prodigal and admonishes his obedient older son to do the same. Perhaps nowhere else in the Central Section do ancient hermeneutics play such an important role. Depending on 'how one reads' the Law (cf. Lk. 10.26), the prodigal could be condemned, or he could be forgiven. The forgiving father recognizes that the prodigal's return and repentance have wiped the slate clean. His compassionate hermeneutics become a model for Luke's readers.

The parable of the rich man and Lazarus (Lk. 16.19-31) flies in the face of ancient conventional wisdom. Surely a man who lives like a king is blessed of God, while one could be equally certain that the sins of Lazarus the beggar have finally caught up with him. Yet, not so. At his death Lazarus is taken to Paradise and placed in the bosom of Abraham. At his death the rich man is sent to Hades. According to the Deuteronomy hypothesis, this parable lies opposite the legislation concerning the treatment of the poor (Deut. 24.6–25.3). If the poor are treated with compassion, Israel will be blessed (Deut. 24.13, 19). But if the wealthy oppress the poor, it will be held as a sin against them (Deut. 24.15). In the Lukan context the parable warns that wealth in itself is no

---

1. See Wall, 'Martha and Mary', pp. 144-50.

2. See Sanders, 'Election in Luke's Great Banquet Parable', pp. 247-71 (pp. 106-20 in rev. edn).

3. See J.D.M. Derrett, 'Law in the New Testament: The Parable of the Prodigal Son', *NTS* 14 (1967), pp. 56-74.

certain indication of salvation. Indeed, it is not, if those who possess it are insensitive to the poverty of their neighbor.

The parable of the ten lepers (Lk. 17.11-19), which according to the Deuteronomy hypothesis lies opposite the legislation concerning leprosy (Deut. 24.8-9), offers another challenge to assumptions about election. The lepers are healed and directed to show themselves to the priests, as the law commands, but only one of them returns to thank Jesus. The point of the pericope, especially in view of its placement in the Central Section, is to show that piety is sometimes exemplified by those not usually thought of as pious. As in the case of the good Samaritan, so here again we have a Samaritan whose conduct wins Jesus' approval.

The parable of the Pharisee and the publican brings the Central Section to a fitting end by summing up what is for Luke the essence of the gospel message, as it pertains to the question of election: anyone, no matter how far estranged from the covenant of Moses, can repent and be brought back to God. If there is genuine repentance, genuine faith, acts of charity and expressions of thanksgiving, then restoration is possible. This can happen, Luke believes, through the message of the 'prophet like Moses' (Deut. 18.15-19; cf. Acts 3.22-23; 7.37). Just as obedience to Moses' teaching would assure possession of the promised land and prosperity within it, so obedience to Jesus' teaching will assure entry into the kingdom of God and great reward.

Lingering Questions

In my judgment, the results of the above study are suggestive, but they are not conclusive. Several questions remain that will have to be addressed if the Deuteronomy hypothesis is to be defended persuasively. First, the respective theological thrusts of Luke's Central Section and Deuteronomy 1–26 have to be carefully analysed. Is James Sanders correct in his assessment that both revolve around the ethic of election? If he is, then an important rationale for the Evangelist's construction of the Central Section has been established. That election questions are the primary driving force in the Central Section seems clear enough, but are these the questions that drive Deuteronomy 1–26? Perhaps they are, but further analysis is required.

Secondly, what is there about Lk. 10.1 that would claim the reader's or hearer's attention and cause him or her to think of Deuteronomy 1? In other words, is there present in the opening lines of Luke 10 something that indicates that Deuteronomy is mirrored by the contents of the Central Section? Lk. 10.1 reads: 'After these things the Lord appointed seventy others and he sent (ἀπέστειλεν) them by twos before his face (πρὸ προσώπου αὐτοῦ) into every city (εἰς πᾶσαν πόλιν) and place where he was about to come'. This opening verse recalls nothing from the opening verses of Deuteronomy 1, until we come to vv. 21-22: 'Behold the Lord your God has delivered up to you the land before your face (πρὸ προσώπου ὑμῶν). Go up and take possession of it, as the Lord, the God of your fathers, commanded you. Fear not, nor be faint hearted. And you all came to me and said, "Let us send (ἀποστείλωμεν) men before us, and let them traverse the land for us, and bring us word which we way we should go up, and to what cities (τὰς πόλεις εἰς ἅς) we should come".'

These parallels are suggestive, but they are not conclusive. Had Deuteronomy 1 explicitly referred to Moses' appointment of the 'seventy' (as in Exod. 24.1, 9; Num. 11.16-25; the latter passage, along with Deut. 18.18-23, is alluded to in Deut. 1.9-18) the case for the Deuteronomy hypothesis would be greatly strengthened. As it is, Deut. 1.23 goes on to speak of the appointment of the 'twelve spies'. Reference to the 'seventy' certainly has a Mosaic ring to it, but in itself Deuteronomy 1 is not brought to mind. Are there interpretive traditions that link Deuteronomy 1 with Moses' appointment of the seventy?

As I see it, these appear to be the tough, lingering questions that must be faced by proponents of the Deuteronomy hypothesis, if this hypothesis is to prove itself. Should the hypothesis prove to be valid, then interpreters of the Lukan Gospel will be in a position not only to understand better the arrangement and order of the Central Section, but to understand better many of the various pericopes that make up this portion of Luke.

Part V

THE GOSPEL OF JOHN

JOHN'S USE OF SCRIPTURE[*]

†A.T. Hanson

The purpose of this essay is to work out as far as we can the significance of the Fourth Evangelist's use of Scripture, illustrating conclusions reached in a previous publication.[1] We shall have to discuss various questions concerning John's methods which have been raised by scholars in the field of Johannine studies, and we shall find that we are inevitably faced, as we are at every point in the Gospel, with the question of historicity. I must, however, note one area which I shall not be looking at in this essay; although John's use of Scripture certainly has a very important bearing on his Christology, I cannot explore this issue here. It seems that the questions we find ourselves faced with now fall into six divisions of unequal length.

I

First, we must ask whether John's treatment of Scripture in his Gospel can legitimately or usefully be described as midrash. As we shall be seeing, this is a term which a number of scholars have used in order to describe John's technique. We can look particularly at two articles on the subject of midrash. The first is by Renée Bloch, in the *Supplément au Dictionnaire de la Bible*.[2] Bloch begins by defining midrash as 'an edifying and explanatory genre close to Scripture'. The book of Wisdom from ch. 10 onwards is a midrash on the exodus events and their

*   The present essay is a slightly revised version of what appeared as ch. 14 in A.T. Hanson, *The Prophetic Gospel* (Edinburgh: T. & T. Clark, 1991), pp. 234-53.

1.   See Hanson, *The Prophetic Gospel*, esp. chs. 1–13 (pp. 1-233).

2.   R. Bloch, 'Midrash', *DBSup*, V, cols. 1263-81; ET 'Midrash', in W.S. Green (ed.), *Approaches to Ancient Judaism I* (BJS, 1; Missoula, MT: Scholars Press, 1978), pp. 29-50.

sequel.[1] Midrash must begin from Scripture, however far it develops its
theme thereafter.[2] What Bloch calls '*midrash aggada*' seeks, she says,
'to define the meaning of the stories and events of history'.[3] She has no
doubt therefore but that midrash as a literary genre existed before New
Testament times: 'Nothing could be more wrong than the idea that
midrash is a late creation of rabbinic Judaism'.[4] Inside the Bible the
books of Chronicles provide an example of midrash; so does Psalm 78,
and indeed the entire book of Deuteronomy itself.[5] Bloch insists that
there is a particularly close relationship between apocalyptic and midrash.
The Palestinian Targum, she adds, is very close to midrash, and may
indeed have been originally based on a number of homilies on Scripture.
When she turns to the New Testament she finds many examples of
midrash: 'all forms of midrash are found in the New Testament'.[6] There
is plenty of midrash, for example, in Matthew's Gospel. And, not
surprisingly, she finds midrash in the Fourth Gospel: 'The symbolism of
the Fourth Gospel, its interest in the meaning of names, its penchant for
word-plays etc., are also related to certain midrashic tendencies'. She
also compares 'the contemporized application of many biblical texts in
the Johannine passion narrative'.[7]

Thus Bloch would have no hesitation whatever in putting large
sections of the Gospel into the category of midrash. On the basis of her
definition of midrash, however, it is doubtful whether it would be illuminating to apply the term to John's distinctive technique of biblical interpretation. A term that can apply equally to considerable parts of the Old
Testament and the New is not likely to help very much if we are trying
to define what is distinctive about John's usage.

We turn now to Roger Le Déaut, whose article is written in the form
of a book review.[8] He says that midrash had not developed into a literary genre by New Testament times. He claims that there are two

---

1.   Bloch, 'Midrash', p. 29.
2.   Bloch, 'Midrash', p. 31.
3.   Bloch, 'Midrash', p. 34.
4.   Bloch, 'Midrash', p. 37.
5.   Compare the theory of J. Weingreen, who in his book *From Bible to Mishna*
(Manchester: University of Manchester Press, 1976) suggested that Deuteronomy
should be regarded as a sort of mishnah on the older versions of the Torah.
6.   Bloch, 'Midrash', p. 48.
7.   Bloch, 'Midrash', pp. 48-49.
8.   R. Le Déaut, 'Apropos a Definition of Midrash', *Int* 25 (1971), pp. 259-82.

features which are characteristic of all forms of midrash. The first is that it must start from the text of Scripture; and the second is that it seeks to serve the community by making Scripture contemporary.[1] One cannot tie midrash down to precise forms, and Le Déaut asks: 'At what moment does a text cease to be a midrash when the biblical reference recedes further and further into the background until it finally disappears?'[2] Le Déaut is quite ready to apply the term 'midrash' to some passages in the New Testament, but in such passages Jesus had been substituted for Scripture. The New Testament writers, he says, used midrashic techniques. Le Déaut usefully considers the relation of midrash to targum and to haggada. It is not always easy, he says, to distinguish midrash from targum. Both seek to make the biblical text contemporary. And haggada is often synonymous with midrash.[3] Finally Le Déaut refuses to attempt a definition of midrash. It is, he thinks, too all-embracing and varied for the possibility of an adequate definition.

Le Déaut would thus discourage us, as Bloch does, from the belief that anything much would be gained by describing John's distinctive technique of scriptural interpretation as midrash. We may welcome his assertion that John uses 'midrashic techniques', but so do other writers of the New Testament. Obviously John is well acquainted with the methods of Jewish exegesis of Scripture and uses them himself. But this is hardly surprising. After all, New Testament writers had no other starting place when they set out on the enterprise of reinterpreting Scripture in a christocentric sense. We have yet to find an adequate definition of what is peculiar to John in his treatment of Scripture.

A number of scholars have used the word 'targum' in describing John's technique. M. Black, quoted by Le Déaut, described the Gospel as 'an inspired "targumising" of an Aramaic sayings tradition'.[4] We need not dispute about the supposition of an Aramaic original for the Gospel. This is a theory which would find few supporters today. But Black's phrase does suggest that John had a written Gospel before him to which he proceeded to apply 'targumizing' techniques. It must be confessed that what scholars have discovered of John's use of Scripture

1. Le Déaut, 'Definition of Midrash', pp. 264, 270, 275, 282 n.
2. Le Déaut, 'Definition of Midrash', p. 273.
3. Le Déaut, 'Definition of Midrash', pp. 278-79, 281.
4. Le Déaut, 'Definition of Midrash', p. 280. The quotation is from M. Black, *An Aramaic Approach to the Gospels and Acts* (Oxford: Clarendon Press, 3rd edn, 1967), p. 151.

does not seem to support this theory. It is no doubt true that John is often reinterpreting the original teaching of Jesus to make it applicable to the conditions of his day. If this is targumizing, then John is a targumizer. But a targum cannot exist without an original text, and we do not for the most part know what the original text was, in what form it existed, and whether or not John was consciously trying to supersede it by means of his 'targum'. B. Olsson also suggests that the nearest parallels to the Fourth Gospel are to be found in the Targums.[1] This is putting the claim in a milder and more acceptable form. I have sometimes found, in my examination of John's use of Scripture, that the form of the text of Scripture found in the Targums comes closest to John's meaning. But this is not the same thing as saying that he was writing a targum. We find B. Lindars making a very similar claim. John, he says, often bases his writing on genuine teaching material of Jesus, but 'his manner of using the material proceeds along the lines of targumic exegesis'.[2] We may therefore reasonably conclude that targumic methods are used in the Gospel and even that some parts of the Gospel look like a targum. But this is not the same thing as saying that the Gospel *is* a targum.[3]

Olsson suggests at one point that the Gospel may be viewed as a midrash on the Gospel tradition.[4] This is perhaps the nearest we can legitimately come to defining the Fourth Gospel in terms of midrash. But this is not to come very near, because 'the Gospel tradition' was not in John's case one written document, as the Scriptures were to Jewish exegetes. Certainly John was not writing a midrash on any one of the Synoptic Gospels, or all of them taken together, whatever view we take of his relation to the Synoptics. In writing a midrash one always had clearly in mind the text or texts of Scripture which one was expounding. But John does not cite the text on which he is elaborating. On the

---

1. B. Olsson, *Structure and Meaning in the Fourth Gospel: A Text-Linguistic Analysis of John 2:1-11 and 4:1-42* (ConBNT, 6; Lund: Gleerup, 1974), p. 282.

2. B. Lindars, 'Traditions behind the Fourth Gospel', in M. de Jonge (ed.), *L'Evangile de Jean: Sources, rédaction, théologie* (repr.; BETL, 44; Leuven: Peeters, 1987 [1977]), pp. 109-24, here p. 115.

3. B.D. Chilton (*Targumic Approaches to the Gospels* [Studies in Judaism; Lanham, MD and New York: University Press of America, 1986], p. 125) rightly cautions against calling the Gospels 'targums'. He prefers to speak of the Gospel as 'cognate with' (rather than 'identical to') the Targums.

4. Olsson, *Structure and Meaning in the Fourth Gospel*, pp. 284-85.

contrary, he attributes his interpretation directly to Jesus himself. If he is writing 'midrashic haggada', that is, commentary and embroidery of an incident in the career of Jesus, he always proceeds as if his haggada were identical with the original narrative of the event, so much so that it is normally impossible to reconstruct the outlines of the original event. It is as though Paul, who frequently writes Christian midrashim on texts from Scripture which he quotes, had refrained from quoting the texts altogether, but had directly attributed his interpretations to the inspired authors of Scripture themselves; as though in Rom. 10.6 he had written: 'But Moses says: who shall bring Christ down from heaven?' When Paul writes a midrash on Scripture we know in nine cases out of ten on which text of the Scripture he is expounding. Is John then perhaps writing a midrash not on Scripture, but on the person of Jesus? It is very hard to retain anything of the usual sense of the word if we use it in this way. A midrash must be written on Scripture, not on a person. In any case, John does not seem to distinguish between that on which he is writing a midrash and the midrash itself. I would therefore conclude that, although it is perfectly reasonable to say that John uses midrashic methods, or targumic techniques, and even that he is sometimes writing something very like haggada, it does not throw light on the question of John's use of Scripture simply to say this his Gospel is a midrash.

II

Can we then apply to the use of Scripture in the Gospel other terms which are often used in discussing the New Testament interpretation of Scripture? For example, does John use typology? It is remarkable that G. Reim is inclined to deny that John ever uses typology proper.[1] No doubt what he means is that John is more likely to represent Jesus as superseding in his own person some person or object in the Old Testament than to present that person or object as a type of Christ. It is more accurate, for instance, to say that Jesus as the true place where the people of God should worship supersedes the Temple than to say that the Temple is a type of Christ. Nevertheless in several other instances it seems absolutely accurate to speak of typology in connection with the Gospel.[2] Thus it would be pedantic to deny that in 3.14 John is

---

1. G. Reim, *Studien zum alttestamentlichen Hintergrund des Johannesevangelium* (SNTSMS, 22; Cambridge: Cambridge University Press, 1974), p. 265.

2. Several scholars agree: R.N. Longenecker, *Biblical Exegesis in the Apostolic*

presenting the lifting up of the bronze serpent in the wilderness as a type of Christ's crucifixion. In ch. 4 the well in the wilderness mentioned in Num. 21.16-18 is, among a number of other figures culled from Scripture, presented as a type of Christ, the source of living water. Similarly, though in ch. 6 the manna is unfavorably compared with the bread of life which is Jesus, it would be perfectly true to say that the manna is used as a type of Christ. The Jews' murmuring against Jesus in 6.41 is meant to recall the murmuring of the Israelites against Moses in the wilderness period, so that the murmuring in Scripture becomes a type of the Jews' murmuring against Jesus. In 8.35 the contrast of the Son and the slave is a reference to Genesis 21; when this is unpacked Isaac must be regarded as the type of Christ, as he is in Gal. 4.29. In ch. 10 we cannot deny a reference to the 'shepherd' passages in Ezekiel 34 and 37; but in those chapters not only is God presented as the true shepherd, but a future prince of the Davidic dynasty occupies this position also. One could of course say that this in John's eyes is a prophecy of Jesus, who is certainly presented as Israel's true king. But his Davidic origin is not emphasized, and it would probably be more accurate to say that the Davidic ruler is a type of Christ. The figure of Jesus as the vine in 15.1-10 depends for its significance on various passages in Scripture where Israel is depicted as a vine. This could perhaps be described as an instance of Jesus superseding an Old Testament figure, but if Jesus is regarded by John as the true Israel, then Israel as presented in Scripture can hardly be anything but a type of Christ, even though an imperfect type. In exactly the same way, John's presentation of Jesus during his passion as the paschal lamb is certainly typology. Here John is closer to Hebrews; but the author of Hebrews, though he regarded the types in the old dispensation as inferior to the reality of the new, can surely be legitimately described as employing extensive typology.

This view is supported by R.H. Smith in an article published in 1962.[1] He says that 3.14 is a clear example of typology. But he then proceeds to trace a very elaborate scheme of typology whereby a great many

---

Period (Grand Rapids: Eerdmans, 1975), pp. 152-57; J.W. Drane, 'Typology', *EvQ* 50 (1978), pp. 195-210; L. Goppelt, *Typos: The Typological Interpretation of the Old Testament in the New* (Grand Rapids: Eerdmans, 1982); C.A. Evans, 'Typology', in J.B. Green, S. McKnight and I.H. Marshall (eds.), *Dictionary of Jesus and the Gospels* (Leicester and Downers Grove, IL: Inter-Varsity Press, 1992), pp. 862-66.

1. R.H. Smith, 'Exodus Typology in the Fourth Gospel', *JBL* 81 (1962), pp. 329-42.

events connected with Moses in Exodus have their counterpart in the Fourth Gospel. The scheme grows more and more improbable as he proceeds until we reach a position where the plague on the cattle in Exodus 9 corresponds to the official's son being cured in Jn 4.43-44; and the plague of boils that follows the cattle plague in Exodus 9 corresponds to the healing of the man at the pool of Bethzatha in John 5. It seems that typology is in danger here of becoming allegory.

Does John ever use allegory? The difference between typology and allegory is that in typology there is an intrinsic connection between the type and the fulfillment, whereas in allegory the connection is purely arbitrary. We must admit that John does sometimes use allegory. The scriptural background to John the Baptist in 5.35 is purely allegorical; there is no intrinsic connection between the Baptist and a lantern. The play on the name Shiloh, whereby it recalls a passage in Genesis 49, seems very close to allegory. There seems no intrinsic connection between something that happened at a pool called Siloam and a messianic prophecy in Genesis. The same perhaps could be said about Gabbatha, the pavement, in 19.13. If John is indeed meaning to recall the occasions upon which λιθόστρωτον occurs in what he regards as a significant context in the LXX, the connection is so remote as to deserve to be called allegory rather than typology. Perhaps the same could be said for the description of Jesus' burial in 19.39. John appears to be anxious to link this event up with various texts in Scripture, no matter how remote the connection. But on the whole, instances of the use of allegory in the Gospel are rare and obscure. They in no way justify the wholesale use of allegory in the church fathers' exegesis of Scripture.

There is one element in John's use of Scripture that distinguishes him sharply from most Jewish exegesis, and that is the element of eschatology. This is only what we might expect, since his exegesis is christocentric and the messianic age is the end time. John, like all the writers of the New Testament, regarded Scripture as consisting very largely of prophecy. It had been written down, as Paul says in 1 Cor. 10.11 and the author of 1 Peter implies in 1 Pet. 1.10-12, for our benefit. Hence John approached Scripture expecting to find in it prophecies about Christ. He employed midrashic methods certainly, but he employed them in the interests of eschatology. So Scripture is used by him for halaka, for help in living according to God's law, not merely for haggada, for elaboration and embroidery of events in salvation history in order that we might understand its significance for us. He used Scripture in order to show that it had been fulfilled in the career of Jesus Christ and in the experience of the early church. This motif takes precedence of all others in his interpretation.

III

I have just mentioned salvation history. It is therefore relevant to enquire next what part salvation history plays in John's interpretation of Scripture. By salvation history I mean the belief that God's dealings with his people, from the call of Abraham until the coming of the messiah, should be regarded as a history of salvation; and that therefore one may expect a certain pattern in God's dealings with his people which will be reflected in what happens in the messianic age. In this sense John's exegesis of Scripture is not atomistic: he is not content to cite or echo individual texts from Scripture, isolated from their context and viewed simply as miraculous examples of prediction fulfilled. Scripture was being fulfilled in the career of Jesus, according to John, against the background of the saving events of the old dispensation, and those saving events are never quite forgotten. They are always there like the backcloth in a play.

This is not to say that there is some scheme of salvation history running through the Gospel, so that the Gospel manifests a continuous and progressive exegesis of Scripture. On more than one occasion I have drawn attention to the fact that John is not going through Scripture in order in his composition of his Gospel. All attempts to prove that there was some sort of scriptural system in the background, such as the learned attempt of Professor A. Guilding,[1] break down in the end.

Nevertheless, in the background all the time is salvation history. I will briefly indicate how this appears from my completed examination of the Gospel. In 1.14-18 the Word is represented as having appeared to Moses on the rock at Sinai. The same Word has now appeared in the person of Jesus Christ. We are reminded that revelation has been in some sense continuous since that clearest of all revelations under the old dispensation, and we are given to understand that the Father never has been seen or heard but by means of the Word. Then in 1.35-51 we are brought back to an earlier period, the revelation of the Word to Jacob at Bethel. There is a sort of typology here, for at one point (1.31) the

---

1. A. Guilding, *The Fourth Gospel and Jewish Worship* (Oxford: Oxford University Press, 1960).

Baptist seems to be the fulfillment of the type of Jacob. But undoubtedly the pre-existent Word is identified with the appearance of God to Jacob at the top of the ladder reaching up to heaven. The theme of the Word as the apprehensibility of God is resumed at 5.37, where not only are the theophanies under the old dispensation attributed to the Word, but also the occasions on which Moses or the Israelites were reported as hearing God's voice. It seems probable that one of the passages lying behind Jesus' mysterious utterance in 7.38 is the story of the riven rock in the wilderness. If this is the case, then the rock is a type of Christ; but it is more likely that John is thinking in the same way as Paul does in 1 Cor. 10.4, and that he regards the Word as having been the author of the life-giving water from the rock.

In 8.35, as I have indicated above, Isaac is probably regarded as the type of Christ in the story of the rejection of Hagar and Ishmael in Genesis 21; so once again we are brought back to an incident in salvation history. Certainly in 8.39-59 there is a very extensive reference to salvation history, the earliest event chronologically speaking that John has yet dealt with. That is the visit of the three angels to Abraham narrated in Genesis 18. One of them is identified with the pre-existent Word. It is because of this that Jesus can claim to have seen Abraham. This is particularly striking because Jesus is represented as actually recalling an event that happened hundreds of years before he was born—something quite incompatible with the actual historical Jesus. If I am right in my interpretation of 10.35-36, we have here a reference to another event in salvation history, the Word addressing Israel just after the revelation on Sinai, as narrated in Psalm 82 interpreted according to Jewish traditional exegesis.

Then in 12.37-41 we have one of the latest events in salvation history of which John speaks, Isaiah's vision in the Temple.[1] The Word has conversed with the prophet and foretold the unbelief with which the incarnation would be greeted. Once more we see the Word portrayed as the visibility of God. I have suggested that in 13.18a there is an echo of the rebellion of the Korahites narrated in Numbers 16.[2] If so, we are back at the wilderness period again, for Jesus uses the words that God is recorded as using then. In looking at 14.8-9 I proposed a general

---

1.   Unless the conjecture is correct that at 19.23-24 John has Zech. 3.1-5 in mind, which would bring us down to an event in salvation history that took place after the exile. See Hanson, *The Prophetic Gospel*, pp. 209-10.

2.   Hanson, *The Prophetic Gospel*, pp. 172-75.

reference to the theophanies under the old dispensation, from Genesis 32 onwards.[1] He who appeared was the Word, the eternal mode by which the Father is shown. And finally in 19.29 we certainly have a reference to the paschal lamb, originally slain at the very moment of the exodus.

There is, then, no *scheme* of salvation history lying behind the Gospel, but it is impossible to deny that salvation history is in the background throughout. Indeed the awareness of salvation history is essential for John's Christology. The theophanies under the old dispensation afford him the opportunity of claiming that the appearance of the Word in Jesus Christ was no bolt from the blue, but was the culmination of a series of appearances of the Word in Israel's history. Without salvation history John could never have arrived at his all-important concept of the pre-existence of the Word.

IV

We now turn to one of the most interesting and remarkable aspects of John's use of Scripture, the occasions on which he has apparently introduced on the basis of Scripture some episode or some piece of teaching that seems to have no other basis in history. Since I have traced about 50 instances of this during my examination of the Gospel,[2] I cannot refer to them all, and will look only at some of the most eminent examples. For purposes of discussion I shall divide the examples into teaching and episodes, although an example can combine both, as for instance at 1.41, 45. I shall begin with six occasions on which John has apparently attributed to Jesus teaching based solely on Scripture.

At 3.13-15 the reference to the lifting up of the serpent in the wilderness can hardly be based on the actual teaching of Jesus. John seems to have introduced it and attributed it to Jesus in order to bring out the full significance of the cross as the means of universal salvation. There can be no doubt but that John must have believed that the incident of the bronze serpent was intended by God to foreshadow the cross. Because of this John felt justified in putting this piece of teaching in Jesus' mouth. A little later in 3.31-36 I have traced a passage in Scripture as the original inspiration, Isa 26.12-21. Once again, we have a passage which could hardly fit the situation of the historical Jesus. It assumes a higher Christology than could possibly have been held during Jesus' lifetime.

1. Hanson, *The Prophetic Gospel*, pp. 179-82.
2. Hanson, *The Prophetic Gospel*, pp. 21-233.

The historical Jesus is the last person whom we would expect to claim to have received the Spirit without measure (3.34). John believes that he has found in Scripture a passage which gives him hints and clues about the true status of the Son. A third example will be found in 5.35, a passage already cited as an example of allegory. John finds in Exod. 27.20-21 and Ps. 132.17 what he believes to be prophetic references to the role of the Baptist and without hesitation represents Jesus as describing the Baptist in terms drawn from these passages.

In 6.44 Jesus says that the Father draws to Jesus those who are to be raised up on the last day. I have proposed that this sentence is inspired by Jer. 31.2-3.[1] There is little likelihood that this verse is based on some actual teaching of Jesus, who would be more likely to claim that the Father draws the elect to himself. It is more probable that John has picked out this passage from Jeremiah, seen in it a prophecy of the attraction of the elect to Jesus, and attributed it to Jesus. Similarly in 7.24 Jesus warns his hearers not to judge by appearances. We have seen here an echo of the messiah's role in Isa 11.3.[2] This seems to be another instance of John's turning what he regarded as a prophecy of Jesus into a logion which he attributes to Jesus himself. As a last example we may consider 16.8-11; I have argued that here a description of the Paraclete's activities in the time after the resurrection of Christ is based on Isa. 42.1-9.[3] It is in the last degree unlikely that the historical Jesus would have given any such detailed instruction about the activity of the Holy Spirit. John has taken a passage from his favorite prophet which he believed gave prophetic information about the Holy Spirit and attributed it to a Jesus whom he represents as being omniscient.

So much for teaching based on Scripture alone. We now turn to actual episodes in the Gospel which seem to have the same basis. A good example to begin with occurs at 2.14, where it looks as if the sheep and oxen, which John alone of the Evangelists includes among the livestock cleared out from the Temple by Jesus, come from Ps. 8.8 and not from history. Jesus, John believed, must have driven out sheep and oxen also because Scripture foretold that he would. As we approach the passion, these scripturally based incidents become more frequent. One such occurs at 10.24. The Jews surround Jesus, just as the Psalmist's enemies surrounded him in Ps. 118.11, and he dispels them in the name

1.   Hanson, *The Prophetic Gospel*, pp. 89-90.
2.   Hanson, *The Prophetic Gospel*, pp. 97-99.
3.   Hanson, *The Prophetic Gospel*, pp. 188-89.

of the Lord, as Jesus does the Jews. A very striking example of this meets us in connection with Jesus' prayers at 11.33-42 and 12.27-32. I have argued that the content of these prayers, including the strong emotion that accompanied them, is inspired by Psalms 42, 43 and 86.[1] John feels justified, on the basis of the prayers in these three Psalms, to tell us not only what Jesus prayed but also how. He was confident that it must have happened this way because so it was foretold in Scripture. An interesting example of this habit of John's occurs in 12.19. The Pharisees remark that the whole world has gone after Jesus. I have argued that this sentence is based on Job 21.32-33.[2] John has seen here a prophetic sentence about Jesus, and has not hesitated to attribute it to his enemies.

My last four examples are all taken from the narrative of the passion, death and resurrection of Jesus. At 18.6 those who would arrest him fall to the ground. I have suggested that John has invented this incident on the basis of Pss. 56.10 and 109.6.[3] It was appropriate that it should happen. Scripture has encouraged him to believe that it did, so it goes into his narrative. Then at 19.17 it looks as if John has ignored the part of Simon of Cyrene and has deliberately represented Jesus as carrying his own cross because in Isa. 53.11 it was prophesied that the Servant of the Lord, whom John identified with Jesus, should bear the sins of many. At Jesus' burial (19.39) John represents Nicodemus as providing a vast quantity of myrrh and aloes because he wishes to give Jesus a burial worthy of a king, as depicted in various passages in Scripture, such as Song 4.14-15; Ps. 45.9; 2 Chron. 16.14; Isa. 11.10. And finally, the movements of Mary Magdalene at the empty tomb when she encounters the risen Lord in 20.14-18 seem to have been determined by Song 5.5-6 and 3.4 rather than by any historical tradition known to John. The fact that Mary Magdalene was one of the witnesses of the risen Lord was no doubt part of John's historical tradition; but because he believed that Scripture had foretold how Mary should encounter the risen Jesus, he felt justified in basing his narrative on Scripture rather than on historical tradition.

In the nineteenth century some scholars accused John of having written a Gospel in which he freely invented both teaching and incidents which he attributed to Jesus according to his arbitrary choice. They made the Fourth Gospel out to be sort of a historical novel, wherein

1. Hanson, *The Prophetic Gospel*, pp. 153-62.
2. Hanson, *The Prophetic Gospel*, pp. 164-65.
3. Hanson, *The Prophetic Gospel*, pp. 201-203.

conversations and episodes were freely invented in order to bring out the effect that the author wished to achieve. We can surely say that this is not what happened. John does not feel himself free arbitrarily to invent conversations and incidents in the life of Jesus. One might almost define a law, or at least a general principle, in connection with the Fourth Gospel: John only inserts teaching, conversations, and incidents that have no basis in his historical tradition if he believes he has justification in Scripture for doing so. This imposes a limit on what he writes of non-historical material,[1] and it means that this material must be closely related to his Christology. The Johannine Evangelist is aware that his picture of Jesus is different from that presented in the earlier tradition. But he goes beyond that tradition in part at least because he believes that Scripture authorizes him to do so. Thus Scripture, far from being used merely as illustrative material in his work, is part of its very woof and warp.

V

In my book *The New Testament Interpretation of Scripture* I devoted some pages to a class of scriptural allusions in the Gospel which I described as being places where Scripture can be shown to have influenced John's narrative.[2] I there gave five examples of this usage, but I added 'it may well be that a further study of the text would reveal more'. In fact this happened; besides the five which I referred to there,[3] I have discovered another eleven examples at least. Some of these I have already referred to as passages where John has based teaching on Scripture alone, not on any tradition of Jesus' own teaching. Quite often in the course of this work I have used the word 'inspirational' for such passages. It is perhaps the most appropriate word, since while John in writing them has certainly been inspired by the words of Scripture, he

---

1.   Of course this does not exclude the possibility that some of the material which John received in his tradition may in fact have been largely legendary, even though John believed it to be genuine history. The events lying behind such narratives as the wedding at Cana of Galilee and the raising of Lazarus are so obscure that we have no way of pronouncing upon their historicity.

2.   A.T. Hanson, *The New Testament Interpretation of Scripture* (London: SPCK, 1980), pp. 166-71.

3.   Cf. Jn 1.30-31 and 43-51; 10.24 with 11.41 and 12.13; 11.11-13; 12.1-8; 12.19 and 32.

uses no direct citations. Nor do these cases constitute allusions that any well-instructed reader might be expected to recognize; see for instance the allusion to the bronze serpent in 3.14-15, where an incident in salvation history is mentioned without any actual quotation from the narrative of the event.

The other eleven cases that I have detected are as follows: 3.31-36, where John is influenced by Isa. 26.12-21; 4.31-38, where the influence is Isa. 58.10-11; 6.44, where we can detect Jer. 31.2-3 in the background; 6.45, where we can find traces of Isa. 54.13; 6.60-71, which seem to have been influenced by Psalm 60 and Isa. 43.8-13; 7.18, where we can find Isa. 55.5-6; 10.8, where I have detected the influence of Hos. 6.11–7.1; 10.28-30, where the influence is Isa. 43.12-13; 15.18-19, which seems to be inspired by Isa. 66.5; 16.8-11, which depends on Isa. 42.1-9; and 20.14-18, where Song 5.5-6 and 3.4 seem to be in the background.

It might seem significant that all of the eleven examples above, with the exception of the last, are passages of teaching, not of action. However, when we turn back to the five passages to which I referred in *The New Testament Interpretation of Scripture*, a different picture appears. Of these five, no less than four come from places in the Gospel where action rather than teaching is being related. In the pages devoted to this subject in *The New Testament Interpretation of Scripture* I asked the question: 'why does John use Scripture in this way?'[1] I suggested that he does so because he believes that the events or teachings that he relates are in fact the fulfillment of the scriptural passages that have inspired him as he relates them. And I went on to conclude that John must have believed that the events really took place: 'The events have not been altered so as to agree with Scripture'. In the light of my further investigation of such passages, I am inclined to qualify this conclusion. The situation, as it seems to me, is rather that John as he read his Bible was struck by the appropriateness of certain passages to his own understanding of Jesus, and therefore saw in them divinely inspired information about the messiah. He even believed that sometimes Scripture provided information about events in Jesus' career for which there was no other evidence, as for example the guards in the garden falling to the ground, or Nicodemus bringing enough myrrh and aloes for a king's burial. He was therefore emboldened to include in his Gospel teaching

---

1. Hanson, *New Testament Interpretation*, pp. 170-71.

and incidents drawn wholly from Scripture. He did not make any explicit allusion to Scripture as he wrote because the connection existed purely in his mind and he was not writing in this context to make any polemical or apologetical point. He was not saying, as Matthew does: 'These things were done in order that the saying of the prophet Isaiah might be fufilled'. He was, perhaps, writing in this context mainly for himself or for the initiated few.

There is an analogy here with the author of the book of Revelation. John the Divine never openly quotes Scripture, but his work is soaked in Scripture. Scriptural images, allusions and phrases occur with the greatest frequency. Nor is John the Divine attempting to prove anything by scriptural allusion, as on occasion both Paul and the author of the First Gospel were. John the Divine regarded himself as a prophet. His vivid, disturbing and dramatic descriptions of what is to come for the world and for the church are laid before the reader to be judged on their own merits. He believed himself to be inspired by the Holy Spirit. It was for the reader to judge whether this was true or not. On the whole the response of the church through the ages has been to accept the claim and to appreciate the value of his visions. The author of the Fourth Gospel comes before us in much the same way. He has based his Gospel upon Scripture and has allowed the writing of it to be influenced by Scripture on almost every page. Like the author of Revelation, he believed that he had rightly understood the true meaning of Scripture, and he sets it down in terms not of an apocalypse but of a Gospel. Just as St John the Divine believed himself to be under the inspiration of the Holy Spirit, so John's use of Scripture in the context we are discussing can approximately be called 'inspirational'. I prefer this to the alternative epithet 'charismatic', because 'charismatic' suggests something outside the control of reason. But John's use of Scripture is, judged by his own standards, perfectly reasonable. We can see a consistent Christology emerging. The author of the Fourth Gospel is a prophet who decided to write a Gospel, with all the limitations and conditions that this implies, instead of an apocalypse. It is a prophetic Gospel. Indeed the author of the Fourth Gospel fits very well the role of the 'mystical sage' which J. Barton claims is the nearest equivalent to prophet afforded by the age.[1]

1.   J. Barton, *The Oracles of God: Perceptions of Ancient Prophecy in Israel after the Exile* (London: Darton, Longman & Todd, 1986), p. 126.

VI

We must now give proper attention to what Johannine scholars have said about John's use of Scripture. We can begin with A. Loisy, who is so often the first to hit on an idea which later scholars exploit. He writes: 'The prophecies, instead of simply being the announcement of actual facts, are an element in the allegorical combination'.[1] I take exception to the word 'allegorical', which Loisy uses simply as if it meant 'non-literal'. But he has made a valid point: the scriptural passages which John quotes, or echoes, or alludes to, are a constitutive element in his presentation of his Gospel. L. Goppelt claims, quite rightly no doubt, that in the Gospel Jesus fulfills the destiny of the Servant of the Lord. Later he makes another relevant comment: 'Christ is still compared with the saviour of the OT, but he is presented exclusively as their Lord, and no longer as their antitype'.[2] This is the feature referred to by other scholars also, whereby Christ does not so much fulfill as supersede scriptural foreshadowings. Great scholars cannot be equally brilliant in all branches of New Testament research; it must be admitted that Bultmann was not at his best when exploring the scriptural background to the Fourth Gospel. His statement that 'Proof from prophecy plays a scanty role' (in the Gospel) is an unfortunate one.[3] It is true only in the sense that, as I have indicated above, John does not, like Paul or the author of the First Gospel, frequently point to prophecy fulfilled in the career of Jesus or argue by means of scriptural proofs. But scriptural prophecy, as we have seen, plays an overwhelmingly important part in his Gospel. Summarizing C.K. Barrett's brief but influential study of 1947, T.F. Glasson comments: 'The Evangelist does not rely mainly on quotations and proof-texts, but he has, so to speak, absorbed the whole of the Old Testament into his system'.[4] I would emphasize the phrase 'the whole of the Old Testament' in light of Reim's claim, examined below, that John only had access to a very limited range of Old Testament books. F.-M. Braun makes the same point when he remarks on the wide range

1.   A. Loisy, *Le Quatrième Evangile* (Paris: Picard, 1903), p. 80.

2.   Goppelt, *Typos*, p. 194.

3.   R. Bultmann, *Theology of the New Testament* (2 vols.; New York: Charles Scribner's Sons, 1955), II, p. 5.

4.   T.F. Glasson, *Moses in the Fourth Gospel* (SBT, 40; London: SCM Press, 1963), p. 36 n. 1. See C.K. Barrett, 'The Old Testament in the Fourth Gospel', *JTS* 48 (1947), pp. 155-69, esp. p. 168.

of Old Testament quotations and allusions which are to be found in the Gospel; and he can write of 'la masse des allusions tacites'.[1]

As we might expect, E.D. Freed has a number of comments to make about John's use of Scripture. About his use of the text of Scripture he writes: 'John...draws from his memory of various texts, or combination of texts and sources, a quotation to suit his purpose'.[2] Freed of course confined his study to explicit citations in the Gospels; but there is a certain danger in accusing any New Testament writer of quoting from memory. We cannot be dogmatic about which source John is using. He may sometimes have access to a non-LXX version. He may translate directly from the Hebrew. He may be influenced by a targumic tradition. Later Freed makes a remark which is certainly confirmed by my researches: 'As one trained in the Jewish Scriptures, John shows a thorough acquaintance with them and in a creative way adapts them to suit his theological purpose'.[3] It might perhaps be more accurate to add that there are occasions on which John adapts his Gospel or his Christology to suit the scriptural text. I cannot possibly accept Freed's suggestion that ἡ γραφή ('the Scripture') in 7.42 refers to the Gospels of Matthew and Luke.[4] The question of whether John was even acquainted with Matthew and Luke is an open one. The suggestion that he regarded them as Scripture is surely anachronistic. Freed rightly concludes from his investigations that an analysis of John's scriptural citations is no help at all in identifying sources behind the Gospel.[5] I heartily endorse his conclusion: 'I believe that this study lends additional evidence for the view that John is certainly later than the Synoptics regardless of the date of composition for either'.[6] But I cannot agree that John's school 'felt the need among other things to strengthen and defend the Synoptic presentation of Jesus through the use of additional O.T. text'.[7] We cannot

---

1. F.-M. Braun, *Jean le Théologien. II. Les grandes traditions d'Israël* (Paris: Gabalda, 1964), p. 226.
2. E.D. Freed, *Old Testament Quotations in the Gospel of John* (NovTSup, 11; Leiden: Brill, 1965), p. 6.
3. Freed, *Old Testament Quotations*, p. 20.
4. Freed, *Old Testament Quotations*, p. 51.
5. Freed, *Old Testament Quotations*, p. 126. W. Rothfuchs (*Die Erfüllungszitate des Matthäus-Evangeliums: Eine biblische-theologische Untersuchung* [BWANT, 88; Stuttgart: Kohlhammer, 1969], p. 154) comes to the same conclusion.
6. Freed, *Old Testament Quotations*, p. 129.
7. Freed, *Old Testament Quotations*, p. 130.

be sure that John is aware of any of the Synoptic Gospels, though contemporary scholarship seems to be veering towards the view that he knew Mark. But he was not dependent on any of them and we never detect him attempting to correct them. If for 'the Synoptic presentation about Jesus' we substitute the words 'the earlier tradition about Jesus', we are nearer the truth, though John can hardly be said to have been anxious to defend this so much as to modify and heighten it.

E. Käsemann's judgment of John's attitude to Scripture is this: 'He did not despise the use of the Old Testament even though he can get along without it in large sections and he always puts it in the shadow of his traditions about Jesus'.[1] This is a misleading account: only in chs. 9 and 17 is there an absence of Scripture references, though in both chapters there are definite links with Scripture. John cannot possibly get on without the Old Testament; far from being overshadowed, it is constitutive for his Gospel. E. Cothenet has made the most illuminating suggestion that the role of the Paraclete is to show how the scriptural texts apply to Jesus; and he quotes R. Schnackenburg to the effect that the task of the Paraclete is to make the Christ of faith transparent in the earthly Jesus.[2] R.T. Fortna claims that John reproduces the Old Testament very inaccurately and inexactly, to which I would apply what I demonstrated above apropos of a similar remark by Freed. Later we encounter a truly astonishing statement about John's use of Scripture: 'there is no deliberate use of the Old Testament such as one finds either in the Gentile gospels of Mark and Luke or in Matthew's elaborately Jewish proof-texting'.[3] It is true of course that John does not use the Old Testament as does any one of the Synoptists, but to say that there is no deliberate use of the Old Testament is absurd. John deliberately chose Scripture as the basis of his Gospel.

Reim, in his learned work on John's use of the Old Testament to which I have already referred, has much to say that is of interest for our

---

1. E. Käsemann, *The Testament of Jesus* (Philadelphia: Fortress Press, 1968), p. 37.

2. E. Cothenet, 'Témoinage de l'Esprit et interprétation de l'écriture dans la corpus johannique', in *La vie de la parole: De l'Ancien au Nouveau Testament* (P. Grelot Festschrift; Paris: Desclée de Brouwer, 1987), pp. 367-77, here pp. 372, 396.

3. R.T. Fortna, *The Gospel of Signs: A Reconstruction of the Narrative Source Underlying the Fourth Gospel* (SNTSMS, 11; Cambridge: Cambridge University Press, 1970), pp. 12, 223.

purposes. He concludes, together with most of those who have studied John's use of Scripture, that John must have been able to use the Hebrew text.[1] He notes how often John makes allusions (*Ausspielungen*) to the Pentateuch.[2] Reim, however, makes certain statements about which parts of Scripture were available to John to which I must take exception. He claims that John did not have access to the book of Psalms but only to certain individual Psalms, such as Psalm 69; that he did not use the Song of Solomon. And he doubts whether John had Isaiah 40–55 before him, since his echoes never exactly agree with the text of the LXX.[3] If there is any value in my earlier examination of this Gospel,[4] these claims must be discounted. John was an avid student of Isaiah[5] (what reason have we to think that what we today call Second Isaiah would have been available separately to early Christians?). He did know the Song of Solomon, and echoed it on occasions. He ranged freely through the Psalms. Indeed, from reading the Gospel one gains the impression not of a peripatetic missionary like Paul, but of a learned scribe, at the centre of a school, with access to more than just the Scriptures. Reim concludes this part of his work by saying that he doubts whether John had any Old Testament text before him. All his references to Scripture came from his tradition.[6] When we consider how many allusions, echoes and implicit references to Scripture have been detected in the Gospel, this is a totally unacceptable conclusion. John had access to the full range of Scripture, and use his facility freely for his purpose.

The exchange in *New Testament Studies* between B. Lindars and P. Borgen provides some useful observations that pertain to our discussion as it has developed thus far.[7] Lindars is writing about the use of the Old Testament by early Christians generally and he remarks: 'The use of the

---

1.   Reim, *Studien zum alttestamentlichen Hintergrund*, p. 96.

2.   Reim, *Studien zum alttestamentlichen Hintergrund*, p. 109.

3.   Reim, *Studien zum alttestamentlichen Hintergrund*, pp. 161, 162, 183.

4.   Hanson, *The Prophetic Gospel*, pp. 21-233.

5.   Cf. F.W. Young, 'A Study of the Relation of Isaiah to the Fourth Gospel', *ZNW* 46 (1955), pp. 215-33; C.A. Evans, 'Obduracy and the Lord's Servant: Some Observations on the Use of the Old Testament in the Fourth Gospel', in *idem* and W.F. Stinespring (eds.), *Early Jewish and Christian Exegesis: Studies in Memory of William Hugh Brownlee* (Homage, 10; Atlanta: Scholars Press, 1987), pp. 221-36.

6.   Reim, *Studien zum alttestamentlichen Hintergrund*, p. 188.

7.   B. Lindars and P. Borgen, 'The Place of the Old Testament in the Formation of New Testament Theology', *NTS* 23 (1976), pp. 59-66.

Old Testament is primarily a mode of expression for Christian thought'. He sums the subject up thus:

> The place of the Old Testament in the formation of New Testament theology is that of a servant, ready to run to the aid of the gospel whenever it is required, bolstering up arguments, and filling out meaning through evocative allusions, but never acting as the masters or leading the way, nor even guiding the process of thought behind the scenes.[1]

This, as it seems to me, is to go too far. It gives the impression that the New Testament writers could make Scripture mean whatever they liked. But, in fact, Scripture in the Fourth Gospel at least acts as a control upon John. He allows it to influence his narrative; he relies on it to provide him with much of his Christology. It is not merely his servant. At times it seems to be his mentor. Borgen, rightly in my opinion, disagrees with Lindars's sentiments here. The Scriptures, he says, have authority for New Testament writers. The Scriptures 'created many of the theological issues which were taken up in the New Testament'.[2] He sums it up admiringly in a note: 'Since Moses wrote about Jesus, the Evangelist and the Johannine community regarded the Scriptures as valid *sources* to [sic] the words and works of Jesus, together with the Gospel-tradition received from the disciples. If so, then in John's Gospel traditions are interpreted and recast from exegetical insights into the Old Testament'.[3]

I conclude this essay with a few comments concerning some recently published works. D.J. Moo remarks that 'John evidences little interest in the Servant conception',[4] a view which is surely refuted by much that we have already discussed. D.M. Smith believes that the Scripture citations in John's passion narrative are more traditional and belong more to the main primitive tradition than do the citations in the rest of the Gospel.[5] There is much truth in this, but this does not preclude John from using his own Scripture material as well. See my expositions of 18.5-6; 19.5; 19.13; 19.17; 19.25-27; 19.30; 19.36-37.[6] J.A.T. Robinson

1. Lindars and Borgen, 'Place of the Old Testament', pp. 64, 66.
2. Lindars and Borgen, 'Place of the Old Testament', pp. 68, 70.
3. Lindars and Borgen, 'Place of the Old Testament', pp. 73 n.
4. D.J. Moo, *The Old Testament in the Gospel Passion Narratives* (Sheffield: Almond Press, 1983), p. 356.
5. D.M. Smith, *Johannine Christianity* (Columbia: University of South Carolina Press, 1984), pp. 89-90.
6. Hanson, *The Prophetic Gospel*, pp. 201-24.

in his posthumously published book thinks that John's use of Scripture 'has a very primitive ring'.[1] This is one of those judgments that it is very difficult to assess. The most primitive examples of Scripture citation we know of come from Paul. John, though he uses a good deal of scriptural material that is also used by Paul, treats it in quite a different manner. I cannot see that there is anything about it that could put it in the earliest post-Easter period; on the contrary, it gives the impression of being the fruit of a long period of meditation and study.

Last of all we must pay attention to an important article by D.A. Carson. He makes a very true statement when he writes that 'The [Fourth Gospel's] christology and eschatology can both be grounded in the Old Testament'.[2] He notes my distinction made in *The Living Utterances of God* between texts in Scripture which John received from tradition and those which he discovered for himself;[3] and very reasonably comments that it is difficult to prove which is which.[4] Nevertheless, I think we can make the effort. For example, those texts in the passion narrative which I listed immediately above seem to me to be John's own discoveries. They are set in the midst of texts which he received from tradition.[5] Carson well remarks that in the Gospel Jesus not only fulfills Old Testament themes but also replaces them. And Carson very finely adds that John 'does not treat the OT with scorn or rejection; he views it with reverence, treating it as the "giver" of revelation that anticipates the new revelation occurring in Jesus'.[6] That word 'anticipates' must be taken in its strictest sense. According to John, the great figures of the old dispensation knew a great deal about the new.

Now that we have thoroughly examined and assessed the significance of John's use of Scripture, we ought to be able to frame some sort of an answer to the question: what is the relation between Scripture and the

---

1. J.A.T. Robinson, *The Priority of John* (London: SCM Press, 1985), p. 311.

2. D.A. Carson, 'John and the Johannine Epistles', in *idem* and H.G.M. Williamson (eds.), *It is Written: Scripture Citing Scripture* (B. Lindars Festschrift; Cambridge: Cambridge University Press, 1988), pp. 245-64, here pp. 246-47.

3. A.T. Hanson, *The Living Utterances of God* (London: Darton, Longman & Todd, 1983), pp. 113-15.

4. Carson, 'John and the Johannine Epistles', p. 248.

5. For a different assessment of the function of John's quotation formulas, see C.A. Evans, 'On the Quotation Formulas in the Fourth Gospel', *BZ* 26 (1982), pp. 79-83.

6. Carson, 'John and the Johannine Epistles', p. 256.

Fourth Gospel? What sort of a Gospel is it? It could perhaps be said of the Synoptic Gospels that they are quasi-historical accounts of the life of Jesus, helped out by fairly frequent recourse to prophecy in the Old Testament. But this will hardly serve as a description of the Fourth Gospel. For the author of the Fourth Gospel Scripture is not just a prop, an addition. It is constitutive for this work. Indeed we may guess that one of the main reasons that he wrote his Gospel was that he wanted to show to what extent the career and person of Jesus Christ was the fulfillment of Scripture. Could we not then, borrowing a phrase which I have already used, call John's work 'the prophetic Gospel'? Far more than any of the other three, this Gospel is concerned with Scripture and the fulfillment of Scripture. The author of the Fourth Gospel must have been regarded by his own circle as a prophet in the sense that he excelled at understanding to what extent the prophecies of Scripture have been fulfilled in Jesus. Perhaps this is something of what Clement of Alexandria meant when he called it 'the spiritual Gospel'. It was the Holy Spirit, everyone agreed, who had inspired the Scriptures. John's Gospel was composed partly at least to show how the Holy Spirit had intended that the Saviour should live and teach, and how Jesus Christ had fulfilled this divinely inspired programme.

THE OLD TESTAMENT IN THE FOURTH GOSPEL[*]

Martin Hengel

The Prophetic 'Scriptures' and the Earliest Church

The three most important apologists of the second century, Justin (*Dial. Tryph.* 3.1), Tatian (*Orat. ad Graec.* 29.2) and Theophilus of Antioch (*Ad Autolycum* 1.14-15), report that they were led to the Christian faith through study of the 'prophetic Scriptures'. By 'prophetic Scriptures' they mean the Old Testament Scriptures, the Law, the Prophets and the Hagiographies, which were all understood as inspired works of the ancient prophets of Israel. All three were philosophically educated pagans before they became Christians. The reading of the Septuagint brought about the turning point in their lives that united them as Christians to the God of (the history of) Israel. Justin testifies to the Jew, Trypho (as well as against Marcion): 'We believe that our God is none other than your God, and moreover, that it is he who led your fathers out of Egypt' (*Dial. Tryph.* 11.1). His pupil, Tatian, confesses that he was 'led to faith by the straightforward clarity of the language...the foreknowledge of future events, the excellent quality of the precepts and the concept of the government of the universe by one Lord' (*Orat. ad Graec.* 29.1). A Hellenistic Jew might have said the same things.

Another apologist, Melito of Sardis, making the first Christian pilgrimage to the Holy Land we know, gathered information concerning the titles and names of the books of the Old Covenant, that is, the Jewish canon. He is the first to use the formula 'Old Testament' for the Scriptures, and produced 'excerpts' (ἐκλογαί) from these books (Eusebius, *Hist. Eccl.* 4.26.14). We see from this how 'Jewish' early Christianity still remained, well into the second century, even after the

---

[*]   Lecture given at the meeting of the European Association of Jewish Studies in July 1987 in Berlin and as Kenneth Clark lecture in October 1987 in Duke University, Durham, NC. A much more extensive version appeared in German, 'Die Schriftauslegung des 4. Evangeliums auf dem Hintergrund der urchristlichen Exegese', *JBT* 4 (1989), pp. 249-88.

church had long become 'Gentile Christian'. This was kept alive through the continual recourse to the inspired 'Holy Scriptures'. The attempts of gnostic teachers to undermine the authority of the Old Testament and its picture of God were bitterly resisted. The Septuagint remained, indeed became, the Holy Scripture of the church. The (quoting Harnack) 'acute secularization—or, as the case may be, the Hellenization of Christianity [presented] in the gnostic thought'[1] did not succeed. There arose rather, under the influence of Old Testament models, a kind of assimilation of the early Catholic church to the synagogue communities, in the forms of worship service, church structure and general ethos. Among earlier liberal Protestants above all, this was seen—without doubt unjustly—as a defeat. The Old Testament, as the book of the holy history of Israel, became the church's teacher on the road through its own new history. For the one Lord spoke in it just as he spoke ultimately in the Jesus traditions.

This brings us back to the beginnings: the life and death of Jesus of Nazareth and its eschatological-messianic significance, accompanied from the beginning by interpretive allusions to the Scriptures that go back to Jesus himself. Already for him the time for the fulfilment of the prophetic promise had dawned. Thus, for example, Lk. 16.16: 'The law and the prophets were until John; since then the good news of the kingdom of God is preached, and every one enters it violently'. The messianic present is superior to the time of preparation announced by the prophets, and becomes the interpretive rule for the ancient texts: 'Blessed are the eyes that see what you see, for many of the prophets and kings wished to see what you see, and saw it not' (Lk. 10.23). Or more radical still, the antitheses of the Sermon on the Mount: 'You have heard that it was said to the ancients...but I say to you...'. The fulfilment could now and again lead to criticism. This is, as far as I can see, something new in the ancient Jewish sources, although we must suppose that during the unsettled time between the Maccabean rebellion and the three great Jewish wars, an eschatological exegesis of Scripture was more frequent than our (accidentally preserved) sources reveal. We see clear preliminaries to this in the interpretation in Daniel 9 of the seventy-year exile of Jeremiah 25 as 'seventy weeks of years' until the eschatological tribulations of the present, or the Essene interpretation in the Pesharim, 'at the end of days', which goes back to the Teacher of Righteousness, 'whom God enabled in the midst of the community to

---

1.   A. von Harnack, *Dogmengeschichte* (Tübingen: Mohr [Paul Siebeck], 4th edn, 1888), I, pp. 249-50.

interpret all the words of his servants the prophets' (1QpHab 2.8-9). By contrast, the dawn of the time of salvation was for Jesus already a present event, and the early Christians looked back on the coming of the messiah as the surety of salvation. At best one might refer to R. Akiba's identification of the 'Star of Jacob' in Num. 24.17 with Bar Koziba, but this is a disputed special case. This messianic-enthusiastic understanding of the present is typical of early Christianity and is decisive for its exegesis, as shown, for example, by Paul's citation from Isaiah 49: 'At the acceptable time I have listened to you, and helped you on the day of salvation' (2 Cor. 6.2). This 'day of salvation' has now come!

The rigorous reference of the eschatological fulfilment to the present brought about a reorientation. The view in traditional Jewish exegesis that the Torah, given to Moses on Sinai by God, stood at the centre, with the prophets as its expositors, was reversed: the entire Scriptures came to be regarded as prophecy looking forward to fulfilment. Moses became the first of the prophets. The story of God's judgments during the forty years of wilderness wanderings was written, according to Paul, for the admonishment of God's people in the 'last times': 'Now these things happened to them as a warning (τυπικῶς), but they were written down for our instruction, upon whom the end of the ages has come' (1 Cor. 10.11). This resulted in a reorientation of the use of Scripture. If we tally the verbatim citations with introductory formulas, according to the 25th edition of the Nestle–Aland text, we get the following results: Psalms 55; Isaiah 51; Deuteronomy 45 (of which 14 are from the Decalogue and love commandment); Exodus 23 (of which 10 are from the Decalogue); Minor Prophets 21; Genesis 16; Leviticus 14 (of which 7 are from the love commandment); Jeremiah 9; Proverbs 4; Ezekiel, Numbers and 2 Samuel 2 each. That is, approximately 60 per cent of all unambiguous Old Testament citations are taken from three books: Psalms, Isaiah and Deuteronomy. The Psalter, that is, the inspired collection of David's songs, became the most important book of prophecy for early Christianity.

This eschatological interpretation of Scripture received central importance for the dialogue with contemporaries. It was necessary to prove that the greatest offence, the scandal of the crucifixion of the messiah Jesus, was a fulfilment of the 'prophetic' Scriptures.

The motivating power of this messianic interpretation lay in the new experience of the prophetic Spirit. That means that a new 'enthusiastic'— one might even say 'tantalizingly undomesticated'—exegesis was set over against the tradition-bound interpretation of the established religious groups. Over against the widespread view that the prophetic Spirit had vanished from Israel since the time of Ezra, the Jewish Christians, appealing to Joel 3, claimed that with the elevation of the Crucified One to the right hand of God, the Spirit, promised for the end time, had been poured out on his church, and that, therefore, they alone were in a position to interpret correctly the Spirit-given prophecies: πνευματικὰ πνευματικοῖς συγκρίνοντες, 'interpreting spiritual truths with spiritual gifts', as Paul says in 1 Cor. 2.13.

This goes back to the beginnings of the first community in Jerusalem, as shown by the ancient confession formula that originated there: 'that the Messiah died for our sins *according to the Scriptures* ...and that he was raised on the third day *according to the Scriptures*' (1 Cor. 15.3-4, my emphasis). Of the texts intended by κατὰ τὰς γραφάς, Isaiah 53 certainly had a special significance, along with the suffering Psalms, 22, 69, 118, Zech. 12.10-12, among others. Citation of the texts was often freely made, for example, through the combination of different verses. According to the most recent investigation, Paul, who had been educated as a scribe, altered 52 out of 95 citations. Here we must suppose that he quoted from memory during dictation, and occasionally let his knowledge of the Hebrew text show through. But Paul's scribal education was rather the exception. The Jesus movement was chiefly a movement of simple people, Galilean fishermen, craftspeople and farmers. Scholarship was initially alien to them.

It was probably the new, provocative, messianic-charismatic interpretation, pointing toward present fulfilment, that impressed the hearers among the people. Mark calls Jesus' first synagogue sermon 'a new teaching—with authority'. Matthew puts this with sharper polemic at the end of the Sermon on the Mount: 'for he taught them as one who had authority, and not as their scribes' (Mt. 7.28). What was here said of Jesus in later times is valid also for the earlier Christian preaching and its prophetic interpretation of Scripture.

This method concentrated primarily on selected portions of text. At first there was no systematic, progressive, verse-by-verse exegesis of larger contexts or entire books. That would have required a fixed typological-allegorical method—a result of later gradual development. Predominant was a charismatic eclecticism which concentrated on particular themes and texts. We find the first thoroughgoing commentaries on Old Testament books at the beginning of the third century from Hippolytus (typically, on the Song of Songs and Daniel), and then—suddenly in grand style—from Origen, the first 'scientific' exegete of the ancient church.

John, the Evangelist

At the turn of the first century we see a significant change. The 'freelance' teachers with their charismatic interpretation of Scripture recede into the background. They are replaced by church office-holders, probably first originating in Jerusalem, who bear responsibility for 'correct' scriptural exegesis. The background of this radical change is easily traced. In the later decades after 70, as Gentile Christians made their presence in the church felt, radical enthusiastic-gnosticizing groups questioned both the authority of Scripture and the earthly existence of Jesus. They appealed to secret teachings of the Risen One or the free activity of the Spirit working among them.

The Johannine corpus came into being about this time, around AD 100, in Asia Minor: the three letters enter directly into this conflict, but without quoting the Old Testament itself directly; the Apocalypse, full of Old Testament paraphrases, and the first Christian writing claiming the same inspiration as the prophetic books, insists on being read (1.3)—like the Old Testament—in the church service as the last of all prophetic books (22.7, 10, 18-19).

The Fourth Gospel, the most mysterious writing of the New Testament, is of a completely different character. It was published posthumously by the author's pupils. This John was the head of an influential school in Ephesus. He knows the Synoptic Gospels, but views them critically as insufficient, and sees himself as widely distanced from them. His historical environment is still disputed. Because of its dualisms between light and darkness, God and the world, and the numerous 'revelation speeches', in which the Son sent from the Father proclaims himself, the Gospel was long viewed as a half-Gnostic work. The Qumran finds, however, have destroyed the credibility of these Gnostic theories. The supposition that behind the Johannine corpus stood a half-heretical conventicle on the periphery of the church is also misleading. The author, as head of a school, is a free, self-assured teacher (in that respect like the author of the First Gospel), who was in earlier times at home in the Jewish-Christian milieu of Palestine, or more precisely, in the Jerusalem aristocracy. Unlike Matthew, he knows as yet no definite ecclesiology or church office, but rather the free fellowship of disciples led by the Spirit-Paraclete, and is thereby still rooted in the early period of the church. On the other hand, the preparation of the trinitarian dogma, gradually crystallizing only after the middle of the second century, forms his high Christology with the deeply profound unity of the Father, Son and Spirit-Paraclete.

Israel and the Scriptures

It is strange that the question of John's interpretation of Scripture has been left rather in the shadows of research interests. One finds hardly excursuses on this question in the commentaries, and in many there is the tendency to play down the use of the Old Testament because of the Gnosis hypothesis: the citations are ascribed in part either to a source, or a church redactor who wanted to make the Gospel acceptable to the church at large by 'doctoring it up'. Standing over against this is the singular unity of the Johannine vocabulary and style. Inseparably bound up with the question of use of Scripture is the view of Israelite-Jewish 'salvation history'.

We begin here with a disputed text. In 4.22 Jesus says to the Samaritan woman at Jacob's well, 'You worship what you do not know; we worship what we know, *for salvation is from the Jews*' (my emphasis). In the recent German Protestant commentaries this is readily dismissed as a gloss from a church redactor since—so R. Bultmann[1]—the Evangelist 'doesn't view the Jews as the people of God's possession and salvation'. Indeed the Jews, that is, the spokesmen and leaders of the people with whom Jesus disputes, appear as representatives of the κόσμος—but both expressions, 'Jews' and κόσμος, are included in the typically Johannine dialectic, which cannot simply be set aside. The world, the 'cosmos', is at the same time God's creation that he loves and the Jews, or Israel, are the people of his possession. Jesus' Jewishness is especially emphasized by John, because the messiah (only John uses the Aramaic word in the New Testament—twice) comes from Israel. Further, in Jn 10.34-36 at the climax of the conflict where Jesus is accused of making himself to be God, it is clearly stated that God's Word long ago came to Israel:

---

1. R. Bultmann, *Das Evangelium des Johannes* (Göttingen: Vandenhoeck & Ruprecht, 11th edn, 1950), p. 139 n. 6.

> [Jesus answered them;] Is it not written in your law, 'I said, you are gods'? If he called them gods to whom the Word of God came (and Scripture cannot be broken), do you say of him whom the Father consecrated and sent into the world, 'You are blaspheming', because I said, 'I am the Son of God'?

This passage is fundamentally important for the Johannine understanding of Israel and the Scriptures. First of all, he designated (as do Paul and the rabbis occasionally) a Psalm passage (82.6) as 'your law' in the sense of *pars pro toto*: the entire Scripture is Torah and was given to Israel first. The rabbis use the same passage to prove Israel's special worth. Further, it is clearly said that God's word, which is contained in Scripture, came to Israel, and that 'Scripture cannot be broken'. Through the address of the λόγος τοῦ θεοῦ Israel receives its unique importance. The argumentation amounts to a conclusion *a minore ad maius*: if God calls even Israel 'gods', how can the one chosen and sent by God be accused of blasphemy when he says, 'I am the Son of God'?

This text is illuminated by the Prologue which, in extremely concentrated form, relates the entire salvation history from the very beginning, ἐν ἀρχῇ, *bᵉreʾšît* to the epiphany of the Logos ἔνσαρκος in the present. In Jn 1.11 the revelation of the Logos, the Word of God that brings judgment and salvation to Israel, is paraphrased: 'He came to his own, and his own received him not'. However, this is not valid for all: 'But to all who received him, who believed in his name, he gave power to become children of God'. There were already some in ancient Israel who believed in God's word and thereby became 'children of God'.

John names four men as paradigms for the reception and witness of the λόγος τοῦ θεοῦ in Israel, who at the same time bear witness to the Son of God become human: Abraham, Isaiah, Moses and John the Baptist. The appeal to Abraham is preceded by an extremely sharp polemic, the interpretation of which, together with statements by Paul and Matthew, was to have in later centuries catastrophic consequences. The authors, who wrote then during a period of powerlessness and persecution, cannot be held responsible for the later Christian abuse of their statements.

The Johannine Jesus recognizes that his opponents are 'descendants' (σπέρμα) of Abraham, but that they are not really 'children' (τέκνα) of Abraham because they do not do his works (8.37-41). 'Sonship' (*Kindschaft*), according to him, is not determined by physical descendancy but by the actual conduct of one's life. But they seek to kill him and therefore reveal by their deeds their true origin: 'you are of your father, the devil, and your will is to do your father's desires. He was a murderer from the beginning' (8.44). Behind this is the ancient story from Genesis 3 and 4: the devil brings death to humankind and Cain, the first murderer (cf. 1 Jn 3.12), is his son. The closest Jewish parallel to this type of language is the reference to the 'Sons of darkness' and of Belial from Qumran, which includes both the Gentiles and rebellious Israel. The reaction of the opponents is no less cutting: Jesus is a demon-possessed Samaritan (8.48). Here, as there, the polemical language of dualism is employed.

Against his adversaries, Jesus claims Abraham himself as witness to his being sent by the Father: 'Your father Abraham rejoiced that he was to see my day; he saw it and was glad' (8.56). This seeing the 'day' of Jesus presupposes a knowledge of the Jewish tradition of Abraham's future vision, according to Gen. 15.2-20, as it appears in the *Apocalypse of Abraham* and the rabbinic texts: the day of Christ becomes thereby identical with the Day of Yahweh, God's eschatological epiphany, and Abraham is a believing witness to the revelation of salvation in the Son.

Isaiah also has a Christ-vision, and through it becomes a witness to Christ. John sets two Isaiah citations at the end of Jesus' public ministry (12.38-41). First, there is the question in the Servant Song, 'Lord who has believed our report?' (Isa. 53.1). Next, there is the saying about Israel's impenitence (mentioned six times in the New Testament) in the visionary call of the prophet: Jesus and his messengers fare no better than the greatest of Israel's writing prophets. The unbelief of God's people is grounded in God's mystery. But we are given an illuminating clue: 'Isaiah said this because he saw his [that is, Christ's] glory and spoke of him'. It was not the Father whom Isaiah saw in his visionary call (Isa. 6), for no one can see God, but the pre-existent Son in his heavenly glory. Isaiah speaks of the Son not only here, but throughout his entire book of prophecy.

Concerning Moses, we notice first of all that his name is mentioned more frequently than by the Synoptics or Paul, eleven times in all. Of course, one must differentiate: the opponents, in contrast to the 'seducer' of the people (7.12), Jesus, make their appeal to Moses. They describe themselves as disciples of Moses, to whom God himself had spoken (9.28-29). Over against this, the Evangelist emphasizes that full salvation will only be given through the incarnate Logos. 'Thus already in the Prologue, 'the Law was given (ἐδόθη) through Moses; grace and truth (*ḥesed we-ʾemet*) came through Jesus Christ' (1.17).

This 'superiority' motif surfaces again in the 'true bread' saying in connection with the feeding of the five thousand (ch. 6). Despite the feeding miracle, the listeners demand a sign—as in the exodus: 'Then what sign do you do, that we may see, and believe you?... Our fathers ate the manna in the wilderness; as it is written, "He gave them bread from heaven to eat"'. To this Jesus answers, 'it was not Moses who *gave* you the bread from heaven; my Father *gives* you the true bread from heaven' (6.30-32). Here John follows, as P. Borgen has shown,[1] a schema that we find in midrash, but also in Philo, in the formula *'al tiqra... 'ālla*. Moses is not the giver (rather, God alone, in unified activity with the Son), nor can the preterite tense ἔδωκεν = *nātan* for God's activity be read. The verb corresponds instead to the present participle *nōtēn* = διδούς (v. 33; cf. διδωσιν, v. 32): he gives (is giving) the true bread from heaven, in the Son. Though the fathers ate the manna in the wilderness and still died there, the Son gives, as the 'bread of life', victory over death and eternal life (6.48-51).

Moses appears in a more positive light as co-author of Scripture. Thus, in the testimony of Philip to Nathanael, 'We have found him of whom Moses in the law and also the prophets wrote, Jesus of Nazareth, the Son of Joseph' (1.45). In the conversation with Nicodemus, Jesus refers Moses' saving activity to his own fate: 'And as Moses lifted up the serpent in the wilderness, so must the Son of Man be lifted up, that whoever believes in him may have eternal life'. The bronze serpent fastened to a high pole (*nes* = σημεῖον, Num. 21.8) is a type of the Crucified One (3.14-15).

The law of Moses and the Prophets thus become witnesses for the truth of the sending of the Son, and even for his fearful death. Therefore the lawgiver himself, to whom the leaders of the people appeal, becomes the prosecutor:

> Do not think that I shall accuse you to the Father; it is Moses who accuses you, on whom you set your hope. If you believed Moses, you would believe me, for he wrote of me. But if you do not believe his writings [again, *a minore ad maius*], how will you believe my words? (5.45-47).

What I have said about Moses is valid also for the concepts νόμος and γραφή. Both appear in John more often than in the other Gospels. Like the person of Moses, the law is also an object of controversy. It is used

---

1.   P. Borgen, *Bread from Heaven* (NovTSup, 10; Leiden: Brill, 1965), pp. 61-69.

to accuse Jesus, but also for his defence and to make counter-accusation. 'Did not Moses give you the law? Yet none of you keeps the law' (7.19). The distance of the Johannine community from the law is clearly seen when the Jews speak of 'our law' (7.51; cf. 12.34; 19.7), while Jesus refers to it as 'your law' (18.17; 10.34 cf. 15.25). Although the Fourth Gospel originated from a Jewish-Christian author, it appeals to the Gentile Christian communities even more strongly than the Syrian Gospel of Matthew. The 'law' question, so acute in Paul, is in John no longer important. As 'law', that is, as lifestyle determined by numerous commandments, it is the property of the Jews. Jesus himself concentrates his one binding directive to the disciples on the one 'new commandment' of love (13.34). Nonetheless, the law is a part of Scripture. Indeed, it is practically identical with the expression γραφή, which is decisive for John: he uses it twelve times—the same as Paul, and three times more than Matthew. That he uses the singular—in contrast to Paul, except for one instance—shows how important for him the christologically founded *unity* of the Scriptures is. In the one instance where he uses the plural, γραφαί, he is referring to the Jews concerning the range and diversity of Scripture: 'You search the Scriptures, because you think that in them you have eternal life; and it is they that bear witness to me' (5.39). This is found at the end of a larger section (5.31-40) dealing with the testimony on behalf of Jesus: he does not bear witness to himself since such a testimony would be invalid—others do this for him. One could call on the Baptist, but Jesus is not dependent on human testimony. He has a better witness, namely the works that the Father has given him to do, that is, his signs. At the same time, however, the Father himself bears witness to him through his Word. Indeed, his Word does not 'abide' in Jesus' opponents because they do not believe in the One whom God has sent. This word is identical with the 'Scriptures' in which they seek eternal life, the very goal that eludes them because they will not hear its testimony. The reference to the *graphai* stands as the climax at the end of the life of argumentation: God himself bears witness through the Scriptures (γραφαί) to the One he has sent. In their entirety they are prophecy for the sending of the Son.

Remembering and Understanding through the Spirit

As God's personal testimony to the Son, the γραφή has supertemporal significance: it has already spoken to God's people, and has been heard by some. It illumines, indeed determines, the way of Jesus even to the cross, and clarifies this way to the disciples *only after* Easter. At the end of the Cleansing of the Temple, placed by John at the beginning of Jesus' ministry (ch. 2), we read: 'His disciples remembered that it was written, "Zeal for thy house will consume me"' (2.17). The perfect of the Hebrew text is here changed into a future (καταφάγεταί με). The reference to Jesus' death in this citation from Psalm 69 becomes thereby just as unambiguous as the previous testimony of the Baptist to the 'Lamb of God who takes away the sin of the world', behind which stand Isaiah 53 and Exodus 12. After the demand by the Jewish authorities that he prove with a sign his right to the forcible cleansing of the Temple, there follows the enigmatic statement about tearing down the Holy Place which he will rebuild again in three days. The Evangelist interprets this as 'the temple of his body', the death and resurrection of Jesus: 'When therefore, he was raised from the dead, his disciples remembered that he had said this; *and they believed the Scripture and the word which Jesus had spoken*' (2.22, my emphasis). Jesus' statement about himself and the Word of Scripture, clearly Ps. 69.10, stand side by side complementing one another. Not until after Easter do the disciples understand the messianic testimony of the Scriptures and believe in him—the same goes for Jesus' own word.

This motif of post-Easter remembering, which according to the farewell speech is a work of the Spirit-Paraclete who 'reminds' the disciples of Jesus' words (and that means his interpretation of Scripture, as well), meets us again at the end of Jesus' final entry into Jerusalem. Here, with recourse to the Hebrew text, John cites Zech. 9.9 in shortened form: 'Fear not, daughter of Zion; behold, your king is coming, sitting on an ass's colt' (12.15). At first the disciples do not understand the event: 'but after Jesus was glorified, then they remembered that this had been written of him and that they had done this to him' (that is, as in the Synoptics, that they had set Jesus on the donkey). John simply presupposes the Synoptics here. It is the Spirit-Paraclete who awakens in the disciples the memory of the prophetic Word (itself produced by the Spirit), and, with that, the meaning of their former actions. 'To remember' means here real, deep, 'creative' understanding through the Spirit, who 'teaches all things' and 'brings to remembrance' Jesus' Word (14.26), which, like the γραφή, 'bears witness' to Jesus (15.26) and thereby 'guides into all truth' (16.13).

In his portrayal of the imparting of the Spirit, which (unlike Luke's great Pentecost depiction) becomes the climax of the Risen One's first appearance to the disciples, John makes conscious use of the second creation account in Genesis 2. After Jesus commissions the disciples, 'As the Father has sent me, even so I send you...he breathed on them, and said to them, "Receive the Holy Spirit"'. The New Testament *hapax legomenon, ἐνεφύσησεν*, appears in Gen. 2.7 as the translation of the *wayippaḥ* at the animation of Adam: God 'breathed into his nostrils the breath of life (ἐναφύσησεν εἰς τὸ πρόσωπον αὐτοῦ πνοὴν ζωῆς); and man became a living being'. Only the Spirit renews and illuminates the uncomprehending, fearful hearts of the disciples, making them into new creatures born from above (3.3, 5), so that they can truly understand the words and work of Jesus, as well as the Word of Scripture. For the very reason that, during the earthly life of Jesus, the disciples' understanding was mistaken, the later, Spirit-informed Christology—which, as John well knows, comes from the messianic testimony of Scripture and not from traditional Jesus-logia—can be unreservedly attributed to Jesus as self-testimony, even supplanting the older Jesus-tradition.

On this point the Fourth Gospel is radically different from its true opposite, the First Gospel. There Jesus is the messiah of Israel from the house of David, who, as the ultimate expounder of the Torah, is a superior antitype to Moses, and also, as in Deuteronomy, combines a broad, ethical paraenesis with an impressive warning of judgment. The multi-faceted citation of the Old Testament is put completely at the service of this portrayal of Jesus. The Spirit motif recedes into the background: ethical obedience, not pneumatic enthusiasm, counts. At the commissioning of the disciples at the end of the Gospel, along with making disciples of and baptizing the nations, they are instructed to enjoin the commandments of Jesus in their teaching: 'teach them to observe all that I have commanded you (ἐνετειλάμην, from ἐντέλλομαι = *ṣiwwa*)' (Mt. 28.20). There is nothing said here about the Spirit. Christ is rather present in his teaching (28.20b; 18.20). Despite the origin of both Gospels from Jewish-Christian Palestinian authors, their knowledge of Aramaic (which is especially important to John), their Hebraizing style, their knowledge of Jewish halakah and haggadah, the two are very different. These considerable divergences, which go back to the very beginnings of the church, are themselves an indirect indication of the astonishing spiritual variety in the Judaism of the first century—a variety carried over into earliest Christianity.

The Citation of Scripture and its Introductory Formulas

John uses the names of Abraham and Moses, and the expressions νόμος and γραφή, more often than Matthew, who refers more to the Prophets, Isaiah and David. Israel's salvation history, which is formed from Scripture, is used by both to good effect, even if in very different ways. Most apparent is the difference in the number of *unambiguous* Scripture quotations. The Nestle–Aland 26th edition counts 19 such citations in John, of those, 17 with introductory formulas, and a further c. 200 marginally noted allusions and parallels. Matthew, on the other hand, the Jewish-Christian scribe, has 87 citations and c. 400 parallels. In accordance with his esoteric, indirectly suggestive style, the emphasis in John (in contrast to Matthew) is on 'allusions'. He prefers the bare, terse clue or allusion, the use of metaphor or motif, to the full citation. Nonetheless it is profitable to examine briefly a few citations. Their distribution corresponds to the demonstrated preference in early Christianity: eight from the Psalms, six from Isaiah, three from the Pentateuch, and two from the Minor Prophets.

The citation introductions are themselves striking. John makes here a fundamental distinction between the formulas in the first part of the Gospel, chs. 1–12, Jesus' public ministry in Israel, and the second part, after 12.38 with the farewell speeches and the Passion. In the first part, in Jesus' speeches and disputes, the participle γεγραμμένον ἐστίν, or something similar, appears five times (2.17; 6.31, 45; 10.34; 12.14). 'That which is written' is the authoritative 'higher court'.

The new formula of the second part appears first at the end of Jesus' public ministry, in connection with the explanation for his lack of success (12.37-41). 'Though he had done so many signs before them, yet they did not believe in him; *it was that the word spoken by the prophet Isaiah might be fulfilled* (ἵνα ὁ λόγος Ἡσαΐου τοῦ προφήτου πληρωθῇ)'. The citation from Isa. 53.1 follows as the predestined consequence: 'Therefore they could not believe, for Isaiah again said...' —and then comes the citation from Isa. 6.9-10 concerning the obstinacy of Israel. With this double 'fulfilment' citation, which clarifies the problematic failure of Jesus among his people as the fulfilment of the prophetic Word and therefore the will of God, the Evangelist prepares the way for the Passion. Until now Jesus—and, in a few cases, his opponents—had appealed to the authority of 'that which is written'. In view of the severe problem presented by the messiah's failure and

Passion, from here forward we read exclusively of 'fulfilment'. However, there is more involved here than John's apologetic motives for overcoming a great problem. He indicates already in the Baptist's testimony to the Lamb of God (1.29) *Jesus' death* as the true salvation event, in which the 'humanization' of the Son of God is consummated. This consummation is foreshadowed in Scripture.

The reference to Scripture in the depiction of Jesus' death is striking in its wording and suggestive as the climax of the entire Gospel:

> After this Jesus, knowing that all was now finished (τετέλεσται, from τελέω), said to fulfil Scripture (ἵνα τελειωθῇ ἡ γραφή), 'I thirst'. A bowl full of vinegar stood there; so they put a sponge full of vinegar on hyssop and held it to his mouth. When Jesus had received the vinegar, he said, 'It is finished' (τετέλεσται); and he bowed his head and gave up his spirit (19.28-30).

Only here in the entire Gospel does the Evangelist speak of a τελειοῦν of the Scriptures, an increase over the previous formulaic πληροῦν, which expresses the 'ultimate fulfilment' of all christological prophecy in the Scriptures, which in turn reach their goal in the death of Jesus. The Evangelist consciously placed this ἵνα τελειωθῇ ἡ γραφή between the twice-occurring τετέλεσται, Jesus' knowledge that the end had come in v. 28, and his death cry in v. 30. With Jesus' death the 'work of saving the world', which the Father had entrusted to him by sending him into the world, is 'finished'. His 'exaltation' (ὑψωθῆναι) and 'glorification' (δοξασθῆναι), foretold about him in Isa. 53.12, occur paradoxically in the deepest humiliation. It is presupposed here that the reader knows the Scripture from Ps. 69.22, 'and for my thirst they gave me vinegar to drink'. The thirst of the Crucified One is at the same time an expression of his creatureliness and his antidocetic character; the same goes for the sinking of his head in death. Indeed, in the report of Jesus' death, the antidocetic significance of Jn 1.14, 'and the Word became flesh' (paradoxically offensive for the educated person of antiquity), is expressed once again. In the severe expression σάρξ, *baśar*, the death of Jesus is already contained *in nuce*—just as Brahms's *Requiem* expresses Isa. 40.3: 'for all flesh is as grass...'

But I would go a step further: the Gospel begins with ἐν ἀρχῇ, the very beginning, before the six days of creation. Jesus dies in the evening of the sixth day of the week and thereby finishes God's work—I refer once more to the twice-occurring τετέλεσται, and Franz Rosenzweig's 'Death as the Consummation of Creation' (*Der Tod als Vollendung der*

Schöpfung). At the beginning of Jesus' prayer for the disciples (ch. 17) we read: 'I have finished the work (ἔργον) that you gave me to do (ποιεῖν)'. There is a clear allusion in all this to Gen. 2.2 (LXX): 'And on the sixth day God finished his works (ἔργα) which he had done (ἐποίησεν)'. God's work of creation and salvation, which begins with ἐν ἀρχῇ in Gen. 1.1 and Jn 1.1, is 'finished' in the death of the Son on Golgotha at evening of the sixth day. There follows, according to Jn 19.31, the enigmatic 'great Sabbath' (*šabbat säl päsaḥ*)—for the dead Jesus, it is a 'day of rest' in the grave. One might refer here to a widespread Jewish haggadah, according to which the first human couple was created on the sixth day, and at the tenth hour—about the time of Jesus' death—sinned. This means that the Son 'finishes' the work of God's creation, which had been upset, indeed destroyed, by human sin.

At the beginning of the 'fulfilment citations' we have a double citation in John 12—so also at the end. Indeed they are the last words of Scripture in the Gospel furnished with an introduction. Preceding this are the breaking of the legs (*crurifragium*) of the two men crucified with Jesus, the spear thrust in Jesus' side, and the testimony of the eye-witness, who is presented as the beloved disciple and author himself: 'and he knows that he tells the truth—that you also may believe. For these things took place that the Scripture might be fulfilled, "Not a bone of him shall be broken"' (cf. vv. 32-37). This scriptural word is probably a mixed citation from several texts that signifies Jesus as the 'true Passover Lamb'. This characteristic justifies John (alone of the Gospel writers) in putting the death of Jesus on the evening of the fourteenth of Nisan. At the same time a connection with the Baptist's testimony in 1.29 and 36 is made: the Baptist is Jesus' witness at the beginning, the unknown disciple and author (as he tells us), his witness at the end.

As with the double citation in 12.38-40, the second part is introduced by πάλιν: 'and again another Scripture says, "They shall look upon him whom they have pierced"'. This citation from Zech. 12.10 follows the Hebrew text; it appears again in Rev. 1.7. There, and in Justin as well, the ὄψονται refers to the parousia. This future characteristic is probably already there in John: the Zechariah citation, therefore, not only means the concrete fulfilment of a christological prophecy, but contains at the same time a future pronouncement of judgment (cf. 8.28; 4.36).

Concluding Remarks

I will now summarize. From what has been said, it is clear that Johannine scriptural proof within the framework of the Gospel's dominating Christology has a greater significance than has generally been recognized. But with that we have gained only a few small insights. Time will not allow us to examine the wide field of allusions with its diverse references to Jewish haggadah. There would, no doubt, be a great deal here to discover. In John the reference to Scripture carries its own weight throughout. The ordering of the citations is not a chance result of using different sources, but is part of a well-considered, unified plan. This is seen especially in the connection of Scripture citation and Jesus' words, with the Spirit-informed 'remembering' of the disciples, and further, the fulfilment citations after the beginning of the Passion, with the unique τελειωθῇ at the climax of the Gospel in 19.28-30. Many of these citations have their origins in disputations with Jewish opponents; others have their *Sitz im Leben* in the discussion within the school. Far fewer of the Scriptural references are found in the Synoptic tradition as well, and even these have been reworked by the Evangelist.

The majority of references demonstrate the originality of John's christological interpretation of Scripture, an impression strengthened by the allusions. The ability to examine and correct Septuagintal formulations based on his knowledge of the Hebrew text presupposes certain scribal knowledge. Two points are significant here: the apologetic-polemical exchange with Judaism, which, because of deeply-rooted dependence, expressed a very painful process of detachment, and the strong reference to Jesus' Passion as the consummation of divine salvation history. This runs through the story like a thread, from the first chapter on, and makes it impossible to characterize the Fourth Gospel as 'gnosticizing' and 'naively docetic'.

To the Judaist who comes fresh from artful rabbinic exegesis, the Johannine way with Scripture may appear strange, while the one familiar with Philo, Qumran or Jewish mysticism will feel more at home with it. One thing remains certain: phenomenologically, despite its conflict with the Judaism of its time (that is, the tragic but unavoidable detachment process, which forces us as Christians today to self-critical reflection)— the Fourth Gospel is to be understood primarily from the Jewish sources of its period and it is at the same time the climax of the new, extremely bold, christological thought at the very end of the apostolic age.

CAN TRADITIONAL EXEGESIS ENLIGHTEN LITERARY ANALYSIS OF THE FOURTH GOSPEL? AN EXAMINATION OF THE OLD TESTAMENT FULFILMENT MOTIF AND THE PASSOVER THEME

Stanley E. Porter

Literary studies of the biblical text abound, and their number is increasing in what appears to be almost exponential numbers. The fact that literary analysis has become such a popular exegetical method has led to a certain, perhaps necessary, independence from traditional historical-critical exegesis, that is, exegetical method concerned with issues of sources, origins, backgrounds and the like. Literary studies have become so numerous, however, that they have taken on an independence that, at least in the past, has threatened to fragment biblical studies. Traditional exegetes have their sections at scholarly conferences, while those interested in literary questions people their sections; and journals are published that cater (sometimes exclusively) to one type of exegetical method. It is only recently that there have been several studies that have attempted to redress this imbalance by including more traditional exegesis as a part of literary analysis of the text.

It is my contention, however, that much greater *rapprochement* is needed between these two disciplinary factions, and that even those literary studies that attempt to include traditional exegesis within their literary method could benefit still more from it. We are probably beyond the threat of creating an unbridgeable chasm between the two methods, but more needs to be done to bring these two exegetical positions into meaningful discussion, to alleviate the mutual suspicion that often pervades attempts to bring the two into dialogue. In particular, it is my impression that several of the recent studies that attempt to bring traditional exegesis into the literary equation only do so in a superficial way, one that does not shed as much light upon the text as it could, and as a result probably does more to perpetuate stereotypes of each side than to increase mutual understanding and development of a more comprehensive exegetical method. In this paper, I wish to do three things. First, I will survey how two recent treatments of the Fourth Gospel have handled one dimension of traditional exegetical method, that is, the use of Old Testament background, in particular the Passover theme as it relates to the Old Testament fulfilment motif. It will be seen that although there is reference to this theme in these two recent literary treatments, there is a general failure to appreciate the theme's significance as one that in conjunction with the Old Testament fulfilment motif binds together the entire Gospel. Secondly, I will establish the importance of the fulfilment motif and the Passover theme in the Fourth Gospel, noting especially how they converge in ch. 19. Thirdly and lastly, I will return to the two literary treatments of the Fourth Gospel and briefly show how a literary-historical analysis that gives full weight to the significance of the Passover theme not only would have added to the historical understanding of the text, but would have enhanced literary understanding as well.

Two Recent Literary-Historical Treatments of the Fourth Gospel

Two literary-historical treatments of the Fourth Gospel appeared in 1992 that provide foils for the major emphases of this paper. The first is by Mark W.G. Stibbe, entitled *John as Storyteller: Narrative Criticism and the Fourth Gospel*.[1] In this study, Stibbe focuses upon John 18–19, claiming that his monograph 'is a first on two accounts: it is the first scholarly, book-length study of John 18–19 in English...and the first comprehensive narrative-critical study of these chapters'.[2] The second study is by Margaret Davies, entitled *Rhetoric and Reference in the Fourth Gospel*.[3] In this study, Davies 'attempts a comprehensive reading of the Fourth Gospel, as a particular kind of narrative written at the end of the first century or at the beginning of the second, which makes sense of its theology, anthropology and history within that period'.[4] Each author makes high claims for their respective treatments of the Fourth Gospel. It is reasonable to think, on the basis of the statements above, that Stibbe would treat in some significant detail most of

1. SNTSMS, 73; Cambridge: Cambridge University Press, 1992.
2. Stibbe, *John as Storyteller*, p. 95.
3. JSNTSup, 69; Sheffield: JSOT Press, 1992.
4. Davies, *Rhetoric and Reference*, p. 7.

the relevant scholarly issues raised by these two chapters, 18 and 19, as well as analysing them from a critical standpoint. For Davies, it is also reasonable to think, on the basis of her statement, that her reading, while perhaps not as detailed as Stibbe's for any given section, would deal in a significant way with the major issues of the Gospel, especially those germane to its narrative construction as a historically-conditioned piece of writing.

In an effort to accomplish his purposes, Stibbe structures his volume in two parts, the first concerned with defining the method of narrative criticism that he purports to use to analyse the Fourth Gospel. His method focuses upon four sub-strategies, which he labels practical criticism,[1] genre criticism, sociological criticism and narrative-historical criticism. In the second part, after having defined his method, he applies each of these criticisms to John 18–19. Davies takes a similar approach. Part one of her book defines aspects of the rhetoric of the Fourth Gospel, part two elucidates key concepts and metaphors, and part three addresses the issue of historical reference in the Fourth Gospel. As can be seen from this brief analysis of the contents of these books, each one attempts to find a way to include at least three major categories of discussion. These include treatment of the self-consciously literary dimensions of the text (practical criticism, genre criticism and rhetorical criticism for Stibbe, and structuralism and reader-response criticism for Davies), discussion of major concepts and themes that appear in the text, and recognition of the historical-critical dimensions of the text. According to the standards that Stibbe and Davies have set for themselves, any element in the text of the Fourth Gospel that could be argued to have significance on all three levels would appear to warrant significant discussion. As evidenced by the inclusion of the Passover theme in their analyses, these two authors agree as to its significance.

In the light of the assumption that the Passover theme is so significant, it is warranted to see exactly how it is discussed by these two critical studies. Stibbe has three sections in which he makes significant reference

---

1.   Practical criticism is a form of criticism that has its roots in the work of the British scholar I.A. Richards, and is a version of formalism or what was once called the New Criticism. Despite its struggle to survive in the theoretical literature on literary criticism, practical criticism is still widely practised in English and literature departments throughout the English-speaking world, if not further abroad. For a summary of this method, see W.S. Scott, *Five Approaches of Literary Criticism* (New York: Collier, 1962), pp. 179-244.

to this idea.[1] In his practical criticism of John 18–19, in the section on 'The slaughter of the lamb. John 19.16b-42', Stibbe is concerned to re-create the Johannine chronology of Jesus' death, concluding that 'the execution of Jesus took place on the day of Preparation, the *'ereb pesah'*. The theological significance of this chronology Stibbe finds more difficult to assess. Recognizing that 'It has often been pointed out that the evangelist's dating of the crucifixion means that Jesus is crucified at the same time as the paschal lambs are being slaughtered in the temple precincts by the Jewish priests', Stibbe finds 'some poignancy in this coincidence of occurrences'. He then briefly cites some possible evidence for Jesus as the paschal lamb, including reference to the lamb of God in 1.29 and paschal nuances in language describing Jesus' execution. He concludes that 'In the light of these details, I suggest that narrative chronology is here inseparable from narrative Christology, that the importance of John's story time derives from the fact that Jesus is implicitly depicted as the true paschal lamb',[2] one of the themes in this final section of the passion narrative. The weakness of this defence must be noted. It is made without actual citation of the Old Testament quotations in Jn 19.36 and 37, and without reference to any other passages in the Gospel apart from 1.29, resulting in a very tenuous argument for the Passover theme.

In his narrative-critical approach to John 18–19, Stibbe goes into more detail. In the section on 'narrative and gospel', he first refers to how the author of the Gospel has 'configured time', creating what Stibbe calls the 'passover plot'. By this he means allusions in John 18–19 to the death of Jesus as 'the final and sufficient passover sacrifice', including mention of the hyssop branch (19.29), citation of the Old Testament in 19.36 and, most of all, 'John's use of story time'.[3] This manipulation of time includes three references to the Passover (2.13, 6.4 and 11.55) and three references in ch. 19 (vv. 14, 31 and 42). Later in the same section, Stibbe refers to four of the Old Testament allusions in the passion narrative being quotations (19.24, 29, 37a, 37b [read 36 and 37 according to *UBSGNT*[3, 4]]). He explicates their use by saying that the effect is to orientate

---

1. Stibbe's book has only a names and subjects index, which makes location of individual verses difficult.

2. Stibbe, *John as Storyteller*, p. 115.

3. Stibbe, *John as Storyteller*, p. 191.

the reader to an understanding of the crucifixion as a revelation of God's purpose in history. Everything that happens to Jesus at the cross is a fulfilment of aspects of the overall OT story... The testimonies in act three from Psalm 21.19, Psalm 68.22, Psalm 33.21/Exodus 12.46 and Zech. 2.10 create the impression that the crucifixion of Jesus is both the greatest demonstration of human disorder and the supremest manifestation of divine providence.[1]

These generalities may be true, but they do little to establish the specific exegetical significance of the Passover theme as it is used throughout the Gospel, or of any of the quotations referred to, including those in Jn 19.36 and 37.[2]

Davies has several more references to the Passover theme and the use of the Old Testament in her treatment. Referring to the characteristics of the Passover theme in the Fourth Gospel, she recounts these as the timing of his death (19.14), the presence of hyssop (19.29), the failure to break Jesus' legs (19.31-33) and removal of his corpse before morning (19.38).[3] What is noteworthy here is that she lists the same characteristics each time, specifically those in ch. 19, although the mention and treatment of the Old Testament is not significant in her references. In her chapter on the genre of the Fourth Gospel, Davies does have a sizeable section on 'The Fourth Gospel and its Scripture'. Here she refers to Zech. 12.10, the passage quoted at Jn 19.37, but only to point out the difficulties in establishing the source of the quotation. In fact this section begins by emphasizing the difficulty in working with the Old Testament because of the open canon in the first century CE. Whereas she also points out that the quotations in Jn 19.36, 37 are made by the narrator, she does not draw any further upon any of these quotations in explicating Old Testament parallels to Jesus, where she concentrates upon Exodus–Deuteronomy and 1 and 2 Kings. This is even though Exod. 12.10 (LXX), 46 and Num. 9.12, all Pentateuchal passages, are often thought to be the source of the quotation in John 19.36. In other

1.   Stibbe, *John as Storyteller*, p. 195. He is referring to the language of C.H. Dodd (*Historical Tradition in the Fourth Gospel* [Cambridge: Cambridge University Press, 1963]) when he mentions 'testimonies'.

2.   Stibbe does a much better job of explicating these topics in his commentary on John, as will be noted and critiqued below (*John* [Readings; Sheffield: JSOT Press, 1993]), but even here it is not a sustained or developed treatment. One might have expected in a technical monograph, however, a fuller exposition of such crucial topics.

3.   Davies, *Rhetoric and Reference*, pp. 24, 234, 305, 355; cf. p. 71.

words, there is no serious attempt by Davies to come to terms with the importance of the Passover theme as it is developed throughout the Fourth Gospel or the significance of the Old Testament quotations in Jn 19.36 and 37.

The Significance of the Old Testament Fulfilment Motif and the Passover Theme in the Fourth Gospel

Little systematic attention has been given to the use of the Old Testament in the Fourth Gospel, especially at Jn 19.36, 37 as seen in the larger context of the entire Gospel, nor to the sustained treatment throughout the Gospel of the Passover theme. These two factors—the use of the Old Testament and development of the Passover theme—work together in the Fourth Gospel to create a pattern that is worth exploring not only from a traditional exegetical standpoint but from a distinctive literary standpoint. Although commentators virtually always take note of the citation of the Old Testament in Jn 19.36, 37, usually to dispute which text is cited in v. 36, few go much further to explore the significance of the citations for the entire Gospel. This significance will be explored here in terms of three categories: (1) how the quotations in Jn 19.36, 37—the final quotations from the Old Testament in the Fourth Gospel—bring to an end a series of references introduced by fulfilment formulas; (2) how they are the final quotations in a group of quotations surrounding the death of Jesus; and (3) how they are the final climactic quotations in establishing the Passover theme in the Fourth Gospel, a theme that is often not given its due in terms of how it is developed throughout the Gospel. Thus, in the death of Jesus, as climactically defined by the Old Testament quotations, the Old Testament fulfilment motif and the Passover theme converge. The way that these two threads are created and woven together merits further discussion.

1. The use of allusions to or direct quotations of Old Testament passages in the Fourth Gospel is probably more complex than most realize, but there are a number of patterns with regard to quotation formulas that bear mentioning.[1] Evans has discussed the quotation formulas in the

---

1.   See C.A. Evans, 'On the Quotation Formulas in the Fourth Gospel', *BZ* 26 (1982), pp. 79-83; and more recently his *Word and Glory: On the Exegetical and Theological Background of John's Prologue* (JSNTSup, 89; Sheffield: JSOT Press, 1993), esp. pp. 172-77. See also D.A. Carson, 'John and the Johannine Epistles', in D.A. Carson and H.G.M. Williamson (eds.), *It is Written: Scripture Citing Scripture:*

Fourth Gospel, where he has noted a significant division between quotations in 1.23–12.16 being 'regularly introduced or alluded to with "it is written", or the like, while in 12.38–19.37 [they are] regularly introduced with the formula "in order that [the Scripture or what was spoken] be fulfilled"'.[1] This pattern is even more regular than most scholars recognize. Not only does it appear that all direct quotations of the Old Testament in the Fourth Gospel are introduced by a formula, but, apart from 1.23 and 12.13, neither passage of which is spoken by Jesus, within the first section (1.23–12.16), coinciding with the book of signs (chs. 2–11),[2] every direct quotation of the Old Testament is introduced by use of the perfect participle of γράφω, γεγραμμένον (2.17; 6.31, 45; 10.34; 12.14; the plural form of the participle is used similarly to refer back to a previously cited quotation in 12.16). Other non-perfect forms of γράφω are used in a quotation formula when no specific citation is produced (1.45; 5.46; 7.42; 8.17). In the second section (12.38–19.37), virtually all of the quotations, as well as the allusions, are introduced by formulas using the aorist passive subjunctive of πληρόω, πληρωθῇ (12.38-40; 13.18; 15.25; 17.12; 18.9, 32; 19.24, 28; 19.36-37). 12.39 and 19.37 do not not use this verb, but these do not constitute exceptions since, as Evans and others have pointed out, they 'are to be understood as extensions of the respective formulae in 12.38 and 19.36 (as is also indicated by the presence of the linking word πάλιν)'.[3] It is further to be noted that the initial and final quotations in this second section are double quotations, that is, they cite two Old Testament passages linked together. The only exception to the use of the subjunctive of πληρόω is 19.28, where τελειωθῇ is used between two other cognate forms, one reporting Jesus' knowledge regarding his 'end' and the other quoting his cry that the 'end' had come (τετέλεσται; 19.30).[4] (19.28 is not a direct quotation; neither are 17.12; 18.9, 32.) Most of the quotations and allusions are from the author or narrator of the Gospel, the exceptions being 13.18, 15.25 and 17.12. Evans has well summarized

---

Essays in Honour of Barnabas Lindars (Cambridge: Cambridge University Press, 1988), p. 247.

1. Evans, *Word and Glory*, pp. 175-76.

2. See C.H. Dodd, *The Interpretation of the Fourth Gospel* (Cambridge: Cambridge University Press, 1953), p. 289.

3. Evans, *Word and Glory*, p. 176.

4. M. Hengel, 'The Old Testament in the Fourth Gospel', *HBT* 12.1 (1990), p. 33; cf. Evans, *Word and Glory*, p. 176.

the use of the Old Testament by the Fourth Gospel: 'The function of the Old Testament in the Fourth Gospel, as seen in the formal quotations, is not ad hoc but is systematic and progressive, showing that Jesus' public ministry (1.29–12.36a) conformed to scriptural expectations and requirements, while his Passion (12.36b–19.37) fulfilled scriptural prophecies'.[1] The result of this patterning, it can be argued, is that although there may be a number of other allusions to the Old Testament in the Fourth Gospel, the author typically sees Jesus' ministry as in some way specifically foreshadowed in the Old Testament, as borne out by the typical use of a standard formula (γεγραμμένον) for introducing direct quotations. In the death of Jesus, however, the author sees the Old Testament as fulfilled, as revealed by his consistent use of πληρωθῇ for all direct quotations.

2. The significance of the quotations in Jn 19.36, 37 needs to be further explicated. It is within ch. 19 alone that three direct quotations of the Old Testament are said to be fulfilled in the death of Jesus, and the quotations in vv. 36 and 37 form a suitable climactic double quotation. In ch. 12, there are four direct quotations of the Old Testament (12.13, 15, 38, 40); however, the author does not treat them in the same way as the quotations in ch. 19. Chapter 12 is a transition chapter between the conclusion to Jesus' ministry and the beginning of his passion, the citation in 12.13 is not introduced by an 'it is written' formula, and the quotation in 12.15 is the final quotation of the first section of the Gospel, both introduced and concluded with a formula using the perfect participle (vv. 14, 16). Thus, the double quotation of 12.38, 40, linked by the connective πάλιν, is the first of the fulfilment quotations of the second section of the Gospel. The double quotation appropriately introduces the fulfilment motif that continues into ch. 19.[2] In ch. 19, the fulfilment motif is continued through the three direct quotations, each seen by the author as fulfilment of the Old Testament. The author not only alludes to the Old Testament in 19.28 (introduced by the word τελειωθῇ) but quotes the Old Testament three times directly, one a single quotation and one a double quotation. 19.24 and 19.36 each are introduced by the fulfilment formula, with 19.37 attached to v. 36 by πάλιν.

Whereas it is uniformly believed that the author of the Fourth Gospel cites Zech. 12.10 at Jn 19.37, there has been much discussion regarding which text is being cited and from which version at Jn 19.36. There

1. Evans, *Word and Glory*, p. 174.
2. See Hengel, 'Old Testament in the Fourth Gospel', pp. 32, 34.

have been two major proposals: a Pentateuchal text, in particular Exod. 12.10 (LXX), 46 or Num. 9.12, or Ps. 33.21 (34.20 MT). Some scholars argue that the Psalm quotation lies behind this passage,[1] others that the passage(s) from the Pentateuch are being cited,[2] and others that both sets are being drawn upon.[3] The evidence points to at least some reference to the Pentateuchal quotations, although there may be secondary reference or allusion to Ps. 33.21/34.20. The reasoning for the Pentateuchal solution is seen on two levels: linguistic and contextual.[4] The Psalm passage and John's quotation use the third person singular passive voice verb, with an impersonal subject provided in the context ('one' with reference to bones, or ὀστοῦν). In other respects, however, the Pentateuchal passages are more appropriate to the Johannine quotation: use of the singular for bones, ὀστοῦν, although it is the subject of the verb in John but the object in the Pentateuchal quotations; singular personal possessive reference, αὐτοῦ; and word order of subject (John) / object (Pentateuch)–negation–verb–prepositional phrase. There are still

---

1. See, for example, Dodd, *Interpretation*, pp. 230-38; *idem, Historical Tradition*, pp. 42-44; R. Bultmann, *The Gospel of John: A Commentary* (trans. G.R. Beasley-Murray *et al.*; Philadelphia: Westminster Press, 1971), p. 677 n. 1; R. Schnackenburg, *The Gospel according to St John* (trans. K. Smyth *et al.*; 3 vols.; New York: Crossroad, 1968–82), III, pp. 191-92. Usually mentioned in support of this proposal is the use of the passive voice of the verb and the use of Psalm quotations in the Fourth Gospel.

2. See, for example, G. Reim, *Studien zum alttestamentlichen Hintergrund des Johannesevangeliums* (SNTSMS, 22; Cambridge: Cambridge University Press, 1974), p. 52; E. Freed, *Old Testament Quotations in the Gospel of John* (NovTSup, 11; Leiden: Brill, 1965), p. 113.

3. See, for example, C.K. Barrett, 'The Old Testament in the Fourth Gospel', *JTS* 48 (1947), p. 175; B. Lindars, *New Testament Apologetic: The Doctrinal Significance of the Old Testament Quotations* (London: SCM Press, 1961), p. 96; A.T. Hanson, *The Prophetic Gospel: A Study of John and the Old Testament* (Edinburgh: T. & T. Clark, 1991), pp. 218-22; B.G. Schuchard, *Scripture within Scripture: The Interrelationship of Form and Function in the Explicit Old Testament Citations in the Gospel of John* (SBLDS, 133; Atlanta: Scholars Press, 1992), pp. 138-40; cf. Bultmann, *John*, p. 677; C.K. Barrett, *The Gospel according to St John: An Introduction with Commentary and Notes on the Greek Text* (Philadelphia: Westminster Press, 2nd edn, 1978), p. 558, who think that the Evangelist may have had the Pentateuchal quotations in mind but that his source was referring to Ps. 34; cf. *idem*, 'The Lamb of God', *NTS* 1 (1954–55), pp. 210-18, esp. p. 211.

4. See D.J. Moo, *The Old Testament in the Gospel Passion Narratives* (Sheffield: Almond Press, 1983), pp. 314-16, and bibliography cited there.

several divergences, including use of the second person plural in Exod.
12.10 and 46, and the third person plural in Num. 9.12, although the last
is closer to Jn 19.36.[1] The second criterion is context. Besides the
Passover context (developed throughout the Gospel, as will be shown
below),[2] and although Psalms regarding the suffering of the righteous
are used in the passion account, the Pentateuchal quotations are more
germane, since Ps. 33.21/34.20 refers to the presentation of the living
rather than to what happens to the one who is to be the victim, whether
alive or dead. It is probably pushing the evidence to argue further that
the unbroken bones were a symbol created by the author of the Fourth
Gospel to foretell Jesus' resurrection and the failure of the grave to hold
him.[3] More likely is that the passage is to be seen in terms of fulfilment
of the Passover theme.[4] Regarding whether the MT or LXX is being
quoted,[5] it is not necessary to establish this here, so long as it is plausibly
agreed that the author is referring to the Old Testament, which is
beyond doubt,[6] and probably to the Pentateuchal passages, each of
which appears in a Passover context. The citation in Exod. 12.10 from
the Passover account is as likely as any, although this cannot be proven
beyond doubt.

3. Although they do not take time to develop the Passover theme in
any significant way in their monographs, and certainly do not develop
the idea in relation to the Old Testament citations in Jn 19.36, 37, Stibbe
and Davies do refer obliquely to the importance of the Passover theme
in the Fourth Gospel. To his credit, Stibbe does mention the Passover
theme at several places in his recent commentary. On 1.29-34, he states,
'there is evidence in John's story of a rich Passover symbolism. The

---

1. Note that Num. 9.12 LXX[A] and Exod. 12.46 LXX[A] read συντρίψεται.

2. See Reim, *Studien*, pp. 52-53; J.H. Bernard, *A Critical and Exegetical Commentary on the Gospel according to St John* (ed. A.H. McNeile; 2 vols.; Edinburgh: T. & T. Clark, 1928), II, p. 651.

3. So D. Daube, *The New Testament and Rabbinic Judaism* (London: Athlone Press, 1956), p. 309; Dodd, *Historical Tradition*, p. 44; Lindars, *Apologetic*, p. 96; and Schuchard, *Scripture within Scripture*, p. 139.

4. Moo (*Old Testament*, p. 316) creates an unnecessary disjunction between the factuality of the *crucifragium* (the breaking of a victim's bones) and Jesus' depiction as the Passover lamb.

5. On the MT see Reim, *Studien*, p. 90; Moo, *Old Testament*, p. 315; on the LXX see Schuchard, *Scripture within Scripture*, pp. 133-40; B. Lindars, *The Gospel of John* (NCB; London: Marshall, Morgan & Scott, 1981), p. 590.

6. Although see Freed, *Quotations*, pp. 109-14, who is undecided.

whole of the Gospel could be described as a *Passover plot* in that it moves through the three Passover festivals in 2.13, 6.4 and 13.1.'[1] On 19.16b-42, and speaking about the author's implicit commentary, he mentions several symbolic details, including the hyssop (19.29) used to spread the blood of the Passover lamb on the door lintels, and the three references to its being the day of preparation (19.14, 31, 42) as coordinating events with the slaughter of the lambs. This 'in turn creates an implicit commentary on the death of Jesus as the perfect paschal sacrifice, and shows how narrative chronology and narrative Christology are inseparable in John'.[2] But how implicit is the commentary? Perhaps it is as veiled as it is to Stibbe because the evidence he examines is quite narrow. Thus although he recognizes the potential importance of the Passover theme for developing his theological-historical interpretive agenda, there is no further effort to show how this might work.

The evidence of a Passover theme in the Fourth Gospel, it seems to me, is stronger than many recognize. The Passover theme essentially states that Jesus is seen by the author of the Fourth Gospel as the suitable and in fact ideal or perfect Passover victim. Since the animal sacrificed at Passover symbolized deliverance from the angel of death as well as redemption from the oppression of Egypt, which leads to the exodus and, eventually, entrance into Canaan, there are several supporting themes in the Fourth Gospel that could be cited as giving further support for the Passover theme. These would include reference to Moses, the leader of the people during the course of these events (1.17, 45; 3.14; 5.45, 46; 6.32; 7.19, 22, 23; 8.5; 9.28, 29),[3] and possibly even reference to the serpent raised by Moses in the desert (3.14). As important as these are, they cannot be pressed here, except as they impinge on the exegesis below. More to the point, although not significant without further elucidation (see below), is reference to the Passover either directly or as a 'feast' (πάσχα is used in 2.13, 23; 6.4; 11.55 bis; 12.1; 13.1; 18.28, 39; 19.14; and ἑορτή is used with reference to the Passover in 2.23; 4.45; 5.1; 6.4; 11.56; 12.12, 20; 13.1, 29). The Fourth Gospel directly refers to the Passover ten times, which is more than any other New Testament book (the closest being Luke with seven

---

1. Stibbe, *John*, p. 35.
2. Stibbe, *John*, p. 196.
3. See T.F. Glasson, *Moses in the Fourth Gospel* (SBT, 40; London: SCM Press, 1963); and W.A. Meeks, *The Prophet-King: Moses Traditions and the Johannine Christology* (NovTSup, 14; Leiden: Brill, 1967), esp. pp. 228-30.

and Matthew and Mark with four each). Although Stibbe admits to what he calls a 'passover plot', he confines his discussion to chs. 1 and 19 and mention of the temporal references in 2.13, 6.4 and 13.1.

The significant literary and critical evidence for the Passover theme in the Fourth Gospel, however, is far more significant than Stibbe, Davies and most other commentators admit.[1] It is this evidence that I wish to analyse here. There are six major passages interspersed throughout the Gospel that make it possible to establish the significance of the theme. It is not appropriate here to argue in detail regarding every dimension of each passage, but it is worth noting the significant features that do establish the theme.

a. Jn 1.29-36, especially vv. 29, 36.[2] This passage contains two significant acclamations (vv. 29 and 36), in which John the Baptist refers to Jesus as 'the lamb (ἀμνός) of God'. These are the only two uses of ἀμνός in the Fourth Gospel (out of only four in the entire New Testament; see also Acts 8.32 and 1 Pet. 1.19). These two references appear in concentrated fashion at a crucial initiatory point in the narrative, marking the Gospel's as well as John the Baptist's introduction of Jesus and the commencement of Jesus' ministry (1.19–12.16). The question for most interpreters, however, is what John the Baptist's words mean. A number of alternatives to understanding the 'lamb' reference have been suggested.[3] These include the apocalyptic lamb of

---

1. Even among those who admit to the Passover theme in the Fourth Gospel, few see it in chapters other than 1 and 19. Those who go beyond those passages in a significant way include: L.L. Morris, *The New Testament and the Jewish Lectionaries* (London: Tyndale Press, 1964), pp. 64-72; J.K. Howard, 'Passover and Eucharist in the Fourth Gospel', *SJT* 20.1 (1967), pp. 329-37. There have been notable disputants, including Dodd, *Interpretation*, pp. 230-40. Despite the fairly widespread mention of the Passover theme by commentators, there has not been thorough discussion of this idea at many of the places where I argue that it appears. Perhaps one reason many have not followed it as thoroughly as it appears to be present in the Gospel is because of the statement of R. Kysar (*The Fourth Evangelist and his Gospel: An Examination of Contemporary Scholarship* [Minneapolis: Augsburg, 1975], p. 140) that though evident the Passover motif tends to be exaggerated. To the contrary, I do not think that it has been appreciated as fully as it appears throughout the Gospel.

2. See Bernard, *John*, I, pp. 43-47.

3. For a summary of the positions, see G.L. Carey, 'The Lamb of God and Atonement Theories', *TynBul* 32 (1981), pp. 101-107; Bultmann, *John*, pp. 95-97; and L.L. Morris, *The Gospel according to John* (NICNT; Grand Rapids: Eerdmans, 1971), pp. 144-47.

Revelation and apocalyptic literature (e.g. Rev. 5.6, 8, 12, 13; ch. 6; 7.14, 17; 14.1, 4, 10; 15.3, although Revelation uses ἀρνίον; *T. Jos.* 19.18-19; *1 En.* 89–90),[1] the sacrifice of Isaac in Genesis 22 (see e.g. v. 8),[2] the daily sacrifice or some other sacrifice of a lamb for an offering in the Old Testament (e.g. Lev. 7.1-7; 14.1-32; Num. 6.1-21),[3] the 'son of God' on the basis of the parallel with Jn 1.34,[4] the Suffering Servant of Isaiah 53,[5] or some combination of these. For example, Glasson notes that the church fathers combined the serpent of Jn 3.14, noted above as possibly suggesting Passover imagery, the outstretched hands of Moses and the offering of Isaac as prefiguring Jesus' crucifixion (e.g. Tertullian, *Answer to the Jews* 10). This kind of interpretive linkage, though a bit extreme, perhaps not only supports a sacrificial view of Christ's death from the standpoint of the early church, but possibly links the cross with Isaac's sacrifice (perhaps already done by Paul; see Rom. 8.32) and with the Passover.[6] It is not appropriate to offer a thorough critique of each of these theories here, however. It is more important to note that, in the eyes of most interpreters, the 'lamb' includes at least some reference to the Passover,[7] often stated in terms of the writer of the Fourth Gospel

---

1. Dodd, *Interpretation*, pp. 230-38; R.E. Brown, 'Three Quotations from John the Baptist in the Gospel of John', *CBQ* 22 (1960), pp. 295-97; G.R. Beasley-Murray, *John* (WBC, 36; Dallas: Word Books, 1981), pp. 24-25; cf. J.C. O'Neill, 'The Lamb of God in the Testaments of the Twelve Patriarchs', *JSNT* 2 (1977), pp. 2-30.

2. Glasson, *Moses*, p. 100.

3. See Davies, *Rhetoric and Reference*, p. 234.

4. N.R. Petersen, *The Gospel of John and the Sociology of Light: Language and Characterization in the Fourth Gospel* (Valley Forge, PA: Trinity Press International, 1993), p. 26; *contra* D.A. Carson, *The Gospel according to John* (Grand Rapids: Eerdmans, 1991), p. 149.

5. Evans, *Word and Glory*, pp. 182-83; M. Turner, 'Atonement and the Death of Jesus in John—Some Questions to Bultmann and Forestell', *EvQ* 62.2 (1990), pp. 119-22. As Evans (p. 182 n. 2) points out, this theory is not dependent upon the idea that Aramaic טליא, which can be rendered 'servant' or 'lamb', was mistranslated as ἀμνός instead of παῖς. Those who have argued this include D.J. Ball, 'Had the Fourth Gospel an Aramaic Archetype?', *ExpTim* 21 (1909–10), pp. 91-93; C.F. Burney, *Aramaic Origins of the Fourth Gospel* (Oxford: Clarendon Press, 1922), pp. 104-108; and J. Jeremias, 'ἀμνός', *TDNT*, I, pp. 339-40.

6. Glasson, *Moses*, pp. 98-99; *contra* Carey, 'Lamb of God', p. 103, who argues that explicit atonement theory regarding the sacrifice of Isaac does not occur until *Barn.* 7.3.

7. See V. Taylor, *Jesus and his Sacrifice: A Study of the Passion-Sayings in the Gospels* (London: Macmillan, 1937), pp. 226-27; Barrett, *John*, pp. 176-77;

understanding the reference in Passover terms, even if John the Baptist's understanding was in terms of, for example, some other form of imagery.[1] Although ἀμνός is not used in Exodus 12 to refer to the Passover animal (πρόβατον is used), in other places in the LXX ἀμνός is used, such as Num. 28.19 (see also Exod. 29.38-41; Lev. 9.3; 12.6; 14.10; with reference to other sacrifices).[2] This verbal correspondence, the association of the lamb with the sacrificial system, the significance of the Passover in this system, and the function of both in John's or the Gospel's and later Jewish thought (see below), all point toward Jesus as the Passover lamb. Howard is probably right in saying that this early episode serves as an introduction to the idea of Jesus as the Passover lamb as a motif that is continued throughout the book.[3]

Perhaps more important in establishing the Passover theme than the simple reference to the lamb, however, is the further comment attributed to John the Baptist, that Jesus is the lamb 'who takes away the sin of the world' (1.29). Some commentators have been surprised at this statement, because it seems to imply that Jesus' death is seen by the author of the Fourth Gospel as in some way substitutionarily sacrificial. This certainly appears to be the case, and for two reasons. The first is that the author appears to be invoking the Suffering Servant motif of Isaiah 53 (see vv. 4, 5, 6, 7, 8, 10, 12).[4] The author shows knowledge of Deutero-Isaiah at several points in the Gospel (including quotation at Jn 1.23 of Isa. 40.3, and at Jn 12.38 of Isa. 53.1), as Young has pointed out,[5] but

---

R.E. Brown, *The Gospel according to John* (2 vols.; Garden City, NY: Doubleday, 1966), I, p. 295 n. 9; Lindars, *John*, p. 109; Carey, 'Lamb of God', p. 111; Moo, *Old Testament*, pp. 312-14; Carson, *John*, p. 150; Evans, *Word and Glory*, pp. 181-82; Davies, *Rhetoric and Reference*, *passim*.

1. On this question, see E.W. Burrows, 'Did John the Baptist Call Jesus "The Lamb of God"?', *ExpTim* 85 (1973–74), pp. 245-47.

2. Davies, *Rhetoric and Reference*, p. 234.

3. Howard, 'Passover and Eucharist', p. 332. See also Barrett, *John*, p. 176, although he notes that 'The reference cannot have been drawn directly from Judaism, since in Judaism the lamb sacrificed at passover does not take away sins. The probable source of John's thought and language is the Paschal interpretation of the last supper and the eucharist.'

4. See J. Morgenstern, 'The Suffering Servant—A New Solution', *VT* 11 (1961), pp. 406-31, esp. p. 425, who sees the Suffering Servant as a single individual rather than a corporate entity.

5. F.W. Young, 'A Study of the Relation of Isaiah to the Fourth Gospel', *ZNW* 46 (1955), pp. 215-33; cf. also Stibbe, *John*, p. 35.

the reference in Jn 1.29 is apparently more specifically focused. In Isa. 53.7, the 'servant of the Lord' (note similar phrasing with 'lamb of God', a phrase found only here and in Jn 1.36)[1] is the ἀμνός who makes no noise and does not open its mouth before its shearers. Although in his commentary Stibbe sees 'evidence in John's story of a rich Passover symbolism',[2] he does not appreciate the full force of these references, in part because he divides up Jn 1.29-42 at vv. 34 and 35, rather than seeing vv. 29 and 36 as part of a single literary unit. Jesus is twice directly equated in this early episode of the Gospel with the lamb of God. This equation moves beyond the language of Isa. 53.7, where the Suffering Servant is said to be *like* a lamb, to represent Jesus directly as the sacrificial victim. In his first appearance Jesus is depicted as one whose life is sacrificial in nature, and the sacrifice is characterized as one that takes away the sin of all people (cf. Acts 8.32). The Johannine language is an expansion of the Isaianic language (cf. Isa. 53.11-12). In Isa. 53.7 it is the ἀμνός that is shorn, but the author of the Fourth Gospel apparently takes what is said of the Isaianic comparison with the sheep and applies it to the Suffering Servant who bears (φέρει) the sins of Israel. Jesus is said in the Fourth Gospel to be the one who takes away (ὁ αἴρων) the sin of the world (cf. 1 Jn 3.5, although with plural 'sins'; see also Jn 11.49-52).[3] φέρω and αἴρω overlap semantically in extrabiblical Greek, although not apparently in the LXX (see Exod. 28.38; 34.7; Num. 14.18; 1 Sam. 15.25; Mic. 7.18, where removal of guilt is spoken of, rendered by forms of αἴρω in the LXX).[4] Thus, the language of Jn 1.29 and 36 intensifies and expands what is said of the

1.   See Schnackenburg, *John*, I, p. 300, but not requiring mistranslation of Aramaic טליא.

2.   Stibbe, *John*, p. 35.

3.   Carey, 'Lamb of God', pp. 199-200; Schnackenburg, *John*, I, p. 298; Brown, 'Three Quotations', p. 296 n. 14 (cf. 1 Jn 3.5, 8); Evans, *Word and Glory*, p. 183; *contra* G.E. Ladd, *New Testament Theology* (Grand Rapids: Eerdmans, 1975), p. 43 n. 35. The point is not dependent on it, but there is some evidence that reference is being made by the author of the Fourth Gospel to the LXX version of Isa. 53, which refers to ἁμαρτίας ἡμῶν rather than 'sickness' in v. 4, gives κύριος παρέδωκεν αὐτὸν ταῖς ἁμαρτίαις ἡμῶν for 'the Lord caused to fall upon him the iniquity of us all' in v. 6, and employs vicarious language in v. 10. *Contra* S.K. Williams, *Jesus' Death as Saving Event: The Background and Origin of a Concept* (HDR, 2; Missoula, MT: Scholars Press, 1975), pp. 112-14.

4.   See B.F. Westcott, *The Gospel according to St John* (repr.; Grand Rapids: Eerdmans, 1973 [1881]), p. 20.

lamb, moving it beyond simply taking sin upon itself, but removing sin as a concept (taking the singular form to represent sin in its collective sense) and this for the entire world, not just for Israel.[1] Secondly, the reader should not be unduly surprised by this kind of language, since Paul had already made such an explicit equation between Jesus and the Passover lamb when he equated the death of Jesus with the Passover sacrifice (see 1 Cor. 5.7). Paul's usage illustrates that a sacrificial understanding of Jesus' death had precedent in earlier Christianity, which the author of the Fourth Gospel apparently takes up in similar terms. Although the original Passover sacrifice may not have been seen as sacrificial, it apparently became so early on (see Num. 28.22; Ezek. 45.21-25).[2] Stibbe concludes rightly that 'The suggestion is that Jesus is the true passover Lamb, the Lamb of God who takes away the sin of the world'.[3] For most who mention the Passover theme, this passage and 19.31-37 are the only ones discussed at length. However, the theme is more pervasive in the Gospel, as subsequent discussion shows.[4]

b. Jn 2.13-25. The second major passage to illustrate that the author of the Fourth Gospel views Jesus as the Passover sacrifice is the incident of his cleansing the temple. The indications are several. First, the author states at the outset that it was 'near the passover of the Jews' (2.13) that Jesus entered Jerusalem and went to the temple. This significant event, apparently placed by the author at the outset of Jesus' ministry, is thus coordinated with the Passover. Stibbe in his commentary recognizes that

1. Westcott (*John*, p. 20) emphasizes the idea of 'taking away' as a conscious substitution and expansion on the LXX, with the singular 'sin' treating sin as a unity.

2. See Howard, 'Passover and Eucharist', p. 332, who cites these and other passages to show a link between sin offerings and Passover. Later Judaism apparently continued this idea (see *Exod. R.* 15.12 [on Exod. 12.6], in which the blood of the Passover sacrifice is said to be atoning blood). See G. Dalman, *Jesus-Jeshua: Studies in the Gospels* (trans. P. Levertoff; London: SPCK, 1929), p. 167.

3. Stibbe, *John*, p. 35. *Contra* Bultmann, *John*, p. 96; Barrett, *John*, p. 68; Brown, *John*, I, pp. 60-61, who do not see the death as sacrificial. Cf. G.A. Barton, ' "A Bone of him shall not be Broken", John 19.36', *JBL* 49 (1930), pp. 13-19, who sees the death as sacrificial, but based on a cannibalistic background.

4. B.H. Grigsby ('The Cross as an Expiatory Sacrifice in the Fourth Gospel', *JSNT* 15 [1982], p. 54 and nn. 37, 38) notes that equation of the Passover lamb with the Suffering Servant is found elsewhere in the New Testament and early Christian literature: see 1 Pet. 2.22-25, where ideas of Isa. 53.1-12 are developed in a Passover setting; and Justin Martyr, *Dial. Trypho* 111: ἦν γὰρ τὸ πάσχα ὁ χριστὸς ὁ τυθεὶς ὕστερον ὡς καὶ Ἡσαίας ἔφη αὐτὸς ὡς πρόβατον ἐπι σφαγὴν ἔχθη.

this reference, the first of three to the Passover (cf. 6.4 and 13.1), is significant, with these references 'important in the creation of a sense of plot (beginning, middle and end)'.[1] But Stibbe does not go far enough in reference to the Passover. Not only is there reference in 2.13, but there is reference to the Passover again in 2.23 at the close of the incident narrated here. This inclusio usefully surrounds the intervening events of Jesus' temple cleansing with explicit reference to the Passover, so that it is seen that Jesus' temple actions are to be understood in terms of Passover activities. Furthermore, Stibbe's statement suggests that his understanding of plot is simply related to the marking of events. Plot, however, is better understood as concerned with the motivation for these events. In this sense, equation of Jesus with the Passover lamb is not simply a plot marker but potentially a major motivating factor for Jesus' actions throughout the entire Gospel, including his actions in the temple. In section a. above it was seen that Jesus was depicted from the outset of his ministry as the 'lamb of God' who serves as a sacrifice for the sin of the world, and his entire ministry once introduced in this way needs to be seen in this light. Thus, the Passover theme itself begins at the outset of Jesus' ministry, and does not end until his death (see below on ch. 19), with further events throughout the Gospel specifying this relationship, including not only 2.13, 6.4 and 13.1 but other places as well to be noted below. Secondly, what Jesus does in this episode in the temple is depicted by the author as instituting a new Passover, one with Jesus as the focus rather than the old institution. This is indicated in several ways. In graphic fashion Jesus drives those selling the animals, including the sheep (πρόβατα) and cattle (βόας), out of the temple (πρόβατον is the more usual term for sheep, and the one used in the Exodus 12 account of the institution of Passover; see vv. 3, 4, 5, 21, and 32, where cattle are mentioned also). Then, through a series of interchanges with the leaders who interrogate him, Jesus is depicted as transferring himself by reference to his own body into the equation as the substitute for the temple sacrificial system, that is, the temple system oriented toward the Passover sacrifice. He tells them to destroy 'this temple' (ναὸν τοῦτον) and he will raise it in three days. The author tells us that Jesus was speaking of 'the temple of his body' (τοῦ ναοῦ τοῦ σώματος αὐτοῦ), a clear reference to his death.[2] As W.D. Davies says, 'John places the Cleansing of the Temple very early in his Gospel, in

---

1. Stibbe, *John*, p. 49.
2. Cf. Stibbe, *John*, p. 52.

2:13-25, to signify that a New Order had arrived. The "Holy Place" is to be displaced by a new reality, a rebuilt "temple (*naos*)," which John refers to as "the temple of his body"...'[1] The author is thus telling his readers that Jesus' death is the new temple institution, and one that renders the old no longer serviceable.

c. Jn 6.1-14 and 22-71. The next episode that helps to establish the Passover theme is John 6. Not only does the author state that the events of the chapter, in particular Jesus' feeding of the five thousand, take place near the time of the Passover (6.4),[2] as Stibbe and others have noted, but there are other substantial reasons as well. First, there is much critical agreement (perhaps even verging on consensus) that this chapter was a form of Christian Passover haggadah, possibly read as a lectionary at Passover celebrations.[3] Secondly, there are several Moses–Exodus allusions that help to create a Passover milieu by reference to images often associated with Passover. For example, there is reference to divine provision through the heavenly manna of the exodus. This is seen in particular in: Jn 6.4-5,[4] when, after mentioning that it was Passover, in

---

1. W.D. Davies, *The Gospel and the Land: Early Christianity and Jewish Territorial Doctrine* (Berkeley: University of California Press, 1974), pp. 289-90; cf. R.H. Lightfoot, *St John's Gospel: A Commentary* (ed. C.F. Evans; Oxford: Clarendon Press, 1956), p. 114. Davies sees the temple incidents of Jn 8 and 9 as continuing this theme. See also Davies, *Rhetoric and Reference*, pp. 231-33.

2. See Lindars, *John*, p. 240.

3. P. Borgen, *Bread from Heaven: An Exegetical Study of the Concept of Manna in the Gospel of John and the Writings of Philo* (NovTSup, 10; Leiden: Brill, 1965), esp. pp. 1-27. The haggadah theory is supported by: supposed verbal parallels with the Old Testament, the Passover haggadah about manna, extrabiblical writers such as Philo, and the text of Jn 6. The lectionary theory is based on less substantial evidence and more on inference, sometimes drawn from later textual evidence. See also A. Guilding, *The Fourth Gospel and Jewish Worship: A Study of the Relation of St John's Gospel to the Ancient Jewish Lectionary System* (Oxford: Clarendon Press, 1960), pp. 58-68; Brown, *John*, I, p. 245. It has been criticized by Morris, *Lectionary*, pp. 64-72; U. Schnelle, *Antidocetic Christology in the Gospel of John: An Investigation of the Place of the Fourth Gospel in the Johannine School* (trans. L.M. Maloney; Minneapolis: Fortress Press, 1992), pp. 194-208, esp. p. 196 n. 128. See Grigsby, 'Cross as an Expiatory Sacrifice', p. 67 n. 25, for further discussion.

4. Schnackenburg (*John*, II, p. 14) notes that this reference is 'not chronological but theological': 'John, however, is alone in explicitly mentioning the nearness of the Passover... For him the importance of the bread discourse is that it introduces the theme of manna, which is important in the Jewish lessons for Passover time.' Schnackenburg (*John*, II, p. 440 n. 2) notes further that 'since manna does not appear

v. 5 Jesus lifts up his eyes (heavenward?), sees a large, hungry crowd and makes provision for them to eat bread; vv. 31-33, where, when asked for a sign, Jesus says that the Jewish people of a previous generation ate the manna from heaven in the desert, but that it is not Moses but God the Father who gives the true bread from heaven, which is the one who comes down from heaven, Jesus alluding to himself;[1] vv. 34-38, where Jesus equates himself with the bread that comes down from heaven, after the people have apparently recognized his capability in this regard and asked him to give to them this bread; and vv. 48-51, when, reiterating more explicitly what he has said above, Jesus not only calls himself the living bread that comes down from heaven and guarantees life, but equates this bread with his flesh, which he says will be given for the life of the world (v. 51), an invocation of sacrificial imagery in terms of the Passover theme. It has been pointed out above (and by numerous interpreters of this passage) that the Fourth Gospel emphasizes the role of Moses, the leader of the exodus and the instigator of Passover, and so allusion to the manna of the exodus is in keeping with the Passover theme. But Jesus goes further and equates himself with this heavenly bread, and sees this bread as sacrificial. Thus, thirdly, Jesus himself is depicted as making his sacrificial death even more explicit in vv. 53-58, where he explicates the idea of the bread coming down from heaven in terms of eating his flesh and drinking his blood.[2] Not only does this language reflect exodus language (cf. 1 Cor. 10.3-4), but it is sacrificial and makes direct appeal to Passover practices in terms of Last Supper imagery, imagery probably maintained throughout the chapter but especially focused on the feeding miracle (see Exod. 12.7, 22; 1 Cor. 10.6-22).[3]

as a theme in early Christian Easter homilies we must go back to the Jewish Passover haggada'. See Guilding, *Fourth Gospel*, pp. 61-62; Dodd, *Interpretation*, p. 333; *contra* Morris, *John*, p. 342 n. 12.

1. Westcott (*John*, p. 102) notes that 'bread from God' in 6.33 is similar in phrasing to 'lamb of God' in 1.29, 36, indicating that it comes directly from God.

2. See Howard, 'Passover and Eucharist', p. 334. πίνειν τὸ αἷμα is unique to John in the New Testament (6.54, 56); and τρώγειν τὴν σάρκα, also unique to John, is used apparently exclusively by him for the Last Supper (6.54, 56, 57, 58; 13.18). See also Bernard, *John*, I, p. 210; and Schnackenburg, *John*, II, pp. 56-59, who debates the critical issues related to 6.52-59, especially regarding their relation to the previous discourse.

3. As Carson states (*John*, pp. 268-69) regarding the reference to the Passover in 6.4 in terms of the context of this chapter and its relation to the Passover, 'the

d. Jn 11.47–12.8. In ch. 11 there is an incident in which the leaders of the Jewish people, represented by the words of Caiaphas the high priest, are depicted as pointing specifically to Jesus as the sacrificial victim. In the light of the controversy caused by Jesus, Caiaphas states that he thinks that it is better that 'one man die for the people' than that the whole nation be destroyed (v. 50). The scene is full of dramatic and verbal irony: on the one hand, the reader is told by the author that Jesus is being referred to in his sacrificial role as creating the unified children of God (vv. 51-52), whereas the high priest says what he does with specific reference to the death of Jesus saving the Jewish people, or in particular its leaders, from destruction at the hands of the Romans; and on the other hand, Caiaphas's wording creates an equation that captures the function of the Passover sacrifice, a least as seen by the author of the Fourth Gospel, in that it is the substitutionary death of the one victim (the 'lamb of God') that prevents the destruction by sin of an entire people.[1] Although the preposition ὑπέρ is used, the substitutionary idea is paramount. This is seen in two ways. First, the preposition ὑπέρ is used with a substitutionary sense consistent with usage during the Hellenistic period. When an amanuensis was employed to write for someone illiterate, a line was often appended by the scribe to indicate that he had written 'for' (ὑπέρ) someone incapable of writing.[2] Secondly, the context is clearly substitutionary, in which Caiaphas sees the single individual as providing a substitute for the nation, so that destruction will come only to one. This sense of the one taking the place

---

connections become complex: the sacrifice of the lamb anticipates Jesus' death, the Old Testament manna is superseded by the real bread of life, the exodus typologically sets forth the eternal life that delivers us from sin and destruction, the Passover feast is taken over by the eucharist (both of which point to Jesus and his redemptive cross-work). "The movement from the miracle to the discourse, from Moses to Jesus (vv. 32-5, cf. i. 17), and, above all, from *bread* to *flesh*, is almost unintelligible unless the reference in v. 4 to the Passover picks up i. 29, 36, anticipates xix. 36 (Exod. xii. 46; Num. ix. 12), and governs the whole narrative" ([E.] Hoskyns [and F.N. Davey, *The Fourth Gospel* (2 vols.; London: Faber & Faber, 1940), I,] p. 281).' This may also allude to the Suffering Servant ascent–descent motif. See G.C. Nicholson, *Death as Departure: The Johannine Descent–Ascent Scheme* (SBLDS, 63; Chico, CA: Scholars Press, 1983).

    1. Cf. Stibbe, *John*, pp. 130-31.
    2. S.E. Porter, *Idioms of the Greek New Testament* (Biblical Languages: Greek, 2; Sheffield: JSOT Press, 2nd edn, 1994), pp. 118-19; Lindars, *John*, p. 406.

of the whole is what is taken up by the author in explaining the meaning of Caiaphas's statement.

There are two further references to the approaching Passover in 11.55 and 12.1. The first is a general reference to the Passover and the second places the following events six days before the Passover. The effect of these two explicit time markers is to link Caiaphas's words with Jesus' being anointed at Bethany by Mary (12.1-8), and then to link both of these events with Jesus' impending death. The author makes sure that the reader understands Jesus' anointing as following on from Caiaphas's words and in anticipation of Jesus' death in Jerusalem, when he depicts Jesus as stating that the purpose of Mary's action was to prepare Jesus' body for burial (v. 7). Thus Jesus is further depicted as the Passover victim being prepared for sacrifice.[1]

e. Jn 13.1–17.26. Whereas the first part of the Gospel (chs. 1–12) covers a number of years in Jesus' life (two and a half by Culpepper's reckoning), chs. 13–19 depict a time period of approximately 24 hours.[2] This latter series of prolonged events that terminates in Jesus' death begins with what is probably best seen as a Passover meal that Jesus partakes of with his disciples (chs. 13–17). It has been debated in many quarters whether this is a Passover meal, largely because of the chronological difficulties between the Synoptic and Johannine accounts of the final days of Jesus' life. This is not the place to discuss the chronological issues, except to say that they are not easily resolved. Nevertheless, it appears fairly clear that in the light of the overwhelming similarities between the Synoptic and Johannine accounts the meal depicted in John 13–17 is seen by the author of the Fourth Gospel as a Passover meal, or at least as one that is infused with numerous Passover elements.[3] What is

---

1. Schnackenburg (*John*, II, p. 366) misses entirely the significance of the temporal reference.

2. R.A. Culpepper, *Anatomy of the Fourth Gospel: A Study in Literary Design* (FFNT; Philadelphia: Fortress Press, 1983), p. 72.

3. The strongest case for equating the meals in the Synoptic Gospels and the Fourth Gospel is probably made by J. Jeremias (*The Eucharistic Words of Jesus* [NTL; London: SCM Press, 1966], pp. 56-82, esp. p. 81). See also R.E. Brown, 'The Problem of History in John', *CBQ* 24 (1962), p. 5, who argues for a meal with Passover features. On chronology, the strongest advocates for two calendars being in use in Palestine are A. Jaubert (*La date de la cène: Calendrier biblique et liturgie chrétienne* [EBib; Paris: Gabalda, 1957]; 'Jésus et le calendrier de Qumrân', *NTS* 7 [1960–61], pp. 1-30; 'The Calendar of Qumran and the Passion Narrative in John', in J.H. Charlesworth [ed.], *John and the Dead Sea Scrolls* [New York: Crossroad,

often less well established are the clear indications of Jesus' being depicted as the Passover lamb in several episodes of these chapters. The indications that should be taken into account are the following. First, 13.1 sets the scene by saying that just before the time of the Passover Jesus realized what would happen to him.[1] This verse probably serves as a heading for chs. 13–17. The author continues by stating that in the light of Jesus' knowledge and compassion, at the 'Passover' dinner (13.4), he did and said a number of things. Secondly, among the words that Jesus is said to have uttered were words regarding his being the true vine (15.1-10). The vine image probably suggests the wine consumed at the Passover celebration, having apparently just been consumed in the events of the narrative above (see 13.2, 4, 26, 30).[2] More than that, however, the language that is used in chs. 15–17 is reminiscent of the 'bearing' and 'taking away' language of 1.29 (see section a. above), and the glory language (e.g. Jn 12.23, 28; 13.31-32) that refers to Jesus' death on the cross (Jn 12.16).[3] In ch. 17, the entire scene is brought to a close by Jesus' prayer for himself and his followers. The concept of glorification (see 17.5) seems to have been inspired by the Suffering Servant passages of Isaiah, especially ch. 53 (see Jn 12.38, 41), which are used at the outset of Jesus' ministry to establish him as not only the one who suffers but the one who dies as a sacrificial lamb (1.29; cf. v. 36; see section a. above). In Jesus' prayer, as the meal draws to a close, it is perhaps not too much to see Jesus offering a new prayer of

---

1990], pp. 62-75) and E. Ruckstuhl (*Chronology of the Last Days of Jesus: A Critical Study* [trans. V.J. Drapela; New York: Desclée, 1965]); see also N. Walker, 'Pauses in the Passion Story and their Significance for Chronology', *NovT* 6 (1963), pp. 16-19; K.A. Strand, 'John as Quartodeciman: A Reappraisal', *JBL* 84 (1965), pp. 251-58. They have been opposed by G. Ogg, 'Review of Mlle Jaubert, *La Date de la Cène*', *NovT* 34 (1959), pp. 149-60, besides numerous commentators.

1. J. Rendel Harris ('The Early Christian Interpretation of the Passover', *ExpTim* 38 [1926–27], pp. 88-90) cites the use of μεταβῇ in Jn 13.1 as an allusion to the Passover since Philo describes the exodus using similar language, but this is pretty thin evidence. See Glasson, *Moses*, pp. 97-98.

2. Howard, 'Passover and Eucharist', p. 335; Bernard, *John*, II, p. 478. Cf. Isa. 5.1-7; 27.2-11. Note also that this probably extends and applies to Jesus' language regarding Israel as the true vine (for example Jer. 2.21; 12.10-13; Ezek. 15.1-8; 19.10-14; Hos. 10.1; Ps. 80.8-16). See Hoskyns and Davey, *Fourth Gospel*, II, pp. 559-60.

3. Evans, *Word and Glory*, p. 180.

blessing and consecration for the Passover feast—one that he himself is about to re-enact as its victim.[1]

f. Jn 19.13-42, especially vv. 14, 29, 31, 36-37, 42. In the light of what has been argued above, it should not come as unexpected that the author draws out the Passover theme in the actual depiction of Jesus' death. Many commentators are willing to concede Passover elements in this scene, but have failed to realize the force such a depiction would have because they have failed to see how the theme has been developed throughout the Gospel. This passage is, therefore, not a simple equation of Jesus with the Passover victim on the basis of only the points of correlation mentioned in this particular passage, but a climactic scene that brings to decisive conclusion a major thematic element developed throughout the Gospel. There are a number of factors in this passage to consider in establishing the importance of the Passover theme, all of which point to the double quotation in vv. 36-37 as the climactic statement regarding this theme. The first factor is the temporal references with regard to the day on which Jesus died. 18.28 and 39 say that it is the evening of the day before Passover; 19.14 says that it is the preparation for Passover (παρασκευὴ τοῦ πάσχα); and 19.31 and 42 say that it is the day of preparation (either for Passover or Sabbath, since the two seem to have fallen on the same day, so far as the author's account is concerned).[2] Throughout the Fourth Gospel there is correlation of events in Jesus' ministry with events surrounding Passover (see above), and the same is true in the passion account, where there is direct correlation of specific events concerning Jesus' death with the events surrounding the Passover celebration. Not only is the mention of the specific timing important, but the repetition unites the account. Jn 18.28 and 39 prepare the reader for the specific chronology of events in ch. 19, and the crucial events surrounding Jesus' death are linked on three occasions with the day of preparation, once at the beginning, once in the middle and once at the end (19.14, 31, 42). The significance of this linkage lies in the fact that the day of preparation was the day on which

1.   See Howard, 'Passover and Eucharist', p. 336.

2.   See Barrett, *John*, p. 555, who claims that there is a significant difference between v. 14 and vv. 31 and 42, on the basis of which day is being referred to. Cf. Schnackenburg, *John*, III, p. 264; Carson, *John*, p. 604. Stibbe (*John*, p. 191) takes them all as referring to Passover.

the Passover sacrifices were killed.[1] Thus Jesus' death not only is seen to occur on the day on which the Passover sacrifice was made but is equated with that sacrifice itself by virtue of its contemporaneity.

Secondly, Jesus is sentenced to death by Pilate at noon (the eighth hour, according to the Jewish chronography),[2] the hour at which the slaughter of the Passover lambs was to begin (19.14; cf. Exod. 12.6).[3] The presentation by Pilate of Jesus for death is accompanied both by the indication of the day, which is repeated twice more in the account, as noted above, and by the indication of the specific hour. This could be a coincidence, but it is an uncanny one that coordinates well with what is known of Passover practice, and points to Jesus' impending death as being interpreted in the light of the Passover. This has the same symbolic significance as the cleansing of the temple.[4] As Bultmann states, 'The end of the Jewish cultus, or the uselessness of its further observance, is thereby affirmed'.[5]

Thirdly, specific events associated with Jesus' actual death are perhaps best interpreted in terms of the Passover.[6] For example, in Exod. 12.22 and Jn 19.29 the hyssop branch is mentioned. There has been much

---

1. G.B. Gray, *Sacrifice in the Old Testament: Its Theory and Practice* (Oxford: Clarendon Press, 1925), p. 388.

2. There is some textual dispute regarding the time of Jesus' death, but readings for the sixth hour are almost certainly designed to bring the Fourth Gospel into harmony with the Synoptic accounts.

3. Gray, *Sacrifice*, pp. 388-89; Brown, *John*, II, p. 833; Barrett, *John*, p. 545.

4. See Beasley-Murray, *John*, p. 341, who states: 'The place, the day, and the hour are all mentioned, for the Evangelist is conscious of the momentous nature of the event now taking place...It is the sixth hour (noon) of the Preparation Day; at this hour three things take place: Jews cease their work, leaven is gathered out of the houses and burned, and the slaughtering of the Passover lambs commences. The Passover festival, for all practical purposes, now begins...The Evangelist's thought is plain: Passover is the great celebration of Israel's deliverance from slavery by God's almighty power; then it was that he showed himself as King, and they became his people. In this celebration the Jews gathered before Pilate are about to play a decisive part in the fulfillment of the Passover, a second Exodus, wherein God would achieve an emancipation for all nations, not for Israel alone, giving them life in the promised land of his eternal kingdom. The crucial hour of destiny for Jew and Gentile has arrived'.

5. Bultmann, *John*, p. 677.

6. On issues of chronology seen in terms of Passover practice, see Grigsby, 'Cross as an Expiatory Sacrifice', pp. 54-56 and notes. He shows that the Passover theme is essentially unaltered by the various chronologies proposed.

debate regarding what the hyssop branch was and, if it was a small, weak plant (as it seems to have been), how it could be used to lift the sponge to Jesus' lips. If anything, these difficulties, as well as the apparently conscious departure from the Synoptic use of κάλαμος (Mk 15.33; Mt. 27.49),[1] point to the author's intentionally including this item to correlate it with the use of the hyssop branch at Passover (cf. Heb. 8.19, where blood, water and hyssop are related; see below). They are described in the Passover and John 19 accounts as serving similar functions, that is, the hyssop branch is used to form a connection between the sacrificial victim and those for whom it or he is the sacrifice.[2] In Jn 19.34, the blood and water of Jesus that flow out when he is stabbed by the soldier may be reminiscent of the flow of blood and fluid out of the sacrificial animal (Exod. 12.7, 22). There are several later rabbinic passages that describe the proper sacrifice in terms of the flow of blood and water or fluid. The idea appears to be that the blood was supposed to flow like water (the καί may be epexegetic, 'blood even water [fluid]') to prevent congealing.[3] Furthermore, Jesus' body is not allowed to stay on the cross until the next morning (19.31, 38), just as the remains of the Passover meal were not to be left until the next day but burned (Exod. 12.19).[4]

Fourthly, the scene is brought to a close by the two quotations (double quotation) from the Old Testament in vv. 36 and 37. The first is probably a quotation of Exod. 12.10 (LXX), 46 or Num. 9.12 (although less likely, Ps. 33.21 has also been suggested), both from Passover accounts. The second quotation is from Zech. 12.10. The first is introduced by John's fulfilment formula, which as noted above he uses throughout the second half of the Gospel (the exception is 19.28). Although the second quotation begins with πάλιν ἑτέρα γραφὴ λέγει,

---

1. Barrett, *John*, p. 553; Grigsby, 'Cross as an Expiatory Sacrifice', p. 57; *contra* Schnackenburg, *John*, III, p. 284; Bultmann, *John*, p. 673 n. 5; Dodd, *Historical Tradition*, pp. 123-24 n. 2.

2. See Lev. 14.6-7; Num. 19.6; Ps. 50.9, where hyssop is related to cultic sprinkling. Barrett (*John*, p. 553) says that 'the fact that hyssop could hardly be used in the manner described is not one that would greatly concern the evangelist'.

3. J.M. Ford ('"Mingled Blood" from the Side of Christ [John XIX. 34]', *NTS* 15 [1968–69], pp. 337-38) also finds reference to the meaning 'spurting' rather than dripping blood in ἐξῆλθον εὐθὺς αἷμα, but this is less clear. See also Beasley-Murray, *John*, pp. 353-58, for medical explanations. *Contra* Stibbe, *John as Storyteller*, pp. 115-16.

4. Davies, *Rhetoric and Reference*, pp. 234, 305, 355.

rather than πληρωθῇ, the two are apparently meant to be taken together, with the second a further passage taken in support of the sacrificial imagery, here referring to the piercing of Jesus. This is the second compound quotation in the Fourth Gospel, the first having begun the passion section of the Gospel and the 'fulfilment' quotations (12.38–19.37). Although Davies contends that the author of the Fourth Gospel is never explicit about referring to Jesus' death as related to the Passover except at this particular point, perhaps in the light of the evidence marshalled above it is better to see these quotations as simply making explicit in a summative way a major theme that has been developed throughout the Gospel. It is not so much an issue of whether an explicit quotation is used to prove that the sacrificial Passover imagery comes from the Old Testament as whether there has been sustained and consistent use of recognizable Passover language throughout. It is my contention that this has been the case at several significant junctures in the unfolding Gospel account. At the outset of Jesus' ministry he is proclaimed the sacrificial lamb of God, introducing a theme that is maintained and developed throughout the Fourth Gospel. At several significant junctures in the ministry of Jesus the author reaffirms Jesus' role as Passover victim. Then at the climactic events leading up to and including his death, he brings the passion story to a close by citing in double, emphatic fashion Old Testament quotations that make the sacrificial Passover death not only specific but virtually undeniable. This particular double quotation not only brings the Passover theme to its fitting conclusion, but also brings the author of the Fourth Gospel's series of Old Testament quotations to an end, both at the death of Jesus. The quotations in vv. 36 and 37 are to be seen therefore as final fulfilment statements that bring the entire course of plot development to a close. A primary motivation for the action of the story is Jesus' death as a substitute and replacement for the Passover sacrifice, seen in his fulfilling various features of that sacrifice.

Implications for Recent Literary-Historical Analysis of the Fourth Gospel

This defence of the Passover theme in the Fourth Gospel has implications for recent literary-historical analysis of the book. To show its particular relevance, the two works reviewed above may be examined again.

Davies's treatment is not to be minimized, in that she recognizes the importance of various allusions to the Passover within the Fourth Gospel, especially in chs. 1 and 19. However, she does not place these factors at the heart of her analysis, apparently because she does not think that a reader would have recognized these features apart from explicit quotation of Old Testament passages. As she says,

> There are, however, some surprising omissions of details. When Jewish feast [sic] are named, their ceremonies are not described, even when they provide the themes of discourses or are pertinent to details in the narrative. For example, of the features which link the sacrifice of the Passover lamb and Jesus' death...only the third [failure to break the bones of Jesus' legs] is made explicit (19.36) and the others have to be discovered from Exodus 12.[1]

But is this logic sound? Might it not also be argued that the mention of the feast in the narrative, especially a feast mentioned as often as the Passover is (ten times), would imply that the reader already had sufficient knowledge to make sense of the reference in the narrative context? Davies apparently does not think so. This apparently accounts for why, although the Passover features of the account in ch. 19 are mentioned at least four times in her discussion, she never develops the discussion. For example, with regard to 'Symbolic References to Time' as part of the author's effort to establish focus, as part of her literary treatment Davies does not treat the several significant temporal references to the Passover.[2] She recognizes that the Passover is the single most important feast and that it is correctly mentioned in relation to the chronology of the other feasts (this topic arises when establishing the accuracy of depiction of the various Jewish practices, where Davies refers only to the incidents of ch. 19 in terms of Passover),[3] but fails to see not only its cultural-historical but its symbolic and narrative value. If the above analysis is correct, depiction of Jesus as the Passover lamb and reference to the Passover at crucial junctures in the narrative not only illustrate an accurate depiction of these practices (as Davies asserts), but are crucial markers to point to Jesus' death as representing the death of the Passover lamb. The reader is then well prepared by chs. 2, 6, 11, 13, 15 and 17 to arrive at ch. 19, with its climactic treatment.

Similarly, when dealing with the use of Scripture in the Fourth Gospel, Davies discusses it as a literary phenomenon, but one that she minimizes especially as it relates to the Passover theme. Here she cites

---

1. Davies, *Rhetoric and Reference*, p. 24; see also p. 355.
2. Davies, *Rhetoric and Reference*, p. 24.
3. Davies, *Rhetoric and Reference*, p. 305.

only Zech. 12.10 to claim that it may be based upon the Hebrew text. Then she discusses various figures such as Moses, Elijah and Elisha, as well as a number of topics, in terms of Scripture. She claims that she shows 'how far the motifs, vocabulary, arrangement and genre of the Fourth Gospel are explained by reference to Scripture'.[1] It strikes me as odd that a treatment of these motifs and so on, would neglect the Passover theme, in the light of the evidence of the parallels above. There is the further difficulty that the criteria she sets regarding explicit reference as requisite for understanding a concept cannot be applied to Moses, Elijah and Elisha, since there is nothing more than allusive reference to events in their lives. In neglecting the Passover theme, therefore, Davies has overlooked a motif that she recognizes as historically plausibly represented in the Fourth Gospel and that could enhance literary appreciation of the text. She apparently misses this opportunity because she fails to explore the historical-cultural dimensions to the theme in conjunction with their literary presentation.

Stibbe's volume too could seriously benefit from considering anew the relationship between literary and historical-critical study. Stibbe focuses upon the former, without due regard for the latter. First, in his practical criticism of John 18–19, Stibbe applies what he calls narratology or narrative criticism to John 18–19. In his assessment of previous research, he notes that one of the important contributions in this area could be in the area of theology and Christology, although 'what has been omitted by narrative critics is a careful consideration of the relationship between theological purpose and the narrative form'.[2] Although Stibbe does note several of the details cited above regarding ch. 19 when he affirms that 'The idea of the death of Christ as a paschal sacrifice is therefore one theme in this final act of John's passion narrative',[3] three factors are worth noting. The first is that he does not deal significantly with the Old Testament quotations at Jn 19.36, 37, apart from saying that the fact that Jesus' legs were not broken 'is redolent of Exodus 12.46'.[4] The second is that apart from reference to 1.29 he does not mention any other significance of the Passover theme in the earlier portion of the Gospel, except to note reference to three

---

1.   Davies, *Rhetoric and Reference*, p. 88.
2.   Stibbe, *John as Storyteller*, p. 12.
3.   Stibbe, *John as Storyteller*, p. 15.
4.   Stibbe, *John as Storyteller*, p. 115; cf. p. 19.

Passovers as a number pattern.[1] The third is that he does not deal with the Old Testament fulfilment quotations, brought to their conclusion in the double quotation at 19.36, 37. It would have enhanced his integration of theological and narrative interpretation especially in terms of plot[2] to have noted that reference to Jesus as the Passover lamb comes as the theological or christological culmination of two separate lines of development, including on the one hand the establishment through several key scenes that Jesus is seen by the author as the Passover sacrifice, and on the other hand the fulfilment motif with regard to the Old Testament quotations finalized and summarized in the double quotation at Jesus' death in 19.36, 37. Both of these lines of development are used by the author to structure the narrative pattern of the work, and are used to bring two important theological lines together at the crucial moment of Jesus' death on the cross. This would also enhance Stibbe's discussion of characterization in the Fourth Gospel, a subject he introduces but does not pursue in terms of the Passover theme.[3] Jesus' character, at least as seen and described by the author throughout the Fourth Gospel, is that of the Passover victim, from his first announcement by John to his hanging lifeless on the cross. This provides motivation for a number of the incidents and discourses discussed above. When he offers his practical criticism of John 18–19, and in particular of 19.16b-42, which he labels 'the slaughter of the lamb',[4] Stibbe concentrates upon the flow of blood and water from Jesus' side when discussing the symbolism of the narrative structure, plot and theme.[5] This is not the central image of the Passover theme. Other items mentioned would have enhanced his discussion of symbolism, including especially the explicit quotation of the Old Testament regarding the breaking of the bones of the victim.

Secondly, Stibbe's discussion of genre is essentially a defence of structuralism from the Proppian perspective that concentrates on plot. The theoretical chapter is probably the least convincing in argumentation, since it summarizes the views of others more than outlines an approach to structure. In the applied chapter, Stibbe goes well beyond the text to try to argue for a structural understanding of the Fourth Gospel. This

1.   Stibbe, *John as Storyteller*, p. 17.
2.   Stibbe, *John as Storyteller*, pp. 26-27.
3.   Stibbe, *John as Storyteller*, pp. 24-25.
4.   Stibbe, *John as Storyteller*, p. 113.
5.   Stibbe, *John as Storyteller*, pp. 117-19.

chapter is perhaps the best for illustrating the importance of the consideration of historical factors even in literary exegesis, and more particularly the place of the Old Testament. Using the archetypal approach of Northrop Frye, Stibbe finds in John 18–19 a Dionysian tragedy about Jesus. After a rather weak attempt to justify John as open to analysis using the categories of tragedy,[1] there is an equally problematic exposition of Euripides' *Bacchae*.[2] When applied to John 18–19, the correlations are superficial. This helps Stibbe to realize, or at least to assert, that with the humiliation of Jesus, John

> subverts the conventions of the tragic mythos. As Euripides's play clearly shows, the unrecognized god, at the moment of greatest conflict with the city's authorities, rises up to bring nemesis upon them. In John's story, Jesus allows himself to suffer the punishment which, in literary and in moral terms, the reader regards as belonging to the Jews.[3]

One of the major plot shifts that Stibbe must account for is the movement from Dionysius's being equated with Christ in the first two sections of chs. 18–19, during which he is arrested and then interrogated by Pentheus, as was Jesus by Pilate, to Pentheus's becoming the victim who is killed and equated with Jesus in the third section. Whereas Dionysius is the unrecognized god, just as Jesus is in the Fourth Gospel, it is Pentheus the stubborn and voyeuristic king torn apart by his own mother who is the victim. These parallels simply do not fit. As seen above, it would have been much clearer, and much more easily verified, to have looked to the Old Testament imagery of the Passover sacrifice to establish the character and nature of the events related in the crucial third section of chs. 18–19. Rather than being forced to argue for

---

1. Note his own internal inconsistency. On p. 129 in *John as Storyteller* Stibbe rebuts the argument that a Jewish Gospel cannot be analysed with the categories of Graeco-Roman phenomena by claiming that 'John's gospel is not a pure Jewish work exempt from Greek literary characteristics'. However, on p. 24, Stibbe asserts that two narrative theorists are better than another 'because they are Hebrew narrative theorists', and hence better guides 'for interpreting so markedly Jewish a gospel' as the Fourth Gospel.

2. One of the major problems is that Stibbe takes essentially an uncritical view of Euripides' play, not dealing with any of the many critical problems bound up with its interpretation, including self-reference by the divine protagonist and the issue of who is the tragic hero. There are other historical-critical issues of significance, including the Asian or oriental origins of the Bacchus cult and its relation to Greek religion.

3. Stibbe, *John as Storyteller*, p. 144.

superficial similarities with a king who has lost the sympathy of the audience, as Pentheus has, it would have been easier for Stibbe to have seen the Johannine plot developing out of the theme of Jesus as Passover victim. Instead of the animal sacrificed for the people, Jesus comes as the singular sacrifice who effects forgiveness not only for the sins of the Jewish people but for the sin of the entire world. Stibbe's concluding point, that the author of the Fourth Gospel has subverted his literary tradition, is correct, but this applies better to seeing Jesus as the Passover lamb than seeing him as a Euripidean tragic hero. Whereas the temple cultus was based upon the repeated yearly and ongoing practices of sacrifice, including the Passover, Jesus is depicted by the author of the Fourth Gospel as the victim who by his cleansing of the temple and his death as the Passover victim signals the end of the establishment system.[1]

In his final section,[2] Stibbe is concerned to establish the relationship between history and narrative, tracing the material in the Gospel back to its source, which he believes has a certain inherent narrative quality about it. He rightly begins from the agreed-upon facts of Jesus' death, which are found in all four Gospels, but then turns to some of the points of tension. He attempts to answer (with varying degrees of success) objections raised to the historical narrative quality of various portions of the text. Believing that he has answered these objections satisfactorily, Stibbe sets out what he believes is close to the original source used by the author of the Fourth Gospel, derived from an eyewitness Judaean. Thus John's passion story is derived from an independent tradition, not from the Synoptic Gospels. In this source, it is to be noted, Stibbe includes the double quotation at 19.36 and 37 of Exod. 12.10 (LXX), 46 or Num. 9.12 and Zech. 12.10. However, in another recent analysis, von Wahlde has concluded that this material could not have belonged to the earliest material, but rather to the third stage of redaction, because it contains the beloved disciple's witness.[3] This is not the place to decide this issue, except to say that several of the significant features of the text do demand explanation, and perhaps a redactional tendency is the best one to account for them. The quotations that are cited in vv. 36 and 37

1. U.C. von Wahlde, *The Earliest Version of John's Gospel: Recovering the Gospel of Signs* (Wilmington, DE: Michael Glazier, 1989), p. 149 n. 165.

2. I am not treating Stibbe's sociological approach, since that falls outside of the general concerns of this paper.

3. Von Wahlde, *Earliest Version*, p. 149 n. 165.

are unique to the New Testament, not cited by any other Gospel author in terms of Jesus or his crucifixion. When this is taken in conjunction with the words of John the Baptist at 1.29 and 36 announcing that Jesus is the 'lamb of God, who takes away the sin of the world', again words unique to this Gospel, it makes it increasingly likely that the Passover theme was not part of the earliest narrative-historical material of the Gospel but was instead part of the early interpretation of the events of Jesus' life and death. This then helps us to appreciate rather than detracts from the storyteller's artistry, something Stibbe says that he wishes to take note of.[1] This is what Stibbe says to some extent, when he empha-sizes John's creation and use of what he calls his 'passover plot': 'There are a number of passover allusions in John 18–19 which support the argument that John wants us to see the death of Jesus as the final and sufficient passover sacrifice'.[2] He then lists a number of the features in ch. 19, as well as several of the references to Passover throughout the Gospel. Although he emphasizes the symbolic nature of the time citations, he fails to exploit the use of the Old Testament quotations in terms of bringing the significant plot lines to a convergent conclusion.

Conclusion

This paper has addressed in a specific way the larger issue of how two recent literary-historical treatments of the Fourth Gospel make use of a theme that has usually been addressed from the standpoint of traditional exegesis. The example of the use of the Old Testament fulfilment motif in conjunction with the Passover theme has been utilized in order to give concrete force to the argument. The exegesis, conducted along tradi-tional lines, although sensitive to literary factors, well illustrates that more recent exegetical methods emphasizing literary and literary-historical criteria not only have nothing necessarily to fear from traditional exegesis but can in fact benefit from such investigation. It has been shown, I believe, that the Old Testament fulfilment motif and the Passover theme converge in ch. 19 of the Fourth Gospel, especially in the events of the cross and the final hours of Jesus' life. It is there that he is seen in a final and summative way as the fulfilment of the Old Testament and as the true and perfect Passover lamb. This convergence of concepts, analysed above especially on the basis of evidence drawn from the Old Testament

1.   Stibbe, *John as Storyteller*, p. 189.
2.   Stibbe, *John as Storyteller*, p. 191.

in the light of Jewish religious practice, speaks directly to several literary issues, including plot, character and motivation. When both literary and historical factors are considered, it seems that an important theme and motif—ones not fully explicated in terms of the force that they have throughout the Gospel—can be appreciated.

THE QUOTATION OF SCRIPTURE
AND UNBELIEF IN JOHN 12.36B-43

John Painter

Quotation Formulae and Text

In John there are seventeen uses of scripture quotation formulae (1.23; 2.17; 6.31, 45; 7.38, 42; 10.34; 12.14-15, 38, 39-41; 13.18; 15.25; 17.12; 19.24, 28, 36, 37) and one identifiable quotation (by the crowd) without quotation formula (12.13). Of these formulae, three quotations cannot be identified with a known scriptural passage (7.38-39; 17.12; 19.28) and one saying is a general appeal to Scripture without being an actual quotation (7.42). In addition there are three appeals to Scripture which do not use quotation formulae and do not involve actual quotations (1.45; 5.39, 46). Normally the person quoting Scripture identifies it as such by the quotation formula; so John the Baptist (1.23); the crowd or part of it (6.31; 7.42; 12.13); Jesus (6.45; 7.38-39; 10.34; 13.18; 15.25; 17.12); the narrator (2.17; 12.14-15, 38, 39-41; 19.24, 36, 37); but on one occasion the narrator identifies the word of Jesus (Διψῶ) as the fulfillment of the Scripture (19.28). In this way a profound interpretation is given to what otherwise could be understood as very ordinary events. The only book mentioned by name is that of the prophet Isaiah (1.23; 12.38, 39, 41),[1] though the law (1.45; 10.34; 15.25) and the prophets are mentioned collectively (1.45; 6.45) and together in 1.45. Frequently the appeal is to what is written (γεγραμμένον, 2.17; 6.31; 12.14) and this can be combined with reference to the law (10.34; 15.25), or the prophets (6.45). Appeal is also made to the Scripture (ἡ γραφή, 7.38, 42; 13.18; 17.12; 19.24, 28, 37). Quotations of Scripture are used to

---

1. In 12.38, 40 (41) it is the narrator who quotes Isa. 53.1 and 6.10 while in 1.23 John the Baptist quotes Isa. 40.3, though these words are the words of the narrator in the Synoptics. This sparing use of the specific quotation of a book might suggest that the context of Isaiah is significant for the use of the quotations in Jn 12.

establish controversial positions such as the role of John the Baptist as witness to Jesus and the messiahship of Jesus.

The fulfillment formula, 'that the Scripture may be fulfilled', or some variation (ἵνα πληρωθῇ, 12.38; 13.18; 15.25; 17.12; 19.24, 36; ἵνα τελειωθῇ, 19.28), most clearly demonstrates the apologetic intention in John's use of Scripture quotation which exemplifies the *pesher* method widely known to us from the Qumran texts.[1] In such interpretation what is spoken of in Scripture is declared to be fulfilled in current events. In the farewell and passion story Jesus uses the formula to introduce quotations (Jn 13.18; 15.25; 17.12), as does the narrator in the passion story (Jn 19.24, 28, 36, 37) and in a more expanded form concerning general unbelief, identifying the word of the prophet Isaiah (12.38). The fulfillment formula in 12.38 refers not so much to the quotation in 12.38 as to the quotation in 12.40.[2]

In John those events most damaging to the cause the Evangelist wished to promote are explicitly shown to be fulfillments of Scripture. The two most troublesome events[3] to be accounted for are the unbelief of the Jews and the rejection and crucifixion of Jesus. The rejection of Jesus is shown to be foretold, not only in a general sense but in terms of detailed fulfillment, including his betrayal by Judas, and the fulfillment formulae are concentrated in the account of these events. Indeed, of the seven remaining quotations beginning with 13.18,[4] which predicts the scandalous betrayal of Jesus by Judas, only 19.37 does not use a fulfillment formula, and its predictive nature, using the future tense (ὄψονται) from Zechariah, makes clear that we are here dealing with fulfillment in the events of the crucifixion, so that the verse is covered by the fulfillment formula of 19.36. The unbelief of the Jews is also shown to be the fulfillment of Scripture. This means that all nine quotations from Jn 12.38 are *specifically* presented as Scriptures fulfilled in

---

1. See B. Lindars, *New Testament Apologetic: The Doctrinal Significance of the Old Testament Quotations* (London: SCM Press, 1961), esp. pp. 15-17, 266-70.

2. The application of the fulfillment formula of 12.38 to 12.40 is the subject of further discussion below.

3. Indeed these could be viewed as two aspects of the same event because John portrays the rejection and crucifixion of Jesus as an expression of the unbelief of the Jews. But the unbelief of the Jews has ongoing consequences for the Johannine community and is singled out for special attention (9.22; 12.36b-43; 16.2; 20.19).

4. The focus of predictive statements on this event shows how scandalous it was for the Evangelist and his readers; see Jn 6.64, 71; 13.11, 18; 17.12.

the events narrated.[1] Given that the unbelief of the Jews is the underlying cause of the rejection of Jesus and that the crucifixion is the
epitome of unbelief, the unbelief of the Jews constitutes the primary
scandal for the Evangelist, and this theme is to be my focus.

The text used by the Evangelist in his quotation of Scripture has been
examined carefully in the major commentaries[2] and in the monograph
by E.D. Freed.[3] My concern is concentrated on the quotations in Jn
12.38, 40.[4] The quotation in 12.38 is identical in wording with the LXX.
The opening word (κύριε) has no basis in the Hebrew text, confirming
that John drew here on the LXX. Determining whether the Hebrew or
LXX provided the quotation of Isa. 6.10 in Jn 12.40 is more complex
because here John agrees with no known form of Isaiah, differing quite
radically from the Hebrew, the LXX, the Targums, and other quotations of
this text in the New Testament. The exact quotation in Jn 12.38 suggests
that the freedom of quotation in 12.40 manifests deliberate modifications
by the Evangelist in the interest of expressing his chosen meaning.[5]

Interpretations of Isaiah and Unbelief in John

The problem in view in Jn 12.37-40 is this: why was unbelief the response
to the many signs performed by Jesus and why did the Evangelist make

1.   Fulfillment can be asserted in the mere quotation of Scripture without
fulfillment formula, as it is in 12.14-15. That being the case the cluster of fulfillment
formulae from 12.38 on might indicate a special cluster of *testimonia*, such as was
suggested by Rendel Harris (*Testimonies* [2 vols.; Cambridge: Cambridge University
Press, 1916–1920], esp. I, p. 18). Alternatively it can be argued that the apologetic
motif is more strongly asserted in these texts through the explicit use of fulfillment
formulae and this indeed seems to be the case.

2.   See especially C.K. Barrett, *The Gospel according to St John* (London:
SPCK; Philadelphia: Westminster Press, 2nd edn, 1978); R.E. Brown, *The Gospel
according to John* (AB, 29, 29a; 2 vols.; Garden City, NY: Doubleday, 1966–70);
R. Schnackenburg, *The Gospel according to St John* (3 vols.; repr.; New York:
Crossroad, 1987 [1980]).

3.   *Old Testament Quotations in the Gospel of John* (NovTSup, 11; Leiden: Brill,
1965), pp. 82-130.

4.   On these texts, see also C.A. Evans, *To See and Not Perceive: Isaiah 6.9-10
in Early Jewish and Christian Interpretation* (JSOTSup, 64; Sheffield: JSOT Press,
1991), esp. pp. 129-35.

5.   R. Schnackenburg (*John*, II, p. 415) rightly notes that 'The analysis shows
clearly that the form of the quotation derives from no-one but the evangelist, who has
tailored the text for his purposes'.

use of Isa. 53.1 with 6.10 in dealing with this problem? In response to the second part of this question Evans has argued 'that the evangelist was aware of the vocabulary common to both Isaianic passages (i.e., 6.1-13 and 52.13–53.12)'.[1] He refers particularly to the use of ὑψοῦν and δοξάζειν. There may be something in this but the evidence is not convincing. The reference to 'the arm of the Lord' is appropriately identified with the signs of Jesus but it is the question 'Who has *believed*…?' that suggests the use of Isa. 53.1 in the context of the discussion of unbelief in response to the signs. This crucial Johannine term is missing from the key passage in Isaiah 6 but is used in Isa. 53.1.

The long-prevailing view is that, in the quotation of Isa. 6.10, John (12.40) has given expression to a predestinarian view, attributing the unbelief of Israel or the Jews to the purpose and activity of God. Commentators on Jn 12.40 are virtually unanimous that 'God is . . . the author of the blindness';[2] 'God is expressly called the author of hardening'.[3] Thus C.K. Barrett has written:[4] 'Signs do not suffice if God does not give men eyes to see…It can hardly be questioned that John meant that the hardening of Israel was intended by God'.[5] While this statement falls short of affirming a predestinarian point of view, it was clearly intended in this sense and this is soon confirmed: 'The divine predestination works through human moral choices, for which men are morally responsible'.

The treatment of Craig Evans falls short of clearly affirming a predestinarian point of view but probably was intended to convey this meaning:

> The evangelist then cites LXX Isa. 53.1 verbatim implying that Jewish unbelief was predicted in the scriptures. However, according to vv. 39-40 this unbelief is not only predicted, but is actually produced by

1. Evans, *To See and Not Perceive*, p. 133.
2. W. Schrage, *TDNT*, VIII, p. 292.
3. K.L. Schmidt and M.A. Schmidt, 'σκληρόω, κτλ', *TDNT*, V, p. 1026.
4. *St John*, pp. 430-31.
5. For 'intended' we could substitute 'predestined'. To illuminate the discussion Barrett (*St John*, p. 430) calls attention to the appendix on predestination in Schnackenburg, *John*, II, pp. 259-74. There Schnackenburg argues that 'A predestination of those who belong to Jesus and his community of faith is unmistakable' (p. 264). With regard to Jn 12.40 Schnackenburg argues that the Evangelist has altered the wording so that 'the action of God is more strongly emphasized' (p. 271). So it is argued that the 'Jewish rejection of God…leads into the mystery of the divine decree' (p. 274).

God:... 'He [God] has blinded their eyes...' The telic force of the Isa. 6.10 quotation is plainly evident...Jesus' signs result in obduracy because that is what the scriptures predict and what God makes happen.[1]

E.D. Freed explicitly asserts that 'Their unbelief is explained as predestined by God himself and fulfills what Isaiah had prophesied concerning Jesus'.[2]

Yet some of those who adopt a predestinarian view qualify this in various ways. Schnackenburg is at pains to emphasize that it is a puzzle that the divine decree 'does not remove the obscurity of human guilt'.[3] This same point was emphasized by Barrett and it is featured at length in Schnackenburg's Excursus, 'Personal Commitment, Personal Responsibility, Predestination and Hardening'. Here Schnackenburg treats the case of Judas and notes that with

> the remark that Satan entered into Judas (13.27; cf. 13.2), the traitor becomes an unhappy figure, who seems to be burdened by a 'doom', a destiny waiting for him particularly. On the other hand, John suspects him of a moral defect: he is a 'thief' who embezzles the money from the common fund (12.6). The area of darkness between being chosen and being rejected has not been reduced.[4]

Barrett is also aware that any understanding of predestination in John must be nuanced if it is to be adequate and warns:

> That on the other hand his [the evangelist's] words were not the cut and dried statement of a philosophical theology appears at once from the exceptions immediately introduced at v. 42 (ὅμως μέντοι), and indeed the existence of Jewish Christians, such as Peter and the beloved disciple.[5]

The qualifications of Barrett and Schnackenburg are enough to make the reader aware that it is far from clear precisely what is asserted by those writers who conclude that Isaiah and John teach that unbelief was caused by God. To say that such unbelief was predestined by God implies that there is no anterior cause lying behind the decree of God. Although Schnackenburg and Barrett use the language of predestination of both believers and unbelievers they are reluctant to remove the human moral responsibility for belief or unbelief. Barrett agrees with

---

1. *To See and Not Perceive*, pp. 132, 135, and see pp. 130, 132-35.
2. *Quotations*, p. 84, and see pp. 84-88, 122.
3. *John*, II, p. 274.
4. *John*, II, p. 263.
5. *St John*, p. 431.

Schnackenburg and quotes E.C. Hoskyns to the effect that the changes to the quotation of Isa. 6.10 in Jn 12.40 'are best explained by the intention of the writer of the gospel to emphasize the judgment as the action of God'.[1] To set this action in the context of the judgement of God implies that God is already responding to the human reality! Thus we have, hidden within the statements of those who assert that the unbelief of Jn 12.39-40 was caused by God, two quite different positions: (1) there is no anterior cause than the decree of God; and (2) God's action is already to be seen as his judgment as a response to human reality.

Following Schnackenburg's treatment of moral responsibility is a discussion of the most dualistic passage in John, where there is a division of people into two classes, those who belong to Jesus and those under the influence of God's opponent. Even here, however, Schnackenburg's interest is to show 'that, even in this descent from the devil, the moral aspect dominates. Such people *show* themselves by their behaviour to be such as are not "of God"'. He goes on to say:

> As in the idea of hardening in 12.39, so too here we have the hard saying 'You cannot hear my word'... and the immediate reason given is their descent from the devil, but in the same breath Jesus says 'and your will is to do your father's desires' (vv. 43-44). Are these desires in them because their father is the devil, or is the statement just deduced from their behaviour and not meant so literally? The previous train of thought... tells decisively in favour of the second.

Clearly Schnackenburg's primary aim is to show that deterministic language does not exclude moral responsibility. He concludes that the argument of two lines of descent does not signify

> an unavoidable fate, since they are not released from responsibility for their actions... An ordinance from all eternity, under which God divided people in advance into two classes, good and evil, chosen and rejected, is never even mentioned in John, though it cannot be denied that we are brought very close to the edge of such an idea.[2]

Schnackenburg does not seem to be aware that in bringing together a discussion of Jn 8.38-47 and 12.36b-42 he has raised another issue. He treats the dualistic material as if it were straightforwardly an example of the problem of predestination and fails to recognize that these passages

---

1. *St John*, p. 431, citing E.C. Hoskyns, *The Fourth Gospel* (ed. F.N. Davey; 2 vols.; London: Faber & Faber, 2nd edn, 1947), II, p. 502.

2. *John*, II, p. 264.

raise the question of whether the cause of the failure to hear in John 8 is not also the cause of blinding in Jn 12.40. When treating Jn 12.40 he says categorically,

> Of a reference to the devil as agent there is no sign at all; neither in 8.44, where non-believers are regarded as children of the devil because of their lusts, nor in the more closely related reference to the overthrow of the ruler of this world in 12.31 is any such activity ascribed to God's opponent.[1]

Schnackenburg gives too little weight to the fact that Jesus has told the Jews that they are children of the devil in a way that implies that this is the explanation of their failure to hear his word, Jn 8.43-44. That this understanding was implied by their failure to believe does not reduce its force or destroy its meaning. The force of the implication arises from the struggle to explain the origin of unbelief, which may have no other evidence to support it than unbelief itself and the circumstances in which it was expressed. Those circumstances include the tradition within which the unbelief is evaluated and the rejection experienced by the Johannine community, which is understood to be in continuity with the rejection of Jesus. A number of other difficult problems are obscured by Schnackenburg's discussion. In particular he has failed to take seriously the influence of the power of evil in determining human destiny.

Various alternatives need to be examined in the light of this discussion and John's modifications to Isa. 6.10. Those modifications necessitate distinguishing the cause of obduracy from the agent of healing. The alternatives can be set out as follows:

1. God has blinded the eyes of the Jews so that they are unable to believe and Jesus cannot heal them.
2. The prophet has blinded their eyes so that they are unable to believe and Jesus cannot heal them.
3. The Evangelist or his Gospel has caused blindness so that God or Jesus cannot heal them.
4. Jesus has blinded their eyes so that they are unable to believe and God cannot heal them.
5. The signs have blinded their eyes so that they are unable to believe and Jesus cannot heal them.
6. The prince of this world, the power of darkness, has blinded their eyes so that they are unable to believe and Jesus cannot heal them.

---

1.   *John*, II, p. 416.

1. The prevailing interpretation of Jn 12.40 needs to be modified in the light of John's changes to the wording of Isa. 6.10. In the Masoretic Text of Isa. 6.10 it is God who instructs the prophet to be an instrument of 'obduracy' and the change to the first person singular future indicative active (καὶ ἰάσομαι αὐτούς) in the LXX probably does not change the sense of the 'divine' passive of the Hebrew because God is the speaker and therefore the one who would heal. Consequently it is correct to say that God is both the cause of obduracy and the one who would heal. But in Isaiah it could hardly be said that the obduracy was predestined. It is rather the consequence of the judgment of God in response to faithlessness. In John, however, the cause of obduracy is expressed by verbs in the third person singular while the speaker is the one who would heal, as is shown by the use of the first person singular. As, it seems, God (or the pre-existent Jesus)[1] is the speaker, he cannot be the cause of obduracy. If the pre-existent Jesus is the speaker it is linguistically possible that God could be the cause of hardening, but this would strain the Johannine view that God and Jesus act as one.

2. Given that in Isaiah God commands the prophet to perform this task, could it be that the prophet is the cause of obduracy while God is the one who would heal the people? Against this interpretation, however, is the recognition that it would be strange if the prophet were made to speak of himself as 'he' because in 12.41 the narrator specifically notes that Isaiah spoke these words when he saw his (Jesus') glory. More seriously, the blinding work of the prophet does not provide any explanation of why the Jews failed to believe in response to the signs of Jesus.

3. Although the Evangelist has introduced the conflict of his own situation into the telling of the story of Jesus, as J.L. Martyn has shown, it is unlikely that he or his Gospel is thought to be the cause of blindness. This would not explain why the response to Jesus' signs was unbelief or why the Evangelist's account of the signs of Jesus in the Gospel was written to produce belief (Jn 20.30-31), and he would hardly write of himself as 'he'.

4. Given that in Jn 12.36b-37 the Evangelist is writing in the third person singular of the activity of Jesus it is possible that it is Jesus who 'has blinded their eyes and has hardened their heart', and that the

---

1. The narrator notes (Jn 12.41) that Isaiah spoke these words when he saw his glory. Naturally to speak of Jesus as pre-existent is misleading but Jesus in John assumes a continuity of identity in the 'I am' of Jn 8.58. But the name 'Jesus' presupposes the λόγος made flesh.

change to the third person singular perfect indicative active was to make this sense possible. But this interpretation sets Jesus in opposition to God, who would heal. It could be argued that Jesus, like the prophet, was fulfilling the purpose of God in producing obduracy. But the Johannine form of the text emphasizes the conflicting activity of blinding and healing that would, in a way uncharacteristic of John, formally set Jesus in opposition to God. According to Jn 12.41, however, the pre-existent Jesus is the speaker, so that the 'I will heal them' of 12.40 is spoken by him. Thus he cannot be the one who has blinded them.

5. Evans argues that the fulfillment formula (Jn 12.38) shows that (according to John) the unbelief in response to Jesus' signs (12.37) was prophesied, and 'according to vv. 39-40 this unbelief is not only predicted, but is actually produced by God',[1] using the signs of Jesus to cause the obduracy which resulted in unbelief.[2] That the unbelief was prophesied is soundly argued on the basis of the fulfillment formula in Jn 12.38, but Evans is mistaken in thinking that the fulfillment formula there refers specifically and exclusively to the quotation of Isa 53.1. All that this quotation does is to introduce the question concerning *belief*. It does not predict unbelief. Rather the theme of unbelief is introduced in Jn 12.39 and the cause of this is set out in the quotation of Isa. 6.10 in Jn 12.40. Thus it seems that the fulfillment formula of Jn 12.38 refers specifically to the text quoted in 12.40, while the quotation of Isa. 53.1 introduces the vocabulary of belief not found in Isa. 6.10. Evans argues that the cause of obduracy is complex because the signs were used to fulfil the purpose of God.

It could be argued that the signs[3] have caused blindness so that God or Jesus could or would not heal the Jews. The tradition of Deut. 29.2-4 could be thought to support this view:[4] 'You have seen all that the Lord did before your eyes in the Land of Egypt…the signs (LXX σημεῖα)… but to this day the Lord has not given you a mind to understand, or eyes to see, or ears to hear'. But this interpretation also has its problems. In Deuteronomy it is not the signs of Moses that produced obduracy but God who withholds the understanding. An alternative argument to support the view that the signs are the cause of blindness is that, if in Isaiah the prophet's activity causes the hardening, and in Mark 4 the

---

1. *To See and Not Perceive*, p. 132.
2. *To See and Not Perceive*, p. 135.
3. The neuter plural σημεῖα takes a singular verb.
4. Thus Evans, *To See and Not Perceive*, p. 135.

parables are the instruments used to cause blindness, in John 12 it is the signs themselves that perform this function and were intended to do so. But the question raised by 12.39 is why the people failed to believe *in spite of the signs*. According to John, the signs made the failure to believe the more surprising and reprehensible because the signs were the most obvious basis for belief (10.38). If the question is 'Why did the signs not lead to belief?', the answer that the signs blinded those before whom they were performed hardly seems to be an adequate answer. That God blinded them to the signs would make sense except that such a reading is made less likely by the changes the Evangelist has made to the text he has quoted.

Views 1–5 generally assume a predestinarian point of view. In Isaiah, however, the activity of the prophet is the instrument of the judgment of God in response to faithless Judah. Consequently the action of the prophet is not to be understood in the normal predestinarian sense because that action is already a response to faithlessness. The same can be argued of the use of the quotation in relation to the parables of Jesus in Mark 4. There the disciples are given 'to know the mystery' while those 'outside' (τοῖς ἔξω) are not. For them the parables do not bring perception and understanding. This falls short of asserting that the outsiders have been so determined. Their outside position is a manifestation of faithlessness and for them the parables have become instruments of judgment. But for the disciples Jesus expounds the meaning of the parables. The quotation of Isa. 6.10 in Jn 12.40 can be understood along similar lines. The signs offer the opportunity for outsiders to become insiders. For those who remain outside the signs become instruments of judgment. It may be that in John the status of outsiders remains for those who, although they believe on the basis of the signs, refuse to confess this openly. For them the signs become signs of judgment causing spiritual blindness and hardness of heart. While this view has much to commend it, and evidence to support it can be gathered from the Gospel, there is contrary evidence[1] and a more persuasive alternative can be suggested.

---

1.   Evans (*To See and Not Perceive*, p. 135) argues that 'in John it is Jesus' ministry of signs' that brings about the blindness. He notes, however, 'that John does not say that Jesus' signs actually cause obduracy. He only states that Jesus' signs result in obduracy because that is what the scriptures predict and what God makes happen.' But surely this is incorrect. If the question is 'why did they not believe on the basis of the signs?' it is the obduracy that prevents belief. The statement of Jn

6. The case for seeing the cause of unbelief in response to the signs of Jesus to be the power of darkness has not been given adequate attention. For example, Schnackenburg argues that John 'attributes the blinding and hardening to God directly and without disguise. Of a reference to the devil as agent there is no sign at all.'[1] This is hardly an adequate exploration, but at least Schnackenburg mentions this possibility, if only to dismiss it instantly as do both Walter Bauer and Rudolf Bultmann who simply insert in parentheses 'not the devil' and give as reference for this view Cyril of Alexandria.[2] It is not considered at all by most commentators.

The Power of Darkness

There are several lines of evidence in support of this view not considered by Schnackenburg or others who dismiss the view:

1. The context in John
2. The evangelist's changes: to the tense, person and voice of the verbs in the text quoted; by omission or use of alternative language
3. The comparative relevance of the dualistic worldview of first-century Judaism
4. The support of Clement of Alexandria and Origen.

12.37 (indicating that in spite of the signs they did not believe) is somewhat absurd if it is the signs that cause obduracy, thus causing unbelief. If the signs are the cause of unbelief the statement should read that they did not believe *because* Jesus had done so many signs in their presence. Other contrary evidence will be set out below.

1. *John*, II, p. 416.
2. W. Bauer, *Das Johannesevangelium* (Tübingen: Mohr, 1933), p. 165; R. Bultmann, *The Gospel of John* (Oxford: Basil Blackwell, 1971), p. 453 n. 2. R.L. Tyler ('The Source and Function of Isaiah 6.9-10 in John 12.40', in J.E. Priest [ed.], *Johannine Studies: Essays in Honor of Frank Pack* [Malibu, CA: Pepperdine University Press, 1989], p. 207 n. 4) wrongly attributes Bultmann's reference to Cyril of Jerusalem. He also criticizes my earlier presentation of the case for interpreting Jn 12.40 in reference to the devil (*John: Witness and Theologian* [London: SPCK, 1975], pp. 74-76) on the grounds that the question of which text John used is not dealt with and the acceptance of the dualistic interpretation is not necessary. But discussion of which text John used does not help because John used neither LXX nor any known Hebrew text, and most scholars agree that John is responsible for the changes. While the interpretation might not be strictly necessary, it takes the changes seriously. If John did not want to change the meaning, why did he change the reading of the text?

The Context in John

Macro-Context. The quotations (12.38, 40) fall in a passage (Jn 12.36b-43) dealing with unbelief which provides a summary conclusion to the 'public ministry' of Jesus (Jn 1–12). The summary passage, understood in isolation, gives the impression of the failure of Jesus' mission even though this is qualified in a somewhat paradoxical way. The qualification puts in question the impression of failure, as does a study of the context. It is then apparent that the summary is a transition to the passion narrative.

The more immediate context is John 11–12. John 11 features the sign of the raising of Lazarus and its consequences. The immediate consequence of the raising of Lazarus is stated in 11.45-46: 'Therefore many of the Jews coming to Mary and seeing what he did believed in him; but certain of them went to the Pharisees and told them what Jesus did'. What is described here is a divided response[1] to the sign of the raising of Lazarus, though the stress is on the consequent belief which is stated first, is the response of 'many' (πολλοὶ) and is re-emphasized by restatement in 12.11. Overwhelming belief in response to the signs of Jesus, especially the raising of Lazarus, is stressed in what follows. But if many believed, some of the Jews who saw what Jesus did reported this to the Pharisees and a council meeting was convened to respond to the question: 'What shall we do because this man does many signs? If we permit him [to go on in] this way all will believe in him' (11.47-48).[2] The result was a 'plot' to put Jesus to death (11.53). Consequently Jesus was not able to go about openly, although the crowd going up to Jerusalem for Passover were seeking (ἐζήτουν) him and questioned whether he would appear at the feast in the light of the decision to arrest him (11.54-57). The impression is of overwhelming belief in Jesus in response to the sign of the raising of Lazarus but also of a determined plot to arrest and execute him by the powerful minority associated with the Sanhedrin. These opponents were blind to the significance of the

---

1. While the 'some of them' (τινὲς δὲ ἐξ αὐτῶν), who went to the Pharisees in 11.46, could refer to those of the Jews who believed, that is, some of those who believed, it is more likely that it refers directly to the Jews. Many of the Jews who saw what he did believed; some of the Jews who saw what he did (an implied minority) went to the Pharisees.

2. It could be argued that recognition of the signs performed by Jesus without acknowledging belief in him turns the signs into signs of judgment. But Jesus' opponents were also capable of denying the actuality of his signs (9.18).

signs except that they saw in the one who performed them a threat to the survival of the nation as it was.

In the account of the anointing at Bethany (12.1-8) many of the features of the Synoptic accounts appear. What was an independent tradition (see Mt. 26.6-13 and Mk 14.3-9) has been caught up into the saga concerning Lazarus by locating the event in the presence (perhaps at the house of) Lazarus, Martha and Mary and by naming Mary as the the woman who anointed Jesus. Distinctively, John has Mary anoint the feet of Jesus rather than his head, thus suggesting a parallel with the washing of the disciples' feet in Jn 13.1-20.[1] That parallel is to be set alongside the raising of Lazarus and the resurrection of Jesus. The anointing in John keeps Lazarus in the picture and the narrator reminds the readers that the great crowd of the Jews had come out not only on account of Jesus but also to see Lazarus and that through him many of the Jews believed in Jesus. Consequently the plot was not only to kill Jesus but Lazarus also (12.9-11; cf.11.53, 57). Again overwhelming belief is portrayed as the response to the sign of the raising of Lazarus, but with a powerful minority determined to kill not only Jesus but Lazarus also.

Apparently the anointing was followed ('on the next day') by Jesus' entry into Jerusalem (12.12-19). The great crowd (12.9, 12) that came out from Jerusalem is thus portrayed as those who have come to believe, especially through hearing of the *sign* of the raising of Lazarus from the crowd that had been present at the time and had borne witness to it (12.17-18). As Matthew does, John makes use of Ps. 118.25-26 and Zech. 9.9,[2] though the order of quotation is reversed and Zech. 9.9 is used in a more abbreviated form. Characteristically, in John the narrator turns the significance of this event to the benefit of the disciples.[3] Although they did not understand the event at the time, when Jesus was glorified they remembered that these things were written of him and done to him (12.16 and cf. Jn 2.22). Yet the incident returns to the

---

1. Mary is here portrayed as the ideal disciple, doing for Jesus what in Jn 13 Jesus calls on his disciples to do for each other. Given that Mary, along with Martha and Lazarus, is said to be loved (ἠγάπα) by Jesus (Jn 11.5) her role in the anointing and the way this notable event is used to identify the family at Bethany is as strong a basis (from within the Gospel itself) for identifying her with the beloved disciple as there is for so identifying anyone alse.

2. Mark and Luke make use only of Ps. 118.

3. Compare Jn 2.11, 22.

perspective of the crowd and the assessment of the Pharisees that 'the world has gone out after him' (12.17-19). That assessment recalls the basis of the decision to arrest and kill Jesus. It is because, unless he is prevented from continuing as he is, all will believe in him with catastrophic consequences (11.48).

The assessment that 'the world has gone out after him', already evidenced in the crowd that went out to meet him, is further verified by the coming of the Greeks seeking Jesus (12.20-26). Their coming, with the request to see Jesus, is the signal for Jesus to announce that 'The hour has come for the Son of Man to be glorified' and to enunciate the principle of abundant life only through death, which would be demonstrated in his own death which, like 'the footwashing', was to be the paradigm for the lives of his disciples. In what follows (12.27-36a) Jesus and the narrator explore the significance of the hour that has now arrived. It is the hour of death and glorification at the same time (12.27-28). It is also the hour of the judgment of this world and the casting out of the prince of this world (12.31). Having spoken of his death in terms of glorification and judgment Jesus now speaks conditionally: 'if I am lifted up (ἐὰν ὑψωθῶ) I will draw all people to myself' (12.32). The narrator informs the readers that this is an image of the manner of Jesus' death (12.33). At this point the crowd is reintroduced and they note that Jesus has referred to his death as a departure. This is used as an objection to the messianic interpretation of the Son of Man.[1] Jesus' response is to change the idiom to the transitory presence of the light which creates the possibility of the people's leaving the darkness and, by believing in the light, becoming 'sons of light' (12.35-36a). Thus, in the passage immediately preceding the use of the quotations dealing with unbelief, Jesus has spoken of (1) the coming of the hour as the time of the judgment of this world and the casting out of the prince of this world; (2) the consequence of his own being lifted up as the moment of drawing all people to himself; and (3) the presence of the light as the time of the opportunity for belief. To this we can add the reiterated motif running through John 11–12 that the majority openly believed on the basis of the sign of the raising of Lazarus, and it is this widespread

---

1.   The crowd assumes that Jesus' 'I' saying can be transposed into a Son of Man saying, that 'Son of Man' is a messianic designation, and that 'lifting up' refers to Jesus' death as departure. The last point is particularly surprising because the reader has to be informed of this meaning by the narrator, who does not normally supply information that is known to the characters in the story (apart from Jesus).

open belief which causes the powerful minority to plot the death of Jesus and that of Lazarus as well.

The public ministry of Jesus concludes (Jn 12.44-50) with his solemn call (ἔκραξεν καὶ εἶπεν) to believe in him as the one sent by the Father. He returns to the image of the light coming into the world so that every one who believes in him should not remain in the darkness. Consequently 12.36b-43 is framed on either side by the call to believe in Jesus as the light and as the only way to be delivered from the darkness (12.35-36a, 44-46). Thus 12.36b-43 occurs in the context of the theme of the conflict of the light and the darkness.

Micro-Context. When Jesus called on his hearers to believe in the light that they might become sons of light the narrator surprisingly indicates (12.36b) that Jesus hid himself from them. Those from whom he hid seem to be the many who believed through the sign of the raising of Lazarus (11.45, 47-48; 12.11, 17-18) and the Greeks who came seeking him (12.20-26). In the background is the plot to arrest Jesus and put him to death (11.46-53, 55-57). The motif of Jesus' hiding himself must recall this, as is confirmed by Jn 12.37, which asserts: 'But although he had done so many signs (τοσαῦτα δὲ αὐτοῦ σημεῖα) in their presence they did not believe in him'. This ignores the dominant motif running through Jn 11.1–12.36a, which is the belief of the many. Now it is asserted that unbelief was the response to Jesus' ministry in spite of the signs. The quotations from Isaiah are then given to support this conclusion.

First, Isa. 53.1 is introduced by a fulfillment quotation formula:[1] 'In order that the word of Isaiah the prophet might be fulfilled which he said, "Lord, who has believed our report? And to whom is the arm of the Lord revealed?"' It is sometimes argued that the 'report' is to be understood as the teaching of Jesus and that 'the arm of the Lord' refers to the divine action in the signs of Jesus.[2] But appeal to the words of Jesus makes little sense at this point, since it is clear that they consti-tute a more serious stumbling block for belief than the signs (or *works,* as Jesus refers to them, 10.38), and the quotation formula identifies this

---

1. The fulness of this formula should be compared with Jn 15.25. Lindars (*Apologetic,* pp. 266-70) rightly identifies the application of this text from the past to what was for John the events of the present as *pesher* interpretation, now commonly known to us in the texts from Qumran.

2. Thus Barrett, *St John,* p. 431, and Freed, *Quotations,* pp. 84-85.

saying as the word of the prophet Isaiah, who refers to 'our report'. Consequently it is more likely that here reference is only to the signs of Jesus, specifically referred to in Jn 12.37, and indirectly in 12.38 as 'the arm of the Lord'. While the saying is introduced by a fulfillment quotation formula there is nothing to be fulfilled in the question of 12.38. It has been used because it specifically raises the question 'who has *believed*?' The subject under discussion, introduced in 12.37, is the failure to *believe* in spite of the signs. The question, 'and to whom is the arm of the Lord revealed?', understood in relation to the signs, asks who has perceived the signs as the saving acts of God. Failure to perceive them as such is the basis of unbelief. But how could they fail to perceive in the signs of Jesus, done before their very eyes, the arm of the Lord in action?

Jn 12.39-41 goes further than 12.37, which simply states that 'they did not believe'. Now it is said that 'Because of this (διὰ τοῦτο) they *could not* believe, because (ὅτι) again Isaiah said...' The initial 'Because of this' may seem to look back to the quotation of Isa. 53.1 but we have seen that this quotation gives no explanation for the unbelief in the face of Jesus' signs. Rather the διὰ τοῦτο is taken up in the ὅτι clause, 'because again Isaiah said'. Thus the failure to believe is actually taken up in the quotation of Isa. 6.10 (in Jn 12.40) which provides the reason why they could not believe.[1] At this point John was wrestling with the reality of the unbelief of the Jews. Some consolation may be found in the recognition that Isaiah provides evidence that they could not believe. Isa. 6.10 does not, however, refer to belief. Rather, as we have seen, John introduces the theme of belief by quoting Isa. 53.1 in association with Isa. 6.10. Blind eyes and hardened hearts made it impossible to see the signs and consequently made belief impossible. The narrator asserts (12.41) that the glory of the pre-existent Jesus (λόγος) was seen by Isaiah (cf. Abraham in Jn 8.56) who thus bore witness to Jesus. Thus the context of Isaiah is important as the paradigm for understanding what was happening in the Evangelist's day. Just as the witness of the prophet to the glory of the eternal λόγος was met with unbelief, so was the witness of the Evangelist to the glory of the incarnate λόγος. Unbelief in the Evangelist's day is interwoven with the theme of unbelief in response to the signs of Jesus, giving the impression that this was the pervasive response in Jesus' day.

1.   Thus the fulfillment formula of Jn 12.38 applies more to the quotation of 12.40 than 12.38.

In spite of this[1] John goes on to assert that 'many of the rulers believed in' Jesus (12.42), apparently contradicting, or at least qualifying 12.37, 39. The qualification reflects a return to the perspective of Jesus' ministry, where the response of belief was common. Even this is qualified by the shadow of the later situation and it is noted that they did not *confess* that belief openly because they did not wish to be cast out of the synagogue, putting in question the validity of that belief, though John does not hesitate to say of these rulers that 'they believed in him [Jesus]'. Here fear (cf. Jn 9.22) is not said to inhibit the confession of faith but love of 'the praise of men' rather than praise from God (Jn 12.43). In a sense we have here an artificial alternative, because the rulers who had believed feared the power of the Pharisees who could have them cast out of the synagogue. The explanation that they preferred 'the praise of men' gives the basis for their unmentioned fear. They feared the loss of 'praise from men'. These rulers are said to have believed but the Evangelist qualified this by indicating they were unwilling to confess their belief openly. There is no doubt that they are presented as believers because they are made an exception (ὅμως μέντοι) to the assertion that 'they were not able to believe'.

Qualifying the Obvious. Some qualifications must be made to the assertion that 'they were not able to believe'.

1.   The disciples, who were Jews, are depicted in the process of coming to authentic faith, towards which they move after the passion and resurrection of Jesus.
2.   Immediately before and after this announcement of unbelief Jesus called for belief (Jn 12.35-36a, 44-50), apparently with the expectation that such belief remained a possibility.
3.   Belief appears to be the mass and open response to Jesus as a consequence of the sign of the raising of Lazarus (Jn 11.45-46, 47-48; 12.9-11, 12-19).
4.   Jn 12.42 introduces a heavily qualified (ὅμως μέντοι καὶ) exception to the assertion that 'they were not able to believe': 'Nevertheless however even from among the rulers many believed in him'. True, this belief is then qualified by the indication that these rulers would not confess their faith openly because they preferred 'praise from men' to praise from God.

---

1.   The exceptional nature is brought out by the use of ὅμως μέντοι.

But the Evangelist does not hesitate to say that they 'believed' and he sets out this belief as an exception to the assertion 'they were not able to believe'.

5. John was combining two sets of data: tradition from the ministry of Jesus in which he openly gained a large popular following, and the reality of the situation of his own time in which the Jews not only were not believers but were active opponents of believers. Intimidation was one reason for the reluctance of many to believe openly (9.22; 12.42; 16.2).

If Jesus' activity was aimed at calling forth belief, what, according to John, was it that prevented that belief? In Isa. 6.10 God is thought to be the speaker, but in Jn 12.41 the revelation is thought to be of the pre-existent Jesus.[1] Given that the pre-existent Jesus is the speaker in Jn 12.40 it is he who would heal the Jews, although this was prevented by their failure to be turned to him as a consequence of being blinded and hardened. On this reading it could be God who has blinded and hardened them so that Jesus may not heal them.[2] While this reading has some appeal, and support for a predestinarian view can be found in other parts of the Gospel, the world of thought that surfaces in the Gospel, the immediate and broader contexts in the Gospel[3] and the modifications John has made to the text from Isaiah all suggest an alternative view.

The Evangelist's Changes

Changes to the tense, person and voice of the verbs in the text quoted in Jn 12.41 draw attention to the opposition between the one who has blinded and hardened and the one who would heal. Whether the Evangelist has used the Hebrew, LXX, or some other version, or has quoted from memory, possibly influenced by Targumic interpretation, cannot be answered with certainty. It is sufficient to say that the quotation of Isa. 6.10 in Jn 12.40 does not agree with the LXX, the Hebrew or any of the other New Testament quotations of the text. Like the LXX John concludes the quotation with καὶ ἰάσομαι αὐτούς,[4] thus using

---

1. The two uses of αὐτοῦ do not clearly refer to Jesus, but the αὐτόν of 12.42 does and it is inconceivable that the person in view has changed.

2. Thus Schnackenburg, *John*, II, p. 415.

3. Associated themes that emerge from the consideration of the context should be taken into account, especially Jn 3.19-21; 9.39-41; 12.31-32, 35-36a, 46.

4. For Hoskyns (*The Fourth Gospel*, II, p. 502) the use of these words confirmed that John was using the LXX.

the verb in the first person singular future indicative active in place of the passive of the Hebrew. Given that in Isaiah God is understood to be the speaker, the use of the first person singular in the LXX is a correct interpretation of the divine passive in the Hebrew. John's view emerges in 12.41-42, which identifies Jesus rather than God with the one revealed. Unique to John also are the changes to the verbs at the beginning of the quotation, from the imperative mood to the third person singular perfect indicative active, thus setting the action in the past (though the consequences remain) rather than the future and distinguishing the agent of the past action (blinding) from the action of Jesus who would heal them. Although most interpreters attribute these changes to the Evangelist too little attention has been paid to them, because it is assumed that the changes were not intended to make any material difference to the use of the quotation. Yet they necessitate the distinction of the one who has blinded from the one who would heal.

Secondly, language introduced or excluded by the Evangelist is a clue to the origin of the obduracy. First, it is regularly noted that John omits the reference to hearing. According to Evans, 'Throughout the fourth gospel emphasis is placed on seeing rather than hearing...'[1] This is hardly convincing when the concentration on discourse material is remembered, and this perspective can be summed up in Jesus' words, 'Truly truly I say to you, the one who hears my words and believes on the one who sent me has eternal life...' (Jn 5.24). More to the point, Evans draws attention to the significance of 'the immediate context in which Jesus has healed a blind man'. The use of τυφλός in John 9 may have suggested the use of the verb τετύφλωκεν in Jn 12.40. But this is not altogether convincing, given that three lengthy chapters lie between that chapter and the use of τετύφλωκεν.

Given that the issue at stake is the failure of the signs to lead to faith, the emphasis on blindness is appropriate. Does this mean that they failed to believe because, being blind, they were unable to see the signs? Certainly there were those who were sceptical of the actuality of the signs (Jn 9.18), and Jn 6.26 has been interpreted as if it denied that those who sought Jesus were able to see his signs, explaining why they failed to believe in him: 'Truly truly I say to you, you seek me not because you saw signs, but because you ate of the loaves and were satisfied'. But this is a mistaken reading. Jesus did not deny that the crowd that sought

---

1.   *To See and Not Perceive*, p. 129.

him had seen the signs (referred to 6.2, 14). It is not a different crowd from the one that followed him and was fed by him. They had eaten of the loaves and been satisfied (6.26). If the people mentioned in 6.14 saw the sign (of the feeding) it is hardly likely that the Evangelist intended the reader to think that the crowd as a whole knew nothing about it. The Evangelist has a different point to make. The people in the crowd knew of the sign and were aware that they had benefited from it. They followed Jesus because they wished for a repeat performance from which they would again benefit. They looked for another sign. Thus, 'sign' has various levels of meaning in John. It means first, 'a mighty work' or what we might call a 'miracle'.[1] Clearly those who opposed Jesus recognized that he performed many signs (11.47), one of which was the raising of Lazarus (12.9-11). For the Evangelist, however, the signs were more than simply 'mighty works' and some of those who saw them were aware of this.

Those who saw the sign of the feeding recognized that it signified something about Jesus. In this, according to the Evangelist, they were right. But they were not right in what they thought was signified and this is shown by Jesus' rejection of the attempt to make him king (6.14-15). Thus, even for those who perceive that the signs point to the significance of Jesus, there is the question of whether the perception is right. Naturally, for John, the correct perception is believing perception which corresponds with his own view.

The Evangelist has substituted the blinding of the people for the shutting of their eyes. Either way they do not see, so that the change might not seem significant. But blindness is a more serious problem because those who shut their eyes may open them. In the context of the ancient world 'blindness' normally refers to the total and permanent loss of sight. Blindness was generally considered to be incurable.[2] It was a state over which the blind had no control. Given the parallel with the hardening of the heart it is clear that the language of blindness is used metaphorically, even though the eyes are specifically mentioned. But because the Evangelist has changed the language of closing the eyes to that of blinding, his purpose would seem to be to bring out the

---

1. Reluctance to use the term 'miracle' is an indication that the term has no exact equivalent in the first century. The modern understanding of miracle owes much to the discussion of David Hume. See *An Inquiry Concerning Human Understanding* (1748), esp. section 10, 'Of Miracles'.

2. Schrage, *TDNT*, VIII, pp. 271, 273.

seriousness of the situation. Indeed, in normal terms, blindness was a hopeless condition.

In the Masoretic Text the prophet is instructed to 'shut' the people's eyes, while in the LXX the people shut their own eyes, thus portraying them as being responsible for their own failure to see. In John it is affirmed that 'he has blinded their eyes' (τετύφλωκεν αὐτῶν τοὺς ὀφθαλμοὺς). If John is using the LXX he has moved from describing a voluntary action of the people to the portrayal of a destructive act committed upon them by a third party. The notion of being blinded is, as we have seen, much more negative than the shutting of eyes. Those who shut their eyes may open them again but those who are blind are not able to see. According to John, God's purpose in creation is not for eyes to be blind, an issue that almost surfaces in Jn 9.2. Rather, in John, it is God who makes the blind to see (Jn 9 and see Isa. 35.4-6).

The notion of blinding is somewhat sinister and the rare use of τυφλοῦν in the LXX, where it is used only three times, suggests that we need to account for the introduction of the term at this point in John. This impression is confirmed by the rare use of τυφλοῦν in the New Testament. The verb is used only three times, in Jn 12.40, 2 Cor. 4.4 and 1 Jn 2.11, and these uses are mutually clarifying.

According to Paul in 2 Cor. 4.4, 'the god of this world has blinded the minds (ἐτύφλωσεν τὰ νοήματα)[1] of the unbelievers, to keep them from seeing the light of the gospel of the glory of Christ, who is the image of God'. Here Paul addresses the problem of unbelief and concludes that the fault lies neither with the gospel, nor with those who preach it, but with Satan, who has blinded those who, as a consequence, are unable to believe. They do not believe because Satan has blinded them.

In 1 Jn 2.11 the writer asserts that it is 'the darkness [that] blinded his eyes' (ἡ σκοτία ἐτύφλωσεν τοὺς ὀφθαλμοὺς αὐτοῦ): 'The one hating his brother is in the darkness and walks in the darkness and does not know where he goes, because the darkness blinded his eyes'. The language of 1 John is closer to the Gospel than 2 Corinthians, though both 1 John and 2 Corinthians use the aorist tense while the Gospel uses the perfect tense. But in both John and 1 John it is eyes that are blinded and both use the idiom of 'walking in the darkness'. The notion of blinded eyes rather than minds is more a difference of idiom than

---

1.   In 2 Cor. 4.4 it is τὰ νοήματα that are blinded while in Jn 12.40 the hardened heart is not able to perceive (νοήσωσιν).

meaning because neither the Gospel nor 1 John is dealing with physical blindness at this point. In the Gospel this is confirmed by the way that, in the quotation of Isa. 6.10, blinded eyes are in parallel with hardened heart, and the failure to see with eyes with the failure to perceive (νοήσωσιν) with heart. Thus John is not far from the notion of the blinding of the minds (νοήματα), though his use of 'heart' rather than 'mind' reveals a more Semitic train of thought.[1] What is clear is that God is not the agent of blinding in either 2 Corinthians or 1 John. In 2 Corinthians the agent is the god of this world and in 1 John the agent is the darkness.[2]

In the LXX ἐπαχύνθη is used to signify the hardening of the heart of the people, but John uses ἐπώρωσεν. In this instance the variation does not seem to be significant because there is a group of terms, including these two, rightly translated as 'to harden'. Schmidt draws attention to the interchangeability of these terms in Luther's translation and confirms the correctness of this through a study of interchangeable readings.[3] In this instance it is not possible to show any intent in the change of term. Thus the emphasis falls on the blinding, which is clarified by the description of the hardening of the heart, which destroys the possibility of the perceiving heart. What we are talking of here is a spiritual blindness of which eye and heart have become symbols.

In John the god of this world (the prince of this world) is the power of darkness (Jn 12.31; 14.30; 16.11). Having mentioned the prince of this world in 12.31, attention is drawn to the blinding effect of walking in the darkness (Jn 12.35-36a and see 1 Jn 2.11). In Jn 12.35-36a Jesus announced that the light (he himself, 8.12; 9.5) was to be present for but a short time and exhorted his hearers to walk in the light while it was with them so that the darkness would not overtake them (ἵνα μὴ...καταλάβῃ). Those who refuse to believe in the light have been overcome by the darkness. But the light has not been overcome by the darkness (οὐ κατέλαβεν, Jn 1.5), rather Jesus himself has overcome the world (Jn 16.33). Consequently Jesus called on his hearers to believe in the light so that they might become 'sons of light' (12.36a). But 12.36b-41 indicates that the power of darkness had its sway and they could not believe, although, as we have seen, this is qualified. Following

1.   See J. Behm, 'νοέω, κτλ', *TDNT*, IV, p. 950.
2.   Compare here Eph. 6.12; Col. 1.13; 1 Jn 5.19; Lk. 8.12; and from Qumran 1QM 13.1–14.9; 1QS 3.13-26, esp. 3.20-24.
3.   Schmidt and Schmidt, 'σκληρόω', p. 1023.

the announcement of the failure to believe, Jesus is depicted as again calling for belief (12.44) and announcing: 'I have come into the world as light, that every one believing in me should not remain in darkness' (12.47). He goes on to speak of those who hear and keep his words, which is a characterization of those who have been rescued from the power of darkness. Thus immediately on either side of the reference to 'He has blinded their eyes' the Evangelist portrays Jesus speaking of himself in terms of the light in conflict with the power of darkness which overcomes those who walk in it; and it is clear that the power of darkness is to be understood in terms of the prince of this world mentioned in 12.31.

The Comparative Relevance of First-Century Judaism

Although the predestinarian view dominates the interpretation of Jn 12.39-40, I have noted that this is frequently severely qualified. In dealing with the comparison of Jewish ideas Schnackenburg notes that

> Judaism tends to stress human free will because of the obligation to observe the Law...The idea of God's fore-ordinance is not, indeed, unknown to the rabbis, but it does not abolish human freedom...The two ideas are left side by side unconnected and hardly interpreted...The idea of predestination was thus familiar to rabbinic Judaism, but hardly influential.[1]

His discussion of the Qumran texts is complex. On the one hand he acknowledges that 'the idea of God's foreknowledge, his plan and his predestination is strongly expressed'.[2] There are, in the texts, many predestinarian expressions of God's initiative. Schnackenburg's understanding of predestination as expressed in the texts is also severely qualified:

> Care is necessary in presuming a belief in absolute predestination ('*ante praevisa merita*'), since in other passages the free decision to join the community (of salvation) is stressed (cf. 1QS 1.11; 5.1, 6, 8, 10, 21-22; 6.1-14; 9.17), members are responsible for their actions, and even their apostasy does not seem impossible (1QS 7.18-24). Of the non-elect it is said...that God knew (beforehand) their works (CD 2.7-8). Did God

---

1. *John*, II, pp. 265-66.
2. *John*, II, p. 267.

make his decrees in foreknowledge of the works of men ('*scientia media*')? It must be wrong to expect such theological precision or even to look for any clear doctrine of predestination.[1]

He is right in insisting that we should not expect to find a philosophically argued and consistent doctrine of predestination either in the Qumran texts or in John.[2] His main concern is to qualify the understanding of predestination in the texts to take account of human freedom and moral responsibility. It is questionable that conflicting emphases should be reconciled in this fashion.

More seriously, by assimilating the dualism to a predestinarian perspective Schnackenburg tends to underplay the force of the dualism at Qumran. His suggestion that in the dualistic section (1QS 3.13–4.26) the emphasis on predestination is even stronger than elsewhere is surprising and in need of careful examination . He argues that 'Even outside the dualistic section (1 QS III.13-IV.26)...the idea of God's foreknowledge, his plan and his predestination is strongly expressed';[3] and 'in the section dealing with the two spirits...the deterministic attitude appears in a much stronger form'.[4] Here we find a confusing identification of dualistic determinism with divine predestination. But the very point of the dualism is to distance God from the cause of evil. Consequently Schnackenburg's approach tends to underplay the force of the dualism at Qumran by subordinating it to the teaching on predestination. While it is true that in John and the Qumran texts all things have their origin in God, nevertheless a significant dualism is sustained.

In John there is no specific reference to the origin of the darkness or the devil, the prince of this world, but in 1QS 3.18-20 it is expressly affirmed that God *appointed* the two spirits and in 3.25 that he created them. In this same passage, however, it is said that God loves the one and delights in its works and loathes the other and hates its ways (3.26–4.1) and in the mystery of his understanding has ordained an end to it

---

1.   *John*, II, p. 268. Schnackenburg comes to a similar conclusion concerning the understanding of predestination in John. Barrett (*St John*, pp. 430-32) is in agreement with Schnackenburg.

2.   R.E. Brown thinks that the determinism of Qumran is neither logically nor speculatively developed; 'The Qumran Scrolls and the Johannine Gospel and Epistles', in K. Stendahl (ed.), *The Scrolls and the New Testament* (New York: Harper & Brothers, 1957), esp. pp. 189-91.

3.   *John*, II, p. 267.

4.   *John*, II, p. 269.

(4.18). Consequently the passage appears to be concerned to affirm the eschatological triumph of God, grounding this in his sovereign power, rather than to make God responsible for evil. In John the power of darkness remains a mystery while in 1QSerek the role of the Spirit of Falsehood/Angel of Darkness is expressly said to be a mystery in the plan of God (אל רז).[1] In neither is God explicitly made responsible for the darkness or falsehood, and the statements concerning control are directed towards the assurance that an end of the darkness or falsehood has been determined by God.[2]

J.H. Charlesworth, like Schnackenburg, interprets the dualism of Qumran in predestinarian terms because the two spirits are subject to God. Charlesworth does not qualify his understanding of predestination at Qumran to take account of human freedom and responsibility but explicitly asserts that 'to join the community was not a free act of choice but an appointed task carried through by one predestined by nature to be a son of light (3.18)'.[3] While this conclusion might be possible on the basis of a consideration of 1QS 2.13–4.26 in isolation,[4] it ignores explicit indications that to join the community was an act of free choice: 'He shall admit into the Covenant of Grace all those who have freely devoted themselves to the observance of God's precepts' (1QS 1.7-8); 'All those who freely devote themselves to His truth shall bring all their knowledge, powers, and possessions into the Community of God' (1QS 1.11-12).

The discussion of the 'fountain of light' and the 'source of darkness' in 1QS 3.18-20 is *not* explicitly set in a context which makes clear that the source of darkness is purposed by God. In other words, dualistic determinism is not expressly equated with divine predestination and if it were it would destroy the purpose of the dualism, which is to distance God from the source of darkness and the Angel of Darkness who leads all the children of falsehood astray.[5] The conclusion that should be

---

1.   1QS 3.23; 4.6, 18.

2.   Jn 12.31; 1QS 4.18.

3.   *John and Qumran* (London: Geoffrey Chapman, 1972), pp. 79-80. Thus he also understands dualistic determinism in terms of divine predestination.

4.   This section does not deal with conditions of entry into the community. Thus such a conclusion must be drawn from related themes. But if in 1QSerek conflicting themes appear side by side an extrapolation along these lines is precarious, especially when it is opposed to explicit statements elsewhere.

5.   In 1QS 3.18-20 the Spirit of Truth is identified with the Prince of Light and

drawn from this is that there is an unresolved tension in the texts
between the dualism and belief in the one sovereign God. In terms of the
present, although the two Spirits were created by God, it is said that
God 'loves the one everlastingly and delights in its works for ever; but
the counsel of the other he loathes and for ever hates its ways'. The
tension, which is recognized as a mystery, is unresolved in relation to the
origin of the source of darkness and the activity of the Spirit of
Falsehood, although there is a promised eschatological resolution: 'But
in the mysteries of His understanding, and in His glorious wisdom, God
has ordained an end of falsehood, and at the time of the visitation He
will destroy it for ever' (1QS 4.18).

Although Schnackenburg assimilates the dualistic determinism of
Qumran to his understanding of divine predestination, which is qualified
to take account of human freedom and responsibility, he finds it
necessary to distance John from the teaching at Qumran. 'We need not
spend any more time on this doctrine of the two spirits, however, since
in its statements it goes far beyond what can be found in John...' This
judgment needs to be questioned, not only because in 1 Jn 4.2, which
should be understood in relation to the Johannine tradition if not by the
same author as the Gospel, the Spirit of Error[1] is mentioned, but also
because of the role of the darkness and the devil, the prince of this
world, in John.

That the Qumran texts contain more fully developed passages on the
role of the two spirits than John does not mean that John's dualistic
statements should not be taken seriously. Charlesworth argues that the
dualism has been used symbolically by John and the devil has been
demythologized.[2] Such an interpretation demythologizes the Evangelist's
language, which is an option for the modern interpreter, but not the
meaning of the Evangelist, who accounted for the struggle he experienced in terms of dualism. According to Charlesworth the dualism of

the Spirit of Falsehood with the Angel of Darkness, as is shown by the way it is said
that 'those born of the *truth* spring from a fountain of light' and are called 'the
children of righteousness' who 'are ruled by the Prince of Light and walk in the ways
of light', while 'those born of *falsehood* spring from a source of darkness' and 'are
ruled by the Angel of Darkness and walk in the ways of darkness'. Further, in 1QS
3.25 the two Spirits are referred to as the Spirits of Light and Darkness.

1.   This title is more or less a Greek equivalent of the Semitic Spirit of
Falsehood. Compare the role of Error in the *Gospel of Truth*.

2.   *John and Qumran*, pp. 92-93.

Qumran has been assimilated into a monotheistic determinism. Consequently Charlesworth argues for a rigorous determinism in the Qumran texts, but says in regard to John: 'We conclude, therefore, that no doctrine of predestination is put forward in this Gospel, nor is there any strong emphasis on determinism. Man's destiny is balanced between God's sovereign initiative and man's response'.[1]

Schnackenburg also assimilates the dualism into a deterministic view but balances this with an emphasis on human freedom and responsibility even at Qumran. If in contemporary Jewish sources the ideas of divine sovereignty and human freedom appear side by side in an unconnected way, as Schnackenburg argued, is it not possible that this is true also of the dualistic and monotheistic statements in John and the Qumran texts? If this is the case the dualistic statements should be taken seriously and not simply absorbed into a predestinarian view which is then qualified by statements about human freedom and moral responsibility.

In the Qumran texts the Spirit of Falsehood not only has led astray all the children of darkness but is active among the children of light also. So also in John it is not only the Jews as the opponents of Jesus who are led astray by the devil; even Judas, one of the twelve, is turned into the one who would betray Jesus by the devil who enters his heart (Jn 13.2). Consequently there is a more strongly dualistic reading of some parts of the Qumran texts as well as the Gospel of John.

The Qumran texts contain the writings of the sect and it would be a mistake to think of them as a homogeneous whole without tensions and even conflicting views. They were the product of the understanding of the sect over the course of a couple of hundred years and not the writing of a single person. Even 1QS should not be seen as a homogeneous document. It brings together the beliefs of the sect. Consequently we should not be surprised to find blatant and unresolved tensions there. The two Spirits can be characterized in terms of the division between the sect as the 'sons of light' and the world as the place of darkness. This aspect is dominant in 1QS 3.13–4.26. But because the members of the sect also experienced the struggle with the darkness there is also the recognition that even they had to struggle with the deceptions of the Spirit of Falsehood. In all of this the two Spirits are understood in apocalyptic terms as supernatural powers. Alongside these uses we find a more psychological use of the term 'spirit' which impinges on the area

---

1.   *John and Qumran*, p. 95.

in which the apocalyptic use occurs. Here every person is characterized by the spirit given by God, so that people are determined by the spirit 'of their lot'. While this understanding is characteristic of the *Hodayoth* (Hymn Scroll) approximations to it are found in 1QS 4.20-23.

For the purpose of our discussion it is the apocalyptic understanding of the two Spirits that is important. It corresponds quite closely to the understanding of the Spirit of Truth in John and the role of the devil that is found there. Against this background a dualistic interpretation of Jn 12.40 is not improbable.

The dualism of the Qumran texts and John probably provides evidence of the influence of an Iranian *Weltanschauung*.[1] It may be that the Iranian dualism was already subject to a monotheistic principle,[2] although this might have been a consequence of the dualism being mediated through Judaism. Which of these views is adopted makes little difference to the interpretation of John. We can conclude that for the Evangelist the belief in one supreme and good God is held in tension with the acknowledgment of a deadly, dualistic conflict between the forces of good and evil, in which humankind is also called to play a part. In this context the possibility that the power that blinded and prevented people from believing was the power of darkness must be carefully examined.

The Support of Origen and Cyril of Alexandria

The understanding of the devil as the agent of blinding and hardening in Jn 12.40 has the support of Origen[3] and Cyril of Alexandria.[4] Given that

---

1.   This view has the support of such scholars as K.G. Kuhn, W.F. Albright, F.M. Cross and H. Ringgren. See W.F. Albright, 'Recent Discoveries in Palestine and the Gospel of John', in W.D. Davies and D. Daube (eds.), *The Background of the New Testament and its Eschatology* (C.H. Dodd Festschrift; Cambridge: Cambridge University Press, 1956), pp. 153-71; F.M. Cross, *The Ancient Library of Qumran and Modern Biblical Study* (London: Duckworth, 1958); K.G. Kuhn, 'Johannesevangelium und Qumrantexte', in A.N. Wilder *et al.* (eds.), *Neotestamentica et Patristica* (O. Cullmann Festschrift; NovTSup, 6; Leiden: Brill, 1962), pp. 111-22; H. Ringgren, 'Qumran and Gnosticism', in U. Bianchi (ed.), *Le Origini dello Gnosticismo* (NumSup, 12; Leiden: Brill, 1967), pp. 379-84.

2.   This is the view of R.C. Zaehner, *The Dawn and Twilight of Zoroastrianism* (London: Weidenfeld & Nicholson, 1975), pp. 50-51.

3.   Fragment XCII (GCS, 554ff.); M. Wiles, *The Spiritual Gospel: The Interpretation of the Fourth Gospel in the Early Church* (Cambridge: Cambridge University Press, 1960), p. 109; J. Blank, *Krisis: Untersuchungen zur johanneischen*

Greek was their language and they were not unorthodox dualists but believers in one God, their reading of Jn 12.40 must carry considerable weight. Since Augustine, who emphasized the sovereignty of God in interpreting this verse, their line of interpretation has been overlooked. But the interpretation of Origen and Cyril of Alexandria has the support of a contextual reading and is consistent with a reading of the dualistic sections of the Qumran texts. That John has the power of darkness in mind in Jn 12.40 is also suggested by the relationship of John 12 to the Gethsemane account in Luke. There, in response to the act of betrayal by Judas and the actual arrest, Jesus is recorded as saying, 'but this is your hour, and the power of darkness' (Lk. 22.53). Although the arrest narrative does not come until John 18, Jn 12.27 is related to the Synoptic prayer in Gethsemane and in what follows in Jn 12.31-36 Jesus speaks of his conflict with the prince of this world and the conflict of the light with the darkness.

Conclusion

In common with Paul (2 Cor. 4.4), the first letter of John (2.11) and the sectarian writings of Qumran, John recognized that, although God is in control of the whole of creation, the power of darkness and falsehood cannot be overlooked. It is likely that this viewpoint was reinforced by the bitter struggle between the Johannine community and the synagogue, although the links between John and the Qumran texts suggest that the language of dualism was integral to the Evangelist's worldview.[1] The significance of the language should not be reduced to an indication of the social situation of the community, signaling its sectarian conscious-ness. The sectarian consciousness reinforced the validity of this language but the dualistic language makes clear that the power of evil is real and is opposed to God.

The Gospel presupposes the reality of the power of darkness. It is because of the pervasive power of darkness in the world created by the λόγος that the λόγος became flesh. But the incarnation by itself did not overcome the power of darkness. Consequently Jesus' ministry is portrayed as an assault on the power of darkness (3.19-21; 8.12; 9.5,

---

Christologie und Eschatologie (Freiburg: Lambertus, 1964), pp. 304-305.

4.   See *PG* 74.96-97.

1.   See my *The Quest for the Messiah: The History, Literature and Theology of the Johannine Community* (Edinburgh: T. & T. Clark, 1991), ch. 2.

39-41; 12.35-36a, 46). That assault is portrayed as a struggle leading up to a decisive assault (Jn 12.31-33).[1] In the struggle, in which the signs of Jesus play a decisive role, 12.36b-43 informs the reader that the signs failed to be decisive in the assault on the darkness. In spite of the many signs Jesus did before the people they failed to believe in him. But how could this be? The Evangelist's answer is that they were unable to believe because the prince of this world, the power of darkness, had blinded their eyes and hardened their hearts. The purpose of this statement is to make clear that the decisive conflict is yet to take place, in the immediate future (see 12.31-33). Jesus' ministry of signs was not without significance and, even with the recognition that the signs were not decisive, the Evangelist indicates that 'even of the rulers many believed' (12.42). Though this is true the reader is reminded of the power of darkness because the values of these believers were corrupted by the darkness (1 Jn 2.11), and they loved the 'glory of men' rather than the glory of God (12.43). Because of this they were unwilling to confess their faith openly. Coming at the end of Jesus' ministry the concluding summary (12.36b-43) serves to reinforce the critical nature of the lifting up of Jesus as the judgment of the world and of the prince of this world.[2]

---

1.   See my *Quest*, pp. 124-28, and 'Theology and Eschatology in the Prologue of John', *SJT* 46 (1992), pp. 512-38.

2.   The finished Gospel recognizes that the power of darkness continues to confront the believers in the world even after the death and resurrection of Jesus. For this reason the Farewell discourses look to the role of the Paraclete/Spirit of Truth to continue the judgment of the world (see 16.4b-11) and Jesus prays that the disciples, left in the world, will be kept from the corrupting power of darkness (Jn 17).

BETRAYAL AND THE BETRAYER:
THE USES OF SCRIPTURE IN JOHN 13.18-19

J. Ramsey Michaels

The Fulfillment Quotations in Matthew and John

The formula 'that it might be fulfilled' (ἵνα or ὅπως πληρωθῇ) in connection with a quotation from Jewish Scriptures is commonly associated with Matthew's Gospel because of eight occurrences of the formula in Matthew (1.22; 2.15, 23; 4.14; 8.17; 12.17; 13.35; 21.4).[1] John's Gospel, however, is not far behind with five such citations (Jn 12.38; 13.18; 15.25; 19.24, 26),[2] plus two others in which the cited words are not Scripture but sayings of Jesus recorded earlier in the Gospel (Jn 18.9, 32). In addition, both Matthew and John contain passages in which the formula (or something close to it) occurs, but without the citation of a specific text (Mt. 26.54, 56; Jn 17.12, and possibly 19.28; see n. 2 below). Of these, Mt. 26.54 and Jn 17.12 do not come as comments of the Gospel writers, but are placed on the lips of Jesus. In the case of the third (Mt. 26.56), it is difficult to tell whether Jesus or Matthew is the intended speaker. In Matthew's tradition (Mk 14.49) it was clearly Jesus.

John, however, is the only Gospel writer who places the distinctive fulfillment formula *with a specific citation* directly on Jesus' lips, and he

---

1. Two other citations (Mt. 2.17 and 27.9) use a slightly different formula, 'then was fulfilled' (τότε ἐπληρώθη), possibly to avoid attributing the evil acts of human beings to divine intention.

2. Another possible example is 19.28, where the most important ancient manuscripts (B and others) have a different verb (τελειωθῇ), which other manuscripts have changed to the more common πληρωθῇ. The first hand of P⁶⁶, however, omits the fulfillment formula altogether, and it is possible (*if* the formula is part of the text) that its reference is not to Jesus' words 'I am thirsty' in the immediate context, but more generally to the fulfillment of Scripture in all that has been accomplished (see πάντα τετέλεσται in v. 28a, and τετέλεσται in v. 30). This would place it in a category similar to that of Jn 17.12, except not on the lips of Jesus.

does so twice (Jn 13.18, 15.25).[1] These two citations are attributed to Jesus, while the other three (12.38; 19.24, 36), like all of Matthew's citations, are comments by the Gospel writer. Thus Jn 13.18 and 15.25 are unique within the New Testament, forming a pair within the Johannine farewell discourses: 'He who eats my bread has lifted his heel against me' (13.18, citing Ps. 41.10), and 'They hated me without cause' (15.25, citing Ps. 35.19 or 69.5).

The Context of John 13.18-19

The contexts of the two Johannine quotations are linked by a pronouncement common to both, 'a servant is not greater than his master', introduced in 13.16 by the Johannine formula, 'Amen, amen, I say to you', and self-consciously repeated in 15.20: 'Remember the word which I said to you, "a servant is not greater than his master"'. A form of this pronouncement is known also from the Synoptic tradition: 'A disciple is not above the teacher, nor a servant above his master' (Mt. 10.24). John in the context of 13.18-19 shows familiarity with the first as well as the second half of this double pronouncement: 'You call me teacher (διδάσκαλος) and master (κύριος), and you say well, for I am. If I, then, your master and teacher, have washed your feet, you too ought to wash each other's feet' (13.13-14). He follows this with 'a servant is not greater than his master' (v. 16a), and then introduces still a third parallel example: 'nor an apostle greater than the one who sent him' (v. 16b). While the first two of these 'greater/lesser' pronouncements are aptly illustrated by the preceding narrative of the footwashing, and focus on the responsibilities of the disciples toward one another, the third looks beyond this setting to the disciples' world mission. The theme of 'sending' is continued in v. 20: 'Amen, amen, I say to you, the one who receives whomever I send receives me, and the one who receives me receives him who sent me' (in the Synoptic tradition, compare Mt. 10.40; Lk. 10.16).

Taken together, the 'Amen, amen' sayings in Jn 13.16 and 20 carry out a transition from mutual ministry *within* the believing community to a ministry directed *outward* to the world. Here and elsewhere in John's

---

1.   The closest parallel to this phenomenon is Lk. 4.21, where Jesus, after quoting from Isa. 61, announces, 'Today this Scripture is fulfilled (πεπλήρωται) in your ears', but in this case he does not claim that something happened or would happen specifically 'in order to fulfill' (ἵνα πληρωθῇ) a text of Scripture.

Gospel (cf. 4.38, 17.18), Jesus can speak of his mission to the world as if it has already begun. In this sense his disciples are already 'apostles' (a word occurring in John only in 13.20). Yet the sending in the proper sense does not occur until Jn 20.21-22: '"Just as the Father has sent me, so I am sending you." And having said this he breathed on them and said to them, "Receive the Holy Spirit. Whosoever sins you forgive are forgiven them, and whosoever sins you retain are retained."'

This post-resurrection mission to the world is apparently the mission to which Jesus refers in Jn 13.16 and 20. John has placed the Scripture citation about betrayal (v. 18), with its application (v. 19), strategically between the twin 'Amen, amen' sayings of vv. 16 and 20. These two pronouncements frame the citation so as to give it a temporal setting in the post-resurrection mission of the disciples. In the course of their mission, Jesus' disciples will experience betrayal by some in their own number. Because many commentators understand vv. 16 and 20 as somewhat parenthetical,[1] they fail to see the interpretive spin that these verses give to the Scripture citation and its application. But if anything is parenthetical in this account, it is vv. 18-19 themselves, not the 'Amen, amen' pronouncements which precede and follow them.[2] The thrust of vv. 12-17 and of v. 20 is positive: a clear statement of the disciples' responsibilities to each other and to the world (vv. 12-16), accompanied by a beatitude (v. 17) and a promise (v. 20). The section would read smoothly if vv. 18-19 were left out. Verses 18-19, introduced by the words 'I am not speaking of all of you' (v. 18a), are a negative warning qualifying the immediately-preceding beatitude, 'Now that you know these things, you are blessed if you do them' (v. 17). Jesus cautions that *not all* the disciples know, or will know, 'these things', and that consequently not all will be 'blessed'. The words correspond to the phrase 'but not all' in the preceding section (v. 10b), which the narrator

1. Rather typical is the remark of E. Haenchen: 'Verse 20 does not belong to this context at all; it is loosely connected with verse 16 by means of the catchword "send..."' (*John 2: A Commentary on the Gospel of John Chapters 7-21* [Hermeneia; Philadelphia: Fortress Press, 1984], p. 110). R. Schnackenburg attributes vv. 16 and 20 to an editor, but undercuts his own proposal with the candid admission that v. 20 at least is characteristically Johannine in style. His explanation that 'It might... have been possible for an editor to take over the evangelist's particular way of expressing himself' is less than convincing (*The Gospel according to St John* [New York: Crossroad, 1982], III, p. 25; compare III, p. 403 n. 70).

2. Cf. F. Godet, *Commentary on the Gospel of John* (New York: Funk & Wagnalls, 1886), p. 253.

immediately explained in one of his characteristic asides to the reader as referring to the individual who would betray Jesus (v. 11).[1]

This time there is no such narrative aside. The question is whether the narrative aside of v. 11 ('For he knew the one who would betray him; that is why he said that "You are not all clean"') is somehow still in effect, or whether the Scripture cited in v. 18 should be understood in the framework of the 'Amen, amen' pronouncements of vv. 16 and 20. Most readers have tacitly assumed that it is still in effect, probably because Jesus goes on to speak explicitly of Judas Iscariot in vv. 21-30. Ernst Haenchen goes so far as to comment that the Scripture citation 'awkwardly presupposes what is said in verses 21ff., and thereby destroys the tension with which the text is obviously concerned'.[2] If we do *not* assume that the narrative aside is still in effect, then vv. 18-19 are not referring to Judas in particular, but to the phenomenon of betrayal in general within the Christian community. On this reading, the disciples— and by extension the readers of the Gospel—are those who will experience in the course of their world mission the full impact of the words 'He who eats my bread has lifted up his heel against me' (v. 18).

The prophecy begins to focus explicitly and exclusively on Judas only in 13.21, where Jesus abruptly brings his warning to bear on the present and immediate future: 'Amen, amen, I say to you that one *of you* will betray *me*' (my emphasis). This provokes an immediate and intense reaction from the gathered disciples (vv. 22-25). There was no such reaction to the Scripture citation and the accompanying warning in vv. 18-19. But now the truth of John's narrative aside in v. 11 ('For he knew the one who would betray him') comes to full realization.

The latter is the last in a series of such asides referring to Judas Iscariot (these include 6.64, 'For Jesus knew from the beginning...who the one is who will betray him'; 6.71, 'He meant Judas son of Simon Iscariot, for he, who was one of the Twelve, would betray him'; also

---

1.   Among older studies of the narrative asides in John, see A.E. Garvie, *The Beloved Disciple: Studies of the Fourth Gospel* (London: Hodder & Stoughton, 1922), pp. 14-29; M.C. Tenney, 'The Footnotes of John's Gospel', *BSac* 117 (1960), pp. 350-64. Among recent works, see R.A. Culpepper, *Anatomy of the Fourth Gospel* (Philadelphia: Fortress Press, 1983), especially pp. 15-49; G. van Belle, *Les Parenthèses dans l'Evangile de Jean* (Leuven: Peeters, 1985); C.W. Hedrick, 'Authorial Presence and Narrator in John', in J.E. Goehring *et al.* (eds.), *Gospel Origins and Christian Beginnings* (Sonoma, CA: Polebridge Press, 1990), pp. 75-93.

2.   Haenchen, *John 2*, p. 109.

12.4, 6 and 13.2).[1] With the help of these narrative asides, the reader is informed of two things: that Judas will betray Jesus, and that Jesus knows this in advance. The disciples within the story are not privy to this information. They cannot hear the narrator's side comments to the reader. All they have to go on is the mysterious grim pronouncement, 'One of you is a devil' (6.70b), and the puzzling words to the disciples after the footwashing, 'and you are clean, but not all' (13.10b). It is impossible to tell what they made of those. Therefore they have no decisive reason to link the Scripture citation in 13.18 to a coming betrayal of Jesus by one of their number. When Jesus says, 'From now on I tell you before it happens (λέγω ὑμῖν πρὸ τοῦ γενέσθαι) so that when it happens you may believe that I am' (v. 19), the disciples will hear it not in relation to Jesus' coming betrayal and death (about which they know nothing), but in relation to the dangers and deceptions of their world mission. In itself, the saying has much the same import as Jesus' words in the Synoptic eschatological discourse, 'But you must watch out, for I have told you all things in advance' (προείρηκα ὑμῖν πάντα, Mk 13.23; compare Mt. 24.25). Later in John's Gospel itself, in a context of predictions of expulsion from synagogues and of martyrdom, Jesus will say, 'But I have spoken these things to you so that when their hour comes you may remember that I told you' (16.4a).

What all this suggests is that the Scripture citation in Jn 13.18 is functioning at two levels. To the disciples within the story it looks beyond the story, as a prophecy of betrayal in the course of their coming mission. This meaning is signaled by the traditional sayings framing the citation, in vv. 16b and 20 respectively. Yet *to the reader* the citation anticipates a fulfillment within the story, as it predicts Jesus' personal betrayal at the hands of Judas. The disciples 'catch up' with the readers in v. 21, when Jesus tells them explicitly that one of them will betray him.

The question we are left with is this: does Jesus' disclosure in v. 21 supersede the meaning of the citation as the disciples would have heard it (that is, in reference to their future mission to the world)? Does their perception simply amount to one of many Johannine misunderstandings by various participants in John's story?[2] Or do *both* interpretations

---

1. See Godet, *John*, p. 253.

2. On these misunderstandings, see Culpepper, *Anatomy*, pp. 152-65. They are part of the larger theme of irony in John's Gospel, on which see D. Duke, *Irony in the Fourth Gospel* (Atlanta: John Knox, 1985), and G. O'Day, *Revelation in the*

retain their force? Is Jesus, by his use of Scripture, making both a general assertion that the disciples will experience betrayal in the course of their mission by some of their own number, and at the same time a specific assertion that Judas Iscariot will betray him to death?

Synoptic Parallels

The theme of betrayal in the setting of the disciples' mission is conspicuous in certain discourses of Jesus in the Synoptic Gospels.

Betrayal and Divisions in Families

In the same chapter of Matthew in which he says 'A disciple is not above the teacher, nor a servant above his master' (Mt. 10.24), Jesus speaks of divisions within families:

> Do not think that I have come to throw peace on the earth. I have not come to throw peace, but a sword. For I have come to split a man against his father, and a daughter against her mother, and a bride [or daughter-in-law] against her mother-in-law—and a man's enemies shall be those of his own household (Mt. 10.34-36).

The parallel passage in Luke is slightly different:

> Do you think I am here to give peace in the earth? No, I tell you, but rather division. For from now on there will be five in one house divided; they will be divided three against two and two against three, father against son and son against father, mother-in-law against her daughter-in-law, and daughter-in-law against the mother-in-law (Lk. 12.51-53).

Both versions draw loosely on the language of Mic. 7.6, but there is no formal quotation or mention of fulfillment.

Betrayal and Hatred

In the immediate context of the Matthean pronouncement 'A disciple is not above the teacher, nor a servant above his master' (Mt. 10.24), Jesus makes two explicit predictions about what is in store for his disciples, one concerned with betrayal and one with hatred: 'But brother will *betray* (παραδώσει) brother to death, and father child, and children will rise against parents and put them to death' (Mt. 10.21); 'And you will be *hated* (μισούμενοι) by all for my name's sake. But the one who endures to the end will be saved' (Mt. 10.22). In Mark the same combination of

Fourth Gospel (Philadelphia: Fortress Press, 1986).

being betrayed and being hated—in exactly the same words—occurs in the setting of Jesus' final eschatological discourse (Mk 13.12-13; cf. also 13.9, with its echoes in Mt. 24.9-10).

The twin themes of betrayal from within and hatred from without correspond closely to the themes of the two key Scripture citations in Jn 13.18 ('He who eats my bread has lifted up his heel against me') and 15.25 ('They hated me without cause'). That John had such Synoptic (or Synoptic-like) passages in mind in his construction of 13.12-20 is clearly shown by his use of a saying similar to Mt. 10.24b in v. 16 and a saying similar to Mt 10.40 in v. 20. That pronouncements of this sort are still at work in the context of 15.25 is shown by the explicit repetition of 13.16 in v. 20a, as well as by such statements as 'If the world hates you, you know that it hated me first' (v. 18), and 'If they have persecuted me, they will persecute you; if they have kept my word, they will keep yours' (v. 20b; compare Mt. 10.25b: 'If they have called the master of the household Beelzebub, how much more his household servants?').

All these parallels suggest that the two Scripture quotations about betrayal and hatred in Jn 13.18 and 15.25 respectively can be legitimately read either as references to the experience of Jesus in his passion, or as prophecies of troubles facing the disciples in the course of their world mission.

The Betrayal by Judas

Neither of the Johannine quotations can be found in the Synoptic tradition, either in connection with the disciples' experience of betrayal or with Jesus' betrayal at the hands of Judas. As we have seen, only Mic. 7.6 plays a role in connection with the former and that not as an actual quotation. At most, there is a very faint echo of the Psalm text quoted in Jn 13.18 in Jesus' prediction of his betrayal according to Mark. The prediction is given in Mk 14.18 and Mt. 26.21 in exactly the same words as in Jn 13.21 (except for a single instead of a doubled 'amen'): 'Amen, I say to you that one of you will betray me' (εἷς ἐξ ὑμῶν παραδώσει με). Although the verb παραδώσει in this pronouncement vaguely recalls the παραδώσει of Mt. 10.21 and Mk 13.12, there is nothing in Mark or Matthew linking the two contexts. Only the Johannine tradition brings them together. Mark, however, qualifies the reference to 'one of you' with an additional phrase, 'the one who eats with me' (ὁ ἐσθίων μετ' ἐμοῦ, Mk 14.18b). This phrase is widely understood as an allusion to Ps. 41.10,[1] but it is doubtful that a connection would have been seen were it not for the explicit fulfillment quotation in Jn 13.18.[2] The existence of the added phrase in Mark, however, reinforces the common tendency to read Jn 13.18-19 exclusively in the light of 13.21, as simply an alternate prediction of Judas' treachery. There is reason, I suggest, to call this tendency into question.

The Form of the Quotation in John 13.18

The text of Ps. 41.10 in the MT is as follows:

גם־איש שלומי ׀ אשר־בטחתי בו
אוכל לחמי
הגדיל עלי עקב:

> Even my bosom friend in whom I trusted,
> who ate of my bread,
> has lifted up the heel against me (NRSV, 41.9).

The LXX text (40.10 LXX) is somewhat different:

καὶ γὰρ ὁ ἄνθρωπος τῆς εἰρήνης μου, ἐφ' ὃν ἤλπισα,
ὁ ἐθίων ἄρτους μου, ἐμεγάλυνεν ἐπ' ἐμὲ πτερνισμόν·

> For even the man of my peace, in whom I trusted,
> the one who eats my loaves, was lifting heel against me.

Jn 13.18 picks up only the latter half of the verse: ὁ τρώγων μου τὸν ἄρτον ἐπῆρεν ἐπ' ἐμὲ τὴν πτέρναν αὐτοῦ (lit., 'the one who eats

---

1.   See for example W.L. Lane, *The Gospel according to Mark* (Grand Rapids: Eerdmans, 1974), pp. 502-503; R.H. Gundry, *Mark: A Commentary on his Apology for the Cross* (Grand Rapids: Eerdmans, 1993), p. 827. Also C.H. Dodd, *Historical Tradition in the Fourth Gospel* (Cambridge: Cambridge University Press, 1963), p. 36; R.E. Brown, *The Gospel according to John (xiii–xxi)* (AB, 29a; Garden City, NY: Doubleday, 1970), p. 571.

2.   The Markan phrase has nothing in common with Ps. 41.10 except ὁ ἐσθίων ('the one who eats'). The words 'with me' (μετ' ἐμοῦ) show no evidence of coming from the Psalm, and simply anticipate v. 20 ('the one who dips with me the dish') with its parallel in Mt. 26.23 (cf. also Lk. 22.21). The only real argument from Mark's context for an allusion to Ps. 41 is the statement in 14.21 that 'the Son of Man goes as it is written of him' in Scripture (Brown, *John*, p. 571), but this could be a purely general reference to Scripture, as in the Matthean parallel (26.24; see also Mark's generalized reference to Scripture fulfillment in 14.49).

my[1] bread has lifted his heel against me'). The citation differs from the LXX in its use of ὁ τρώγων instead of ὁ ἐθίων for 'the one who eats', its use of the singular ἄρτον, 'bread' (in agreement with the MT) instead of ἄρτους, 'loaves', and its use of the aorist ἐπῆρεν, 'has lifted', instead of the imperfect ἐμεγάλυνεν, 'was magnifying', or 'lifting'. It differs from both the MT and the LXX in referring to 'his' heel (αὐτοῦ) instead of simply 'the heel'.

τρώγειν is probably John's distinctive substitute for the present tense of ἐθίειν, which never occurs in this Gospel. Much has been written on the phrase ὁ τρώγων, which occurs five times in John where ὁ ἐθίων might have been expected—not only here but also 6.54, 56, 57 and 58, in the setting of Jesus' 'bread of life' discourse. Notice in particular the parallel in word order between 'the one who eats my bread' (ὁ τρώγων μου τὸν ἄρτον) in our quotation and 'the one who eats my flesh' (ὁ τρώγων μου τὴν σάρκα) in 6.54 and 56 (in a context which assumes that 'the bread which I will give is my flesh for the life of the world', 6.51c). Yet it is difficult to know what the point of the parallel might be. Is Jesus saying in one place that the eating of his 'flesh' (or bread representing his flesh) guarantees salvation, and in another that one of those eating will betray him, so that in fact there is no such guarantee? More likely, it is simply a matter of Johannine style, which prefers τρώγειν to ἐθίειν as the present tense of the verb 'to eat'.[2]

The Time of Fulfillment and the Time of Realization

It is natural to suppose that Jesus himself is taking on the role of the speaker to whom the 'me' and the 'my' refer in the citation of Ps.

---

1. Brown (*John*, p. 554) argues for the originality of μετ' ἐμοῦ, instead of μου in John's quotation (with P⁶⁶, ℵ, A, D, and the majority text), yielding the translation 'He who feeds on bread within me' (*John*, p. 549). But this is likely an assimilation to the Synoptic tradition (see above, p. 466 n. 2). The simple μου (with B, C, L and others) is both the more difficult reading and the one more in keeping with the text of the Psalm (cf. B.M. Metzger, *Textual Commentary on the Greek New Testament* [London and New York: United Bible Societies, 1971], p. 240). Brown's effort to defend μετ' ἐμοῦ as a translation of the Hebrew is strained.

2. With other New Testament writers, John uses φαγεῖν for the aorist, but as Dodd notes (*Historical Tradition*, p. 37 n. 1), 'although in grammars this is conventionally given as the aorist of ἐσθίειν they are of course different verbs. In John φαγεῖν serves rather as the aorist of τρώγειν, and βεβρωκέναι serves as perfect (vi.14).'

41.10, just as Jesus is the 'me' and the 'I' and the 'my' in the Psalm citations in Jn 15.25 and 19.24 (cf. 2.17). It could even be argued that the 'I am' (ἐγώ εἰμι) of v. 19b is intended to confirm this identification: 'That you may believe when it happens that I am [the one referred to in the Psalm]'. More likely, however, the ἐγώ εἰμι is (like all other occurrences of that expression in John's Gospel) far wider in its reference: 'that you may believe when it happens that I am [what I claim to be]'. The mention of a future moment of verification recalls Jesus' promise to his enemies in 8.28 that 'when you lift up the Son of Man, then you will know that I am' (ἐγώ εἰμι). The moment of verification is clear in 8.28. The verification will take place when Jesus is 'lifted up' on the cross. Here the verification, although accented by the contrast between 'before it happens' (πρὸ τοῦ γένεσθαι) and 'when it happens' (ὅταν γένηται), is less clearly defined. When exactly will the disciples come to believe that Jesus is who he claims to be on the basis of the accuracy of his prediction of betrayal? When exactly is Ps. 41.10 fulfilled, so far as they are concerned?

Rudolf Bultmann rightly interprets v. 19 in the light of several other verses in the Johannine farewell discourses in which Jesus tells the disciples certain things in advance so that when they take place the disciples will 'believe' (14.29), or 'not be scandalized' (16.1), or simply 'remember' what he told them (16.4).[1] The parallels between 13.19 and 14.29 are especially close:

13.19: ἀπ' ἄρτι λέγω ὑμῖν πρὸ τοῦ γενέσθαι, ἵνα πιστεύσητε ὅταν γένηται ὅτι ἐγώ εἰμι.
From now on I tell you before it happens, so that when it happens you may believe that I am.

14.29: καὶ νῦν εἴρηκα ὑμῖν πρὶν γενέσθαι, ἵνα ὅταν γένηται πιστεύσητε.
And now I have told you before it happens, that when it happens you may believe.

In 14.29 the time of realization is after the resurrection, when Jesus has gone to the Father (see v. 28). In 16.1 and 4 the time is also after Jesus' resurrection, when the disciples are being expelled from synagogues and put to death (see v. 2).

These parallels suggest that in 13.19 as well as 14.29 the time of

---

1.   R. Bultmann, *The Gospel of John: A Commentary* (trans. G.R. Beasley-Murray; Philadelphia: Westminster Press, 1971), p. 478 n. 3.

realization is post-resurrection, in the setting of the disciples' mission to the world. Bultmann makes the significant comment that in v. 19 the Gospel writer

> does not refer to Jesus' prior knowledge in order to overcome the difficulty caused by a single fact, which is what Judas' betrayal is. On the contrary, just as the allusion to the betrayer is intended to shake the disciple's assurance and to draw attention to a possibility he always has to face, so too the difficulty that the Evangelist is concerned with is the ever present one, that there are disloyal disciples. It is this, fundamentally, that Jesus knows beforehand: it is a matter of fact, which springs from the nature of revelation, that is to say, from its relation to the world. We are not of course told here as clearly as we are later (16.1, 4, 32f; 14.29) that Jesus' foreknowledge is of this kind.[1]

These remarks of Bultmann seem to have had little impact on subsequent discussion of this passage, but they are profoundly important, not only because of the parallels he cites with other passages in the farewell discourses but because of the clear allusions to the disciples' future mission in vv. 16b and 20.

None of this changes the fact suggested earlier in this article that the Scripture citation in Jn 13.18 refers *both* to betrayal in general and to Judas the betrayer in particular. Bultmann was not denying the reference to Judas, nor is it possible to do so. What his comment does suggest is that there is as much value in the disciples' understanding of the Scripture citation in Jn 13.18 and Jesus' explanation of it in v. 19 as there is in the reader's understanding of it after the fact and in light of Jesus' passion. The disciples' hearing of the text of the Psalm, while limited, is not simply a misunderstanding to be set aside, like Peter's mistaken notion that he needed a bath all over (v. 9).[2] The reader must remember that his or her own understanding, to the extent that it is colored by the many narrative asides that have preceded the citation,[3] is also limited. These 'helps to the reader' do not always enrich or broaden the nuances of the text (as they seem to do, for example, in Jn 2.21-22). Often they have the opposite effect of closing out certain options, and as readers it is important for us to keep all options—at least all legitimate ones—open.

---

1. Bultmann, *John*, p. 478. See also my own brief discussion in *John* (New International Biblical Commentary, 4; Peabody, MA: Hendrickson, 1989), pp. 244-45.

2. See Haenchen, *John*, p. 109.

3. Cf. Godet, *John*, p. 253.

This means that we should allow ourselves to read this text through the eyes of Jesus' disciples on the scene as well as through our own eyes. When we do, we sense something of the drama of the transition from vv. 18-20 to vv. 21-30. In vv. 18-20 Jesus predicts that when he sends his disciples into the world there will be grim experiences of betrayal, but that through these they will come to realize that he is who he claims to be. In v. 21b, after a dramatic pause in which he 'was troubled in spirit' (v. 21a), Jesus solemnly testifies with a third 'Amen, amen' formula (following on from the two in vv. 16 and 20), to the effect that 'This future is now! One of you—right here at this table—will betray me!' The shock produced by this announcement is clearly described in vv. 22-30, but these verses also make it unmistakably clear that the disciples did *not* at that time realize either who the betrayer was, or in what the betrayal consisted, or much of anything about Jesus' identity or intention. This is amply demonstrated not only by their bewilderment in vv. 27-29 but by their puzzled questions at many points in the farewell discourses that follow. Even though the Psalm citation in v. 18 now has at least a provisional fulfillment, the moment of realization for the disciples still has not come when the chapter ends.

When does the moment of realization come? It is not an easy question. To ask it is much the same as asking when the disciples came to understand the significance of Jesus' washing their feet. Jesus said to Peter, 'What I do, you do not know now, but you will know after these things' (13.7). When is 'after these things'? Is it when he asked the disciples, 'Do you know what I have done to you?' (13.12)? Is it when he says to them, 'Now that you know these things, blessed are you if you do them' (13.17)? Or is it at some indefinite time after his resurrection? Is it somewhere inside the story, or outside and beyond the story, or is it both? Similarly, when do the disciples see Jesus again, as he promises them in the farewell discourses (14.19, 16.19)? Inside the story, in his resurrection appearances (20.20, 29), or beyond the story, in the coming of the Paraclete—or even in Jesus' eschatological coming? Finally, what are 'the things to come' which the Paraclete will announce to Jesus' disciples (16.13)? Are they the events of Jesus' passion (18.4), or are they the future in general? In each instance, it is hard to avoid the conclusion that the realization of the promise is in some sense *both* within and beyond the story as told in John's Gospel. Again and again, certain signs in Jesus' ministry or in connection with resurrection appearances are used to point to continuing post-resurrection realities.

There is one more example with particular bearing on Jn 13.18-19. When does the promise come true that Jesus' disciples are kept safe and united so that none of them is lost (6.39, 10.28)? Is it within the story, either during Jesus' ministry (17.12) or specifically at the arrest (18.8-9), or is it beyond the story, in the course of the disciples' world mission (17.11, 15)? This promise is linked to Judas's betrayal by the statement of Jesus in 17.12 that the disciples' safety and unity has one explicit exception: 'none of them is lost except the son of destruction, that the Scripture might be fulfilled'. Most commentators assume (probably correctly) that 'the Scripture' in mind here is Ps. 41.10, the same Scripture quoted explicitly in 13.18. Rudolf Schnackenburg sees the influence of 13.18-19 both here[1] and in 18.5, where Judas is mentioned (rather awkwardly) as being present at Jesus' arrest, when Jesus said 'I am' (ἐγώ εἰμι, vv. 5-8) and the soldiers who had come to arrest him 'drew back and fell to the ground' (v. 6). In the latter instance, Schnackenburg comments significantly that 'the moment has now arrived when Jesus' prophecy in the supper room is fulfilled, that the one eating his bread lifts his heel against him (13.18); the disciples are to believe, when it happens, that Jesus rightly says: ἐγώ εἰμι (13.19)'.[2]

This passage may indeed be a sign, so far as the readers of the Gospel are concerned, of Jesus' decisive revelation as the One he claimed to be, but there is no evidence in the context that the disciples saw anything significant in the scene. From their perspective, the realization promised in Jn 13.19 was still future. Whatever Jesus may have meant here by 'I am'—simply 'I am Jesus of Nazareth', or 'I am all I claim to be'— none of the disciples responds in faith to his self-disclosure. For them the realization of the promise of 13.19 lies outside the parameters of the Johannine story proper, when they learn the hard lesson that in their mission and in their communities no less than in Jesus' mission and Jesus' community of disciples, some of those who eat their bread will lift up the heel against them. For them, Jn 13.18-19 will be one of the many

---

1.   Schnackenburg, *St John*, III, p. 182; also C.K. Barrett, *The Gospel according to St John* (Philadelphia: Westminster Press, 2nd edn, 1978), p. 509. Bultmann generalizes 'the son of destruction' (in keeping with his generalizing interpretation of 13.18): 'if a member of the community is lost, then he never was a true disciple'. He does this, however, only with reference to a pre-canonical source, not the Gospel writer himself, who related the phrase solely to Judas (*John*, p. 504 n. 2). Bultmann is less convincing here than on 13.18-19 (see Schnackenburg, *St John*, III, p. 436 n. 48).

2.   Schnackenburg, *St John*, III, p. 224.

things—along with hatred, expulsion from synagogues and martyrdom—which Jesus had spoken about 'so that when their hour comes you may remember of them that I told you' (16.4). When all these troubles come to pass, they can take comfort in knowing that Jesus foresaw everything from the beginning, and consequently that he is the 'I am'—all that he claimed to be.[1]

Conclusion

My purpose in this article has been to show that the two Johannine fulfillment citations placed on the lips of Jesus are not to be understood *solely* as self-references to Jesus' ministry and passion. They can be read either as that, or as prophecies of the experience of Jesus' disciples after his departure. They invite the disciple to put himself or herself in the place of the 'I' or 'me' in the Psalm in a way in which Jn 19.24, for example, does not.[2] I have concentrated mainly on the citation in 13.18-19, because of someone's (the author's? the implied author's? the narrator's?) persistent efforts, by the use of 'narrative asides', to focus the reader's attention exclusively on Judas and on Jesus' passion. Most conspicuously, as we have seen, the aside in 13.11 ('for he knew the one who would betray him; that is why he said, "You are not all clean"') tends to predetermine the way one reads vv. 18-19.

It is not necessary to condemn this narrator or narrative voice as

---

1.   Cf. the test for prophets in Deut. 18.22 (NRSV): 'If a prophet speaks in the name of the Lord but the thing does not take place or prove true, it is a word that the Lord has not spoken'. Also, cf. God's own claim to veracity in Isa. 46.8-11 (NRSV): 'Remember this and consider, recall it to mind, you transgressors, remember the former things of old; for I am God, and there is no other; I am God, and there is no one like me, declaring the end from the beginning and from ancient times things not yet done, saying, "My purpose shall stand, and I will fulfill my intention"... I have spoken and I will bring it to pass; I have planned, and I will do it'.

2.   By its very nature, the casting of lots for Jesus' clothing (19.23-24) is a procedure not likely to be duplicated in the experience of the disciples! The same is probably true of 19.28 if in fact 'I thirst' is to be understood as a Scripture citation (see n. 2 on the first page of this article). This is not the case, however, in 12.38, where the question 'Lord, who has believed our report?' is as applicable to the disciples in their mission as to Jesus (cf. Rom. 10.16). The classic case of ambiguity about whether a 'Scripture' (whatever it might be!) refers to Jesus or a disciple is 7.38, where the debate over the source of 'rivers of living water' will probably never be settled.

'unreliable' in order to insist that it does not represent the *only* legitimate way to read the text. When Jesus says, 'And you are clean, but not
all' (v. 10b), or 'I am not speaking about all of you; I know whom I
have chosen' (v. 18a), it is not certain from these actual words that Jesus
is thinking of just one exception.[1] Is it not possible that such pronouncements as 'You are clean, but not all', or 'I know whom I have
chosen'[2] could apply to the state of the Christian community always and
everywhere—or at least in a wide range of times and circumstances?
Later in John's Gospel, Jesus will tell his disciples without qualification
that 'You are clean because of the word which I have spoken to you'
(15.3), and yet almost in the same breath warn that 'If anyone does not
remain in me, he is thrown outside like the branch and is withered, and
they are gathered and thrown into the fire, and he is burned' (15.6).
This too suggests that the horizons of the text 'He who eats my bread
has lifted up his heel against me' are somewhat wider than the single
tragedy of Judas Iscariot.[3]

The companion quotation in Jn 15.25 requires less discussion. In itself
the text 'They hated me without cause'[4] refers to the experience of
Jesus, not only in his passion but throughout his ministry. Yet it is placed
in a context predicting that the disciples will be hated by the world
exactly as Jesus was (vv. 18-21). Jesus adds the corollary that those who
hate him hate his Father as well (vv. 23, 24b), thus defining themselves
once and for all as sinners (vv. 22, 24a; cf. 9.41). The world hates Jesus
and his Father and his disciples all for the same reason—they are not 'of
the world' (ἐκ τοῦ κόσμου), and the world only loves its own (15.19;
cf. 17.14). The thrust of the passage as a whole, however (not only

---

1. The *Good News Bible* makes just such an assumption with its imprecise
renderings, 'All of you are clean—all except one', in v. 10b, and 'All of you, except
one, are clean', in v. 11b.

2. The principle that the Christian community, though firmly established, is less
than perfect is at least intimated in 2 Tim. 2.19-21, introduced by the dictum 'The
Lord knows those who are his' (v. 19).

3. Brown (*John*, pp. 675-76) explicitly points out the parallel between Judas and
the fruitless branches of 15.6: 'In the atmosphere of the Last Supper Judas may be
thought of as a branch that did not bear fruit; he is now a tool of Satan and belongs to
the realm of darkness (xiii.2, 27, 30)'.

4. This quotation could come from either Ps. 35.19 or 69.5, where the phrase in
question is exactly alike, whether in Hebrew (חנם שׂנאי), Greek (ἐμίσησάν με
δωρεάν), or the NRSV ('those who hate me without cause'). John's text differs only
in using an indicative verb instead of a participle.

15.18-25, but 15.18–16.4 in their entirety) is not to make the point that Jesus and his Father are hated, but to warn the disciples that *they* will be hated. While *in itself* Jn 15.25 refers to Jesus' experience, *in its broader context* it refers to the disciples, inviting them to put themselves in the place of the 'me' who is the object of hatred in the relevant passages from the Psalms (35.19 and 69.5).

In these ways the Gospel of John has used Scripture citations to put together its own distinctive version of Jesus' Synoptic prophecies that 'brother will betray brother to death', and that 'you will be hated by all for my name's sake' (Mt. 10.21-22 = Mk 13.12-13). Jesus in this Gospel, no less than in the others (though in slightly different words), tells his disciples, 'You then must watch out, for I have told you all things ahead of time'.

INDEXES

INDEX OF REFERENCES

OLD TESTAMENT

Genesis		18.14	22, 154, 156	9	364
1	58, 210	21	154, 156,	11.15	296
1.1	394		161, 363	12	390, 409,
1.9	226	21.1-3	157, 159		422
1.27	60	21.1	154, 157,	12.3	412
1.31	210		159	12.4	412
2	58, 254, 391	25.19	154	12.5	412
2.2	394	25.21	159	12.7	414, 420
2.7	391	25.23	141	12.10	400, 404,
2.24	57, 58	25.32	141		405, 426
3	387	28	25	12.12	23
3.1	47	29.31-32	160	12.19	420
3.4	47	30.6	152	12.21	412
3.13-15	47	32	367	12.22	414, 419,
3.15	75	35.19	171		420
4	387	38.6-14	142	12.29	296
12.1-3	317	38.9	153	12.32	412
15.2-20	387	38.24	142	12.46	400, 404,
15.3	153	38.27-30	136		405, 423,
16	154, 161	41.29	142		426
16.7-8	161	41.53	142	14	215-24,
16.11	161, 284	46.3	142		227, 229,
17	156, 161	48.5	141		232, 233
17.8	317	48.7	171	14.1	217, 218
17.14-15	156	49.8-10	141	14.2	217, 218
17.16	152	49.11	142	14.3	220
17.19	153, 156,	49.26	120	14.4	219, 220
	161	49.27	350	14.5	220
17.21	156			14.6	219
18	154, 156,	*Exodus*		14.7	219
	161, 223,	3.6	73, 141	14.8	220
	366	4.19	169	14.9	217, 219
18.10	156	4.22	168	14.10	218, 219
18.11	159	6.23	142	14.11	220

14.12	218	34.5-9	231	25	241
14.13	218, 219	34.5	295	25.1-4	48
14.15	218	34.6-7	205	27.17	16, 19
14.16	217	34.7	410	28.19	409
14.17	219, 220			28.22	411
14.18	219	*Leviticus*		35.16-21	63
14.19	73	7.1-7	408		
14.20-21	329	9.3	409	*Deuteronomy*	
14.20	220, 295	10.9	22	1–26	342, 354
14.21	217, 220, 232	12.6	409	1	355
		14.1-32	408	1.9-18	355
14.22	217	14.6-7	420	1.19-25	343
14.23	217, 219	14.10	409	1.21-22	355
14.24	218-20, 222, 224	18.13	59	1.23	355
		18.16	40	2.1–3.3	343
14.26	217	19.18	196, 272-74, 276-78, 352	3.3-7	343
14.27	217			3.23-27	343
14.28	217, 219			4.5-8	343
14.29	217	20.10	60	4.9-10	330
14.30	217, 218	20.21	40	4.32-40	343
14.31	218, 219	21.17-23	353	4.34	224, 225
15.2	226	23.29	302	4.35	196
16.22	339	23.43	329	5.1–6.24	343
19.5	331	25	337	5.3	330
19.6	331	25.10	337	5.6	273, 274, 278
20	272	25.21	339		
20.13-15	17	25.23	337	5.17-20	17
21.12	61			6.3	20
22.7	300	*Numbers*		6.4-9	275
23	71, 89, 206	1.7	143	6.4-5	20, 275
23.7-8	99	2.3	143	6.4	196, 200, 211, 272
23.20-24	69	5.1-22	274		
23.20-23	71, 89	6.1-21	408	6.5	196, 275-77, 352
23.20-22	205, 206, 208	6.3	21		
		7.12-18	143	7.1-16	343
23.20-21	208	9.12	400, 404, 405, 426	7.2	352
23.20	43, 71, 73, 208			7.4	352
		10.13-14	143	7.11	352
23.21	205, 208	10.34	295	7.16	352
23.22	206, 207	11.16-25	355	8.1-3	343, 352
24.1	355	12.8	239	8.4-20	343
24.9	355	14.18	410	9.1–10.11	343
27.20-21	368	15.37-41	275	9.10	330
28.38	410	16	366	10.12-15	343
29.38-41	409	19.6	420	10.16–11.7	343
32.10-12	48	21.8	388	11.2	340
33.15	73	21.16-18	363	11.13-21	275
33.18-23	231	24.17	287, 382	11.26-28	343

12.1-16	343	26.12	346	*1 Samuel (1 Kingdoms)*	
12.17-32	343	27.25	99	1	126, 161
13.1-5	343	29.2-4	437	1.6	153
13.6-11	343	29.16-28	48	1.11	22, 125, 153
13.12-18	343	30.15	332	1.22	124
14.22	346	30.19	332	2–3	154
14.28	343	30.20	332	2.1-10	124
15	337	31.10-13	326	2.1	125
15.1-18	343	32.11	291	2.7	125
15.9-11	339	32.33	47	2.10	286
15.12	339	32.43	89	2.20	124
15.19-23	343	33.17	286	2.26	124
16.1–17.7	343	34.1	273	3.1-18	124
16.19	99			3.19	124
17.8–18.22	343	*Joshua*		3.35	286
18.15-19	354	1.15-18	136	11–15	241
18.15-18	181	3–4	30, 241	15	241
18.15	286, 316	3.13	31	15.21	241
18.16	340	3.16	31	15.25	410
18.18-23	355	4.24	296	16.18	286
18.18	286	6.25	143	17.12	286
18.22	472			17.58	286
19.15	17	*Judges*		20.6	286
20.1-9	343	3.9	286		
20.5-7	353	3.15	286	*2 Samuel (2 Kingdoms)*	
20.10-20	343	13	126, 128,	5.2	106, 134,
21.15–22.4	343		161		153, 164
21.15-17	353	13.3	161	5.7	286
21.18-21	353	13.5	122, 126,	5.9	286
21.22-23	298		128, 161	7	123, 124
24.1-4	58	13.7	121, 122,	7.8	153
24.1	59		175	7.9	123
24.4	61	14.6	127	7.11-14	123
24.6–25.3	343, 353	16.13	161	7.12-16	151, 153,
24.8-9	353	16.17	121, 122,		154
24.13	353		128, 175	7.13-14	286
24.15	353			7.13	123, 140
24.19	353	*Ruth*		7.14	123, 155,
26	342-52	1.1	143		156
26.1-19	343-45	2.11-12	144	7.16	123
26.2	348-50	2.11	291	16.10	286
26.5-19	225	3.5-6	144	22.3	286
26.5-10	351	4.11-12	144	23.1	286
26.6-7	350, 351	4.11	135		
26.7-8	346, 347	4.12-13	144	*1 Kings (3 Kingdoms)*	
26.8	225, 351	4.12	142, 152	1.17	296
26.9	349	4.13	152	3.6	296
26.10	348, 350	4.18-22	142	8.25	296

9.9-18	231	*Job*		43	369

9.9-18 231
11.13 265
17 341
17.23 319
17.24 340

2 Kings (4 Kingdoms)
1.8 33, 46, 108
1.10 23
1.12 23
2.8 30, 36, 37
2.13-14 30
5.8 341
5.10 37
5.14 49
24.1-5 145

1 Chronicles
2.1-10 142
2.19-24 145
3.10-16 144
11.2 106, 153
12.23 296
16.34 209
17.16 296

2 Chronicles
5.13 209
16.14 369
18.28 16
24.18 48
36.6 145
36.21-22 133
36.21 145
36.22 145

Ezra
2.2 145
3.2 145
5.2 145

Nehemiah
8 325, 329
8.8 325, 329
10 330
12.1 145

Job
9.8 217, 221, 222
9.11 222
21.32-33 369

Psalms
1 249-52, 254, 255, 263, 265, 268, 269
1.1 250, 252, 253
1.3 251-53, 268
1.4 53
1.6 268
2 164, 285
2.6-7 153, 155
2.7 153, 155, 156, 288, 299
6.4 25
6.5 25
8.8 368
16 297, 299
16.8-10 297
17.8 291
21.9 18
21.19 18, 297, 400
22 383
22.2 18
22.8-9 297
22.19 24
31.5 297
31.6 24
33.21 400, 404, 405, 420
34.20 404, 405
35.19 460, 473, 474
36.8(7) 291
41 466
41.6 21
41.10 460, 466, 468, 471
42 369
42.5 18

43 369
45.9 369
50.1-2 349
50.9 420
51 349
56.10 369
57.2(1) 291
61.5(4) 291
61.13 17
68.22 400
69 376, 383, 390
69.5 460, 473, 474
69.10 390
69.22 297, 393
69.26 18, 292
75.5 286
75.6 286
75.11 286
77.19 226, 227
78.2 177
80.8-16 417
82 366
82.6 386
86 369
89.4 140
89.26-27 156
89.27-30 153
89.27-28 154
89.27 155, 156
91.4 291
103.12 17
104.3 295
109.1 24
109.6 369
110 76, 154, 164, 183, 200-202, 295-98
110.1-3 153
110.1 76, 155, 200, 201, 204
110.3 155, 156
110.4 76, 155
113.12 23
117 292

117.25   50
117.26   17, 292
118   292, 293, 298, 383, 441
118.1   209
118.11   368
118.25-26   441
118.26   18, 24, 50, 68, 208, 292
123.9   154
130.8   133
132.11   297, 333
132.17   286, 368
137.9   301
140.3   47
148.1   18
148.14   286

Proverbs
5.18-19   62
10.1   64
23.22   64
24.12   17
26.6   64

Song of Songs
3.4   369, 371
4.14-15   369
5.5-6   369, 371

Isaiah
3.26   301
4.3   122, 127, 128
4.4   51, 53
5.1-7   417
5.24   36
6   432
6.1-13   432
6.9-10   19, 304, 321, 392
6.9   23
6.10   429, 431-38, 444, 446, 450
6.13   50
7–11   164

7   152, 153
7.10-15   161
7.10-14   151
7.14   105, 125, 126, 128, 130, 134, 149-55, 160, 161, 163, 164, 168, 284
8.8   153
8.14-15   287
9   152, 153, 184
9.1-2   153
9.2   22
9.5-6   150, 151, 153, 155, 160, 161, 164
9.5   151-54, 156, 157, 161
9.6   152, 154
9.18–10.5   48
10.15-19   48, 53
10.33–11.4   50, 53
10.33-34   48
11   128, 144, 150, 152, 153
1.1-10   287
11.1   120, 122, 127, 128, 135, 174
11.3   368
11.8   47
11.10   369
13.6-16   48
13.10   18, 20
13.14   48
14.13-15   23
14.29   47
19.1   295
24.18   48
26.12-21   367, 371
26.19   17, 23, 180
27   263

27.1   229
27.2-11   417
27.12-13   53
28.13-16   287
28.21-22   302
29.1-4   301
29.6   51
29.14   302
29.18-19   180, 290
29.18   16, 22
30.6   47
30.10   100
30.16-17   48
30.23-26   53
30.27-28   51-53
31.5   291
32.15   51, 130
33.10-12   36
33.15   99
34.2   47
34.4   18, 20, 24
34.8   48
34.10   53
35.4-6   449
35.4   180
35.5-7   290
35.5-6   16, 68, 180
37.20   25
40–66   288
40–55   376
40   89, 300
40.1-5   45, 70
40.3-5   288, 335
40.3   25, 33, 42, 43, 45, 46, 53, 69, 393, 409, 429
40.5   43, 44
40.10   70
40.11   70
40.24   53
40.15-24   70
41.8   288
41.15-16   53
42.1-9   368
42.1   97, 155, 288, 336
42.6   128

42.7	180	61	180, 289, 460
42.18	16, 68, 180	61.1	23, 68, 180, 287, 290, 298
43.20	97		
43.25	205		
44.3	51		
44.22	205	61.2-3	339
45.4	97	61.2	180
46.8-11	472	63.9	73
49	382	65.23–66.8	154
49.6	120, 128, 300, 302	66.5	20
		66.9	154
51.1-3	49, 53	66.15	51
51.1	49	66.24	53, 54
51.9-10	227		
51.9	229	*Jeremiah*	
52.13–53.12	432	2.21	417
52.14-15	52-54	4.11-12	53
53	269, 295, 390, 408, 409, 417	5.21	19, 98
		6.6-21	301
		6.16	17
53.1-12	411	7.11	98, 238, 243, 246
53.1	387, 392, 409, 429, 432, 437, 443, 444	7.16-20	48
		7.25	98
		7.33-34	99
53.4	109, 191, 409, 410	7.34	32
53.5	409	8.1-2	99
53.6	409, 410	8.13-22	301
53.7	409, 410	8.13	238
53.8	409	10.25	47
53.10	409, 410	12.7	292
53.11-12	410	12.10-13	417
53.11	369	14.13-16	98
53.12	393, 409	15.7	53
54.1-10	154	16.9	32
55.3	299	17	249-55, 263, 268
56.7	238, 243, 245, 246	17.1-4	253
56.8	333	17.4	253
57.4	47	17.5-7	254
58.6	289	17.6	253
58.7	58	17.8	252, 253
58.10-11	371	17.9	253
59.5	47	17.10	252
60.1-3	287	17.14	253
60.21	175	18.2-3	98
		22.5-6	292
		22.5	292

22.30	145
23.1-6	98
23.3	333
23.5	123, 174, 287
25	381
25.4	98
25.6	48
25.10	32
31	169
31.2-3	368
31.6-7	128
31.6	120
31.15-22	172
31.15-20	131
31.15	131, 171
31.16	171
31.20	172
31.31-34	73, 173
32.21	224, 225
33.7-9	100
33.7-8	154
33.11	32
33.14	82
33.15	123, 174, 287
33.21-22	140
36.30	145
38.15	98, 171
39.7-9	98
46.22-23	48
48.44	48
50.13	47
Lamentations	
4.7	120
Ezekiel	
4.1-2	301
8.6	292
11.23	292
13	100
15.1-8	48, 417
19.10-14	417
20.5	97
21.31	347
22	48
29.21	286

31.12	48	*Hosea*		*Obadiah*	
34	363	4.6	98	14	48
36.25-27	52	6.6	16, 17		
37	363	8.13	168	*Micah*	
39.29	51	9	240	1.10-16	127
40–48	254	9.3	168	2.12	333
43.3	239	9.10-17	235, 236,	3.5-8	100
45.21-25	411		238-47	3.9-12	98
47	249, 254,	9.10-13	241	4.1-4	97
	269	9.10	238-42, 244	4.2	97
47.1-12	252, 253,	9.15-16	241	4.7	154
	264	9.15	239-41,	5.1-3	106, 139,
47.10	264		243, 245		150, 151,
47.12	268	9.16	238-43		153, 154,
		10.1	417		164
Daniel		10.8	24	5.1-2	286
2.34	293	11	168, 169	5.1	130, 131,
2.44	293	11.1-11	172		151, 164,
7	201, 203,	11.1	96, 130,		167, 168
	205, 206,		131, 154,	5.2-4	151
	208		167, 168	5.2	151
7.4	20	11.2	168	5.3	130, 151,
7.6	17	11.3	168		164, 168
7.9-11	48	11.5	168	5.10-15	48, 292
7.9	202, 203,	11.7	168	7.1	238
	205, 206	11.8	173	7.6	16, 23, 464,
7.10	51, 208				465
7.12	21	*Joel*		7.15	292
7.13-14	202-204	2	297	7.18	207, 410
7.13	18, 21, 24,	2.1-2	48		
	51, 68, 295	2.4	18	*Nahum*	
7.14	202, 203,	2.28-29	51	3.10	301
	205, 208	3.1-5	335		
7.22	208	4.18	256	*Habakkuk*	
7.23	202, 203	4.19-20	256	1.5	299, 302
7.26	208			3.17-18	154
7.27	203, 205,	*Amos*		3.18	22
	208	3.7	174		
9	381	5.12	99	*Zephaniah*	
9.9	205	5.19	48	1.15	48
9.26	73	7.2-3	241	1.18	48
10.5-6	206	7.5-6	241	2.2-3	48
10.13	202	7.8	232	3.8	48
10.21	202	7.10-17	100		
11.22	73	8.2	232	*Haggai*	
12.1	202	8.11-14	291	2.8	337
		9.1	48		
		9.11	303		

Zechariah		Malachi		3.2-3	35
1.15	47	1.1-2	141	3.2	76
1.16	73	1.6–2.9	69	3.3	35
2.10	400	2.1-3	98	3.5	69
3.1-5	366	2.5	81	3.6	69
3.8	123, 174, 287	2.8	81	3.7-15	69
		2.10-16	69	3.13-14	17
4.11-14	73	2.10	81, 337	3.16-18	69
6.9-14	73	2.13-16	39, 40	3.19-24	34
6.12	123, 174, 287	2.14-16	58	3.19-20	35
		2.14	81	3.19	40
9.9	292, 390, 441	2.17	69, 73	3.20	287
12.10-12	18, 383	3–4	89	3.22-24	328
12.10	394, 400, 403, 420, 423, 426	3	181	3.22	19
		3.1-8	71	3.23	320
		3.1-3	34, 36, 39, 40	3.23-24	71, 336
13.4	33, 46	3.1-2	35, 68	3.24	36-38, 40
14.4	266	3.1	22, 33, 36, 40, 43, 50, 66-73, 75-79, 83, 86-88, 90, 182, 290	4.1-4	69
14.5	266, 267			4.1	48, 49, 53
14.8	256			4.4	81
14.9	210			4.5-6	72, 182
14.16-19	97			4.5	46, 69, 71, 73, 76, 77, 79, 80, 83-88, 90
14.21	40	3.2-4	69		

APOCRYPHA

1 Maccabees		35.22	17	48.4	323
3.6	24	36.24	62	48.5	319, 323
3.48	29	44–50	317	48.6	319, 323
4.8-9	29	44.19-21	317	48.8	318, 323
		44.19	317	48.9	318, 323
2 Maccabees		44.20	317	48.10	36-38, 181, 320, 323
2.27-29	338	44.21	317		
3.24	296	45.1-5	317	48.11	318, 324
3.38	296	45.1	317	48.12	318, 324
9.8	296	45.4	317	48.15-16	320
15.8-9	29	48	308, 310, 313, 314, 316-21, 323, 324	48.15	314, 318, 324
Judith				48.16	319, 324
11.19	16	48.1-16	308-10, 312, 314, 316-18, 320, 321	Tobit	
Sirach				8.6-7	63
4.1	20				
13.18-19	62	48.1	319	Wisdom	
25.25	62	48.3	319, 323	7.25	296
34.25	49				

NEW TESTAMENT

Matthew

1–2   133, 135, 154, 175, 177, 178
1.1-17   132, 138
1.1   135, 140, 147, 153
1.2-17   101
1.3   142
1.9   144
1.16   140, 145-49
1.17   128, 139, 146
1.18-25   132, 140, 146, 156, 161, 163
1.18-24   101
1.18-21   141
1.18   148, 162
1.19   95, 162
1.20   104, 146, 148, 162
1.21   105, 126, 133, 153, 173
1.22-23   130
1.22   459
1.23   105, 110, 126, 128, 130, 134, 146, 153, 154, 161
1.24   134, 144
2   118, 125, 131
2.1-12   132, 165, 166
2.1   164
2.2   107
2.4-6   134
2.5-6   106
2.6   96, 130, 151, 153, 164
2.8   154

2.9   154
2.11   107, 114, 154
2.12-13   107
2.12   104
2.13-23   132, 167, 168
2.13   104, 154, 169
2.14   154
2.15   96, 131, 154, 259
2.16   112
2.17   120, 171, 459
2.18   98, 131, 170-72
2.19   104, 114
2.20-21   169
2.20   154, 169
2.21   154
2.22   104
2.23   116, 120, 121, 126, 127, 129, 135, 173, 175, 259
3.2   184, 188, 191, 192
3.3   43, 108, 184
3.4   33, 46, 108
3.7-12   43
3.7-10   44, 47, 105
3.7   38
3.8   38, 48
3.9   48, 49, 96, 172
3.10   48, 49
3.11-12   49, 108
3.11   68, 180, 184
3.12   184
3.14   39
3.16   127
3.17   110, 153, 155

4.7   334
4.9   114
4.14   459
4.15-16   153
4.16   184
4.17   184, 188, 191
4.18-22   105
4.23-25   105
4.23   334
4.25   334
5–7   96, 109, 327
5.12-13   168
5.17-20   191
5.22   64
5.28   65
7.12   278
7.19   48
7.23   16
7.28   68, 383
8–10   68
8–9   187
8.1–9.38   109
8.1-4   191
8.5-13   191
8.11-12   172
8.14-17   191
8.17   459
8.19-20   110
9.8   99
9.10-13   105
9.13   16, 17
9.14-15   191
9.36   16
10   187
10.16-25   169
10.21-22   474
10.21   464, 465
10.22   464
10.24   460, 464, 465
10.25   465
10.32-33   185
10.34-36   464
10.35-36   16

11–13	68	12.14-15	19	21.9	17, 20, 97
11	78, 85, 90, 192	12.17	459	21.13	98
11.2-19	68, 188, 189	12.42	96, 183	21.18-22	257, 268, 269
11.2-10	182	12.48-50	96	21.19	264
11.2-6	66, 68	13	327	21.43	98
11.2-3	185	13.10-17	177	22.13	172
11.2	185, 188	13.13	98	22.32	141
11.3	39	13.32	17	22.34-40	278
11.4	46	13.34-35	177	22.37-38	20
11.5-6	66	13.35	459	22.37	275
11.5	16, 75, 180	13.42	17, 172	22.39	278
11.6	181	13.50	172	22.41-46	97, 183
11.7-15	68	13.51-52	177	23	110
11.7-11	66	13.53	68	23.8	96
11.7-8	185	13.54-58	340	23.12	347
11.9-10	190	13.57	336	23.23	346
11.10-14	80, 86	14.15-21	96	23.29	18
11.10	43, 44, 66-68, 70-72, 75, 77, 79, 80, 82, 191	15.1-2	95	23.34	98
		15.26	172	23.37	172
		15.32-39	339	23.39	50
		15.32-38	96	24–25	327
11.11-12	190	16.14	89	24.3	114, 263, 266
11.11	68, 79, 90, 182-85, 191	16.27	17		
		17	85	24.9-14	169
11.12-15	66	17.1-8	110	24.9-10	465
11.12-14	89	17.3	96	24.25	463
11.12-13	66, 179, 188	17.4	110	24.29	18
11.12	68, 180, 186, 187, 191	17.5	96	24.30	18
		17.6	114	24.51	172
		17.10-13	46	25.30	172
11.13-14	46	17.10-12	50	25.31	266, 267
11.13	69, 79, 179, 182, 184, 187-92, 194, 262	17.10-11	17	26.1	68
		17.12-13	79	26.6-13	441
		17.12	72	26.14-16	99
		17.13	72	26.21	465
11.14	38, 50, 69, 71, 79, 82	17.20	257	26.23	466
		18	327	26.24	71, 466
11.15	69	18.18	204	26.28-29	267
11.16-19	66, 68, 189	18.20	391	26.28	173, 199
11.19	127, 172, 188, 189	19.1	68	26.53	266, 267
		19.2-9	55	26.54	459
11.20-24	68	19.11-12	60	26.56	459
11.25-30	68	19.18-19	17, 20, 24, 274	26.69	18
11.28	75	19.28	97, 262	27.9	459
11.29	17, 75	19.30	262	27.10	98
12.6	183	21.2	142	27.19	104, 108, 112
12.7	17	21.4	459		

27.20	169	3.4	209	10.18	196-98, 209
27.25	98, 172	4	437, 438	10.19	20, 24
27.35	18, 21, 24	4.12	19	10.21	209
27.37	107	4.32	19	10.35-40	262
27.43	18	4.35-41	223, 230	10.46-52	262
27.45	112	4.39	223, 228,	10.40	201
27.46	18, 21, 112		230, 233	10.45	208
27.49	420	5.19-20	201	11	78, 236, 239
27.51	112	6.1-6	340	11.3	201
27.52-53	99, 108	6.4	336	11.9	20, 25, 50,
27.53	113	6.15	46		68, 201, 208
28	114	6.17-18	40	11.12-21	235-40,
28.2-3	113	6.34	19		242-45, 248
28.2	113	6.45-52	214, 215,	11.13-14	239
28.5	114		220, 230,	11.13	242, 244,
28.12	99		232		259, 260,
28.16	97	6.45	214, 221		264, 267
28.17	107	6.46	232	11.14	242
28.18-20	107, 185	6.47	217, 220,	11.15-17	239
28.19	101, 110		223, 233	11.15-16	244
28.20	114, 134,	6.48	214, 217,	11.15	235
	391		220, 222,	11.16	245
			231, 232	11.17	243-45
Mark		6.49	217, 218,	11.20-21	239
1.2	43, 208		231	11.20	243, 261
1.3	43	6.50	218, 219,	11.21	261
1.6	33, 46		231	11.22-25	238, 245,
1.7-8	49	6.51	219, 221,		246
1.15	201, 334		223, 228,	11.24-25	245
1.24	121, 175,		230, 232,	11.27	197
	209		233	11.28	246, 270
1.39	334	6.52	214, 220,	12.28-37	201, 208
2	203		221	12.28-34	196, 198,
2.1-12	201, 203-	7.3-4	199		200, 210
	205, 208	8.1-10	339	12.28-31	270-78
2.5-10	199	8.18	19	12.29-30	20
2.5	199	8.38	202, 203,	12.29	196
2.6	199, 204		206	12.31	274
2.7	196, 197,	9.3	206	12.32-33	270
	204, 205,	9.11-13	46, 50	12.32	196
	208	9.11	19, 39	12.34	197, 211
2.10–7.5	199	9.13	38	12.35-37	197, 200
2.10	199, 202,	9.14-29	320	12.35	197
	204, 205,	9.48	20	12.36	204
	208	10.3-12	55	12.38-41	271-73,
2.12	199, 204,	10.4	20		276, 278
	205	10.5	61	12.39	275
2.17	197, 198	10.17-22	198	12.41	275

13.9	465	1.52	124, 319	4.1	336
13.12-13	465, 474	1.54	288	4.3	285
13.12	465	1.67-79	285	4.9	285
13.14	20	1.68	22, 285	4.14	336
13.23	463	1.69	285, 286	4.16-30	289
13.24-25	20	1.70	285	4.16-18	294
13.26	21, 202	1.71	286	4.16	118, 326
13.28-30	262	1.72-73	285	4.18	290, 336
13.32	201	1.76-79	83	4.21	263, 336, 460
14.3-9	441	1.76	22, 38	4.22	340
14.18	465	1.78-79	286	4.25-27	301
14.34	21	1.79	22	4.41	285, 289
14.36	201	2	287, 317	6.20	339
14.49	459, 466	2.1-5	340	6.23	306
14.62	21, 200, 202	2.4-5	350	6.26	306
15.33	420	2.4	286	7	290
15.34	21, 201	2.11	286, 295	7.4-5	341
		2.22	124	7.9	300
Luke		2.26	286	7.13	295
1-2	294	2.29-31	287	7.14-15	323
1	161, 285, 287	2.30	286	7.15	319
1.1-4	314, 322	2.32	300, 303	7.16	291, 341
1.1	314	2.34-35	287	7.18-35	188
1.3-4	315	2.34	124	7.19	50
1.3	321	2.36-38	124	7.20	39, 292
1.4	282, 315	2.40	124	7.22	22, 290, 338
1.14-17	284	2.41-51	124	7.27	43, 44, 71, 290
1.15	21	2.52	124	7.28	290
1.17	22, 38, 83, 320, 323, 336	3.1-3	335	7.35	188, 189
1.27	154	3.4-6	288, 335	8.10	23
1.28	126	3.4	43	8.29	285
1.31-35	286	3.6	300	9-19	305, 306
1.31	123	3.7-9	43, 44, 47, 301	9-13	301
1.32-33	284, 303	3.7	38	9.7-8	291
1.32	123, 154, 284	3.8	38, 48, 49	9.13-17	339
1.33	123, 154	3.9	48, 49	9.18-19	291
1.35	123	3.15-18	43	9.20	291
1.37	154	3.15-17	290, 292	9.28	323, 350
1.38	154	3.16-18	49	9.30-31	323
1.45	149	3.16	50	9.35	285, 288, 291, 292, 294
1.46-55	285	3.22	285, 288, 290, 291, 336	9.51-18.14	342
1.46-48	124	3.34	289	9.51-56	319
1.46	22	3.38	139, 289	9.54	23, 323
1.48	22	4	290	10.1-3	343
		4.1-13	289		

10.1	295, 354, 355	13.15	295	18.38	293		
10.4-16	343	13.19	23	18.40	293		
10.15	23	13.22-35	343	19.8	295		
10.16	460	13.22-30	343	19.35-38	292		
10.17-20	343	13.27	24	19.38	20, 24, 68, 292, 294		
10.21-24	343	13.29	300				
10.23	324, 381	13.31	343	19.41-44	301, 306		
10.25-28	278, 343	13.33-35	321	20	295		
10.25	324	13.34-35	301	20.16	300, 301		
10.26	352, 353	13.35	24, 50, 68, 291, 292, 294	20.17	293		
10.27-28	324			20.41-44	295		
10.27	20, 270, 275, 352	14	300	21	314, 318		
		14.1-14	343	21.20-24	320		
10.28	352	14.1-6	338	21.20	324, 338		
10.29-37	343	14.5	338	21.23-24	314, 318		
10.36-37	352	14.11	347	21.23	314		
10.38-42	343, 352	14.13	338	21.26	24		
10.39	295	14.15-24	343, 353	21.27	295, 318		
10.41	295	14.23	300	22.21	466		
11.1-13	343	14.25-35	343	22.29-30	323		
11.14-26	343	15.1-32	343	22.30	24		
11.27-28	343	15.11-32	353	22.37	295		
11.29-36	343	16.1-18	343	22.53	457		
11.29	336	16.13	338	22.69	24, 295, 296		
11.37–12.12	343	16.15	338	23	297		
11.37-52	301	16.16-17	192	23.28-31	301		
11.37	338	16.16	179, 187, 188, 190-93, 381	23.34	24, 297		
11.39	295			23.35	297, 317		
11.41	193			23.36	297		
11.42	193	16.17	192, 193	23.46	24, 297		
11.47-51	321	16.19–18.8	343	24.19	109		
12.13-34	343	16.19-31	353	24.21	261		
12.13-21	340	16.29-31	321	24.26-27	296		
12.33	338	17.5-6	295	24.26	294		
12.35-48	343	17.11-19	354	24.27-44	75		
12.35	23	18.1-14	338	24.27	193		
12.42	295	18.6	295	24.43-47	294, 296		
12.49-53	301, 343	18.9-14	342-44, 346, 351	24.44	194		
12.51-53	464						
12.53	23	18.9	347, 351	*John*			
12.54–13.5	343	18.10	350	1–12	392, 416, 440		
13	292, 300, 302	18.11	347, 350				
		18.12	346	1.1	394		
13.6-9	48, 301, 343	18.13	347	1.5	450		
13.6	338	18.14	347, 351	1.11	386		
13.10-21	343	18.20	20, 24	1.13	136		
13.10-17	338	18.22	338	1.14-18	365		
				1.14	393		

1.15	68	2.22	390, 441	6.31	392, 402, 429
1.17	388, 406	2.23	406, 412	6.32	388, 406
1.19–12.16	407	3.3	391	6.34-38	414
1.20-27	47	3.5	391, 410	6.39	471
1.21	37, 46, 72	3.13-15	367	6.41	363
1.23–12.16	402	3.14-15	371, 388	6.42	165
1.23	25, 43, 44, 45, 409, 429	3.14	362, 363, 406, 408	6.44	368, 371
1.25	72	3.19-21	446, 457	6.45	371, 392, 400, 429
1.27	68	3.27-30	47		
1.28	36	3.28-36	39	6.48-51	388, 414
1.29–12.36	403	3.31-36	367, 371	6.51	414, 467
1.29-42	410	3.34	368	6.52-59	414
1.29-36	39, 407	4	363	6.53-58	414
1.29-34	405	4.22	385	6.54	414, 467
1.29	393, 394, 399, 407, 409, 410, 414, 417, 423	4.31-38	371	6.56	414, 467
		4.36	394	6.57	414, 467
		4.38	461	6.58	414, 467
		4.43-44	364	6.60-71	371
		4.44	336	6.64	430, 462
1.30-33	49	4.45	406	6.70	463
1.30-31	370	5	364	6.71	430, 462
1.31	365	5.1	406	7.12	387
1.34	408, 410	5.18	199	7.18	371
1.35-51	365	5.24	447	7.19	406
1.35	410	5.31-40	389	7.22	406
1.36	394, 407, 410, 414, 417	5.35	364, 368	7.23	406
		5.37	366	7.24	368
		5.39	389, 429	7.27	166
1.41	367	5.45-47	388	7.38-39	429
1.43-51	370	5.45	406	7.38	366, 429, 472
1.45	181, 367, 388, 402, 406, 429	5.46	402, 406, 429	7.41-42	165
		6	363, 388, 413	7.42	374, 402, 429
1.46	135			7.51	389
1.51	25	6.1-14	413	8	435
2–11	402	6.2	448	8.5	406
2	390	6.4-5	413	8.12	450, 457
2.11	441, 457	6.4	399, 406, 407, 412-14	8.17	402
2.13-25	411, 413	6.5	414	8.28	394, 468
2.13	399, 406, 407, 411, 412	6.14-15	448	8.35	363, 366
		6.14	68, 448	8.37-40	386
2.14	368	6.19	218	8.38-47	434
2.17	390, 392, 402, 429, 468	6.22-71	413	8.39-59	366
		6.26	447	8.43-44	435
		6.30-32	388	8.44	387, 435
2.21-22	469			8.48	387

8.56	387, 444	11.55-57	443	12.35-36	442, 443,
8.58	436	11.55	399, 406,		445, 446,
9	375, 447,		416		450, 458
	449	11.56	406	12.36–19.37	403
9.2	449	11.57	441	12.36-43	430, 440,
9.5	450, 457	12	394, 403,		443, 458
9.18	440, 447		429, 438,	12.36-42	434
9.22	430, 445,		457	12.36-41	450
	446	12.1-8	370, 416,	12.36-37	436
9.28-29	387		441	12.37-41	366, 392
9.28	406	12.1	406, 416	12.37-40	431
9.29	406	12.4	463	12.37	437, 439,
9.39-41	446, 458	12.6	433, 463		443-45
9.41	473	12.7	416	12.38–19.37	402, 421
10	363	12.9-11	441, 445,	12.38-41	278, 387
10.8	371		448	12.38-40	394, 402
10.24	368, 370	12.9	441	12.38	392, 402,
10.28-30	371	12.11	440, 443		403, 409,
10.28	471	12.12-19	441, 445		417, 429-
10.33	199	12.12	406, 441		31, 437,
10.34-36	385	12.13	25, 370,		440, 444,
10.34	389, 392,		402, 403,		459, 460
	402, 429		429	12.39-41	429, 444
10.35-36	366	12.14-15	429, 431	12.39-40	434, 437,
10.38	438, 443	12.14	392, 402,		451
10.40-42	183		403	12.39	402, 429,
10.40	36	12.15	390, 403		437, 438,
11–12	440, 442	12.16	402, 403,		445
11.1–12.36	443		417, 441	12.40	403, 429-
11	440	12.17-19	442		32, 434-40,
11.5	441	12.17-18	441, 443		444, 446,
11.11-13	370	12.19	369, 370		447, 449,
11.33-42	369	12.20-26	442, 443		456, 457
11.41	370	12.20	406, 442	12.41-42	447
11.45-46	440, 445	12.23	417	12.41	417, 429,
11.45	443	12.27-36	442		436, 437,
11.46-53	443	12.27-32	369		444, 446
11.46	440	12.27-28	442	12.42	445, 446,
11.47–12.8	415	12.27	25, 457		458
11.47-48	440, 443,	12.28	417	12.43	445, 458
	445	12.31-36	457	12.44-50	443, 445
11.47	448	12.31-33	458	12.44-46	443
11.48	442	12.31-32	446	12.44	451
11.49-52	410	12.31	435, 442,	12.46	446, 458
11.50	415		450, 451	12.47	451
11.51-52	415	12.32	370, 442	13–19	416
11.53	440, 441	12.33	442	13–17	416, 417
11.54-57	440	12.34	389	13.1–17.26	416

13	441	14.19	470		427, 472
13.1-20	441	14.26	390	18	457
13.1	406, 407,	14.28	468	18.4	470
	412, 417	14.29	468, 469	18.5-8	471
13.2	417, 433,	14.30	450	18.5-6	377
	455, 463	15–17	417	18.5	471
13.4	417	15.1-10	363, 417	18.6	369, 471
13.7	470	15.3	473	18.8-9	471
13.9	469	15.6	473	18.9	402, 459
13.10	461, 463,	15.18–16.4	474	18.17	389
	473	15.18-25	474	18.28	406, 418
13.11	430, 462,	15.18-21	473	18.32	402, 459
	472, 473	15.18-19	371	18.39	406, 418
13.12-20	465	15.19	473	19	397, 400,
13.12-17	461	15.20	460		403, 420,
13.12	470	15.22	473		422, 427
13.13-14	460	15.23	473	19.5	377
13.16	460-63,	15.24	473, 474	19.7	199, 389
	465, 469,	15.25	389, 402,	19.13-42	418
	470		429, 430,	19.13	364, 377
13.17	461, 470		443, 459,	19.14	399, 400,
13.18-20	470		460, 465,		406, 418,
13.18-19	460-62,		468, 473		419
	466, 471,	15.26	390	19.16-42	399, 406,
	472	16.1	468, 469		424
13.18	366, 402,	16.2	430, 446,	19.17	369, 377
	414, 429,		468	19.23-24	366, 472
	430, 460-	16.4-11	458	19.24	399, 402,
13.19	681,4653,	16.4	463, 468,		403, 429,
	468, 469,		469, 472		430, 459,
	471, 473	16.8-11	368, 371		460, 468,
13.20	460-63,	16.11	450		472
	465, 466,	16.13	390, 470	19.25-27	377
	469, 470	16.19	470	19.26	459
13.21-30	462, 470	16.33	450	19.28-30	393, 395
13.21	462, 463,	17	87, 375,	19.28	393, 402,
	465, 466,		394, 417,		403, 420,
	470		458		429, 430,
13.22-30	470	17.5	417		459, 472
13.22-25	462	17.11	471	19.29	367, 399,
13.26	417	17.12	402, 429,		400, 406,
13.27-29	470		430, 459,		418, 419
13.27	433		471	19.30	377, 393,
13.29	406	17.14	473		402, 459
13.30	417	17.15	471	19.31-37	411
13.31-32	417	17.18	461		
13.34	389	18–19	597-99,		
14.8-9	366		423-25,		

19.31-33	400	2.40	301	13.47	302
19.31	394, 399,	3	298, 302,	15.11	303
	406, 418,		315, 316	15.16-17	303
	420	3.1	350	15.21	28, 326
19.34	420	3.13	323	17	298
19.36-37	377, 402,	3.14-26	291	18.6	324
	405, 418	3.20-23	323	18.9-10	281
19.36	399-403,	3.22-23	316, 321,	18.12-17	281
	405, 420,		354	19.4	68
	421, 423,	3.23	301, 302,	20	303
	424, 426,		324, 340	20.21	303
	429, 430,	4.4	339	20.23	281
	460	4.11	298	20.24	303
19.37	399-403,	4.25-26	298	20.25	303
	420, 421,	5.31	298	21.11	281
	423, 424,	5.36-37	338	22.15	303
	426, 429,	5.36	30	23.5	300
	430	6.1	44	26	303
19.38	400, 420	6.3	339	26.17-18	303
19.39	364, 369,	7	315, 316	27	304
	422	7.22	109	27.23-25	281
19.42	399, 406,	7.23-29	322	28.24-28	324
	418	7.35	322	28.24	324
20.14-18	371	7.37	316, 321,	28.26-27	303
20.19	430		340, 354	28.31	304, 324
20.20	470	7.38-41	321		
20.21-22	461	7.51-52	321	*Romans*	
20.29	470	8	298, 300	1.3-4	159
20.30-31	436	8.32	407, 410	3.25	199
		9.15	303	3.30	199, 200
Acts		10	298, 300,	4.13	317
1–2	318, 323,		303	8.32	408
	324	10.9	350	9.12-13	141
1.1	316	10.36-43	305	10.6	362
1.3	338	10.36	298	10.16	472
1.6-8	338	10.38	298	13.9	274
1.8	304, 323,	10.42	298	15.4	170
	324, 338	10.43	299	16.27	200
1.9	324	11.27-30	281		
1.9-11	318, 323,	12	169	*1 Corinthians*	
	324	12.25	281	2.13	383
2	236, 298,	13	299-301,	5.7	411
	302, 318		315, 316	8.4	198
2.14-40	297	13.14-41	335	8.6	198, 199
2.14-37	335	13.15	28	9.9-10	80
2.17-18	323	13.16-39	302	10	78
2.28-36	303	13.23	317	10.3-4	414
2.36	298	13.45-46	324	10.4	366

10.6-22	414	2.5	200	4.2	454
10.11	234, 364,	2.8	331	5.19	450
	382	6.15-16	200		
13.8	239			*Jude*	
15.3-4	383	*2 Timothy*		25	200
15.3	199	2.19-21	473		
15.28	210	2.19	473	*Revelation*	
				1.3	384
2 Corinthians		*Titus*		1.4	68
4.4	449, 457	1.12	181	1.7	394
6.2	382			1.8	68
		Hebrews		1.13-14	206
Galatians		1.6	89	5.6	408
3.16	140	2.5	317	5.8	408
3.20	199, 200	7.1-10	80	5.12	408
4.21-31	80	8.19	420	5.13	408
4.23	140, 156	10.37	68	6	408
4.26	74	11	82	6.13	21
4.28	140	11.31	143	7.14	408
4.29	140, 156,	12.22-29	74	7.17	408
	363			11.8	169
		James		12.15	229
Ephesians		2.8-13	274	13.1-10	229
1.3	74	2.19	200	14.1	408
2.6	74	2.25	143	14.4	408
2.19	74			14.10	408
4.6	200	*1 Peter*		15.3	408
5.31	63	1.10-12	75, 83, 364	19.10	75, 89
6.12	450	1.19	407	21–22	87
		2.22-25	411	22.1-12	265
Colossians				22.7	384
1.13	450	*1 John*		22.10	384
		2.11	449, 450,	22.18-19	384
1 Timothy			458		
1.17	200				

PSEUDEPIGRAPHA

1 Enoch		*2 Baruch*		11.1-4	206
14.19	51	41.3-4	291		
45.3	208			Aristeas, *Ep.*	
62.5	203	*4 Ezra*		229	270
69.29	203	1.30	291		
71	204	3.1	145	*Jub.*	
89–90	408	13.10-11	51	1.23	51
90.20-27	48			4.1	145
		Apoc. Abr.		5.10-16	48
		10–11	206	7.20	270

15.16	157	23.5	157	*T. Dan*	
15.34	48	23.7	157	5.3	270
16.3	140	23.8	157, 158		
16.12-13	157	42–43	161	*T. Iss.*	
16.16-17	140	50–51	161	5.2	270
17.3	317			7.6	270
19.21	317	*Ps.-Phoc.*			
20.2	270	3–21	275	*T. Jos.*	
22.14	317			19.18-19	408
32.18	317	*Pss. Sol.*			
32.34	171	11	338	*T. Judah*	
36.7-8	271	17	338	1.3	141
36.10	48	18	338	24.5-6	174
41.22	142				
		Sib. Or.		*T. Levi*	
Odes		2.196-97	51	4.4	287
1	105	2.203-205	51	18.3	287
12	105	2.252-54	51		
46–48	105	3.54	51	*T. Naph.*	
		4.165	37	8.9-10	270
Ps.-Philo, LAB				8.9	271
8.4	158	*T. Benj.*			
12.10	273	3.3	270		

QUMRAN

CD		3.25	452, 454	*1QSa*	
2.7-8	451	3.26–4.1	452	1.10-11	59
2.12	52	4.6	453	2.5-22	353
4.2	48	4.18	453, 454	2.11	156]
4.20–5.2	59	4.20-23	456		
4.20-21	40	4.21	51, 52	*1QM*	
5.8-11	59	5.1	451	1.11	296
6.4-5	48	5.6	451	1.14	296
8.16	48	5.8	451	4.4	296
		5.10	450	4.12	296
1QS		5.12	48	6	296
1.7-8	453	5.21-22	450	7.4-6	353
1.11-12	453	6.1-14	450	10.5	296
1.11	451	6.24-27	64	11.6	287
2.13–4.26	453	7.18-24	451	13.1–14.9	450
2.15	48	8.12-14	45		
3.3-9	38	9.11	181	*1QH*	
3.13–4.26	452, 455	9.17	450	2.9	48
3.13-26	450	9.19-20	45	3.17	47
3.18-20	452, 453	10.20	48	3.29-32	51
3.20-24	450			5.27	47
3.23	453			14.24	48

1QpHab		*4QTest*		2.1	123
2.8-9	382	12	287	2.5	123
7.5	33				
		4QpPs 37		*11QTemple*	
4QFlor		3.1	48	49.18-20	52
1.10-12	123			50.14-15	52
1.11	287	*4Q246*		57.17-19	40
		1.1	123		
		1.7	123		

TARGUMS

Targ. Onq. Lev.		*Targ. Ps.-J.* Deut.		2.10	125
19.18	277	26.6-7	350		
				Targ. Joel	
Targ. Ps.-J. Exod.		*Targ.* 1 Sam.		1.14	350
24.12	271	2.7-10	125		
		2.8	125		

MISHNAH

m. Ab.		*m. Giṭ.*		*m. Šeq.*	
1.1	325	9.10	59	2.5	72
1.5	64				
		m. Ma'as. Š.		*m. Soṭ.*	
m. B. Meṣ.		1.5	349	7.8	326
1.8	72	5.10-15	343	9.15	72
3.4	72	5.10	343		
3.5	72	5.12	349	*m. Tam.*	
				5.1	275
m. B. Qam.		*m. Meg.*			
10.1-2	350	4.5	327	*m. Ṭoh.*	
		4.6	326, 327	7.6	350
m. Bikk.					
1.1–3.12	343	*m. Ned.*		*m. Yad.*	
1.1	343	3.4	350	4.6	331
1.2	351				
1.5	350	*m. Pes.*		*m. Yom.*	
2.2	349	10.4	351	4.1-2	197
m. 'Ed.		*m. Sanh.*			
8.7	72	3.3	351		

TALMUDS

b. 'Abod. Zar.		*b. B. Qam.*		*b. Ber.*	
16b	118	82a	326	12a	275

21b	331	*b. Pes.*		*b. Ta'an.*	
28b	349	106a	329	12a	348
34b	262			16b	197
47b	275	*b. Šab.*			
		30b	264	*y. Ber.*	
b. Gۭit.				4.2	349
90b	40	*b. Sanh.*			
		38b	202, 203,	*y. Šeb.*	
b. Ket.			207, 296	35d	259
111b	264	43a	118		
		58a	58	*Der. Er. Rab.*	
b. Meg.		103a	118	2.11	350
3a	33, 329				
31a	327	*b. Šebu.*		*Sop.*	
31b	327	39a	351	14.14	331
32a	331				
32b	327				

TOSEFTA AND MIDRASHIM

t. Meṣ.		*Num. R.*		*Sefer-ha-*	
8.26	351	13.2		Zikkronot	163
		(Num. 7.12)	162		
t. Ṭoh.				*Sifra Lev.*	
8.5-6	351	*Cant. R.*		§239	
		1.2 §2	271	(Lev. 23.43)	329
Gen. R.					
17.3		*Mek. Exod.*		§260	
(Gen. 2.19)	58	14.16-21		(Lev. 26.3)	329
65.21 (Gen.		(Beš. §5)	329		
27.22)	210	14.31		*Sifre Deut.*	
81.3		(Beš. §7)	317	§34 (Deut.	
(Gen. 35.4)	350	15.17-21		6.5-6)	275
		(Shir. §10)	163	§297 (Deut.	
Exod. R.		15.22		26.1-2)	350
1.13 (Exod.		(Vayas. §1)		§298 (Deut.	
1.15)	162	23.19		26.2)	349
1.19		(Kaspa §5)	350	§301 (Deut.	
(Exod. 2.1)	163			26.5-11)	350
15.12 (Exod.		*Mek. SbY. Exod.*		§301 (Deut.	
12.6)	411	15.22	326	26.9)	349
32.4 (Exod.					
23.21)	207	*Chronicle of*		*Tanḥuma, Mišpatim*	
32.4 (Exod.		*Moses*	163	§18	207
23.22)	206, 207				

PHILO

Abr.		106-10	273		
208	270	106	272	*Spec. Leg.*	
		108-10	272	1.1	271
Cher.		121	272	2.63	270
12-15	103			4.141	275
42-52	159	*Leg. All.*			
44-45	159	3.219	158	*Virt.*	
46	160			95	270
47	160	*Mut. Nom.*			
		7	209	*Vit. Cont.*	
Dec.				68	59
19-20	271	*Somn.*			
50	272	1.149	209	*Vit. Mos.*	
51	272	2.127	28	1.155	317

JOSEPHUS

Ant.		4.8.22		*Apion*	
2.9.2–4		§§242-43	347	2.17 §175	28
§§205-23	161	5.1.3 §16	31		
2.9.3		13.11.2 §311	181	*War*	
§§210-16	162, 163	15.10.5		1.5.2 §110	348
2.9.4 §217	163	§§373-78	181	2.7.3 §111	170
2.16.5		18.5.2		2.8.7 §139	271
§§347-48	31	§§116-19	38, 42	2.8.12 §159	181
3.5.8 §101	273	20.5.1		6.5.3	
4.8.13 §212	275	§§97-98	30	§§300-309	32, 181
				6.5.4 §312	29
				7.8.1 §260	271

LATER JEWISH WRITERS AND WRITINGS

Cave of Treasures		Moses ben Maimonides		*Yad, Hilhoth Sabbath*	
29.1-2	158	*Morek Nebukim*		29.1	329
		2.13	147		

LATER CHRISTIAN WRITERS AND WRITINGS

Apos. Const.		11	277	*Benedict*	
2.5.36	277			*Regula*	
		Aristides		4.1-7	277
Aquinas		*Ep.*		4.2-7	275
De decem parae.		15.3-5	274		
4	277				
4.11	273				

Calvin
Inst.
2.8.11   277
2.8.52-53   273

Chrysostom
Hom. on Matt.
37.3   184

Cyprian
De dom. orat.
28   277

Didache
1.2   277
1.3-6   274

Eusebius
Hist. Eccl.
4.26.14   380

Gospel of Thomas
§31   336

Gregory of Nyssa
Vit. Mos.
2.48   274

Irenaeus
Adv. Haer.
4.16.3   273, 277
5.33.3   264

Epideixis
87   277

Justin
1 Apol.
16.6   277

Dial. Tryph.
3.1   380
11.1   380
67   103
111   411

Methodius of Olympus
Symp.
8.13   275

Ps.-Clem.
Hom.
12.32   277
13.15.1   63

Prot. Jas.
9.2   340
13.1   340
16.1   340

Tatian
Orat. ad Graec.
29.1   380
29.2   380

Tertullian
Adv. Jud.
4   274

Adv. Marc.
4.18   184

Theophilus of Antioch
Ad Autolycum
1.14-15   380

GRECO-ROMAN WRITERS

Cicero
On Divination
1, 23, 47   106

Dio Cassius
53.1.3   112

Dio Chrysostom
80(30), 11   112

Diodorus Siculus
16.66.3   106
17.10   105
17.49.5   108
17.50.6   108
17.112.2-4   106
17.112.4-5   107
19.7-9   105

Diogenes Laertius
3.1   101
3.2   104
4.6-11   109
4.9   109
4.10   110
4.11   108

Dionysius of Halicarnassus
6.13   114

Hermogenes
Progymnasmata
37   101, 103
38   108

Homer
Iliad
5.4-6   110
9.443   109

18.205-206   110
20.129-31   113
22.358-60   105
22.393-94   102
24.169-70   113
24.169   113
24.170   113

Odyssey
10.383-85   109
16.172-79   113

Lucan
Civil War
7.205-206   113

Lycurgus
Against Leocrates
86 (158)   111

Ovid
Metamorphoses
6.699   112

On Love
1.8.17-18   112

Pausanias
8.23.6-7   108

Pliny the Elder
Hist. Nat.
16.40   259

Pliny the Younger
Ep.
10.96   274

Plutarch
Alexander
2.1-6   104

Alcibiades
23   104

Cicero
1–2   105

Demetrius
12.3 (894)   112

Demosthenes
1–2   106

Greek Questions
22 (296d)   108

Moralia
718b   103

Numa
4, 3-4   103

Polybius
3.112.8   112

Ps.-Callisthenes
3.33.26   106, 112

Ps.-Demetrius
On Style
267   111

Thucydides
1.139.4   109

Tibullus
1.2.45   112

Vergil
Aeneid
2.801   106

INDEX OF AUTHORS

Achtemeier, P.J. 213, 215, 228, 230, 320
Aland, B. 15
Aland, K. 15
Albright, W.F. 117, 188, 260, 275, 456
Allan, G. 117, 128
Allen, R. 82
Allen, W.C. 183
Allison, D.C. 44, 46, 50, 51, 59, 72, 117, 118, 128, 129, 179, 180, 202, 205
Almqvist, H. 103
Ambrozic, A.M. 204
Anderson, B.W. 67
Anderson, H. 19, 278, 334
Archer, G.L. 70
Argyle, A.W. 257
Arndt, W. 48, 100, 104, 107, 110, 111, 219, 224
Aune, D.E. 105, 181

Bacchiocchi, S. 262
Bagatti, B. 37
Baker, D.L. 73, 79, 82, 84, 88
Baldi, D. 36
Balentine, S.E. 118
Ball, D.J. 408
Balz, H. 334
Bamberger, B.J. 143, 144
Bammel, E. 193
Banks, R. 191
Barnett, P.W. 30
Barrett, C.K. 25, 199, 280, 373, 404, 408, 409, 411, 418-20, 431-33, 443, 452, 471
Barth, G. 119
Barton, G.A. 411

Barton, J. 372
Bartsch, H.W. 244, 258, 260
Bauer, B. 244
Bauer, W. 48, 100, 104, 107, 110, 111, 219, 439
Beale, G.K. 67, 75
Beare, F.W. 258, 260
Beasley-Murray, G.R. 404, 408, 419, 420, 468
Becker, J. 35, 49, 50
Beecher, W.J. 83
Beker, J.C. 210
Belle, G. van 462
Berger, K. 56, 63
Bergman, I. 109
Bernard, J.H. 405, 407, 414, 417
Best, E. 118
Betz, O. 334, 336
Bieler, L. 103
Birdsall, J.N. 237
Black, D.A. 75
Black, M. 28, 48, 95, 117, 118, 325, 360
Blank, J. 456
Bligh, J. 342
Bloch, R. 358, 359
Blomberg, C.L. 74, 344
Bock, D.L. 21, 282, 288, 297
Borgen, P. 376, 377, 388, 413
Bornkamm, G. 119
Bourke, M.M. 120
Bovon, F. 315
Boyarin, D. 283, 311, 312
Branscomb, B.H. 278
Braumann, G. 193
Braun, F.-M. 374
Braun, H. 62

Brawley, R.L. 283, 289, 311, 317
Briggs, C.A. 250
Bright, J. 250
Brodie, T.L. 310, 311
Brooke, G.J. 336
Brown, R.E. 46, 84, 103, 117, 118,
    408-11, 413, 416, 419, 431, 452,
    466, 467
Brownlee, W.H. 38, 335
Bruce, F.F. 74, 77, 335
Brunec, M. 184
Buber, S. 142
Buchanan, G.W. 253, 254, 261-63, 265
Büchsel, F. 347
Bultmann, R. 66, 212, 231, 238, 373,
    385, 404, 407, 411, 419, 420,
    439, 468, 469
Burney, F.C. 408
Burrows, E.W. 409
Buss, M. 241

Cadbury, H.J. 316
Cangh, J.M. van 119
Carey, G.L. 407, 409, 410
Carroll, R.P. 95
Carson, D.A. 16, 42, 78, 84, 85, 118,
    186, 189, 280, 378, 401, 408,
    409, 414, 418
Catchpole, D.R. 296
Cathcart, K.J. 243
Charlesworth, J.H. 416, 454, 455
Chilton, B.D. 28, 66, 67, 75, 78, 81, 83,
    333, 334, 346, 361
Chirichigno, G.C. 70
Coleman, R.O. 16, 119
Collins, A.Y. 262
Collins, J.J. 202, 204
Conzelmann, H. 194
Cope, O.L. 119, 188
Cothenet, E. 375
Cotter, W.J. 238, 260
Cranfield, C.E.B. 274, 278
Crenshaw, J.L. 342
Cripps, R.S. 99, 100
Cross, F.L. 146
Cross, F.M. 34, 456
Crump, D.M. 99
Culler, J. 309

Cullmann, O. 127, 184, 340
Culpepper, R.A. 238, 416, 462, 463

Dahood, M. 250
Dalman, G. 411
Danker, F.W. 48, 94, 100, 104, 107,
    110, 111, 193, 219
Darr, K.P. 255
Daube, D. 32, 58, 63, 405, 456
Dautzenberg, G. 193
Davey, F.N. 415, 417, 434
Davids, P.H. 274
Davies, M. 397, 398, 400, 408, 409
Davies, W.D. 44, 46, 50, 51, 59, 117,
    118, 128, 129, 179, 180, 202,
    205, 412, 413, 420, 422, 423, 456
Delitzsch, F. 89
Denis, A.-M. 214-16
Denonn, L.E. 238
Derrett, J.D.M. 61, 62, 213, 260, 265,
    342, 353
Descamps, A. 334
De Vries, S. 82
DeYoung, J.B. 86, 87
Dibelius, M. 66, 212, 230
Didier, M. 119
Díez Macho, A. 224
Dobschütz, E. von 237
Dockery, D.S. 75
Dodd, C.H. 44, 46, 236, 402, 404, 407,
    408, 414, 420, 466, 467
Donahue, J.R. 342
Dowd, S.E. 238
Drane, J.W. 363
Dreyfus, F.-P. 88
Drury, J. 342
Duke, D. 463
Dunn, J.D.G. 43, 52, 180, 199, 200,
    274
Dupont, J. 57

Edwards, J.A. 237, 277
Efird, J. 19, 118
Egner, R.E. 237
Eichrodt, W. 87
Ellis, E.E. 19, 75, 77, 118, 238, 304
Eltester, E. 116, 118, 137, 334
Elwell, W. 74

Ernst, J. 42, 46, 47, 51, 180
Evans, C.A. 19, 23, 39, 74, 124, 235,
    236, 308, 309, 342, 344, 363,
    376, 378, 401-403, 408-10, 417,
    431, 432, 437, 438
Evans, C.F. 293, 342, 343, 413

Faiersten, M.M. 72
Falk, Z.W. 58
Farmer, W.R. 264
Felten, J. 101
Ferguson, E. 320
Fewell, D.N. 241
Fichtner, J. 48
Finkel, A. 326, 332, 334, 335
Finkelstein, L. 225, 226, 325
Fishbane, M. 32, 120, 236, 239, 245,
    336
Fitzmyer, J.A. 39, 40, 52, 53, 72, 121-
    23, 192, 293, 315, 347, 349, 350
Fleddermann, H. 214, 231, 232
Foakes-Jackson, F.J. 117, 316
Foerster, G. 326
Ford, J.M. 229, 420
Fortna, R.T. 199, 375
France, R.T. 28, 75, 79, 117, 327, 334,
    344
Freed, E.D. 25, 374, 404, 405, 431,
    433, 443
Freedman, H. 210
Friedlander, G. 227
Frizzell, L. 329
Fuller, R. 34

Gärtner, B. 117, 215, 223, 229, 233
Garvie, A.E. 462
George, A. 334
Gerhardsson, B. 216
Gese, H. 135, 137, 151, 176, 177
Gill, J. 276, 277
Gingrich, F. 98, 100, 104, 107, 110,
    111, 219, 224
Ginzberg, L. 72
Glasson, T.F. 373, 406, 408, 417
Glazier-MacDonald, B. 40
Gnilka, J. 129-31, 160, 172, 197, 199,
    209, 278
Godet, F. 461, 463, 469

Goehring, J.E. 462
Golomb, D.M. 125
Goppelt, L. 79, 82, 363, 373
Gordon, R.P. 243
Goulder, M.D. 327, 342
Grabbe, L.L. 325
Grässer, E. 19, 238
Gray, G.B. 419
Gray, R. 30
Green, J.B. 119, 189, 363
Green, W.S. 312, 313, 358
Greenberg, M. 254
Greene, T.M. 310
Grigsby, B.H. 411, 413, 419, 420
Grossfeld, B. 350
Grundmann, W. 260
Guilding, A. 327, 365, 413, 414
Gundry, R.H. 16, 44, 57, 61, 69, 71,
    75-78, 81, 89, 117-21, 127, 128,
    179, 183, 257, 466
Gunkel, H. 250
Gunneweg, A.H.J. 135
Gutmann, J. 325

Hachlili, R. 325
Haenchen, E. 461, 462, 469
Häfner, G. 187
Halleux, A. de 334
Hanson, A.T. 15, 42, 358, 378
Hanson, J.S. 30, 366-71, 376, 404
Harnack, A. von 381
Harrington, D.J. 125, 258
Harris, R. 236, 417, 431
Harrison, E.F. 74
Hartman, L. 119
Harvey, A.E. 56, 64, 65
Hasel, G.F. 67, 81, 82, 86, 87
Hay, D.M. 201
Hedrick, C.W. 462
Heil, J.P. 212, 221, 227, 231
Heinemann, J. 327
Hengel, M. 44, 402, 403
Henry, M. 276, 277
Herrenbrück, F. 342
Herz, J. 333
Heschel, A.J. 330
Hiers, R.H. 260-62, 264-66
Hill, D. 334

Hillyer, N. 16, 75, 119
Hirsch, E.D. 67, 83
Hoffmann, P. 193
Hollenbach, P. 39, 42
Holtz, T. 21, 280
Hommel, H. 222
Hooker, M.D. 206, 209
Horsley, R.A. 28, 30
Horst, P. van der 275
Hoskyns, E. 415, 417, 418, 434, 446
Howard, G. 120
Howard, J.K. 407, 409, 411, 414, 417, 418
Hubbard, R.L. 74
Hughes, J.H. 72
Hughes, P.E. 89
Hume, D. 448
Hurtado, L. 199, 200, 204, 206
Hurty, S. 86, 87
Huttenmeister, F. 325
Hyatt, J.P. 250
Hyvernat, H. 258

Jacoby, F. 102
Jaubert, A. 416
Jellinek, A. 265
Jepson, A. 17
Jeremias, J. 49, 180, 349, 408, 416
Johnson, L.T. 274, 316
Johnson, S.E. 259, 278
Johnson, S.L. 79
Johnston, R.M. 262
Jonge, M. de 361
Juel, D. 235

Kaiser, W. 67, 72-74, 76, 79, 83, 84
Käsemann, E. 375
Kee, H.C. 19, 215, 230, 238, 240
Keil, C.F. 70
Kelber, W. 214
Kelsey, D.H. 67
Kermode, F. 235
Kimelmann, R. 197
Kirkpatrick, A.F. 250
Kittel, G. 142
Klein, W.W. 74, 75, 85, 87
Kloppenborg, J.S. 34
Klostermann, E. 190

Knight, D. 311
Köhler, L. 87
Kosch, D. 193
Kraeling, C.H. 35
Kraft, R.A. 120
Krause, D. 241
Krentz, E. 116
Kretschmar, G. 60
Kuhn, K.G. 456
Kümmel, W.G. 193
Kurz, W.S. 320
Kysar, R. 407

Ladd, G.E. 410
LaGrange, M.-J. 259
Lake, K. 117, 316
Lambrecht, J. 44
Lane, W.L. 257, 278, 466
Lapide, P. 56, 213, 232
Lauterbach, J.Z. 226
Le Déaut, R. 359, 360
Lehmann, K. 136
Lehmann, O.H. 146
Leisegang, H. 103
Levenson, J.D. 254
Levey, S.H. 125, 333
Levine, L.I. 197, 326
Lewy, H. 266
Lewy, J. 266
Lightfoot, J. 348
Lightfoot, R.H. 413
Lindars, B. 15, 118, 361, 376, 377, 404, 405, 409, 413, 415, 430, 443
Lohmeyer, E. 209, 212, 230-32, 278
Loise, L.A. 238
Loisy, A. 121, 373
Longenecker, R.N. 15, 73, 75, 77, 78, 81, 118, 200, 336, 362
Lovering, E.H. 283, 293, 311
Lührmann, D. 231
Lull, D.J. 305
Luz, U. 97-99, 117, 128-33, 135, 165, 168, 172, 174, 185
Lyonnet, S. 117

Maher, M. 224
Mai, H.-P. 309
Malbon, E. 218

Malchow, B. 34, 73
Maloney, L.M. 413
Mann, C.S. 188, 260
Mann, J. 154, 238
Manson, T.W. 300
Marcus, J. 197, 198, 200-203, 208
Marshall, I.H. 42, 44, 49, 51, 53, 78, 118, 119, 193, 363
Martinez, F.G. 254
Martyn, J.L. 72, 436
Maurer, C. 49
May, H.G. 254
Mays, J.L. 241
McConnell, R.S. 16, 119
McKnight, S. 74, 119, 363
McLaughlin, G.A. 258
McNamara, M. 224
McNeile, A.H. 183
Médebielle, A. 117
Meeks, W.A. 199, 320, 406
Meier, J.P. 42, 187, 257
Merklein, H. 193
Metzger, B.M. 467
Meyer, H.A.W. 258, 260
Meyers, E.M. 325
Mickelsen, A.B. 82
Mielziner, M. 222
Millar, F. 28, 95, 326
Miller, M.P. 180
Miller, P.D. 271
Moessner, D.P. 305
Moo, D.J. 84, 85, 118, 377, 404, 405
Moore, E. 186
Moore, G.F. 117, 127
Morgan, R. 25
Morgenstern, J. 266, 409
Morris, L. 327, 407, 413, 414
Mounce, R.H. 258
Mulder, M.J. 28, 32, 119, 328, 336
Murphy-O'Connor, J. 37
Mussies, G. 122
Myers, C. 238

Nellessen, E. 120
Nestlé, E. 15
Neugebauer, F. 296
Neusner, J. 312, 313, 332, 334
Newsom, C. 240

Neyrey, J.H. 119, 228-30
Nicholson, G.C. 415
Niditch, S. 254
Nielsen, E. 272, 273
Nineham, D.E. 278, 342
Nolland, J. 52, 344
Norden, E. 103
Norton, G.J. 120
Noth, M. 88

O'Day, G. 463
O'Neill, J.C. 183, 408
O'Rourke, J.J. 16, 84, 119
Oberweis, M. 120
Ogg, G. 417
Olsson, B. 361
Osborne, G.R. 87

Packer, J.I. 85
Painter, J. 457, 458
Pannenberg, W. 80, 82
Parker, P. 36
Patte, D. 259
Payne, J.B. 73
Payne, P.B. 83
Peek, W. 110
Percy, E. 193
Perri, C. 313
Perrin, N. 193
Perot, C. 28
Perrot, C. 154, 158, 327
Pesch, R. 45, 46, 116, 119, 120, 128, 133, 134, 136, 142, 146, 154, 169, 175, 197, 202, 209, 278
Petersen, E. 103
Petersen, N.R. 408
Petuchowski, J.J. 328
Pfister, F. 113, 114
Pisano, S. 120
Plett, H.F. 309
Plevnik, J. 204
Porter, S.E. 415
Potterie, I. de la 215
Priest, J.E. 439
Puech, E. 254

Rabe, H. 101
Rabin, C. 122

Rad, G. von 79, 80, 82, 88, 241, 273
Rahlfs, A. 94
Reeg, G. 325
Reicke, B. 334
Reif, S.C. 196, 197
Reim, G. 25, 362, 376, 404, 405
Reitzenstein, R. 103
Rembry, J. 117
Rese, M. 280, 281
Richard, E. 316
Richards, I.A. 398
Ridderbos, H.N. 258
Ringe, S.H. 337
Ringgren, H. 21, 456
Robinson, J.A.T. 35, 36, 72, 377, 378
Robinson, T.H. 257
Rosenzweig, F. 393
Rothfuchs, W. 119, 374
Rowdon, H.H. 186
Rowley, H.H. 76
Rubinkiewicz, R. 206
Ruckstuhl, E. 417
Rudin, J.A. 75
Rudolph, W. 241
Rüger, H.P. 117, 127
Russell, B. 237, 238
Russell, D.S. 82

Sabourin, L. 257
Safrai, S. 122
Saldarini, A.J. 125
Salmon, G. 278
Sanders, E.P. 30, 48, 49, 56, 60
Sanders, J.A. 120, 175, 180, 329, 334,
     342, 352, 353
Sarna, N.M. 250
Sawyer, J.F.A. 251
Schaeder, H.H. 117, 128
Schenke, L. 133
Schimanowski, G. 151
Schlosser, J. 182
Schmidt, K.L. 432, 450
Schmidt, M.A. 432, 450
Schnackenburg, R. 130-32, 316, 375,
     404, 410, 413, 414, 416, 418,
     420, 431-34, 446, 451, 452, 461,
     471
Schneider, G. 316

Schnelle, U. 413
Schrage, W. 325, 432, 448
Schreiner, J. 171
Schrenk, G. 186
Schroer, H. 135
Schuchard, B.D. 25, 404
Schulz, S. 193, 334
Schürer, E. 28, 95, 325
Schürmann, H. 44, 193, 334
Schweizer, E. 116, 121, 127, 130, 175,
     244, 258, 278
Scobie, C.H.H. 51
Scott, W.S. 398
Seebass, H. 87
Segal, A.F. 196, 200, 206-208
Shanks, H. 326
Shepherd, T. 237
Shires, H.M. 15, 118
Silva, M. 78
Slater, W.F. 258
Sloan, R.B. 337
Smith, D.M. 66, 118, 377
Smith, R.H. 363
Snodgrass, K.R. 45, 75, 89, 288, 335
Snoy, T. 213, 214
Soares Prabhu, G.M. 117, 118, 120,
     128
Spicq, C. 186
Stanton, G. 119
Starcky, J. 39
Steck, O. 311
Stegner, W.R. 216, 230
Stein, S. 226
Steinmann, A.E. 100
Stendahl, K. 16, 66, 71, 76, 77, 118,
     119, 121, 126, 137, 336, 452
Stern, M. 122
Stibbe, M.W.G. 397-400, 405-407,
     409-12, 415, 418, 423-27
Stinespring, W.F. 376
Strand, K.A. 417
Suhl, A. 19
Suriano, T. 230
Swete, H.B. 278
Swetnam, J. 186

Talbert, C. 280, 281, 310
Talmon, S. 119

Tannehill, R.C. 315, 316, 319, 334
Tannenbaum, M. 75
Tasker, R.V.G. 258, 259
Tatum, W.B. 117
Taylor, D.B. 117
Taylor, V. 205, 213, 258, 261, 278, 408
Taylor, W.R. 250
Telford, W.R. 237, 238
Tenney, M.C. 462
Thomas, K.J. 57
Tov, E. 119, 120
Trompf, G.W. 321
Turner, M.M.B. 189, 408
Tyler, R.L. 439
Tyson, J.B. 319

Usener, H. 103, 106, 108, 110

Van Segbroeck, F. 119
Vawter, B. 84
Verhoef, P. 73, 82
Vermes, G. 28, 56, 59, 95, 325, 349
Vögtle, A. 137, 316
Vorster, W.S. 19
Vriezen, T.C. 87

Wacholder, B.Z. 337
Wahlde, U.C. von 426
Walker, N. 417
Wall, R.W. 342, 353
Walters, S. 126
Waltke, B.K. 74

Ward, J. de 119, 120
Watson, T. 276
Webb, R.L. 35, 42, 49-51, 53
Weingreen, J. 359
Weir, J. 73, 82, 83
Wenham, D. 274, 327, 334, 344
Wenham, J. 73
Westcott, B.F. 410, 411, 414
Westermann, C. 79, 80, 88, 222
Wetstein, J. 112
Wikenhauser, A. 316
Wilcox, M. 118
Wiles, M. 456
Williams, S.K. 410
Williamson, H.G.M. 16, 42, 78, 118, 180, 378, 401
Willis, J.T. 342
Wills, L.M. 96
Wilson, R.M. 75, 118
Wink, W. 35, 47, 184
Wise, M.O. 122
Wolff, H.W. 82, 241
Woodbridge, J.D. 78, 84, 85

Yoder, J.H. 337
Young, F.W. 376, 409

Zaehner, R.C. 456
Zakowitsch, J. 143
Zerwick, M. 184
Zolli, E. 117
Zuckschwerdt, E. 117, 128

JOURNAL FOR THE STUDY OF THE NEW TESTAMENT

Supplement Series

1 THE BARREN TEMPLE AND THE WITHERED TREE
William R. Telford

2 STUDIA BIBLICA 1978
II. PAPERS ON THE GOSPELS
Edited by E.A. Livingstone

3 STUDIA BIBLICA 1978
III. PAPERS ON PAUL AND OTHER NEW TESTAMENT AUTHORS
Edited by E.A. Livingstone

4 FOLLOWING JESUS:
DISCIPLESHIP IN THE GOSPEL OF MARK
Ernest Best

5 THE PEOPLE OF GOD
Markus Barth

6 PERSECUTION AND MARTYRDOM IN THE THEOLOGY OF PAUL
John S. Pobee

7 SYNOPTIC STUDIES:
THE AMPLEFORTH CONFERENCES OF
1982 AND 1983
Edited by C.M. Tuckett

8 JESUS ON THE MOUNTAIN:
A STUDY IN MATTHEAN THEOLOGY
Terence L. Donaldson

9 THE HYMNS OF LUKE'S INFANCY NARRATIVES:
THEIR ORIGIN, MEANING AND SIGNIFICANCE
Stephen Farris

10 CHRIST THE END OF THE LAW:
ROMANS 10.4 IN PAULINE PERSPECTIVE
Robert Badenas

11 THE LETTERS TO THE SEVEN CHURCHES OF ASIA IN THEIR LOCAL
SETTING
Colin J. Hemer

12 PROCLAMATION FROM PROPHECY AND PATTERN:
LUCAN OLD TESTAMENT CHRISTOLOGY
Darrell L. Bock

13 JESUS AND THE LAWS OF PURITY:
TRADITION HISTORY AND LEGAL HISTORY IN MARK 7
Roger P. Booth

14 THE PASSION ACCORDING TO LUKE:
THE SPECIAL MATERIAL OF LUKE 22
Marion L. Soards

15 HOSTILITY TO WEALTH IN THE SYNOPTIC GOSPELS
Thomas E. Schmidt

16 MATTHEW'S COMMUNITY:
THE EVIDENCE OF HIS SPECIAL SAYINGS MATERIAL
Stephenson H. Brooks

17 THE PARADOX OF THE CROSS IN THE THOUGHT OF ST PAUL
Anthony Tyrrell Hanson

18 HIDDEN WISDOM AND THE EASY YOKE:
WISDOM, TORAH AND DISCIPLESHIP IN MATTHEW 11.25-30
Celia Deutsch

19 JESUS AND GOD IN PAUL'S ESCHATOLOGY
L. Joseph Kreitzer

20 LUKE
A NEW PARADIGM (2 Volumes)
Michael D. Goulder

21 THE DEPARTURE OF JESUS IN LUKE–ACTS:
THE ASCENSION NARRATIVES IN CONTEXT
Mikeal C. Parsons

22 THE DEFEAT OF DEATH:
APOCALYPTIC ESCHATOLOGY IN 1 CORINTHIANS 15 AND ROMANS 5
Martinus C. de Boer

23 PAUL THE LETTER-WRITER
AND THE SECOND LETTER TO TIMOTHY
Michael Prior

24 APOCALYPTIC AND THE NEW TESTAMENT:
ESSAYS IN HONOR OF J. LOUIS MARTYN
Edited by Joel Marcus & Marion L. Soards

25 THE UNDERSTANDING SCRIBE:
MATTHEW AND THE APOCALYPTIC IDEAL
David E. Orton

26 WATCHWORDS:
MARK 13 IN MARKAN ESCHATOLOGY
Timothy J. Geddert

27 THE DISCIPLES ACCORDING TO MARK:
MARKAN REDACTION IN CURRENT DEBATE
C. Clifton Black

28 THE NOBLE DEATH:
GRAECO-ROMAN MARTYROLOGY
AND PAUL'S CONCEPT OF SALVATION
David Seeley

29 ABRAHAM IN GALATIANS:
EPISTOLARY AND RHETORICAL CONTEXTS
G. Walter Hansen

30 EARLY CHRISTIAN RHETORIC AND 2 THESSALONIANS
Frank Witt Hughes

31 THE STRUCTURE OF MATTHEW'S GOSPEL:
A STUDY IN LITERARY DESIGN
David R. Bauer

32 PETER AND THE BELOVED DISCIPLE:
FIGURES FOR A COMMUNITY IN CRISIS
Kevin Quast

33 MARK'S AUDIENCE:
THE LITERARY AND SOCIAL SETTING OF MARK 4.11-12
Mary Ann Beavis

34 THE GOAL OF OUR INSTRUCTION:
THE STRUCTURE OF THEOLOGY AND ETHICS
IN THE PASTORAL EPISTLES
Philip H. Towner

35 THE PROVERBS OF JESUS:
ISSUES OF HISTORY AND RHETORIC
Alan P. Winton

36 THE STORY OF CHRIST IN THE ETHICS OF PAUL:
AN ANALYSIS OF THE FUNCTION OF THE HYMNIC MATERIAL
IN THE PAULINE CORPUS
Stephen E. Fowl

37 PAUL AND JESUS:
COLLECTED ESSAYS
Edited by A.J.M. Wedderburn

38 MATTHEW'S MISSIONARY DISCOURSE:
A LITERARY CRITICAL ANALYSIS
Dorothy Jean Weaver

39 FAITH AND OBEDIENCE IN ROMANS:
A STUDY IN ROMANS 1–4
Glenn N. Davies

40 IDENTIFYING PAUL'S OPPONENTS:
THE QUESTION OF METHOD IN 2 CORINTHIANS
Jerry L. Sumney

41 HUMAN AGENTS OF COSMIC POWER:
IN HELLENISTIC JUDAISM AND THE SYNOPTIC TRADITION
Mary E. Mills

42 MATTHEW'S INCLUSIVE STORY:
A STUDY IN THE NARRATIVE RHETORIC OF THE FIRST GOSPEL
David B. Howell

43 JESUS, PAUL AND TORAH:
COLLECTED ESSAYS
Heikki Räisänen

44 THE NEW COVENANT IN HEBREWS
Susanne Lehne

45 THE RHETORIC OF ROMANS:
ARGUMENTATIVE CONSTRAINT AND STRATEGY AND PAUL'S
DIALOGUE WITH JUDAISM
Neil Elliott

46 THE LAST SHALL BE FIRST:
THE RHETORIC OF REVERSAL IN LUKE
John O. York

47 JAMES AND THE Q SAYINGS OF JESUS
Patrick J. Hartin

48 TEMPLUM AMICITIAE:
ESSAYS ON THE SECOND TEMPLE PRESENTED TO ERNST BAMMEL
Edited by William Horbury

49 PROLEPTIC PRIESTS
PRIESTHOOD IN THE EPISTLE TO THE HEBREWS
John M. Scholer

50 PERSUASIVE ARTISTRY:
STUDIES IN NEW TESTAMENT RHETORIC
IN HONOR OF GEORGE A. KENNEDY
Edited by Duane F. Watson

51 THE AGENCY OF THE APOSTLE: A DRAMATISTIC ANALYSIS OF PAUL'S
RESPONSES TO CONFLICT IN 2 CORINTHIANS
Jeffrey A. Crafton

52 REFLECTIONS OF GLORY:
PAUL'S POLEMICAL USE OF THE MOSES–DOXA TRADITION IN
2 CORINTHIANS 3.12-18
Linda L. Belleville

53 REVELATION AND REDEMPTION AT COLOSSAE
Thomas J. Sappington

54 THE DEVELOPMENT OF EARLY CHRISTIAN PNEUMATOLOGY
WITH SPECIAL REFERENCE TO LUKE–ACTS
Robert P. Menzies

55 THE PURPOSE OF ROMANS:
A COMPARATIVE LETTER STRUCTURE INVESTIGATION
L. Ann Jervis

56 THE SON OF THE MAN IN THE GOSPEL OF JOHN
Delbert Burkett

57 ESCHATOLOGY AND THE COVENANT:
A COMPARISON OF 4 EZRA AND ROMANS 1–11
Bruce W. Longenecker

58 NONE BUT THE SINNERS:
RELIGIOUS CATEGORIES IN THE GOSPEL OF LUKE
David A. Neale

59 CLOTHED WITH CHRIST:
THE EXAMPLE AND TEACHING OF JESUS IN ROMANS 12.1–15.13
Michael Thompson

60 THE LANGUAGE OF THE NEW TESTAMENT:
CLASSIC ESSAYS
Edited by Stanley E. Porter

61 FOOTWASHING IN JOHN 13 AND THE JOHANNINE COMMUNITY
John Christopher Thomas

62 JOHN THE BAPTIZER AND PROPHET:
A SOCIO-HISTORICAL STUDY
Robert L. Webb

63 POWER AND POLITICS IN PALESTINE:
THE JEWS AND THE GOVERNING OF THEIR LAND 100 BC–AD 70
James S. McLaren

64 JESUS AND THE ORAL GOSPEL TRADITION
Edited by Henry Wansbrough

65 THE RHETORIC OF RIGHTEOUSNESS IN ROMANS 3.21-26
Douglas A. Campbell

66 PAUL, ANTIOCH AND JERUSALEM:
A STUDY IN RELATIONSHIPS AND AUTHORITY IN EARLIEST CHRISTIANITY
Nicholas Taylor

67 THE PORTRAIT OF PHILIP IN ACTS:
A STUDY OF ROLES AND RELATIONS
F. Scott Spencer

68 JEREMIAH IN MATTHEW'S GOSPEL:
THE REJECTED-PROPHET MOTIF IN MATTHAEAN REDACTION
Michael P. Knowles

69 RHETORIC AND REFERENCE IN THE FOURTH GOSPEL
Margaret Davies

70 AFTER THE THOUSAND YEARS:
RESURRECTION AND JUDGMENT IN REVELATION 20
J. Webb Mealy

71 SOPHIA AND THE JOHANNINE JESUS
Martin Scott

72 NARRATIVE ASIDES IN LUKE–ACTS
Steven M. Sheeley

73 SACRED SPACE
AN APPROACH TO THE THEOLOGY OF THE EPISTLE TO THE HEBREWS
Marie E. Isaacs

74 TEACHING WITH AUTHORITY:
MIRACLES AND CHRISTOLOGY IN THE GOSPEL OF MARK
Edwin K. Broadhead

75 PATRONAGE AND POWER:
A STUDY OF SOCIAL NETWORKS IN CORINTH
John Kin-Man Chow

76 THE NEW TESTAMENT AS CANON:
A READER IN CANONICAL CRITICISM
Robert Wall and Eugene Lemcio

77 REDEMPTIVE ALMSGIVING IN EARLY CHRISTIANITY
    Roman Garrison
78 THE FUNCTION OF SUFFERING IN PHILIPPIANS
    L. Gregory Bloomquist
79 THE THEME OF RECOMPENSE IN MATTHEW'S GOSPEL
    Blaine Charette
80 BIBLICAL GREEK LANGUAGE AND LINGUISTICS: OPEN QUESTIONS IN
    CURRENT RESEARCH
    Edited by Stanley E. Porter and D.A. Carson
81 THE LAW IN GALATIANS
    In-Gyu Hong
82 ORAL TRADITION AND THE GOSPELS: THE PROBLEM OF MARK 4
    Barry W. Henaut
83 PAUL AND THE SCRIPTURES OF ISRAEL
    Edited by Craig A. Evans and James A. Sanders
84 FROM JESUS TO JOHN: ESSAYS ON JESUS AND NEW TESTAMENT
    CHRISTOLOGY IN HONOUR OF MARINUS DE JONGE
    Edited by Martinus C. De Boer
85 RETURNING HOME: NEW COVENANT AND SECOND EXODUS AS THE
    CONTEXT FOR 2 CORINTHIANS 6.14–7.1
    William J. Webb
86 ORIGINS OF METHOD: TOWARDS A NEW UNDERSTANDING OF JUDAISM AND
    CHRISTIANITY—ESSAYS IN HONOUR OF JOHN C. HURD
    Edited by Bradley H. McLean
87 WORSHIP, THEOLOGY AND MINISTRY IN THE EARLY CHURCH: ESSAYS IN
    HONOUR OF RALPH P. MARTIN
    Edited by Michael Wilkins and Terence Paige
88 THE BIRTH OF THE LUKAN NARRATIVE
    Mark Coleridge
89 WORD AND GLORY: ON THE EXEGETICAL AND THEOLOGICAL
    BACKGROUND OF JOHN'S PROLOGUE
    Craig A. Evans
90 RHETORIC IN THE NEW TESTAMENT
    ESSAYS FROM THE 1992 HEIDELBERG CONFERENCE
    Edited by Stanley E. Porter and Thomas H. Olbricht
91 MATTHEW'S NARRATIVE WEB: OVER, AND OVER, AND OVER AGAIN
    Janice Capel Anderson
92 LUKE: INTERPRETER OF PAUL, CRITIC OF MATTHEW
    Eric Franklin
93 ISAIAH AND PROPHETIC TRADITIONS IN THE BOOK OF REVELATION:
    VISIONARY ANTECEDENTS AND THEIR DEVELOPMENT
    Jan Fekkes
94 JESUS' EXPOSITION OF THE OLD TESTAMENT IN LUKE'S GOSPEL
    Charles A. Kimball

95 THE SYMBOLIC NARRATIVES OF THE FOURTH GOSPEL:
    THE INTERPLAY OF FORM AND MEANING
    Dorothy A. Lee

96 THE COLOSSIAN CONTROVERSY:
    WISDOM IN DISPUTE AT COLOSSAE
    Richard E. DeMaris

97 PROPHET, SON, MESSIAH
    NARRATIVE FORM AND FUNCTION IN MARK 14–16
    Edwin K. Broadhead

98 FILLING UP THE MEASURE:
    POLEMICAL HYPERBOLE IN 1 THESSALONIANS 2.14-16
    Carol J. Schlueter

100 TO TELL THE MYSTERY:
    ESSAYS ON NEW TESTAMENT ESCHATOLOGY IN HONOR OF
    ROBERT H. GUNDRY
    Edited by E. Schmidt and Moisés Silva

101 NEGLECTED ENDINGS:
    THE SIGNIFICANCE OF THE PAULINE LETTER CLOSINGS
    Jeffrey A.D. Weima

102 OTHER FOLLOWERS OF JESUS:
    MINOR CHARACTERS AS MAJOR FIGURES IN MARK'S GOSPEL
    Joel F. Williams

103 HOUSEHOLDS AND DISCIPLESHIP:
    A STUDY OF MATTHEW 19–20
    Warren Carter

104 THE GOSPELS AND THE SCRIPTURES OF ISRAEL
    Edited by Craig A. Evans and W. Richard Stegner